Memory and Identity in the Syriac *Cave of Treasures*

Jerusalem Studies
in Religion and Culture

Editors

Anthony Grafton (*Princeton University*)
David Shulman (*Hebrew University of Jerusalem*)
Guy Stroumsa (*Hebrew University of Jerusalem*)

VOLUME 26

The titles published in this series are listed at *brill.com/jsrc*

Memory and Identity in the Syriac *Cave of Treasures*

Rewriting the Bible in Sasanian Iran

By

Sergey Minov

BRILL

LEIDEN | BOSTON

The Library of Congress Cataloging-in-Publication Data is available online at http://catalog.loc.gov
LC record available at http://lccn.loc.gov/2020044644

Typeface for the Latin, Greek, and Cyrillic scripts: "Brill". See and download: brill.com/brill-typeface.

ISSN 1570-078X
ISBN 978-90-04-44550-5 (hardback)
ISBN 978-90-04-44551-2 (e-book)

Copyright 2021 by Sergey Minov. Published by Koninklijke Brill NV, Leiden, The Netherlands.
Koninklijke Brill NV incorporates the imprints Brill, Brill Hes & De Graaf, Brill Nijhoff, Brill Rodopi, Brill Sense, Hotei Publishing, mentis Verlag, Verlag Ferdinand Schöningh and Wilhelm Fink Verlag.
Koninklijke Brill NV reserves the right to protect this publication against unauthorized use. Requests for re-use and/or translations must be addressed to Koninklijke Brill NV via brill.com or copyright.com.

This book is printed on acid-free paper and produced in a sustainable manner.

манăн аннене, Нина Якимовăна, халалласа

Хватит, покружились мы здесь,
как звонкие монеты серебряные,
поклонимся, – согнемся пред вами,
как белые деньги бумажные.
ГЕННАДИЙ АЙГИ, *Тридцать шесть вариаций
на темы чувашских и татарских народных песен*

Contents

Acknowledgements IX
Abbreviations and Conventions XI

Introduction 1

1 **Genre, Date, and Provenance of CT** 18
 1 Content and Genre 18
 2 The State of the Text 26
  2.1 *Direct Textual Witnesses* 26
  2.2 *Indirect Textual Witnesses* 28
  2.3 *The "Original" Text of CT* 32
 3 Date of CT 36
  3.1 *Terminus ante quem* 38
  3.2 *Terminus post quem* 38
 4 Milieu of CT 40
 5 Concluding Observations 44

2 **Categorizing the Jewish "Other"** 49
 1 The Jewish Background of CT 55
 2 Apologetics: The Genealogy of the Virgin Mary 60
 3 Polemic: Anti-Judaism and the Passion Narrative 71
  3.1 *Jews as the Killers of Christ* 72
  3.2 *Demonization of the Jews* 74
  3.3 *Anti-Jewish Revision of the Canonical Passion Narrative* 77
  3.4 *The Jews and the Instruments of Jesus' Execution* 79
  3.5 *The Sponge-Bearers as Jews* 85
 4 Polemic: Supersessionism 87
  4.1 *Rhetoric of Supersessionism* 89
  4.2 *Supersessionist Exegesis of the Old Testament* 101
  4.3 *Supersessionist Revision of Biblical History* 121
 5 Concluding Observations 130

3 **Categorizing the Iranian "Other"** 142
 1 The Customs and Beliefs of the "Persians" 145
  1.1 *The Cult of Fire* 145
  1.2 *The Cult of the Horse* 152
  1.3 *Close-Kin Marriage* 163
  1.4 *Astrology* 177

2   Iranian Kingship   190
       2.1   *Nimrod*   190
       2.2   *Cyrus*   218
       2.3   *The Magi*   223
  3   Concluding Observations   247

4 **Identifying the Syriac Christian "Self"**   254
  1   The Ethnonym "Syrians"   255
       1.1   *Territorial Aspects of* Suryāyā   259
       1.2   *Linguistic and Cultural Aspects of* Suryāyā   263
       1.3   *The Confessional Aspect of* Suryāyā   266
  2   Syriac Primacy: The Language   271
  3   Syriac Primacy: The People   283
  4   The Figure of Abgar   290
  5   Attribution to Ephrem   294
  6   Concluding Observations   300

General Conclusion   310

Bibliography   317
Index of Scriptural References   390
Index of Ancient Sources   394

Acknowledgements

This book is a reworked version of my thesis in Comparative Religion which I have submitted for the degree Doctor of Philosophy at the Hebrew University of Jerusalem in the year 2013.

It was, however, the Ratisbonne Pontifical Institute in Jerusalem, where my Israeli odyssey started two decades ago. I am most thankful to the members of the Congregation of the Religious of Our Lady of Sion, as well as to such external lecturers as Pesach Schindler, Alon Goshen-Gottstein, and Ada Spitzer, who were the first to introduce me into the field of Jewish studies. Fortuitously, it was one of these teachers, Petra Heldt, who "infected" me with curiosity in Syriac Christianity. Moreover, I owe a deep debt of gratitude to Elio Passeto, the former vice-rector of the Institute, for his goodwill and unfaltering support that made my stay in Israel possible.

Later on, at the Hebrew University of Jerusalem, I was fortunate to have had the opportunity of studying under such renowned scholars as Michael E. Stone, Menahem Kister, Isaiah M. Gafni, Lee I. Levine, Israel J. Yuval, David Satran, and several others, who taught me how to approach intellectually the intertwined worlds of Judaism and Christianity in their formative periods. I am also grateful to Shraga Assif, who kindly let me join his class of Classical Syriac even before I was officially enrolled as a student.

My deepest expression of gratitude goes to my two *Doktorväter*, Serge Ruzer and Guy G. Stroumsa. It was their wise guidance, unwavering faith in me, and ever-present readiness to help that made it possible to bring this project to fruition.

A special expression of appreciation is reserved for Brouria Bitton-Ashkelony, the former director of the Center for the Study of Christianity at the Hebrew University, whose kind support and encouragement were a source of strength and inspiration throughout this and several other academic ventures. Fortunately for me and for the whole community of *syriacisants*, it was her long-term strategic vision that made the ongoing online project "Comprehensive Bibliography on Syriac Christianity" possible.

I also appreciate very much the help and support that I have received from those among my colleagues and friends from Jerusalem and all over the world, who have read various parts of this book and offered their insights and corrections, especially Sebastian P. Brock, Lorenzo Perrone, Tal Ilan, Geoffrey Herman, Māra Poļakova, Yonatan Moss, Nikolai Seleznyov, Muriel Debié, and Alice Croq. I am especially indebted to Michael Shenkar and Yuhan S.-D. Vevaina, whose expertise in things Zoroastrian saved me from many embarrassing mistakes in the relevant chapter. Needless to say, any errors of fact or judgment that one may come across in the book are mine and solely mine.

I have also greatly enjoyed discussing different matters related to my research with Aryeh Kofsky, Craig Morrison, Clemens Leonhard, István Perczel, Reuven Kiperwasser, Julia Rubanovich, Michael Schneider, Yakir Paz, Miriam Goldstein, Daniel Barbu, Emiliano Fiori, Salam Rassi, Simcha Gross, and David Taylor. Moreover, I feel a deep sense of gratitude to friends who supported me on this path,—Lolita Tomsone, Michael Rand, Natasha and Leonid Ostrovsky, and Laura Slater.

I would like to offer my sincere appreciation to the Dolabani Fund for Syriac Studies in Oxford that provided me with a grant for academic proofreading of the book's manuscript, and to Katharine Handel, who had carried out this arduous task. Finally, I owe thanks to the editors of "Jerusalem Studies in Religion and Culture" Series for accepting my book to be published in what feels like its proper home.

Last but not least, I would like to express my eternal gratitude to my mother Nina, without whose love and support this long journey there and back again would not be possible.

Abbreviations and Conventions

Abbreviations

AB	*Analecta Bollandiana*
BSGRT	Bibliotheca scriptorum Graecorum et Romanorum Teubneriana
BSOAS	*Bulletin of the School of Oriental and African Studies*
CCSL	Corpus Christianorum Series Latina
CHRC	*Church History and Religious Culture*
CSCO	Corpus Scriptorum Christianorum Orientalium
CSEL	Corpus Scriptorum Ecclesiasticorum Latinorum
GCS	Die griechischen christlichen Schriftsteller
HTR	*Harvard Theological Review*
HUCA	*Hebrew Union College Annual*
JECS	*Journal of Early Christian Studies*
JJS	*Journal of Jewish Studies*
JSS	*Journal of Semitic Studies*
LCL	Loeb Classical Library
OC	*Oriens Christianus*
OCA	Orientalia Christiana Analecta
OCP	*Orientalia Christiana Periodica*
OLA	Orientalia Lovaniensia Analecta
PdO	*Parole de l'Orient*
PG	Patrologia Graeca = *Patrologia cursus completus: series graeca*, edited by J.-P. Migne, 162 vols (Paris, 1857–1886).
PO	Patrologia Orientalis
PTS	Patristische Texte und Studien
ROC	*Revue de l'Orient chrétien*
SC	Sources chrétiennes
TSAJ	Texts and Studies in Ancient Judaism
TTH	Translated Texts for Historians
TUGAL	Texte und Untersuchungen zur Geschichte der altchristlichen Literatur
VC	*Vigiliae Christianae*
VT	*Vetus Testamentum*
WUNT	Wissenschaftliche Untersuchungen zum Neuen Testament
ZAC	*Zeitschrift für Antikes Christentum*
ZDMG	*Zeitschrift der Deutschen Morgenländischen Gesellschaft*

Conventions

Most of the abbreviations of the titles of works by ancient writers used throughout the book may be found in *The SBL Handbook of Style*, edited by Patrick H. Alexander et al. (Peabody, Mass.: Hendrickson Publishers, 1999).

For transcribing Syriac, I use a slightly modified version of the simplified transcription system outlined by Sebastian P. Brock and adopted by the Library of Congress.[1]

The Peshitta version of the Old Testament is quoted according to the edition *The Old Testament in Syriac according to the Peshiṭta Version*, 18 vols. (Leiden: Brill, 1966–2019).

Unless indicated otherwise, all translations of Syriac and other ancient texts in the book are mine.

---

1 The description is available online at https://www.loc.gov/catdir/cpso/romanization/syriac.pdf.

Introduction

Since the very beginning of Christianity, the Bible formed a backbone of the new religion. The belief in a revealed Scripture, held by Christians, set in motion complex dynamics that affected the life and culture of Roman society on many levels, engendering what Guy Stroumsa has aptly called the "scriptural universe" of ancient Christianity.[1] Scholars interested in the religious, cultural, and social impact of the Bible in late antique Christendom tend to focus, for the most part, on literary works or material evidence coming from the Greco-Roman world. One should not forget, however, that the boundaries of the Christian scriptural universe extended beyond those of the Roman empire. In this book, I intend to venture into one of the less explored corners of this universe by discussing the crucial role that reception of the Bible played in the cultural history of the Syriac Christians who lived in the territory of the Sasanian empire.[2]

With that goal in mind, I am going to explore some aspects of the formation of collective memory and identity among Syriac-speaking Christians of Sasanian Mesopotamia with a focus on the parabiblical composition known as the *Cave of Treasures* (hereafter referred to as CT). CT presents its readers with an extended narrative retelling of the biblical history of salvation that begins with the creation of the world and ends with Pentecost. Although ascribed to the famous fourth-century poet and theologian Ephrem the Syrian, it was composed much later, at the end of late antiquity. My choice of this work as the main topic of this investigation was determined by its unique character as the most developed attempt to co-opt the textual strategy of Biblical rewriting for the purposes of anti-Jewish polemic in the Syriac literary tradition, as well as by the fact that it stands at the watershed between the late antique and medieval periods and effectively serves as a milestone marking the transition to a new, ethnically-marked, discourse of identity among Syriac Christians.

In order to adequately apprehend CT's character as a vehicle of group memory and identity, it is necessary to situate the Christian community behind this composition as accurately as possible within the world of late ancient Christianity. Merely characterizing this work in general terms as a product of Syriac Christian culture would hardly suffice, as we need a more precise

---

[1] Stroumsa 2016.
[2] For a general introduction to the history and culture of Syriac Christians, see Brock et alii 2011; Briquel-Chatonnet & Debié 2017; King 2019.

understanding of the historical circumstances of the group that was responsible for its production.

What may be said with absolute certainty is that CT is undoubtedly of Christian origin and that it was originally composed in the Syriac language. Beyond this, there is disappointingly little explicit information that may allow scholars to contextualize it. Thus, nothing is known about the real author of the composition. Although in the majority of manuscripts CT's authorship is ascribed to Ephrem the Syrian, this attribution does not stand the test of scholarly scrutiny. Moreover, we do not have any direct information on the exact date or location of CT's composition, or on the Christian community that produced it. Any clues to the work's date and provenance must be deduced from its content.

It is not an easy task to situate CT within the diverse world of late antique Syriac Christianity. There seems to be a general agreement among scholars that it was composed sometime during the fifth or sixth century by a Syriac-speaking author who lived within the confines of the Sasanian empire. Operating on the basis of this consensus, I will attempt to contextualize CT more accurately. As I argue in chapter 2, this work was most likely produced during the time period between the middle of the sixth century and the first decades of the seventh. Furthermore, some internal and external considerations allow me to propose that CT's author belonged to a West Syrian, i.e. Miaphysite, confessional milieu.[3] Upon a close examination of CT, it becomes clear that the socio-cultural context of late Sasanian Iran is of primary importance for understanding the particular identity politics pursued by its author, a member of a Christian minority group entangled in a complex relationship with the dominant Iranian culture.

The long and rich history of the Christian presence in the territories controlled by Iranian dynasties, first the Parthians and then the Sasanians, can be traced back to perhaps the second century.[4] Although our sources for this

---

3 Throughout this book the term "Miaphysite" refers to those Christians of the late antique Middle East who rejected the Christological formula of the Council of Chalcedon (451); for general information, see Atiya 1968, pp. 167–235; Frend 1972. I use the label "West Syrian" to refer to the Syriac-speaking part of the anti-Chalcedonian movement (formerly known as "Jacobites"). While the majority of this faction was comprised of the followers of Severus of Antioch, it also included several other groups, such as the partisans of Severus' opponent Julian of Halicarnassus, known as "Phantasiasts" or "Aphthartodocetes." The label "East Syrian" designates members of the Church of the East, until recently often referred to as "Nestorians."

4 For a general introduction to the history of Christianity in Iran during late antiquity, see Asmussen 1983; Herman 2019; the most comprehensive treatment remains Labourt 1904. On the beginnings of Christianity in Iranian Mesopotamia, see Taylor, D.G.K. 2019, pp. 79–83.

period are very limited, it appears that under Parthian rule, the Christians living in their domain enjoyed a relative peace. Their situation, however, changed dramatically when the new Sasanian dynasty came to power in the year 224.[5] The subsequent history of Christians in Iranian lands was marked by a series of persecutions; or, at least, that is what the literature produced by the Christians of Iran, such the acts of the Persian martyrs written mostly in Syriac,[6] wanted its readers to believe. The most memorable of these outbreaks was the "Great Persecution" of Shapur II (r. 309–379), the true extent of which, however, is still debated by scholars.[7] There is no reason to doubt that there were occasional outbursts of violence from the Sasanian rulers against their Christian subjects, even if their extent was exaggerated in the latter's memory. This hostility was motivated, on the one side, by religious considerations, such as the Zoroastrian priesthood's zeal for defending their religion's prestige, and, perhaps to a greater degree, by the fear that Christians would collude with the Roman enemies of Iran on the other. Yet notwithstanding this, we see that their condition began to normalize and improve from the first decades of the fifth century, when Yazdgird I (r. 399–420) launched the policy of accommodating Christians in the empire by formally recognizing the Church at the council gathered in the year 410 at Seleucia-Ctesiphon.[8] After this, during the fifth and sixth centuries, and until the demise of Sasanian rule in 637, Christians became more and more integrated into the workings of Sasanian society, so that we hear about them being present at the royal court, serving in the army, and embarking on diplomatic missions to the Roman empire.

To understand the position of Syriac Christians in Sasanian society, one should also take into account such an important factor as their strained relationship with the well-established and influential Jewish community of Mesopotamia. From the fourth century on, we see Syriac Christian writers engaged in a constant polemic against Jews and Judaism, especially about the correct interpretation of the Bible. Similarly to what scholars observe in other Christian societies of late antiquity, anti-Judaism constituted a major driving force in the development of collective identity among the Christians of Mesopotamia. The central role of this factor for understanding workings of the identity discourse in CT is confirmed by the author himself, as he explicitly declares his work to be an exercise in anti-Jewish apologetic.

---

5 For general information on the Sasanians, see Christensen 1944; Daryaee 2009. On their policy towards Christians, see Labourt 1904, pp. 258–315; Brock 1982a; Rist 1996; Panaino 2004c; Herman 2014; Payne 2016a.
6 For a chronologically arranged inventory of this corpus, see Brock 2008a, pp. 77–95.
7 See Wiessner 1967; Mosig-Walburg 2005; Smith, K.R. 2016.
8 See Vergani 2017; McDonough 2008b.

The historical time frame of CT's composition was a formative period in the history of Syriac Christianity, crucial for the development of its two main branches, East Syrian and West Syrian.[9] This process was conditioned by the Christological pronouncements of the two Church councils that took place in the Roman empire during the fifth century: the Council of Ephesus, held in 431, eventually led to a fundamental break with the Church of the East in the Sasanian empire, whereas the Council of Chalcedon, held in 451, resulted in the Christians of the Roman empire splitting into two major factions: Chalcedonians, or Dyophysites, and anti-Chalcedonians, or Miaphysites. The sixth century saw the rise of the Miaphysite commonwealth, which encompassed several Eastern provinces of the Roman empire, most importantly Egypt and Syria, as well as territories of neighboring states such as the Sasanian empire, Aksumite Ethiopia, and the Nubian kingdoms.[10]

When we attempt to reconstruct the confessional map of the Christian world of the Sasanian empire during CT's time, the picture that emerges is complicated. While the Church of the East seems to be the dominant Christian confession throughout the empire until the middle of the sixth century, after the anti-Chalcedonian circles within the Roman empire had failed to reverse the official policy of supporting Chalcedon endorsed by Justinian I (r. 527–565), we observe a steady spread of Miaphysitism in the territories controlled by the Sasanians, especially in Northern Mesopotamia. As a result of this expansion, which culminated in the establishment of a separate Miaphysite hierarchy in the year 628 with Takrit as its center, we see West Syrian Christians playing a prominent role in Iranian society during the last decades of Sasanian rule. The extended occupation of the Eastern Roman provinces of Egypt and Syria, with their large Miaphysite communities, by Khosrow II's troops during the Byzantine–Sasanian war of 602–628, which must have significantly altered the balance of power between West Syrians and East Syrians within the Sasanian empire, contributed to the rise in the importance of this faction.[11]

Characterized by dramatic changes of fortune, the history of the Iranian Christians has attracted considerable attention from scholars. Much of the previous scholarship on Christianity in the Sasanian empire, however, gravitates toward one of two main poles: either that of the theological developments among the Syriac Christians of Iran, i.e. the formation of the distinctive "Nestorian" doctrine, or that of their troubled relationship with the authorities.

---

9   For a brief overview, see Menze 2019. On some important aspects of this process, see Brock 1982a; Menze 2008; Reinink 2009; Wood 2010.
10 See Frend 1972, pp. 255–315; Fowden, G. 1993, pp. 100–137; van Rompay 2005.
11 On Khosrow's policy of neutrality towards Christians in his empire, see Greatrex 2003.

As far as the latter is concerned, the primary focus was usually on the doleful history of persecutions waged by Sasanian rulers against their Christian subjects. While this interest is understandable, one of its detrimental side effects is that it can make one fall all too easily into the trap of forming a somewhat distorted picture of the Christian minority's place within Iranian society during late antiquity, in which the dominant motifs would be those of isolationism and staunch antagonism.[12] The focus on the audacious experience of the "Persian martyrs," as they are represented in their Syriac acts, caused scholars to overlook other, positive aspects of Christian interaction with Iranian society and culture. As a result, the problem of Christian–Iranian acculturation has received remarkably scant attention in much of the previous scholarship.[13]

The changes in this situation began relatively recently, so that one observes a substantial increase in scholarly interest in the integrative dimension of Christian–Iranian interaction in the context of the Sasanian empire. Several recent works have pursued this avenue of inquiry. Thus, Joel Walker, in his study of the early seventh-century *Acts of Mār Qardagh*, has demonstrated how Sasanian epic tradition influenced the work of a Syriac Christian hagiographer.[14] In his monograph, Richard Payne shows how during the sixth and seventh centuries, the East Syrian elites of the Sasanian empire sought to articulate their Christian identity in terms of Iranian culture, while striving to participate in Iranian social practices.[15] In addition to these monographs, there are a number of recent scholarly contributions that touch upon different aspects of the profound influence exercised by Iranian society and culture on the Syriac-speaking Christians.[16]

A preliminary observation that may be made on the basis of these studies is that acculturation was an important part of the Syriac-speaking Christian minority's strategic reaction to its prolonged exposure to Iranian culture within the confines of the Sasanian empire. The cumulative effect of recent scholarship on that subject underscores the need for a more balanced attitude to the question of relations between the Christian minority of the Sasanian empire

---

12   On this, see Payne 2015, pp. 10–16.
13   Among the rare exceptions are Taqizadeh 1940 and Widengren 1960.
14   Walker 2006, esp. pp. 121–163.
15   Payne 2015. See also Payne 2012.
16   See Hutter 2003; McDonough 2005; Suermann 2007; Schilling 2008; Jullien, Ch. 2009; Becker 2009; Panaino 2010; Jullien, F. 2015. The fundamental research on linguistic borrowing from Middle Persian into Syriac by Claudia Ciancaglini provides rich evidence of the familiarity of Syriac Christians with different aspects of Iranian culture. See Ciancaglini 2008.

and the dominant Iranian society and its culture, one that would put a greater emphasis on the integrative aspects of Christian–Sasanian interaction.

Looking for analogies, what comes to mind is the major methodological paradigm shift that has been taking place recently in the field of Jewish studies. There, the traditional view of Jewish history under Christian rule during late antiquity and the Middle Ages as a *historia lacrimosa* with the predominant leitmotifs of oppression and survival gave way to more complex models that take into account the Jews' cultural integration into Christian societies and mutual influences between the minority and majority cultures.[17] It is about time for a similar focal adjustment to be systematically carried out in research on Christian communities in the Sasanian empire. Further analytical efforts are necessary in order to reimagine this minority group not as merely powerless victims of the hostile regime, but as active agents of history who participated in a wide range of social, political, and cultural processes that took place in Iranian society and whose stand vis-à-vis the dominant culture was thus not limited to that of antagonism and denunciation.

It was during the last decades of the past century that the concept of collective identity—that is, how people experience themselves as members of various groups, which was primarily developed in the academic domains of sociology and social anthropology—transcended the confines of social sciences and became an important heuristic tool in the hands of historians. The usefulness of this notion for understanding ancient societies is confirmed by numerous works of scholars of the Greco-Roman world, as well as those of Jewish and Christian antiquity.[18] Yet although there are a considerable number of studies on the development of Christian identity during late antiquity and the Middle Ages, until recently, this field has been dominated by research confined mostly to the boundaries of Greek- and Latin-speaking parts of the Christian world.

There is a relative lack of systematic scholarly attention when it comes to the issues of identity formation in non-Western Christian groups such as Copts, Syrians, Ethiopians, Armenians, Arab Christians, and some other communities. As far as Syriac Christianity is concerned, the situation is somewhat better. There is a growing body of scholarly literature on the emergence and evolution of collective identities among Syriac Christians throughout the

---

17   Cf. Boyarin 2004; Yuval 2006; Elukin 2007; Chazan 2010.
18   Cf., for example, Hall 1997; Stenger 2009; Goodblatt 2006; Lieu 2004; Buell 2005; Johnson, A.P. 2006.

different periods of their history.[19] In that regard, the Leiden research group's pioneering work on the formation and development of West Syrian communal identity should be singled out.[20]

Important as they are, these studies do not yet present us with a sufficiently full picture of how Syriac Christian identity developed throughout the centuries, as they are either limited in time-span or deal with only one segment of the Syriac-speaking world, or with only one aspect of the complex phenomenon of collective identity. In view of this, the task of providing a comprehensive and systematic account of the formation of Syriac-speaking Christian identity, beginning with the period of late antiquity, has yet to be accomplished.

A necessary preliminary step towards that goal, I believe, involves the analysis of the dynamics of identity formation on the level of separate key authors or literary compositions. Many of the previous studies of Christian identity in general and Syriac Christian identity in particular have focused on processes and trends that cut across a variety of authors, texts, and other bodies of evidence. Although epistemologically legitimate, this approach runs the risk of turning a blind eye to the importance of individual agency in shaping collective identities. In my opinion, it should be balanced by placing the analytical focus on individual authors in a more consistent and in-depth manner.

At the outset, some clarifications are also necessary concerning the use of the term "identity," which has become a buzzword in the academic community as well as in society in general.[21] People evoke identity when they want to make sense of themselves, of what they do, and of what they have in common with others and how they differ from them. It is customary among scholars to distinguish between individual and collective identity. However, given that the human mind and selfhood do not exist outside of relationships, this distinction should be understood not as absolute, but rather as reflecting the opposite ends of a continuum, constituted on one side by the self-image of a particular person and on the other by its public image, when "each is constructed in terms of the other and in terms of her perceived similarity or difference to others.

---

19 See several articles by Fergus Millar on the sociolinguistic aspects of Syriac Christian identity in the late Roman empire, reprinted in Millar 2015; the collective volume edited by van Ginkel et alii 2005; Menze 2008; Wood 2010; Debié 2015; Becker 2015; Smith, K.R. 2016; Tannous 2018a.

20 For a description of this project and its results, see ter Haar Romeny 2004; ter Haar Romeny 2005a; ter Haar Romeny et alii 2009, and other publications in this issue of *Church History and Religious Culture*; ter Haar Romeny 2012; Immerzeel 2009; Snelders 2010.

21 For a general introduction to the burgeoning field of identity studies, see Alcoff 2003; Woodward 2004; Jenkins 2008.

The difference is who is doing the perceiving, who is doing the constructing."[22] What underlies the logic of all identification, whether personal or collective, is the dialectics of similarity and difference.

Although personal identities can only be realized within the framework of collective ones, for analytical purposes, it still remains useful to distinguish between individuality and collectivity when speaking about identity. In the most general terms, collective or social identity may be described as "a person's awareness of being a member of a group."[23] As there are many modes of self-definition, each person ascribes multiple collective identities to themselves which can be based on criteria such as gender, kinship, territory, social position, occupation, education, religion, ethnicity, culture, or nationality. Regardless of which of these criteria are chosen, the building of a collective identity involves social groups achieving a certain cohesion and continuity through the process of associating oneself with other individuals or reference groups so that one comes to adopt their objectives and values and to share their experience.

It is now a commonplace in social thought that collective identity is never a given, but is always a result of discursive construction. The contemporary social constructionist perspective on group identity underscores its transactional and situationally flexible character. I find particularly useful the basic processual model of the construction of identity advocated by Richard Jenkins.[24] In his opinion, instead of conceiving "identity" as a fixed and stable characteristic that human groups possess, we should rather speak of the ongoing and open-ended process of "identification," understood as "the production and reproduction during interaction of the intermingling, and inseparable, themes of human similarity and difference."[25]

According to the conceptual framework that Jenkins outlined, any group identity should be analyzed as an outcome of the simultaneous dialectic of similarity and difference, conceived as the interrelated moments of internal—external definition through inclusion and exclusion. The internal aspect of this phenomenon finds its expression in the process of "collective internal definition," i.e. the group's self-identification, while the external does so in the process of "collective external definition," i.e. the categorization of the group by others.[26] It should be noted that the movement of collective internal definition

---

22 Jenkins 2008, p. 73.
23 Malina 2007, p. 103.
24 Jenkins 2008.
25 Jenkins 2008, p. 118.
26 See Jenkins 2008, pp. 102–111.

is also twofold, as it involves not only self-identification, but also categorization of others.

As has just been mentioned, there are various strategies of identification that can be employed in order to achieve group cohesion. While focusing on the most fundamental "Christian" dimension of the collective identity constructed by CT's author, I will first of all analyze those strategies that articulate collective difference using a religious framework, such as the narrative politics of self-assertion vis-à-vis Jewish and Zoroastrian "others." In addition to this, I will take seriously the "Syriac" aspect of CT and pay attention to a complementary strategy of collective internal definition employed in our composition; namely, its author's use of ethnic reasoning. This latter point demands further elucidation.

Rooted in the modern preoccupation with cultural, ethnic, and national diversity, attentiveness to ethnicity as an important dimension of identity in intercultural situations is cultivated by scholars in various fields of the humanities and social sciences. Students of ancient societies and cultures, including those of the Mediterranean and Near Eastern world, have not remained oblivious to this intellectual challenge. The last years have seen an increasing amount of academic studies that delve more deeply into the workings of ethnic, racial, and nationalistic identities in these regions.[27]

However universalistic and inclusive the original vision of Christianity might have been, judging by Paul's famous proclamation that in Christ "there is no longer Jew or Greek, ... slave or free, ... male or female" (Galatians 3:28), the religious movement inaugurated by Jesus and his disciples was never uniform. As the followers of the new faith increased in number, inner-Christian tensions and factionalism began to play an increasingly important role. There was more than one line of fissure along which Christians would split into distinctive, often mutually competitive or even antagonistic groups. Scholars have singled out a wide range of factors that worked as key catalysts of internal division throughout the history of Christianity, such as those related to confessional, political, cultural, territorial, linguistic, and several other forms of self-identification. As has been made clear by several recent studies, ethnic self-understanding and self-definition should be regarded as one of the major driving forces in the

---

27   On ethnicity in the ancient Near East, including ancient Israel, see Limet, 2005; Grosby 2002; Killebrew 2005. For the Greco-Roman world, see Herring 2009; Hall, J.M. 1997; Bilde et alii 1992; Isaac 2004. For important contributions on ethnicity in ancient Judaism, see Cohen, Sh.J.D. 1999; Goodblatt 2006.

development of a sense of collective selfhood among Christians, beginning from the very early period of the new religion's existence.[28]

But what do scholars mean when they speak about "ethnicity"? In accordance with the constructionist perspective, which is almost universally accepted in social studies, ethnic identity, much like any other identity, is considered not as a "natural" fact of life, but as "something to be actively proclaimed, reclaimed, and disclaimed through discursive channels."[29] There are many definitions of ethnicity in the social sciences that compete with or complement each other. While a full discussion of this field would demand a separate study, I will limit myself to pointing out the two main methodological approaches to ethnic identity that have gained currency in modern scholarship.

On the one hand, some scholars try to establish a limited number of specific ideological constructs whose presence would definitively mark a given collective identity as ethnic. One of the most prominent proponents of such an approach to ethnicity is Anthony Smith. In his influential work *The Ethnic Origins of Nations*, Smith singles out six characteristics of ethnic identity that distinguish it from other forms of collective identity: a collective name, a common myth of descent, a sense of shared history, a distinctive shared culture, an association with a specific territory, and a sense of communal solidarity.[30]

This methodological approach, however, was met with a well-founded criticism on the part of those scholars who instead prefer to speak about a "polythetic" definition of ethnicity. From the perspective of this conceptual framework, none of the elements that may define the ethnic group, such as physical features, language, religion, or culture (including a myth of common descent or shared history), is either a necessary or a sufficient criterion for considering such an identification to be ethnic. This approach to ethnicity has been advocated, among others, by Walter Pohl, who claims that there is only one element which seems to be specific to ethnicity: "Whatever distinctive features serve as 'boundary markers,' they are perceived as expressions of an innermost self, an ingrained common nature."[31] In Pohl's opinion, while most social identities have a point of reference—i.e. the common denominator that defines the community—outside the group, it is only in the case of ethnic identity that "the principle of distinction and the symbolic essence of the community are thought to lie in the human group itself."[32] A conceptually

---

28   See Byron 2002; Buell 2005; Johnson, A.P. 2006; Hodge 2007.
29   Hall, J.M. 1997, p. 182.
30   See Smith, A.D. 1986, pp. 22–31.
31   Pohl 2012, p. 10.
32   Pohl 2012, p. 10.

related view of ethnicity has recently been expressed by Aaron Johnson. In his examination of ethnic argumentation in the works of Eusebius of Caesarea, this scholar proposes that the only *sine qua non* for defining ancient ethnicities is claims made by ancient authors vis-à-vis peoplehood, i.e. "that a people are said to constitute an *ethnos*—whatever the markers of difference that are employed to distinguish them from other peoples."[33]

An important point Pohl makes is that ethnic identification rarely occurs in its pure form, since "it has to attach itself to other, more tangible forms of community—a homeland, state, army or religion."[34] Accordingly, ethnicity can hardly ever be studied on its own, but only as one of several forms of identification through which all historical group identities are aggregated, such as territorial, political, religious, and some others. The main task of a student of social identity is thus to establish the strategies of group identification that operate in the particular case of the community under study; the discursive channels through which they are produced and negotiated; and how they interact with each other.

It is this minimalist and process-oriented approach to ethnicity that I will use in my study. In what follows, I analyze CT not as an expression of an existing Syriac Christian identity, but as a historically conditioned site of production and negotiation of a new form of Christian collective identification. Insofar as CT conforms to the minimal requirement of ethnicity—that is, it exhibits an awareness of "Syriac" peoplehood, testified by the author's use of the ethnonym *Suryāyē*, "Syrians"—I shall also approach collective identity in this work from the conceptual angle of ethnic identification.

Consequently, instead of attempting to measure the ethnic argumentation that CT's author employs by the standards of a fixed list of features that comprise the preconceived "ideal" ethnic identity, my task is to explore the narrative strategies of collective identification as they are actually operative in this composition. Using Jenkins' terminology, the primary focus of my attention in this study of Syriac Christian identity is the process of "collective internal identification." I intend to demonstrate that CT marks a new stage in the history of the development of Syriac Christian identity, as its author creates an original ethno-religious model of Christian group identity in which he brings together religious and ethnic strategies of collective identification. To achieve that objective, I am going to examine how his construction of the narrative of the foundational past addresses the themes of difference and similarity by

---

33 Johnson, A.P. 2006, pp. 29–30.
34 Pohl 2012, p. 10.

categorizing others, such as "Jews" and "Persians," and by identifying his own group of "Syrians."

In my analysis of CT as a testimony to the formation of a Christian collective identity within a particular West Syrian faction of Syriac Christianity, I am especially indebted to the conceptual approach of the Leiden research group on identity formation among Syrian Orthodox Christians.[35] The general model of the development of West Syrian collective identity during late antiquity and the Middle Ages proposed by these scholars envisages this process as a gradual shift from a religious to an ethno-religious modus of identification. In a publication that presents the main results of this research project, Bas ter Haar Romeny singles out the seventh century as the crucial period in this convoluted process, since it was during that time that "the Syriac Orthodox developed from a religious association to a community that gradually acquired the sense of being an ethnic community."[36] It is this framework of the historical development of West Syrian identity that I find most useful and methodologically suitable for my own research. My adoption of the Leiden group's approach in this investigation is also warranted by the emphasis that it places on biblical interpretation as a particularly important vehicle in the process of identity formation among West Syrians.[37]

The main objective of this study is to examine how CT's author participated in the multifarious process of identity formation by offering his own vision of Syriac Christian collective identity, deeply rooted in the biblical past, in which cultural and religious elements were closely interwoven. As can be seen from CT's content, the primary purpose of its narrative is to preserve the memory of the distant past, encompassing events from the Old and New Testaments. This enables us to analyze this work from the methodological angle of memory studies, a relatively new field of research that explores the ways in which people, either individuals or groups, construct a sense of the past.[38]

The modern rediscovery of memory in sociology is closely connected with the name of the French sociologist Maurice Halbwachs, who was one of the first to call attention to the social aspect of human memory and who argued that memory was a specifically social phenomenon.[39] One of Halbwachs' lasting contributions to the conceptual apparatus of social sciences and the

---

35 For references to their publications, see n. 20 above.
36 ter Haar Romeny 2012, p. 196.
37 See ter Haar Romeny 2004; ter Haar Romeny et alii 2009, pp. 384–388.
38 For a general introduction, see Whitehead 2009; Misztal 2003; Erll 2011; Kattago 2015.
39 See Halbwachs 1925, 1941.

humanities was the notion of "collective memory," which presupposes a give-and-take relationship between personal memory and the memory of the collective to which a person belongs. According to Halbwachs, every human group comprising any given society develops a memory of its own past that serves as a foundation for its distinctive identity. Addressing the past is thus an indispensable element of a group's collective memory, which in its turn is a necessary prerequisite for a stable collective identity. Human groups predominantly base their awareness of their unity and uniqueness on events that took place in the past, either remote in time or not so distant.

The particular direction within memory studies that has the most relevance for our case is related to the notion of "cultural memory," which was developed more than two decades ago by Jan Assmann, a German Egyptologist.[40] In his elaboration of Halbwachs' ideas and those of other sociologists about collective or social memory, Assmann distinguishes between its two basic types: "communicative" and "cultural" memory.[41] The former comprises "memories related to the recent past," i.e. "historical experiences in the framework of individual biographies" that rely on everyday communication and are handed down within a limited time horizon. In distinction from this biographical memory, "cultural memory" has a strong foundational character as it relates to origins and accumulates residues of much more distant pasts. According to Assmann, cultural memory does not strive to preserve the past as it was, but transforms it by condensing it into symbolic figures of memory. Doing so in order to make the past relevant for explaining the present, cultural memory "transforms factual into remembered history, thus turning it into myth."[42]

It is this focus on the mythical history of origins that makes this second type of collective memory a key factor in the formation of group identities. This aspect of cultural memory was highlighted by Assmann himself, who noted that its main function is "to keep the foundational past alive in the present, and this connection to the past provides a basis for the identity of the remembering group."[43] In his discussion of discursive channels of cultural memory in society, Assmann points out that it functions through a variety of "institutionalized mnemotechnics," both linguistic and nonlinguistic.[44]

In the case of literate societies, it is the practice of history writing that constitutes one of the most powerful and sophisticated linguistic mnemotechnics

---

40   See Assmann 2011, esp. pp. 15–141.
41   Assmann 2011, pp. 35–41.
42   Assmann 2011, p. 38.
43   Assmann 2011, p. 38.
44   Assmann 2011, p. 37.

in the service of cultural memory. Historical writing is here evoked not in the narrow sense of historiography as a specifically defined literary genre, but in the broad sense envisioned by the Dutch historian Johan Huizinga, who defines history as "the intellectual form in which a civilization renders account to itself of its past."[45] The contribution of this type of intellectual creativity, which can express itself in a wide range of literary genres including but not limited to historiography, chronography, mythography, genealogy, biography, hagiography, and parabiblical writing, to the processes of developing and maintaining of collective identities, is attracting more and more attention among scholars of ancient Christianity.[46]

My book contributes to this field of research by conceptualizing CT as an exercise in the construction of cultural memory. This methodological choice is justified by the fact that in his work, our Syriac Christian author deals with the foundational past of myth, in Assmann's sense of the word. Taking this into consideration, I intend to explore how CT's author resorts to the textual strategy of Biblical rewriting and reshapes the master narrative of Christianity's foundational past, enshrined in the writings of the Old and New Testaments, in line with the perceptions and needs of his contemporary reality.

The central role played by historiographical literature and related strategies of appealing to the past in the development of collective identities among Syriac-speaking Christians of late antiquity and the Middle Ages has received increasing attention in the recent academic literature.[47] In his discussion of the use of history by the famous seventh-century West Syrian theologian Jacob of Edessa, Jan van Ginkel singled out three main functions of historical writing in the context of Christian identity-building.[48] First of all, the writing of history is meant to create a sense of continuity within a Christian community through forging a connection with the formative period of Church history, i.e. the days of Christ and his immediate disciples. In addition to this, the past was commonly evoked in order to affirm the antiquity of a group vis-à-vis its rivals, Christian and non-Christian alike, in accordance with the cultural conventions of the ancient world, where the argument from antiquity, i.e. the belief that the most ancient traditions are the most authoritative, enjoyed great popularity. Finally, the third important aspect of historical writing in the service of collective identity finds its expression in the establishment of boundaries with

---

45 Huizinga 1936, p. 9.
46 See, for instance, Cameron 2001; Lieu 2004, pp. 62–97; Mendels 2004; Castelli 2004; Stroumsa 2005.
47 See Morony 2005; van Ginkel 2005, 2008; Debié 2009, 2016; Weltecke 2009; Payne 2012.
48 van Ginkel 2005, pp. 72–73.

other groups, whether within the fold of Christian coreligionists or outside of it. In the course of my investigation, I shall pay attention to each of these three aspects and to how they interplay with each other in the original narrative of the biblical past created by CT's author.

In the search for an appropriate framework for discussing issues related to the development of a collective identity among the Christians of the Sasanian empire, including the author of CT and his community, another important methodological point should be made. Throughout most of their history, Syriac-speaking Christians lived under the political domination of other ethnic or religious groups, regardless of how demographically significant they might have been in a given territory. This is true for both the late Roman empire and Sasanian Iran, as well as for various Islamic polities that came to rule over the Middle East in their stead. This situation of permanent political, religious, and often cultural subjugation inevitably exerted a profound impact on how Syriac Christians conceived of themselves and of their society in general. This impact can be assessed if we turn to the critical methods developed within the field of postcolonial studies, which enable us to recognize how cultural forms reflect the dynamics of power relationships between dominating and dominated groups in a given society.[49] Engendered by the intellectual critique of imperialism in the aftermath of the anti-colonial struggles of the past century, the postcolonial turn in the humanities primarily focuses on the critique of hegemonic discourse. This critique operates by shedding light on "the power of hegemonic cultures to shape discourse while illuminating the increasingly autonomous self-representation of previously marginalized societies, ethnic groups and literatures."[50]

Although the field of postcolonial studies developed from primarily focusing on the modern period, students of the ancient and medieval world are increasingly finding its insights useful for describing cultural dynamics in pre-modern societies. However, the spread of its methods in these academic circles shows an uneven pattern of distribution, so that when it comes to the world of late antiquity, the majority of the research is concentrated on the Roman empire,[51] whereas the dynamics of imperial hegemony and its discontents within the Sasanian realm remain virtually unexplored.[52] It could be particularly fruitful

---

49 For a general introduction to postcolonial theory, see Young 2003; Loomba 2015; Bachmann-Medick 2016, pp. 131–173.
50 Bachmann-Medick 2016, p. 132.
51 Cf. Draper 2004; Sommer 2012; Leander 2013; Labahn & Lehtipuu 2015.
52 Regarding the empire's Jewish minority, see now Gross 2017.

to examine the culture of Syriac Christians, a perennial subaltern group, from this theoretical angle. However, while postcolonial theory has already gained a certain currency among students of ancient and medieval Christendom, scholars of Syriac Christianity seem to be slow to recognize its explanatory potential.[53]

I believe that turning to the instruments and insights of postcolonial studies may enrich our understanding of the processes of identity formation among Syriac Christians during late antiquity and later periods. In CT's case, this approach seems to be particularly relevant for analyzing how its author makes use of Iranian themes and imagery. By evoking the postcolonial concept of cultural hybridity in connection with the representation of Iranian royal figures in CT,[54] I hope to facilitate a new way of thinking about the culture of the Syriac-speaking Christians of the Sasanian empire.

The heart of this book, comprised by chapters 2 to 4, provides a close examination of the three most significant strategies of collective identification that CT's author employs in his reworking of the biblical past. The first two are concerned with establishing difference, primarily conceived in religious terms. One of them, analyzed in chapter 2, is directed against the Jewish "other" and manifests itself in a pronounced anti-Jewish stance that characterizes the work as a whole. The second strategy, discussed in chapter 3, is expressed in the author's close engagement with the Iranian "other," which is pursued on different levels, both as a polemic against Zoroastrianism and as a creative appropriation of ideas and images primarily related to the domain of Iranian kingship. The third major strategy of identification, analyzed in chapter 4, is internally oriented and involves argumentation based on ethnic reasoning, which our author used in order to promote a peculiar vision of Syrian uniqueness that elevates his community not only over the non-Christian "others," but also over the rest of the Christian world. In order to establish the extent of CT's author's originality in his reliance on these strategies of identification, they are examined in the diachronic context of other writings produced by Christians during late antiquity.

My primary concern in focusing on these three aspects of collective identity in CT is to expose their role as main factors in its author's creation of an up-to-date version of Christian cultural memory that would meet the needs of

---

53 This trend, however, is starting to change. See the recent contributions by Becker 2015; Georgia 2018; Loosley 2018. For some useful observations, see also Brock 1982a; Becker 2009; Panaino 2010; Payne 2012.
54 See section 2 of chapter 3 below.

his community. Each of these chapters ends with concluding observations in which its particular findings are put into the broader context of the cultural and socio-political dynamics of late antique Mesopotamia. By attempting to articulate the possible relationship between the cultural and the social in CT, I follow the lead of Alon Confino, who, in an insightful critique of memory studies, calls scholars to ground the notion of collective memory within a rigorous theoretical framework by using it "as an explanatory device that links representation and social experience."[55]

[55] Confino 1997, p. 1402.

CHAPTER 1

Genre, Date, and Provenance of CT

Since every collective identity emerges as a response to particular historical, political, and socio-cultural circumstances, in order to be able to adequately comprehend it, it is necessary to contextualize all of its discursive channels with the greatest possible precision. In this preliminary chapter, I am going to clarify this aspect of CT by addressing the complicated set of issues related to identifying its genre, date, and original milieu.

1   Content and Genre

CT offers its readers an extended retelling of biblical history that begins with the creation of the world and ends with Pentecost. In its title, the authorship of the work is ascribed to Ephrem the Syrian, the famous fourth-century Syriac poet and theologian. Although this identification certainly cannot be accepted as true, it is important to help us to understand the agenda of CT's real author,[1] whose identity is unknown.

The main organizing principle of CT's narrative is the division of the time-span from Adam to Jesus into six large sections, in accordance with the six thousand years into which the entire course of human history is supposedly divided. The narrative thus presents the history of salvation, which encompasses 5500 years and spans from the beginning of the first millennium to the middle of the sixth millennium, following the general sequence of events as they unfold in the canonical narratives of the Old and New Testaments. The first thousand years (chs. 1–10) cover the period from the first day of the creation of the world to the rule of Jared (Gen 5:15–20). The second thousand years (chs. 11–17) describe the events from Jared's reign to Noah and his family boarding the ark during the Flood (Gen 7:7). The third thousand years (chs. 18–24) deal with the period from the Flood up to the rule of Reu (Gen 11:18–21). The fourth thousand years (chs. 25–34) describe the period from Reu's reign to the rule of Ehud, son of Gera (Judg 3:15–26). The fifth thousand years (chs. 35–42) cover the time-span from the rule of Jabin of Canaan (Judg 4:2–24) to the second year of the reign of the Persian king Cyrus. The concluding section of CT (chs. 42–54) covers the five hundred years from the second year of Cyrus' reign

---

1   On this, see section 5 of chapter 4 below.

to the birth of Christ and culminates in a detailed account of the execution and resurrection of Jesus.

CT's author offers a condensed and rather peculiar version of the Christian *Heilsgeschichte*, which has no immediate precedents in Christian writings from late antiquity. CT's unique literary character has been noted by scholars such as Sebastian Brock, who characterizes it as a "highly idiosyncratic work."[2] Although CT's author presents his work as a genealogical composition,[3] the scope of the information that he chooses to include in it is much wider and goes far beyond what one might expect from such a description. Since it deals with the past, CT could be generally described as a historiographical composition. A more precise generic classification of this work, however, would involve a close analysis of its literary structure and a comparison of it with other compositions that possess similar formal traits, a task that would require a separate investigation. Moreover, such an inquiry would face a considerable challenge if the inherently dynamic and fluid nature of ancient literary genres, including that of historiography, was taken into consideration.[4] In what follows, I will merely briefly discuss the most important genre-defining features of CT.

First of all, we should take note of the work's self-identification as "the book on the succession of generations" (*ktābā d-ʿal yubāl šarbātā*) incorporated into its title (CT 1.1).[5] The authenticity of this characteristic is confirmed by explicit statements made by the author later in the narrative that the primary purpose of his entire literary endeavor was to provide his audience with a correct genealogy from Adam to Christ.[6] Within the narrative of CT, the noun *yubālā*, "propagation, origin, course, succession, tradition," is used to refer to different kinds of genealogical lines, which include (a) the "royal succession" (*yubālā d-malkutā*), CT 33.8 (cf. also CT 39.10); (b) the "succession in the genealogy of Jesus Christ" (*yubālā b-iliduteh d-Yešuʿ mšiḥā*), CT 33.16; (c) the "succession of the children of Israel" (*yubālā da-bnay Isrāēl*), CT 34.1; and (d) the "succession of priests" (*yubālā d-kāhnē*), CT 42.7. The exact phrase "succession of

---

2 Brock 1999, p. 334.
3 On this, see below.
4 This point was stressed in connection with the Greco-Roman tradition of historical writing by Marincola 1999. For a useful discussion of instability of historiographical genre, see also Roest 1999.
5 Here and in what follows, the Syriac text of CT is given according to ms. British Library, Add. 25875 (= Or^A of Ri's classification, which I will follow in order to refer to the manuscripts used in his edition), unless specified otherwise. For an explanation of this textual choice, see section 2.3 below. The chapter and verse division follows Ri's 1987 edition.
6 Cf. CT 44, esp. 13–51, where the whole genealogical succession, comprised of sixty-three families, is presented as a list, and 54.16–17.

generations" also appears in CT 44.1–5, which mentions the triple destruction of the Jews' genealogical books.

The claim of being first and foremost a genealogical work makes CT a *sui generis* composition, as it has no immediate analogues among Syriac or other Christian literary traditions of antiquity. The most obvious precedents in that regard would be the genealogical lists in the Old Testament (cf. Gen 5; Gen 11:11–32; 1Chr 1–9) and the genealogies of Jesus in the Gospels.[7] CT's connection to the biblical genealogical tradition becomes even more apparent if we consider that the Syriac author uses the nouns *šarbātā* and *tawldātā* (a cognate of the Biblical Hebrew technical term *tôlēdôt*, "generations") synonymously, as can be seen from such phrases as "the true succession of the generations of their fathers" (*yubālā šarirā d-tawldātā d-'abāhāyhun*) in CT 44.8 or "the succession of the generations of David" (*yubālā d-tawldātēh d-Dawid*) in CT 44.49. Although CT's author was not the first Christian writer who attempted to solve problems related to establishing a correct genealogy for Jesus,[8] the particular literary format he employed sets his project apart from other attempts made in that direction.[9]

When trying to determine CT's intertextual affinity, we should take into account that its author, who was hiding behind the name of Ephrem, does not claim to have produced his work in a complete vacuum. In order to buttress his claim of being an unrivaled expert in genealogical knowledge, able to present a correct line of succession from Adam to Jesus, he makes vague references to works by some earlier writers, both Jewish and Christian. On several occasions, he claims his superiority vis-à-vis some unspecified "ancient writers" (*maktbānē qadmāyē*).[10] In CT 42.6, he asserts his superiority over "the writers of the Hebrews, Greeks, and Syrians" (*maktbānē d-'Ebrāyē wa-d-Yawnāyē wa-d-Suryāyē*), who were active before Nebuchadnezzar's destruction of Jerusalem.[11] In an even more detailed statement in CT 44.8–16, the narrator reproaches both the "many writers" (*maktbānē sagi'ē*) among the Jews and "our own writers, the children of the Church" (*maktbānē dilan bnay 'idtā*)

---

7   On this genre, see Johnson, M.D. 1969; Robinson, R.B. 1986; Levin 2001.
8   These problems arose from discrepancies between the two versions of Jesus' genealogy found in the New Testament, i.e. in the Gospel of Matthew (Mt 1:2–17) and the Gospel of Luke (Lk 3:23–38). See Johnson, M.D. 1969, pp. 139–256; Brown 1993, pp. 57–95.
9   For earlier and more intellectually sophisticated attempts, see Julius Africanus' *Letter to Aristides* (ed. Guignard 2011) and the *Gospel Questions and Solutions* by Eusebius of Caesarea (ed. Pearse 2010).
10 Cf. CT 15.4; 24.11; 33.1; 44.1.
11 A similar list appears in CT 44.14, where the author points out the inability of "the Greek writers, and the Hebrew writers, and even the Syriac writers" (ܠܐ ܡܟܬܒܢܐ ܝܘܢܝܐ ܘܠܐ ܥܒܪܝܐ ܘܐܦܠܐ ܣܘܪܝܝܐ) to provide the correct genealogical information.

for their incompetence, claiming that he is the one who is able to supply the correct genealogical information thanks to "the grace of Christ." However, in none of these cases does CT's author provide the writers' names or the titles of the works with which he claims to be acquainted, the only exception being CT 17.22, where he explicitly relies on the authority of "the seventy wise writers" (*šabʿin maktbānē ḥakimē*), i.e. the translators of the Septuagint, for the chronology of Noah's boarding of the Ark.

The author's choice to divide the whole course of biblical history into the six millennia as the main organizing principle of the narrative betrays his indebtedness to the concept of *septimana mundi*, i.e. the "world-week," a specifically Christian version of the general chronological approach known as millenarianism.[12] According to this doctrine, which gained considerable currency among Christian intellectuals and is connected with the names of such third-century writers as Hippolytus of Rome and Julius Africanus, the whole time-span of human history is divided into seven periods, each lasting 1000 years. The notion of *septimana mundi* is based on a typological interpretation of the creation week in Genesis 1, where the six days of creation represent the time of this world, while the seventh day of Sabbath rest signifies the eschatological future of the world to come.

As far as the general notion of *septimana mundi* is concerned, there is a certain affinity between CT and earlier Christian historiographical works such as Julius Africanus' *Chronography*.[13] However, there seems to be insufficient ground to speak of a direct influence of Africanus on CT. The principal difference between the two compositions is that whereas the main driving force behind Africanus' project is an attempt to harmonize two different chronological systems, biblical and classical, with its succession of Olympiads, the Syriac author is completely uninterested in the Greco-Roman chronographical tradition and exclusively bases his chronology on the biblical sequence of events.

Furthermore, CT's author's use of the Creation as the starting point of his narrative and the fact that it encompasses the subsequent world history in a linear manner bring his work close to the genre of "universal history" or "world chronicle," a specific form of Christian historiography that enjoyed considerable popularity during late antiquity.[14] The genre of Christian world chronicle

---

12 On this aspect of CT, see Leonhard 2001, pp. 285–287. On the development of this notion, see Daniélou 1948; Luneau 1964. On its popularity in Syriac Christian tradition, see Witakowski 1990a; Bruns 2002.
13 For an edition of all surviving textual witnesses of this work, see Wallraff et alii 2007.
14 See Momigliano 1983; Croke 1983; Adler 1989; Allen 2003; Wallraff 2011.

that apparently begins with Julius Africanus developed based on Greek chronographical writing and the Jewish Hellenistic tradition of historiography. In distinction from the classical forms of Greco-Roman historiography, history in these writings was interpreted within a universalist Christian framework that was based on the Bible as the most important and authoritative source of historical knowledge. Covering the widest possible time-span, from the beginning of time to contemporary events, the Christian authors of these works sought to uncover how a divine and providential plan was unfolding throughout the course of human history.

The narrative of CT, which begins with the Creation and presents the subsequent history of the world in a linear manner, shares its general organizing principle with these works. There are, however, significant differences as well. Thus, contrary to the common practice of other Christian chronographers, CT's author does not attempt to integrate recent events into his work, as he stops at Pentecost and does not extend his narrative to the later period of Christian history. Moreover, even in the part of human history that he does cover, the scope of our author's attention is not nearly as universal as that of his Greek- and Latin-writing writers, since he makes almost no attempt to supplement his narrative using non-biblical sources systematically.

CT's author builds his composition by creatively amalgamating accounts from both the Old and New Testaments into a new coherent narrative. This new idiosyncratic version of Christian sacred history features a considerable amount of material that is not found in the two canonical collections. Some of these traditions may be traced back to classical, Jewish, or Zoroastrian sources, or to the various strands of the earlier tradition of Christian biblical interpretation, whereas the origins of some others are difficult to establish with certainty.[15] Our author's selective blending of canonical and extra-canonical material within the general framework of the biblical master narrative allows us to characterize his work as a representative of the broadly defined category of "rewritten Bible/Scripture" or parabiblical writing.

This quasi-genre—or better say textual strategy, the appropriate designation and precise formal characteristics of which are still hotly debated by scholars, has its beginning in Jewish literary and exegetical creativity in the Second Temple period.[16] Among its earliest specimens are such compositions as the *Book of Jubilees*, Josephus' *Jewish Antiquities*, the *Genesis Apocryphon*,

---

15 One of the most notable among the latter is the figure of Yonṭon, Noah's fourth son (CT 27.6–11). For attempts to explain this tradition, see Gero 1980; Toepel 2006.

16 For general information, see Alexander, Ph.S. 1988; Falk 2007; Crawford 2008; Zahn 2020.

and several others writings from Qumran, in which biblical material is refashioned with a greater or lesser degree of modification into new narratives that serve the particular agendas of their authors and communities. A similarly "free" approach to the canonical texts was also adopted at a very early stage by many Christian authors, who would naturally extend it to the New Testament writings as well.[17] As far as the complicated problem of the relationship between these texts and their canonical prototypes is concerned, I find particularly useful the theoretical model developed by Hindy Najman, who, in a seminal discussion of early Jewish reworkings of biblical narratives such as the *Book of Jubilees* and 11QTemple Scroll, has proposed that they were produced not in order to replace Scripture, but that their authors were thereby seeking to participate in the authoritative "Mosaic discourse" by providing the appropriate interpretative context in which canonical scriptural traditions could be properly understood.[18]

The authors of scriptural paraphrases sought to safeguard the authoritative message of canonical texts by transforming them into literary forms suitable for their own times and cultures. It is very often the case that the alterations of canonical narratives by their later emulators reveal a surplus of meaning that reflects new developments in the self-understanding of their authors or communities of readers. By retelling biblical history, while assuming the name of Ephrem, CT's author aimed to provide his community with an accessible and authoritative version of sacred history, which at the same time would address the new challenges that it faced.

Another literary characteristic of CT that has great significance for understanding it from a functional genre perspective is the marked presence of an apologetic element in this composition. This aspect of CT is made explicit in the narrator's claim that he undertook the work of providing the accurate genealogy of Jesus and Mary in order to defend his coreligionists against the Jews, who would challenge Christians in the matter of Mary's descent (CT 44.1–2). The integral character of the apologetic tendency in CT is confirmed by the abundant presence of anti-Jewish polemic scattered throughout the work.[19]

Apologetics—that is, the explanation, justification, and defense of a person's or group's system of beliefs—was one of the major fields of intellectual activity in the multiconfessional world of the late ancient Near East, where

---

17 See Roberts 1985; Thomas 2003; Green, R.P.H. 2006; Czachesz 2010.
18 Najman 2002, pp. 41–69. See also the discussion of this problem in Brooke 2005; Petersen 2007.
19 Both these aspects are analyzed in detail in chapter 3.

various religious groups, such as Jews, Christians, Zoroastrians, and "Pagans," vied for power and influence.[20] While a variety of literary and non-literary media could be and actually were used for that purpose, the apologetic use of history writing became one of the most sophisticated and efficient tools in such inter-communal power struggles.[21] The importance of this particular intellectual practice for the development and maintenance of collective identities in antiquity was rooted in "the pre-modern perception of culture which explicitly and implicitly regarded the imagined past as the sole legitimate basis for appraising the legitimacy of the present and envisioning or shaping the future."[22]

In his seminal monograph on the beginnings of the use of history writing for apologetic purposes, Gregory Sterling singled out a subgenre of "apologetic historiography" within the ethnographic and historiographical literature of the Hellenistic and early Roman world, to which he assigned works by ancient writers such as the Babylonian Berossos, the Egyptian Manetho, and the Hellenistic Jewish historians Demetrios, Artapanus, Eupolemos, and Flavius Josephus, as well as the Christian author of Luke–Acts. According to Sterling, all these historical compositions should be categorized as representatives of this genre because they present "the story of a subgroup of people in an extended prose narrative written by a member of the group who follows the group's own traditions but Hellenizes them in an effort to establish the identity of the group within the setting of the larger world."[23]

The theory of "apologetic historiography" that Sterling developed has recently been subjected to further refinement by Todd Penner, who suggests that it would be more appropriate to analyze the apologetic dimension of these and some other Greco-Roman historical works as being rooted in the attempts to articulate collective history in terms of the epideictic mode of rhetoric, when an author would present his own tradition in a praiseworthy manner, while disparaging other competing traditions.[24]

---

20 For general information about Jewish and Christian apologetics in antiquity, see Droge 1989, esp. pp. 12–48; Alexandre 1998; Edwards, M.J. et alii 1999. For important methodological observations on this literature, see Bernjam 2001; Cameron 2002a; Johnson, A.P. 2006, pp. 1–24.
21 An in-depth analysis of the beginning and the earliest representations of apologetic historiography in Jewish and Christian traditions is provided by Sterling 1992. On the use of this genre by Christians in antiquity, see also Penner 2004; Burgess 2006; Kofsky 2000.
22 Aune 2006, p. 13.
23 Sterling 1992, p. 17.
24 See Penner 2004, pp. 138–142, 229.

Penner's suggestion brings us close to the methodological approach of those scholars of early Christian literature who argue that apologetics in antiquity should not be considered a distinctive literary form that can be precisely defined in terms of genre characteristics, but rather as a "type of argumentation" which is found across a variety of literary forms and which came into existence "as a response to a situation of competition," whether real or imagined.[25] As Aaron Johnson outlined this approach in his recent study on the apologetic argumentation employed by Eusebius of Caesarea, "apologetic writings were defined ... not so much by genre ... but by shared concern, a *Tendenz* or strategy of identity formulation and world-construction."[26]

An important issue that often arises in academic discussions of apologetic literature is the question of its relationship to works of a polemical nature. While it has been customary for scholars to draw a clear line between these two corpora, a number of recent studies on early Christian apologetics demonstrate that "the dividing line between apologetic and polemic is not clearcut."[27] Thus, Tessa Rajak, in her examination of Justin's anti-Jewish *Dialogue with Trypho*, justly emphasizes that the polemical element "is intrinsic to defending one's own side in apologetic literature."[28] In light of these considerations, it seems more promising to approach these two categories not as though they are mutually exclusive, but as a pair of dialectical poles that constitute a field within which intellectuals in antiquity would defend the truth of their own system of collective beliefs as opposed to those of outsiders, giving preference to more irenic or more aggressive mode of argumentation in accordance with the particular situation in which they found themselves.

The significance of apologetic (and polemical) works for understanding the dynamics of Christian group identification can hardly be overestimated.[29] The primary task of Christian apologists—that is, the defense of Christian doctrines and practices against the hostile criticisms of Jewish or "pagan" others—inevitably involved the representation of a Christian collective identity, defined through contrast with these groups. Designed to persuade, these texts did so by operating within the framework of the binary model of self-identity, where "the negation of collective others serves simultaneously to assert the self."[30] Moreover, they exerted a dynamic force on their audience, not only through providing counterarguments against supposed opponents, but

---

25 Cameron 2002a, pp. 221–222.
26 Johnson, A.P. 2006, p. 5.
27 Cameron 2002a, p. 224.
28 Rajak 1999, p. 61.
29 On this, see Johnson, A.P. 2006, pp. 1–10.
30 Lieu 2004, p. 271.

by actually shaping the beliefs which they allegedly defended. Averil Cameron has emphasized this aspect of apologetic discourse, relying on Bourdieu's sociological theory of cognitive structures that are involved in the construction of the social world, as she argues that it has an important function of not merely sustaining a world of belief, but of creating it anew: "'Christianity,' 'Hellenism' and 'Judaism' are not fixed entities; rather, apologetic writings themselves create the respective identities which they purport to defend or attack."[31]

Analyzed along these lines, CT emerges as a representative of the mixed genre that fuses together genealogical, chronographical, and historiographical literary strategies in the crucible of the apologetical mode of writing. Its author aims to arm his intended audience with an expedient summary of the history of salvation that will enable them to build up their cultural self-confidence in the face of rival claims over the biblical past made by the Jews. A sophisticated and multi-dimensional composition, CT emerges as a fascinating and unique example of literary creativity among Syriac-speaking Christians of Syria–Mesopotamia, where the competition between Jews and Christians in late antiquity would engender a great variety of literary forms that the latter would use in their polemic against the former.

2   The State of the Text

CT's text is available to us through a wide range of textual witnesses: direct ones, represented by the Syriac manuscripts, and indirect ones, the most important of which are the ancient translations of it into other languages. In what follows, a concise overview of this evidence is offered.

2.1   *Direct Textual Witnesses*

The Syriac text of CT survives in a considerable number of manuscripts; Su-Min Ri's standard critical edition lists thirty-five,[32] and there are at least fifteen more.[33] Together with these witnesses, the total number of the existing Syriac manuscripts of the work amounts to fifty, bearing witness to its popularity among East and West Syrians during the early modern period.

---

31   Cameron 2002a, p. 223.
32   For the list and description, see Ri 1987, v. 1, pp. vi–xxii. Manuscripts Bruxelles, Museum Bollandianum, Syr. 737 and Mardin, Library of the Chaldaean Bishop of Mardin, #83 are the same.
33   See Minov 2021b.

As in the case of almost every antique text, we do not possess the autograph of CT. The oldest Syriac manuscripts that contain it, i.e. Or^B (British Library, Add. 7199) and Oc^C (Mingana Syr. 588), are dated to the sixteenth century; that is, they were produced almost a millennium after the work itself had been composed. Furthermore, the existing manuscripts of CT exhibit a high level of textual fluctuation, resulting both from unintentional corruption and scribal errors and from intentional changes that manifest themselves in numerous omissions, alterations, and additions.

The latter development might be regarded as an inevitable outcome of CT's peculiar genre status. A specimen of "rewritten Bible" literature, this composition can be relegated, together with other Jewish and Christian apocryphal works, to the general category of "evolved literature." This term was coined by Robert Kraft, who, in a discussion of the Jewish apocryphal and pseudepigraphic writings that were adopted and further reworked by Christians, characterizes them as belonging to a *sui generis* type of literature that was "not 'authored' in any normal sense of the word but *evolved* in stages over the years."[34] As Johannes Tromp notes in connection with the *Life of Adam and Eve*, such writings "underwent continuous change, by addition, by omission, by corruption and conjecture, as well as by drastic revision. Each new copy of such a writing became, in turn, the object of renewed adaptation and redaction."[35]

This is also true for CT, since its textual tradition is characterized by a comparable degree of fluidity, so that no version is identical to another. CT's textual fluidity becomes even more pronounced in the case of the ancient translations of the work into other languages.[36] All of this poses a considerable challenge to the practical task of establishing the "original" text of CT. The first scholar to undertake this task was the German orientalist Carl Bezold, who, from 1883 to 1888, published an edition of the Syriac text of CT, together with a German translation and an ancient Arabic version.[37] Bezold's edition presents an eclectic Syriac text of CT, reconstructed on the basis of four manuscripts: Or^{ABSV}.[38] Although this edition played an important role in bringing CT to the attention of the scholarly community, it has now become seriously outdated. Its main shortcoming is the limited textual basis that Bezold used, as he had access only to four Syriac manuscripts of CT.[39]

---

34 Kraft 1975, p. 185.
35 Tromp 1997, p. 26.
36 On this, see section 2.2 below.
37 Bezold 1883–1888. On the Arabic version, extracted from the *Apocalypse of Peter to Clement*, see section 2.2.2.1 below.
38 See Bezold 1883–1888, v. 2, pp. v–vii.
39 For additional critical comments on Bezold's edition, see Götze 1922, pp. 5–22.

A century later, a new attempt to provide a satisfactory critical edition of CT was made by Su-Min Ri, who also produced a French translation of the work.[40] Ri prepared the Syriac text on the basis of the nineteen manuscripts that were available to him.[41] Although he acknowledges that "le texte de la *Caverne des trésors* ne possède qu'un seul archétype, une seule version originale, en syriaque,"[42] in his edition, Ri does not attempt to recover this "original" text of CT. Instead, he chooses to divide all the Syriac manuscripts that he examined into two main recensions: Eastern, comprised of three smaller subgroups (Or^{HM}, Or^{AF} and Or^{BCDELOPSUV}), and Western, comprised of two subgroups (Oc^{abc} and Oc^{de}). The primary criterion for this division is the confessional provenance of the manuscripts, deduced, apparently, from their script: the East Syrian Estrangelo for the Eastern recension and the West Syrian Serto for the Western recension.[43] Within each of the two recensions, Ri singles out a base manuscript: Or^M (Mingana Syr. 11) for the Eastern and Oc^a (Vatican Syr. 489) for the Western, which are accurately reproduced, while variant readings from other manuscripts are given in the critical apparatus.[44]

It should be mentioned that besides Bezold's German and Ri's French translations, there are several other renditions of CT's Syriac text into modern languages, such as English, Spanish, Greek, and Polish.[45]

2.2 Indirect Textual Witnesses

In addition to the Syriac text of CT, there are a number of translations of this work into several other languages of the Christian Orient: Arabic, Georgian, Geez, and Coptic. These textual witnesses can be divided into two main groups: independent versions, which present the entire text in relation to the Syriac original, and incorporated versions, where CT is either wholly or partially incorporated into another composition.

---

40 Ri 1987.
41 For a description and comments, see Ri 1987, v. 1, pp. vi–xx.
42 Ri 1987, v. 1, p. xxiii.
43 See Ri 1987, v. 1, p. vi.
44 In doing this, Ri claims to be following the editorial principles outlined in Draguet 1977.
45 English: Budge 1927 and Toepel 2013 translate Or^A; Spanish: González Casado 2004 translates both recensions of Ri's edition; Greek: Grypeou 2010 translates Bezold's text; Polish: Tronina & Starowieyski 2011 translate the Eastern recension of Ri's edition (Or^M). The German translation of CT, found in Riessler 1928, pp. 942–1013, does not seem to be derived from a Syriac original, but from Bezold's German translation.

2.2.1 Independent Versions

2.2.1.1 *Christian Arabic Version I*

Georg Graf, in his monumental *Geschichte der christlichen arabischen Literatur*, listed several manuscripts that feature a translation of the complete text of CT into Arabic.[46] The oldest of them seems to be Borgia Ar. 135, possibly dated to the fourteenth century.[47] While in this manuscript the work's title is lost, in other manuscripts it is often given as the *Book of the Cave of Treasures* (*Kitāb maghārat al-kunūz*). Unfortunately, none of these textual witnesses of CT has been edited so far, nor is there a satisfactory text-critical examination of them. Until this task is accomplished, not much can be said about the possible date of this translation, as well as about its relationship to the version of CT incorporated into the *Arabic Apocalypse of Peter* (see below).

In his commentary on CT, Su-Min Ri offers a detailed description of an important Karshuni witness of this version from manuscript Mingana Syr. 32, dated to the year 1675.[48] The manuscript's colophon indicates that it was translated into Arabic from Syriac. According to Ri, this version contains a significant amount of additional material that is not attested in other textual witnesses of CT.[49] In terms of this version's relationship to the main versions of CT, Ri situates it "half-way" between the incorporated version of the *Arabic Apocalypse of Peter* and the Western recension of the Syriac original.[50]

2.2.1.2 *Georgian Version*

Another independent version of CT is preserved in Georgian. A critical edition of this work was published by Ciala Kourcikidzé on the basis of nine manuscripts, the oldest of which, Kutaisi State Historical Museum 128, is dated to the fifteenth or sixteenth century.[51] It is accompanied by a French translation by Jean-Pierre Mahé.[52]

---

46 Graf 1944–1953, v. 1, p. 199.
47 Produced in a Maronite milieu, this codex is made of two different parts. The dating of the second part, in which CT appears, is debatable. Its colophon (f. 275r) gives the year 1695 without mention of era. While some scholars interpret it as given according to the Seleucid era, making thus the date 1384 (Tisserant 1924, p. 17), others take it to be according to the Gregorian calendar (Moukarzel 2014, p. 250). I am grateful to Alice Croq for clarifying this point to me.
48 Ri 2000, pp. 57–61. See also Mingana 1933–1939, v. 1, col. 87. Ri's attempt to replace the date given by Mingana, i.e. 1675, by 1575 should be dismissed as based on a misreading of the manuscript.
49 Ri 2000, p. 60.
50 Ri 2000, p. 61.
51 Kourcikidzé 1993.
52 Mahé 1992.

The Georgian version covers the entire text of the Syriac original. In addition to this, it incorporates the text of the apocryphal *Testament of Adam* into chapter 6. Regarding the origins of this version, Mahé, who based his claim on the transcription of proper names, argued that it was translated into Georgian not from a Syriac but rather from an Arabic *Vorlage*, which in its turn was different from the incorporated version of the *Arabic Apocalypse of Peter* in that it was closer to the Syriac original.[53] According to Kourcikidzé, it is not unlikely that this translation was made during the ninth or tenth century.[54] In his discussion of the Georgian version, Ri noted its closeness to the Western Syriac recension of CT.[55]

2.2.2 Incorporated Versions

2.2.2.1 *Christian Arabic Version II*

The earliest composition that incorporates a significant part of CT's narrative is the Arabic apocryphal work entitled the *Book of the Revelations* (*Kitāb al-mağāl*) or the *Book of the Rolls* (*Kitāb al-mağāll*), known also as the *Arabic Apocalypse of Peter*.[56] In this work, the apostle Peter entrusts his disciple Clement with knowledge of the heavenly secrets, revealed to him by Christ himself, that include prophecies about the early Christian kings and the appearance of Islam, descriptions of heaven and hell, a discourse about Antichrist, and a revelation about the annulment of the Law of Moses. The *Apocalypse*, which contains several features pointing to a Syrian provenance,[57] was most likely composed during the ninth or tenth century.

The first section of this long composition presents a narrative whose content corresponds to chapters 1–44 of the Syriac version of CT. The Arabic text of this part of the *Apocalypse* has been published twice, once by Carl Bezold and once by Margaret Gibson, who also provided an English translation.[58] The

---

53 See Mahé 1992, pp. xxv–xxvi.
54 Kourcikidzé 1993, p. vi. Cf. also Avalichvili 1927–1928, p. 383, who puts this translation in the context of the official identity politics pursued by the early rulers of the Georgian Bagratid dynasty, who sought to establish a genealogical connection with the ancient Jewish kings.
55 Ri 2000, p. 62.
56 On this work, see Graf 1944–1953, v. 1, pp. 283–292; Grypeou 2013; La Spisa 2014. For a discussion of its title, see La Spisa 2014, p. 513. So far, the Arabic text of the *Apocalypse* has not been published in its entirety. For a partial facsimile edition, together with an English translation (except for the section from CT), see Mingana 1931.
57 See Roggema 2007, p. 137.
58 Bezold 1883–88; Gibson 1901. Gibson's text has been republished, accompanied by an Italian translation and commentary, by Battista & Bagatti 1979; for its Spanish translation, see Monferrer-Sala 2003, pp. 61–119.

earliest textual witness of the *Apocalypse* seems to be the manuscript that Gibson chose for her edition, i.e. manuscript Sinai Ar. 508, written in the tenth century, if not earlier. It should be noted that the Arabic text of this version does not exactly correspond to the text of the Syriac original, as it features many omissions and additions. Moreover, similarly to the Georgian version, it incorporates the text of the *Testament of Adam*.[59]

2.2.2.2   *Ethiopic Version*

Another Christian work that contains material from CT is the Ethiopic Pseudo-Clementine pseudepigraphon that is entitled the *Book of Clement* (*Mäṣḥafä Qälemənṭos*) in Geez.[60] It is a seven-book compendium that comprises a variety of apocryphal, apocalyptic, and canonical materials. This composition was put together no later than the fourteenth century by combining different works, most of which were translated into Geez from Arabic. The first book of *Qälemənṭos* (1.1–2) incorporates material corresponding to chapters 1–37 of CT's narrative.[61] As has been argued by Alessandro Bausi, the immediate source upon which *Qälemənṭos'* compiler drew for this section was the *Arabic Apocalypse of Peter*.[62]

2.2.2.3   *Coptic Version*

Material from CT is also found in the Coptic composition entitled the *Homily of Cyril of Jerusalem on Mary Magdalene*.[63] In this work, an account of Mary's life is offered, beginning with her early youth. The main textual witness of the *Homily* is manuscript IFAO Copt. 27, published together with a French translation by René-Georges Coquin and Gérard Godron, who date it to approximately the eleventh or twelfth century.[64] While there is no doubt that Cyril, the famous fourth-century bishop of Jerusalem, was not the author of this work, there is still no scholarly agreement on the question of the *Homily*'s exact provenance, or on whether it is an original Coptic composition or a translation from another language such as Greek or Arabic.[65]

The passages from CT appear in the part of the *Homily* in which the author presents the archangel Gabriel's revelation to Theophilus, the steward of Mary

---

59   See Gibson 1901, pp. 13–17 [trans.].
60   On this work, see Bausi 2010; Cowley 1978.
61   There is still no critical edition of this part of *Qälemənṭos*. For a French translation of this section, see Grébaut 1911–1913.
62   Bausi 1992, pp. 18–21.
63   On this work, see van den Broek 2013, pp. 105–111.
64   See Coquin & Godron 1990, p. 170.
65   On this, see van den Broek 2013, pp. 110–111.

Magdalene, concerning the fulfillment of the scriptures and the dispensation of Christ, from the creation of Adam until the present time. Folios 4v°–10v° of IFAO Copt. 27 very closely reproduce material from chapters 2 to 6 of CT.[66] An additional two folios of the *Homily*, found in manuscript Pierpont Morgan M 665(4), contain material from chapters 44, 47, and 48.[67] As to the question of the immediate source of the material from CT in the *Homily*, it still remains to be established whether it was translated into Coptic directly from Syriac or from an intermediary Greek translation.[68]

2.3 The "Original" Text of CT

While Ri's edition has become a standard reference work in the field, some words of caution should be spoken regarding its value for those who are concerned with the "original" text of CT. It significantly expands the textual basis of CT in comparison with Bezold's edition, making data from several important manuscripts available to us. At the same time, this edition suffers from several shortcomings which considerably limit its usefulness.

To begin with, Ri does not attempt to answer the question of which of the two recensions into which he divided all the textual witnesses of CT stands closer to its "original" text. In his recent monumental commentary on CT, he also expresses doubts about the possibility of establishing the priority of one recension over another.[69] It is thus left to the reader to determine whether any given reading belongs to the original stratum of the composition or not. Another obvious weakness of Ri's edition lies in its relatively limited textual basis, as it takes into account only half of the Syriac manuscripts of CT that are now known to exist. Moreover, some scholars have seriously criticized the editorial principles that Ri adopted, claiming that they considerably undermine the value of his work. According to Alessandro Bausi, Ri's "criteria for the classification of the mss. are totally unsatisfactory."[70]

It is not possible to embark upon a systematic and comprehensive criticism of Ri's edition within the framework of this book. I shall limit myself to merely pointing out the two editorial decisions that he made that compromise the quality of his work at the most basic level. First of all, one can hardly accept Ri's decision to group all the Syriac manuscripts of CT into two separate recensions based not on proper text-critical considerations that take their mutual

---

66 See ed. Coquin & Godron 1990, pp. 184–196 [Copt.], 204–210 [trans.].
67 First published by Poirier 1983, they were re-edited in Coquin & Godron 1990, pp. 197–198 [Copt.], 210–212 [trans.].
68 See Coquin & Godron 1990, p. 169.
69 See Ri 2000, p. 86.
70 Bausi 2006, p. 544; cf. also Bausi 2008, p. 24, n. 17.

interrelations into account, but on the superficial criterion of the form of their script. Second, equally deplorable is Ri's failure to recognize the importance of manuscript Or^A. The latter point deserves to be elaborated in some detail, because I believe that this witness is crucial for an adequate understanding of the textual history of CT and for establishing the work's earliest stratum.

Manuscript Or^A, i.e. British Library, Add. 25875, is a collection of apocryphal, hagiographical, and historiographical writings written down by the East Syrian priest Homo, son of Daniel of Alqosh, in 1709 and 1710.[71] CT is the first composition in this collection and occupies folios 3v–50v. This textual witness drew the attention of scholars dealing with CT during the earliest period of research on this work and is one of the four Syriac manuscripts that Bezold used for his edition. The importance of Or^A was later stressed by Albrecht Götze, who gave it a place of precedence in his stemma of CT's manuscripts.[72] In a similar vein, Ernest Wallis Budge chose this textual witness as the basis for his English translation of CT, praising it as "the best ... of all the known manuscripts" and expressing astonishment at Bezold's decision not to use it as the base text for his edition.[73]

In his edition, however, Ri decided to disregard these opinions and relegated the evidence from Or^A to the critical apparatus, having chosen Or^M as the base text for the Eastern recension, to which Or^A is also related. As he explains, the reason for this decision was that Or^A bears traces of contamination from the readings found in Or^F, which in its turn is a result of conflating the manuscripts of the Eastern (first subgroup, i.e. Or^HMD) and Western (fourth subgroup, i.e. Oc^abc) recensions, as well as of reworking on the basis of the Peshitta version of the Old Testament.[74] Unfortunately, Ri makes no effort to substantiate this allegation, which has far-reaching consequences for his editorial strategy.

This claim, however, does not do justice to the place of Or^A in the textual tradition of CT. Whether Ri was right regarding the amalgamate character of Or^F, upon which Or^A supposedly depends, is in need of a more thorough examination. At the moment, I shall only note that there is textual evidence that invalidates his characterization of Or^A as a combination of Or^HMD and Oc^abc. For instance, in CT 24.19, there is a list of the descendants of Shem, which certainly comprises an integral part of the work,[75] that is only preserved in Or^A and Oc^d.

---

71 See description in Wright, W. 1870–1872, v. 3, pp. 1064–1069.
72 See Götze 1922, p. 12.
73 Budge 1927, pp. xi–iii.
74 Ri 1987, v. 1, p. x.
75 Cf. CT 24.21, where the territories controlled by Shem's sons are listed.

In addition to this, I would like to offer several text-critical observations that demonstrate the superiority of Or^A over the rest of the Eastern manuscripts in general and over Or^M in particular. The most significant textual feature that sets Or^M apart from Or^A is the extended lacuna in CT 36.10–41.10,13–22 that skips the entire period of the divided Israelite monarchy until the time of the exile. This omission, which is most likely due to a homoioteleuton, is found in all the Eastern manuscripts except Or^A and Or^F. It has been convincingly argued by Clemens Leonhard that this section, which appears in the Western recension and in the Georgian version of CT, is an integral part of the original work and not a later addition, as Ri suggested.[76]

A similar although smaller lacuna is found in CT 44.12–13a, where Or^A is the only Eastern manuscript to preserve the part of the author's argument regarding his supremacy over other Christian writers, which is also attested in the Western recension and the Georgian version. Another example of such omission is provided by CT 2.6–14, where Or^A is the only Eastern manuscript to contain a detailed description of the creation of Adam from the four elements and of his beautiful appearance, which closely corresponds to the Western recension. A similar omission is found in CT 2.25, the passage describing the angelic veneration of Adam, which among the Eastern manuscripts appears only in Or^A, but is preserved in the Western recension and the Georgian version. Likewise, all the Eastern manuscripts save Or^A omit the second half of CT 4.5 that describes how Satan flew to Paradise inside a serpent, which does appear in the Western recension and the Georgian version.

In addition to these examples, there are instances when Or^A is the only Eastern manuscript to preserve correct original readings. For example, in the genealogical list in CT 43.15, all the Eastern manuscripts give "Eliud" as the name of Zerubbabel's son, whereas only Or^A and Or^F, as well as the Western recension and the Georgian version, feature the correct form "Abiud" mentioned in Matthew 1:13.

Furthermore, there are a considerable number of instances when Or^M features readings that are undoubtedly inferior to those of Or^A and other Eastern witnesses. For example, in CT 21.19, Or^M erroneously ascribes the words from Acts 5:30–31 to the apostle Paul, while Or^A and the rest of the Eastern manuscripts correctly attribute them to Peter. The superiority of Or^A and other Eastern manuscripts over Or^M may be observed in the case of CT 3.6 and CT 35.18, where the latter lacks one member of the originally tripartite schemes in both cases. Thus, in CT 3.6, Or^A, along with the majority of the Eastern and all of the Western manuscripts, offers three etymologies of Satan's names,

---

76 See Leonhard 2001, pp. 274–275.

whereas Or^M omits one of them.⁷⁷ Likewise, in CT 35.18, Or^A, together with the majority of the Eastern and all the Western manuscripts, presents the names of all three envoys sent by Nimrod to Balaam, while Or^M gives the names of only two of them. Besides this, in CT 52.1b–6a, Or^M lacks the passage that contains the biblical proof-text of Psalm 118:27 and the beginning of the following genealogical list, which are preserved in the majority of the Eastern manuscripts, including Or^A, as well as in the Western recension.

These observations demonstrate the fundamental superiority of Or^A over Or^M, and thus lend additional support to Leonhard's earlier suggestion that Or^A and Or^F "contain the original text of the eastern tradition."⁷⁸ In my opinion, it is absolutely essential that this textual witness receive proper attention as the best candidate for the *codex optimus* in a future critical edition of CT's Syriac text, at least among the manuscripts of the Eastern recension, if not for the work as a whole.

At this point, I would like to emphasize that Or^A as such should by no means be equated with the "original" text of CT. As good as this textual witness is, similarly to all existing manuscripts of CT, it also exhibits traces of textual corruption and contamination during the process of transmission within the East Syrian milieu. One of the most striking expressions of the latter phenomenon is the presence of two mutually exclusive theological agendas in this manuscript: East Syrian and West Syrian, the former being expressed in the explicit anti-Miaphysite polemic and the latter in the recognizable traces of Miaphysite Christological doctrines.⁷⁹ The interpretation of the scriptural "garments of skin" (Gen 3:21) being made from the bark of trees in CT 4.22, which is only attested in Or^A, should most probably also be characterized as a later East Syrian addition.⁸⁰

In light of all these considerations, the inadequacy of Ri's edition becomes apparent. In the absence of a viable alternative, however, one has no choice but to operate on the basis of his work. In this situation, one satisfactory solution to the problem of CT's "original" text would be to rely in the first place on those readings that are attested in both recensions of Ri's edition. Taking this methodological principle as a given, in most such cases that follow, the Syriac text of CT is quoted according to Or^A. All other instances, when the "original"

---

77 The name *šīʿdā*, explained as a derivative of the verb *ʾeštdi*.
78 Leonhard 2001, p. 271.
79 For a detailed discussion, see sections 3.2 and 4 below.
80 This exegetical tradition appears for the first time in the commentary on Genesis by Theodore of Mopsuestia (5th c.); see Tonneau 1953, p. 60. Due to Theodore's authority, it gained popularity among the East Syrians; cf. Narsai, *Homilies on the Creation* 4.248–249; ed. Gignoux 1968, pp. 624–625; John bar Penkāyē, *Chronicle* 1; ms. Mingana Syr. 179, fol. 6v.

stratum of CT may be preserved in the readings limited to one recension or even to one textual witness, will be evaluated on a case-by-case basis.

3 Date of CT

Since the last decades of the nineteenth century when the original Syriac text of CT was made available to European scholars by Carl Bezold, a number of opinions on the date of this work have been expressed. In his edition, Bezold himself suggests the sixth century as the time of the work's composition, although without giving any detailed argumentation to substantiate this claim.[81] In a review of Bezold's edition, his teacher, Theodor Nöldeke, accepted the latter's opinion.[82] This date was also supported by Ernst Wallis Budge, who, in the preface to his English translation of CT, noted that "it is now generally believed that the form in which we now have it is not older than the VIth century."[83] The authors of the two most influential handbooks of Syriac literature, Rubens Duval and Anton Baumstark, also date CT to the sixth century.[84]

One of the first attempts to argue for an earlier composition date for CT was made by Jacob Bamberger, who dated it to the fourth century on the basis of its supposed indebtedness to the Jewish Adam literature and its origins in "Ephrem's school."[85] Later on, Albrecht Götze, the first scholar to undertake a thorough examination of CT, suggested that an early version of this work, which he labeled the *Urschatzhöhle*, was composed around the middle of the fourth century in Jewish Christian circles, and that it was later reworked by an East Syrian writer during the sixth century.[86] Götze's main arguments for dating the *Urschatzhöhle* to the fourth century are the following: (a) the closeness of CT's ideology to Gnostics and Ebionites; (b) the dependence of CT's chronology on that of Julius Africanus; (c) the influence of Aphrahat on CT; and (d) Ephrem's ignorance of this work. This theory enjoyed considerable popularity. Thus, in his fundamental work on Jewish apocryphal literature, Albert-Marie Denis claims that the core of CT existed in the fourth century as a polemical anti-Jewish work produced by Jewish Christians.[87]

---

81 See Bezold 1883–1888, v. 1, p. x.
82 See Nöldeke 1888.
83 Budge 1927, p. xi.
84 See Duval 1907, p. 81; Baumstark 1922, p. 95.
85 See Bamberger 1901, p. 25.
86 See Götze 1922, p. 91.
87 See Denis 2000, v. 1, p. 31.

Götze's hypothesis was adopted and further developed by Su-Min Ri, who proposed in a number of publications that the core of CT was composed in the third century. For example, in the preface to the French translation of CT, Ri suggested that it fits the context of "interfaith" discussion in third-century Caesarea Maritima, where Origen lived and taught.[88] Later, in an article dealing with the parallels between CT and Ephrem's writings, Ri came to the conclusion that the latter was dependant on the former and knew it "par cœur," even before he became a Christian. Ri found support for this bold claim in the supposed connection between CT and such early Christian writers as Irenaeus of Lyon, Justin the Martyr, Melito of Sardis, Julius Africanus, and Hippolytus.[89] That would point to an even earlier date than c. 350 as Götze suggested. Ri maintains this date in his monograph on CT, where he gives the end of the second to the beginning of the third century as the time of the work's composition.[90] Ri's theory that CT had early origins gained a certain popularity among Syriacists.[91]

It has been recently put to a thorough examination by Clemens Leonhard, who exposed the weakness of Ri's arguments in favor of an early date for CT.[92] Leonhard has persuasively demonstrated that CT should be read as a coherent literary unit and that no distinct textual layer such as Götze's *Urschatzhöhle* can be securely distinguished within it.[93] He has also examined several important themes that appear in CT—such as the traditions concerning the burial of Adam on Golgotha and the death and burial place of the prophet Jeremiah, as well as the use of the Peshitta text of the New Testament, the millennial concept, the influence of the cult of relics, and the importance of Syriac identity—from a diachronic point of view.[94] As a result, Leonhard comes to the conclusion that CT could not have been composed before the fourth century and that the most likely date of its composition would be the fifth or sixth century.

As I find Leonard's arguments against the theory of CT having early origins proposed by Götze and Ri fully convincing, I am not going to discuss them here and I will take his suggestion of the fifth to sixth century as the probable date of the work's composition as an initial working hypothesis for my own investigation. In what follows, I will briefly summarize the detailed discussion of CT's date that I published earlier elsewhere.[95]

---

88 See Ri 1987, v. 2, pp. xxii–xxiii.
89 See Ri 1998, pp. 82–83.
90 See Ri 2000, pp. 555–557.
91 Cf. Tubach 2003, pp. 193–194; Witakowski 2008, p. 815.
92 See Leonhard 2001.
93 Leonhard 2001, pp. 261–277.
94 Leonhard 2001, pp. 277–288.
95 Minov 2017, pp. 133–149.

3.1 Terminus ante quem

The most secure *terminus ante quem* for CT is provided by the *Apocalypse of Pseudo-Methodius*. This anonymous apocalyptic work was written in Syriac not long after the Arabic conquest of Northern Mesopotamia, around the year 690 or 691, somewhere in the vicinity of Siṇǧār, a region about 100 kilometers southeast of Nisibis.[96] There are several instances where the author of this work exhibits closeness to or acquaintance with CT. The most telling instance of CT's influence on the *Apocalypse* is the story of Yonṭon, the fourth son of Noah born after the Flood, who is portrayed as the inventor of astronomy and the instructor of Nimrod. This peculiar tradition which first appears in CT (27.6–20) is also used by the author of the *Apocalypse* (3.2–8).[97] This and several other instances of the *Apocalypse*'s author being acquainted with CT gives us the year 690 as a secure *terminus ante quem* for our work.

I believe, however, that there is additional evidence that might allow us to push the date of CT's composition to an even earlier period. Thus, the description of King Sasan's founding of a Zoroastrian fire temple in Azerbaijan in CT 27.4–5, alluding to the famous Sasanian cultic center Ādur Gušnasp in West Azerbaijan, seems to suggest that our author was writing before the destruction of this temple by Heraclius' troops in the year 623.[98] Taking this evidence into consideration, as well as CT's author's significant use of Iranian ideas and images,[99] and the absence of any references to the Arabic conquest, Islam, or Arabs in general in CT, it seems reasonable to date this work to the pre-Islamic period and to propose the first two decades of the seventh century as its *terminus ante quem*.

3.2 Terminus post quem

A major obstacle for establishing CT's *terminus post quem* is its author's literary strategy, as he reworks his wide range of sources so thoroughly that any traces of his indebtedness to previous writers are erased. Nevertheless, there are still a number of motifs and traditions in CT that might be of help in this regard.

One of them is the use of the name of Sasanian monarch Pērōz for the construction of the name of one of the Magi in CT 45.19. It seems reasonable to accept the suggestion made by Witold Witakowski that Pērōz's rule (459–484)

---

96   For the critical edition of the *Apocalypse*, see Reinink 1993. On the *Apocalypse*'s date and provenance, see Brock 1982b, pp. 18–19; Reinink 1993, v. 2, pp. v–xxix. See also Alexander, P.J. 1985 on this work.
97   On this tradition, see Gero 1980; Toepel 2006b.
98   On this temple, see below chapter 3, pp. 155–156.
99   On this, see chapter 3.

serves as a *terminus post quem* for this tradition.[100] A similar case is that of the relic of the "tunic" of Christ, mentioned in CT 50.8–12. Michel van Esbroeck, who traces the development of the legend of Christ's tunic, argues that it was put into circulation in Byzantine Palestine during the last two decades of the fifth century.[101] These observations provide us with the last two decades of the fifth century as one *terminus post quem* for CT.

Further support for a relatively late dating of CT is found in the description of the sacrifice of Isaac in CT 29.8–14. Clemens Leonhard, who has analyzed the textual evidence for this pericope, has convincingly argued in favor of the primacy of the version in manuscript Or^{F} from the Eastern recension as the earliest recoverable text.[102] This passage contains an unusual description of the circumcision of Jesus on the eighth day, according to which "nothing has been cut off him according to the order of human nature" during this procedure.[103] A very similar description of Jesus' circumcision appears in CT 46.16–18, in all the manuscripts of the Eastern recension, including Or^{A}:

> In truth, Joseph circumcised him according to the Law. But he performed the circumcision in such a way that nothing was cut off from him. For like iron that passes through and cuts the rays of fire while cutting off nothing, so likewise Christ was circumcised while nothing was cut off from him.[104]

Leonhard has suggested that this unusual depiction of Jesus' circumcision reflects a Christological position that was characteristic of one particular group within the broad spectrum of sixth-century Christianity, the so-called "Aphthartodocetes" or "Phantasiasts."[105] This radical strand within the Miaphysite movement was characterized by its adherence to the ideas of Julian of Halicarnassus regarding the original incorruptibility of Christ's body.[106] As I have argued elsewhere, for the present moment, this radical Miaphysite interpretation of Jesus' circumcision, opposed by theologians such as Severus

100 Witakowski 2008, pp. 815–816.

101 See van Esbroeck 1994, pp. 233–242. Unfortunately, the author does not take into consideration the form of the legend of the tunic found in CT.

102 See Leonhard 2004.

103 Or^{F}: ܠܐ ܐܬܦܣܩ ܡܢܗ ܡܕܡ ܐܝܟ ܛܟܣܐ ܐܢܫܝܐ.

104 Or^{A}: ܒܫܪܪܐ ܕܝܢ ܐܝܟ ܕܒܢܡܘܣܐ ܓܙܪܗ ܝܘܣܦ. ܒܪܡ ܠܗ ܠܓܙܘܪܬܐ ܥܒܕ ܟܕ ܡܕܡ ܡܢܗ ܠܐ ܐܬܦܣܩ. ܐܝܟ ܦܪܙܠܐ ܓܝܪ ܕܥܒܪ ܘܦܣܩ ܠܙܠܝܩܐ ܕܢܘܪܐ. ܟܕ ܡܕܡ ܠܐ ܦܣܩ ܠܗ. ܗܟܢܐ ܐܦ ܡܫܝܚܐ ܐܬܓܙܪ. ܟܕ ܡܕܡ ܡܢܗ ܠܐ ܐܬܦܣܩ.

105 Leonhard 2004, pp. 22–25.

106 On Julian and his followers, see Draguet 1924; Grillmeier & Hainthaler 1995, pp. 79–111; Kofsky 2013.

of Antioch and Philoxenus of Mabbug, should be better categorized not as "Julianist," but as "Eutychian," after Eutyches of Constantinople.[107] What is pertinent to the present argument is that this particular tradition, identical to the stance on Jesus' circumcision found in CT, does not seem to be attested before the first decade of the sixth century. Its presence in CT, then, could be used to argue in favor of the beginning of the sixth century as another *terminus post quem* for the work.

There might also be an additional avenue for future research on the date of CT based on linguistic profiling. This approach would entail an assessment of the vocabulary used by the author of CT and its further comparison with that of other Syriac authors. I was not able to pursue this line of research, because it should be based on a new critical edition of CT which would take all of its textual witnesses into account and it would also require a comprehensive and searchable digital corpus of all Syriac texts from late antiquity and the early Middle Ages that does not currently exist.[108] There are, however, several preliminary observations, derived from the pioneering work of Sebastian Brock on the diachronic aspects of Syriac word formation,[109] that testify to the possible usefulness of this approach. For instance, the adjective *kāhnāyā*, "priestly," used in CT 4.1, is attested for the first time in a homily by Jacob of Serugh (6th c.) and becomes common among Syriac authors only during the seventh century.[110]

4   Milieu of CT

As stated above, I will not deal with the hypothesis of the *Urschatzhöhle*, first proposed by Albrecht Götze and then stretched to a breaking point by Su-Min Ri. It has already been convincingly refuted by Clemens Leonhard, and even more arguments against it could easily be added. There is no need, thus, to discuss here the hypothesis of Jewish Christian origins of CT, which is closely linked to this theory and is mostly supported by scholars who accept the early dating

---

107   Minov 2017, pp. 140–146.
108   An important first step in this direction is the recently launched Digital Syriac Corpus project, https://syriaccorpus.org/index.html.
109   See Brock 1990, 2003, 2010.
110   Brock 2010, p. 114. In a personal communication, Sebastian Brock observed that the same might be applied to the adjective *šiʾdānitā*, "diabolical," in CT 11.10, which, although found in Philoxenus' works, becomes widely attested only during the late sixth/early seventh century. Cf. also Brock's observations on the phrases *praš hu leh* (CT 3.3) and *magen ba-btultā* (CT 5.8) in the Eastern recension of CT; BROCK 2008b, p. 557.

of the work.¹¹¹ In light of the modern state of knowledge of Jewish Christianity, there is nothing at all in our composition's theological or socio-cultural outlook that might be regarded as a sufficient basis for making such a claim.

The most widely held opinion on the origins of CT is that it was composed in an East Syrian milieu. This hypothesis was likewise introduced by Götze, who proposed the sixth century as the time of the "final redaction" of CT and suggested an East Syrian provenance for its editor.¹¹² This opinion was adopted by many scholars, and to this day it is arguably the most prevalent point of view on the origins of our work.¹¹³ This theory, however, has its weak points.

The main support for the proponents of the theory that CT had an East Syrian provenance comes from the explicit anti-Miaphysite statements found in two passages of the Eastern recension, CT 21.19 and 29.10. These passages attack some unidentified "heretics" who supposedly believe that it is possible for the divinity to experience suffering. Here, there is an immediately recognizable accusation of *theopaschism*, a stock argument from the arsenal of anti-Miaphysite polemic employed by East Syrian polemicists.¹¹⁴

The question arises as to whether this polemic should be regarded as authentic, i.e. pertaining to the work's original stratum, or as a later addition. As I have argued in detail elsewhere, there are several reasons that make the latter option more plausible.¹¹⁵ A number of text-critical considerations have brought me to the conclusion that none of the passages in the Eastern recension of CT that feature anti-Miaphysite polemic should be taken as evidence in a discussion of the confessional background of the work's original stratum. Both CT 21.19 and 29.10 of the Eastern recension exhibit features that bear witness to their substantial reworking during the process of transmission within the East Syrian milieu.

To these two cases could be added more passages which convey distinctive East Syrian theological ideas and images in the manuscripts of the Eastern recension, but which are absent from the manuscripts of the Western recension or express West Syrian theology. One such case is CT 51.18–19, where a paraphrase of John 19:34 is offered.¹¹⁶ In all the East Syrian manuscripts of this passage, the blood and water that come from Jesus' side pierced by the lance are said to be "unmixed," while all Western manuscripts express precisely the opposite idea, i.e. that they were "mixed."

---

111   See Götze 1922, p. 91; Ri 2000, pp. 577–582.
112   See Götze 1922, pp. 90–91.
113   Cf. Vosté 1939, p. 80, n. 1; Denis 2000, v. 1, p. 31; Toepel 2006, pp. 6–7.
114   See Chediath 1982, pp. 71–75.
115   See Minov 2017, pp. 151–160.
116   For a discussion, see Minov 2017, pp. 160–162.

It is clear, then, that the manifest East Syrian traditions found in the Eastern manuscripts of CT cannot serve as proof of the work's East Syrian provenance, and that new criteria for establishing the confessional affiliation of the original text from which both the West and East Syrian recensions derive should be established. It appears that the safest avenue for such an inquiry would be to rely only on those traditions that (a) are attested in the manuscripts of both recensions, or (b) conform to the criterion of dissimilarity.

While the former principle is self-evident, the latter deserves to be explained in some detail. The most striking instance of what one might call "inner-recensional" dissimilarity is presented by the appearance of the idiosyncratic radical Miaphysite view on the circumcision of Jesus in the manuscripts of the Eastern recension (CT 29.8–14, 46.16–18). The importance of this specific tradition for understanding the process of CT's textual growth cannot be overestimated. The presence of this exclusively Miaphysite tradition in the Eastern recension cannot be explained as an isolated case of a later textual addition, since it is attested in *all* the manuscripts of this recension. Accordingly, we must assume that it was present in the lost prototype from which all the East Syrian manuscripts are ultimately derived.

This fact gives us serious reason to challenge the consensus that CT was of East Syrian origin. In fact, some scholars have already opted in favor of a West Syrian provenance for this work. Ernest Budge was the first to raise such a possibility. In the introduction to his English translation of CT, he states that "the writer was certainly a Syrian Jacobite who was proud of his native language."[117] As an illustration of his thesis, Budge points out several examples where CT's author affirms the priority of the Syriac language (i.e. CT 24.9–11; 53.25–26). Important as they are for understanding the cultural background of CT, these passages by themselves, however, can hardly bear the weight of definitive proof when it comes to the author's confessional identity, since the priority of the Syriac language was evoked not only by West Syrians, but also by some Antiochene and East Syrian authors.

To this may be added a recent contribution by Sebastian Brock, who, in his review of Alexander Toepel's book on CT, pointed out several instances of West Syrian traditions that appear there.[118] Besides the identification of the "spirit of God" of Genesis 1:2 with the Holy Spirit in CT 1.4–7, Brock mentions two other cases: (a) the appearance in CT 5.8 (Or^M) of the strikingly West Syrian incarnational formula *magen ba-btultā* and (b) a peculiar syntactic form *praš hu leh*, typical of the West Syrian translation technique, used in CT 3.3 (Or^M) in

---

117 Budge 1927, p. 22.
118 Brock 2008b, p. 557.

order to describe Satan's separation from God. While both these cases conform to the aforementioned criterion of dissimilarity, since both of them appear in manuscripts of the Eastern recension, their absence from the best Eastern textual witness, i.e. Or^A, prevents us from giving them too much weight.

The implausibility of the theory that CT had East Syrian origins becomes even more apparent and the likelihood of its West Syrian provenance receives additional support when one examines the work's exegetical affinity. Since CT's author's primary goal was to produce an interpretative paraphrase of the biblical narrative, it comes as no surprise that he did not pursue it in a vacuum, but relied upon the previous tradition of scriptural exegesis. One may thus attempt to uncover and analyze those exegetical traditions that he inherited from his predecessors. I believe that a careful examination of such embedded exegetical material offers an additional possibility to establish the author's confessional milieu by allowing us to situate him within the West or East Syrian exegetical tradition.

Besides early exegetical material that comprises a common pool of exegetical lore that was shared by the authors belonging to both the West Syrian and East Syrian traditions, CT includes a number of exegetical traditions that gained currency in the Syriac-speaking milieu later on, during the fifth and sixth centuries. In an earlier article, I examined several cases when the exegetical traditions embedded into CT manifest the author's distance from the East Syrian exegetical tradition and his closeness to the West Syrian one.[119] The most conspicuous examples of this kind are (a) the interpretation of the "spirit of God" of Genesis 1:2 as the Holy Spirit in CT 1.4–7; (b) the interpretation of Noah's drunkenness (Genesis 9:20–27) that combines a Noah–Christ typology with anti-Jewish rhetoric in CT 21.18–22; (c) the vegetarian interpretation of the "locusts" in John the Baptist's diet (Matthew 3:4) in CT 48.3; and (d) the elaborate Adam–Christ typology in CT 48.12–30.

The argument that CT's author was close to the West Syrian tradition is enhanced still further by two instances of dissimilarity between the work's exegetical background and the East Syrian tradition. One of them is related to the suggestion made by Alexander Toepel that CT originated in the school of Ḥenana of Adiabene, the famous East Syrian theologian and exegete, who was active during the second half of the sixth century.[120] A close examination of those exegetical traditions in CT that have parallels with what survives from

---

119   Minov 2017, pp. 165–193.
120   Toepel 2006a, pp. 247–248. The most comprehensive account of Ḥenana's academic career along with his exegetical activity is found in Vööbus 1965, pp. 234–317.

the corpus of Ḥenana's writings revealed the absence of any positive evidence of Ḥenana's influence on our composition.[121]

Even more significant is exegetical dissimilarity between CT and Theodore of Mopsuestia. Theodore played a most important role in the formation of the East Syrian exegetical tradition.[122] His proficiency as a scriptural exegete was widely recognized among East Syrians as a result of his works being translated into Syriac during the first decades of the fifth century and studied in the schools of Edessa and, afterwards, Nisibis. Theodore's supreme authority as "the interpreter" (*mpašqānā*) reached its pinnacle after it was formally recognized as such by the decisions of several East Syrian synods (Išoʿyahb I in 585 CE; Sabrišoʿ in 596 CE; Gregory I in 605 CE) that conferred a quasi-canonical status upon his writings. That this was not merely lip service is confirmed by the fact that Theodoret's impact is discernable in virtually all East Syrian writers who addressed scriptural themes and issues, beginning with Narsai in the fifth century.

While claiming East Syrian origins for CT, one might thus expect to find at least some traces of Theodore's influence in this work. Contrary to this, however, we are faced with the fact that several important for the East Syrian theology themes which are deeply rooted in Theodore's thought and which could be found in the majority of East Syrian works from late antiquity and the early Middle Ages are absent from CT.[123] Among these, we should particularly mention the notion of God's pedagogical attitude towards his creation, especially the human race, based on Theodore's conception of the divine education (παιδεία), the purpose of which is to prepare humans in this *katastasis* of mortality for the future *katastasis* of immortality.

5   Concluding Observations

In order to obtain reliable information about CT's date, a wide range of evidence, internal as well as external, has been examined. As a result of this investigation, the time-span between the middle of the sixth century and the first decades of the seventh century has emerged as the most probable date of its composition.

Regarding CT's hypothetical author's cultural and theological milieu, several important points should be stressed. First, speaking in cultural terms, the

---

121 See Minov 2017, pp. 193–195.
122 See Becker 2006, pp. 114–125; Reinink 2009, pp. 239–240.
123 For a detailed discussion, see Minov 2017, pp. 196–200.

most likely geographical location for our Syriac writer is the part of Northern Mesopotamia that was controlled by the Sasanian empire. This is testified by the deep interest he exhibited in various aspects of Iranian culture and religiosity, as well as his intimate knowledge of Iranian realities.[124] Second, several aspects of CT have led me to discard the theory of its East Syrian origins as baseless. Thus, I have pointed out the unsatisfactory textual basis of the distinctively East Syrian traditions that are found in CT. The apparent dissimilarity between CT's author's exegetical background and the East Syrian exegetical tradition, as well as his closeness to West Syrian exegesis on several points, also testify against this theory. The latter observation, taken with the presence of distinctively Miaphysite material in the best Eastern manuscripts of CT, as well as the history of the work's reception, give us sufficient reason to claim a West Syrian provenance for CT's author.

Apparently, the attractiveness of the theory of CT's East Syrian origins is closely related to the commonly agreed presumption of an Iranian provenance for this work. At first glance, it may appear self-evident to suggest that if CT was produced by Syriac-speaking Christians of the Sasanian empire, then they most probably belonged to the East Syrian Church, which comprised the largest ecclesiastical body in Persia during the sixth and seventh centuries. However, this view is undermined by the compelling evidence about the significant presence of the Syriac-speaking Miaphysite community in Sasanian Iran during this period, to the degree that by the time of CT's composition, it constituted an important social and cultural force.[125]

The very beginnings of the West Syrian presence in the Sasanian empire are related to the policy of mass deportations of the Byzantine Christian population practiced by the Persians during their military campaigns against the Roman empire.[126] Thus, in the *Lives of the Eastern Saints* (§58), John of Ephesus describes the forced deportation of the citizens of Amida, including the Miaphysite monks of the monastery of Mār John of Amida, to Persia after the city was taken by Kavad's troops in the year 501/502.[127]

Another important factor that significantly facilitated the growth of the West Syrian community in Sasanian Iran was the anti-Miaphysite persecutions in the Roman empire that were inaugurated by Emperor Justin I immediately after the death of his predecessor Anastasius I (r. 491–518), who was favorably

---

124 This aspect of CT is discussed in detail below, in chapter 3.
125 On this, see Labourt 1904, pp. 217–246; Fiey 1970, pp. 113–143; Morony 1984, pp. 372–380.
126 See Kettenhofen 1996; Morony 2004.
127 Ed. Brooks 1923–1925, v. 3, pp. 217–220. It seems that they were settled in Arragan in the province of Fars; see Fiey 1960.

disposed towards the anti-Chalcedonian cause.[128] From that period on, an influx of West Syrian refugees into the territories controlled by the Sasanians may be observed. For example, Elias, the author of the *Life of John of Tella*, relates how this sixth-century leader of the Miaphysite party flew to Persia, going into hiding in the Siṅğār Mountains in Northern Mesopotamia along with other Miaphysite refugees from the Roman empire.[129] Likewise, the East Syrian author of the *Chronicle of Seert* (2.21), while discussing the beginnings of the Jacobite heresy in the Sasanian empire, mentions the West Syrians, who fled to the Persian territory during Justin's reign.[130]

As a result of these developments, from the middle of the sixth century onwards, there are a growing number of testimonies on the activities of Miaphysite Christians in the Sasanian Iran, especially in Northern Mesopotamia. The importance of Persia's Miaphysite community is reflected in the fact of the establishment of the *maphrianate*, i.e. the "secondary" patriarchate that enjoyed independent ecclesiastical authority in governing the West Syrian Christians under Sasanian rule, in the city of Takrit in the year 628.[131] Some of the West Syrian Christians of Sasanian Iran found their way to the highest levels of Persian society and at times could exercise a considerable degree of influence, as the examples of Shirin, the famous wife of King Khosrow II Parvīz (r. 590–628), and Gabriel of Siṅğār, his court physician, demonstrate.[132]

There are two features that connect CT's author with this particular faction of Syriac-speaking Christianity in Iran. One of them is the appearance of imagery characteristic of radical Miaphysite Christology, espoused by some followers of Julian of Halicarnassus, in the best manuscripts of CT. The presence of the Julianists in Northern Mesopotamia during the late Sasanian period is well attested in ancient sources. Thus, the author of the West Syrian *Chronicle of Zuqnin* (8th c.) relates for the years 548 and 549 how a certain Sergius, one of the Julianist bishops ordained by Eutropius, "rushed to Persia and to the land of the Ḥimyarites," where he had considerable success recruiting followers.[133] In the *Life of John of Tella*, we come across the mention of a Julianist monk living on Mount Siṅğār who disclosed John's whereabouts to the Persians.[134] In a letter from the West Syrian patriarch of Antioch Sergius I (557–561) to the

---

128   See Vasiliev 1950, pp. 221–250.
129   Ed. Brooks 1907, pp. 60–62 [Syr.]. See also *Chronicle of Ps.-Zachariah Rhetor* 10.1; ed. Brooks 1919–1924, v. 2, p. 175.
130   Ed. Scher 1908–1918, v. 3, p. 142.
131   On this institution, see Labourt 1904, pp. 236–241; Fiey 1974–1978.
132   On them, see Labourt 1904, pp. 221–224; Hutter 1998.
133   Ed. Chabot 1927–1949, v. 2, p. 124; trans. Harrak 1999, p. 122.
134   Ed. Brooks 1907, p. 67 [Syr.].

bishops of Persia, the hierarch addresses the canonical question of how to receive those who are returning to the orthodox fold from the "heresy of Julian the Phantasiast."[135] It is also noteworthy that George of Pisidia, a seventh-century Constantinopolitan poet who accompanied Emperor Heraclius during his counter-offensive against the Persians launched in the year 615, found it necessary to attack "the error of Phantasiasts" in the poem describing this campaign.[136]

Another noteworthy aspect of CT that connects this work with the West Syrian circles of Sasanian Mesopotamia is the peculiar polemical tradition found in CT 30.12–13.[137] In this passage, our author reproaches some unidentified "simpletons" (*hedyuṭē*) for believing that the biblical Melchizedek was not a human being, but God, based on his description in Hebrews 7:3 as one "having neither beginning of days nor end of life." The author of CT is here polemicizing against the heterodox group, categorized under the label of "Melchizedekians" in the heresiographical sources of late antiquity. Attested as early as the third century, these Christians apparently regarded Melchizedek as a divine mediator figure, if the reports of their hostile adversaries can be trusted.[138]

At some point, this teaching made its appearance in Syria, where its earliest mention is connected with the name of a certain John of Apamea, who was active during the fifth or early sixth century.[139] Of particular relevance for our discussion is evidence provided by several Miaphysite sources from which it may be inferred that the Melchizedekians were present in Sasanian Mesopotamia during the sixth century and, moreover, that they were a cause for concern among the West Syrians in this region.

The most important of these sources is Sergius I's letter to the West Syrian bishops of Persia mentioned above. In the second question of this letter, the patriarch deals with the canonical problem of receiving those who have rejected the heresy of the "Melchizedekians" (*malkizdeqyānē*), characterized as those who hold the opinion that "Melchizedek is the Son of God."[140] To this may be added the evidence of the encyclical letter sent by the Armenian catholicos

---

135   Ed. van Roey 1975–1976, pp. 218–219.
136   *Expeditio Persica* 1.149; ed. Pertusi 1959, p. 91.
137   This tradition is attested in manuscripts Or^AF of the Eastern recension and all the manuscripts of the Western recension, and should thus be regarded as an integral part of the original stratum of CT.
138   Cf. Hippolytus, *Ref.* 7.36.1; Epiphanius, *Panar.* 4.55.1–9. For more information on this group, see Bardy 1928; Stork 1928.
139   See van Reeth 2000.
140   Ed. van Roey 1975–1976, p. 220: ܒܪܗ ܕܐܠܗܐ ܗܘ ܡܠܟܝܙܕܩ.

Komitas to the West Syrian bishops of the Sasanian empire in the second decade of the seventh century, in which the heresy of the Melchizedekians, who "called Melchizedek God," is anathematized.[141] The resurgence of the Melchizedekian heresy in the late antique Near East during the sixth century finds additional confirmation in the *Chronicle of Zuqnin*. While describing the ecclesiastical crisis that took place in Ethiopia, Ḥimyar, and "India" due to Justinian's refusal to appoint non-Chalcedonian bishops there, the historiographer relates:

> Thus because of the lack of a bishop, there too another heresy was born. And the error [of the Melchizedekites, who presumptuously] claimed that Melchizedek himself was the Christ, established itself.[142]

The residual traces of Julianist Christology and the polemic against the Melchizedekians in CT, as well as its serious engagement with Judaism and Zoroastrianism, allow us to situate its author and his community within the multi-confessional potpourri of Northern Mesopotamia, where such diverse religious groups as the East Syrians, West Syrians of Severian and Julianist persuasions, Melchizedekians, Jews, and Zoroastrians lived alongside each other during the late Sasanian period. Whereas we do not have enough information to establish our author's geographical context with greater certainty, it can be imagined to be much like the region of the Singǎr Mountains, 100 kilometers southeast of Nisibis, where most of these groups were represented during the sixth and seventh centuries.

---

141   See the French translation in van Esbroeck 2001, p. 169.
142   Ed. Chabot 1927–1949, v. 2, p. 112; trans. Harrak 1999, p. 115. Witold Witakowski suggested that the author of the *Chronicle* derived this information from John of Ephesus' *Church History*; see Witakowski 1991, p. 266.

CHAPTER 2

Categorizing the Jewish "Other"

The early Church's particular and deeply entangled relationship with Jews and Judaism was perhaps the most important factor that determined the course of the development of Christian identity for centuries to come.[1] On the one hand, a wide variety of Christian practices and beliefs can be traced back to the Jewish matrix of the new religion, which began as a marginal eschatological movement within the diverse and dynamic world of Second Temple Judaism.[2] On the other hand, the Jews became the paradigmatic negative "other" in relation to whom the Church articulated its identity.[3] Attempting to define Christianity with greater precision, its leaders did so by contrasting Christians and their New Testament to the Jewish people and their Old Testament. The earliest and most significant expression of Judaism's double relevance to Christianity is provided by the New Testament corpus itself.[4]

The historical development of Syriac Christianity also demonstrates a profound impact exercised by these two major factors. Thus, many scholars have recognized the significant role Judaism played in the dissemination of Christianity in the regions of Syria and Mesopotamia, as well as its deep and lasting influence on the doctrines and customs of Syriac-speaking Christians.[5] At the same time, one should not overlook the fact that from the fourth century onwards, polemic against Jews and Judaism becomes one of the most significant concerns of Syriac Christian writers. The rise of anti-Jewish polemic in Syriac is associated with the names of Aphrahat and Ephrem, who were followed by writers such as Isaac of Antioch and Jacob of Serugh.[6] From existing studies of Jewish-Christian relations in Syria–Mesopotamia during late

---

1 For a general overview of Jewish-Christian relations in antiquity, see Simon 1996; Jacobs 2008; Richardson 2006; Gager 1985.
2 See Sanders 1977; Skarsaune 2002; Nickelsburg 2003.
3 On this aspect of Christian anti-Judaism, see Lieu 1996, 2002; Stroumsa 1996; Jossa 2006; Rutgers 2009; Boddens Hosang 2010. For a general overview of *adversus Judaeos* literature, which served as an important (but not exclusive) vehicle of this process, see Williams, A.L. 1935; Hruby 1971; Schreckenberg 1995; Déroche 2012.
4 See, for example, Hakola 2006.
5 For a general picture, see Brock 1979; Drijvers, H.J.W. 1985, 1992; ter Haar Romeny 2005b; Minov 2019b.
6 For a general overview of polemic against Judaism in Syriac, see Fiey 1988; Hayman 1985; Schreckenberg 1995; Williams, A.L. 1935; Becker 2016. For late antiquity, see also Becker 2003; Neusner 1972; Shepardson 2008b.

antiquity, one may reach the conclusion that Judaism was a major factor in the process of the formation of Syriac Christian identity during this period. This is hardly surprising given that the history of the Jewish presence in these regions goes back to the sixth century BCE and that Judaism was already a well-established and influential religion by the time Christianity arrived there.[7]

While many aspects of Jewish-Christian relations in late ancient Syria–Mesopotamia have already been addressed by students of Syriac Christianity, no comprehensive study of CT from this angle has yet been conducted. The only aspect of this work's relation to Judaism that has aroused the interest of scholars so far is the question of the Jewish traditions and sources with which its author might have been acquainted.[8] However interesting this subject may be, in order to understand the author's attempt to promote a particular vision of Christian identity, one should take into account that his retelling of the sacred history of the Old and New Testaments is interspersed with no small amount of polemical references to the Jewish people and/or their religion. From some passages, one might infer that polemic against Judaism was the major driving force behind the entire literary project (cf. CT 44.3–4). Nevertheless, except for occasional unsubstantiated guesses,[9] no research that takes into account all the anti-Jewish material found in CT and puts it into both a diachronic and a synchronic perspective has yet been carried out.

This chapter intends to bridge this gap and to examine those passages in CT where the author engages with Jews and Judaism, whether directly or obliquely. In my examination of this material, I shall pay attention to the problems of the genesis as well as the purpose of particular anti-Jewish motifs and images, combining a source-critical approach with an analysis of narrative and ideological function. In order to contextualize the anti-Jewish material in CT and assess the author's relationship to the previous tradition of polemic against Judaism, it will be examined against the background of the rich trove of anti-Jewish arguments and rhetoric found in the writings of earlier and contemporary Greek, Latin, and Syriac Christian writers. As to the latter, particular attention will be paid to the works of two prominent fourth-century writers who determined the course of the development of anti-Jewish discourse in

---

7   On the beginnings of the Jewish Diaspora in Mesopotamia, see Yamauchi 2002. For a general work covering the history of Babylonian Jewry up to the time of the Islamic conquest, see Neusner 1965–1970. In addition to this, see Segal 1964, Neusner 1976, Gafni 1990a. On the archaeological data (inscriptions), see Noy & Bloedhorn 2004; Ilan 2011.

8   A brief overview of research on this topic is provided below.

9   Cf. Götze 1922, p. 91, who suggests that the core of CT ("Urschatzhöhle") was composed in the middle of the fourth century and reflects the polemic waged by Jewish Christians against traditional Jews.

Syriac to a considerable degree, namely Aphrahat and Ephrem.[10] Other works written in Syriac during the following fifth and sixth centuries which feature polemics against the Jews and their religion will be taken into consideration, such as those of Narsai, Isaac of Antioch, Jacob of Serugh, and some others.

A caveat should be raised regarding our ability to reconstruct the development of anti-Jewish polemic in Syria–Mesopotamia and to situate our author's views on Jews and Judaism within its trajectory, which are seriously limited by the fact that only a part of the *adversus Judaeos* literature that was produced or circulated in this region has survived the vicissitudes of history. Among important anti-Jewish works originally written in Syriac that have been lost, Ephrem's *Treatise against the Jews and Sects* should be mentioned.[11] We know also about another anti-Jewish treatise that was produced later, during the sixth century, by a distinguished East Syrian scholar and head of the famous School of Nisibis, that is the *Disputation against the Jews* by John of Bēt Rabban (not to be confused with his teacher Abraham).[12] The loss of these two compositions is especially lamentable, since due to the closeness in their time of composition and the socio-cultural milieu of Sasanian Mesopotamia to which their authors belonged, they might have provided a particularly useful point of comparison for the anti-Jewish polemic in CT. One should also mention two originally Greek anti-Jewish treatises that were translated into Syriac during late antiquity but are now lost: the five-volume work against the Jews by Eusebius of Emesa (4th c.),[13] and the "two books against the Jews" by Diodore of Tarsus (4th c.).[14] Moreover, the two major anti-Jewish works of John Chrysostom, the *Homilies against the Jews* and the *Treatise against the Jews and*

---

10 On anti-Jewish polemic by Aphrahat, see Neusner 1971; Becker 2002; Koltun-Fromm 2011; for Ephrem, see Botha 1990, 1991; McVey 1990; Shepardson 2008a.

11 It is quoted by Philoxenus of Mabbug in his *Florilegium* against Ḥabib; ed. Brière & Graffin 1982, p. 66, §33. It might also be that when mentioning Ephrem's "Disputation with the Jews," ʿAbdišoʿ of Nisibis is referring to this work; ed. Assemani 1719–1728, v. 3.1, p. 63. Cf. also the testimony of the *Chronicle of Seert* 1.68, where the "book of refutation of the Jews" is listed among Ephrem's works; ed. Scher 1908–1918, v. 2, p. 323.

12 This work is mentioned by Barḥadbešabbā ʿArbāyā, *Cause of the Foundation of the Schools*; ed. Scher 1908, p. 388. It is also mentioned by ʿAbdišoʿ; ed. Assemani 1719–1728, v. 3.1, p. 72. The *Chronicle of Seert* (2.9) refers to it as the "book of refutation of the Jews"; ed. Scher 1908–1918, v. 3, p. 116. On John's career, see Vööbus 1965, pp. 211–222.

13 Mentioned by Jerome, *Vir. ill.* 95. ʿAbdišoʿ refers to it as the "book against the Jews"; ed. Assemani 1719–1728, v. 3.1, p. 44.

14 Mentioned by Barḥadbešabbā ʿArbāyā; ed. Nau 1932, p. 315. This work was apparently translated into Syriac during the fifth century by Maʿna of Shiraz; see Baumstark 1922, p. 105.

the Heathen on the Divinity of Christ, were also rendered into Syriac, but these translations have only survived in fragments, which are still unpublished.[15]

Before moving on, I would like to address an important methodological issue in the research of *adversus Judaeos* literature that concerns the nature of the relationship between the written sources featuring polemics against Judaism and the socio-historical reality of the interaction between Jews and Christians. As a result of keen scholarly interest in the history of Jewish-Christian relations during the second half of the last century, two competing scholarly approaches to understanding anti-Jewish polemic in the works of ancient Christian authors have developed, one of which is socio-historical and the other of which is literary.[16]

The former approach, often referred to as the "theory of conflict," seeks to reconstruct the social background of anti-Jewish texts, assuming that the polemic reflects the situation of a fierce rivalry between the rising Christianity and the thriving and influential Judaism. One of the founding fathers of this theory was Marcel Simon, who in 1948 published a fundamental treatment of Jewish-Christian relations in antiquity entitled *Verus Israel*.[17] In this monograph, Simon opposes the view that during the first five centuries of Christian history, Judaism was isolated and unable to attract outsiders, which was popular among scholars before the Second World War. On the contrary, he maintains that at that time Jews and their religion were "a real, active, and often successful competitor with Christianity."[18] According to Simon, this competition was the main cause of friction between the two religious communities and thus accounts for the vehemence and persistence of anti-Jewish polemic in Christian texts. This theory profoundly altered the perception of Jewish-Christian relations in antiquity and has had a lasting effect on the development of scholarship in this field.[19]

An alternative model of Christian anti-Judaism, which may be called the "identity theory," resulted from both dissatisfaction with certain presuppositions and methods of the "conflict theory" and the general impact of the

---

15 For the former, see ms. British Library, Add. 14623 (dated 822/23); Wright, W. 1870–1872, v. 2, pp. 763–764. For the latter, see ms. British Library, Add. 14604 (7th c.); Wright, W. 1870–1872, v. 2, p. 724.
16 For a brief exposition of these approaches, see Stroumsa 1996, pp. 10–16. A useful overview of the development of scholarly perceptions of Jewish-Christian relations in antiquity during the past century is provided by Murray, M. 2004, pp. 127–152.
17 Simon 1996.
18 Simon 1996, p. 385.
19 Among the important contributions written from this perspective, one should mention Kraabel 1971; de Lange 1976; Wilken 1983.

"linguistic turn" in humanities on the practice of writing history.[20] Proponents of this approach claim that anti-Jewish polemic in the works of ecclesiastical authors must be primarily understood as an inner-Christian discourse that has little to do with external social reality. Rosemary Ruether laid the groundwork for this theory in her influential book *Faith and Fratricide*. She argues that anti-Judaism was not a peripheral phenomenon of Christian thought, but that from the New Testament period onwards, it constituted an intrinsic part of Christian self-identity due to its function as an integral element of classical Christology.[21]

Twenty years later, Miriam Taylor published a book that became a manifesto for the "identity theory."[22] In her work, Taylor wages a sustained attack on Simon's view that Christian anti-Judaism was a reaction to the rivalry between Christians and Jews. In contrast to the "conflict theory," Taylor argues that anti-Judaism was intrinsic to the Church Fathers' project of articulating a new and distinctive Christian identity, and therefore that the Jews mentioned in the works of Christian authors should primarily be regarded as "symbolic figures who play an essential role in the communication and development of the church's own distinctive conception of God's plans for His chosen people, and in the formation of the church's cultural identity."[23] According to this approach, the roots of anti-Judaism lie not in the external reality of Jewish-Christian interaction, but in the internal dynamics of Christian identity building, and so its polemic is aimed against a symbolic rather than a living Judaism. Taylor's position has been subjected to severe (and just) criticism for her attempt to explain *all* anti-Jewish sentiments in Christian literature as the result of inner-Christian discourse.[24] At the same time, there are a number of studies whose authors pursue a similar agenda by focusing on how Christian writers constructed "the Jew" and "Judaism" through their rhetoric instead of asking whether and how this rhetoric could be used as evidence for their attitude to the real Jews and Judaism.[25]

After thesis and antithesis, what should come but synthesis? Recent years have seen a growing number of publications in which scholars seek to find a way beyond this conceptual dichotomy and advocate the need for a new paradigm that surpasses the limitations of both these approaches while retaining and further enhancing their epistemological value. In a seminal article, Guy

---

20   On the latter, see Clark 2004.
21   Ruether 1974.
22   Taylor, M.S. 1995.
23   Taylor, M.S. 1995, pp. 4–5.
24   For a systematic critique of Taylor's book, see Carleton Paget 1997. See also Kinzig 1997; Broadhurst 2005.
25   Cf. Fredriksen 1995; Cameron 2002b; Shepardson 2008.

Stroumsa criticizes the weaknesses of the two approaches, where the "conflict theory" ignores "the autonomous power of theological beliefs and their ability to shape perceptions of the other," whereas the "identity theory" is plagued by ahistoricism, as it tends to misrepresent "Christian discourse" by treating it as if it were "a well-defined and fixed entity, unchanged by historical circumstances."[26] According to Stroumsa, one should pay great attention to the dynamic character of religious identity and focus on "the history of Christian discourse, its transformations throughout the first centuries," in order to understand the genesis and development of Christian anti-Judaism over time.[27]

Among significant practical attempts to develop a new integrative paradigm for conceptualizing Christian polemic against Judaism, one should mention the work of Judith Lieu, especially the monograph *Image and Reality*, in which she explores the treatment of the Jews and Judaism by second-century Christian writers.[28] In her analysis of the Christian presentation of the Jews during this period, Lieu characterizes it as a complex interplay between image and reality. She points out that when Christian authors speak of Jews and Judaism there is, on the one side, "a contemporary reality, one of which, in differing degrees, its authors are aware," and, on the other side, the "image," i.e. the terms in which they speak, which are created and molded by "their own needs, the logic of their own argument, and the tradition they draw on, especially the 'Old Testament.'"[29] The main task of scholars who study this material is thus to try to disentangle this "intertwining of historical experience and theological rationale" that characterizes Christian polemic against Jews while being fully aware of "the encounter between Judaism and Christianity as a meeting not of two strangers, but of two who were irrevocably bound up with each other."[30]

The importance of Lieu's analysis resides in the fact that it emphasizes that when analyzing Christian anti-Jewish literature, one should always strive to recognize that there is a convoluted relationship, which is not always clearly discernible, between the needs of Christian theology and self-definition and the presence of an external reality called Judaism. As per David Brakke's formulation, scholars must work at a "textual/extratextual dialogue" in order "to connect our surviving, primarily textual evidence to its original social world while not only accepting, but even fully appreciating, its nature as textual (that is, literary and rhetorical)."[31]

---

26 Stroumsa 1996, p. 15.
27 Stroumsa 1996, p. 17.
28 Lieu, J.M. 1996. Cf. also Lieu, J.M. 1992.
29 Lieu, J.M. 1996, p. 12.
30 Lieu, J.M. 1992, p. 87.
31 Brakke 2002, pp. 488–489.

With these considerations in mind, I am going to analyze first apologetic (section 2) and then polemical (sections 3 and 4) aspects of CT's attitude towards Jews and Judaism. In the concluding section (5), I will try to look at this material against the broader background of Jewish-Christian interaction in the late antique Near East. Before all that, however, I shall briefly address the related issue of to what extent, if at all, our author was influenced by Jewish tradition in his handling of biblical material.

1 The Jewish Background of CT

After more than 100 years of scholarly interest, CT has acquired a solid reputation as one of the richest depositories of Jewish apocryphal and exegetical traditions among Syriac Christian writings. This image of CT began to form during the first decades of the past century. In the introduction to his English translation of the *Pirke de-Rabbi Eliezer*, Gerald Friedlander lists it among other Christian apocrypha that in his view contain much material in common with this relatively late midrashic work.[32] However, Friedlander is reluctant to see any direct literary connection between this work and these Christian authors, limiting himself to the suggestion that they may all have relied on a common source.[33]

CT's reputation as a cornucopia of Jewish traditions was later reconfirmed by Sebastian Brock. Although he locates this work within the second period of his overall chronological scheme of the Jewish impact on Syriac Christianity (5th to 7th cc.), when "the gap between Syriac Christianity and its Jewish background widened,"[34] Brock nevertheless characterizes it as "the richest source for Jewish traditions."[35] A similar opinion has been voiced by many other students of Syriac literature, who have often assumed that CT's author was acquainted with a variety of Jewish sources, spanning from the Second Temple to the rabbinic period.[36]

Although the question of the Jewish influence on CT has occupied the minds of several scholars, there are not many in-depth investigations dealing with this subject. The first serious attempt to approach it was undertaken by Jacob

---

32 Friedlander 1916, p. lii. Cf. also Budge 1927, pp. xiv, 27.
33 Friedlander 1916, p. lii. For recent attempts to tackle this problem, see Spurling & Grypeou 2007; McDowell 2017, pp. 239–276.
34 Brock 1979, p. 226.
35 Brock 1979, p. 227.
36 Cf. Drijvers, H.J.W. 1985, p. 101; van Rompay 1996, p. 631; Ruzer 2001, p. 268; Hidal 2007, p. 575.

Bamberger at the turn of the last century.[37] In his book, Bamberger attempted to trace a number of exegetical traditions found in CT which in his view had parallels in Jewish, and particularly rabbinic, literature.[38] Unfortunately, Bamberger's approach to CT has several fundamental shortcomings. Firstly, he based his argument on the premise (which is not supported by any facts) that its author was directly acquainted with the *Book of Jubilees*,[39] as well as on a purely speculative claim about the existence of a separate composition entitled the "Book of Adam" (*Sifrā d-Ādām*) in the rabbinic circles of fourth-century Nisibis, with which he was also supposedly acquainted.[40] An even greater fault of Bamberger's approach is that in his assessment of individual traditions from CT in relation to their possible Jewish antecedents, he handled sources in a manner that Samuel Sandmel would later aptly call "parallelomania,"[41] that is, the heaping together of any possible parallels to a given tradition, however superficial they might be. The lack of intelligible criteria of relevance for his parallels, together with the aforementioned misguided assertions, renders Bamberger's study of CT completely obsolete.

The following years saw a number of isolated case studies that sought to uncover traces of influences from Jewish apocryphal or exegetical traditions on the author of CT by focusing on particular motifs or images. Some time ago, Michael Stone suggested, albeit cautiously, that CT may have depended on the primary Adam literature, i.e. the writings comprising the *Life of Adam and Eve* corpus.[42] This suggestion, however, was challenged by Marinus de Jonge and Johannes Tromp, who, listing some traditions common to CT and the primary Adam literature, reached the conclusion that "the claim that the *Cave of Treasures* depends directly on the *Life of Adam and Eve* cannot be substantiated."[43] Recently, Stone's hypothesis has found a supporter in Michael D. Eldridge, who writes about CT's "dependence on the actual *text* of a primary Adam book similar to the *Greek Life* [of Adam and Eve]," taking certain traits in the depiction of Adam's descendants gathered at his deathbed

---

37 Bamberger 1901.
38 The following passages from CT are discussed: 1.22; 2.19–21; 5.1; 5.17–20; 5.21–27; 5.28; 8.2–10; 14.2–3; 16.15–17; 32.14; 34.2, 9; 35.9–10; 35.25–28; 39.6–12; 40.3–6.
39 Bamberger 1901, p. 24.
40 Bamberger 1901, p. 25. Bamberger bases his argument on such phrases as סיפרא דאדם הראשון in *b.Bava Metzia* 85b (cf. also ספרו שלאדם in *Genesis Rabbah* 24.2 and של ספרו אדם הראשון in *Exodus Rabbah* 40.2), which are in fact nothing more than exegetical variations rabbis made on the phrase ספר תולדת אדם, "the book of the generations of Adam" in Gen 5:1.
41 Sandmel 1962.
42 Stone 1992, p. 55.
43 As has been suggested by de Jonge & Tromp 1997, p. 74.

that are supposedly present in both the Greek *Life* 5.3 and CT 6.8, 22 as proof.⁴⁴ It seems that the last word in this scholarly dispute has not yet been said, so Stone's proposal that "the whole question of the exact relationship between the various primary Adam books and *The Cave of Treasures* should be examined once more" still remains in force.⁴⁵

Another case of CT's author being acquainted with contemporary Jewish exegesis has been suggested by Serge Ruzer. While discussing the peculiar traditions about Abel's blood in CT, he comes to the conclusion that they "might bear witness to a contemporary exegetical contact with rabbinic tradition."⁴⁶ Ruzer's argument is based on a supposed correlation between the re-enactment of the oath on Abel's blood taken by every successive generation of Seth's descendants, according to CT,⁴⁷ and those exegetical traditions found in rabbinic literature that derive meaning from the plural form of the noun "blood" in the Hebrew text of Genesis 4:1. Yet however one may regard the results of such a comparative approach, any possibility of a *direct* dependence of CT on the rabbinic texts at hand in this particular case should be safely ruled out.

A possible instance of Jewish influence on CT was sought in the account of Yonṭon, the fourth son of Noah, who was born after the Flood and taught wisdom to the first monarch Nimrod, especially the art of astronomy (CT 27.6–11). The singular character of this figure, who is not attested in any Jewish or Christian source prior to the time of CT, was noted by Stephen Gero, who suggested that "the legend of Yonṭon ... arose within a branch of Mesopotamian Judaism, which adopted a broadly favorable attitude toward Babylonian astrology, and was receptive to local historical lore."⁴⁸ His position, however, was challenged by Witold Witakowski, who, without producing any sustained argument, claimed that the figure of Yonṭon had been invented by the author of CT himself.⁴⁹ The case has been "reopened" by Alexander Toepel, who follows Su-Min Ri's suggestion that the name "Yonṭon" was derived from the biblical figure of Eber's son Yokṭan (Gen 10:25)⁵⁰ and further develops Gero's thesis by arguing that this story should be taken as evidence of CT's author having

---

44   Eldridge 2001, p. 24. Yet Eldridge does not base his far-reaching claim on any philological argumentation that takes the critical edition of the original Syriac text of CT into consideration. In any case, even from the material that he quotes, it can hardly be seen how his argument about CT's *direct* dependence on the Greek *Life of Adam and Eve* might be sustained.
45   Stone 1992, p. 55, n. 42.
46   Ruzer 2001, p. 270.
47   CT 8.13; 8.19; 9.5; 10.5; 12.11.
48   Gero 1980, p. 328.
49   Witakowski 1993, pp. 641, 648. He has been supported by Leonhard 2001, pp. 287–288.
50   Ri 2000, p. 356.

appropriated an otherwise unattested tradition about Yokṭan's transmission of astrological lore that circulated in Jewish Hellenistic circles in the third century CE.⁵¹ As often happens in intellectual history, the scarcity of relevant evidence only exacerbates scholarly curiosity. It seems though that the case is doomed to remain a matter of learned speculation for the time being. In any case, in the context of our research, it is important to point out that none of the scholars discussing the figure of Yonṭon has claimed that our author was directly dependent on any known Jewish source.

In addition to these attempts to recover a Jewish background for CT, scholars have pointed out several other parallels between this work and various Jewish sources, although mostly in a somewhat perfunctory manner.⁵² Moreover, Su-Min Ri, in his comprehensive commentary on CT, suggests a large number of parallels from Jewish literature.⁵³

The problem of CT's Jewish background has recently been addressed by Alexander Toepel, who launched a thorough and systematic source-critical examination of chapters 1–7, which deal with Adam and Seth.⁵⁴ As a result, Toepel has singled out twenty-two exegetical motifs that are either possibly or definitely of Jewish origin.⁵⁵ As his own analysis makes clear, however, most of these motifs are already attested in Greek or Syriac Christian works that predate CT,⁵⁶ and thus cannot be used as evidence of the author's direct acquaintance with Jewish sources. Toepel concludes his study with a statement that the nature of the use of Jewish traditions in CT clearly shows that it is a Christian work.⁵⁷

According to Toepel, among these twenty-two motifs, there are only four that have parallels in Jewish sources but not in earlier Christian ones: (1) the beauty and gigantic size of Adam (CT 2.13ff; 6.2), also found in rabbinic literature; (2) Adam's joyous reaction to the newly created Eve as an allusion to their wedding (CT 3.13), also found in the Samaritan Targum to Genesis 2:24; (3) the "garments of skin" of Genesis 3:21 as the actual skin of the human body (CT 4.23), also found in Philo's *Quaest. in Gen.* 1.53; (4) the legend of Cain's murder of Abel as an outcome of the conflict over marriage to their twin sisters

---

51 Toepel 2006a, pp. 242–245.
52 See Anderson 1988, 1989, 2000; Brock 1979, pp. 227–228; van Rompay 1993, p. 631.
53 Ri 2000.
54 Toepel 2006b.
55 See Toepel 2006b, pp. 242–243 for the list, which includes the following passages: CT 1.3; 1.9–10; 1.21; 1.22; 1.25; 2.2; 2.6–9; 2.12; 2.13ff; 2.20f; 3.1–7; 3.13; 4.1; 4.4f; 4.23; 5.5; 5.19–32; 6.1; 6.2f; 6.9; 7.11,18.
56 Toepel 2006b, pp. 243–244.
57 Toepel 2006b, p. 244.

(CT 5.19–32), also found in rabbinic literature.[58] However, in none of these cases does Toepel succeed in substantiating his general assertion that the author of CT was at least sometimes *directly* dependent on Jewish sources.[59]

Due to the limitations of space, I will refrain from an in-depth analysis of these exegetical traditions; instead, I will briefly point out some shortcomings in Toepel's handling of these cases which render them unsuitable to be used as arguments to support his thesis. In case #1, while the author of CT does describe Adam's body as exceedingly glorious and beautiful, he never explicitly refers to its gigantic dimensions, contrary to Toepel's opinion.[60] Likewise, case #2 cannot bear the weight that Toepel placed on it, since it is built on the unjustified narrowing of the broad semantic range of the Syriac verb *ḥdy* (Pe "to rejoice"; Pa "to make happy," "to greet") in CT 3.13 to the particular act of marital consummation.[61] In case #3, I fail to see how the brief reference to God's creation of the garments of skin, which were spread "over" the already existing material "body of pains" according to CT 4.22–23, is related to Philo's philosophical interpretation of this biblical image as a symbolic reference to the human body. As for case #4, the motif of Cain's murder of Abel as a result of their conflict over their twin sister(s) found in CT 5.19–32 also appears in Christian sources, some of which are unquestionably earlier than CT.[62]

To summarize these attempts to identify CT's Jewish background, it can be concluded that for the most part, those originally Jewish motifs and images that do appear in this composition reached its author through the mediation of earlier Christian works. So far, no convincing evidence has been provided for our author's *direct* acquaintance either with contemporary rabbinic traditions of scriptural exegesis or with ancient Jewish compositions that were popular in certain Christian circles such as *Jubilees*, *1 Enoch*, the *Life of Adam and Eve*, or the works of Philo and Josephus. In light of all this, one wonders whether the presence of a relatively limited amount of Jewish traditions, mostly borrowed from earlier Christian sources, makes CT deserving of its widespread reputation as a cornucopia of Jewish lore. In my opinion, this image of CT largely

---

58   Toepel 2006b, p. 244.
59   Cf. Toepel 2006b, p. 244: "Der Verfasser verwendet eine Anzahl von jüdischen Motiven, die er z.T. von christlichen Autoren, z.T. direkt aus jüdischen Quellen übernimmt."
60   Even if it were true, this suggestion could hardly be used to support Toepel's thesis, since the notion of Adam's gigantic dimensions is also attested in Christian sources. Cf. the Gnostic mythological system described in Irenaeus, *Adv. haer.* 1.30.6; Greek *Questions of Bartholomew* 1.21–22 (ed. Wilmart & Tisserant 1913, pp. 187–188); Armenian *Question* 3 (ed. Stone 1996, p. 119).
61   Toepel 2006b, pp. 108–109.
62   Cf. the doctrine of the Archontics in Epiphanius, *Panar.* 3.40.5.4; *Testament of Adam* 3:5.

emerged in response to the peculiar mixed genre of this work, which blends chronography, historiography, scriptural exegesis, apologetics, and polemics in a way unusual for Christian literature of late antiquity and certainly unique for Syriac literature.

2 Apologetics: The Genealogy of the Virgin Mary

In chapter 44, the author goes to considerable lengths discussing the genealogy of the Virgin Mary, with a view to rebuffing the accusations made against her by the Jews. Within the general flow of the narrative, this chapter follows the account of the Jews' return from their captivity in Babylon under Ezra's leadership (ch. 43). The author concludes this account with a statement that the genealogies of the later Israelites have been lost by the "scribes" (CT 43.13). At the same time, he claims that he himself possesses knowledge of the correct genealogy and presents a list of the succession of families that goes from Zerubbabel to Christ (CT 43.14–25).

This genealogical digression is continued in the next chapter, which opens with the statement that the failure of the "early writers" to establish the correct genealogy of their fathers served as a pretext for the Jews to challenge Christians on the matter of Mary's descent (CT 44.1–2):

> The Jews pressed the sons of the Church very strongly to show them the fathers of the blessed Mary in the order of the succession of their families, and for the sons of the Church to be diligent, in order to investigate the succession of the families of their fathers and to show them the truth.[63]

The author also relates that an apparent reason behind the Jews' supposed request was that they "call Mary an adulteress" (CT 44.3).[64] Accordingly, the main rationale behind his genealogical enterprise is explicitly stated as "to shut up the mouths of the Jews," who as a result would come to "believe that Mary was of the seed of the house of David and of Abraham" (CT 44.4).[65]

---

63 Or^A: ܐܠܨܘ ܗܘܘ ܝܗܘܕܝܐ ܛܒ ܠܒܢܝ̈ ܥܕܬܐ ܕܢܚܘܘܢ ܐܢܘܢ ܐܒܗ̈ܘܗ̇ ܕܛܘܒܢܝܬܐ ܡܪܝܡ܂ ܒܛܟܣܐ ܕܫܪ̈ܒܬܗܘܢ܂ ܘܢܬܚܦܛܘܢ ܐܝܟ܂ ܠܒܢ̈ܝ ܥܕܬܐ ܕܢܒܨܘܢ ܥܠ ܫܘܘ̈ܕܥܐ ܕܫܪ̈ܒܬܐ ܕܐܒܗ̈ܝܗܘܢ ܘܢܚܘܘܢ ܐܢܘܢ ܫܪܪܐ܀

64 Or^A: ܡܛܠ ܕܓܝܪܬܐ ܩܪܝܢ ܗܘܘ ܠܗ̇ ܠܡܪܝܡ܂

65 Or^A: ܘܣܟܡ ܐܟܘܬ ܦܘܡܗܘܢ܂ ܕܝܗܘܕ̈ܝܐ܂ ܘܡܗܝܡܢܝܢ܂ ܕܡܪܝܡ ܐܝܬܝܗ̇ ܡܢ ܙܪܥܗ ܕܒܝܬ ܕܘܝܕ ܘܕܐܒܪܗܡ܂

He then offers an explanation of how the Jews' present lack of adequate genealogical knowledge came about. A decisive role in the loss of this information is ascribed to the three destructions of Jewish books, including those under Antiochus IV Epiphanes and Herod, as a result of which no "table of succession of the generation of their fathers" has survived (CT 44.5–11). The author continues by deploring the inability of previous "Greek," "Hebrew," and "Syrian" writers to provide a correct and complete table of succession of the sixty-three generations from Adam to Christ, which would include information not only about the male line of ancestors, but about their wives as well (CT 44.12–14).

At this point, an explicit statement is made about what he considers to comprise his unique contribution to the treasure of Christian knowledge. In a rhetorical address to his projected interlocutor "Nāmusāyā," the author asserts that due to divine assistance, he is the first Christian writer able to "write down the true table of succession" of the sixty-three generations of Christ (CT 44.15–20). This claim is followed by the list of Jesus' ancestors, beginning with Adam (CT 44.21–47). According to this list, Mary was the daughter of Joseph's uncle, while both of them trace their descent from King David via their grandfather Mathan.

At the conclusion of his genealogical deliberations, our author notes that the marriage between Mary and her paternal cousin Joseph was providentially prearranged by God, who "knew that Mary would be certainly persecuted by the Jews" (CT 44.48),[66] and reassures Nāmusāyā once more of the Davidic lineage of the Virgin (CT 44.49).

As the author explicitly declares in CT 44.3–4, his entire genealogical project is a response to the Jews' alleged claim about Mary being an "adulteress" (*gayārtā*). Although extremely laconic, this formulation of the Jews' resentment of Mary allows us to identify it as a reference to the well-known anti-Christian polemical topos of Jesus as the illegitimate offspring of Mary's liaison with a man other than her official husband Joseph.[67]

The earliest undisputable attestation of this accusation against Jesus' mother comes from Origen's apologetical work *Against Celsus*. One of the charges brought against Christianity by the second-century Roman philosopher Celsus that Origen strives to refute is expressed in the following observation about circumstances of Jesus' birth:

---

66 Or^A: ܒܪܗ ܕܡܪܝܡ ܡܢ ܓܝܪܘܬܐ ܕܓܝܪܬ ܗܘܐ ܝܕܥ.
67 See Meier 1991, pp. 216–219; Brown 1993, pp. 534–542; Shoemaker 1999, pp. 788–798.

> The mother of Jesus is described as having been turned out by the carpenter who was betrothed to her, as she had been convicted of adultery and had a child by a certain soldier named Panthera.⁶⁸

The primary purpose of this polemical strategy is to discredit Jesus by claiming, contrary to the canonical narrative of the Gospels, that he was an illegitimate child and thus to deprive him of any claim to authority.

This anti-Christian argument most likely originated in a Jewish milieu, since Origen explicitly refers to Celsus having received it from a Jewish informant. This charge is associated with Jews in another early work, the apocryphal *Acts of Pilate* (2:3–5), where the Jews accuse Jesus before the procurator of being "born of fornication" (ἐκ πορνείας γεγέννησαι).⁶⁹ Taking into consideration the time when Celsus' work was produced, i.e. c. 177–180 CE, it could be suggested that the accusation challenging Mary's marital integrity was formulated around the middle of the second century. This polemical motif may, however, have been even older, and such allegations against Jesus' mother might have already been made in the first century. Thus, it has been argued by several scholars that the story of Mary's extramarital affair with Panthera was already circulating during the last decades of the first century and that it lies behind the story of the miraculous conception of Jesus which was propagated at that time by the authors of the canonical Gospels.⁷⁰

The charge of Jesus' illegitimate birth gained considerable popularity and became a stock motif in the tradition of Jewish polemic against Christianity. Its traces may be found in the corpus of rabbinic literature, where Jesus is occasionally referred to as *Ben Pandira*, "son of Panthera."⁷¹ The story of Mary falling victim to sexual assault by a neighbor, who beguiled her by acting as if he was her husband, forms an essential part of the caricatured account of Jesus' career in the *Toledoth Yeshu*, a Jewish "anti-Gospel" that was written during the early Middle Ages but contains many motifs and themes that go back to late antiquity.⁷²

---

68 *C. Cels.* 1.32: ἐν ᾗ ἀναγέγραπται ἡ τοῦ Ἰησοῦ μήτηρ ὡς ἐξωσθεῖσα ἀπὸ τοῦ μνηστευσαμένου αὐτὴν τέκτονος, ἐλεγχθεῖσα ἐπὶ μοιχείᾳ καὶ κύουσα ἀπό τινος στρατιώτου Πανθήρα τοὔνομα; ed. Marcovich 2001, p. 33; trans. Chadwick 1965, p. 31. Cf. also *C. Cels.* 1.28; 1.69.
69 Ed. Tischendorf 1876, pp. 224–227.
70 Cf. Rokeah 1969, p. 14. A similar position is taken by McKnight 2003; Chilton 2007.
71 Cf. *t.Hullin* 2:23–24; *t.Sotah* 5:9; *y.Avoda Zara* 2:2 [40d]; *y.Shabbat* 14:4 [14d]; *b.Sanhedrin* 43a; 67a; 106a; *b.Shabbat* 104b. For analysis of this material, see Horbury 1971, pp. 402–408; Schäfer 2007, pp. 15–24.
72 For an edition and translation of different recensions, see Meerson & Schäfer 2014; on the story of Mary's seduction, see v. 1, pp. 45–56. For general information on this composition, see also Horbury 1971; Di Segni 1985.

The accusation of Jesus' illegitimate birth was certainly known in Syria–Mesopotamia and was accordingly a matter of concern for the local Christians. Ephrem alludes to this charge on several occasions. In the *Hymns on Nativity*, while speaking about the reward that Joseph would have deserved due to his acceptance of the pregnant Mary, the poet exclaims:

> For who could convince a just man to carry the hateful son of adultery (*bar gawrā*) and to be pursued from one place to another?[73]

Moreover, Ephrem often refers to the "slander" to which Mary was subjected by the Jews on account of Jesus' conception and birth, as for example in the following passage:

> Moses has already exposed how slanderous they were, for although cloths of virgins are possessed by their families, they have accused them and killed them. How much more they slandered the mother of the Son![74]

Likewise, in his description of the verbal abuse to which Jesus had been subjected by his "crucifiers," the author of the *Book of Steps* relates that "they called him son of adultery (*bar gawrē*) and a deceiver."[75] Jacob of Serugh, in the *Homily on the Presentation of Our Lord in the Temple*, constructs a dialogue between Mary and Symeon the Righteous in which she urges him to defend her from the false accusations made by the Jews on account of her having given birth to Jesus and relates that "I had been reckoned as an adulteress (*gayārtā*) on account of Him."[76]

In order to better understand the author of CT's motivation for rebuffing this particular motif from the repertoire of anti-Christian mockery, one should take into account that as a result of the success of Jewish polemical efforts, the negative image of Mary as an adulteress was propagated among other communities of the late ancient Near East. Of particular relevance in this respect is the evidence of Zoroastrian polemic against Christianity.

---

73 *De Nat.* 2.11; ed. Beck 1959, p. 16; trans. McVey 1989, p. 78.
74 *De Nat.* 14.13; ed. Beck 1959, p. 79; trans. McVey 1989, p. 143. Cf. also *De Nat.* 6.3; Ephremian *Commentary on the Diatessaron* 2.1.
75 *Lib. Grad.* 22.11; ed. Kmosko 1926, col. 660; trans. Kitchen & Parmentier 2004, pp. 260–261. Cf. also *Lib. Grad.* 27.1.
76 Ed. Bedjan 1905–1910, v. 5, p. 462; trans. Kollamparampil 1997, p. 154. Similar rhetoric appears in another Marian work by Jacob, the *Homily on the Holy Mother of God and Everlasting Virgin Mary and against Those, who Blaspheme and Say that She Did Not Remain Virgin after her Delivery*; ed. Bedjan 1902, pp. 688–690.

A decisive proof that Zoroastrians were acquainted with this argument and were making use of it to challenge Christians by the time of CT comes from the *History of Vardan and the Armenian War*, an Armenian historiographical work ascribed to Ełišē Vardapet. Composed during the fifth or, as some scholars argue, the sixth century, it narrates the history of the armed uprising of the Christian Armenians against the Persians during the reign of Yazdgird II (r. 439–457). Chapter 2 of the *History* contains an exchange of letters between Mihr-Narseh, the grand vizier (Mid. Pers. *wuzurg framādār*) of Yazdgird,[77] and the Armenian high clergy. In his letter, incorporated *in toto* into the *History*, the vizier seeks to demonstrate the superiority of Zoroastrianism over Christianity. One of the absurd beliefs of the Christians that he denounces is their claim that "God who created heaven and earth came ... and was born of some woman called Mary, whose husband was Joseph." Instead, he points out that Jesus "was son to a certain Banturak by an illicit intercourse."[78] In their reply to the vizier, the Armenian bishops rebuff this and other accusations while reproaching him, among other things, for not referring to Jesus with his proper name "Jesus Christ," but calling him instead "the son of Pʻandurak."[79] The Armenian versions of the name of Jesus' supposed father, *Bantʻurak* and *Pʻandurak*, are nothing but slightly corrupt forms of "Pandira," known to us from rabbinic sources.

A similar polemical argument appears in the *Škand Gumānīg Wizār*, a Middle Persian apologetic treatise composed during the ninth century by Mardān-Farrox, which offers a systematic critique of various religions, including the Christian faith.[80] At the beginning of chapter 15, which deals with Christianity, its author relates the story of Jesus' birth, in which he introduces Mary by saying that she lived among the Jews in Jerusalem where she "was known for her loose companionship" (*dušabāgīh āšnāg būd*).[81] From the following narrative, in which Mary is asked to explain the fact of her unexpected pregnancy and does so by referring to her encounter with the Archangel Gabriel, one can infer that the main intent of this passage was to cast doubt on the sexual integrity of Jesus' mother and thus on his own descent.

As the case of Ełišē's *History* makes clear, the negative portrayal of Mary presented there goes back to the pre-Islamic period of Zoroastrian polemic against Christianity. We can also learn about the close familiarity of the "pagan" inhabitants of the Near East with this anti-Christian slur during late

---

77   For him, see Daryaee 2012.
78   Ed. Ter Minasyan 1957, p. 26; trans. Thomson 1982, p. 79.
79   Ed. Ter Minasyan 1957, p. 38; trans. Thomson 1982, p. 90.
80   On this work, see Cereti 2001, pp. 79–86.
81   Ed. and trans. Taillieu 2004, pp. 132–133. See also Gignoux 2008, pp. 61–63.

antiquity from the fact that it was apparently known in the Arabian milieu in which the Qurʾān was produced. There, in *Sūrat an-Nisāʾ* (4:156), the Jews are criticized for uttering "a great slander (*buhtānan ʿaẓīman*) against Mary."[82] The polemical allegation of Mary's sexual misconduct also seems to reverberate in the Mandaean legends about a certain "Meryey," a positive female figure who had left Judaism for Mandaeism and was consequently accused of sexual licentiousness by her parents and former coreligionists.[83]

As one turns to the particular apologetic strategy chosen by the author of CT in order to refute the Jewish charge against Mary, namely providing a genealogical list which demonstrates her Davidic lineage, a question arises as to its relevance to the topic under discussion. It should be pointed out that by the time of CT's composition, Christian apologetes had developed a number of strategies to counter Jewish attempts to undermine the Christian belief that Mary had conceived and given birth to Jesus while remaining a virgin. Besides a straightforward rejection, more sophisticated ways of handling this accusation were invented. Thus, the author of the *Protevangelium of James* (16:1–3) introduced a story about Mary successfully passing the biblical ordeal of *sotah* (Num 5:11–31) into his account of her life as a means of proving her marital integrity.[84] Some authors defended Jesus' virginal birth by pointing to the story of the creation of Eve from Adam's side as a relevant precedent.[85] As to the story of Panthera, several ancient authors understood this patronym as relating to Jesus' grandfather on Joseph's side.[86] Others, like Eusebius, interpreted the name Panthera symbolically, on the basis of the supposed ability of the animal of the same name to lull its prey with its fragrance.[87]

The author of CT, however, chooses to defend Mary's honor by providing her with a Davidic genealogy. At first glance, this line of defense appears to be incoherent. It misses the point, since from a properly halakhic point of view, such argumentation is of little relevance; that is, Mary could be of a proper Davidic lineage and still be vulnerable to the accusation of adultery, which

---

82   Cf. *Qurʾān* 24:16, where the same phrase, i.e. the "great slander," appears in the context of the defense of Muhammad's wife Aisha against an accusation of sexual immorality.
83   Cf. *Book of John* 34–35; ed. Häberl & McGrath 2020, pp. 164–181. See also Buckley 1993.
84   Cf. also the Syriac version of *Transitus Mariae*; ed. Lewis 1902, pp. 38 [Syr.], 23 [trans.].
85   Cf. Ephremian *Commentary on the Diatessaron* 2.2–3. For an explicitly anti-Jewish use of this argument, see Jacob of Serugh, *Homilies against the Jews* 1.66–86; ed. Albert 1976, p. 48. As to the possibility of Jews being aware of this line of reasoning, see the story of the polemic between R. Simlai and some *minim* in *y.Berakhot* 9:1 [12d]; see Kister 2001, pp. 56–57.
86   Cf. Epiphanius, *Panar.* 78.7.5; *Doctrina Iacobi* 1.42.
87   *Ecl. proph.* 3.10; ed. Gaisford 1842, p. 111.

would render Jesus' descent illegitimate. In order to comprehend the driving force behind our author's apologetic efforts, we should pay attention to the issue of Mary's lineage in the context of Jewish-Christian polemics in antiquity.

The New Testament contains many passages that either note Jesus' Davidic descent or use the title "son of David" when referring to him.[88] Yet when the Gospels' authors give details of Jesus' Davidic lineage, they establish it through Joseph (Mt 1:2–16; Lk 3:23–38). At the same time, the canonical writings of the New Testament provide no information about Mary's descent, except for a brief mention that her relative Elizabeth was "a descendant of Aaron" (Lk 1:5, 36). Speculations about the identity of Mary's ancestors began at a very early stage. From the second century on, the belief in the Davidic lineage of Jesus' mother becomes a popular notion among Christian authors.[89] In the Syriac tradition, this notion might also have been in circulation at this time, in the *Diatessaron* version of Luke 2:4–5.[90] We see it embraced by two fourth-century writers, Aphrahat and Ephrem. The former relates that "Jesus was born from Mary, the virgin, from the seed of the house of David."[91] According to Ephrem, "Joseph, the son of David, espoused himself with the daughter of David."[92]

Our author was not the first Christian writer who had recourse to the motif of the Davidic lineage of Mary or Jesus in the context of a polemic against Judaism. This subject is raised in several texts of the *adversus Judaeos* tradition. As early as the second century, Tertullian, in his apologetic composition *Against the Jews*, asserts that the virgin from whom Christ was to be born "must derive her lineage of the seed of David (*ex semine Dauid*)," quoting Isaiah 11:1–2 as a proof-text.[93] In several works that claim to depict actual debates between Jews and Christians, the former raise doubts about the Davidic descent of Jesus or Mary. Thus, in the *Dialogue of Simon and Theophilus*, the Jew asks his Christian interlocutor to demonstrate how Jesus "was born from the seed of David in the city of Bethlehem." In his reply, the Christian quotes Isaiah 11:1–2 as the proof-text for Mary's descent "from the seed of David."[94] In another dialogue between Timothy and Aquila, the Jew tries to corner the Christian by

---

[88] Cf. Mt 1:1,6,17; 9:27; 12:23; 15:22; 20:30–31; 21:9,15; 22:42–45; Mk 10:47–48; 11:10; 12:35–37; Lk 1:27–32; 3:31; 18:38–39; 20:41–44; Acts 2:25–31; 13:22–23,34–37; Rom 1:3–4; 15:12; 2 Tim 2:8; Rev 3:7; 5:5; 22:16. For a discussion, see Meier 1991, pp. 216–219.

[89] Cf. *Protevangelium of James* 10:1; Justin Martyr, *Dial.* 43.1; 45.4; 100.3; Ireneaus, *Adv. haer.* 3.21.5; Tertullian, *De carne Christi* 22.

[90] See Quispel 1975, pp. 160–161. For an overview of different views on Mary's genealogy among Syriac Christians, see Brock 2006.

[91] *Dem.* 23.20; ed. Parisot 1907, col. 64; trans. Valavanolickal 2005, v. 2, p. 279.

[92] *De Nat.* 2.13; ed. Beck 1959, p. 16; trans. McVey 1989, p. 79.

[93] *Adv. Jud.* 9.26; ed. Kroymann 1954b, p. 1372; trans. Thelwall 1870, p. 233.

[94] *Altercatio Simoni et Theophili* 15; ed. Varner 2004, pp. 104–105.

pointing out the apparent contradiction between the two Christological titles of Jesus, "son of God" and "son of David."[95] One also finds selections of biblical proof-texts intended to demonstrate Jesus' Davidic descent in several *testimonia* collections, which served as handbooks of sorts for Christian polemicists against Judaism.[96]

The considerable attention these polemicists paid to the defense of the Davidic lineage of Jesus and Mary raises a question as to whether the Jews' hostile inquisitiveness about Mary's Davidic descent in CT reflects a contemporary Jewish argument against Christianity. The apparent absence of anti-Christian polemic based on denial of the Davidic descent of Jesus or his mother in genuine Jewish sources from late antiquity seems to contradict this interpretation. However, besides the already quoted Christian sources, there is additional evidence that makes us seriously entertain such a possibility.

A remarkable testimony of the antiquity of the anti-Christian argument based on a repudiation of Jesus' Davidic pedigree comes from the polemical treatise *Against the Galileans* by Emperor Julian. As a part of his attack on the Christian use of biblical proof-texts, the emperor endeavors to demonstrate that the prophecy about the coming of a Messiah from the "royal house of David" in Genesis 49:10 could not be applied to the figure of Jesus, the "son of Mary." According to Julian, since Jesus "was not born of Joseph but of the Holy Spirit," he has no right to claim the former's Davidic lineage through Judah.[97] It is not clear whether the emperor invented this argument himself or whether he was relying on the already existing tradition of the *adversus Christianoi* polemics by pagans or Jews. Given his close ties with the Jewish establishment of Palestine, the latter scenario does not seem impossible.

A more explicit example of Jews challenging Christians regarding Mary's Davidic lineage is found in the *Teaching of Jacob, the Newly Baptized*. This Christian work, written in Greek during the late 630s or early 640s, purports to tell the story of a certain Jacob who converted from Judaism to Christianity and found himself engaged in protracted disputes with his former coreligionists as a result.[98] At some point in the verbal exchange between Jacob and the Jews, who try to dissuade him from embracing Christianity, they arrive at the subject of Jesus' Davidic lineage.[99] Jacob relates how after having examined

---

95 *Dialogue of Timothy and Aquila* 35; ed. Varner 2004, pp. 218–221.
96 Cf. Ps.-Epiphanius, *Testimony Book* 7; ed. Hotchkiss 1974, pp. 28–31; Ps.-Gregory of Nyssa, *Testimonies against the Jews* 2.7; ed. Albl 2004, pp. 18–21.
97 *C. Gal.* 253D–261E; ed. Wright, W.C. 1913–23, pp. 394–397. For more on this passage and its impact, see Cook 2000, pp. 289–290.
98 On this work, see Dagron & Déroche 1991, pp. 17–46.
99 *Doctrina Iacobi* 1.41–42; ed. Dagron & Déroche 1991, pp. 130–135.

the Scriptures, he had become persuaded of the Messiahship of Jesus, who was born of Mary, "daughter of Joachim from the tribe of Judah." This statement triggers a Jew named Isaac's promise to renounce his ancestral religion if Jacob will demonstrate Mary's Davidic lineage to him. While challenging Jacob on this issue, Isaac makes explicit mention of the fact that in the New Testament, Jesus' Davidic descent is only established through Joseph. In his reply to Isaac, Jacob relates a story about his meeting with a certain "great Jewish scholar of the law" from Tiberias who revealed to him Mary's correct genealogy, which traces her lineage back to David. From Jacob's account, it follows that the Tiberian Jew regarded this genealogical information as a useful tool in polemic against Christians, who improperly exalt Mary as the "mother of God" and believe that she "is from heaven."

This testimony reinforces our suggestion that the denunciation of Mary's Davidic lineage comprised a genuine polemical strategy in the repertoire of Jewish arguments used against Christianity in antiquity. The reliability of the *Teaching of Jacob* as a source of authentic information on Jewish attitudes towards Christians is strengthened by the fact that in distinction from many other fictional dialogues between Jews and Christians, this composition evinces a much more intimate knowledge of post-biblical Judaism.[100]

A conclusive proof that such an argument was indeed used by the Jews for the purposes of polemic against Christianity is found in a thirteenth-century anti-Christian composition, the Hebrew *Sefer Niẓẓaḥon Yašan*. Among other arguments against Christianity, its author seeks to undermine the Christian claim that "Jesus' genealogy can be traced to kings" and for this purpose goes into a detailed examination of the New Testament accounts of Jesus' descent.[101] According to the author of the *Niẓẓaḥon*, the common Christian belief that Joseph was not Jesus' biological father renders the Davidic lineage of the former in the Gospels irrelevant for establishing the latter's identity. It would be more persuasive, he argues, if Christians were able to demonstrate the royal lineage of Jesus on the basis of Mary's genealogy, but this is impossible on the grounds of the New Testament itself:

> Rather than telling us the genealogy of Joseph, he should have told us that of Mary by saying that so-and-so begat so-and-so until "So-and-so begat Mary who gave birth to Jesus." The fact that this was not done

---

100 See van der Horst 2009.
101 Ed. Berger 1979, pp. 106 [Heb.], 167 [trans.].

shows that they did not know Mary's genealogy and that she was not of royal descent.[102]

On another occasion, the author also refutes Christian attempts to save the situation and to secure a Davidic pedigree for Mary by making her a "relative" (Heb. *qərōḇāh*) of Joseph.[103]

Notwithstanding its late date, the *Niẓẓaḥon* can help us to reconstruct what might have been a driving force behind the anti-Marian disposition ascribed to the Jews in CT and the *Teaching*. Because of the elliptical manner in which these Christian authors present Jewish attempts to deny Mary a Davidic lineage, the nature of the polemic edge of the argument vis-à-vis the Christian doctrine is not entirely apparent. However, as the anti-Christian argumentation presented in the *Niẓẓaḥon* makes clear, Mary's Davidic descent becomes significant once Joseph is left out of the picture as a merely legal (and not biological) father of Jesus. In that case, Mary's genealogy would remain the only possible avenue for defending the Christian claim that Jesus was a descendant of David according to the flesh. By denying Mary a Davidic pedigree, Jewish polemicists against Christianity would achieve several objectives. They would not only completely undermine the long-standing Christian tradition of interpreting the Old Testament prophecies about the Davidic Messiah as being fulfilled in Jesus (cf. Gen 49:10; 2 Sam 7:12–14; Is 9:6–7), but they would also cast doubt on Jesus' royal authority as a cornerstone of traditional Christology.[104] It was against these or very similar attacks that the author of CT was attempting to build a line of defense by constructing his genealogy of Jesus' mother.

There may also be an additional dimension to the apologetic agenda pursued by the author of CT in his defense of Jesus' genealogy. As has been noted earlier, on several occasions in this section and later on he makes his fictive narrator Ephrem turn to the interlocutor, addressed as ܢܡܘܣܝܐ / NMWSY', who is characterized as "my brother" or "our brother."[105] Whereas it is not difficult to decipher the form NMWSY', which should most probably be read as *Nāmusāyā*, establishing the exact meaning of this name and its connotations in the context of CT poses certain difficulties.

---

102   Ed. Berger 1979, pp. 106 [Heb.], 167 [trans.].
103   Ed. Berger 1979, pp. 61 [Heb.], 107 [trans.].
104   Cf. the standard title *malkā mšiḥā*, "King Messiah," applied to Jesus in Syriac tradition. See Brock 2007.
105   Cf. CT 44.17,19,49,53; 45.1,13; 47.6; 48.5; 49.20; 50.19; 51.11; 52.14; 53.11,21.

The first translator of CT into a modern language, Carl Bezold, interpreted it as being derived from the Greek personal name Νεμέσιος.[106] However, as has been correctly pointed out by Paul de Lagarde, in that case, one would expect to find the regular spelling of this name in CT, such as ܢܡܣܝܘܣ.[107] On the one hand, one could still build a case for *Nāmusāyā* in CT to be a distorted form of the Greek "Nemesios," as follows. The first irregularity in its spelling, the appearance of the letter *waw* in the name's stem, finds a counterpart in the way the name "Nemesios" is spelled as ܢܡܘܣܝܘܣ in one of the letters of the East Syrian patriarch Timothy I (eighth to ninth cc.).[108] Likewise, the second irregularity, the gentilic ending -*āyā* instead of the expected -*os*, could also be explained away by referring to similar cases, such as, for instance, the rendering of the Greek personal name "Porphyrios" not as ܦܪܦܘܪܝܘܣ, but as ܦܪܦܘܪܝܐ by the Syriac translator of the *Commentary on Ecclesiastes* by Theodore of Mopsuestia.[109]

On the other hand, an alternative solution to the riddle of the name of Ephrem's addressee has been proposed by several scholars, who note that it exactly corresponds to the well-attested Syriac adjective *nāmusāyā*, "legal, lawful," a derivative of the noun *nāmusā*, "law" (from Gr. νόμος).[110] This connection has already been explored by De Lagarde, who points out that the cognate Arabic adjective *šarʿī*, "legal," was occasionally used for referring to jurists and suggests that *Nāmusāyā* in CT stands for "ein Lehrer des jüdischen Gesetzes."[111] A similar position was taken by Paul-Hubert Poirier, who discovered the independent plural form *nāmusāyē*, referring to (Muslim) "legists," in the works of Barhebraeus and proposed that *Nāmusāyā* in CT would be better understood not as a personal name, but as a substantivized adjective meaning "légiste" or "spécialiste de la loi."[112]

If correct, this interpretation of the name of Ephrem's addressee can help us to better understand the apologetic strategy of the author of CT, who introduces a fictive Jewish interlocutor into the narrative in order to lend greater credibility to his arguments. In doing so, he might have been inspired by the

---

106   Bezold 1883–1888, v. 1, p. 54 *et passim*.
107   de Lagarde 1888, p. 843.
108   *Letter* 43.11; ed. Heimgartner 2012, v. 1, p. 68. Cf. also the spelling ܢܡܣܝܢܘܣ for "Nemesianus" used by Barhebraeus; ed. Séd 1981, pp. 396–397.
109   Ed. Strothmann 1988a, pp. 1–2. Cf. also the nominal form "Elustriya," which refers to the governor of Harran during the first half of the seventh century in the still-unpublished Syriac *Life of Theodosius of Amida* according to Palmer 1990, pp. 165–167.
110   For examples, see Brock 2010, pp. 113–114.
111   de Lagarde 1888, p. 832.
112   Poirier 1995, pp. 117–118. Cf. also Ri 2000, pp. 101–102.

literary genre of *adversus Judaeos* dialogues, where such straw opponents were a standard literary device, beginning with the famous work of Justin the Martyr. This scenario seems particularly plausible in light of his proneness to paronomastic word-play.[113]

Yet there are certain difficulties which must be overcome by those who want to set this interpretation of the figure of *Nāmusāyā* in CT on firmer ground. The most serious problem is posed by the fact that the narrator refers to him as "my/our brother." This form of address only makes sense if the author conceived this figure to be one of Ephrem's fellow Christians. And indeed, in CT 44.17, *Nāmusāyā*'s Christian identity is expressed in a more explicit manner, when he is addressed as "our brother in Christ" (*'aḥun ba-mšiḥā*). Poirier attempted to resolve this apparent contradiction by suggesting that Ephrem's addressee was in fact a Jewish Christian.[114] However, given the absence of any reliable evidence for the actual presence of Jewish Christianity of whatever kind in Northern Mesopotamia during the time of CT's composition, this explanation generates more problems than it purports to solve.

3   Polemic: Anti-Judaism and the Passion Narrative

The story of Jesus' crucifixion, found in all four canonical Gospels, stands at the pivotal point of the New Testament account of his life. The authors of the Gospels present Jesus' gory end as the inevitable result of his prolonged conflict with the Jewish establishment, represented by Pharisees, scribes, and priests. This conflict culminates in a conspiracy against him by the Jerusalemite chief priests, which leads to his arrest and execution on a cross. Many scholars have pointed out an anti-Jewish bias that underlies the canonical accounts of Jesus' last days and testifies that from the earliest times, Christian belief in the death of the Messiah became the very crux of the Jewish-Christian divide.[115] The anti-Jewish elements of the canonical Passion accounts were promptly recognized and further expanded by subsequent generations of Christians.

Like many Syriac Christian writers before him, the author of CT was a natural and faithful heir to this legacy and contributed to its further development and propagation. The following section examines the anti-Jewish material that

---

113   Cf. the triple explanation of Satan's names in CT 3.6; the pun Eve-*ḥewyā*, "serpent" in CT 4.12, discussed in Minov 2010, pp. 92–93; the case of Sasan-*susyā*, "horse" in CT 27.4–5, discussed in section 1.2 of chapter 3.
114   Poirier 1995, p. 118.
115   See articles by Ch.P. Anderson, L. Gaston, E. Buck and D. Granskou in Richardson & Granskou 1986.

appears in chapters 49–53 of CT, in which our author advances an extended and inventive retelling of the canonical Passion narrative.

3.1 Jews as the Killers of Christ

Among the most prominent anti-Jewish arguments deployed in CT is the notion of the Jews as the killers of Christ. This imagery appears more than once in this work. For instance, in CT 51.12, the Jewish people are described as "the congregation of the crucifiers" (*knuštā d-zāqupē*). In CT 53.12, the author mentions "the Jews who crucified him" (*yihudāyē d-zaqpuhi*). In CT 53.26–27, he refers to Abgar, the legendary first-century king of Edessa, who "wanted to take Jerusalem and destroy it because the Jews had crucified Christ."[116] The king's behavior is evoked here as proof that contrary to the Jews, as well as the Greeks and the Romans, the Syrians are not guilty of Jesus' murder.[117]

Blaming the Jews for Jesus' crucifixion and death was the most common and powerful charge in the repertoire of Christian polemic against Judaism.[118] This accusation had already appeared in the writings of the New Testament corpus, including its earliest layers.[119] An anti-Jewish tendency appears throughout the accounts of the Passion in the Gospels, whose authors agree in shifting the blame for the death of Jesus from the Romans to the Jews. It reaches a climax in the Gospel of Matthew, where not only is Pilate portrayed as exculpating himself of any responsibility for the death of Jesus, but also the Jewish "people as a whole" is made to call a blood curse upon themselves and their descendants (Mt 27:24–25). In their presentation of the Passion, all four canonical Gospels share the same basic point: Jewish misanthropy and depravity caused the death of Jesus.

Although the New Testament clearly presents some Jews as bearing responsibility for Jesus' death, neither Paul nor the authors of the Gospels are eager to engage in a *sustained* condemnation of the entire Jewish nation as the murderers of God's Messiah. This step, however, was quickly taken by Christians, already by the second century. Many scholars single out Melito of Sardis as one of the most outspoken advocates of this approach. In his work *On Pascha*, where this second-century bishop from Asia Minor recounts the biblical story

---

116   Or^A: ܟܕ ܨܒܐ ܐܘܪܗܝ ܘܢܣܚܘܦ ܠܐܘܪܫܠܡ ܥܠ ܕܙܩܦܘܗܝ ܝܗܘܕܝܐ ܠܡܫܝܚܐ.

117   For a detailed discussion of this argument, see section 3 of chapter 4.

118   On the development of this notion, see Cohen, J. 1983, 2007; Davis 2003.

119   The apostle Paul had already espoused this notion in his comparison of the afflictions of the Christians in Asia Minor to those experienced by their coreligionists in Palestine, persecuted by "the Jews, who killed both the Lord Jesus and the prophets" (1Thes 2:14–15). Likewise, the author of the Acts of the Apostles repeatedly reproaches the Jews for having "crucified and killed" Jesus (cf. Acts 2:23, 36; 4:10, 27; 5:30; 10:39; 13:27–28).

of the Exodus and the Passover, Melito takes this anti-Jewish accusation to a new level, as he lashes out with extraordinary hostility at the Jewish people as the only party responsible for the death of Christ while leaving the Romans completely out of the picture.[120] From Melito's time onwards, the idea of the Jews' collective responsibility for the murder of Christ becomes a commonplace in Christian theology.

Syriac Christians certainly did not remain alien to this trend and they embraced the rhetoric of the Jews' responsibility for Christ's death at an early stage. One of the earliest attestations of this anti-Jewish motif in the Syrian milieu comes from the *Didascalia Apostolorum*, a third-century Greek composition that was translated into Syriac during the fourth century. The author of the *Didascalia* exhorts his audience to fast on Fridays because "on [this day] the people killed themselves in crucifying our Savior."[121] A very similar accusation is made by Aphrahat, who relates regarding the Jews that "when they crucified Jesus, the true lamb, the murderous people died through his killing."[122]

The charge of Christ's murder is one of the recurring anti-Jewish themes in the works of Ephrem. For instance, in the *Hymns on Virginity*, the poet castigates the Jewish people for their jealousy of Jesus which led them to kill him:

> By means of death they silenced You. Your death itself became endowed with speech; it instructs and teaches the universe. The scribes knew that by You the writings of Moses would be dispersed in the inhabited earth. Although they fastened You on a cross, Your cross explained the scripture.[123]

In the *Nisibene Hymns*, Ephrem exclaims that "death did not crucify Jesus, but the people (*'amā*)."[124] Likewise, in the *Homily on Our Lord* (§6), he explains that "Israel crucified our Lord" on the charge of turning the people away from the worship of one God into idolatry.[125]

The popularity and widespread impact of this anti-Jewish charge in the regions of Syria–Mesopotamia during late antiquity is also confirmed by the fact that the denigrating label *zāqupē*, "crucifiers," is attested as one of the

---

120 Cf. *Peri Pascha* 72–99; ed. Hall, S.G. 1979, pp. 38–57. See also Werner 1966; Wilson 1986.
121 Syr. *Didasc.* 21: ܩܛܠ ܠܗ ܥܡܐ ܕܙܩܦܘ ܠܦܪܘܩܢ; ed. Vööbus 1979, v. 2, pp. 215 [Syr.], 200 [trans.].
122 *Dem.* 21.10; ed. Parisot 1894, col. 960; trans. Valavanolickal 2005, v. 2, p. 212. Cf. also *Dem.* 21.15–20.
123 *De Virg.* 8.22–23; ed. Beck 1962, p. 31 [Syr.]; trans. McVey 1989, p. 300.
124 *Carm. Nis.* 67.2; ed. Beck 1963, p. 106 [Syr.].
125 Ed. Beck 1966, p. 5 [Syr.]; trans. Mathews & Amar 1994, p. 281.

most widespread terms for referring to the Jews in Syriac literature from that period.[126] It may be seen at once from his choice of words when referring to the Jews that the author of CT was a faithful heir to this centuries-long legacy of blaming the Jewish people for Jesus' death. An additional confirmation of his indebtedness to this tradition is found in the reference to the anti-Jewish outburst made by King Abgar in CT 53.26–27. The most likely literary source from which our author became acquainted with this story is the fifth-century Syriac composition known as the *Teaching of Addai*. Like many other Syriac writers, the author of this apocryphal narrative places the responsibility for Jesus' crucifixion on the Jews.[127] To enhance the image of Edessa as a champion of Christianity, he forges a story about how King Abgar, having heard about this crime from the apostle Addai, wished to launch a military operation against the Jewish people and abandoned his plan only because of the possible political complications with the Romans.[128]

3.2 Demonization of the Jews

To enhance the image of the Jews as the murderers of Christ, the author of CT infuses his retelling of the Passion narrative with the rhetoric of demonization. For example, in CT 51.12–13, he launches the following invective against the Jewish people:

> The congregation of the crucifiers became a deserted vine; its daughters—bitter grapes, and its sons—bitter clusters. Their head was Caiaphas, the evil asp, and they were all evil dragons, and all of them were filled with the venom of Satan, who is the evil dragon.[129]

The drawing of a close connection between the Jews and Satan was one of the most popular stock motifs in the repertoire of Christian polemics against Judaism. The roots of this anti-Jewish motif go back to the New Testament itself. According to the Gospel accounts, Judas decides to betray Jesus under the influence of Satan, who has possessed him (Lk 22:3; Jn 13:2, 27). Even more

---

126 Cf. Ephrem, *De Virg.* 38.11, *De crucif.* 5.14, *De fid.* 87.10, *et passim*; *Teaching of Addai* (ed. Howard 1981, pp. 43 [Syr.], 87 [trans.]); *Acts of Mār Mari* 33 (ed. Harrak 2005, pp. 76 [Syr.], 77 [trans.]); *Judas Kyriakos Legend* (ed. Drijvers & Drijvers 1997, pp. 42–43 [Syr.], 60–61 [trans.]); *Acts of Mār Qardagh* 29 (ed. Abbeloos 1890, p. 37).
127 Cf. ed. Howard 1981, pp. 6, 11, 27, 29, 37–38 [Syr.]; 13, 23, 55, 59, 75–77 [trans.].
128 Ed. Howard 1981, pp. 6, 37–38 [Syr.]; 13, 75–77 [trans.].
129 Or^A: ܗܘܬ ܟܪܡܐ ܣܕܝܬܐ ܟܢܘܫܬܐ ܕܙܩܘܦܐ. ܒܢܬܗ ܥܢܒܐ ܡܪܝܪܬܐ. ܘܒܢܝܗ ܣܓܘܠܐ ܡܪܝܪܐ ܘܪܝܫܗܘܢ ܩܝܦܐ ܚܘܝܐ ܒܝܫܐ. ܘܟܠܗܘܢ ܗܘܘ ܬܢܝܢܐ ܕܐܟܠܩܪܨܐ ܕܗܘܝܘ ܬܢܝܢܐ ܒܝܫܐ.

important is John 8:39–47, where Jesus is presented as rebuking "the Jews" for not accepting his message and accusing them of harboring murderous intentions against him with the following words: "You are from your father the devil, and you choose to do your father's desires" (8:44). These scriptural passages laid a foundation for the proliferation of the anti-Jewish rhetoric of demonization in the works of later Christian writers.

Among Syriac authors, the notion of a close association between the Jews and Satan is expressed by Ephrem, who calls them "the sons of the Evil One" (*bnay bišā*) in his *Hymns on the Nativity*.[130] The imagery of the Jews as an instrument Satan used to attack Jesus is evoked by Narsai, who in the *Homily on Passion* rebukes the "sons of Abraham" for serving as "armor for the deceiver."[131] In the *Homily on the Friday of the Passion*, Narsai's contemporary Jacob of Serugh presents a developed picture of Satan assigning each of the different representatives of the Jewish people that took part in the murder of Jesus, i.e. the scribes, elders, Pharisees, Sadducees, Caiaphas, Annas, Herod, and Judas, his or their particular course of action.[132]

The author of CT's use of serpentine metaphors with regard to the Jews constitutes an additional rhetorical strategy aimed at emphasizing the close connection between them and Satan, who is often portrayed as a serpent or dragon in ancient Jewish and Christian sources.[133] The derogatory use of anguine imagery in relation to the Jews is already attested in Ephrem's works. Thus, in the *Hymns on the Unleavened Bread*, the poet resorts to a metaphor based on the natural phenomenon of a serpent's yearly renewal through the shedding of its skin in order to castigate the Jewish people, who fail to mend their evil inner nature: "The people is renewed outwardly in form but in their heart dwells deadly bile."[134] The relationship of such anti-Jewish serpentine rhetoric to the figure of Satan becomes evident in the following verse, where Ephrem likens the Jews to the serpent of Genesis 3:1–15: "It (i.e. the people) resembles that ancient serpent, who cunningly gave us the fruit of death."[135]

This anti-Jewish imagery is related to those passages in the New Testament where John the Baptist or Jesus castigates some groups within the Jewish people, such as the Pharisees, Sadducees, or scribes, by referring to them as "snakes" or a "brood of vipers."[136] As happened with many other New Testament passages

---

130 *De Nat.* 3.8; ed. Beck 1959, p. 21; trans. McVey 1989, p. 85.
131 Ed. McLeod 1979, pp. 110–111.
132 Ed. Rilliet 1986, p. 616; trans. Kollamparampil 1997, p. 283.
133 Cf. Rev 12:9, where Satan is characterized as the "great dragon" and the "ancient serpent."
134 *De azym.* 18.9; ed. Beck 1964, p. 33 [Syr.]; trans. Walters 2011, p. 82.
135 *De azym.* 18.10; ed. Beck 1964, p. 34 [Syr.]; trans. (modified) Walters 2011, p. 82.
136 Cf. Mt 3:7; 12:34; 23:33; Lk 3:7.

featuring polemics against a certain group or faction within the Jewish people, later Christian writers did not miss an opportunity to expand their frames of reference and apply them to the Jewish people as a whole, thus amplifying their anti-Jewish message. One example of this anti-Jewish hermeneutics of decontextualization is the author of the *Commentary on the Diatessaron*, a text which has been ascribed to Ephrem, who treats the derogatory phrase "race of vipers" addressed to the Pharisees and Sadducees in Matthew 3:7 as relating to the entire people of Israel.[137]

There is an additional intertextual reference behind the serpentine image of the Jews in CT 51.12–13. This passage forms a part of a bigger textual unit, CT 51.1–17, in which the author offers a developed anti-Jewish interpretation based on the biblical imagery of the vineyard.[138] One of the scriptural proof-texts the author uses is Deuteronomy 32:32–33, quoted in CT 51.9–10 in order to demonstrate the deteriorated spiritual state of the Jewish people, metaphorically described as a vineyard:

> Christ knew that the prophecy of Moses who prophesized about them and said, "Their grapes are grapes of gall, their clusters are bitter. Their poison is the poison of the dragon, and their head also is that of an evil asp," had been fulfilled in them.[139]

It is evident from his choice of vocabulary that the author of CT modeled the anti-Jewish invective of CT 51.12–13 on the pattern set in Deuteronomy 32:32–33. By doing so, he fundamentally altered the meaning of these biblical verses, which in their original setting are directed not against the people of Israel, but against its enemies. An earlier example of a similar use of this scriptural text in the context of polemic against Judaism is found in the writings of Aphrahat, who resorts to the vine and vinegar symbolism of Deuteronomy 32:32 in his anti-Jewish exposition based on the New Testament parable of the Wicked Husbandmen.[140]

It might also be significant for understanding the genesis of this anti-Jewish imagery in CT that the antipathetic portrayal of the Jews as being filled with Satan's venom, couched in a language very similar to that of CT 51.12–13, is found in the works of Jacob of Serugh. Thus, in the *Homily on the Friday of the*

137 *Comm. Diat.* 3.8; trans. McCarthy 1993, p. 77.

138 This is analyzed in detail below.

139 Or[A]: ܝܕܥ ܗܘܐ ܡܫܝܚܐ ܕܐܫܬܠܡܬ ܠܗ ܒܟܠܗܘܢ ܢܒܝܘܬܗ ܕܡܘܫܐ ܕܐܬܢܒܝ ܥܠܝܗܘܢ ܘܐܡܪ. ܕܥܢ̈ܒܝܗܘܢ ܥܢ̈ܒܝ ܡܪ̈ܪܐ. ܘܣܓ̈ܘܠܝܗܘܢ ܡܪ̈ܝܪܐ ܠܗܘܢ. ܚܡܬܐ ܕܬܢܝܢܐ ܚܡܬܗܘܢ. ܘܐܦ ܪܫܗܘܢ ܕܦܬܢܐ ܗܘ ܒܝܫܐ.

140 *Dem.* 5.21; ed. Parisot 1894, col. 225; trans. Valavanolickal 2005, v. 1, p. 115.

CATEGORIZING THE JEWISH "OTHER"

Passion, which presents a description of the Jews who accused Jesus before Pilate, the poet relates that "from their hearts they vomit bitterness, and their lips pour out the filth of the dragon."[141]

3.3 Anti-Jewish Revision of the Canonical Passion Narrative

In order to reinforce the general accusation of the Jews as the killers of Christ, the author of CT substantially reworks several details of the canonical account of Jesus' execution. The main thrust of this reworking is to present those violent actions against Jesus—which according to the New Testament narrative were undertaken by the Romans or some undefined agents—as having been performed by the Jews.

For instance, according to the canonical narrative, after Jesus had been crucified, it was the Roman soldiers who divided his clothes among themselves.[142] However, contrary to this description, our author relates in CT 49.11 that

> when the Jews crucified Christ on the tree of the cross, they divided his garments among them beneath the cross, as it is written.[143]

A similar claim about the Jews taking part in the division of Jesus' garments is made in CT 50.4:

> The Jews and the soldiers, who were the servants of Herod and Pilate, were struggling together to rend the tunic of Christ, to divide it among them.[144]

Another anti-Jewish modification of the canonical account of the Passion in CT concerns the "crown of thorns" that was woven and put on Jesus' head by the Roman soldiers.[145] In his narrative, however, our author seems to imply that this action was performed by the Jews. Although CT 50.1 states that "they wove a crown of spikes of thorn bushes, and set it upon His head"[146] and the author does not specify who was responsible for this, from the explicit references to the Jews in the preceding (49.11) and following (50.4) sentences, one

---

141   Ed. Rilliet 1986, p. 614; trans. Kollamparampil 1997, p. 283.
142   Cf. Mt 27:27,35; Mk 15:15,24; Jn 19:23–24.
143   Or^A: ܟܕ ܙܩܦܘܗܝ ܝܗܘܕܝܐ ܠܡܫܝܚܐ ܥܠ ܩܝܣܐ ܕܨܠܝܒܐ. ܦܠܓܘ ܢܚܬܘܗܝ ܒܝܢܬܗܘܢ ܬܚܝܬ ܨܠܝܒܐ ܐܝܟ ܕܟܬܝܒ.
144   Or^A: ܝܗܘܕܝܐ ܕܝܢ ܘܐܤܛܪܛܝܘܛܐ ܗܢܘܢ ܕܐܝܬܝܗܘܢ ܡܫܡܫܢܐ ܕܗܪܘܕܤ ܘܦܝܠܛܘܤ. ܡܬܟܬܫܝܢ ܗܘܘ ܥܡ ܚܕܕܐ ܕܢܤܕܩܘܢ ܟܘܬܝܢܗ ܕܡܫܝܚܐ ܕܢܦܠܓܘܢܗ ܒܝܢܬܗܘܢ.
145   Cf. Mt 27:27,29; Mk 15:15,17; Jn 19:2.
146   Or^A: ܘܓܕܠܘ ܠܗ ܟܠܝܠܐ ܡܢ ܩܨܐ ܕܚܒܘܪܐ ܘܤܡܘ ܒܪܫܗ.

may conclude that they were likewise the perpetrators of this hostile action. Furthermore, the Jews' responsibility for this deed can be inferred from the supersessionist passage in CT 50.16 where the making of the "crown of thorns" is mentioned together with the construction of the cross and the rending of Jesus' tunic as the means by which the three spiritual offices were taken away from the Jewish people.

As noted above, these two examples of intentional alterations to the New Testament narrative by the author of CT are clearly a result of the anti-Jewish bias that causes him to exaggerate the role the Jews played in the execution of Christ. Another aspect of such a partial approach to the Passion account manifests itself in the fact that he largely omits the Romans from his retelling of the story of Jesus' condemnation and execution. This hermeneutic strategy was not invented by our author. Allison P. Hayman points out that such passages should be regarded as a continuation of the tendency "to shift onto the Jewish People as a whole the blame for accusing and condemning Jesus" that is already attested in the canonical version of the Passion narrative.[147]

One of the early advocates of this anti-Jewish reworking of the Passion account is Melito of Sardis, who on several occasions accuses the Jews of providing the nails, ropes, gall, vinegar, and the crown of thorns for the crucifixion.[148] Among Syriac writers, we may already find this strategy at work in the works of Ephrem. For example, in the *Hymns on the Unleavened Bread*, he contradicts the canonical account of John 19:34, according to which it was one of the Roman soldiers who pierced Jesus' side with a spear, as he ascribes this deed to the Jews: "And the people (ʿamā), while eating that unleavened bread, stabbed the Son with a lance in Nisan."[149]

As for the origins of the two particular anti-Jewish motifs used by the author of CT, the image of the Jews taking part in the division of Jesus' "tunic and cloak" (*kutinēh w-peḷyunēh*) is found in the poem *On the Pasch of Our Lord* by Cyrillona, another fourth-century poet.[150] The notion of the crown of thorns being made by the Jews is also well attested in Syriac sources. Already before the time of CT's composition, several Syriac writers had ascribed the responsibility for providing this instrument of Jesus' torture to the Jews. Thus, Aphrahat, in an extended anti-Jewish interpretation of the parable of the Wicked Husbandmen, accuses the leaders of the Jewish people that "they

---

147 Hayman 1985, p. 429. Cf. John 18:12–13, where "the officers of the Jews" assist the Roman soldiers in arresting Jesus.
148 Cf. *Peri Pascha* 79, 93; ed. Hall 1979, pp. 42–43, 50–53.
149 *De azym.* 18.4; ed. Beck 1964, p. 33 [Syr.]; trans. (modified) Walters 2011, p. 80.
150 Ed. Griffin 2016, pp. 122–123.

plaited thorns which grew in the vineyard and placed them on the head of the Son of the Lord of the vineyard."[151] Similarly, Jacob of Serugh, in the *Homily on the Transfiguration*, accuses the "daughter of the Hebrews" of providing the instruments for Jesus' execution, relating among other things that "she plaits a crown (*gādlā klilā*) and mingles vinegar and mixes it with gall."[152]

3.4 *The Jews and the Instruments of Jesus' Execution*

The "crown of thorns" was not the only implement of Jesus' execution that was provided by the Jews according to CT. Another anti-Jewish motif that puts a strong emphasis on the Jews' active participation in Jesus' murder focuses on the origins of the wooden beams from which his cross was made. This appears in an account that begins in CT 50.20–21:

> And when the sentence of death had been passed on our Lord by Pilate, they hastily went into the sanctuary and brought out from there the (carrying) poles of the ark of the covenant, and out of them they made the cross for Christ. Verily, it was just that these pieces of wood which used to carry the covenant should also carry the Lord of the covenant.[153]

After Jesus' death and the removal of his body from the cross by the councilor Joseph, the brother of Nicodemus, the Jews hurriedly proceed to restore the beams of the cross to their place in the Temple (CT 53.6):

> And when he had taken down the body of our Lord from the cross, the Jews ran and took the cross, and brought it into the Temple, because it was the bearing poles of the ark of the covenant.[154]

As he explains how Jesus' death was foretold in the Old Testament in CT 53.11–15, the author relates once more that "the bearing poles of the ark of the service

---

151 *Dem.* 5.22; ed. Parisot 1894, col. 229; trans. Valavanolickal 2005, v. 1, p. 117.

152 Ed. Bedjan 1905–1910, v. 2, p. 367; trans. Kollamparampil 1997, p. 224.

153 Or[A]: ܘܟܕ ܐܬܦܣܩܬ ܐܦܘܦܣܝܣ ܡܢ ܦܝܠܛܘܣ ܥܠ ܡܪܢ ܙܪܝܙܝܢ܂ ܐܣܬܪܗܒܘ ܘܥܠܘ ܠܒܝܬ ܡܩܕܫܐ܂ ܘܐܦܩܘ ܡܢ ܬܡܢ ܠܩܝ̈ܣܐ ܗܠܝܢ ܕܩܒܘܬܐ܂ ܘܥܒܕܘ ܡܢܗܘܢ ܨܠܝܒܐ ܠܡܫܝܚܐ܂ ܘܟܐܢܐܝܬ ܓܝܪ ܗܘܐ ܠܗܘܢ ܕܗܠܝܢ ܩܝ̈ܣܐ ܕܫܩܠܝܢ ܗܘܘ ܒܗܘܢ ܕܝܬܩܐ ܗܢܘܢ ܢܫܩܠܘܢ ܠܡܪܗ ܕܕܝܬܩܐ܂

154 Or[A]: ܘܟܕ ܐܚܬܗ ܠܦܓܪܗ ܕܡܪܢ ܡܢ ܨܠܝܒܐ܂ ܪܗܛܘ ܝܗܘ̈ܕܝܐ ܘܢܣܒܘܗ ܠܨܠܝܒܐ ܘܐܥܠܘܗܝ ܠܗܝܟܠܐ܂ ܡܛܠ ܕܩܝ̈ܣܐ ܕܩܒܘܬܐ ܐܝܬܝܗܘܢ ܗܘܘ܂

of God" and "the veil of atonement of the sanctuary" were used in the execution of Jesus.[155]

The most salient feature of this expansion of the canonical account of Jesus' Passion is the direct connection between the cross and the wooden poles that bear the Ark of the Covenant (Ex 25:13–15, 27–28). This extra-canonical story is most likely a product of our author's narrativization of an exegetical tradition that treated the poles of the Ark of the Covenant figuratively, as a symbol or type of the cross. It thus reflects a more general hermeneutic strategy of Patristic biblical exegesis in which any wooden object mentioned in the Old Testament could legitimately be interpreted as referring to Jesus' cross. One can observe this principle at work in the *Mēmrē on the Blessing of the Table*, which is attributed to Ephrem. In one of these homilies, the wooden "pole" (*qupā*) upon which the Israelite spies carried the cluster of grapes during their foray into the Land of Canaan (Num 13:23) is interpreted as a symbol of the Cross: "The cluster through the pole (*qupā*) showed the mystery of the beautiful cross."[156]

This anti-Jewish motif seems to be unique to our author. The most popular mode of figurative handling of the Ark of the Covenant among Christian authors in late antiquity was to treat it as a Mariological or ecclesiological symbol. It was only on very rare occasions that the Ark itself and/or its poles were related to Jesus' cross, figuratively or otherwise.

One of the first Christian writers to make a connection between the Ark of the Covenant and Jesus' cross was Ephrem, who, in the *Hymns against Julian* (3.10–12), draws a parallel between the Roman campaign against the Sasanians under Constantius II and Julian and the Israelite conquest of the Promised Land under Joshua. As he does so, the Syrian poet compares the defeat suffered by the Roman army at the hands of the Persians with the Israelites' failure at the battle of Ai (Josh 7:1–26), while noting regarding the former that "instead of the ark of the covenant (*'ārunā*), they were carrying the Cross."[157] There are additional examples of a similar symbolic treatment of the Ark of the Covenant in the context of military confrontations between Romans and Persians. For instance, George of Pisidia (7th c.), in his poem on the restitution of the relic of the Holy Cross from Persian captivity by Emperor Heraclius, likens it to the Ark

---

155 Or^A: ܘܗܘܐ ܐܝܟ ܕܩܡܘ ܥܠܘܗܝ ܠܡܩܛܠܗ ܩܡܘ ܒܗ ܟܠܗܘܢ ܡܕܡ ܕܡܬܩܪܐ ܩܝܣܐ܂ ܘܐܦ ܥܠ ܩܝܣܐ ܕܐܠܗܐ ܩܡܘ ܠܡܩܛܠܗ܂ ܘܐܦ ܦܪܣܐ ܕܚܘܣܝܐ ܕܒܝܬ ܩܘܕܫܐ܂.
156 Ed. Mariès & Froman 1959, p. 189, ln. 22.
157 *C. Jul.* 3.12; ed. Beck 1957a, p. 84; trans. Lieu & Lieu 1989, p. 120.

of the Covenant. While extolling the relic as the holy weapon that enabled the emperor to vanquish the Persians, the Byzantine writer states that thanks to Heraclius, "the cross was seen by the enemies as a new ark."[158] A different approach to bringing together the Ark and the cross is taken by another seventh-century author, Isaac of Nineveh. In one of the homilies from the "Second Part" of his œuvre, which is dedicated to the mystery of the cross, the East Syrian mystic draws a close parallel between the Ark of the Covenant and the cross as the two loci in which the power of God mysteriously resides: "The limitless power of God dwells in the Cross, just as it resided in an incomprehensible way in the Ark (*qibutā*)."[159] Considered against the background of these two types of figurative use of the Ark of the Covenant in Syriac Christian tradition, the approach of CT's author, who resorts to a symbolic association of the Ark with the cross for the particular purpose of anti-Jewish polemic, stands out as unique and innovative.

Aside from ascribing the provision of the material for the cross to the Jews, our author associates them with another instrument of Jesus' execution, the "veil of atonement" (*šušepā d-ḥusāyā*), mentioned in CT 53.11 without any further explanation as to its origins and function. However, notwithstanding its elliptical description, it is possible to identify this apparently cultic object as the "scarlet robe" from the part of the canonical Passion narrative in which the soldiers make a mockery of Jesus as an impostor "king of the Jews" and dress him in caricatured royal paraphernalia that include this garment.[160]

At first sight, the connection between the "veil of atonement" of CT 53.11 and the "scarlet robe" of the New Testament is far from obvious. In order to understand how the two objects are related to each other, one has to turn to the earlier tradition of the interpretation of Jesus' Passion by Syriac authors.

Ephrem appears to be one of the first Christian writers to understand the "scarlet robe" of Jesus as an element of the Temple's inner furniture that the Jews furnished for his execution. As he elaborates the subject of Jesus' Passion in the *Hymns on the Unleavened Bread*, the poet relates that "the priests took the veil (*šušepā*) of pure scarlet from the sanctuary and threw (it) upon him."[161] Ephrem places this action in close relation to the canonical story of the Jews who tried to corner Jesus with a politically charged question on the legitimacy

---

158   *In Restitutionem S. Crucis* 73–74; ed. Pertusi 1959, p. 228.
159   *Hom.* 11.4; ed. Brock 1995, pp. 44 [Syr.], 54 [trans.].
160   Mt 27:27–31; Mk 15:16–20; Jn 19:2–5. In the Peshitta version of NT, this clothing is rendered thus: Matthew 27:28: *klamis da-zhuritā* for χλαμύς κοκκίνη; Mark 15:17: *'argwānē* for πορφύρα; John 19:2: *naḥtē d-'argwānā* for ἱμάτιον πορφυροῦν.
161   *De azym.* 5.6; ed. Beck 1964, p. 11 [Syr.]. Cf. also *De crucif.* 4.3.

of paying taxes to the Romans,[162] and explains that the Jewish priests did this in order to accuse Jesus before the Romans of attempting to usurp royal status.

It has been suggested by J. Edward Walters that this exegetical tradition came into existence due to the verbal affinity between the description of the "purple cloth" (*naḥtā d-'argwānā*) that should cover the sanctuary's altar according to Numbers 4:13 and those New Testament passages that use similar vocabulary for the "scarlet robe" of Jesus, such as the Old Syriac (Sinaitic) version of Matthew 27:28 that renders it as the "clothes of scarlet and purple" (*naḥtē da-zḥuritā wad-'argwānā*).[163] It should be added here that the reading *naḥtē d-'argwānā* for the "scarlet robe" may already be present in the Syriac version of Tatian's *Diatessaron*, as shown by its Arabic translation (ch. 50), where the soldiers dress Jesus in "purple garments" (*ṭiyāb urǧuwān*).[164]

As a result of Ephrem's influence, this elaboration of the Passion story became a popular theme among Syriac authors. As may be expected, it appears in the Passion section of the Ephremian *Commentary on the Diatessaron*.[165] Closer to the time of CT, Jacob of Serugh also makes use of this motif. In the *Homily on the Friday of the Passion*, he expounds at length how after Jesus' arrest by Pilate, the Jewish priests devised a plot against him by trying to make him touch a holy object from the Temple so that he would be liable for the death penalty (cf. Num 4:15).[166] According to Jacob, the priests "brought the veil of the sanctuary (*šušepē d-qudšā*) and made a tunic of purple (*klamis d-'argwānā*) and decked out on our Lord in mockery" for this purpose.[167]

These examples demonstrate that by the time of CT's composition, the anti-Jewish motif that interpreted the scarlet robe of Jesus' Passion as being made of the sacred curtain that the Jews had brought from the Temple was already entrenched in the Syriac tradition of New Testament exegesis. It is remarkable that both Ephrem and Jacob of Serugh chose to denote this material object with the noun *šušepā*, as this is contrary to the normal use of this word in the Peshitta version of the Old Testament, where it is never used to refer to the curtain of the Ark of the Covenant or of the Temple in general.

It thus becomes obvious that by mentioning the "veil" (*šušepā*) as an instrument of Jesus' execution, the author of CT is relying on this anti-Jewish tradition. In contrast to Ephrem and Jacob of Serugh, however, he chooses to convey

---

162 Mt 22:15–22; Mk 12:13–17; Lk 20:20–26.
163 Walters 2011, p. 34, n. 49. Cf. also *'argwānā* in OS Mark 15:17 and *naḥtē d-'argwānā* in Peshitta of John 19:2.
164 Ed. Ciasca 1888, p. 191, ln. 2.
165 *Comm. Diat.* 20.17; trans. McCarthy 1993, pp. 301–302.
166 Ed. Rilliet 1986, pp. 618–620; trans. Kollamparampil 1997, pp. 285–286.
167 Ed. Rilliet 1986, p. 619; trans. Kollamparampil 1997, p. 285.

the notion of this object's cultic origins by using the noun *ḥusāyā*, "atonement," in order to specify what kind of covering it was. In the Old Testament Peshitta, this noun is most often used for rendering the Hebrew noun *kappōreṯ*, "mercy seat," a golden object that rested on the Ark of the Covenant (Ex 25:17–21; Lev 16:13–15). Occasionally, it was used for referring to the Holy of Holies as a whole, as in 1 Kings 6:5, where the Hebrew noun *dəḇīr* is translated as *bēt ḥusāyā*. In view of this, it is possible to conclude that the phrase "the veil of atonement" in CT 53.11 refers to the *parokhet*, i.e. the thick curtain that separated the Temple's innermost sanctuary, where the Ark of the Covenant was kept from the rest of the structure (Ex 36:35–36; Lev 16:12–16). This suggestion is strengthened by the fact that in CT 53.12, immediately after referring to "the veil of atonement," the author offers a supersessionist interpretation of it in which he refers to "the breast-piece of judgment," a sacred object that was kept inside the Ark.[168]

It should finally be noted that while the identification of Jesus' scarlet robe as the Temple curtain is a result of purely extra-canonical development, the connection between this artifact and the Jews does have some basis in the New Testament account. On the one hand, in three out of the four versions of the story of Jesus' Passion in the Gospels, it is the soldiers under Pilate's command who dress Jesus in the scarlet robe.[169] However, according to Luke 23:11, it was Herod and his soldiers who clothed Jesus with the "splendid robe" (ἐσθῆτα λαμπράν) before sending him back to Pilate.[170] This detail may serve as a starting point for the emphasis of the Jewish origins of this instrument of Jesus' execution by both Ephrem and other Syriac authors.

We have seen how the author of CT expands the canonical account of the Passion by introducing the imagery of the Jews as the suppliers of instruments for inflicting capital punishment upon Jesus such as the cross and the scarlet robe. By doing so, he attempts to achieve several objectives. First of all, in this way, he enhances the image of the Jews as the killers of Christ. Moreover, by associating these instruments of torture with the Temple of Jerusalem, he undermines this powerful symbol of Jewish religiosity.

It is legitimate to regard these extra-canonical additions to the Passion story as emerging from an inner-Christian hermeneutic that was operational in the

---

168 On this, see section 4.2.4 below.
169 Cf. Mt 27:27; Mk 15:15–16; Jn 19:1–2.
170 While in the Old Syriac (Curetonian) version of Luke this phrase is translated close to the Greek as "fair garment" (*naḥtā šapirā*), in the Peshitta version it is harmonized to the "scarlet garment" (*naḥtā da-zḥuritā*).

gradual process of amplifying the repertoire of anti-Jewish rhetoric. Yet one should not remain oblivious to possible external factors that may have contributed to the development and spread of these particular anti-Jewish motifs among Syriac Christians during late antiquity. Thus, it is noteworthy that both these anti-Jewish images focus on cultic objects that are directly related to the Ark of the Covenant. In assessing this phenomenon, one should take into account the fact that the Ark and its curtain enjoyed a high symbolic value among the Jews in antiquity. These cultic symbols were carried over into the context of the synagogue in the form of *aron ha-qodeš*, the Torah ark, an ornate cupboard in which the Torah scrolls were housed, and *parokhet*, the veil that was spread in front of the Torah ark.[171] As has been suggested by Erwin Goodenough, in synagogues these items served as numinous objects, whose function was analogous to that of a statue in the inner shrine of a pagan temple.[172]

What is even more interesting is that there are indications that the Christians were not only aware of the high prestige of these objects among the Jews, but even found them attractive as powerful agents of holiness. Important evidence for this phenomenon comes from the anti-Jewish work of John Chrysostom, in which he castigates his fellow Christians for venerating synagogues as holy places on account of the Bible scrolls that were kept there.[173] One might infer from Chrysostom's rhetoric that the Torah ark was considered and venerated as a symbolic equivalent of the Ark of the Covenant.[174] To this, one should add evidence for the veneration of the Torah and the ark by the Jews of South Arabia. The Syriac Christian author of the *Book of the Himyarites* represents the Jewish king Dhū Nuwās swearing "by Adonai, and by the ark, and by the Torah."[175] This literary testimony is supported by archaeological material from this region, as for example a Jewish Aramaic signet ring from Ẓafār that features images of the Torah scroll and the ark.[176] In light of this evidence, it seems likely that by drawing a connection between the sacred prototypes of the Torah ark and its veil and the execution of Jesus, Ephrem and those Syriac authors who followed in his footsteps waged a war against the visible and powerful symbols of the

---

171 See Hachlili 1998, pp. 76–77; Schenk 2006, pp. 8–85.
172 Goodenough 1953–1968, v. 4, pp. 99–144, v. 12, pp. 83–86. See also Levine 2005, pp. 368–369.
173 Cf. *Adv. Jud.* 1.5.2–8; 6.7.1–7.
174 Cf. esp. *Adv. Jud.* 6.7.2: "What sort of ark (κιβωτός) is it that the Jews now have, where we find no propitiatory (ἱλαστήριον), no tables of the law, no holy of holies, no veil (καταπέτασμα), no high priest, no incense, no holocaust, no sacrifice, none of the other things that made the ark of old solemn and august?" PG 48, col. 914; trans. Harkins 1979, pp. 172–173.
175 ܐܪܘܢܐ ܘܐܘܪܝܬܐ ܘܡܪܝܐ; ed. Moberg 1924, pp. 7a [Syr.], cv [trans.]. Although the main word for the Ark of the Covenant in the Peshitta is *qibutā*, sometimes *'ārunā* is also used for this purpose (cf. 1Sam 6:13; 1Kg 8:1).
176 See Robin 2004, pp. 849, 890.

contemporary Jewish tradition, which possessed a modicum of attraction in the eyes of at least some of their coreligionists.

3.5 The Sponge-Bearers as Jews

Another important augmentation of the canonical Passion narrative which serves the purpose of polemic against Judaism appears in CT 51.1–17. In this long passage, the author presents a developed anti-Jewish exposition that opens with the assertion that the Jews gave Jesus "vinegar and gall in a sponge" (51.1).[177] He continues by explaining the vinegar metaphorically, as a symbol of the spiritual deterioration of the Jewish people, the originally "good vineyard" (*karmā ṭābā*) which had however turned "from goodness to wickedness" (*men taqnutā l-bišutā*) (51.2,4). Furthermore, he describes the Jews as the "wicked heirs" (*yārtē bišē*) who neglected the vineyard and crucified its true "heir," i.e. Christ, while offering him their "sour wine" mixed with the "impurity of their wickedness" (51.5–7). In the following section, 51.8–14, the author dwells on the theme of the malice and ungratefulness of the Jewish people and presents the episode of the vinegar-soaked sponge as a fulfillment of the biblical prophecy, relying on Psalm 80:8–15 and Deuteronomy 32:6,32–33 as scriptural proof-texts. The section concludes with a general supersessionist explanation according to which the Jews caused themselves to lose God's spiritual gifts of royalty, priesthood, and prophecy by offering Jesus a drink by means of a sponge (51.15–17).

In order to unravel the elaborate web of intertextual allusions from which this anti-Jewish explication is woven, let us focus on the two scriptural points of reference that have crucial relevance for understanding the author's polemical strategy, namely the image of the vinegar-soaked sponge and the metaphor of the vineyard.

The entire exposition is constructed as a midrash on details of the canonical Passion narrative such as the act of offering Jesus a drink in the form of a sponge soaked in "vinegar" or "sour wine" (Gr. ὄξος; Syr. *ḥalā*) while he was hanging on the cross.[178] It is noteworthy that the author mentions "gall" (*mrārē*) as another component of this drink alongside "vinegar." By doing so, he blends together two different incidents from the canonical Passion account. The "gall" forms a part of another beverage, the "sour wine mixed with gall" (ὄξος μετὰ χολῆς μεμιγμένον)[179] that the Roman soldiers offered to Jesus *before* nailing him to the cross, which he refused to drink according to Matthew 27:34 (cf. also Lk 23:36).

---

177   Or^A: ܚܠܐ ܘܡܪܪܐ ܒܐܣܦܘܓܐ.
178   Cf. Mt 27:47–48; Mk 15:35–36; Jn 19:28–29.
179   In the Peshitta version of Matthew, this phrase is rendered as ܚܠܐ ܕܚܠܝܛ ܡܪܪܐ.

It should be noted that none of the New Testament passages that features Jesus being offered the vinegar-soaked sponge explicitly mentions the Jews as the perpetrators. Moreover, the original meaning of the action is unclear, since it could be understood in two completely different ways: as intending to cause the crucified Jesus more suffering, or contrariwise as aiming to alleviate his agony.[180] All this notwithstanding, our author interprets this incident with the clear intention of representing the Jewish people in a negative light. Not only does he explain the offering of vinegar to Jesus as a malevolent act, but he places responsibility for it on the Jews. The anti-Jewish message of this image finds an additional expression in the section's conclusion, where it is incorporated into the author's general supersessionist scheme of the three gifts.[181]

Another important intertextual frame of reference for the anti-Jewish exposition of CT 51.1–17 is provided by the New Testament parable of the Wicked Husbandmen, which appears in all the synoptic Gospels.[182] The author of CT integrates several basic elements of this parable into his retelling of the sponge episode in order to construct a sort of spiritual genealogy for the vinegar drink offered to Jesus. Through this procedure, and by altering the parable's polemical intention from one criticizing only the Jewish leadership (as was its original setting) to one that targets the Jewish people as a whole, the author enhances its anti-Jewish message.

The author's deployment of these two New Testament images provides us with additional evidence for how deeply he was rooted in the earlier tradition of anti-Jewish polemic on Syrian soil. The image of Jews as the bearers of the vinegar-soaked sponge was very popular among Syriac writers.[183] For example, the Ephremian *Commentary on the Diatessaron* reprimands the Jewish people for their ingratitude towards God using this imagery: "He had nourished her with choicest food and honey, but she gave him gall (*mrārā*). He had given her pure wine, but she offered him vinegar in a sponge (*ḥalā b-'espugā*)."[184] Likewise, Jacob of Serugh, in the *Homily on the Transfiguration*, relates how the Jewish people, personified as "the daughter of the Hebrews," among other instruments for Jesus' execution "mingles vinegar and mixes it with gall."[185] Isaac

---

180   See Heidland 1968.
181   This anti-Jewish motif is discussed in section 4.1.1 below.
182   Mt 21:33–41; Mk 12:1–12; Lk 20:9–19.
183   It is also well attested in the works of Greek and Latin authors. Cf. Hippolytus, *Dem. adv. Jud.* 1, 5 (PG 10, col. 788–789); Cyril of Alexandria, *Comm. in Ioan.* 12 (ed. Pusey 1872, v. 3, pp. 93–94); Augustine, *Serm.* 218.11. On the Latin Christian tradition, see Jordan 1987.
184   *Comm. Diat.* 18.1; ed. Leloir 1963, p. 204; trans. McCarthy 1993, p. 269.
185   Ed. Bedjan 1905–1910, v. 2, p. 367; trans. Kollamparampil 1997, p. 224. Cf. also Jacob's *Homilies against the Jews* 1.315–317 (ed. Albert 1976, p. 64); *Homily on the Two Goats* (ed. Bedjan 1905–1910, v. 3, p. 278).

of Antioch, in the *Homily against the Jews*, presents a contrast between the nations whose custom is to "give wine" to a convicted murderer and the Jews, who gave Jesus "vinegar to cause him additional pain."[186]

Indebted to this tradition, our author was also not original in resorting to the symbol of the people of Israel as a vine or vineyard for the purposes of anti-Jewish polemic. Imagery based on the vine symbolism of the Old and New Testaments was one of the most powerful and popular vehicles for ecclesiological discourse in Syriac Christian tradition.[187] Such images were also often evoked in the context of anti-Jewish polemic, foremost among them being the parable of the Wicked Husbandmen. An early example of its use for such a purpose is found in the Pseudo-Ephremian *Sermon against the Jews Given on Palm Sunday*. Among other supersessionist images and metaphors, it features a description of the people of Israel as the vineyard that once "increased" but is now barren and yields only wild clusters, so that its owner, i.e. God, decided to stop watering it with spiritual streams and "in their place was planted the Vine that grew among the nations."[188]

By bringing together these two polemical motifs, i.e. the image of Jews as the sponge-bearers and the anti-Jewish interpretation of the parable of the Wicked Husbandmen, our author followed an already established tradition of polemical utilization of this evangelical story. These two motifs appear together in Aphrahat's *Demonstration on Wars*, which offers a developed supersessionist interpretation of this parable according to which the vineyard of the Jewish people has been replaced by the vineyard of Christ and his followers.[189] At one point, Aphrahat weaves the image of the vinegar-soaked sponge into his retelling of the parable by relating how the son of the vineyard's master "was thirsty and sought drink from them and they gave to him the vinegar (*ḥalā*), but he did not wish to drink."[190]

4   Polemic: Supersessionism

The construction of the negative image of the Jewish people as the killers of Christ was not an end in itself for the author of CT. Rather, this anti-Jewish imagery serves as a necessary prerequisite for him to develop a general

---

186   Ed. and trans. Kazan 1961–1965, p. 53.
187   See Murray, R. 1975, pp. 95–130.
188   Ed. Beck 1970, p. 58 [Syr.]; trans. Morris 1847, p. 64. A similar interpretation of this parable appears in the Ephremian *Commentary on the Diatessaron* (16.19); trans. McCarthy 1993, pp. 252–253.
189   *Dem.* 5.21–22; ed. Parisot 1894, cols. 225–232.
190   *Dem.* 5.22; ed. Parisot 1894, col. 229; trans. Valavanolickal 2005, v. 1, pp. 116–117.

perspective on the relationship between Judaism and Christianity, which in his case takes the form of supersessionist theology. Known also as the theology of replacement, this Christian doctrine is based on the belief that the Jewish people and religion had been completely superseded by the Christian people and religion.[191] According to this teaching, the rejection of Jesus and his message, which culminated in his crucifixion and death, became a turning point in the history of the Jewish people, after which the old law of Judaism was replaced with the new law of Christianity. As a punishment for their willing participation in Jesus' execution, God disowned the Jews as his chosen people and installed in their place a new "spiritual Israel," that is, the Church of the Christians. In the realm of religious practice, one of the most important manifestations of this doctrine was the abolishment of the greater part of the biblical commandments and laws, which became irrelevant as faith in Christ came to be considered as the only avenue for obtaining God's blessing and assistance.

The theology of replacement was deeply ingrained in Christian thought and practice, and its earliest expressions are already present in the New Testament corpus.[192] Notwithstanding some notable exceptions such as the Jewish-Christian "dual-covenant" theology, a more inclusive position upholding the covenantal status of the people of Israel and the Church equally,[193] it was supersessionism that provided the main ideological framework for the development of Christian thought on the Jewish people and Jewish-Christian relations.

Supersessionist doctrine became a fundamental cornerstone in the development of theology among Syriac-speaking Christians, with its strong emphasis on the superiority of the Church from the "nations" (*ammē*) over the Jewish "people" (*amā*).[194] Among the earliest proponents of this teaching on Syrian soil was the author of the *Didascalia*, who cites several scriptural proof-texts meant to demonstrate that "God had abandoned the people of the Jews and the temple, and has come to the church of the gentiles."[195] Another early advocate of this doctrine among Syrians was Aphrahat, who devoted an entire

---

191 For a general presentation, see Ruether 1974, pp. 124–165; Simon 1996, pp. 76–97; Soulen 1996, pp. 1–18, 25–56.

192 For Paul's letters, cf. Rom 9:6–33; Gal 4:21–31; for the Gospels, cf. Mt 21:33–43; 23:34–39; Jn 12:37–43; cf. also Acts 13:46; 18:6; 28:25–28.

193 The foundations of this theology were laid by Paul in his epistle to Romans (cf. 3:1–4; 9:1–5; 11:1–32). Cf. also Pseudo-Clementines (*Hom.* 8.5–7; *Rec.* 4.5) as well as the views of some unidentified Christians, against whom the author of the *Letter of Barnabas* (4.6–7) polemicizes. See Sigal 1983; Marcus 2012, pp. 385–389.

194 See Murray, R. 1975, pp. 41–68; Darling 1987; Neusner 1971, pp. 158–175.

195 Syr. *Didasc.* 23; ed. Vööbus 1979, v. 2, pp. 226 [Syr.], 209 [trans.].

treatise to the subject of the "peoples which have taken the place of the people" (*ʿammē da-hwaw ḥlāp ʿamā*).[196] Aphrahat presents an impressive array of scriptural proof-texts aiming to refute the Jews, who boast of being "the people of God and the children of Abraham," and demonstrating that they had been rejected by God while the "peoples who are from all languages" had taken their place. On another occasion, the Persian sage expresses his view on the relationship between the two covenants, in complete agreement with the tenets of supersessionism: "Aged and antiquated are the works which are in the Law and they are for destruction. For, from the time the new was given, the old was made obsolete."[197]

Even a superficial perusal of CT reveals that its author fully endorsed this perspective on Jewish-Christian relations, already deeply entrenched among Syriac Christians, as the theology of supersessionism may be found permeating his work on different levels. In what follows, various expressions of this anti-Jewish aspect of our work will be analyzed, including discussion of their genesis and function.

4.1 *Rhetoric of Supersessionism*

4.1.1 The Three Gifts

The most prominent of the supersessionist motifs scattered throughout CT is the notion of the three spiritual "gifts" (*mawhabātā*), namely kingship, priesthood, and prophecy, which originally belonged to the Jewish people but were taken from them by God as a punishment for their rejection of Christ. The author traces the notion of God's three spiritual gifts to the human race to the very beginning of its history. According to CT 2.18, Adam, who was created in Jerusalem and granted the highest authority over all other creatures, "was made king, and priest, and prophet."[198] These three endowments were kept and further transmitted through the generations of Adam's posterity. Thus, in the scene of Methuselah's deathbed testament in CT 16.8, the patriarch informs Noah and his progeny that

> these three measures of blessing which God gave to your father Adam shall serve as leaven, and shall be kneaded into your seed, and into the seed of your children, and they are kingship, priesthood, and prophecy.[199]

196 *Dem.* 16; ed. Parisot 1894, cols. 760–783; trans. Valavanolickal 2005, v. 2, pp. 127–138.

197 *Dem.* 2.6; ed. Parisot 1894, col. 60; trans. Valavanolickal 2005, v. 1, p. 45.

198 Or[A]: ܘܬܡܢ ܐܬܥܒܕ: ܡܠܟܐ ܘܟܗܢܐ ܘܢܒܝܐ.

199 Or[A]: ܘܗܠܝܢ ܬܠܬ ܦ̈ܣܐܢ ܕܒܘܪܟܬܐ ܕܝܗܒ ܐܠܗܐ ܠܐܕܡ ܐܒܘܟܘܢ. ܢܗܘ̈ܝܢ ܚܡܝܪܐ ܘܢܬܬܠܫ̈ܢ ܒܙܪܥܟܘܢ ܘܒܙܪܥܐ ܕܒܢ̈ܝܟܘܢ. ܗܘ ܕܝܢ ܡܠܟܘܬܐ ܘܟܗܢܘܬܐ ܘܢܒܝܘܬܐ.

In the course of history, the three gifts were passed on to the people of Israel through the mediation of its greatest spiritual leaders, as is reported in CT 50.13–14:

> Three precious gifts, than which there is nothing more valuable, were given to the Jews in the times of old, namely, kingship, priesthood, and prophecy: prophecy through Moses, priesthood through Aaron, and kingship through David.[200]

The most dramatic turning point in the history of the transmission of the three gifts is constituted by the Jews' rejection of Christ. The author presents Jesus' Passion as the fateful event which resulted in these three tokens of spiritual blessing being removed from the Jewish people and appropriated by Christ. The fact that the notion of the transition of spiritual authority from Jews to Christians is repeated throughout his work on several occasions bears witness to its importance to our author. Thus, it is sketchily formulated in CT 50.15–16:

> These three gifts which the generations and families of the children of Israel had enjoyed for years were taken from them in one day; and they were despoiled and became alienated from these three: from prophecy by the Cross, and from priesthood by the rending of the tunic, and from kingship by the crown of thorns.[201]

The author returns to this imagery once more in CT 51.15–17, in order to elucidate details of Jesus' execution such as the sponge soaked in wine that he was given to drink from while hanging on the cross.[202] According to him, this sponge served as a symbolic instrument that removed God's spiritual gifts from the Jewish people:

> They did not give Him to drink from a cup, but from a sponge, so that they might show that the blessing of their fathers had been wiped away from them. For this is evident: when a vessel is empty and there is no wine in it, they wipe and wash it with a sponge. Likewise it is with the Jews:

200 Or[A]: ܬܠܬ ܡܘܗ̈ܒܬܐ ܡܝܩܪ̈ܬܐ ܗܠܝܢ ܕܠܝܬ ܕܡܝܬܪܢ ܡܢܗܝܢ ܐܬܝܗܒܘ ܗܘܘ ܠܝܗ̈ܘܕܝܐ ܡܢ ܩܕܝܡ. ܡܠܟܘܬܐ ܘܟܗܢܘܬܐ ܘܢܒܝܘܬܐ. ܢܒܝܘܬܐ ܒܝܕ ܡܘܫܐ. ܘܟܗܢܘܬܐ ܒܝܕ ܐܗܪܘܢ. ܘܡܠܟܘܬܐ ܒܝܕ ܕܘܝܕ.

201 Or[A]: ܗܠܝܢ ܬܠܬ ܡܘܗ̈ܒܬܐ ܕܒܗܝܢ ܐܬܦܢܩܘ ܗܘܘ ܕܪ̈ܐ ܘܫܪ̈ܒܬܐ ܘܫܢ̈ܝܐ ܕܒܢ̈ܝ ܝܣܪܝܠ. ܘܒܚܕ ܝܘܡܐ ܐܫܬܩܠ ܡܢܗܘܢ. ܘܐܬܦܠܣܘ ܘܗܘܘ ܢܘܟܪ̈ܝܐ ܡܢ ܬܠܬܝܗܝܢ. ܢܒܝܘܬܐ ܒܝܕ ܙܩܝܦܐ. ܘܟܗܢܘܬܐ ܒܨܪܝܗ ܕܟܘܬܝܢܐ. ܘܡܠܟܘܬܐ ܒܟܠܝܠܐ ܕܟܘ̈ܒܐ.

202 Cf. Mt 27:48; Mk 15:36; Jn 19:29.

> when they crucified Christ, with a sponge he wiped away and removed from them kingship, and priesthood, and prophecy, and anointing, and gave them to Christ, while the vessels of their bodies remained broken and empty.[203]

The notion of the Jews having been dispossessed of their spiritual gifts is repeated again in CT 52.17–18 in the context of an anti-Jewish interpretation of Daniel's prophecy of the weeks:

> Until the cross of Christ the festivals of the Jews succeeded each other, in priesthood, and kingship, and prophecy, and Passover, but from the time of the cross of Christ and henceforth they have all departed from the Jews, as I have said. And there was no more a king, or a priest, or a prophet, or a Passover among them, as Daniel prophesied about them.[204]

It should be added that it was particularly important for our author to integrate this supersessionist theme into his general vision of a close typological connection between Adam and Christ, based on an understanding of the latter's mission as the restitution of humanity to its glorious state before the Fall. This connection is made explicit in CT 48.29, a passage that forms part of an extended section which establishes a detailed chronological correspondence between the life of Adam and the Passion of Christ:

> On Friday kingship, and priesthood, and prophecy were given to Adam, and on Friday priesthood, and kingship, and prophecy were taken away from the Jews.[205]

The author of CT was by no means the first to deploy the supersessionist motif of the three gifts for the purposes of polemic against Judaism. The idea

203 Or[A]: ܠܘ ܒܪ ܟܗܢܐ ܗܘܐ ܠܗ ܕܢܣܒܬܐ ܐܠܐ ܒܐܣܦܘܓܐ. ܕܐܫܩܝܘܗܝ ܕܐܬܚܫܒܬ ܡܢܗܘܢ ܒܡܘܪܒܬܐ ܕܐܒܗ̈ܬܗܘܢ. ܐܝܟ ܗܝ ܕܐܡܪ ܗܘܐ ܕܒܥܘܬܗ ܘܡܬܒܛܠ ܡܐܢܐ ܡܢ ܣܒܪܐ: ܒܐܣܦܘܓܐ ܡܫܩܝܢ ܘܡܫܝܚܝܢ ܠܗ. ܗܠܝܢ ܐܦ ܢܒܝ̈ܘܬܐ ܟܕ ܘܡܫܚܘܬܐ ܠܡܫܝܚܐ. ܒܐܣܦܘܓܐ ܗܘ ܘܟܠ ܡܢܗܘܢ ܡܠܟܘܬܐ ܘܟܗܢܘܬܐ ܘܢܒܝܘܬܐ ܘܡܫܝܚܘܬܐ ܘܝܗܒ ܠܡܫܝܚܐ. ܘܦܫܘ ܡܐܢ̈ܐ ܕܦܓܪ̈ܝܗܘܢ ܟܕ ܐܬܬܒܪܘܢ ܣܪ̈ܝܩܐ ܘܣܦܝܩܐ.

204 Or[A]: ܥܕܡܐ ܠܙܩܝܦܗ ܕܡܫܝܚܐ ܐܬܚܠܦܘ ܥܐ̈ܕܝܗܘܢ ܕܝܗ̈ܘܕܝܐ ܒܟܗܢܘܬܐ ܘܡܠܟܘܬܐ ܘܢܒܝܘܬܐ ܘܦܨܚܐ. ܡܢ ܙܩܝܦܗ ܕܝܢ ܕܡܫܝܚܐ ܘܠܗܠ ܐܬܦܠܓ ܟܠܗܝܢ ܡܢ ܝܗ̈ܘܕܝܐ ܐܝܟ ܕܐܡܪܬ. ܘܠܐ ܬܘܒ ܗܘܐ ܒܝܢܬܗܘܢ ܡܠܟܐ ܐܘ ܟܗܢܐ ܐܘ ܢܒܝܐ ܐܘ ܦܨܚܐ ܐܝܟ ܕܐܬܢܒܝ ܥܠܝܗܘܢ ܕܢܝܐܝܠ.

205 Or[A]: ܒܥܪܘܒܬܐ ܐܬܝܗܒܬ ܠܐܕܡ ܡܠܟܘܬܐ ܘܟܗܢܘܬܐ ܘܢܒܝܘܬܐ. ܘܒܥܪܘܒܬܐ ܐܫܬܩܠܬ ܡܢ ܝܗ̈ܘܕܝܐ ܟܗܢܘܬܐ ܘܡܠܟܘܬܐ ܘܢܒܝܘܬܐ.

that after the coming of Jesus the succession of kings, priests, and prophets among the Jews came to an end enjoyed a certain popularity among Christian authors long before the time of CT's composition.

Of particular importance for the development of this supersessionist argument was the early Christian theological concept of the "threefold office of Christ" (*munus triplex Christi*). According to this belief, in his person Christ brings together the three great mediatorial offices of biblical Israel: king, priest, and prophet.[206] In its own way, this Christian idea continues and develops ancient Jewish beliefs about the ideal system of tripartite government over Israel that should be carried out by kings, priests, and prophets reflected in chapters 17 and 18 of Deuteronomy. In Jewish tradition, this notion was further developed during the Second Temple period and was later adopted by the rabbis in the imagery of the "three crowns."[207]

Eusebius of Caesarea was one of the earliest proponents of the notion of *munus triplex*. In his *Ecclesiastical History*, he speaks about Christ as "of the world the only High Priest, of all creation the only king, of the prophets the only archprophet of the Father."[208] In the Syriac milieu, this imagery is attested from the late fourth century, when Eusebius' *History* was translated into Syriac.[209] It is also found in Melito's *On Faith*, another work translated into Syriac from Greek at an early date.[210] The importance of this concept for the formation of Christian identity is demonstrated by its appearance in the context of sacramental theology. A number of early Christian sources, including Syriac ones, draw a parallel between the baptismal anointment of Christians and the ritual anointment of kings, priests, and prophets in the Old Testament.[211]

Soon after it was conceived, the image of Christ as the holder of the three spiritual offices was deployed in anti-Jewish polemic, connected with the declaration of the Jewish people's complete and irreversible loss of these same offices. Besides purely theological considerations, a crystallization of this supersessionist argument was greatly facilitated by such empirical facts as the Jews' loss of political autonomy and the cessation of their cult after the destruction of the Temple in 70 CE, as well as the apparent absence of

---

206 On the development of this idea, see Schwemer 2003.
207 Cf. the portrayal of John Hyrcanus by Josephus, *War* 1.68; *Ant.* 13.299–300. In rabbinic sources, the crown of prophecy is replaced by that of Torah. Cf. *m.Avot* 4:13; *Avot de-Rabbi Nathan* A 41; B 48. For more on the notion of the three crowns in the rabbinic corpus, see Cohen, S.A. 1990.
208 *Hist. eccl.* 1.3.8; trans. Lake et alii 1926–1932, v. 1, pp. 32–33.
209 Ed. Wright & McLean 1898, p. 18.
210 Ed. Cureton 1855, pp. 32 [Syr.], 53 [trans.].
211 Cf. Hippolytus, *Trad. ap.* 5; Aphrahat, *Dem.* 23.3.

prophetic activity in their midst. Thus, the fourth-century Pseudo-Clementine *Recognitions* affirm that sin offerings made by Jewish priests had lost their atoning efficacy with the coming of Jesus, since from that time on "the chrism has ceased (*cessavit chrisma*), by which the priesthood or the prophetic or the kingly office was conferred."[212]

This anti-Jewish argument also surfaces in fourth-century Syriac works translated from Greek, such as the Syriac version of the *Recognitions*,[213] as well as in those by native Syriac writers. Among the latter, Aphrahat resorts to it in the *Demonstration on Charity*, where he describes the process of the people of Israel's spiritual demotion as a series of dispossessions that took place after the coming of Christ. Among other offices that the Jews had lost, Aphrahat lists the three "gifts" of CT:

> Because they rejected his kingdom, he took from them the kingdom ... And he offered "a living sacrifice" (Rom 12:1) for us and made obsolete their sacrifices ... He (God) abolished from them visions and prophets for they did not hear the Great Prophet.[214]

Aphrahat raises the subject of the Jews' loss of the three offices on one more occasion. While offering an anti-Jewish interpretation of the prophecy of the weeks from Daniel 9 in *Demonstration* 19, he cites the absence of these three ministries among the contemporary Jews as a proof of the prophecy's fulfillment.[215]

Supersessionist rhetoric based on the motif of the three spiritual gifts also served as a popular anti-Jewish polemical strategy for Ephrem. In the *Homily on Our Lord* (§56), he writes how Christ had taken over the royal, priestly, and prophetic succession of Israel from the Jews:

> He took priesthood from the temple, even though the high priest Annas exercised it. And He also took prophecy, which had been handed down by the righteous, even though Caiaphas used it once to weave our Lord a crown. And he took kingship from the house of David, even though Herod kept the position and functioned in it.[216]

---

212 *Rec.* 1.48.5–6; ed. Rehm & Strecker 1994, p. 36; trans. Smith 1867, p. 175.
213 Ed. Frankenberg 1937, p. 54.
214 *Dem.* 2.6; ed. Parisot 1894, col. 60; trans. Valavanolickal 2005, v. 1, p. 45.
215 *Dem.* 19.11; ed. Parisot 1894, col. 885; trans. Valavanolickal 2005, v. 2, p. 181.
216 Ed. Beck 1966, p. 52 [Syr.]; trans. Mathews & Amar 1994, p. 331. Cf. also *De Nat.* 24.2.

In distinction from CT, no explicit connection between the Jews' loss of the spiritual gifts and Jesus' execution is made in the passages quoted so far. Ephrem, however, comes closer to our work in another of his compositions, the *Hymns on the Crucifixion*, where he establishes a link between Israel's spiritual despoliation and the Passion narrative. In one of these hymns, Ephrem relates that through his suffering, Jesus "took away kingdom, priesthood, and prophecy" from the Jews.[217]

It should be pointed out that whereas the author of CT follows the earlier tradition of anti-Jewish polemic in Syriac by employing the motif of the three spiritual offices that were taken away from Israel, he exercises a certain degree of creativity in handling this imagery, as he integrates it into his own version of the history of salvation.

First of all, the attribution of these three gifts to Adam and the devising of a line of their subsequent transmission from the first man to Christ is, so far, unique to CT. Whereas simultaneous ascribing of these three offices to Christ is attested in other ancient Christian sources, Syriac as well as non-Syriac, their combination in the person of Adam has no apparent precedents in the earlier Christian sources. It appears that our author adapted the traditional motif of the three spiritual offices of Christ to his own needs by transferring it to Adam, in order to strengthen the typological connection between the two that was central for his theology of history. Perhaps it was also our author's indebtedness to the portrayal of Adam in Syriac exegetical tradition that made such a transfer possible. It is noteworthy that whereas the portrayal of Adam as a king or prophet is well attested in other late ancient Christian traditions of biblical exegesis, none of them besides Syriac seems to represent Adam's ministry in Paradise in priestly terms.[218]

Another aspect of the description of the three gifts in CT that may be unique to this work is the connection between them and the detail from the canonical Passion narrative of the sponge soaked in wine, made in CT 51.15–17. None of the Syriac authors from late antiquity whose works have survived seems to connect Israel's loss of the spiritual offices with this particular instrument of Jesus' execution or the New Testament pericopes where it figures. The closest parallel to the role played by the sponge in CT 51.15–17 is provided by the Syriac *Romance of Julian*, whose author resorts to similar imagery in connection with Emperor Julian. At one point, he relates a story about a certain unnamed saint who dreams he sees the emperor standing in the thermal baths of Athens and

---

217   *De crucif.* 4.11; ed. Beck 1964, p. 57 [Syr.].
218   This imagery figures prominently in Ephrem's works; cf. *De Parad.* 3.14, 16–17. For more on this motif in Syriac sources, see Minov 2016, pp. 138–144.

sweating as an angel wipes this pleasant-smelling perspiration from his body with a "sponge of fire" (*'espugā d-nurā*). When the saint asks the angel about the meaning of his actions, he is informed that because "the Spirit of God has departed" from the pagan emperor, "the holy consecration, which he put on in baptism" is now being removed from him.[219] One can see from this description that the author of the *Julian Romance* resorted to the graphic image of the sponge in order to convey the notion of the removal of spiritual gifts from a sinner in a manner similar to that of CT. However, the difference between the two narrative contexts in which this imagery appears, is significant enough to prevent us from making even a tentative judgment on the possible literary relationship between the two works.

4.1.2   Departure of the Holy Spirit

According to CT, the three spiritual offices were not the only loss sustained by the people of Israel as a result of their rejection of Jesus. In CT 50.17, the author augments their departure with that of the Holy Spirit:

> Even that spirit of atonement, which had dwelt in the Temple, in the Holy of Holies, forsook them and departed. And it cleft the curtain of the sanctuary in twain.[220]

In this passage, the author denies Judaism its validity as a religion by declaring that the Holy Spirit had left the Jewish people immediately after Jesus' death on the cross. This event is put into direct connection with a particular New Testament story, namely the miraculous tearing of the Temple curtain that occurred immediately after Jesus breathed his last.[221]

The idea of the Jewish people being completely devoid of the Holy Spirit after the coming of Christ became one of the cornerstones of Christian supersessionist theology at a very early stage. For instance, Tertullian refers disapprovingly to Jewish synagogues, describing them as places "in which the Holy Spirit no longer lingers."[222] Among Syriac writers, we should mention Jacob of Serugh, who while addressing his imaginary Jewish interlocutor in the *Homilies against the Jews* remonstrates against him by saying that "the spirit of Lord has departed from you, O Hebrew!"[223] For Jacob's contemporary, Philoxenus

---

219   Ed. Hoffmann 1880, p. 248; trans. Gollancz 1928, pp. 261–262.
220   Or^A: ܐܦ ܗܘ ܪܘܚܐ ܕܚܘܣܝܐ ܕܗܘܐ ܒܗ ܒܡܩܕܫܐ ܒܩܕܘܫ ܩܘܕܫܐ ܫܒܩ ܐܢܘܢ ܘܥܢܕ. ܘܨܪܝܗܝ ܠܦܪܣܐ ܕܒܝܬ ܩܘܕܫܐ ܠܬܪܝܢ.
221   Cf. Mt 27:51; Mk 15:38; Lk 23:45. On this episode, see Gurtner 2006.
222   *Adv. Jud.* 13.15: *in quibus iam spiritus sanctus non immoratur*; ed. Kroymann 1954b, p. 1388.
223   *Hom.* 5.149; ed. Albert 1976, p. 146.

of Mabbug, this notion serves as a self-evident postulate upon which he builds his speculations about the difference in the postmortem fate of Christians, who enter a state of sleep after their physical death, and that of pagans and Jews, who die permanently because "there is no Holy Spirit (in them), and for this reason when they die they really die, and are not just asleep."[224]

There are also early parallels to this particular modification of the supersessionist notion in CT 50.17, where the Holy Spirit's departure from Israel is connected to the rending of the Temple's curtain. A similar idea is expressed in the *Apostolic Constitutions*, where it is declared concerning the relationship between God and Israel that since "He has forsaken His people, He has also left His temple desolate, and rent the veil of the temple, and took from them the Holy Spirit."[225] Later, Pseudo-Macarius makes use of this motif as he reproaches the Jews by claiming that after the crucifixion of Jesus and the tearing of the Temple's veil, "the Spirit departed from them."[226]

In Syriac literature, this anti-Jewish motif had already appeared in the *Didascalia Apostolorum*, which shares some material with the *Apostolic Constitutions*. This work relates that when God abandoned the Jewish people and its temple, "He rent the curtain, and took away from it the Holy Spirit, and poured it upon those who believed from among the gentiles."[227] This motif is also evoked in the Ephremian *Commentary on the Diatessaron*, where several supersessionist explanations for the incident of the tearing of the curtain are offered. According to one of them, this event symbolically indicated the coming destruction of the Temple, "because his (i.e. God's) Spirit had gone forth from it."[228] The author of the *Commentary* develops this imagery further and presents the rending of the Temple's curtain by the departing Holy Spirit as an act of retribution for the denunciation of Jesus by the Jewish high priest, who tore his garments according to the canonical account of Jesus' trial (cf. Mt 26:65; Mk 14:63).

It might well be that in his use of this anti-Jewish motif the author of CT was inspired by the *Commentary*. The fact that both these writers represent the tearing of the curtain as a result of the direct action of the Holy Spirit on its departure from the Temple speaks in favor of such a suggestion.[229]

---

224 *Homily on the Indwelling of the Holy Spirit*; ed. Tanghe 1960, p. 54; trans. Brock 1987, p. 123.
225 *Const. ap.* 6.5.4; ed. Metzger 1985–1987, v. 2, p. 304; trans. Whiston & Donaldson 1870, p. 147.
226 *Hom.* 17.14; ed. Dörries et alii 1964, p. 175.
227 Syr. *Didasc.* 23; ed. Vööbus 1979, v. 2, pp. 228 [Syr.], 210–211 [trans.].
228 *Comm. Diat.* 21.4; trans. McCarthy 1993, p. 319.
229 It should be noted, however, that the two authors differ in their choice of words for describing this action. While in CT 50.17 we find the verb *sdaq*, in *Comm.* 21.4–6 the verb *ṣrā* is used; ed. Leloir 1963, pp. 208–210.

4.1.3 Cessation of Passover

Another spiritual deprivation that the Jews suffered as a consequence of Jesus' death was the loss of the festival of Passover. The author resorts to this anti-Jewish theme on several occasions. For instance, he makes a general reference to it in CT 43.8–9, right after reporting that the Israelites celebrated Passover after their return to their homeland from their captivity in Babylon:

> These three Passovers had been kept by the children of Israel during the days of their lives: the first—in Egypt in the days of Moses, the second—in the reign of Josiah, the third—when they went up from the land of Babylon. And their Passover has been brought to naught forever.[230]

For a reason that is difficult to comprehend, among all the mentions of it in the Old Testament, our author singles out three particular examples of the celebration of Passover by the Jewish people in a seemingly arbitrary manner as the only cases of its observance during the whole course of Jewish history.[231]

Furthermore, in CT 50.18, which follows the passage mentioning the removal of the three gifts from the Jews and the departure of the Holy Spirit from the Temple, it is related that "the Passover fled away and departed from them, for they never celebrated another Passover in it (i.e. in the Temple)."[232] The author returns to this subject once more in CT 52.17–18, quoted above, where the abolition of Passover among the Jews is likewise mentioned alongside their loss of the three gifts after the crucifixion of Jesus and is said to have occurred in fulfillment of Daniel's prophecy of the weeks.[233]

The biblical festival of Passover was an important topic of anti-Jewish polemic in late ancient Syria–Mesopotamia. In the fourth century, one comes across such writers as Aphrahat and Ephrem in the East and John Chrysostom in the West exercising substantial rhetorical efforts aimed at preventing their Christian congregants from celebrating Passover in accordance with the Jewish calendar, i.e. on 14 Nisan, or from joining the Jews in their celebration of this festival.[234] Apparently, Christian participation in the Jewish rites of Passover continued to be a matter of concern during the sixth century as well. Thus, Severus of Antioch, in one of his *Catechetical Homilies*, warns the newly baptized Antiochenes against adhering to the custom of eating the unleavened

230 Or[A]: ܗܠܝܢ ܬܠܬܐ ܦ̈ܨܚܐ ܐܦܨܚܘ ܒܢ̈ܝ ܝܣܪܐܝܠ ܟܠ ܝܘ̈ܡܝ ܚܝ̈ܝܗܘܢ. ܚܕ ܒܡܨܪܝܢ ܒܝܘ̈ܡܝ ܡܘܫܐ. ܘܐܚܪܢܐ ܒܡܠܟܘܬܗ ܕܝܘܫܝܐ. ܘܬܠܝܬܝܐ ܟܕ ܣܠܩܘ ܡܢ ܐܪܥܐ ܕܒܒܠ. ܘܐܬܒܛܠ ܡܢܗܘܢ ܦܨܚܐ ܕܒܝܬܐ ܠܥܠܡ.

231 Cf. Ex 12; 2 Kg 23:21–23; Ezra 6:18–22.

232 Or[A]: ܘܐܦ ܦܨܚܐ ܥܪܩ ܘܥܒܪ ܡܢܗܘܢ. ܠܐ ܓܝܪ ܬܘܒ ܐܦܨܚܘ ܒܗ ܦܨܚܐ ܐܚܪܢܐ.

233 On this, see section 4.2.6 below.

234 See Shepardson 2008b.

bread sent to them by Jews during the festival.[235] Cyrus of Edessa, another sixth-century author, takes particular care to establish a clear distinction between the Jewish and Christian festivals—which bear the same name, *peṣḥā*, in Syriac—while arguing for the superiority of the latter over the former.[236]

Christian polemicists came up with a number of rhetorical strategies aimed at discrediting the continued Jewish practice of celebrating Passover. One of the most popular lines of attack against this festival was to assert its invalidity after the destruction of the Temple. According to this argument, since the Scripture requires animals to be sacrificed during Passover and such sacrifices could only be legitimately performed in the Temple in Jerusalem, after the Temple's destruction in 70 CE, its celebration became illegitimate. It is this argument that seems to underlie the general supersessionist statements against Passover made in CT.

One of the closest parallels to the anti-Passover rhetoric of CT comes from the *Homilies against the Jews* by John Chrysostom. At one point, Chrysostom draws a contrast between the inspired Fathers of Nicaea, who promulgated new rules concerning the proper manner of Passover celebrations for Christians, and the Jews, who are exiled from their homeland and "celebrate no festival at all" (ἑορτὴν οὐδεμίαν τελοῦντας).[237] Immediately after making this bold claim, Chrysostom endeavors to explain away the obvious fact that both Passover and the Feast of Unleavened Bread are still celebrated by the Jews:

> But there is no feast of unleavened bread among them, nor is there a Pasch. Why is there no feast of unleavened bread among them? Hear the words of the Lawgiver: "You may not sacrifice the Passover in any one of the cities which the Lord your God gives you, but only in the place in which His name shall be invoked." He was speaking about Jerusalem.[238]

This argument is developed in great detail further on, where it is explained that God restricted the celebration of Passover to Jerusalem only and later brought destruction on this city because he "wished to bring this festival to an end."[239] At the core of Chrysostom's attack on the Jews' continued celebration of Passover lies the claim that by destroying the only valid place for the Jews' festival sacrifices, God abolished them altogether. From this, it follows that the

---

235   *Hom.* 43; ed. Brière & Graffin 1971, pp. 92–95.
236   *Explanation of the Pasch* 6; ed. Macomber 1974, pp. 59–64 [Syr.], 51–55 [trans.].
237   *Adv. Jud.* 3.3.6; PG 48, col. 865.
238   *Adv. Jud.* 3.3.6; PG 48, cols. 865–866; trans. (modified) Harkins 1979, p. 57.
239   *Adv. Jud.* 3.3.7; PG 48, col. 866; trans. (modified) Harkins 1979, p. 58.

contemporary Jews' observation of this biblical prescription has no spiritual validity whatsoever and thus should be considered as void.

Another anti-Jewish argument that relates the abrogation of Passover among the Jews to the destruction of the Temple in Jerusalem is found in the works of Syriac writers such as Aphrahat and Ephrem. The former, in the *Demonstration on Passover*, builds his polemic against the Jewish practice of observing this festival on the assumption that according to the prescriptions of the Torah, it is only "before one altar in Jerusalem" that one may lawfully offer the paschal sacrifice (cf. Deut 16:5–6). Accordingly, those among the Jews in the Diaspora who are still continuing this custom following the destruction of Jerusalem and the dispersion of their nation are doing so "in violation of the commandment."[240] Likewise, Ephrem establishes a close nexus between the commandment to celebrate Passover and Deuteronomy 16 in order to claim that the Jews' contemporary celebrations of this festival stand in direct contradiction to God's will as long as they are performed without sacrificial offerings in the temple of Jerusalem:

> For Moses did not allow the people to celebrate their festival wherever they would come. For Moses bound the feast to the sacrifice, and he bound the sacrifice to the holy of holies.[241]

As he develops this theme further, Ephrem adds that "the feast would not happen without the sacrifice."[242] It is in this sense that one should understand the assertion made in CT that the Passover "has been brought to naught forever" among the Jews. Following the same line of thought as Aphrahat and Ephrem, he conceives the destruction of the Temple as a turning point in the spiritual history of the Jewish people. After this event, the Jews' celebration of this festival had no scriptural or spiritual validity, and thus could be justifiably disregarded as fallacious.

4.1.4 Divorce Imagery

Another motif employed by the author to imbue his narrative with supersessionist ideology is the imagery of divorce. In the section dealing with the story of Jesus' crucifixion and death, he expounds at length on the subject of the divine punishment that befell the Jews for this crime and relates, among other things, that (52.1–2)

---

240 *Dem.* 12.3; ed. Parisot 1894, col. 512; trans. Valavanolickal 2005, v. 2, pp. 20–21.
241 *De azym.* 21.3–4; ed. Beck 1964, p. 39 [Syr.]. Cf. also *De azym.* 21.5–7, 21–22, 24.
242 *De azym.* 21.7; ed. Beck 1964, p. 40 [Syr.].

when everything was fulfilled, the divorce document was written for the Synagogue, and she was repudiated and was stripped of the garments of glory.[243]

Representing God's complete repudiation of the Jewish people through the imagery of divorce was by no means new at the time of CT. It was rooted in the biblical understanding of the relationship between God and his chosen people as that of a marital union. Hosea was the first biblical prophet to explicitly use the metaphor of marriage to describe the unique bond between God and Israel (Hos 2:18). This metaphorical language is also found in the writings of other prophets and continued well into post-biblical times, including rabbinic literature.[244] The authors of the New Testament inherited this imagery and adapted it to their own vision of the link between the Church and Christ, presenting Jesus as the "bridegroom" and likening his followers to "bridesmaids."[245] Paul elaborates this imagery further, laying the foundation for the idea of the Church as the Bride of Christ which became one of the key metaphors in the development of ecclesiology.[246]

Of particular relevance for understanding the genesis of the anti-Jewish divorce rhetoric is the inner-biblical evolution of the marital metaphor into the dramatic imagery of the "whoring" Israel, whom God threatens to divorce for her misbehavior.[247] In their mining of the Old Testament for anti-Jewish arguments, Christian authors recognized the subversive power of these metaphors at quite an early stage. Origen was one of the first Christian thinkers to combine the biblical imagery of divorce with a supersessionist understanding of Jewish-Christian conflict. In the *Commentary on Matthew*, while discussing Jesus' saying on divorce from Matthew 19:7–9, he uses this opportunity to offer his vision of the relationship between God and the people of Israel.[248] Origen presents a detailed figurative explanation, representing the Synagogue as an adulterous wife who betrayed her lawful husband Jesus with Satan, prefigured by the robber Barabbas (Mt 27:16–26). As a result, her marriage was terminated

---

243 Or^A: ܘܟܕ ܗܘܐ ܣܥܘܪܐ ܠܗ ܡܪܝܐ. ܐܬܟܬܒ ܠܗ ܠܟܢܘܫܬܐ ܐܓܪܬ ܕܘܠܦܐ ܘܐܫܬܕܝܬ ܡܢ ܠܒܘܫܝ ܫܘܒܚܐ.
244 On this metaphor in the Bible, see Moughtin-Mumby 2008. For later Jewish sources, see Satlow 2001, pp. 44–57.
245 Cf. Mt 9:15; 25:1–13; Mk 2:19–20; Lk 5:34–35.
246 Cf. 1Cor 6:15–17; 2Cor 11:2; Rom 7:1–4; Eph 5:22–32. See also Batey 1971.
247 Cf. Is 50:1; Jer 3:7–9; Ezek 16.
248 *Comm. in Matt.* 14.18–20; ed. Klostermann 1935, pp. 327–334; trans. Patrick 1906, pp. 507–509. Cf. also *Comm. in Matt.* 12.4.

with a "bill of divorce" (τὸ βιβλίον τοῦ ἀποστασίου), while Christ espoused a new wife, summoned from the Gentiles.

The notion of the Church as the Bride of Christ features prominently in Syriac Christian tradition.[249] At quite an early stage, this marital imagery was also adapted to the needs of anti-Jewish polemics, with an emphatic stress laid on the motif of divorce. Thus, in the *Demonstration on Passover*, Aphrahat claims that by celebrating Passover outside Jerusalem, his Jewish opponents transgress the commandment and adds, in order to prove his point, that "a letter of divorce (*ktābā d-šubqānā*) has been written for you."[250] As can be seen from several other passages, in his use of the divorce imagery Aphrahat is strongly influenced by biblical tradition. For instance, on several occasions, he quotes Jeremiah's metaphorical words about the "bill of divorce," issued to the northern kingdom of Israel for its transgressions (Jer 3:8) as a proof-text that demonstrates God's permanent rejection of the Jewish people.[251]

This image became a stock motif in the repertoire of anti-Jewish rhetoric employed by Syriac authors in late antiquity. For instance, the Pseudo-Ephremian *Sermon against the Jews Given on Palm Sunday* depicts God's rejection of the Jewish people as the act of repudiation of an unfaithful wife by a king, who among other things "wrote and delivered her the divorcement (*dulālā*)."[252] Similar imagery appears in the works of Jacob of Serugh, who adjusts it to his own rhetorical needs by transferring the initiative of divorce from God to the Synagogue. In the *Homily on the Sunday of Hosannas* (§§25–30), he compares the reaction of the Jewish inhabitants of Jerusalem to Jesus' entry into the city to that of an "adulterous bride" (*mkirtā gayārtā*) who "desired to give a letter of divorce (*dulālā*) to the Bridegroom, to separate herself from His company [of marriage]."[253]

4.2 Supersessionist Exegesis of the Old Testament

4.2.1 Genesis 8:8–11: Noah's Dove

CT 19.9–12 paraphrases the biblical account of Noah from Genesis 8:6–12, where he sends out two species of birds, a raven and a dove, in order to work out whether the Flood's waters have receded. Having related how the dove returned to the ark with an olive branch in its beak after its second flight, the author concludes this section with the following remark (CT 19.13):

---

249 See Murray, R. 1975, pp. 131–142; Engberding 1937; Graffin 1958.
250 *Dem.* 12.3; ed. Parisot 1894, col. 512; trans. Valavanolickal 2005, v. 2, p. 21.
251 Cf. *Dem.* 15.7; 19.5; 19.11.
252 Ed. Beck 1970, pp. 63–64 [Syr.]; trans. Morris 1847, p. 70.
253 Ed. Rilliet 1986, pp. 596–600; trans. Kollamparampil 1997, p. 271. Cf. also *Homily on the Friday of the Passion* 24; ed. Rilliet 1986, p. 622; trans. Kollamparampil 1997, p. 287.

> That dove, however, depicts for us the two covenants. In the first one the spirit, which spoke through the prophets, did not find a place of rest among that rebellious people, but in the second one it rested on the nations through the waters of baptism.[254]

According to the biblical narrative, Noah sent out the birds four times, the raven once and the dove thrice. After being sent out, the raven did not return to the ark. The dove returned after the first time it was sent, having found no place to land. Sent for the second time, it came back after seven days carrying a freshly plucked olive leaf, which indicated that the earth was emerging from the water. After Noah sent the dove for the third time and it did not return after another seven days, he himself left the ark.

The figure of the dove serves as a pretext for our author to introduce anti-Jewish rhetoric. He does so by interpreting this bird as a prefiguration of the Holy Spirit and its two departures from the ark as symbols of the two covenants, the old and the new. In line with his general theology of supersessionism, the author explains the dove's first return to Noah as an image of God's spirit's abandonment of the Jewish people, and its second return with the olive leaf as an image of God's election of the Gentiles, realized through the sacrament of baptism.

This anti-Jewish interpretation of the figure of the dove from Genesis 8:6–12 seems to have no close analogy in Christian sources prior or contemporary to CT. There are, however, several related exegetical traditions that might help us to understand the genesis of this polemical motif.

Our author develops his typological interpretation based on an older Christian exegetical tradition that regards the dove in Genesis 8:8–11 as a type of the Holy Spirit. A pneumatological understanding of Noah's dove in a baptismal context is ultimately rooted in the New Testament account of Jesus' baptism, where the Holy Spirit descends on him in the form of a dove.[255] It is hardly surprising that the most famous dove from the Old Testament would sooner or later be associated with this tradition. This connection was also facilitated by the strong baptismal associations that the biblical story of the Flood acquired in Christian thought.[256] And indeed, a symbolic and typologi-

254 Or^A: ܗܝ ܕܝܢ ܝܘܢܐ. ܠܬܪ̈ܬܝܗܝܢ ܕܝܬ̈ܩܐ ܨܝܪܐ ܠܢ. ܒܗܝ ܓܝܪ ܩܕܡܝܬܐ ܠܐ ܐܫܟܚܬ ܠܗ ܪܘܚܐ ܗܝ ܕܡܠܠܬ ܒܢܒ̈ܝܐ ܢܝܚܐ ܒܗܘ ܥܡܐ ܡܡܪܡܪܢܐ. ܒܬܪܝܢܐ ܕܝܢ ܕܬܪ̈ܬܝܢ ܐܬܬܢܝܚܬ ܥܠ ܥܡܡ̈ܐ ܒܝܕ ܡ̈ܝܐ ܕܡܥܡܘܕܝܘܬܐ.

255 Mt 3:16, Mk 1:10, Lk 3:22, Jn 1:32.

256 After its first appearance in the New Testament, in 1 Peter 3:20–21, this interpretation of the Flood resurfaces in the writings of many Christian authors. For the references, see Lewis 1978, pp. 114–120, 167–173.

cal connection between the dove sent by Noah and the Holy Spirit is attested from the earliest stages of Christian exegesis. The interpretation of the dove in Genesis 8:8–11 gained wide currency among Christian writers, Latin as well as Greek, from the second century onwards.[257]

In Syriac exegetical tradition, this motif had already appeared in the works of Ephrem. In the *Hymns on Faith*, Ephrem offers a baptismal interpretation of the biblical account of the Flood, where he compares Noah with Christ, the ark with the Church, and the dove with the Holy Spirit that "administers ... her anointing and the mystery (*rāzā*) of his salvation."[258] Later on, we see Jacob of Serugh making use of this exegetical motif when he presents the dove bringing the olive branch to Noah as a type of the Holy Spirit in the context of baptism in the *Homily on the Flood*.[259]

It is noteworthy, however, that in contrast to the author of CT, none of those ancient Christian authors who take Noah's dove to be a symbol of the Holy Spirit seems to resort to this particular typology for the purposes of anti-Jewish polemic. At the same time, several Christian exegetes do interpret the story of Noah sending out the birds in an explicitly anti-Jewish manner.

Among the Christian writers of late antiquity, it is Cyril of Alexandria who offers one of the most developed interpretations of Genesis 8:6–12 along these lines. In the *Glaphyra on Genesis*, he interprets the raven and the dove as prefigurations of different kinds of Christians.[260] According to him, the raven depicts those believers "of the race of Israel" (τῶν ἐξ αἵματος Ἰσραὴλ), who turn back to "the shadows of the Law" even after having accepted Jesus. In order to justify his disapproval of these Christians, who apparently want to continue practicing some biblical commandments, Cyril resorts to the authority of Paul, quoting Galatians 5:4–5. As to Noah sending the dove, while in general it functions as an image of Christ sending saints to the world, the bird's failure to return to its master in Genesis 8:12 prefigures the apostasy of some of them which will take place in the eschatological future.

A comparable anti-Jewish interpretation of Noah's birds appears in the Syriac version of *Physiologus*, according to which "the raven is the likeness (*dmutā*) of the synagogue of the Jews."[261] In the explanation that follows, the author compares the "avarice and carnal gluttony" exhibited by the Jewish people during their wandering in the desert after the flight from Egypt (Num 11:4–5)

---

257 Cf. Tertullian, *De bapt*. 8. For more references and discussion of this tradition, see Lewis 1978, pp. 174–175.
258 *Hymn. de fide* 49.3–4; ed. Beck 1955, p. 155 [Syr.].
259 Ed. Bedjan 1905–1910, v. 4, p. 49.
260 *Glaph. in Gen.* 2; PG 69, col. 69d–72c.
261 Ed. Land 1875, p. 65 [Syr.].

to the ungrateful behavior of the raven, who failed to deliver the message of peace to Noah as a result of its "covetousness of food." On the other hand, the dove that brought the olive branch to the ark is said to be "the image of the Church" (ṣurtā d-ʿidtā).[262]

There is a marked difference, however, between these two cases of anti-Jewish exegesis of Genesis 8:6–12 and the supersessionist typology of CT 19.9–12. Both Cyril and *Physiologus* base their typological interpretation of the biblical narrative on the dichotomy between the raven and the dove, associating Jews with the former. The author of CT, however, follows a completely different line by leaving the raven out of the picture and focusing solely on the figure of the dove. This fact prevents us from considering any of these sources as a direct precursor of the anti-Jewish typology in CT 19.9–12.

It could have been the author of CT himself who invented the anti-Jewish interpretation of the dove episode from Genesis 8:6–12, basing it on the well-established association of Noah's dove with the Holy Spirit. In light of the existing exegetical traditions that attach anti-Jewish rhetoric to the figure of the raven, one might wonder, however, why our author did not follow this seemingly obvious path. It might be speculated that by doing so, he was responding to some particular sensibilities of his intended audience, especially those rooted in the Iranian cultural background. According to Zoroastrian beliefs, the raven (Mid. Pers. *warāy*) belongs to the category of beneficent animals that were created by the deity Ohrmazd.[263] Moreover, alongside several other species of animals and birds, the raven was believed to drive away the demons of impurity from a dead body.[264] These positive connotations of the raven in the context of the Iranian cultural milieu might have been a sufficient reason for our author to avoid drawing a negative image of this bird by associating it with the Jews.

4.2.2 Genesis 9:20–27: The Cursing of Canaan

The biblical account of Noah provides the author with another opportunity for denouncing Jews. In chapter 21, which presents a typological interpretation of the drunken patriarch as the crucified Christ, he explains the episode of Noah's cursing of Canaan in the following manner (CT 21.21–22):

> Now when Noah woke up from his sleep he cursed Canaan, and reduced his offspring to slavery, and scattered his offspring among the nations.

---

262 Ed. Land 1875, pp. 65–66 [Syr.].
263 Cf. Iranian *Bundahišn* 13.22; ed. Pakzad 2005, p. 174.
264 Cf. *Šāyest-nē-šāyest* 2.5; ed. Tavadia 1930, p. 32.

And when our Lord rose from the dead he cursed the Jews, and scattered their offspring among the nations.²⁶⁵

In this brief passage, the author interprets the biblical story of Noah cursing Ham's son Canaan and promising that he would be enslaved to Shem and Japheth (Gen 9:24–27) as a prefiguration of Jesus' actions towards the Jewish people after his resurrection. Here, he presents the message of God's ultimate rejection of the Jews, referring to their dispersal among the nations. The latter statement most likely alludes to the destruction of Jerusalem's Temple in 70 CE.

Since the typological interpretation of Noah as Christ, of which this passage forms a part, has already been analyzed in detail elsewhere,²⁶⁶ I will not discuss all the evidence on the history of this exegetical motif again. To sum it up, the anti-Jewish typological interpretation of Genesis 9:24–27 is well attested in Latin and Greek exegetical traditions from the fifth century on. As has been suggested, there are two main sources from which our author may have become acquainted with the exegetical tradition that combines a Noah–Christ typology with anti-Jewish rhetoric: the tradition of Greek catenae on Genesis and the *Glaphyra* by Cyril of Alexandria.

Regardless of whence he had borrowed this anti-Jewish tradition, it should be noted that the author of CT modifies it in accordance with his own exegetical tastes and polemical needs. Thus, he places a strong emphasis on Jesus' condemnation of the Jewish people after his resurrection, citing their dispersion throughout the nations as an illustration.

The latter notion is closely related to the Christian view of the destruction of Jerusalem and the Temple in 70 CE as a punishment inflicted by God upon the Jews for the death of Jesus. This polemical interpretation of the Jewish national catastrophe was developed by Christian authors very early on. From the second century, it may be found employed by Greek Christian writers as an argument for the legitimacy of Gentile Christianity and for the claim that the place of Jews in God's covenant had now been inherited by the Christians.²⁶⁷ Syriac authors in late antiquity would also occasionally resort to this argument in polemics against Judaism. Thus, Aphrahat says of the "foolish people" of the Jews that because they "did not receive the humble king Christ, he uprooted and

---

265 Or^A: ܘܟܕ ܩܡ ܡܪܢ ܡܢ ܐܝܟܐ ܕܡܝܬ ܠܛ ܐܢܘܢ ܠܝܗܘܕܝܐ ܘܒܕܪ ܙܪܥܗܘܢ ܒܝܢܬ ܥܡܡܐ. ܐܝܟ ܕܒܕܪ ܚܡ ܠܒܢܘܗܝ ܒܝܢܬ ܥܡܡܐ ܒܙܕܩܐ ܕܥܒܕܘܬܐ.

266 Minov 2017, pp. 171–181.

267 Cf. Justin Martyr (*Dial.* 24–26, 52, 109–110), Origen (*C. Cels.* 4.73), Eusebius of Caesarea (*Dem. ev.* 1.1.6, 6.13). For an analysis of this material, see Gregerman 2007, pp. 15–199.

scattered them from their place."[268] Likewise, the author of the Ephremian *Commentary on the Diatessaron* admonishes an imaginary Jewish protagonist to "learn from your demolished city" the true divine identity of Jesus, while pointing out: "Because the sons of Jerusalem are dispersed and scattered among all the nations of the Gentiles, learn who he is who has reunited and gathered all the nations of the Gentiles into the Church."[269]

Whereas none of the earlier writers who interpreted the story of Noah's cursing of Canaan typologically made use of this anti-Jewish motif in this context, the author of CT decided to incorporate it into the traditional typological scheme in order to illustrate and reinforce the notion of God's condemnation of the Jews.

4.2.3 Genesis 29: Leah and Rachel

At the end of chapter 31, a large part of which is devoted to a typological interpretation of episodes from Jacob's life such as the vision of the ladder (Gen 28:11–19) and the meeting with Rachel at the well (Gen 29:1–10), the author offers the following explanation of the patriarch's double marriage (CT 31.26–28):

> And as Jacob served with Laban for seven years, and the one whom he loved was not given to him, so also was it with the Jews, who served Pharaoh, king of Egypt, in slavery, and went out of Egypt—the covenant of the Church, the bride of Christ, was not given to them, but instead the one that has gotten old, and worn out, and corrupted. Now the eyes of the first one, whom Jacob married, were ugly, while the eyes of Rachel were beautiful and her countenance was bright. A veil was laid over the face of the first covenant, so that the children of Israel might not see its beauty. As for the second one, it is wholly light.[270]

The biblical account of Jacob's marriage to the two daughters of Laban, Leah and Rachel (Gen 29:15–28), is here interpreted as a figurative reference to the two crucial moments in the spiritual history of the Jewish people. The author

268 *Dem.* 9.8; ed. Parisot 1894, col. 428; trans. Valavanolickal 2005, v. 1, p. 210.

269 *Comm. Diat.* 20.29; trans. McCarthy 1993, pp. 308–309.

270 Or[A]: ܘܕܦܠܚ ܝܥܩܘܒ ܥܡ ܠܒܢ ܫܒܥ ܫܢܝܢ. ܘܠܐ ܐܬܝܗܒܬ ܠܗ ܗܝ ܕܪܚܡ ܗܘܐ. ܗܟܢܐ ܐܦ ܝܗܘܕܝܐ ܕܝ ܦܠܚܘ ܒܥܒܕܘܬܐ ܠܦܪܥܘܢ ܡܠܟܐ ܕܡܨܪܝܢ. ܘܢܦܩܘ ܡܢ ܡܨܪܝܢ. ܠܐ ܗܝ ܕܝܬܩܐ ܕܥܕܬܐ ܟܠܬܗ ܕܡܫܝܚܐ ܐܬܝܗܒܬ ܠܗܘܢ. ܐܠܐ ܗܝ ܕܥܬܩܬ ܘܒܠܝܬ ܘܐܬܚܒܠܬ. ܕܗܝ ܠܡ ܩܕܡܝܬܐ ܕܢܣܒ ܝܥܩܘܒ ܣܢܝ̈ܢ ܗܘܝ̈ ܥܝ̈ܢܝܗ. ܘܕܪܚܝܠ ܫܦܝ̈ܪܢ ܗܘܝ̈ ܥܝ̈ܢܝܗ ܘܢܗܝܪ ܦܪܨܘܦܗ. ܕܝܬܩܐ ܠܡ ܩܕܡܝܬܐ ܬܫܒܝܬܐ ܫܡܝܟܐ ܗܘܬ ܥܠ ܐ̈ܦܝܗ ܕܠܐ ܢܚܙܘܢ ܒܢ̈ܝ ܝܣܪܝܠ ܫܘܦܪܗ. ܗܕܐ ܕܝܢ ܕܬܪ̈ܬܝܢ ܢܘܗܪܐ ܐܝܬܝܗ ܟܠܗ.

likens the biblical patriarch to the Jewish people, while Leah and Rachel are respectively compared to the old and new covenants. Far from being neutral, this comparison conveys a distinct anti-Jewish message. The figures of the two matriarchs serve as a screen onto which the ideologically charged dichotomy between the two covenants is projected. Our author presents the Law of Moses as inferior to that of Jesus by drawing a contrast between the appearance of Leah and that of Rachel based on the scriptural reference to the former's "weak" eyes (Gen 29:17). True to his supersessionist vision of the two religious traditions, he devalues the Old Testament as obsolete.

The supersessionist message of the Leah–Rachel typology is reinforced further by his use of the imagery of the "veil" (*taḥpitā*) that covered the face of the Mosaic Law and thus prevented the Jews from perceiving its true beauty. This motif alludes to the biblical story of the covering that Moses put on his shining face after he descended from Mount Sinai and communicated God's commandments to the Israelites (Ex 34:29–35).

The typological interpretation of the story of Leah and Rachel by the author of CT is deeply rooted in Pauline thought. In his letters, the apostle lays the foundations for the future supersessionist hermeneutics of the biblical stories of the patriarchs. In order to corroborate his point that the Gentiles prevailed over Israel in obtaining God's favor because of their faith in Jesus, in Romans 9:6–13 Paul presents the examples of Jacob and Esau and the offspring of Hagar and Sarah as reflecting the hermeneutical principle that "the elder shall serve the younger" (Gen 25:23). Our author takes the two matriarchs to be symbols of the old and new covenants in exactly the same manner as Paul treats the figures of Hagar and Sarah in Galatians 4:22–31, where he explains them to be an "allegory" of the "two covenants." The convenience with which the story of Jacob's two wives fits Paul's supersessionist pattern explains the popularity of the Leah—Rachel typology in Christian exegetical tradition. As Leonard Rutgers has aptly noted, this typology became so appealing to Christian readers of Genesis 29 "especially because Rachel, although the younger wife, had taken precedence over Leah. Therefore, it could be argued that there was something deeply and inevitably biblical about the fact that God now favored the younger church over the much older synagogue."[271]

This typological connection had already been explored by Justin Martyr, who argues in the *Dialogue with Trypho the Jew* that Jacob's two marriages should be regarded not as an ordinary action, but as a divinely sanctioned dispensation, intended to carry symbolic and prophetic messages as "types of what Christ

---

[271] Rutgers 2009, p. 97.

would do."272 Following the equation "Leah is your people and the Synagogue, while Rachel is our Church,"273 Justin justifies Jacob's double marriage as a prefiguration of the salvific mission of Jesus, who, in a manner similar to that of the patriarch, acquired two different groups of believers for himself, one from the Jews and one from the Gentiles. This interpretation of the figures of Leah and Rachel became a commonplace in the later Christian tradition of biblical exegesis, both in the West and in the East.274

This typology appears in the works of fourth-century authors in the Syriac exegetical tradition. It seems to be implied in Aphrahat's *Demonstration on Exhortation*, where he provides a long list of scriptural examples meant to illustrate that God's sovereignty expressed itself in different periods of human history when "He has made the small great and treated the proud with contempt."275 Among other examples of God elevating the disadvantaged over the privileged, Aphrahat mentions "the Peoples in the place of the People" and "Rachel in the place of Leah."276 The typological connection between Jacob's wives and the two religious communities is pursued in a more explicit manner by Ephrem. In the *Nisibene Hymns*, he draws a parallel between Laban and Satan and regards the two young maidens that Jacob snatched away from their father to be a "type of the (two) congregations" (*ṭupsā da-knušātā*), i.e. of the Synagogue and the Church.277

A most thorough treatment of this exegetical topos in Syriac literature comes from the pen of Jacob of Serugh, who devoted a separate composition to it, the *Homily on Our Lord and Jacob, and on the Church and Rachel, and on Leah and the Synagogue*.278 In this work, Jacob offers an elaborate exposition of the events of the patriarch's life narrated in Genesis 29, the overall goal of which is to demonstrate that through his actions, "Jacob depicted the entire path of the Son of God."279 Focusing on various aspects of the biblical narrative, the poet seeks to convey the main typological message of Jacob's double marriage, i.e. that "the nation and nations were depicted in Leah and Rachel; the Synagogue and the Church were spoken through the two sisters."280

---

272   *Dial.* 134.3; ed. Marcovich 1997, p. 302; trans. Falls 1948, p. 355.
273   *Dial.* 134.3; ed. Marcovich 1997, p. 302; trans. (modified) Falls 1948, pp. 355–356.
274   Cf. Theodoret of Cyrus, *Quaest. in Gen.* 91; Cyril of Alexandria, *Glaph. in Gen.* 4; Cyprian, *Test.* 1.20; Jerome, *Ep.* 22.21; 123.13; Maximus of Turin, *Con. Jud.* 5; Ambrose, *Jac.* 5.25.
275   *Dem.* 14.33; ed. Parisot 1894, col. 656; trans. Valavanolickal 2005, v. 1, p. 83.
276   *Dem.* 14.33; ed. Parisot 1894, col. 657; trans. Valavanolickal 2005, v. 1, p. 84.
277   *Carm. Nisib.* 32.16; ed. Beck 1961, p. 78 [Syr.].
278   Ed. Bedjan 1905–1910, v. 3, pp. 208–223.
279   Ed. Bedjan 1905–1910, v. 3, p. 218, ln. 18.
280   Ed. Bedjan 1905–1910, v. 3, p. 219, ln. 8–9.

As to the imagery of the veil that covered the face of the Old Testament, the fact that the author of CT chooses the noun *taḥpitā* and not *šušepā*, used for Moses' covering in the Peshitta version of Exodus 34:29–35, betrays his indebtedness to the Pauline tradition of interpreting this scriptural passage. In 2 Corinthians 3:13–16, the apostle attacks the Jews who do not accept his message and evokes the image of Moses' veil in order to explain their inability to perceive the true meaning of the Old Testament.[281] In the Peshitta version of the New Testament, the Greek noun κάλυμμα, which Paul uses for this covering, is rendered not as *šušepā*, but as *taḥpitā*.

Paul's interpretation of Moses' veil gained such wide currency that from the second century on, many Christian authors refer to it as an image of the literal understanding of the Old Testament and to the unveiled faces of those who understand its spiritual sense.[282] One of the first Christian exegetes to combine this understanding of Moses' veil with the typological interpretation of Jacob's marriage was Theodoret of Cyrus. According to him, Jacob was a type of God because "God had two peoples: the elder with a veil (κάλυμμα) over its heart, the younger clad in the beauty of faith."[283] Jacob of Serugh, in the aforementioned *Homily on Our Lord and Jacob*, likewise brings together the two exegetical motifs, as he asserts that "in that veil (*šušepā*), which Moses spread over his face, the cover of Leah, who was older, is prefigured."[284]

Jacob's *Homily* is of particular interest to us as a possible source for the Leah–Rachel typology in CT. Besides the joint appearance of this typological scheme and the notion of Moses' veil, there are some additional features in the way Jacob's two wives are portrayed that our author shares with him. Thus, both authors describe Leah using derivatives of the adjective *sanyā*, "hateful, ugly,"[285] and both of them associate Rachel with "light" (*nuhrā*).[286]

It would be unfair, however, to assume that the author of CT is merely reproducing Jacob's rhetoric in his anti-Jewish handling of the story of Leah and Rachel, or, for that matter, that of any other author quoted above. Indeed, the function performed by this pair of women in his typological scenario is different from that attested in Jacob's *Homily* and in the works of other authors. While for all of them Leah and Rachel embody the two religious communities, in CT they prefigure the two covenants. The same is true of the function of Moses' veil. For instance, for Jacob of Serugh, this covering prevents the

---

281   For analysis of this passage, see Stockhausen 1989.
282   For examples, see Roukema 2006.
283   *Quaest. in Gen.* 91; ed. and trans. Petruccione & Hill 2007, v. 1, pp. 178–179.
284   Ed. Bedjan 1905–1910, v. 3, p. 219, ln. 18–19.
285   For Jacob, cf. ed. Bedjan 1905–1910, v. 3, p. 209, ln. 19 *et passim*.
286   For Jacob, cf. ed. Bedjan 1905–1910, v. 3, p. 221, ln. 4.

ugliness of the Synagogue from being perceived by her bridegroom, i.e. Christ: "Veiled was standing before Adonai the daughter of the Hebrews, and her ugliness was covered by the radiance of Moses and was not evident."[287] For our author, however, the veil shields the inner beauty of the Old Testament from being perceived by the Jews. This understanding of Moses' veil is much closer to the original Pauline exegesis of Exodus 34:29–35, reflected in 2 Corinthians 3:13–16, where Moses' "veil" (*taḥpitā*) prevents the Jewish people from perceiving the true Christocentric message of the "old covenant."

Accordingly, it seems more likely that the author of CT developed this anti-Jewish argument himself, readjusting the traditional supersessionist interpretation of Leah and Rachel as the Synagogue and the Church to the Pauline construction of Moses' veil in 2 Corinthians 3:13–16 and allegorization of Hagar and Sarah as the two covenants in Galatians 4:22–31. CT 31.26–28 thus demonstrates his creative stance vis-à-vis the previous tradition of scriptural exegesis. It might also be added that this readjustment is similar to the way our author handles the story of Noah's dove analyzed above. In both cases, he reworks the traditional typological scheme by shifting the focus from the two communities of believers, the Synagogue and the Church, to the two covenants, the old and the new.

4.2.4   Exodus 28: The "Breast-Piece of Judgment"

The book of Genesis was not the only repository of scriptural themes and images that the author of CT uses for polemics against Judaism. Occasionally, he turns to other biblical books for this purpose. He borrows one such image from the book of Exodus. In CT 53.12, which follows the statement that Jesus was executed with the help of Temple objects provided by the Jews such as the poles of the Ark of the Covenant and the veil of atonement, the author offers an explanation of this extra-canonical tradition:

> This was what God commanded Moses: to make a girdle of judgment and peace: of judgment—for the Jews who crucified Him, and of peace—for the Gentiles who believed in him.[288]

In this passage, the author presents "the girdle of judgment and peace" (*prāzumē d-dinā wda-šlāmā*), a supposedly scriptural artifact that Moses manufactured by divine command, as a symbol of God's discriminating attitude

---

287   Ed. Bedjan 1905–1910, v. 3, p. 219, ln. 20–21.
288   Or^A: ܗܘܐ ܗܟܢܐ ܕܦܩܕܗ ܐܠܗܐ ܠܡܘܫܐ. ܕܢܥܒܕ ܦܪܙܘܡܐ ܕܕܝܢܐ ܘܕܫܠܡܐ܆ ܕܕܝܢܐ܂ ܠܝܗܘܕܝܐ ܕܨܠܒܘܗܝ. ܘܕܫܠܡܐ܆ ܠܥܡܡܐ ܕܗܝܡܢܘ ܒܗ.

towards two groups of people based on their relation to Christ: punishing the Jews, who killed Jesus, and rewarding the Gentiles, who accepted him.

From the author's choice of words for describing this object, it can be seen that he is referring here to the so-called "breast-piece of judgment" (Heb. *ḥōšen mišpāṭ*), a part of the high-priestly attire which, according to Exodus 28:15–24, consisted of a bejeweled rectangular piece of material. In the Bible, this object is associated with judgment because two mysterious objects were kept inside it, the Urim and Thummim, which were mainly used in the context of judicial decision-making among the Israelites (Ex 28:30).[289]

The author of CT refers to this cultic object using the noun *prāzumē*, "girdle." On the one hand, this usage appears to stand in contradiction to the Peshitta version of the Old Testament, where the Hebrew noun *ḥōšen* is usually rendered by Syriac *prisā*, "mantle, cloak" (Ex 28:15, 29:5). It seems, however, that whoever translated Exodus into Syriac was not consistent in his use of equivalents for the Hebrew *ḥōšen*. Thus, on several occasions in the description of the breast-piece, he chooses to translate it not with *prisā*, but with *ḥusāyā*, "atonement" (Ex 28:23–24, 27). There is also at least one instance in the Peshitta where *ḥōšen* is translated with *prāzumā*.[290]

Our author describes the breast-piece as possessing the qualities of "judgment and peace." In doing so, he conflates two different biblical traditions about it. The first part of this phrase comes from the name of the "breast-piece of judgment" itself, which was translated into Syriac as *prisā d-dinā* in Exodus 28:15, 29–30. The second noun, i.e. *šlāmā*, "peace," is borrowed from the description of the Urim and Thummim which were kept inside the breast-piece. The Syriac translator of Exodus 28:30 rendered the Hebrew phrase "Urim and Thummim" (אֶת־הָאוּרִים וְאֶת־הַתֻּמִּים) as *nahirā wa-šlāmā*, "light and peace," understanding *'ūrīm* as being derived from the noun *'ōr*, "light," and *tummīm* from the root *tmm*, "to be whole, complete," the semantic range of which overlaps with that of the Syriac root *šlm*.[291]

The author's choice of these two nouns reflects a conscious hermeneutic strategy on his part, the main purpose of which is to construct a value-laden dichotomy between two aspects of the sacred object that could then

---

289   On this, see van Dam 1997, pp. 154–163.
290   Cf. Ex 28:4, where the phrase *ḥōšen wə'ēpôḏ* is rendered as *prāzumā w-pedtā d-ki'pē*.
291   Cf. also Dt 33:8. A similar approach to explaining the noun *tummīm* is attested in rabbinic sources. Cf. *Targum Pseudo-Jonathan* to Ex 28:30, according to which the words of *'ūrīm* are "enlightening (*manherin*) and make public the hidden things of the house of Israel," while the *tummīm* "fulfill (*mašlemin*) the oracles of the high priest"; ed. Ginsburger 1903, p. 149; trans. M. Maher in McNamara et alii 1994, p. 241. On this tradition, see van Dam 1997, pp. 86–89.

be converted into the general supersessionist opposition between Jews and Christians in their asymmetrical relation to God. Since no comparable interpretation of the high-priestly breast-piece is attested in the works of late ancient Christian writers, our author might have been among the first to infuse this scriptural image with anti-Jewish meaning.

4.2.5 Psalm 118:27: The "Horns of the Altar"

Another scriptural image that provides the author with an opportunity to express criticism of Judaism comes from the book of Psalms. In CT 52.1–2, after the statement that God had annulled his marriage to the "synagogue" of the Jews, he relates regarding the latter that

> she was stripped of the garments of glory, even as in times of old David had, through the Holy Spirit, said about her and prophesied: *unto the horns of the altar*—so far were the festivals of the Jews perpetuated; *unto the horns of the altar*, that is unto the cross of Christ.[292]

This statement is followed by an extended genealogy of Christ, beginning with Adam and extending as far as Jesus' ascent to heaven. After that, in CT 52.14–17, the author repeats the anti-Jewish argument of verses 1–2, albeit in a more developed form:

> Observe, our brother Nāmusāyā, how the generations and families have succeeded each other from Adam and until the Jews, and the Jews also from one (generation) to another until the cross of Christ. From that time and on the festivals of the Jews have ceased, as the blessed David says about them: *Bind our festivals with chains, unto the horns of the altar*. The *chains* are the families which are linked to each other, and the *altar* is the cross of Christ. Until the cross of Christ the festivals of the Jews succeeded each other, in priesthood, and royalty, and prophecy, and Passover, but from the time of the cross of Christ and henceforth they have all departed from the Jews, as I have said.[293]

---

292 Or^A: ܘܐܫܬܠܚܬ ܡܢ ܠܒ̈ܘܫܝ ܫܘܒܚܐ. ܐܝܟ ܕܡܢ ܩܕܝܡ ܐܡܪ ܥܠܝܗ̇ ܕܘܝܕ ܒܝܕ ܪܘܚܐ ܕܩܘܕܫܐ. ܘܐܬܢܒܝ. ܕܥܕܡܐ ܠܩܪܢܬܗ ܕܡܕܒܚܐ ܠܗܪܟܐ ܡܬܬܟܠܝܢ ܥܐܕܝܗܘܢ ܕܝܗܘ̈ܕܝܐ. ܥܕܡܐ ܠܩܪܢܬܗ ܕܡܕܒܚܐ. ܗ̇ܘ ܕܝܢ ܥܕܡܐ ܠܙܩܝܦܗ ܕܡܫܝܚܐ.

293 Or^A: ܚܙܝ ܐܚܘܢ ܢܡܘܣܝܐ. ܕܐܝܟܢܐ ܐܬܬܒܥܘ ܕܪ̈ܐ ܘܫܪ̈ܒܬܐ ܡܢ ܐܕܡ ܘܥܕܡܐ ܠܝܗܘ̈ܕܝܐ. ܘܡܢ ܝܗܘ̈ܕܝܐ ܬܘܒ ܡܢ ܗܕܐ ܠܗܕܐ. ܥܕܡܐ ܠܙܩܝܦܗ ܕܡܫܝܚܐ. ܘܡܢ ܬܡܢ ܘܠܗܠ ܒܛܠܘ ܥܐܕܝܗܘܢ ܕܝܗܘ̈ܕܝܐ. ܐܝܟ ܕܐܡܪ ܥܠܝܗܘܢ ܛܘܒܢܐ ܕܘܝܕ. ܕܐܣܘܪ ܒܥ̈ܐܕܝܢ ܒܫܫܠܬܐ. ܥܕܡܐ ܠܩܪܢܬܗ ܕܡܕܒܚܐ. ܫܫܠܬܐ ܐܝܬܝܗܝܢ ܫܪ̈ܒܬܐ ܕܐܚܝܕܐ ܗܕܐ ܒܗܕܐ. ܘܡܕܒܚܐ ܙܩܝܦܗ ܕܡܫܝܚܐ. ܥܕܡܐ ܠܙܩܝܦܗ ܕܡܫܝܚܐ ܐܬܬܒܥܘ

At the core of these two passages lies an anti-Jewish argument based on the claim that the Jewish festivals were abolished after Jesus' crucifixion. In the second passage, the author combines this motif with the general supersessionist scheme of the "three gifts" discussed above. A similar supersessionist assertion is made in CT 54.3, where it is related that after Christ's resurrection and descent to Sheol, "he abolished the festivals of the Jews."[294] This anti-Jewish argument is closely linked to the notion of the abrogation of the Jewish Passover.

This anti-Jewish argument is supported by a particular biblical verse, the second part of Psalm 118:27—"The Lord is God, and he has given us light. Bind the festal procession with branches, up to the horns of the altar"—quoted in CT 52.15 according to the Peshitta version. This verse is interpreted as a divinely inspired prophecy about the abrogation of the Jewish festivals as the result of a divine punishment for Jesus' death on the cross.

Our author was not the first Christian reader of Psalm 118 to harness the imagery of verse 27 for the purpose of anti-Jewish polemic. An early example of the supersessionist interpretation of the second half of this verse comes from Aphrahat's writings. In the *Demonstration on Charity*, whose main agenda is to prove the supremacy of the double commandment to love God and one's neighbor (Lk 16:31) over the rest of the commandments of the Old Testament, he argues at length that the Mosaic Law was made obsolete after the arrival of Christ. One of the biblical proof-texts Aphrahat evokes to corroborate this point is Psalm 118:27b, of which the first half is quoted, slightly altered to fit the sentence structure: "From the time that he (i.e. Jesus) came, he made obsolete the observances in the Law and from the time that they bound him, the feasts were bound in chains."[295]

Another anti-Jewish interpretation of Psalm 118:27b, similar to that of CT 52.1–17, appears in the homily *On the Holy Resurrection of Christ*, a Greek composition of unknown date and provenance that was transmitted under the name of Epiphanius of Salamis. The author of this work opens with an extended panegyric of Easter, which contains two elements that bring his representation of this festival close to our author's anti-Jewish argument. First of all, he interprets Ps 118:27b as a divinely inspired prophecy about the festival of Easter, i.e. a celebration of the crucifixion and resurrection of Jesus.[296] Furthermore, while presenting the resurrection of Christ as "the true Passover" (τὸ Πάσχα

---

294 Or^A: ܐܠܐ ܕܥܐܕܐ ܕܝܗܘܕܝܐ ܒܛܠ ܐܢܘܢ.

295 *Dem.* 2.6; ed. Parisot 1894, cols. 57–60; trans. Valavanolickal 2005, v. 1, p. 45.

296 αὕτη ἡ ἑορτὴ, περὶ ἧς τὸ Πνεῦμα τὸ ἅγιον παρακελεύεται λέγον· Συστήσασθε ἑορτὴν ἐν τοῖς πυκάζουσιν ὁμοῦ τε καὶ θάλπουσιν, ἕως τῶν κεράτων τοῦ θυσιαστηρίου; PG 43, col. 468.

τὸ ἀληθινὸν) that inaugurated a complete renewal of the world, the homilist imbues his praise of this event with an explicit supersessionist rhetoric, as he claims that on this day Jesus "put an end to the legal Passover of the Jews."[297]

An interesting parallel to the interpretation of the altar horns as a reference to Christ's cross in CT is found in the works of Cyril of Alexandria. In the *Adoration and Worship of God in Spirit and in Truth*, Cyril offers a Christological interpretation of the seemingly unrelated altar for incense offering described in Exodus 30:1–10. Among the other features of this cultic object that allow him to draw a parallel between it and Jesus, Cyril points out that "the horns of the altar, stretched out like hands, prefigure the form of the honorable Cross."[298] This interpretation serves him as an illustration of the general hermeneutic principle that the crucified Christ could be recognized in virtually every scriptural passage.[299]

This evidence demonstrates that the anti-Jewish interpretation of Psalm 118:27b as a prophecy about the resurrection of Jesus and the abolishment of the Jewish festivals was most likely inherited by the author of CT from the previous tradition of scriptural exegesis. A possible clue to the source our author used may be found in the fact that he integrates this anti-Jewish motif into the general supersessionist scheme of the "three gifts." This immediate context of the anti-Jewish argument, based on Psalm 118:27b, very strongly recalls the way in which Aphrahat handles this biblical verse. After he cites it, the Persian sage continues to develop his main point about the irrelevance of the Mosaic Law by illustrating it through the following series of examples that elaborate different aspects of Jewish sovereignty, made obsolete after the coming of Christ:

> He (God) caused to pass from them the judges because they wished to judge the innocent. Because they rejected his kingdom, he took from them the kingdom "for, the one to whom the kingdom belongs had come" (Gen. 49:10). And he offered "a living sacrifice" (Rom. 12:1) for us and made obsolete their sacrifices. And the sons of Israel sat without sacrifices, without altar, without putting on ephod and burning incenses (Hos. 3:4). He (God) abolished from them visions and prophets for they did not hear the Great Prophet.[300]

---

297 ἐν ταύτῃ κατέπαυσε τὸ Πάσχα τοῦ νόμου, καὶ Ἰουδαίων; PG 43, col. 468.
298 Κέρατα δὲ τῷ θυσιαστηρίῳ, καὶ οἱονεὶ χεῖρες ἐκπεπετασμέναι, καὶ τοῦ τιμίου σταυροῦ τὸ σχῆμα προαναπλάττοντα; PG 68, col. 617. Cf. also Alexander the Monk (c. 6th c.), *De inventione Crucis*; PG 87.3, col. 4073.
299 ἐν παντὶ γὰρ τόπῳ Χριστὸς γινώσκεται, καὶ οὗτος ἐσταυρωμένος; PG 87.3, col. 4073.
300 *Dem.* 2.6; ed. Parisot 1894, col. 60; trans. Valavanolickal 2005, v. 1, p. 45.

It is remarkable that this list includes all three of God's original gifts to the Jewish people mentioned by the author of CT in connection with the abolishment of the Jewish festivals in CT 52.17, i.e. royalty, priesthood, and prophecy. This similarity invites us to seriously consider the possibility that in his interpretation of Psalm 118:27b, the author of CT was inspired by Aphrahat.

4.2.6 Daniel 9:26–27: The Prophecy of the Weeks

In the same chapter, which presents a defense of Mary's genealogy, the author addresses another important aspect of Jewish-Christian polemic, the problem of the messianic status of Jesus (CT 44.53–57):

> Observe, O our brother Nāmusāyā, that in the days of Cyrus the fifth thousand (of years) came to an end. And from the thousand (years) of Cyrus until the passion of our Redeemer, the years were in number five hundred, according to the prophecy of Daniel, who prophesied and said, *After sixty-two weeks the Messiah shall be slain.* And these weeks make five hundred years. Behold, from this time the mouth of the Jews is shut, for they have dared to say that the Messiah has not yet come. So, they must do one of two things: either accept the prophecy of Daniel, or say, "We do not accept it." For the prophecy has fulfilled itself, and the weeks have passed, and the Messiah has been killed, and the holy city has been destroyed by Vespasian.[301]

The author is here making an effort to counter Jewish objections to the Christian belief that Jesus is the eschatological Messiah promised to the Jewish people in the Old Testament. In order to do this, he resorts to arguments from Scripture and cites Daniel 9:26 as the main proof-text of the Christian truth. This verse, quoted in a version close to the Peshitta with minor changes to the word order, is meant to demonstrate that Jesus' death and the following destruction of Jerusalem had occurred in exact fulfillment of Daniel's prophecy in 9:26–27.

301 Or[A]: ܚܙܝ ܐܘ ܐܚܘܢ ܢܡܘܣܝܐ. ܕܒܝܘܡܝ ܟܘܪܫ ܫܠܡ ܐܠܦܐ ܕܚܡܫܐ. ܘܡܢ ܐܠܦܐ ܕܟܘܪܫ ܥܕܡܐ ܠܚܫܗ ܕܦܪܘܩܢ ܗܘ̈ܝ ܒܡܢܝܢܐ ܫ̈ܢܝܐ ܚܡܫܡܐܐ ܐܝܟ ܢܒܝܘܬܗ ܕܕܢܝܐܝܠ ܕܐܬܢܒܝ ܘܐܡܪ. ܕܡܢ ܒܬܪ ܫܬܝܢ ܘܬܪܝܢ ܫܒ̈ܘܥܝܢ ܢܬܩܛܠ ܡܫܝܚܐ. ܕܗܘܝܢ ܫܒ̈ܘܥܐ ܗܠܝܢ ܚܡܫܡܐܐ ܫ̈ܢܝܢ. ܗܐ ܡܢ ܗܪܟܐ ܡܣܬܟܪ ܦܘܡܗܘܢ ܕܝܗ̈ܘܕܝܐ. ܡܛܠ ܕܡܡܪܚܝܢ ܠܡܐܡܪ ܕܠܐ ܒܥܓܠ ܐܬܐ ܡܫܝܚܐ. ܚܕܐ ܡܢ ܬܪ̈ܬܝܢ ܐܠܨܐ ܗܝ ܠܗܘܢ. ܐܘ ܕܢܩܒܠܘܢ ܢܒܝܘܬܗ ܕܕܢܝܐܝܠ. ܐܘ ܕܢܐܡܪܘܢ ܕܠܐ ܡܩܒܠܝܢ ܠܗ̇. ܡܛܠ ܕܫܠܡܬ ܠܗ̇ ܢܒܝܘܬܗ. ܘܫܒ̈ܘܥܐ ܥܒܪܘ. ܘܡܫܝܚܐ ܐܬܩܛܠ. ܘܡܕܝܢܬܐ ܩܕܝܫܬܐ ܐܬܚܪܒܬ ܡܢ ܐܣܦܣܝܢܘܣ.

He resorts to Daniel 9:26 once more in the context of anti-Jewish polemic in CT 52.18–19. This verse is quoted there in order to buttress the general supersessionist notion that the Jewish people had been permanently deprived of the three divine expressions of its sovereignty, i.e. kingship, priesthood, and prophecy, as a result of Jesus' crucifixion:

> And there is no more a king, or a priest, or a prophet, or a Passover among them, even as Daniel prophesied concerning them, *after two and sixty weeks the Messiah shall be slain, and the holy city shall be destroyed until the completion of the judgment*, that is to say, for ever and ever.[302]

This anti-Jewish argument is rooted in the overall chronological framework of the author's vision of world history, based on the idea of *septimana mundi*. According to him, the time-span of sixty-two weeks, at the end of which the Messiah will be executed in line with Daniel 9:26, began after the completion of the fifth millennium during the reign of the Persian king Cyrus and lasted 500 years.[303] It should be noted that in his assignment of the completion of the fifth millennium to Cyrus' reign, our author deviates considerably from one of the most influential chronological systems of the late antique Christian East, i.e. that of Julius Africanus, according to which the return of the Jewish people from Babylon and the beginning of Cyrus' thirty-year reign are dated to the year 4942, while the end of the fifth millennium falls in the 19th year of the reign of Darius.[304]

Before discussing the genesis of this anti-Jewish argument, a word should be said about the original context of the biblical prophecy to which our author refers. The main aim of the author of Daniel 9 was to bring a message of hope to his Jewish audience that the ruthless religious persecution that had been launched by the Seleucid monarch Antiochus IV Epiphanes (r. 175–164 BC) was about to end through the agency of God, who is the true master of history.[305]

302 Or[A]: ܘܠܐ ܬܘܒ ܗܘܐ ܒܝܢܬܗܘܢ ܡܠܟܐ ܐܘ ܟܗܢܐ ܐܘ ܢܒܝܐ ܐܘ ܦܨܚܐ ܐܝܟ ܕܐܬܢܒܝ ܥܠܝܗܘܢ ܕܢܝܐܝܠ. ܕܡܢ ܒܬܪ ܫܬܝܢ ܘܬܪܝܢ ܫܒܘܥܐ ܢܬܩܛܠ ܡܫܝܚܐ. ܘܡܕܝܢܬܐ ܩܕܝܫܬܐ ܬܬܚܪܒ. ܥܕܡܐ ܠܫܘܠܡܐ ܕܦܣܩܬܐ. ܗܘ ܕܝܢ ܥܕܡܐ ܠܥܠܡ ܥܠܡܝܢ.

303 This chronological calculation is repeated again in CT 48.5–7.

304 Cf. Julius Africanus, *Chron.*; ed. Wallraff et alii 2007, pp. 224–229. For a discussion of the possible origins of this chronological tradition in CT, see Ri 2000, pp. 509–511. It is noteworthy that some of the scribes of CT were aware of this discrepancy and tried to correct it, as for instance in 48.5–7 Oc[e], where the end of the fifth millennium is presented in accordance with Africanus' system and assigned to the 19th year of Darius.

305 For an analysis of this chapter, see Hartman & Di Lella 1978, pp. 245–254.

With that purpose in mind, he reinterprets Jeremiah's prophecy about the seventy years of exile (Jer 25:11–12, 29:10) as referring to seventy weeks of years, i.e. 490 years. This period of time, which is divided into three unequal parts of seven, sixty-two, and one, most probably began in the year 594 BCE, when Jeremiah uttered the prophecy about the restoration of Jerusalem. The prophecy contains allusions to historical persons and events such as the high priest Joshua ben Jozadak, the murder of the high priest Onias III in the year 171 BCE, and the plunder and desecration of the Temple by Antiochus in c. 167/166 BCE. This elaborate—though somewhat chronologically imprecise—scheme was intended to reassure the distressed community that the end of the period of tribulations was nigh.

The joint mention of the violent demise of the just person referred to as the "anointed one" (Heb. *māšîaḥ*) and the subsequent destruction of the city of Jerusalem and desecration of its sanctuary in Daniel 9:26–27 made it inevitable that Christian readers of this prophecy would sooner or later perceive it as referring to the execution of Jesus and the Romans' destruction of the Jerusalem Temple in the year 70 CE. Indeed, from the second century onwards, this understanding of Daniel 9:24–27 became a common and recurring theme in the Christian tradition of interpreting this biblical book.[306]

One of the first to use this exegetical tradition for the purposes of anti-Jewish polemic was Tertullian, who offers a detailed chronological examination of the time-span from the time of Darius II to Vespasian in order to demonstrate that it corresponds precisely to the 490 years constituting the seventy weeks mentioned in Daniel 9:24–27.[307] This computation was intended to prove that both Jesus' death and the Romans' destruction of the Jerusalem Temple had happened in fulfillment of Daniel's prophecy and thus to buttress his general supersessionist claim that the old law had been replaced by the new.[308] Later, this exegetical argument came to be a stock motif in the repertoire of scriptural *testimonia* used in anti-Jewish works.[309]

It is not clear exactly when and how the messianic interpretation of Daniel 9 entered the Syriac tradition of biblical exegesis. As has been noted by

---

306   Cf. Tertullian, *Adv. Jud.* 8; Clement of Alexandria, *Strom.* 1.21.125–126; Hippolytus, *Comm. in Dan.* 4.31–32; Julius Africanus, *Chron.* (ed. Wallraff et alii 2007, pp. 236–237, 278–285); Jerome, *Comm. in Dan.* 3.9.24; Theodoret of Cyrus, *Comm. in Dan.*, ad loc.. On the origins and development of this tradition, see Beckwith 1981; Knowles 1944; Adler 1996.
307   *Adv. Jud.* 8; ed. Kroymann 1954b, pp. 1356–1364.
308   On this aspect of Tertullian's use of Dan 9:24–27, see Dunn 2002, 2003.
309   Cf. *Dialogue of Timothy and Aquila* 121 (ed. Varner 2004, pp. 80–81); Pseudo-Epiphanius' *Testimony* 5.42 (ed. Hotchkiss 1974, pp. 26–27); *Doctrina Iacobi* 1.22 (ed. Dagron & Déroche 1991, pp. 98–101); *Trophies of Damascus* 4.2.1–4.6 (ed. Bardy 1927, pp. 262–269).

Phil Botha, several subtle changes were introduced into the Peshitta version of Daniel 9:24–27 which prompt a Christian interpretation of this prophecy and thus may be taken as evidence that the translator of this book was a Christian.[310] The existence of a Syriac translation of Hippolytus' *Commentary on Daniel* in which this interpretation of Daniel's prophecy appears should also be taken into account, although the exact date of this translation is not known.[311]

What is certain, however, is that by the fourth century the interpretation of Daniel 9:24–27 as a prophecy about Jesus' death and the Romans' destruction of Jerusalem had become common among Syriac Christians. It appears, for example, in the *Commentary on Daniel* attributed to Ephrem.[312] Among other writings, the Ephremian *Commentary on the Diatessaron* should also be mentioned, where the prophecy of Daniel 9:27 is interpreted as referring to the Romans' desecration of the Jerusalem Temple.[313] This exegetical motif is also attested in Ephrem's indisputably genuine work the *Hymns on the Nativity*, where the poet evokes Daniel 9:24–27 and refers to Daniel as the one who "declared that the glorious Messiah would be slain, and the holy town would be destroyed by His slaying."[314]

Among fourth-century Syriac writers, the most developed example of the use of this exegetical motif for polemic against Judaism is provided by Aphrahat, who deals with the prophecy in *Demonstrations* 17 and 19. In the *Demonstration on the Messiah*, he makes an apologetic effort to defend the central tenet of Christian doctrine against any possible criticism from the Jews. In order to justify the validity of the Christian faith in Jesus as the Son of God and promised Messiah, he presents a number of Old Testament prophecies intended to demonstrate that Christian beliefs conform to Scripture. Among other scriptural proof-texts, Aphrahat quotes (with some omissions) and expounds Daniel 9:26–27.[315] While resorting to this proof-text, the Persian sage not only strives to defend the truth of Christianity by asserting that this prophecy finds its exact fulfillment in the figure of Jesus, but also seeks to discredit the Jews as opposing the prophet's words. For that purpose, he points out the disagreement between the eschatological expectations of the Jews, who hope that "at the coming of Messiah, Israel shall be gathered together by means of him from all regions and Jerusalem shall be built up and inhabited," and the description of Jerusalem's future in the prophecy of Daniel 9:26–27,

---

310   See Botha 2007, pp. 114–118.
311   See the fragments published by de Lagarde 1858, p. 81.
312   Ed. Assemani et alii 1732–1746, v. 2, pp. 221–223.
313   *Comm. Diat.* 18.12; trans. McCarthy 1993, p. 276.
314   *De Nat.* 25.7; ed. Beck 1959, p. 129; trans. McVey 1989, p. 201.
315   *Dem.* 17.10; ed. Parisot 1894, col. 805; trans. Valavanolickal 2005, v. 2, pp. 147–148.

according to which the city will be destroyed in the aftermath of the Messiah's coming and will remain in a devastated condition until the final eschatological consummation.

Aphrahat returns to Daniel 9 once more in *Demonstration* 19, where he elucidates its prophecy at even greater length while building an argument specifically aimed against the Jewish messianic hope of an eschatological gathering of Israel's dispersed and exiled people.[316] Here, Aphrahat does not limit himself to a brief mention of the time-span of sixty-two weeks from Daniel 9:26 as in *Dem*. 17, but goes into the details of the complicated eschatological scenario in Daniel 9 and offers an explanation for all three time-spans (one, seven, and sixty-two weeks) of which the total seventy-week period is comprised in Daniel 9. The main drive of this exegetical exercise is again apologetic, as Aphrahat explicitly states that his purpose is to provide his audience with an appropriate argument with which to counter alternative explanations of this scriptural material by the Jews (*Dem.* 19.12).

There are several elements in the handling of Daniel 9:26–27 that are shared by CT and Aphrahat. For instance, the formulation of the Jews' supposed argument against Christian beliefs, i.e. that "the Messiah has not yet come" (*Dem*. 17.10), is very close to CT in its wording. Moreover, both authors resort to the general polemic strategy of dissociating their Jewish opponents from the legacy of the biblical prophets. Yet these common elements notwithstanding, a similarity between these two cases of anti-Jewish use of Daniel 9:26–27 is not strong enough to claim that the author of CT relied on Aphrahat's writings for this argument. Given the fact that the interpretation of the prophecy of Daniel 9:26–27 as relating to Jesus had become a stock motif in the Christian exegetical tradition of the book of Daniel, as well as a popular proof-text in *adversus Judaeos* literature, by the time CT was composed, it seems difficult to definitively establish the immediate source of this exegetical tradition in CT.

As to the question of the nature of the Jewish argument to which the author of CT seems to be responding in this passage, it should be noted that disproval of Jesus' messianic status seems to play no significant role in the repertoire of anti-Christian polemics scattered throughout the corpus of rabbinic literature.[317] Even in those rare cases where rabbis do comment on the

---

316   *Dem*. 19.9–12; ed. Parisot 1894, cols. 876–888; trans. Valavanolickal 2005, v. 2, pp. 177–181.
317   One possible instance of the rabbis' rebuttal of the Christian belief in Jesus as Messiah is a tradition in the name of Rabbi Abbahu, preserved in the Palestinian Talmud (*y.Taanit* 2:1 [65b]), which ridicules a person who proclaims himself to be God or claims the title of "son of man" (*ben 'ādām*) for himself. The wording in the latter claim evokes the famous messianic figure of *bar 'enāš* from Daniel 7:13 and Jesus' way of referring to himself in an

prophecy of Daniel 9, no anti-Christian bias comes to the fore. An example of this attitude is the early rabbinic chronographic composition *Seder Olam*, where the seventy weeks in Daniel 9 are taken to cover the time-span between the destructions of the first and second Temples.[318] It is noteworthy that although the author of this work discusses several aspects of the Danielic prophecy, including explanations of each of the three periods that comprise the seventy weeks, he chooses to say nothing about the possible identity of the "anointed one" of Daniel 9:26. In addition to this, although he espouses an understanding of Daniel 9:26–27 as a prophecy about the destruction of the second Temple, he remains silent about the role played by the Romans as the agents of its fulfillment.

It appears more likely that in CT 44.53–57 our author is venting his frustration over the Jews' general disposition in still clinging to their own messianic hopes, which seemed illogical to a Christian observer.[319] It was rather common for Syriac Christians in antiquity to stress this point when turning their hostile attention to the Jews and their religion.

The sixth century alone provides us with several examples of Christian disappointment in their obstinate Jewish neighbors and their stubborn adherence to the belief in a future redemption. Thus, Philoxenus of Mabbug in his *Commentary on Matthew*, while attacking Christian heretics who hold incorrect Christological views and denigrating their faith by comparing it to that of the Jews, notes concerning the latter that "the expectation of the Jews to this very day looks to the false Christ."[320] On another occasion, Philoxenus bears a grudge against the Jews, who do not recognize Jesus as the Messiah and "look for Antichrist, the false Messiah."[321] In a similar vein, Jacob of Serugh, in one of his homilies on the Nativity in which he elaborates the idea of Jesus' birth as a fulfillment of biblical prophecies, evokes an imaginary Jewish interlocutor in order to emphasize the groundlessness of the Jewish messianic expectations:

> O Jew, whom are you looking for to come to the earth? For, none other will come again because there is none; keep yourself silent. The Father had a

---

oblique manner as ὁ υἱὸς τοῦ ἀνθρώπου (Mt 8:20 *et passim*). See also Zellentin 2007, which discusses a possible attempt to neutralize the Christian claim of messianic status for Jesus in the Babylonian Talmud (*b.Sukkah* 52a–b).

318 *Seder Olam* 28; ed. Milikowsky 1981, pp. 427–429 [Heb.], 539–540 [trans.].
319 On the messianic component of Jewish eschatological beliefs in late antiquity, see Alexander, Ph.S. 2007.
320 *Comm. in Matt.*, on Mt 16:16–17; ed. Watt 1978, pp. 28 [Syr.], 24–25 [trans.].
321 Ed. Nau 1916, p. 249.

single (Son) and He sent Him as He promised, and behold, Immanuel is with us and He is the Only-begotten.[322]

4.3 Supersessionist Revision of Biblical History

Explicit anti-Jewish rhetoric and exegesis are not the only literary strategies our author uses to convey his supersessionist vision of Jewish-Christian relations. It is possible to discern another subtler dimension of anti-Jewish polemic in his work, one that comes to light when we turn our attention to more general aspects of the representation of the pre-Christian period in CT. Here, there are two additional historiographical strategies at work through which our author advances his anti-Jewish agenda. One of them involves an intentional recomposition of the canonical narrative with the purpose of "de-Judaizing" it. This strategy is complemented and enhanced by a consistent Christianization of the primeval history.

4.3.1 De-Judaization

One aspect of the reworking of the biblical past in CT that poses a challenge to Judaism is that the amount of narrative space allocated to the pre-Abrahamic period of the history of salvation considerably overshadows that of the post-Abrahamic one. Out of the total forty-one chapters covering the whole course of biblical history from Adam to the return of the Jews from their Babylonian exile under Cyrus (chs. 2–42), twenty-six chapters are devoted to persons and events prior to Abraham, whereas only fifteen chapters deal with the rest. The space allocated to the primeval history is thus almost twice as long as that of the entire subsequent period of biblical history.

This ratio stands in striking contrast to the perspective of the canonical corpus of the Old Testament, where the narrative space taken up by the latter historical period greatly exceeds that of the former. Such a pronounced inequality in the distribution of our author's interest is hardly incidental. The focus on the primeval period of humanity's history at the expense of the history of the Jewish people should be regarded as an intentional literary strategy, employed to advance the author's supersessionist agenda. The subversive power of this polemical strategy lies in the oblique manner in which it marginalizes and downplays that part of the shared biblical past presented by the history of the people of Israel.

There is an additional consideration that gives further strength to the suggestion of an anti-Jewish objective behind the peculiar way in which the author recomposes biblical history. An attentive reader of CT may be struck by

---

322   Ed. Bedjan 1902, p. 798; trans. Kollamparampil 1997, p. 119.

the fact that it lacks several episodes of the post-Abrahamic part of the biblical narrative that are of crucial importance for the history and identity of the Jewish people. The most remarkable example of this kind is unquestionably the author's complete silence about such pivotal events in Jewish history as the Exodus from Egypt and the giving of the Law on Mount Sinai. Neither of these milestones in the history of God's providential care for his chosen people is mentioned in chapter 34, where Moses' biography is briefly recounted, nor do they receive substantial attention anywhere else in the work.[323]

Another significant gap in the narrative of CT is that it completely ignores the whole of the Second Temple period of Jewish history. This silence is particularly noticeable in light of the fact that there are several indications that our author was acquainted with sources covering this historical period, such as the books of Maccabees and Josephus.[324] Especially noteworthy is the absence of any reference to the story of the Maccabees, since their heroic accomplishments were well known to Syriac Christians and enjoyed considerable popularity among them.[325]

These omissions should by no means be ignored as incidental. Rather, together with the promotion of the primeval history over the history of the Jewish people, they form a part of the general polemical agenda of CT as an exercise in the genre of "counter-history," aimed against the Jewish version of *Heilsgeschichte*. Introduced by the historian Amos Funkenstein, this term refers to a category of polemical literature that aims at "the distortion of the adversary's self-image, of his identity, through the deconstruction of his memory."[326]

The particular narrative strategy of the deconstruction of Jewish collective memory through omission that the author of CT employs recalls the procedure of silencing in the practice of historiographical writing that has been brought into focus by Michel-Rolph Trouillot. In an investigation into how power operates in the making and recording of history, he demonstrates that any historical production is at once a bundle of what it says and what it does not say, and so any historical narrative should be regarded as "a particular bundle of silences."[327] In his analysis of the phenomenon of silencing in historiography,

---

323   The Exodus is referred to *en passant* in CT 35.9, where God is described as the one "who had delivered them from the servitude of the Egyptians."
324   Cf. his references to the persecution by Antiochus IV Epiphanes (CT 44.6) and to Herod the Great (CT 44.6; 47.20–27).
325   In addition to 1–4 Maccabees, which formed part of the canon in the Syriac Old Testament, see the additional documents published by Bensly & Barnes 1895. See also Witakowski 1994; Brock 2014.
326   Funkenstein 1993, p. 36.
327   Trouillot 1995, p. 27.

Trouillot singles out four main moments or stages during which "silences enter the process of historical production."[328] Placed into this analytical perspective, our author's historiographical method corresponds to the conceptual stage characterized by Trouillot as "fact retrieval," i.e. when a historian selectively retrieves facts from the already existing "archives" with the aim of producing a narrative that reflects his particular perspective.

In the case of CT, the historiographical facts retrieved by its author come from a wide range of "archives," which include the books of the Old and New Testament as well as some later Jewish and Christian writings. In order to deconstruct the aforementioned silences in the narrative that our author presents, it would be useful to examine them in light of the notion of the Old Testament as the depository of Jewish national memory. Analyzed against this background, the particular cases of our historian's selective amnesia can help scholars to contextualize his polemical agenda with greater precision.

A relevant example of rewriting the biblical past in the context of Jewish national memory is provided by Josephus, the famous Jewish historian, who published a monumental compendium of the history of his people, the *Jewish Antiquities*, in Rome around the year 94 CE.[329] As Josephus himself explains, the main purpose of his literary project was to acquaint the Greek-speaking world with the "entire ancient history and political constitution" of the Jews.[330] In line with this apologetic goal, the main body of this work, nineteen out of its twenty-two books, is devoted to the history of the Jewish people proper. At the same time, the events and figures from the pre-Abrahamic period of biblical history occupy less than half of the first book of the *Antiquities*.

For another remarkable example of how the biblical past was put to the service of Jewish identity, one can turn to the frescoes of the third-century synagogue from the city of Dura-Europos on the Middle Euphrates.[331] The synagogue's walls are covered with frescoes that feature heroes and episodes relevant to the national history of the Jewish people: Moses and the Exodus from Egypt, Aaron, Jacob blessing his sons, Elijah, Samuel and David, Mordecai and Esther, and several other scenes taken from the biblical narrative. As has been noted by Marcel Simon, the visual project of the Dura-Europos synagogue celebrates "the history of Israel and, shining through it the Lord's solicitude for the Jews."[332] What strikes a modern observer of this ambitious iconographical

---

328 Trouillot 1995, pp. 26–27.
329 For general information on this work, see Attridge 1975; Feldman 1998.
330 *Ant.* 1.5; ed. Thackeray 1926–1965, v. 4, pp. 4–5.
331 For general information on the synagogue, see Levine 2005, pp. 252–257. For a detailed description of the synagogue's frescoes, see Hachlili 1998, pp. 96–197.
332 Simon 1996, p. 382.

project is the complete absence of images that refer to the primeval period of human history. This absence becomes even more telling in light of the fact that such imagery does appear in the Christian baptistery, located not far from the synagogue.[333] This discrepancy lends additional weight to the approach of those scholars who discern an element of cultural resistance, aimed primarily against the local pagan world, in the celebration of the Jewish tribal history in the iconography of the Dura-Europos synagogue.[334]

A comparison of the author of CT's presentation of the biblical past with that of Josephus' *Antiquities* and with the iconographical program of the Dura-Europos synagogue helps us to discern the subversive power of silencing as a polemical strategy. By allocating more narrative space to the pre-Abrahamic period of biblical history and erasing such triumphant episodes as the Exodus from Egypt, the victory of Esther and Mordecai, the heroic exploits of the Maccabees, and others from its post-Abrahamic period, our author purposefully shifts the focus of the readers' attention from the national history of the Jewish people to the history of humanity. Analyzed in the general context of the anti-Jewish agenda advanced in CT, this strategy might be characterized as an exercise in a systematic "de-Judaization" of the biblical past.

4.3.2 Christianization

In addition to the process of de-Judaization, another strategy may be recognized in our author's revision of the biblical past that advances his polemical agenda by subverting the Jewish character of the Old Testament in a more subtle manner. This strategy is manifested in a pronounced propensity to Christianize the primeval period of biblical history.

In its most visible form, it finds expression in the author's introduction of an assortment of explicitly Christian ideas and images into his retelling of biblical narratives. A substantial part of these additions is comprised of the exegetical traditions that present biblical figures or events as symbols or types of Christ, his Crucifixion, the Church, and the sacraments. It should be noted that nearly all of these Christian motifs concern the period of biblical history before Moses. Below, I offer a provisional inventory of such additions, without going into an analysis of their origins:

– CT 1.4–7: the "spirit of God" of Gen 1:2 is interpreted as the Holy Spirit;
– CT 2.2–3: mention of the Trinity in the context of the creation of Adam;
– CT 2.16: connection between the newly created Adam and Golgotha;
– CT 3.17, 21; 4.1: the Garden of Eden is characterized as "the Holy Church";

---

333 One of its frescoes features a painting of Adam and Eve. See Dirven 2008.
334 Cf. Elsner 2001. For an opposite interpretation of the synagogue's images, see Dirven 2004.

- CT 4.3: the Tree of Life as a prefiguration of the Holy Cross;
- CT 5.7–13: God's promise to Adam to send his Son to redeem him;
- CT 6.17–18: Adam–Christ typology;
- CT 18.2–7: the Ark–Church typology;
- CT 19.5: the Ark moves upon the waters of the Flood following the pattern of the cross;
- CT 21.18: the drunken Noah as a symbol of Jesus' crucifixion;
- CT 28.11: during their meeting (Gen 14:18–20), Melchizedek makes Abraham participate in a quasi-Eucharistic sacrament;
- CT 29.9–10: the ram entangled in the thicket (Gen 22:13) as a symbol of the crucified Jesus;
- CT 31.17–19: Jacob's ladder (Gen 28:12) as a symbol of the Cross, the stone and the pouring of oil (Gen 28:18) as a symbol of the Church and of chrism;
- CT 31.20–24: Jacob's well (Gen 29:10) as a symbol of baptism;
- CT 33.14–15: the reason that Solomon only had a son from Naamah the Ammonite and not from his other wives was to prevent the genealogy of Jesus from being contaminated by the nations forbidden to intermarry with Israel (cf. Deut 7:1–3);
- CT 48.12–30: Adam–Christ typology;
- CT 49.1: Adam–Christ typology

It is certainly legitimate to consider this material as an expression of a fundamental principle of Christian interpretation of the Old Testament: the notion of the unity of the two Testaments.[335] Elegantly articulated in the famous dictum of Augustine, "the New (Testament) is concealed in the Old, and the Old is revealed in the New,"[336] this axiom of theologically based Christian hermeneutics affirms that the God of the New Testament is the same as the God of the Old Testament and that while the latter finds its fulfillment in the former, both bear witness to Christ. By infusing his retelling of the Old Testament narratives with references to Christ and the Church, the author of CT faithfully follows this rule.

There is, however, more to be said about the apologetic and polemic implications of such hermeneutics in CT. In order to better appreciate its subversive power in the context of polemic against Judaism, let us turn to another manifestation of the author's propensity to Christianize the primeval history, namely the creation of a quasi-Christian tradition before Christ. In addition to superficially Christianizing the biblical past through the introduction of explicitly Christian images and notions, he implements this strategy on a deeper

---

335 On this, see de Lubac 1998–2009, v. 1, pp. 225–268.
336 *Quaest. in Hept.* 2.73: *in vetere novum lateat et in novo vetus pateat*; ed. Zycha 1895, p. 141.

level by remodeling several figures from the primeval period in such a way that their behavior embodies Christian attitudes and practices. This aspect of CT's presentation of the biblical past has been noted by Han Drijvers, who observed that it presents Adam, Seth, and several other patriarchs as having knowledge of Christ and thus as "Christians *avant la lettre*, namely, before the Jewish nation came into existence through Moses' activities and law-giving."[337]

Indeed, a closer look at the pre-Abrahamic figures in CT reveals that the author significantly reworked this period of biblical history, constructing an axis of righteousness comprised by such figures as Adam, Seth and his progeny, Noah, and Melchizedek, who are presented as bearers of Christian values. This tendency manifests itself most prominently in the notion of the uninterrupted ministry of unceasing prayer that began in the cave of treasures with Adam himself and was carried on in front of his embalmed body by his descendants up until the time of Melchizedek.[338]

Another outstanding example of the remodeling of primeval figures in accordance with Christian ideals is found in the elaborate description of the course of life pursued by the descendants of Seth on the mountain of Paradise described in CT 7.1–14: following Adam's command in CT 6.14, they live "in all purity and holiness and in the fear of God";[339] they are called "holy" (*qaddišē*), while their wives are "pure" (*dākyān*); since they are free from all vices and exempt from the need to toil and work to survive, their only occupation is "to praise and glorify God, together with the angels."[340] Furthermore, the author models his description of the internal arrangement of the ark during the Flood in CT 18.2–7 after the pattern of a Christian community gathered in a church, where men and women are confined to separate sections of the indoor space so that they will not see each other's faces. Finally, in CT 16.24–28 and 23.19–23, Melchizedek's ministry over the body of Adam deposited on Golgotha is presented in quasi-Eucharistic terms as the offering of "bread and wine" (*laḥmā w-ḥamrā*). The patriarch himself is depicted as a Nazirite (*nazirā*), constituting a role model of Christian anchoretism: he lives alone, practices celibacy, does not shave his hair, and is forbidden to shed the blood of animals.

These examples demonstrate that in his presentation of the primeval period of the history of the human race, our author deliberately chooses to portray several of its main protagonists as paragons of Christian virtues. This

---

337 Drijvers, H.J.W. 1985, p. 101.
338 Cf. CT 5.10–12,17; 6.9–14; 8.1,15; 9.1,7–8; 10.1,8; 13.3–7; 16.12–21,28; 23.13–23.
339 Or^A: ܒܟܠܗ ܕܟܝܘܬܐ ܘܩܕܝܫܘܬܐ ܘܕܚܠܬ ܐܠܗܐ.
340 Or^A: ܕܢܫܒܚܘܢ ܘܢܗܕܪܘܢ ܠܐܠܗܐ ܥܡ ܡܠܐܟܐ.

confessional bias in representing the biblical past is not unique to CT, but is attested in the works of some earlier Christian writers.

One of the most developed manifestations of this attitude is found in the œuvre of Eusebius of Caesarea. This historian pursues a comparable strategy of Christianizing the biblical past in his two major apologetic works, *Praeparatio Evangelica* (7.3–8) and *Demonstratio Evangelica* (1.2–4). Here, Eusebius develops an original model of the history of religions in which he constructs a notion of the true primeval religion of the human race, different from both paganism and Judaism.[341] He characterizes it as a "third form of religion midway between Judaism and Hellenism, ... the most ancient and most venerable of all religions."[342]

According to Eusebius, this was a natural religion, based on knowledge of the Logos of God.[343] It was first practiced during the earliest period of biblical history by a small minority of virtuous human beings such as Enoch, Noah, Seth, Japheth, Abraham, Isaac, Jacob, Joseph, and Job, who are characterized in different places as "godly and holy men of old time," "pre-Mosaic saints," or "friends of God."[344] These virtuous men avoided the polytheistic error of Hellenism, but were not yet subjugated to the particularistic laws of Judaism. In order to strengthen the latter point, Eusebius introduces an artificial distinction between "Hebrews," as he calls these people, and "Jews," whose way of life begins only with the Mosaic legislation.[345]

The most important aspect of Eusebius' model, however, is that for him this primeval true religion was identical to Christianity. At one point, he refers to its adherents as "Christians in fact, if not in name."[346] Accordingly, it was this true faith that "has been preached of late to all nations" by Jesus, who through his life and teaching brought about "a renewal of the ancient pre-Mosaic religion, in which Abraham, the friend of God, and his forefathers are shown to have lived."[347] While a detailed examination of this historical model lies beyond the scope of my investigation, I would like to mention that it is a result of Eusebius' creative confluence of two major themes from the repertoire of

---

341 For a general overview of this scheme, see Kofsky 2000, pp. 100–136.
342 *Dem. ev.* 1.2.9: τὸ μεταξὺ ἰουδαϊσμοῦ καὶ ἑλληνισμοῦ τρίτον ἡμῖν ἀποδεδειγμένον τάγμα, παλαίτατον μὲν καὶ πάντων τυγχάνον πρεσβύτατον; ed. Heikel 1913, pp. 8; trans. Ferrar 1920, v. 1, p. 9.
343 *Hist. eccl.* 1.4.4,12; ed. Lake et alii 1926–1932, v. 1, pp. 40–41, 44–45.
344 *Dem. ev.* 1.2.9; 1.5.2; ed. Heikel 1913, pp. 8, 20; trans. Ferrar 1920, v. 1, pp. 9, 25; *Hist. eccl.* 1.4.4–6; ed. Lake et alii 1926–1932, v. 1, pp. 40–43.
345 Cf. esp. *Praep. ev.* 7.3–8. See Iricinschi 2011.
346 *Hist. eccl.* 1.4.6: ἔργῳ Χριστιανούς, εἰ καὶ μὴ ὀνόματι; ed. Lake et alii 1926–1932, v. 1, pp. 40–43.
347 *Dem. ev.* 1.2.9; 1.5.2; ed. Heikel 1913, pp. 8, 20; trans. Ferrar 1920, v. 1, pp. 9, 25.

Christian apologetics: the argument for the antiquity of Christian belief and the idea of Christians as the "third race" (*tertium genus*).[348]

The unambiguous anti-Jewish agenda behind Eusebius' scheme is important for our subject.[349] He resorts to this not only for the purpose of defending the antiquity of the Christian faith, but also to provide an answer to the question of why Christians, who claim that the writings of the Old Testament are an integral part of their canon of Holy Scriptures, do not follow their legal and ritualistic prescriptions.[350] To justify the Christians' rejection of the Mosaic Law, Eusebius emphasizes its limited scope by claiming that God gave it to the Jews as a disciplinary measure after their apostasy from the true "religion of their forefathers" during their enslavement in Egypt, when the Israelites embraced the corrupt "manners and life of the Egyptians," including polytheism and idolatry.[351] This argument demonstrates the particularistic character of the Mosaic legislation, which cannot thus be regarded as suitable for all nations, but is applicable only to those among the Jews who live in their own land.

Eusebius' apologetic interpretation of the primeval history was taken over by later Christian writers. The same scheme may be found being used by Epiphanius of Salamis, who integrates it into his own vision of the spiritual development of the human race. In the section of his *Panarion* (1.2.3–7) in which he describes this stage of the process as "Scythianism," which follows "Barbarism" and is followed by "Hellenism," he explains that while during this period "there was no Judaism, no Hellenism, no other sect at all," there was "the faith (πίστις) which is now native to God's present day holy catholic church, a faith which was in existence from the beginning and was revealed again later."[352] Following the principle that "the holy catholic church is the beginning of everything," Epiphanius presents Adam as the first proponent of this faith, which exhibited the "image of Christianity" (τοῦ Χριστιανισμοῦ τὴν εἰκόνα), because "without circumcision he was no Jew and since he did not worship carved images or anything else, he was no idolater."[353] After Adam, the main adherents of this religion were Abel, Seth, Enosh, Enoch, Methuselah, Noah, Eber, and Abraham.

---

348   On the former, see Pilhofer 1990; Rhee 2005, pp. 66–69; Buell 2005, pp. 63–93; on the latter, see Lieu 2004, pp. 239–268; Iricinschi 2011.
349   See Kofsky 1996, pp. 71–73; Johnson 2006, pp. 94–125.
350   Cf. *Dem. ev.* 1.3–5.
351   *Dem. ev.* 1.4.6; ed. Heikel 1913, p. 19; trans. Ferrar 1920, v. 1, p. 23.
352   *Panar.* 1.2.3; ed. Holl 1915–33, v. 1, p. 174; trans. Williams, F. 2009, pp. 16–17.
353   *Panar.* 1.2.4–5,7; ed. Holl 1915–1933, v. 1, pp. 174–175; trans. Williams, F. 2009, p. 17.

The popularity of Eusebius' model among Christians in the Orient is corroborated by the apologetic treatise *On God* by Eznik of Kołb, a fifth-century Armenian writer. When he refers to the introduction of paganism during Serug's lifetime, Eznik notes that "up to that moment there existed God-worshippers, and the Church of God existed in the world from the beginning."[354] Moreover, even after this deplorable lapse of the human race, "the worship of God was not entirely lacking," as can easily be seen from the examples of Abraham, Melchizedek, Abimelech, and the friends of Job.[355]

An examination of the author of CT's portrayal of the pre-Mosaic past against this background makes it clear that it developed within the conceptual framework provided by the Eusebian paradigm of Christianity as the primeval religion of humankind.[356] The explicitly apologetic context of this historiographical model in Eusebius' works enables us to perceive the anti-Jewish function of the Christianization of the primeval history as a polemical strategy, which our author consciously pursued in his overall project of a supersessionist revision of biblical history. In a manner similar to that of Eusebius, he projects Christian values and ideas back onto the most ancient period of human history in order to present Christianity as the only true religion, which is innate to mankind and thus superior to Judaism.

We have seen how, in his supersessionist revision of the biblical past, the author of CT resorts to two distinctive narrative strategies that complement and enhance each other: the silencing of the national history of the Jewish people on the one side and the Christianization of the primeval history on the other. This double maneuver forms perhaps a very basic structure of Christian supersessionist hermeneutics, which was not confined to the realm of literature. For example, an interesting structural counterpart to the supersessionist scheme of CT can be found in the urban topography of Jerusalem during the Byzantine period. On the one hand, it reveals the existence of a conspicuously empty urban space in the city on the spot where the Jewish Temple once stood.[357] On the other hand, during this period the city witnessed the creation of a new sacral center, the Church of the Holy Sepulcher, which was manifestly associated with

---

354 *De Deo* 341; ed. Mariès & Mercier 1959, p. 509; trans. Blanchard and Young 1998, pp. 173–174.
355 *De Deo* 342; ed. Mariès & Mercier 1959, p. 509; trans. Blanchard and Young 1998, p. 174.
356 It is also noteworthy that on two occasions when the author speaks about the biblical education of Pērōzad, one of the three Magi (CT 45.16–17, 46.22–25), he refers to "the book of the Hebrews" and "the school of the Hebrews," in a manner evoking Eusebius' "Hebrews" vs. "Jews" dichotomy.
357 See Thorpe 2009.

paradigmatic figures of the primeval history such as Adam.[358] The anti-Jewish implications of this aspect of city planning in Byzantine Jerusalem have been pointed out by Guy Stroumsa, who recognized them as a visual expression of the ideology of supersessionism that "had been symbolized by the relocation of the sanctified locus, from the Temple Mount, whose emptiness should remain striking, visible to all, by the new basilica of the *Anastasis*."[359] Likewise, our author erases the Jewish dimension of biblical history by relocating its sanctified locus from the events of Jewish national history to those of the primeval pre-Mosaic past.

5 Concluding Observations

The assortment of direct and indirect critical references to Jews and their religion analyzed above demonstrates that CT is organized around an extended engagement with Judaism, which takes the dual form of apologetics and polemics. From this rich material, it could be concluded that polemic against Judaism was a major driving force motivating our author in his retelling of biblical history. One should thus take seriously the author's declaration in CT 44.1–4 that he undertook the entire literary project in order to provide an adequate response to the Jews who challenged his coreligionists on the subject of the descent of Mary and, by extension, of Jesus. In his work, however, the author faces this challenge not only by forging an elaborate genealogy for the Virgin, but also by engaging in a sustained attack against Judaism, which is carried out through two principal avenues: the portrayal of the Jews as the killers of Christ and the theology of supersessionism. The latter notion is especially important for understanding the author's agenda, because it provides the general ideological framework within which he operates while reworking the canonical narrative.

The reception history of CT provides additional evidence that this composition was indeed perceived by its readers as a useful tool for polemic against Judaism. For instance, at the conclusion of the first part of his work, which consists of a rather close paraphrase of CT's narrative, the author of the *Arabic Apocalypse of Peter*, a Christian apocryphal composition from approximately the ninth century, puts the following words in the mouth of Clement as an expression of gratitude to his master, the apostle Peter:

---

358   The Christian tradition about Adam's burial on Golgotha is attested as early as the third century. Cf. Origen, *Comm. ser. 126 in Matt.* (PG 13, col. 1777). See Jeremias 2002, pp. 35–43.
359   Stroumsa 2007, p. 292. See also Jacobs 2004, pp. 139–199.

> You have taught me the history of the Old Testament, and instructed me in the genealogies found in it down to the birth of Lady Mary, the daughter of Joachim, to such an extent that I am in a position to refute the Jews in my discussions with them, since by disclosing to me their secrets you have made me versed in their history.[360]

The prominent place occupied by the polemic against Judaism in CT compels us to address two important methodological issues that confront students of *adversus Judaeos* literature: first, the question of to what extent our author was original in his use of the repertoire of anti-Jewish images, exegetical motifs, and narrative strategies, and second, the issue of the relation between the "image" of Judaism he produced and the "reality" of Jewish-Christian interaction in late antique Mesopotamia raised in the introductory part of this chapter.

Concerning the first problem, there is a view that is still popular among scholars that due to its traditional character, patristic anti-Jewish literature is mostly repetitive and derivative in its argumentation. As an example of this attitude, one may quote Rosemary Ruether, who has written regarding the Christian *adversus Judaeos* works produced during late antiquity that "throughout these writings from the second to the sixth century the arguments themselves remain fairly continuous and fixed."[361]

At first glance, it may indeed appear that the findings of this investigation support this view, since it has been demonstrated that the author of CT was deeply rooted in the earlier tradition of anti-Jewish polemics in the Syriac language and that many of the anti-Jewish images and arguments he uses are attested in the works of earlier Syriac authors. Among Syriac writers whose works provide the greatest number of parallels to the anti-Jewish material in CT, one should single out Aphrahat, Ephrem, and Jacob of Serugh.

At the same time, one should not remain oblivious to the fact that our author shows a considerable degree of inventiveness and versatility in advancing his anti-Jewish agenda. His creativity in this area manifests itself on several levels. On the most basic level, his originality can be discerned in his selective approach to the rich repertoire of anti-Jewish themes and arguments that was apparently available to him.[362] He does not feel obliged to furnish his work with all the arguments against Jews and Judaism that were invented by

---

360 Trans. Mingana 1931, p. 100. For the Arabic text of this passage, see Sachau 1899, v. 2, pp. 736–737.
361 Ruether 1979, p. 29.
362 For a similar claim on the originality of Narsai's anti-Jewish polemic, see Frishman 1987, p. 227.

his predecessors, but limits himself to those motifs that appeared to him to be relevant for his particular situation. In that respect, it could be noted that CT features no attacks against such idiosyncratic Jewish practices as circumcision, Sabbath observance, or the keeping of dietary laws, around which a large amount of Jewish-Christian polemics revolved.[363]

Another aspect of our author's individual creativity is that even when relying on the existing stock of anti-Jewish motifs and images, he often does not limit himself to slavishly recycling them, but transforms them in order to integrate inherited material into his own narrative and ideological framework. Moreover, we have seen that on several occasions he seems to advance completely new and original polemical ideas.

Our author's third and probably most original contribution to the tradition of anti-Jewish polemics is his choice of the particular literary form of the "rewritten Bible." Although by the sixth century a wide range of literary genres had already been employed for the purposes of anti-Jewish apologetics or polemics, such as dialogue, tractate, homily, poetry, or collections of scriptural *testimonia*, no Christian writer apart from the author of CT had utilized the paraphrase of biblical history as a tool for waging a sustained attack against Judaism. In fact, the only literary analogs to CT that are known to me come from a much later period and from a different cultural milieu, namely the Slavonic composition known as the *Explanatory Palaea* and some similar Byzantine compositions.[364] By adapting this literary genre to the needs of anti-Jewish polemic, our author proves himself a true innovator in the field of *adversus Judaeos* literature.

Taking these considerations into account, it can be stated that although the point of view of scholars such as Miriam Taylor—who has declared that the main *themes* of anti-Jewish polemics were "repetitive and consistent over centuries"[365]—might still be acknowledged as generally valid, it would be an oversimplification to make a similar claim about *arguments* used by Christian authors for this purpose. The case of CT illustrates very well the original and creative ways in which these themes could be (and were) transformed in

---

363 Among Syriac writers, these three themes figure prominently in the polemical works of Aphrahat (cf. *Dem.* 11, 13, 15) and Jacob of Serugh (cf. *Homilies against the Jews* 2–3 and *Homily on the Separation of Foods*; ed. Akhrass & Syryany 2017, v. 2, pp. 104–112). The Sabbath and circumcision are also the main polemical themes of the only surviving anti-Jewish homily of Isaac of Antioch.

364 On *Palaea*, see Pereswetoff-Morath 2002, pp. 51–53. For Greek analogs, cf. the unpublished work in ms. Paris, Bibliothèque nationale de France, Coisl. 111 (13th c.), described in detail by Istrin 1898, pp. 138–142.

365 Taylor, M.S. 1995, p. 22.

different cultural contexts. Thus, one should take seriously the advice offered some time ago by Marcel Simon that "the monotonous and stereotyped nature of the anti-Jewish literature ought not to be exaggerated."[366] The results of our investigation are congruent with a growing awareness among students of anti-Jewish literature that while many Christian polemicists shared common material, they each employed it in ways that suited their own individual agendas and contributed their own unique understandings and perspectives to it.[367]

Let us turn now to the second methodological challenge posed by the anti-Jewish polemic in CT. We have seen that its author constructs a consistently negative "image" of Judaism by depicting the Jews as Christ-killers and infusing his retelling of the biblical past with supersessionist rhetoric and exegesis. We have seen that by doing so he followed and creatively adapted the previous traditions of *adversus Judaeos* polemic in Syriac. But what was the "reality" of the social and historical circumstances that made our author present his audience with this specific "image"? Why, at this particular time and in this particular place, would a Christian writer allot a considerable amount of narrative space to a polemic against Judaism when recounting the history of the Old and New Testaments? The relevance of this question can be seen from a comparison of CT with a similar literary project by John Malalas, a sixth-century Christian historiographer from Antioch.[368] In his *Chronicle*, which spans the whole course of human history from Adam to Justinian, this historian is more concerned with providing a general chronographical framework that would integrate biblical and Greco-Roman historical traditions than with attacking any particular non-Christian group. Malalas' work demonstrates that anti-Judaism was not an inevitable element in Christian retellings of the biblical past during late antiquity.

There can be little doubt that the intended audience of CT was Christian and not Jewish. One has to ask oneself, then, what needs of the Christian community to which our author belonged he was addressing when he offered it a distinctively anti-Jewish interpretation of the biblical past. At the outset, we should rule out the possibility that he was seeking to attack some other Christian faction by doing this. We do know that anti-Judaism at times served as a tool in inner-Christian conflicts. A good example of such use of anti-Jewish polemic in a Syriac context is provided by Ephrem, who furnished his

---

366   Simon 1996, p. 140.
367   Cf. a recent examination of the anti-Jewish interpretation of Genesis 25:23 by Tertullian in Dunn 1998.
368   For the text, see Jeffreys et alii 1986. For a general introduction, see Jeffreys 2003.

attacks against Arianism by using anti-Jewish imagery.[369] Later, one may come across anti-Jewish rhetoric habitually employed by the Miaphysites against the supporters of dyophysite Christology, Chalcedonian and "Nestorian" alike.[370] However, in contrast to these cases, in which inner-Christian polemical bias is easily discernable, our author does not evince any sustained interest in challenging other groups of Christians.[371] This is consistent with his general agenda of promoting a unifying Syrian Christian identity, reflected in the attribution of his work to Ephrem and in the emphasis on Syriac primacy.[372]

Let us first consider the case of Mary's descent from David. As we have seen, the author states that he composed the Virgin's genealogy in order to refute Jewish accusations of Jesus' illegitimate birth and to demonstrate his mother's Davidic pedigree. Should we regard this explicitly apologetic statement as a mere literary device that enabled our author to introduce the theme of Mary's genealogy, which had nothing to do with the contemporary reality of Jewish-Christian relations but was important to his audience for some other reason? I believe that one would be doing an injustice to the author's intent by taking such an approach. In fact, his resort to this particular apologetic strategy could be understood in the light of contemporary Iranian and Jewish sources. From analyzing them, it becomes evident that while by creating a new version of Mary's genealogy our author indeed strengthens the self-confidence of his Christian audience, he does so in the very particular socio-cultural context of Sasanian Mesopotamia, in which the Jewish presence constituted an important factor.

The strong emphasis on lineage constituted a hallmark of the social organization of the Sasanian empire.[373] The importance of descent was conditioned by the hierarchical division of Iranian society into the three, or from the fifth century on, four social "estates" (Mid. Pers. *pēšag*), that is priests, warriors, peasants, and artisans.[374] As membership of these estates was hereditary, transition from one to another was difficult. The fact that the charge of bringing havoc in matters of genealogies was among the main accusations leveled

---

369 See Shepardson 2008.
370 See van Rompay 1981; Horn 2006–2007.
371 On the rare occasions when he does refer to some unacceptable views held by Christians, such as those of the Melchizedekians in CT 30.11–17, he does so in a rather moderate manner.
372 See chapter 4.
373 Unfortunately, no comprehensive study of this subject has been undertaken to date. For general information on the structure of kinship in the Sasanian period, see Perikhanian 1983a, pp. 50–125; Macuch 2003.
374 See Perikhanian 1983b, pp. 632–633.

by Zoroastrian orthodoxy against the famous sixth-century social reformer Mazdak and his followers, who supposedly deviated from the accepted norms of sexual morality and introduced the custom of women being held in common, highlights the high value ascribed to lineage in Sasanian society.[375] For example, in the *Fārs-nāma* by Ibn al-Balkhī (12th c.), the monarch Khosrow I Anūšīrvān is presented as saying that "in the sect of Mazdak lineage (*nasl*) is not to be preserved, anyone can come from anyone."[376] Consequently, the author of the *Letter of Tansar*, an allegedly sixth-century specimen of Middle Persian *andarz* literature that has been preserved only in the late Persian translation made from an earlier Arabic one, praises the first Sasanian king Ardašīr for being zealous in enforcing strict boundaries between the social classes so that "rank and station might remain fixed for each man and might be registered in books and archives."[377]

This importance of descent was apparently internalized by the Jews who lived in the territories controlled by Sasanians. Scholars of rabbinic literature have noted that a strong emphasis on the purity of lineage forms a distinctive characteristic of the Babylonian Talmud.[378] Arguments based on genealogy were used by the rabbinic elite of Sasanian Babylonia as a weapon in polemic against their fellow Jews and non-Jews alike. Richard Kalmin has demonstrated that Babylonian rabbis resorted to such arguments in attempts to enhance their status vis-à-vis their Palestinian colleagues as well as their non-rabbinic Jewish competitors.[379]

In the Babylonian context, therefore, the issue of descent, and especially of Davidic lineage, could be raised during polemic with non-Jews. The claim of a Davidic pedigree was an important element in the self-identity of the Jewish leadership in Sasanian Babylonia.[380] It was the descent from King David that provided the exilarchs of Babylonia with a basis for claiming a quasi-monarchic authority over the Jewish community. Apparently, they did not hesitate to evoke this elevated status in dealing with non-Jews as well. An interesting piece of evidence for this comes from the *Unique Necklace* of Ibn 'Abd

---

375 See Crone 1991, p. 25; Shaked 1994, pp. 125–127.
376 Ed. Le Strange & Nicholson 1921, p. 87, ln. 11–12.
377 Ed. Minovi & Rezvani 1975, p. 65; trans. Boyce 1968a, p. 44. There is still no consensus among scholars about whether the *Letter*'s core should be dated to the third or the sixth century; for a discussion, see Boyce 1968a, pp. 11–22. It appears that the passages that stress the importance of securing boundaries between the classes reflect sixth-century sensibilities, developed in the aftermath of Mazdak's egalitarian revolt.
378 See Kalmin 1999, pp. 51–60; Rubenstein 2003, pp. 80–101; Oppenheimer 2009.
379 Kalmin 1996.
380 See Goodblatt 1994, pp. 277–311; Herman 2012, pp. 54–59. On the later development of this notion, see Franklin 2013.

Rabbih, a Muslim writer from Spain (10th c.). This Arabic author quotes a story by another Muslim writer, Ibn Lahī'a (8th c.), about Abu'l Aswad, a seventh-century grammarian and poet from Baṣrah. According to this story, one day Abu'l Aswad happened to engage in a conversation with a Jewish "exilarch" (*ra's al-ǧālūt*), who reprimanded him for the murder of Muhammad's grandson Hussein ibn Ali while boasting of the high prestige afforded to him by his own coreligionists: "Between King David and me there is an interval of seventy generations, and still the Jews show me great respect, recognize my claim to royal descent and consider it a duty to defend me."[381] Although the story as a whole may have been invented for the purposes of Shiite propaganda,[382] it is very likely that this Muslim tradition faithfully represents the ideology of the Jewish Babylonian leadership, who based their claim to authority on their supposed Davidic lineage.

It has been argued above that due to the influence of the Jewish tradition of anti-Christian polemic, the negative image of Mary as an adulteress spread among the non-Christian communities of the late ancient Near East. It would be hard to overestimate the subversive power of this sort of anti-Christian argumentation in the context of Sasanian society with its particular stress on lineage purity. That alone would suffice to provoke the apologetic efforts of the author of CT. Moreover, as the evidence on the importance of Davidic lineage for the ideology of the Babylonian exilarchate suggests, the Jews of Sasanian Iran also had good reason to contest the Christian belief in the Davidic descent of Jesus or Mary. In light of these considerations, it seems likely that in his defense of Mary's sexual integrity and Davidic pedigree, our author was first and foremost driven by the desire to provide his coreligionists with an appropriate antidote to the anti-Christian arguments that could be used by their Jewish or, for that matter, Zoroastrian adversaries.

Important as it is, however, the need to defend Mary's reputation alone hardly suffices to account for the ubiquitous presence of anti-Jewish polemic in CT. In order to make sense of this phenomenon, one has to address the general problem of Jewish-Christian relations in Sasanian Mesopotamia during late antiquity. To date, there has been no systematic investigation of this aspect of the social and cultural history of the Sasanian empire.[383] In what

---

381   ed. بيني وبين داود سبعين أباً وإن اليهود إذا رأوني عظّموني وعَرفوا حقّي وأوجبوا حِفظي ; Būlāq 1876, v. 2, p. 309; trans. *apud* Goodblatt 1994, p. 310.
382   See Goldziher 1884, pp. 124–125.
383   Most of the research on Jewish-Christian relations in Iran during late antiquity is focused on the fourth-century figure of Aphrahat; for references, see n. 10 above. To these studies, one should add the important contributions of Neusner 1972 on the role Jews played in

follows, I offer merely a provisional overview of those moments in the history of Jewish-Christian interaction in the Sasanian empire that might be relevant for understanding the conspicuous anti-Jewish character of our work. It must be remembered, however, that our ability to reconstruct these socio-cultural dynamics is significantly impeded by the loss of several important literary witnesses,[384] as well as by the fact that the majority of the preserved Syriac sources that feature anti-Jewish polemic come from the Byzantine-controlled parts of Syria–Mesopotamia.

As has been already mentioned, the founding father of the "conflict theory" of Jewish-Christian relations, Marcel Simon, explained the phenomenon of Christian anti-Judaism by the challenge posed to Christian communities by the attraction of non-Jews to Judaism. According to Simon, the latter phenomenon was a direct result of the active missionary efforts of Jews.[385] This argument was subject to criticism from scholars, who called into the question the existence of an active Jewish mission during late antiquity. However, even if this criticism is justified, the absence of a Jewish mission cannot be used as a decisive argument against the core of Simon's thesis. As Vincent Déroche has rightly emphasized recently, "the lack of a conscious and organized enterprise of proselytism is not a lack of real religious attraction."[386] And indeed, the history of Judaism on the Roman–Persian frontier provides us with several examples of the attractiveness of this religion to various peoples in this region.

Among the earliest examples of Judaism's appeal to the nations of the Iranian cultural area is the Parthian royal house of Adiabene, whose members, Prince Izates and his mother Queen Helen, converted to it during the first half of the first century CE.[387] A less reliable case is found in the *Bibliotheca* of Photius of Constantinople, who refers to "an ancient tradition" according to which Zenobia, the famous third-century queen of Palmyra, "converted from pagan superstition to Judaism."[388]

---

the persecution of Persian Christians by Shapur II, and Becker 2010 on the Jewish and Christian scholarly culture of Sasanian Mesopotamia.

384 Cf. the two sixth-century anti-Jewish treatises by Abraham and John of Bēt Rabban, mentioned at the beginning of this chapter, n. 12.
385 See Simon 1996, pp. 271–305.
386 Déroche 2012, p. 540.
387 This event is described by Josephus, *Ant.* 20.17–96, and mentioned in several rabbinic sources. See Schiffman 1987; Marciak 2014.
388 *Bibl.* 265: ἣν καὶ μεταβαλεῖν εἰς τὰ Ἰουδαίων ἔθη ἀπὸ τῆς Ἑλληνικῆς εισιδαιμονίας παλαιὸς ἀναγράφει λόγος; ed. Henry 1959–1977, v. 8, p. 60; trans. Wilson 1994, p. 254. Cf. also Athanasius, *Hist. Arian.* 71.1, where Zenobia is referred to as Ἰουδαία; PG 25, col. 777. For a discussion, see Millar 1971, p. 13.

The most striking and significant example of the religious vitality of Judaism in the context of the late ancient Near East comes from South Arabia. Jewish monotheism began to gain hold in the kingdom of Ḥimyar during the last decades of the fourth century under King Abīkarib, and gained such a great influence that it brought about a large-scale international conflict during the early sixth century, when the Jewish king Yūsuf Dhu Nuwās launched a persecution against the Christians of his realm.[389] However, even after the defeat of Dhu Nuwās by the Axumite Christian forces in the year 525, the Jews remained the largest religious community in South Arabia until the rise of Islam.

There is additional evidence that demonstrates the attractiveness of Judaism to the inhabitants of the Iranian realm. It comes from the opposite pole of the Roman–Persian frontier, the Caucasus. The Georgian *Martyrdom of Eustathius of Mtskheta* presents a narrative about a Zoroastrian cobbler from Ganzak in Iran, who settled in the Georgian city of Mtskheta around the middle of the sixth century. There, he abandoned his ancestral religion for Christianity, and as a result, he was convicted and executed by the Persian authorities.[390] As Eustathius recounts the story of his conversion, he relates how, dissatisfied with the faith of his fathers, he started attending services both in the Christian church and in the Jewish synagogue in order to decide which faith fitted him best. Although attracted by the beauty of the Christian liturgy, he was still not certain about the right choice and turned to the archdeacon Samuel with a request to explain to him "the faith of the Jews and that of the Christians, and whichever creed be the holier, that I will adopt."[391] It is only after an extended catechetical instruction, in which Samuel gives him an outline of the Christian vision of sacred history and demonstrates that Judaism had been superseded by Christianity, that Eustathius decides to embrace the latter religion. What is striking about this account is that the author of Eustathius' *Vita* presents Judaism and Christianity as two religious options that a discontented Zoroastrian Persian considers to be equally viable and legitimate.

To understand the role played by the Jewish community in the social and political life of Northern Mesopotamia during the sixth century, one should take into account that it was a natural ally of the Persians in their perpetual struggle with the Roman empire for control over the Near East. The earliest evidence of Jewish military support of Iranians against the Romans comes from

---

389 On the spread of Judaism in South Arabia, see Robin 1991, 2004; Rubin, Z. 2000; Gajda 2002, 2010.

390 For an English translation, see Lang 1976, pp. 94–114. For general information, see Tsulaja 1991; Shapira 2008, pp. 202–208.

391 Trans. Lang 1976, pp. 101–102.

pre-Sasanian times, when, in the year 116 CE, the Jews of Northern Mesopotamia took arms in order to prevent the Roman conquest of the region.[392] Later, during the Sasanian period, we hear about Jews serving in the Persian army.[393] From the early sixth century comes the story of the massacre of the Jews of the Roman city of Constantina (Tella), caught in the act of collaboration with the Persians during the city's unsuccessful siege by the troops of Kavadh I in 503.[394] The history of Heraclius' Persian campaign in the third decade of the seventh century contains an episode in which the Jews of Edessa fight against the emperor's brother Theodoric together with the city's Persian garrison.[395]

These actions should be regarded in the context of the Sasanian policies of supporting dissident, especially non-Christian, minorities in the frontier zone, whom the Persians saw as possible allies against the Romans. A good illustration of this policy is found in the story of King Khosrow I's visit to Harran in the year 540, when he returned the prisoners of war from that city without taking any ransom because "most of them are not Christians but are of the old faith" (i.e. pagans).[396] Slightly earlier, in the years 529–30, the Samaritans of Palestine rebelled against the Roman rule while hoping for military support from the Persians.[397] The case of South Arabia, furthermore, provides a prominent example of strategic cooperation between the Sasanians and the Jewish communities of the Roman–Persian frontier. As Glen Bowersock has convincingly demonstrated, the Jewish rulers of Ḥimyar saw themselves as allies of Persia and were regarded as such by the Romans.[398] Bowersock also suggests that the process of transforming the ruling dynasty of Ḥimyar into Jews itself took place under the direct aegis of the Sasanians, who needed a counterbalance to the pro-Byzantine Christian kingdom of Aksum.[399]

Given the attractiveness of Judaism as an ancient and well-established religion and the close political ties between the Jewish community and the Persians, it is no wonder that Jews of the Roman–Persian frontier zone were

---

392 For references and discussion, see Ben Zeev 2005, pp. 191–217.
393 Cf. *Chronicle of Ps.-Zachariah Rhetor* 9.4; ed. Brooks 1919–1924, v. 2, p. 95 [Syr.].
394 Cf. *Chronicle of Ps.-Joshua the Stylite* 58; ed. Wright, W. 1882, pp. 55–56 [Syr.], 47–48 [trans.]. On this episode, see Greatrex 1998, pp. 101–103.
395 Cf. *Anonymous Chronicle of AD 1234*, AG 936; ed. Chabot 1916–1937, v. 1, pp. 235–236 [Syr.]; trans. Palmer et alii 1993, p. 139; Arm. *History of Sebeos* 42; trans. Thomson & Howard-Johnston 1999, p. 95.
396 Procopius, *Bell. pers.* 2.13.7; ed. Dewing 1914–1961, v. 1, pp. 374–375. On this episode, see also Athanassiadi 1999, p. 52.
397 Cf. *Chronicle of Ps.-Zachariah Rhetor* 9.8; ed. Brooks 1919–1924, v. 2, pp. 100–101 [Syr.]; John Malalas, *Chron.* 18.54; Theophanes Confessor, *Chron.* AM 6021/AD 528–529.
398 Bowersock 2004.
399 Bowersock 2004, p. 272.

assertive in their relations with Christians and did not hesitate to resort to violence. For instance, several ancient sources report Jewish support for and at times even active participation in the "Great Persecution" of Persian Christians that was instigated by King Shapur II (309–79).[400] As to the later period, one cannot fail to notice that anti-Christian violence was the logical and inevitable outcome of the spread of Judaism in South Arabia. First, we hear about the Christian priest Azqir, who was arrested for his missionary activities and executed in Najran on the advice of Jewish rabbis in the third quarter of the fifth century.[401] The tense relations between the Jews of Ḥimyar and the local Christians deteriorated further during the first quarter of the sixth century, when King Dhu Nuwās launched a large-scale persecution against the Christian community of Najran.[402]

Turning to our author's geographical milieu, we come across a story of the failed attempt by the Jews of Nisibis to denounce the local Christians before the Persian governor in the Syriac *Life of Mār Yāret the Alexandrian*, apparently a seventh-century composition from Northern Mesopotamia.[403] Another hagiographical work from the same period and region, the Syriac *Martyrdom of ʿAbd al-Masīḥ of Singar*, tells the story of a young convert from Judaism named Asher ben Levi who was murdered by his father.[404] Finally, cases of Jewish violence against the Christian population of Byzantine Palestine in the aftermath of its takeover by the Persian troops in the year 614 should also be mentioned.[405] Of course, one should be aware that the Christian sources are prone to exaggerate the extent of Jewish involvement in these incidents, but to deny them completely on that basis would be incorrect.

400 Cf. *Martyrdom of Simeon bar Sabbae* 12; ed. Kmosko 1907, cols. 806–807; Theophanes Confessor, *Chron.* AM 5817/AD 324–325; *Chronicle of Arbela* 12; ed. Kawerau 1985, pp. 49, 53–54 [Syr.]; Mārī ibn Sulaimān, *Kitāb al-maǧdal*; ed. Gismondi 1896–1899, v. 1, pp. 29–30 [Arab.], v. 2, pp. 25–26 [Lat. trans.]. This and other hagiographic material has been analyzed by Neusner 1972.

401 For the Geez text and Italian translation of the *Martyrdom of Azqir*, see Bausi 2017; secondary literature: Rubin, Z. 1995; Beeston 2005.

402 The main sources are: the Syriac *Book of the Ḥimyarites*; ed. Moberg 1924; two letters of Simeon of Bēt Aršām; ed. Guidi 1881 and Shahîd 1971; the Greek *Martyrdom of Arethas*; ed. Detoraki & Beaucamp 2007. Studies of this material include Ryckmans 1989; van Rompay 1982; Nebes 2010; Beaucamp et alii 2010.

403 For the text and translation of the *Life*, see Minov 2021a. For a discussion of this story, see also Minov 2019a.

404 For the text and translation, see Butts & Gross 2016.

405 For Jerusalem, see *Chronicle of Khuzistan*; ed. Guidi 1903, v. 1, p. 26 [Syr.]; trans. Greatrex & Lieu 2002, p. 235. For Acco-Ptolemais—*Teaching of Jacob* 2.5; ed. Dagron & Déroche 1991, pp. 180–181. On this issue, see Schick 1995, pp. 26–31; Horowitz 1998; Cameron 2002b.

From this evidence, it seems reasonable to assume that Judaism posed a significant religious and social challenge to Christianity in the part of Sasanian Mesopotamia where CT was produced. This suggestion tallies well with the view of Jewish-Christian relations in the Roman–Persian frontier zone during late antiquity that has recently been proposed by Fergus Millar. In a balanced analysis of the dynamics of religious coexistence, competition, and conflict between Judaism and Christianity in the Eastern provinces of the late Roman empire during the fourth and fifth centuries, Millar has argued, providing ample evidence, that "the idea that there was an ideological, or religious, challenge from Judaism was not purely fanciful."[406]

While acknowledging that the author of CT's anti-Jewish polemic cannot be divorced from the social context of inter-communal competition and conflict in the Sasanian empire, it would however be counterproductive to try to contextualize it as a reaction to any particular event. Rather, one should conceptualize the anti-Jewish "image" of the biblical past promoted by CT as an internal response to the "reality" of the particular socio-political situation in which its author's Christian community found itself. Apparently, a key element of this situation was competition between the two religious minorities, Jewish and Christian. It was his coreligionists' perceived vulnerability to the challenges posed by Jews that played the largest role in making our author engage in a large-scale anti-Jewish rewriting of biblical history, seeking, thus, to strengthen their self-image at the expense of their rivals.

---

406 Millar 2004, p. 2. For a similar conclusion on Judaism in fourth-century Syria, see Frishman 1987, p. 228.

CHAPTER 3

Categorizing the Iranian "Other"

The second major strategy of collective identification that influenced CT's author's reworking of biblical narrative finds expression in his close engagement with the culture of Iran. In this chapter, I would like to examine the most important avenues of CT's engagement with Iranian culture and religion, focusing on the instances of direct references to "Persians," whether polemical or not, as well as on some protagonists who are explicitly marked as Iranians. In my analysis, I will pay attention to the problem of the genesis of these motifs and images, including their relation to other Syriac and non-Syriac accounts of Iran and Zoroastrianism, as well as to the question of their narrative and ideological function.

The corpus of Syriac texts produced during late antiquity contains a substantial amount of references to the culture and religion of Sasanian Iran, including anti-Zoroastrian polemic. A comprehensive study of this rich and variegated material is still a desideratum.[1] In order to establish how original CT's author was in his treatment of Zoroastrianism, these texts will be taken into consideration alongside the relevant literary sources in Greek and Armenian.

Before moving on, a caveat should be raised regarding some difficulties in situating CT's author in regard to the previous tradition of writing on or polemic against Persians and their religion among Syriac-speaking Christians. Although the corpus of Syriac Christian literature contains fewer examples of anti-Zoroastrian polemical works in comparison with the number of texts in the *adversos Judaeos* tradition, we know of several written works dealing with this subject that might have been available to a Syriac reader by the time of CT's composition.

The earliest Christian composition of this genre seems to be the short tractate entitled "On Persian Magic and How It Differs from the True Religion," which was written in the fifth century by Theodore of Mopsuestia.[2] As Photius of Constantinople testifies, in the first of the three books that comprised this

---

1   The fullest collection of information on Zoroaster and Zoroastrianism in Syriac sources remains Bidez & Cumont 1938, v. 2, pp. 93–135. See also Gignoux 1984; Panaino 2006. On anti-Zoroastrian polemic, see Bruns 2014; Payne 2016b.
2   Photius, *Bibl.* 81; ed. Henry 1959–1977, v. 1, p. 187. In the entry on Theodore, Photius offers a brief summary of this work.

work, Theodore offered a systematic exposition and refutation of Zoroastrian doctrines. This composition enjoyed a certain popularity among Syriac Christians and was translated into Syriac, as we learn from the *Catalogue* of ʿAbdišoʿ of Nisibis, where it is described as "the two (books) against Magianism."[3] In addition to this, an anti-Zoroastrian tractate was authored by another representative of the Antiochene school, Theodoret of Cyrus, a younger contemporary of Theodore. In one of his letters, when giving a brief list of his literary output, Theodoret mentions a work "against the Magi in Persia."[4] This composition, however, is also lost to us, and there is no evidence that it was ever translated into Syriac.

The genre of anti-Zoroastrian polemic turned out to be even more productive among Syriac-speaking Christians. It is hardly surprising that as far as our evidence shows, all these works were produced by Syriac authors who lived in the territories controlled by the Sasanian empire or, in one case, by their later successors. We know of at least six polemical works in Syriac that dealt with this subject. One of the first compositions of this genre seems to have been penned by Mari the Persian, who was active in the middle of the fifth century and is better known as the addressee of the famous letter of Hiba of Edessa. According to ʿAbdišoʿ's *Catalogue*, he authored a work "against the Magi of Nisibis."[5]

The sixth century saw a proliferation of anti-Zoroastrian polemic appear among the Syriac Christians of the Sasanian relam. Thus, we know of a polemical treatise against the Persian religion that was produced by the East Syrian author Elisha bar Qozbāyē (ob. 510), who was the second director of the School of Nisibis. In the *Cause of the Foundation of the Schools*, Barḥadbešabbā ʿArbayā relates that Elisha wrote "a refutation of the charges of Magianism."[6] The tradition of anti-Zoroastrian polemic in the Nisibene school was further continued by John of Bēt Rabban, another sixth-century director of this institution. ʿAbdišoʿ's description of this scholar's rich literary output mentions a work "against the Magi."[7] Attacking the tenets of Zoroastrian religion was not the exclusive prerogative of East Syrian theologians. According to ʿAbdišoʿ, another

---

3 ܬܪܝܢ ܕܠܘܩܒܠ ܡܓܘܫܘܬܐ; ed. Assemani 1719–1728, v. 3.1, p. 34. For quotations from this composition found in the works of Syriac authors, see Scheinhardt 1968; Reinink 1997.

4 *Ep.* 113: τὰ δὲ πρὸς τοὺς ἐν Περσίδι μάγους; ed. Azéma 1955–1998, v. 3, p. 64. On this work, see Brok 1953.

5 ܠܘܩܒܠ ܡܓܘܫܐ ܕܢܨܝܒܝܢ; ed. Assemani 1719–1728, v. 3.1, p. 172.

6 ܫܪܝ ܕܪܫܝܢ ܕܡܓܘܫܘܬܐ; ed. Scher 1908, p. 387; trans. Becker 2008, p. 153.

7 ܠܘܩܒܠ ܡܓܘܫܐ; ed. Assemani 1719–1728, v. 3.1, p. 72. In the *Chronicle of Seert* 2.9, it is listed as the "Book of Contestation against the Magi" (كتابًا في مناقضة المجوس); ed. Scher 1908–1918, v. 3, p. 116.

sixth-century Syriac author, Aḥudemmēh, who served as the West Syrian metropolitan of Tikrit, also wrote "a book against the Magi."[8]

Apparently, the tradition of polemic against Zoroastrianism did not cease with the demise of the Sasanian empire. In the entry on Bar Sāhdē of Kirkuk, who flourished during the first half of the eighth century, ʿAbdišoʿ lists "a book against the Magi, followers of the doctrine of Zoroaster."[9] For the sake of completeness, it should also be mentioned that according to the information provided by ʿAbdišoʿ, a certain Ara, apparently an East Syrian author about whose floruit and milieu nothing is known, also composed "a book against the Magi."[10]

It is a great loss that not one of the aforementioned works, Greek or Syriac, has survived the vicissitudes of history. As a result, we are left to merely speculate about the possibility that any of these writers influenced the author of CT. This considerably limits our ability to assess our author's originality in his presentation of Iranian beliefs and practices.

Bearing this limitation in mind, in what follows I am going to discuss two main groups of evidence that are of principal importance for understanding CT's author's stance towards Iranian culture. The first group comprises passages dealing with Persian religious and cultural practices. To this group belong all the cases in which the author explicitly refers to "Persians" and their customs, such as the descriptions of the cult of fire (CT 27.1–3) and horse-worship (CT 27.4–5), and the polemics against the institution of close-kin marriage (CT 27.12–16) and astrology (CT 27.17–22). The second group of passages revolves around the institution of the Iranian monarchy. It includes portrayals of several protagonists whose Iranian connection is marked by giving them or their associates unambiguously Iranian names, such as the accounts of Nimrod (CT 24.24–26; 27.6–11; 30.19; 45.2–12), Cyrus (CT 42.11–22), and the New Testament Magi (CT 45–46).

It should be noted that the repertoire of Iranian motifs and images in CT is not limited to these explicitly marked passages. There are also instances in which our author tacitly adopts Iranian religious or mythological ideas. This material is comprised of, but not limited to, such cases as the peculiar ouranological scheme presented in CT 1.8–9, where Rapithwin, a mythological figure from Zoroastrian cosmology, is explicitly mentioned, and the image of Paradise as a cosmic mountain in CT 3.15.[11] Although they are an important

---

8   ܟܬܒܐ ܕܠܘܩܒܠ ܡܓܘܫܐ; ed. Assemani 1719–1728, v. 3.1, p. 193.
9   ܟܬܒܐ ܕܠܘܩܒܠ ܡܓܘܫܐ ܒܢܝ ܬܘܕܝܬܗ ܕܙܪܕܘܫܬ; ed. Assemani 1719–1728, v. 3.1, p. 229.
10 ܠܘܩܒܠ ܡܓܘܫܐ ܟܬܒܐ; ed. Assemani 1719–1728, v. 3.1, p. 230.
11 For a discussion of the Iranian background of these passages, see Minov 2014b and Minov 2016 respectively.

confirmation of the author's close ties with Iranian culture, these examples are outside the scope of the present investigation, since they do not form part of the text's conscious strategy of identity building.

1 The Customs and Beliefs of the "Persians"

1.1 *The Cult of Fire*

The author opens the section dedicated to Nimrod with the following piece of information (CT 27.1–3):

> And in the days of Nimrod, the mighty man, a fire appeared which ascended from the earth. And Nimrod went down, and saw it, and worshipped it. And he established priests to minister there, and to cast incense into it. And from that time the Persians began to worship fire, up until this day.[12]

In this passage, the author offers a concise explanation of the etiology of the Persian cult of fire, linking it to the biblical figure of Nimrod. This tradition is absent from the canonical portrayal of this personage and thus deserves to be examined regarding its origins and function.

According to the tenets of the Zoroastrian religion, believers are expected to worship not only the highest deity Ohrmazd, but also to venerate his material creations and the deities associated with them. One of the most prominent elements of the material world to which such worship belongs is fire, considered to be a son of Ohrmazd and closely associated with the divinity Aša ("Truth" or "Order").[13]

The veneration of fire belongs to the Indo-European matrix of Zoroastrianism and has its origin in the Indo-Iranian cult of the hearth fire. The sacred fire of the Zoroastrians, which was made of wood, was "enthroned" on an altar-like stand and received offerings five times a day. Notwithstanding the limitations of the archaeological evidence, scholars of Iranian religion agree that cultic structures in which activities and rituals connected to fire took place were already in existence during the Achaemenid epoch, to say nothing of the later Hellenistic period.[14] The cult of fire played an even more prominent role in

---

12 Or^A: [Syriac text]
13 On the Zoroastrian cult of fire, see Boyce 1968b; Yamamoto 1979–1981; de Menasce 1964.
14 See Schippmann 1971; Garrison 1999; Shenkar 2007, 2011.

Zoroastrian religious life under the Sasanian kings, who would usually engrave a fire-holder on their coins and mark the beginning of each king's reign with the lighting of his regnal fire.

The prominent place occupied by fire in Zoroastrian devotion did not go unnoticed by external observers. As a result of its high visibility, the worship of fire became the mark of Zoroastrianism par excellence for many classical and Christian authors who referred to the inhabitants of Persia and their religion.[15] This practice was often evoked in order to single the Persians out as a distinctive religious group. For example, in the Syriac *Teaching of Addai*, the native inhabitants of the Persian empire, who were antagonistically disposed towards Christians, are described by the author as "worshippers of fire" (*sāgday l-nurā*).[16] The author of the Manichaean Middle Persian hymn *M 28 I* in the Turfan Collection, while waging a polemic against the Zoroastrians and their religion, refers to them as "those that worship the blazing fire."[17]

Returning to our passage, several features of CT's author's description of the origins of the Persian cult of fire deserve close scrutiny. First of all, it is noteworthy that the invention of this form of worship is ascribed to Nimrod. This idea stands in direct contradiction to the indigenous Zoroastrian tradition, in which the introduction of the veneration of fire is not related to a specific mythological or historical figure. According to Zoroastrian sources, the worship of fire existed long before Zoroaster. In the *Bundahišn*, after the three most sacred fires—Farrōbāg, Gušnasp, and Burzēnmihr—were created by Ohrmazd himself at the beginning of the world, they were worshipped by the primeval rulers Tahmurab and Jam.[18]

It is the non-Zoroastrian sources that bring up the notion that the Persians' fire-worship was introduced at a specific historical moment by a particular person. Ancient writers offered different explanations of its origins. Thus, John Malalas, a sixth-century Christian historiographer from Antioch, ascribed the invention of this practice to the Greek mythological hero Perseus.[19] This tradition seems to go back to the classical period, as Malalas refers to the

---

15   Cf. Nicolaus of Damascus, #90, F 68 (ed. Jacoby 1923–1958, v. 2, pp. 370–373); Strabo, *Geogr.* 15.3.13–15; Dinon *apud* Clement of Alexandria, *Protr.* 5.65.1; Procopius, *Bell. pers.* 2.24.2; Agathias, *Hist.* 2.25.1. On these and other Greco-Roman sources on Zoroastrian fire-worship, see de Jong 1997, pp. 343–350.
16   Ed. Howard 1981, pp. 37 [Syr.], 75 [trans.].
17   *prystynd 'dwr swcyndg*; ed. Boyce 1975a, p. 174.
18   Cf. Iranian *Bundahišn* 18.4–9; ed. Pakzad 2005, pp. 230–232.
19   *Chron.* 2.12; ed. Thurn 2000, pp. 27–28. This tradition appears in the works of later authors influenced by Malalas, such as John of Nikiu (*Chron.* 21.17–19) or the *Chronicon Paschale* (ed. Dindorf 1832, v. 1, p. 73).

second-century Greek writer Pausanias as his source. An alternative version of the beginning of fire-worship is found in the works of Gregory of Tours, another sixth-century Christian historiographer. According to him, Persians were taught to worship fire by Zoroaster, who is identified with the biblical Cush.[20]

The description of the origins of the Persian veneration of fire that most closely resembles the one found in CT is found in the Pseudo-Clementine novel, a Greek composition written in Syria around the third century. The story of Nimrod and fire-worship appears in both main textual witnesses of the Pseudo-Clementines.[21] While there are significant differences between the two narratives, they share a common plot. In both accounts, the founding event of Persian fire-worship is the spectacular death of Zoroaster, a prominent magician, who was deceived by a demon and burnt to ashes by heavenly fire.[22] This supernatural accident gave rise to the post-mortem cult of Zoroaster.[23] It is in the question of how the fire-worship is linked to the veneration of Zoroaster's remains that the two versions diverge. According to the *Homilies*, where Zoroaster is identified with Nimrod (9.4.1), the cult of fire began when the Persians took coals from the heavenly lightning that burned the magician and preserved them with ordinary fuel while honoring this fire as a god.[24] In contrast, the author of the *Recognitions* identifies Zoroaster not with Nimrod, whom he considers identical with the King Ninus found in Greek historiography (4.29.1), but with the biblical Mitzraim, son of Cush (4.27.2–3), said to be active at least two generations earlier (4.28.5). According to the *Recognitions*, the practice of venerating fire took its beginning from Nimrod, who, after he founded the city of Babylon, "migrated to the Persians and taught them to worship fire."[25]

The motif of Nimrod as the founder of fire-worship among the Persians is found in both the Pseudo-Clementines and CT 27.1–3. It should be noted that the Greek version of the Pseudo-Clementines was translated into Syriac

---

20 *Hist.* 1.5; ed. Krusch & Levison 1951, p. 7. For a similar tradition, see the Manichaean Middle Persian *Hymn to the Living Soul* in text *M 95* from Turfan; ed. Boyce 1975a, p. 112.
21 Namely the Greek *Homilies* 9.3–6; ed. Rehm & Strecker 1992, pp. 132–134, and the Latin *Recognitions* 1.30, 4.27–29; ed. Rehm & Strecker 1994, pp. 25–26, 159–161.
22 *Hom.* 9.4.2–5.1; *Rec.* 4.27.4–5.
23 *Hom.* 9.5.2; *Rec.* 4.28.1–2.
24 *Hom.* 9.6.1: Πέρσαι πρῶτοι τῆς ἐξ οὐρανοῦ πεσούσης ἀστραπῆς λαβόντες ἄνθρακας τῇ οἰκείᾳ διεφύλαξαν τροφῇ, καὶ ὡς θεὸν οὐράνιον προτιμήσαντες τὸ πῦρ, ὡς πρῶτοι προσκυνήσαντες ὑπ' αὐτοῦ τοῦ πυρὸς πρῶτοι βασιλείας τετίμηνται; ed. Rehm & Strecker 1992, pp. 133–134.
25 *Rec.* 1.30.7: *et inde migravit ad Persas eosque ignem colere docuit*; ed. Rehm & Strecker 1994, p. 26.

quite early, in the fourth century, and thus might have influenced CT's author.²⁶ However, the differences between the two narratives of the origins of Persian fire-worship are so numerous that it is hardly possible to suggest any direct literary relationship between the two works. Even if CT's author was acquainted with the Pseudo-Clementine account of Nimrod-Zoroaster, he reworked it very thoroughly in order to make it serve his goals. Moreover, there are at least two details in CT's description of the invention of fire-worship that are unique to this work and seem to betray the author's familiarity with the mainstream religious tradition of the Iranian empire.

The first of these features is CT's author's description of the place of origin of the fire that Nimrod venerates. According to him, this fire was "ascending from the earth" (*sālqā men 'arʿā*). In stark distinction from this, most of the Western sources that address the question of the fire's origins, the Pseudo-Clementines, John Malalas, and Gregory of Tours, are unanimous in presenting it as coming from heaven.²⁷ This seemingly insignificant difference between the Western tradition and CT betrays, I believe, the influence of the local context on the Syriac author. Living in Northern Mesopotamia, he was most likely familiar with the phenomenon of the oil fields of northern Iraq, where petroleum, known to the Syrians as *napṭā*, would often rise to the surface of the earth, forming natural wells or springs. Sometimes, these natural reservoirs of crude oil would conflagrate and burn for prolonged periods of time. It comes as no surprise that Zoroastrians, who regarded fire as a manifestation of divine presence in this world, held such places in high esteem.²⁸

There is sufficient evidence to show that the Persians imbued such sites with cultic significance. Thus, 2 Maccabees 1:18–36 narrates a story of the Persian king who, having discovered the fire that had been brought from the destroyed First Temple by the exiled Judean priests and kept burning in the cave with crude oil (νεφθαι), ordered the place to be enclosed, making it sacred (ἱερόν). Later, Strabo describes the "fountain of crude oil" (ἡ τοῦ νάφθα πηγή) and burning "fires" (τὰ πυρά) in the vicinity of the temple of the Iranian goddess Anāhitā located near the city of Arbela in Northern Mesopotamia.²⁹ Finally, in the *Bundahišn*, there is a special category of sacred fires comprised of two natural fires that burn "without nourishment" (*a-xwārišn*), i.e. without artificially

---

26 Cf. the Syriac version of the passage on Nimrod from *Rec.* 1.30.7: ܘܡܢ ܗܕܐ ܠܒܝܫ ܗܘܐ. ܘܗܘܝܘ ܠܡܐ ܕܢܘܡܪܘܕ ܐܬܩܪܝ; ed. Frankenberg 1937, p. 38.
27 Cf. also John of Nikiu, *Chron.* 21.14–19.
28 Occasionally, it might be also a burning spring of natural gas. On one such venerated site in the province of Khuzistan, see Yamamoto 1979–1981, p. 41.
29 *Geogr.* 16.1.4; ed. Jones H.L. 1917–1949, v. 7, p. 196. See also *Geogr.* 16.1.16 for a description of petroleum and its use in Babylonia.

provided fuel.³⁰ Although crude oil is not explicitly mentioned in connection with these fires, it is obvious from their description that the author is referring to flaming natural reservoirs of this substance.

In light of these sources, it seems justified to interpret CT's author's particular assertion of terrestrial, not heavenly, origins for the paradigmatic fire of Zoroastrian worship as a reflection of his intimate knowledge of the regional customs of Iranian piety that were current in the Sasanian-controlled part of Northern Mesopotamia.

Another noteworthy feature of the author's description of the Persian veneration of fire is the mention of the burning of "incense" (*lbuntā*) as a distinctive ritual practice pertinent to this form of worship. In spite of its seeming triviality, this detail should not be ignored as merely a topos that reflects the popularity of incense in the rituals of many ancient religions. In fact, this ingredient is mentioned extremely rarely in the Western descriptions of Zoroastrian ritual practice. I am aware of only one literary source that refers to incense in this context, namely Appian of Alexandria (2nd c.). At some point, this historian describes a typical "ancestral" offering performed by Mithridates IV of Pontus (134–163 BC), a Hellenistic monarch of Persian descent, during his campaign against the Romans. According to Appian, after the king constructs a double pile of dry wood, he pours upon it libations of "milk, honey, wine, oil, and various kinds of incense (θυμιάματα πάντα)" and sets it on fire.³¹ Leaving aside the question of the accuracy of this account,³² a fundamental difference between this ritual and that of CT 27.1–3 should be underscored. While in the case of Mithridates incense forms part of the libation which is poured onto dry wood, according to the ritual scenario implied in the passage from CT, incense alone should be cast directly into the burning fire. This discrepancy prevents us from regarding CT's description of incense-burning as being derived from previous literary traditions of presenting the Persian religion.

As we turn to the Iranian milieu, it becomes apparent that incense (Mid. Pers. *bōy*) played a very important role in Zoroastrian ritual practice. Offering incense to fire is an essential part of the ceremonial of the sacred fire, known among modern Zoroastrians as *bōy dādan*, "incense offering."³³ During this ceremony, which in regularly prescribed circumstances takes place five times

---

30 Iranian *Bundahišn* 18.19–20; ed. Pakzad 2005, pp. 234–235.
31 *Hist. rom.* 12.9 (66); ed. White 1912–1913, v. 2, pp. 362–363.
32 On this, see de Jong 1997, pp. 356–357.
33 See Boyce 1977, pp. 74–75.

a day, the priest goes into the sacred chamber, places one or more pieces of sandalwood on the fire, and recites certain ritual texts.

The importance of incense-offering for Zoroastrians is stressed in a number of literary sources. In the Pahlavi version of the *Ātaš Niyāyišn* (14), the fifth in a group of five daily Zoroastrian prayers, which is addressed to fire, any person who comes to the fire with a supplication is expected to bring incense as an offering.[34] In Ohrmazd's revelation to Zoroaster found in the *Pahlavi Rivāyat* (8c1–2), "offering firewood and incense and oblation (to) the fire" is one of the four best things that a believer may perform in this world, as it is believed to repel demons.[35]

Much like in the previous case, this prominence of incense in Zoroastrian ritual practice, enhanced by the virtual absence of comparable images of Persian rites in the Greco-Roman ethnographical tradition, suggests that the mention of incense-burning in CT 27.1–3 may legitimately be regarded as another mark of the author's immediate acquaintance with the Iranians' religious customs.

Having discussed the possible sources of the presentation of the origins of Iranian fire-worship in CT, let us turn to the question of its narrative function and possible purpose.

On the most obvious level, CT's author provides his audience with information concerning the precise moment in the course of human history when the Persians' veneration of fire came into existence. Given his and his community's Iranian context, this interest in anchoring some specific local customs and practices in the biblical master narrative is quite understandable. In connecting this religious practice to the figure of Nimrod, our author seems to be following an established tradition already attested in the Pseudo-Clementines.

However, one significant peculiarity of the narrative of the origins of fire-worship in CT draws our attention as we compare it with that of the Pseudo-Clementines. In striking distinction from his predecessor, who presents both Nimrod and the Persian veneration of fire in unmistakably negative terms, CT's author portrays both this religious practice and its founder in a rather impartial manner. This non-polemical attitude towards one of the most visible practices of Zoroastrianism stands out as unusual when compared to the majority of Christian works from antiquity that touch upon the Persians' religious customs, where the scolding of the "Magians" for their reverence towards fire and other created elements is one of the recurrent topoi.

---

34 Ed. Dhalla 1908, pp. 166–177.
35 Ed. Williams, A.V. 1990, v. 1, p. 51 [Pahl.], v. 2, p. 11 [trans.].

Polemics against the cult of fire appear quite frequently in the Christian hagiographical works produced in Sasanian Iran. In many of these compositions, the Christian martyrs' refusal to honor fire is presented as one of the major points of contention between them and their Sasanian masters. In the *Acts of Mār ʿAqebšmā*, a martyr under Shapur II, the Mazdean priest accuses the saint that he "does not worship the sun" and "does not honor fire."[36] Polemics against fire-worship are found on several occasions in the *Acts of Mār Qardāg*, where the saint's teacher, the holy man ʿAbdišo, and the saint himself denounce the worship of fire.[37]

Notwithstanding their minority status, Iranian Christians did not limit themselves to passive resistance to this objectionable religious practice: they would sometimes physically attack the places of Zoroastrian fire-worship. Thus, as an immediate result of his embracement of Christianity, the aforementioned Mār Qardāg is said to have forcibly converted the fire temples of his estate into churches, destroying the fire altars.[38] In the opening scene of another text, the *Acts of Mār ʿAbdā*, which gives the story of a bishop martyred under Yazdgird I, representatives of the Iranian nobility and the Zoroastrian clergy turn to the king with a petition against the Christians in which the latter are accused, among other things, that they "insult your gods, and mock fire and water, and overthrow foundations of the fire temple, where we worship."[39] When the king summons the saint and his supporters and interrogates them concerning the accusation of destroying the fire temple and extinguishing the sacred fire, a certain priest named Hašu readily acknowledges the "crime" while denying the divine nature of fire, which according to him "is not a daughter of god, but a handmaid for kings and for men of low estate, for rich and for poor and beggars, and it is born from the dry wood."[40]

Read against the background of this evidence, the account of the invention of the cult of fire in CT 27.1–3 is striking by its absence of any polemical overtones. This silence becomes even more puzzling in light of the fact that our author does not hesitate to raise his voice against some other aspects of Iranian culture, such as, for example, close-kin marriage or prognostication. What made the author, an heir to the heroic history of Christian resistance to the

---

36 ܠܐ ܣܓܕ ܠܫܡܫܐ ܘܠܐ ܡܝܩܪ ܠܢܘܪܐ; ed. Bedjan 1890–1897, v. 2, p. 364.
37 See §§20–21; ed. Abbeloos 1890, pp. 28, 30.
38 See §§38, 47; ed. Abbeloos 1890, pp. 53, 67–68.
39 ܠܐܠܗܝܟ ܡܓܕܦܝܢ ܘܒܢܘܪܐ ܘܒܡܝܐ ܡܒܙܚܝܢ ܘܫܬܐܣܘܗܝ ܕܒܝܬ ܢܘܪܐ ܕܣܓܕܝܢܢ; ed. Bedjan 1890–1897, v. 4, p. 251.
40 ܠܐ ܢܘܪܐ ܒܪܬ ܐܠܗܐ ܗܝ ܐܠܐ ܐܡܬܐ ܗܝ ܕܡܠܟܐ ܘܕܒܢܝ ܚܐܪܐ ܘܕܥܬܝܪܐ ܘܕܡܣܟܢܐ ܘܕܒܝܫܐ ܘܡܢ ܩܝܣܐ ܝܒܝܫܐ; ed. Bedjan 1890–1897, v. 4, p. 252.

religious pressure of the Sasanian empire, refrain from denouncing this principal form of Zoroastrian worship? I believe that a possible key to the solution of this problem should be sought at the intersection of two factors—the radical re-evaluation of Nimrod as a positive figure in Syriac Christianity and the particular ambivalent agenda pursued by CT's author in his dealing with the institution of Iranian kingship. Both of these developments will be analyzed in more detail below, where the question of their relevance to the representation of Iranian fire-worship in CT 27.1–3 is also addressed.

1.2 *The Cult of the Horse*

Immediately after the account of Nimrod's institution of the Iranian cult of fire, CT's author cites another etiological story, which deals with the origins of the Persians' alleged horse-worship (CT 27.4–5):

> And King Sasan found a spring of water in Azerbaijan. And he made a white horse and set (it) over it. And those who bathed (there) used to worship that horse. And from that time the Persians began to worship that horse.[41]

This brief narrative poses several problems of interpretation. One of them concerns the identity of the king responsible for the introduction of horse-worship among the Persians. The textual witnesses of CT contain two different spellings of his name. While all the manuscripts of the Eastern recension and some West Syrian manuscripts (Oc^{de}) have the form SYSN, some of the manuscripts of the Western recension (Oc^{abc}) spell this name as SSN.[42] These two spellings correspond to the two proper names that were current in ancient Iran, *Sīsin* and *Sāsān*. Remaining on a purely text-critical ground, it is difficult to decide which of these two forms reflects the original stratum of CT, since there are instances when manuscripts of the Western recension preserve correct forms in comparison with those of the East Syrian manuscripts, including Or^{A}.[43] In order to solve this problem, both the general onomastic context of Sasanian Iran and the narrative function of the bearer of this name should be taken into consideration.

41 Or^{A}: ܘܐܫܟܚ ܣܝܣܢ ܡܠܟܐ ܥܝܢܐ ܕܡ̈ܝܐ ܒܐܕܘܪܒܝܓܢ ܘܥܒܕ ܣܘܣܝܐ ܚܘܪܐ ܘܣܡ ܥܠܝܗ̇. ܘܐܝܠܝܢ ܕܣܚܝܢ ܡܣܓܕܝܢ ܗܘܘ ܠܗܘ ܣܘܣܝܐ. ܘܡܢ ܗܝܕܝܢ ܫܪܝܘ ܦܪ̈ܣܝܐ ܕܢܣܓܕܘܢ ܠܗܘ ܣܘܣܝܐ.

42 The spelling of the name of "Sasan the weaver" in CT 24.25 provides a similar distribution of these two onomastic forms between the manuscripts of the two recensions. On this figure, see below.

43 Cf. the spelling of the toponym "Heliopolis" in CT 35.21.

CATEGORIZING THE IRANIAN "OTHER" 153

As we turn to the onomastic evidence provided by the epigraphical and literary sources from the Sasanian period, it becomes apparent that the form *Sīsin* was very seldom used as a separate personal name during this epoch. The only known occurrence of it is that of the third-century Manichaean leader "Sisin," who was the immediate successor to Mani as the head of the community.[44] This name is also attested as a theophoric element of rare composite names such as *Asp-Sēsen* or *Sēsen-bād*.[45] At the same time, the form *Sāsān* appears to be well attested as a personal name during this period.[46] First and foremost, it was the name of the eponymous founder of the Sasanian royal dynasty, the father of King Ardašīr I. Moreover, it was not an unpopular name among the Iranian nobility and elites.[47] In light of this evidence, as well as the royal status of the bearer of this name in CT, it seems warranted to conclude that *Sāsān* and not *Sīsin* should be considered the correct form of the king's name in CT 27.4.

As has just been mentioned, the most famous bearer of the name "Sasan" in late ancient Iran was undoubtedly the legendary eponym of the Sasanian dynasty. It is unclear who the historical Sasan was or whether he existed at all. The Iranian historiographical tradition has preserved different versions of the kinship relation between him and Ardašīr I.[48] However, for our present discussion it is important to recall that the figure of Sasan constituted an important element in the royal ideology of the Sasanian dynasty as the first link in the chain of its history. In that role, he became an instrumental figure in the official Sasanian propaganda and its efforts to gain legitimacy for the new Iranian dynasty. Thus, the third-century inscription of Shapur I on Kaʻba-ye Zardošt glorifies him in three languages as "Sasan the lord" (Mid. Pers. *Sāsān ī xwadāy*, Gr. Σασάνου τοῦ κυρίου).[49] In the bilingual Parthian–Middle Persian inscription made by King Narseh at Paikuli in Iraqi Kurdistan after he had successfully ousted his nephew from power in the year 293, it is proclaimed that Ardašīr I's ascension to kingship was the turning point in the history of

---

44   He is referred to as *Sīsin* in Middle Iranian sources (cf. *mry sysn* in the Sogdian fragment M 197 from Turfan; Henning 1945, p. 154) and as *Sisinnios* in Coptic Manichaean texts (cf. *Manichaean Homilies*; ed. Pedersen 2006, p. 82; *Bema Psalms* 235, 241; ed. Wurst 1996, pp. 86, 108). On this figure and his name, see Tardieu 1991; Tubach 1997, pp. 388–390.

45   For examples, see Gignoux 2003, pp. 24, #43; 59, #304. On the theophoric meaning of this name, see Schwartz, M. 1998. See also Gignoux 1998, who discusses the names *Sāsān* and *Sīsīn* in the corpus of Aramaic magical texts.

46   The earliest attestations of this name belong to the Parthian period. For examples and discussion of its etymology, see Livshits 2010, p. 150.

47   For examples, see Gignoux 1986, pp. 156–157, #827; Gignoux et alii 2009, p. 122, ##372c–d.

48   On this, see Frye 1983, pp. 116–117.

49   Huyse 1999, v. 1, p. 49 (§36).

Ērānšahr, when "the gods gave glory and rulership to the family of Sāsān."[50] Sasan is celebrated along similar lines by the author of the late Sasanian *Book of the Deeds of Ardašīr, Son of Pābag*, a Middle Persian romance which relates the first Sasanian monarch's rise to power. At the beginning of this work, there is a story in which Ardashir's great future is heralded by a prophetic dream of Pāpak in which he beholds Sasan endowed with such attributes of royal "sovereignty" (*pādixšāyīh*) as the sun and a white elephant.[51]

This importance of Sasan for the self-image of the ruling royal house did not go unnoticed by those Eastern Christians who had fallen into the political or cultural orbit of Sasanian Iran. The fifth-century Armenian historian Eznik of Kołb says of the royal succession of the ruling dynasty that "from a certain Sasan the Sassanians—from father to son—received in order to this very day the kingship of the Sassanians."[52] The name "Sasan" was also often evoked as the patronym of Ardašīr I. In the *History of the Armenians*, Agathangelos mentions "Artashir, son of Sasan" (Արտաշիր որդւոյ Սասանայ),[53] and in Syriac sources, "Ardashir, son of Sasan" is attested in a seventh-century patristic catena.[54]

Given the prominent status held by the semi-legendary figure of Sasan in the self-image of the ruling Sasanian dynasty, as well as the absence of any other Iranian monarch bearing such a name, the identification of "Sasan the king" in CT 27.4–5 presents no difficulties. The main problem in this regard is a blatant chronological discrepancy, since Sasan lived much later than the biblical Nimrod. This incongruity, however, does not seem to bother CT's author, who resorts to similarly anachronistic interpretations of important figures from Iranian history on several occasions, such as the story of Ardashir in CT 27.12–17 or the account of the New Testament Magi, named after Sasanian kings, in CT 45.18–19.[55] In distinction from the Greek-speaking Christian historiographers of late antiquity, who faced a comparable task of reconciling two different chronologies, biblical and Greco-Roman, CT's author seems to be oblivious to the problem involved, as, in a Procrustean manner, he adjusts the

50 [y]'ztn GDE W hštr-h[wtwyp]y OL twhm ME S'[s]nkn YNTNt; ed. Skjærvø 1983, p. 65, ln. 36.
51 *Kār-nāmag* 1.8–13; ed. Grenet 2003, pp. 54–56.
52 *De Deo* 227: Որպէս եւ ի Սասանայն ումեմնէ' սասանականքն որդի ի հաւրէ կարգաւ առին մինչեւ ցայսաւր զթագաւորութիւն սասանականացն; ed. Mariès & Mercier 1959, p. 479; trans. Blanchard and Young 1998, pp. 131–132. Cf. also Ełišē, *History of Vardan* 1.1 on the Arshacid royal line as "the race of Sasan the Persian" (ազգն Սասանայ պարսկի); ed. Ter Minasyan 1957, p. 6.
53 *Hist.* 18; ed. Thomson 1976, pp. 34–35.
54 Ms. BL Add. 12168; see Wright, W. 1870–1872, #852, v. 2, p. 905, #6.
55 Both of these traditions are discussed in sections 1.4 and 2.3.3 below.

main figures of Iranian history to the framework of his master narrative based on biblical chronology.

Another aspect of the etiological account in CT 27.4–5 that demands clarification is that of the location of the place where the institution of Persian horse-worship supposedly occurs. From the description of the cultic place in this story, i.e. its setting at the body of water in Azerbaijan and its association with the horse, it becomes clear that the author is here alluding to the famous Zoroastrian fire temple of Ādur Gušnasp.[56] The fire Ādur Gušnasp, whose name could be translated from Persian as "the fire of the stallion," was one of the three most important Zoroastrian sacred fires.[57] This fire was associated with the warrior caste and thus with the Iranian kings who belonged to it. During the Sasanian period, Ādur Gušnasp assumed the highest importance among the three fires, functioning as a symbol of imperial power. It was to this temple that Sasanian monarchs would offer expensive donations and go on pilgrimage after coronations in the capital city of Ctesiphon.[58]

The location of the fire temple of Ādur Gušnasp in the West Azerbaijan region of Iran is well documented in a wide range of Zoroastrian and non-Zoroastrian sources. However, since in Zoroastrian religious practice the sacred fires could be moved from one place to another while retaining their names, there is a certain difficulty in establishing the exact location of this temple during the pre-Islamic period.[59] Different sources connect it with the cities of Ganzak and Šīz, as well as with Lake Čēčast. On the basis of this tangled evidence and archaeological data, it is possible to suggest that Ādur Gušnasp was originally located in the city of Ganzak, situated close to the southern shore of Lake Urmia.[60] However, later on, early in the fifth century CE, it was apparently transferred to the city of Šīz, nowadays Takht-i Sulaimān, located 160 km southeast of Lake Urmia. At Takht-i Sulaimān, the remains of a great fire temple that was situated by the lake, formed by a thermal spring, are preserved to this day.[61] The transfer of Ādur Gušnasp is mentioned by the Arab historian al-Masʿūdī, who reports that it was moved from Ganzak to the place called "al-Birka" (i.e.

---

56   J. Marquart seems to be the first to recognize this connection: see Marquart 1907, p. 10.
57   On these fires, see Schippmann 1971; Gyselen 2003. On Ādur Gušnasp, see also Boyce 1985; Humbach 1967.
58   See Christensen 1944, pp. 166–167.
59   In what follows, I rely on the discussion in Boyce & Grenet 1991, pp. 73–81.
60   On this town, see Boyce 2001.
61   For a detailed overview of literary and archaeological evidence on this temple, see Schippmann 1971, pp. 309–357.

"the pond") by the Sasanian king Khosrow I Anūširvān.[62] This theory is also supported by the fact that in the accounts of Heraclius' campaigns in Persia (621–628), when the temple of Ādur Gušnasp was captured and sacked by the Byzantine army, these events take place in the city of Thebarmais and not in Ganzak.[63]

The portrayal of Ādur Gušnasp in CT 27.4–5 seems to fit this second location better, because in Takht-i Sulaimān the temple was situated next to a deep lake formed by the waters of a thermal spring. It is this body of water and not Lake Urmia, which is shallow and maintains a regular temperature, that seems to be reflected in the descriptions of the mythological Avestan Lake Čēčast, upon which Ādur Gušnasp is located, that are found in some Pahlavi compositions.[64] The author of *Zand ī Wahman Yasn* (6.10) speaks about "Ādur Gušnasp on the deep, warm-watered, and anti-demonic lake Čēčast."[65] Likewise, Zādspram's *Anthology* (3.24) relates that Ādur Gušnasp stands on the shores of Lake Čēčast and describes the lake as "salty, warm, without movement, free from animals."[66]

While the identification of the Zoroastrian holy place located in Azerbaijan in CT 27.4–5 as the fire temple of Ādur Gušnasp does not present particular difficulties, another aspect of this story—namely the supposed existence of a statue of a white horse in this location which functioned as an object of cultic worship—is more problematic. The main difficulty that this passage presents is that it is far from clear whether this description reflects the author's familiarity with the actual practice of the cultic use of horse statues among Zoroastrians or whether it is merely a product of his imagination.

The fact that Zoroastrian worship seems to be of a predominantly aniconic character during the Sasanian period, as has been argued by Mary Boyce,[67] speaks in favor of the latter possibility. This theory is based on the testimony of some ancient authors such as Herodotus, who says of Persians that "it is not their custom to make and set up statues (ἀγάλματα) and temples and

---

62   *Murūǧ al-ḏahab* 68; ed. de Meynard et alii 1966–1979, v. 2, p. 398. See also Minorsky 1944, pp. 249, 257.
63   Theophanes, *Chron.* A.M. 6114; ed. de Boor 1883–1885, v. 1, pp. 307–308.
64   On the identification and location of this lake, see Tafazzoli 1992; Boyce & Grenet 1991, pp. 73–78.
65   *ādur gušnasp pad war ī čēčast ī zofr ī garmō-āb ī jud-dēw*; ed. Cereti 1995, pp. 141 [Pahl.], 161 [trans. (modified)].
66   Ed. Gignoux & Tafazzoli 1993, p. 44.
67   See Boyce 1975b. For a balanced up-to-date discussion of this issue, see Shenkar 2014, 2017, who pays attention to the regional differences in approaches to the visualization of the divine within the Sasanian realm.

altars."⁶⁸ These testimonies are reinforced by the almost complete absence of cultic images or statues among the archaeological material from Sasanian Iran. Moreover, even during the earlier pre-Sasanian stages of the Persian religion, when statues could occasionally be used for cultic purposes, they tended to represent native Persian deities such as Anahita in anthropomorphic form and not in the guise of animals.⁶⁹

However, the possibility that CT 27.4–5 somehow reflects an actual Zoroastrian practice of the use of cultic statues of horses cannot be completely ruled out. There is some archaeological and literary evidence that suggests that such practices might have been current in some parts of the Iranian-dominated area. Thus, a visual representation of the deity of the river Oxus (the modern Amu Darya) being worshipped in the form of a horse appears on one of the sixth-century funerary monuments for Sogdian merchants that were discovered in China.⁷⁰ This archaeological testimony of the cultic use of horse statues in Sogdiana is supported by an eighth-century literary source, also from China. In his collection of miscellanea entitled *Youyang zazu*, Duan Chengshi (803–863), a scholar from the Tang Dynasty, describes a fire temple located on an island in the middle of the river Oxus, where there are no cultic images save a bronze statue of a horse.⁷¹ It has been argued by some scholars that this gold-colored horse rising from the river represented the Iranian deity Tištriia.⁷²

Another group of literary testimonies to the practice of horse-worship in Iran is comprised of Eastern Christian works from the sixth and seventh centuries. The earliest of these belongs to Jacob of Serugh, who refers to the horse as an object of worship of the "Indians" in the *Homily on the Fall of Idols*.⁷³ There is some ambiguity as to the precise meaning of the ethnonym in this sentence, because in some manuscripts of the homily it is not "Indians" (*hendwāyē*), but "Huns" (*hunāyē*) who are said to worship the horse. Whatever the correct reading may be, it should be noted that both these ethnonyms refer to the nations that occupy the regions near the eastern borders of the Sasanian empire, so this evidence is, in principle, compatible with that of the Chinese sources.⁷⁴

68 *Hist.* 1.131; ed. Godley 1926–1930, v. 1, pp. 170–171.
69 See de Jong 1997, pp. 350–352; Shenkar 2014, pp. 181–190.
70 See Marshak 2001, p. 240; Grenet 2007, p. 410.
71 See Drège & Grenet 1987.
72 See Drège & Grenet 1987, p. 121. For additional evidence in support of this hypothesis, see Panaino 1990–1995, v. 2, p. 106.
73 ܐܠܗܐ ܐܝܟ ܗܘܘ ܣܓܕܝܢ ܠܣܘܣܝܐ ܗܢܕܘܝܐ; ed. Martin 1875, p. 111, ln. 77–78.
74 Besides their similar spelling in Syriac, confusion of these two ethnonyms might result from the fact that the toponym "India" (*Hindūgān*) in Middle Persian sources occasionally refers to the regions alongside the western borders of China, which were inhabited by Huns. See Akbarzadeh 2010.

One of the earliest unambiguous references to Persian horse-worship comes from a Greek poem on Emperor Heraclius' military expedition against Persia composed by George of Pisidia shortly after the year 622. In this work, the poet, who himself participated in this campaign, ridicules the religious customs of the Persians, among which is mentioned the worshipping of something as reasonless as a horse.[75] Another roughly contemporary reference to the Persian horse cult is found in the *Acts of Anastasius the Persian*, a Byzantine hagiographical composition. This work recounts the story of the life and martyrdom of a Persian soldier, Anastasius, who converted to Christianity during the first decades of the seventh century. He was arrested in Caesarea by the Persians, who captured Palestine in 614, and was offered the chance to renounce his religion and return to Zoroastrianism. While refusing the offer, Anastasius challenged the Persian *marzban* or margrave, who was overseeing the trial, with the following argument: "To which gods do you order me to sacrifice? To the sun, to the moon, to the fire, to the horse (τῷ ἵππῳ), or to those of the mountains and the hills, and any others like these?"[76]

Bernard Flusin, the editor of the *Acts of Anastasius*, suggested that this tradition does not reflect the reality of Iranian religious practice and should be regarded as a purely literary topos from the repertoire of Byzantine anti-Persian polemic.[77] Yet these references to Iranian horse-worship cannot be explained away as merely a popular polemical topos. Firstly, this is contradicted by the fact that no mention of horse-worship is attested in the classical or pre-sixth-century Christian sources that deal with the Persians' religious beliefs.[78] Moreover, Flusin's suggestion does not explain why the motif of Persian horse-worship emerges so prominently within such a relatively narrow time period and does so in the works composed in the immediate aftermath of Heraclius' Iranian campaign, during which many Byzantines, including the author of one such work, had an opportunity to acquire first-hand knowledge of the religion and culture of Sasanian Iran.

Nevertheless, even the combined weight of the evidence of Persian horse-worship provided by Oriental and Byzantine sources is not sufficiently strong to settle the general problem of the possible use of statues of deities

---

75   *Expeditio Persica* 1.23–26; ed. Pertusi 1959, p. 85. For a similar contemporary report, see Theophylact Simocatta, *Hist.* 3.13.14–15, who points out that Persians "elect a horse for worship"; trans. Whitby & Whitby 1988, p. 93. Cf. also John of Nikiu, *Chron.* 95.26.

76   *Acta Anastasii Persae* 23; ed. Flusin 1992, v. 1, pp. 65–67.

77   Flusin 1992, v. 2, p. 239.

78   See de Jong 1997. The horse is also absent from the lists of Persian deities that Christian martyrs were forced to worship in hagiographical sources. See Gray, L.H. 1913–1914, pp. 42–44.

represented as animals in Zoroastrian ritual practice during the Sasanian period once and for all, to say nothing of the particular question of the presence of a cultic horse statue in the temple of Ādur Gušnasp, as is suggested by CT 27.4–5. At the same time, this evidence is suggestive enough to prevent us from ruling out the possibility of this story referring to an actual cultic practice among Zoroastrians with absolute certainty, relying on the scholarly theory of Sasanian "iconoclasm." Only a fresh in-depth re-examination of all available archaeological and literary evidence on Zoroastrian cult in Sasanian Iran can clarify this complicated issue.

For the time being, a safer approach to the story of Persian horse-worship in CT 27.4–5 would be to regard it as a product of its author's imagination. Our author may have invented this motif to serve his own narrative purposes, even if it has little to do with the actual character of Zoroastrian worship. Yet even in this case, we should take into consideration that he may have been influenced by some genuine features of Iranian religiosity when constructing this story. One such feature is the conspicuous place of horses in Sasanian culture.

Horses played a very important role in the culture and religion of Indo-European peoples, including the Iranians.[79] Ritual sacrifices of white horses formed an important element of proto-Indo-European religious tradition, where they were closely related to the institution of kingship. This practice is attested in Vedic India, where the ritual of horse sacrifice was performed at the investiture of a monarch.[80] Likewise, in the Iranian milieu, horses, especially white horses, had been used as sacrificial animals from the time of the Achaemenids.[81]

Among the Iranians, the horse was not only considered to be an appropriate sacrificial offering to the gods, but it could also represent deities. On several occasions, the Avesta refers to the yazatas, who would adopt the form of a white horse. Thus, in the *Bahrām Yašt*, the Old Iranian deity of victory, Vərəθraγna, manifests himself to Zoroaster as "a white, beautiful horse, with yellow ears and a golden caparison."[82] In the *Tištar Yašt*, the yazata Tištriia, identified with the star Sirius, assumes the "shape of a white horse" (Avest. *aspahe kəhrpa aurušahe*) in order to engage the demon Apaoša in battle.[83]

---

79 See Kuzmina 1977; Shahbazi 1987, pp. 728–730; Swennen 2004; Schilling 2008, pp. 200–208.
80 See Kelekna 2009, pp. 113–115.
81 Cf. description of the sacrifices of horses to the sun by Xenophon, *Cyrop.* 8.3.24. See, however, de Jong 1997, p. 361, who questions the authenticity of this tradition. For the Parthian period, see Philostratus, *Vita Apol.* 1.31; Heliodorus of Emesa, *Aeth.* 10.6.
82 *Yašt* 14.3; trans. Darmesteter 1883, p. 233.
83 *Yašt* 8.18, 20, 30; ed. Panaino 1990–95, v. 1, pp. 44–46, 54. Cf. also Iranian *Bundahišn* 6B.8.

The horse's prominent role in Iranian rituals and beliefs is also expressed in their art. It should also be noted that representations of a chariot of winged horses, related to the iconography of the god Mithra, may also be found during the Sasanian period.[84] A considerable number of the seals of Sasanian officials feature images of winged horses.[85] As has been noted by R. Ettinghausen, in Sasanian art, the winged horse "represented the mount of the king and the vehicle of ascension, implying semi-divinity."[86] It is noteworthy that a representation of two winged horses appears on a Sasanian seal which also evokes Ādur Gušnasp.[87] There are also examples of horse statues made of precious metals, such as silver, from this period.[88]

The importance of both the horse and Ādur Gušnasp in the culture of Sasanian Iran is also reflected in the onomastic practices of the Iranian nobility during this period. Theophoric names containing the element "Gušnasp," such as *Ādur Gušnasp, Dād Gušnasp, Mihr Gušnasp* etc., enjoyed considerable popularity among the members of the higher classes, aristocracy and Zoroastrian clergy alike. Such names are well attested in Sasanian inscriptions, including those on bullae and seals, as well as in literary sources from this period.[89] In fact, the practice of using equine elements to derive personal names goes back to the most ancient period of Zoroastrian history.[90]

In view of the horse's high visibility as a religious symbol in the culture of Sasanian Iran, it is not difficult to imagine how a non-Zoroastrian observer who had been exposed to these expressions of Iranian religiosity, such as the author of CT, might arrive at the conclusion that the Persians regarded this animal as divine.

The juxtaposition of the founder of the Sasanian dynasty, the Ādur Gušnasp fire temple, and the cult of the white horse seems to be unique to CT. No comparable tradition is attested in the native Zoroastrian sources. As to the

---

84 See Gyselen 2000.
85 Cf. Gyselen 2007, pp. 308–311, ##IVB/10, IVB/12; pp. 338–339, ##IVD/25, IVD/27; pp. 372–373, ##VI/19, VI/20, VI/21.
86 Ettinghausen 1972, p. 46.
87 See Gyselen 2003, pp. 133–134, fig. 4d.
88 See Fukai 1974. Cf. also the testimony of al-Maʿsūdī, who mentions stone representations of horses decorating the famous fire temple in Istakhr; *Murūǧ al-ḏahab* 68; ed. de Meynard et alii 1966–1979, v. 2, p. 399.
89 See invert indexes in Gignoux 1986, 2003; Gignoux et alii 2009. It remains, however, to be answered whether this element conveyed a purely religious meaning or perhaps also served as a marker of regional or familial identity.
90 For a list of Avestan personal names containing the element *asp*, "horse," see Ambartsumian 2005, pp. 25–28.

etiology of the fire Ādur Gušnasp, its origins may be traced back to the beginning of the world, such as, for instance, in the *Pahlavi Rivāyat* (46.31), where it is related that it was Ohrmazd who "established Ādur Gušnasp in the role of a victorious fire in Ādurbādagān."[91] According to the *Bundahišn*, Ādur Gušnasp was placed in the fire temple at Mount Asnwand in Azerbaijan by the legendary Kayanian king Kay Husraw.[92]

In the Middle Persian literary tradition, Ādur Gušnasp is mentioned in connection with Sasan only once, in the *Book of the Deeds of Ardašīr*. The beginning of this work relates the story of Ardašīr's father Pābag's several prophetic dreams that focus on Sasan. In one of these dreams, he beholds how the three sacred fires, Ādur Farnbāg, Ādur Gušnasp, and Ādur Burzēn-Mihr, are burning in "the house of Sasan."[93] This connection between Sasan and the three great fires of Persia aims to convey the idea of the Sasanian kings as patrons of Zoroastrianism. Yet this account can hardly be taken as a meaningful parallel to CT 27.4–5, since it does not indicate that there is any unique relation between Ādur Gušnasp and Sasan.

Nor do we find any parallels to the story of CT 27.4–5 in those Greek and Roman sources that deal with Zoroastrianism.[94] Even those Christian authors from late antiquity who exhibit an awareness of the existence of this great Zoroastrian sanctuary in Azerbaijan say nothing about its origins or its cultic inventory.[95] No mention of Sasan or the white horse in connection with this temple is found in the later medieval works that refer to it.[96]

An interesting parallel to the account in CT 27.4–5 is found in the eighth-century *Book of Scholia* by the East Syrian writer Theodore bar Koni. In the seventh section of this book, Theodore narrates a story about Zoroaster uttering a prophecy about Christ's future coming in front of his disciples while he was "sitting at the water spring of Glošā d-Ḥorin, the place that was fashioned into the baths by the ancient kings."[97] One of the three disciples who were present at this event is named "Sasan." The most conspicuous element of this narrative that brings it close to CT's story is the connection between Sasan and

---

91 Ed. Williams, A.V. 1990, v. 1, p. 167 [Pahl.], v. 2, p. 75 [trans.].
92 Iranian *Bundahišn* 18.8; ed. Pakzad 2005, pp. 231–232.
93 *Kār-nāmag* 1.10; ed. Grenet 2003, p. 56.
94 They are conveniently collected in Bidez & Cumont 1938; de Jong 1997; Vasunia 2007.
95 Cf. Procopius of Caesarea, *De bell. Pers.* 2.24.1–2; Sebeos, *Hist.* 38 (trans. Thomson & Howard-Johnston 1999, p. 81).
96 For a comprehensive overview of ancient sources that refer to this temple, see Schippmann 1971, pp. 310–325. Unfortunately, he does not include the passage from CT.
97 ܕܟܕ ܗܘܐ ܝܬܒ ܥܠ ܡܒܘܥܐ ܕܡܝ̈ܐ ܕܓܠܘܫܐ ܕܚܘܪܝܢ ܐܬܪܐ ܕܐܬܬܩܢ ܠܒܝܬ ܣܚܘܬܐ; ed. Scher 1910–1912, v. 2, p. 74.

the natural spring that becomes the royal baths. Unfortunately, the otherwise unknown toponym "Glošā d-Ḥorin" leaves us with no clue as to the exact location of the site where these events are supposed to have taken place. Given this, as well as the fact that this account was written considerably later than CT, it has little to offer us when it comes to the question of the possible sources of CT 27.4–5.

It seems reasonable, then, to suggest that the story of King Sasan and the Persian horse cult as it is narrated in CT 27.4–5 is a result of an internal Syriac development. CT's author was apparently the first person to weave together the originally separate traditions of Sasan and the fire temple in Azerbaijan into a coherent etiological narrative. This connection could have been facilitated by the possibility of a paronomastic pun involving the equine connotations of the name of the fire, i.e. Ādur Gušnasp, and the personal name Sasan, since the default word for "horse" in Syriac, i.e. *susyā*, alliterates well with the king's name.

The question that remains to be asked in connection with CT 27.4–5 is that of the authorial purpose behind this etiological account. This narrative functions in a similar way to the story of the origins of the Persian veneration of fire in CT 27.1–3 analyzed above. Both of these stories endeavor to throw light on the origins of those religious practices that are unique to the Persians. In both of them, these forms of worship originate during the formative period of King Nimrod's rule. While the fire cult is introduced by Nimrod himself, the horse cult is invented by his close associate Sasan.[98]

Similarly to the account of CT 27.1–3, the description of Persian horse-worship in CT 27.4–5 is free from any negative connotations. Here, the author likewise presents a blatantly idolatrous practice in an unperturbed manner, without attempting to pass any moral or religious judgment on its value. This is particularly striking if we take into consideration the strong condemnation of idolatry and element-worship that the author wages in CT 25.8–14, where the origins of these religious practices are ascribed to Satan. I believe that, as in the case of the story of Nimrod's invention of fire-worship, this unusually placid attitude towards an Iranian religious practice on our author's part is an outcome of his positive stance towards the institution of Iranian kingship. This story should be viewed in light of his intricate attitude towards the Sasanian dynasty, which in its turn reflects the complex social, cultural, and political

---

98   The connection between Nimrod and Sasan, stressed in CT 24.25–26, is analyzed in section 2.1 below.

dynamics that shaped the development of Syriac Christian identity in the late Sasanian empire.[99]

1.3 *Close-Kin Marriage*

Another reference related to the Persians' religious customs appears after the description of Nimrod's homage to Yonṭon, the fourth son of Noah, who lived in the land of Nodh, located in the East. Having learned wisdom and the art of revelation from Yonṭon, Nimrod leaves the East and returns to his domain. It is there that the following event occurs (CT 27.12–16):

> And when Nimrod went up from the East, and began to use this revelation, and many men marveled at him. And when Ardashir the priest, who ministered to the fire that ascended from the earth, saw Nimrod occupied with these exalted courses, he entreated that demon, who appeared around that fire, to teach him the wisdom of Nimrod. And as the demons are in the habit of destroying through sin those who approach them, that demon said to that priest—"A man cannot become a priest and a Magian unless he has intercourse with his mother, and with his daughter, and with his sister." And Ardashir the priest did thus. And from that time the priests, and the Magians, and the Persians began to marry their mothers, and their sisters, and their daughters.[100]

In this passage, CT's author presents his audience with an etiological story about the peculiar Iranian custom of close-kin marriage (Avest. *xᵛaētuuadaϑa-*; Mid. Pers. *xwēdōdah*).[101] This practice included marriages within the close family circle, that is of a man to his mother, daughter, or sister. The Persians regarded the performance of *xwēdōdah* not only as an acceptable social practice, but as a highly meritorious religious duty which was incumbent on all members of the Zoroastrian community—monarchs and commoners, priests and laymen.

99 The author's attitude to the Sasanian kings is discussed below in section 2.1 on Nimrod and section 2.3 on the Magi of the Gospel of Matthew.

100 Or^A: ܘܟܕ ܣܠܩ ܡܢ ܡܕܢܚܐ ܢܡܪܘܕ، ܘܫܪܝ ܠܡܬܚܫܚܘ ܒܗܕܐ ܓܠܝܢܐ. ܘܣܓܝܐܐ ܡܬܕܡܪܝܢ ܗܘܘ ܒܗ. ܘܐܪܕܫܝܪ ܟܘܡܪܐ ܗܘ ܕܡܫܡܫ ܗܘܐ ܠܢܘܪܐ ܗܝ ܕܣܠܩܐ ܗܘܬ ܡܢ ܐܪܥܐ. ܟܕ ܚܙܐ ܠܢܡܪܘܕ ܕܡܬܗܦܟ ܒܗܠܝܢ ܪܘܡܝܬܐ ܗܠܝܢ ܡܬܚܦܛ ܗܘܐ ܠܗ ܠܗܘ ܫܐܕܐ ܕܡܬܚܙܐ ܗܘܐ ܚܕܪ ܗܝ ܢܘܪܐ، ܕܢܠܦܝܘܗܝ ܚܟܡܬܗ ܕܢܡܪܘܕ. ܘܐܝܟ ܕܐܝܬ ܗܘܐ ܠܗܘܢ ܥܝܕܐ ܠܫܐܕܐ ܕܢܚܒܠܘܢ ܐܝܠܝܢ ܕܩܪܒܝܢ ܠܗܘܢ ܒܚܛܝܬܐ. ܐܡܪ ܠܗ ܗܘ ܫܐܕܐ ܠܗܘ ܟܘܡܪܐ ܗܘ. ܕܠܐ ܠܡ ܡܫܟܚ ܓܒܪܐ ܕܢܗܘܐ ܟܘܡܪܐ ܘܡܓܘܫܐ ܐܠܐ ܟܕ ܢܫܐ ܕܡܫܬܘܬܦ ܥܡ ܐܡܗ ܘܥܡ ܒܪܬܗ ܘܥܡ ܚܬܗ. ܘܥܒܕ ܐܪܕܫܝܪ ܟܘܡܪܐ ܗܟܢܐ. ܘܡܢ ܗܝܕܝܢ ܫܪܝܘ ܟܘܡܪܐ ܘܡܓܘܫܐ ܘܦܪܣܝܐ ܢܣܒܝܢ ܐܡܗܬܗܘܢ ܘܐܚܘܬܗܘܢ ܘܒܢܬܗܘܢ.

101 On this practice, see Bucci 1978; Frye 1985; Macuch 1991; Frandsen 2009; Vevaina 2018.

A strong emphasis on the great importance of close-kin marriage as a religious duty is expressed over and over again in the Middle Persian corpus of Zoroastrian writings.[102] Thus, in the abovementioned passage about the four most meritorious Zoroastrian practices from the *Pahlavi Rivāyat* (8c1–2), it is *xwēdōdah* that is given the greatest importance:

> These (are) the four best things: worship of Ohrmazd the Lord; and offering firewood and incense and oblation (to) the fire; and satisfying (the needs of) the priest; and he who practises *xwēdōdah* with (his) mother or daughter or with (his) sister. And of all those he who practises *xwēdōdah* is greatest and best and foremost.[103]

This high regard for close-kin marriage rests on the belief that practicing it offered an especially effective protection against demonic forces.[104] Thus, *xwēdōdah* was thought to have a unique expiatory power and to be able to procure atonement even in the case of the gravest *marg-arzān* sins that are "worthy of death."[105] In one work, none other than Ahriman himself acknowledges *xwēdōdah* as the most efficacious means against the forces of evil when he tells one of his demonic assistants that a person who performs this duty four times cannot be separated from communion with Ohrmazd and the Ameša Spentas by any means.[106]

The centrality of close-kin marriage was strengthened even further by ascribing universal and even cosmic significance to it. Thus, *xwēdōdah* characterized the primeval uncorrupted condition of humanity, as it was practiced by the first human couple, and it would be restored as the universal norm of human propagation by Saošyant, the future savior, in the eschatological consummation.[107] According to the *Dēnkard*, neglecting this religious duty may exert detrimental effects on the whole order of creation, since "when the virtue of consanguine marriage diminishes, darkness increases and light

---

102 Cf. especially the eighth chapter of the *Pahlavi Rivāyat*; ed. Williams, A.V. 1990, v. 1, p. 48–61 [Pahl.], v. 2, pp. 10–17 [trans.].
103 Ed. Williams, A.V. 1990, v. 1, p. 51 [Pahl.], v. 2, p. 11 [trans.]. Cf. *Hērbedestān* 2.9; ed. Kotwal & Kreyenbroek 1992, p. 33.
104 Cf. *Dēnkard* 3.80; trans. de Menasce 1973, pp. 86–87; *Pahlavi Rivāyat* 8a1, 8e10, 8f3, 8l1; ed. Williams, A.V. 1990, v. 1, pp. 49, 55, 57, 61 [Pahl.], v. 2, pp. 10, 13–14, 16 [trans.].
105 Cf. *Pahlavi Rivāyat* 8b1–3; ed. Williams, A.V. 1990, v. 1, p. 51 [Pahl.], v. 2, p. 11 [trans.]; *Šāyest-nē-šāyest* 8.18; ed. Tavadia 1930, p. 113.
106 *Supplementary Texts to the Šāyest-nē-šāyest* 18.1–4; ed. Kotwal 1969, pp. 76–77.
107 Cf. *Pahlavi Rivāyat* 8a7–9, 8c6; ed. Williams, A.V. 1990, v. 1, pp. 49–51 [Pahl.], v. 2, pp. 10–12 [trans.].

CATEGORIZING THE IRANIAN "OTHER"

diminishes."[108] There were also condemnations of those who dare to prevent faithful Zoroastrians from performing this sacred duty.[109]

While the earliest references to close-kin marriage among the Persians come from the Achaemenid and Parthian periods,[110] there is no doubt that *xwēdōdah* was also practiced during the Sasanian period. For example, in his inscription on the Kaʿba-ye Zardošt, the famous Zoroastrian priest Kartir, who was active in the second half of the third century, mentions as one of his achievements in restoring the Zoroastrian religion that "many close-kin marriages were performed."[111] In the late Sasanian composition *Ardā Wirāz-nāmag*, we are told that the main protagonist of this work, the visionary priest Wīrāz, was married to all seven of his sisters.[112] An additional example of close-kin marriage during the Sasanian period is found in the *Life of Mār Šabbay*, the legendary fourth-century bishop of Merv. According to this composition, the holy man succeeded in converting the wife and son of the Persian king Shapur. When the whole affair became known to the king and he decided to punish the culprits, the former was punished only lightly for her transgression, with the explicit reason for this leniency being that "the queen was not only the wife, but also the sister of the utterly tyrannical king,—this is something pleasing to the Magians, and lawful to their foul (religion)."[113]

The practice of close-kin marriage among the Persians was well known to and, as a rule, denounced by their Western as well as their Eastern neighbors, who occasionally refer to what was, in their view, a bizarre Iranian custom.[114] This ancient enthongraphical convention was later adopted and continued by Christian authors, who would regularly condemn *xwēdōdah* whenever they

---

108 *Dēnkard* 6.C82; ed. Shaked 1979, pp. 172–173.
109 Cf. *Pahlavi Rivāyat* 8k1–2; ed. Williams, A.V. 1990, v. 1, p. 59 [Pahl.], v. 2, pp. 15–16 [trans.].
110 For the Achaemenids, see Herodotus, *Hist.* 3.31. For the Parthians, see Josephus, *Ant.* 18.42–43, and the evidence of Syrian Christian writers such as Tatian, *Orat.* 28 and Bardaisan, *Book of the Laws of Countries*; ed. Cureton 1855, pp. 18, 26, 29, 33 [trans.].
111 *WKBYR ḥwytwtdʾhy klty*; ed. Gignoux 1991, p. 47, §14 [Pahl.], p. 72 [trans.].
112 Ed. Vahman 1986, pp. 82–85 [Pahl.], 192–193 [trans.].
113 ܗܘ ܚܒܪ ܢܨܝܦ ܠܡܠܟܐ܂ ܡܛܠܗܕܐ ܐܠܐ܂ ܐܚܘܬܗ ܠܡܠܟܐ ܗܘܬ ܐܝܬܝܗ ܠܡܠܟܐ ܬܘܒ ܐܠܐ ܐܢܬܬܗ ܒܠܚܘܕ ܠܘ܂ ܠܢܡܘܣܗܘܢ ܛܢܦܐ ܘܫܪܝܐ ܠܡܓܘܫܐ ܫܦܝܪ܂; ed. Brock 2011, pp. 275 [Syr.], 268 [trans.].
114 For negative attitudes towards *xwēdōdah* in Greco-Roman sources, see Xanthus *apud* Clement of Alexandria, *Strom.* 3.11.1; Ctesias *apud* Tertullian, *Apol.* 9; *Ad nat.* 1.16.5; Catullus 90.1; Curtius Rufus 8.2.8, 19; Philo, *De spec. leg.* 3.13; these traditions are analyzed by de Jong 1997, pp. 424–432. For Buddhist critique of this practice, see Silk 2008.

had a chance to discuss the Persian way of life.[115] Syrian and Syriac-speaking Christian writers were no exception in this regard, and beginning with the second-century writer Tatian, we may find different expressions of polemic against this practice. Thus, the third-century philosopher Bardaisan refers disapprovingly to close-kin marriage while waging a defense of the doctrine of free will.[116] Condemnation of *xwēdōdah* is found in Syriac sources from late Sasanian Iran such as Barḥadbešabbā's *Cause of the Foundation of the Schools*, and the *Acts of Pethion, Adurhormizd and Anahid*.[117]

CT's author participates in this trend as he denounces close-kin marriage by ascribing its origins to the demonic forces. In doing so, he follows in the footsteps of the early Christian apologetes and polemicists, among whom one of the most common strategies of delegitimizing those Greco-Roman religious practices and beliefs that did not conform to Christian norms was to present them as originating through diabolic agency.[118] A similar approach to the native religion of the Persians is well attested in Syriac sources.[119]

What is innovative in the manner in which CT denounces Iranian close-kin marriage is not the resort to a general motif of the supposedly demonic origins of this abominable custom, which could be found in the works of other Syriac Christian authors,[120] but the peculiar etiological story that purports to explain how exactly it came into existence. CT's author presents a rather peculiar version of the origins of *xwēdōdah* by explaining it to be the result of a demonic trick played on a specific quasi-historical figure, namely the fire-priest Ardashir. Such a connection between the practice of close-kin marriage and this particular human agent is not attested in any other ancient work and thus deserves to be closely examined.

Ancient sources present us with a wide range of different views about the origins of Iranian close-kin marriage. As we turn to the native Zoroastrian tradition, it becomes apparent that there is no simple answer to this question.

---

115 Cf. Minucius Felix, *Oct.* 31.3; Clement of Alexandria, *Paed.* 1.7.55; Origen, *C. Cels.* 5.27; 6.80; Theodoret of Cyrus, *Quaest. in Lev.* 24; *Ep.* 8.
116 See the references in n. 110 above. Cf. also Pseudo-Clementines (*Rec.* 9.29; *Hom.* 19.19) and Eusebius (*Praep. ev.* 6.10), who made use of Bardaisan's motif.
117 For the former, see Scher 1908, pp. 366–367; for the latter, Bedjan 1890–1897, v. 2, pp. 578, 592. For a German translation of these passages, see Bidez & Cumont 1938, v. 2, pp. 108–111.
118 On this strategy, see Borgeaud 2010.
119 Cf. *Life of Mār Awgen*, where Satan proclaims, as the saint is exorcizing him from a Persian prince, that "even the Magi worship me and I am their God"; ed. Bedjan 1890–1897, v. 3, p. 468.
120 Such as Mār Abā and the author of the *Acts of Pethion, Adurhormizd and Anahid*, on whose reports on the origins of *xwēdōdah* see below.

Sometimes, this practice is traced back to the most ancient period in the history of humanity. Thus, according to some sources, the first act of *xwēdōdah* was performed by Mašyā and Mašyāne, the first human couple, who were brother and sister since they were both descended from the primeval human being Gayōmart.[121] Their union in *xwēdōdah* marriage that resulted in the birth of offspring and the perpetuation of the human race is presented by these Zoroastrian authors in a positive light, as a successful counterattack against the demonic forces (*druz*) who had previously gained the upper hand by killing Gayōmart, aiming to eliminate humanity.

There is, however, a different account of the origins of *xwēdōdah* according to which the first act of close-kin marriage was performed by none other than Ohrmazd himself and had cosmogonical significance, since it resulted in the creation of the sun, moon, and stars. This etiological myth does not appear in its full form in the surviving Pahlavi Zoroastrian sources, but it is well attested in Christian, Armenian and Syriac, sources from the Sasanian period.[122]

Thus, Eznik of Kołb, a fifth-century Armenian writer, refers to the Persian custom of close-kin marriage several times in a lengthy anti-Zoroastrian polemical excursus in his treatise *On God*. At some point, when he recounts the Zoroastrian cosmogonical myth, Eznik relates how the secret of *xwēdōdah*'s efficacy as a means of creating the sun and moon was disclosed to Ohrmazd by the demon Mahmi, who in his turn learned it from Ahriman.[123]

Similar accounts of the cosmogonical function of close-kin marriage are found in two Syriac sources from Sasanian Iran. First, the author of the *Acts of Pethion, Adurhormizd and Anahid*, who wages a polemic against Zoroastrian beliefs, relates that it was Ohrmazd who performed the first act of *xwēdōdah* with his mother, having been taught to do so by the disciples of Ahriman, in order to create light. As a result, the sun came into existence.[124] Another Syriac author who exhibits knowledge of this cosmogonical myth is Mār Abā I, the famous sixth-century East Syrian patriarch, a contemporary of Khosrow I (r. 531–579). In his tractate on the laws of marriage and sexual intercourse, Mār Abā mentions a Zoroastrian tradition according to which the material world came

---

121   Cf. *Dēnkard* 3.80; trans. de Menasce 1973, p. 86; *Dādestān ī Dēnīg* 36.68–69; ed. Jaafari-Dehaghi 1998, pp. 136–137; *Pahlavi Rivāyat* 8a7–8; ed. Williams, A.V. 1990, v. 1, p. 49 [Pahl.], v. 2, p. 10 [trans.].

122   See Panaino 2008.

123   *De Deo* 187; ed. Mariès & Mercier 1959, pp. 470–471; trans. Blanchard & Young 1998, pp. 117–118. Cf. also *De Deo* 158, 189, 191–192, 195.

124   Ed. Bedjan 1890–1897, v. 2, p. 578.

into existence as a result of the sexual intercourse between Ohrmazd and his female relatives, who were spurred to this course of action by the devil.[125]

The surviving corpus of Pahlavi literature bears witness that this cosmogonical myth once formed part of the native Zoroastrian mythological tradition. For example, in the eighth chapter of the *Pahlavi Rivāyat*, where Ohrmazd instructs Zoroaster concerning the utmost importance of *xwēdōdah*, he does so while locked in the loving embrace of the female yazata Spendārmad, whom he introduces as "my daughter and my Queen of Paradise, and the Mother of Creation" (8a4).[126] Moreover, in the *Dēnkard*, we find a close connection being established between *xwēdōdah* and natural light in the declaration that "when the virtue of consanguine marriage diminishes, darkness increases and light diminishes."[127]

Relying on this evidence, both Christian and Zoroastrian, some scholars regard this myth as part of the cosmological system of Zurvanism, a distinctive monist stream within Zoroastrianism that seems to enjoy particular popularity during the Sasanian period.[128] Whether this theory is correct or not, it should be noted that this version of the origins of *xwēdōdah* does not necessarily contradict the one that connects its beginning with Mašyā and Mašyāne. It may be that by performing close-kin marriage, the first human couple was following a universal pattern that was established by the action of their creator Ohrmazd.

As we turn to non-Zoroastrian theories of the origins of Iranian close-kin marriage, we find that several historical or quasi-historical figures were credited with the honor of inventing this custom. According to Herodotus, this practice was introduced to the Persians by the Achaemenid king Cambyses, who fell in love with his sister and married her. While relating this story, Herodotus notices that "before this, it had by no means been customary for Persians to marry their sisters."[129]

Another opinion on this subject is offered by John Malalas, a sixth-century Christian historiographer from Antioch. In his work, Malalas says of Ninus, the son of Kronos who ruled Assyria, that "he had taken his mother Semiramis as

---

125 Ed. Sachau 1907–1914, v. 3, pp. 264–267.
126 *spandarmad ī man duxt u-m kadag-bānūg ī wahišt ud mād ī dāmān*; ed. Williams, A.V. 1990, v. 1, p. 49 [Pahl.], v. 2, p. 10 [trans.].
127 *Dēnkard* 6.C82: *ud ka kirbag ī xwēdōdah be kāhēd tārīkīh be abzāyēd ud rōšnīh be kāhēd*; ed. Shaked 1979, pp. 172–173.
128 See Zaehner 1955, pp. 147–163. This material has recently been discussed by Panaino 2008. For a balanced treatment of the controversial issue of Zurvanism, see Shaked 1994, pp. 17–22; Rezania 2008.
129 Herodotus, *Hist.* 3.31; ed. Godley 1926–1930, v. 2, pp. 40–41.

CATEGORIZING THE IRANIAN "OTHER"

his wife; from him the Persians derive the custom of marrying their mothers and sisters."[130] This tradition is based on the widespread Greco-Roman ethnographical notion of King Ninus, the eponymous founder of Nineveh, being one of the founding figures in the history of the Assyrian and Persian nations.[131]

One opinion about the origins of *xwēdōdah* that enjoyed particular popularity among Christian authors was the attribution of this practice to Zoroaster. This option seems to have been endorsed in the fifth century by Theodoret of Cyrus, who says of Persian close-kin marriage that it is performed in accordance with "the law of Zoroaster."[132] It seems that Eznik of Kołb, mentioned above, also ascribes the invention of this custom to Zoroaster. Eznik gives a euhemeristic reinterpretation of the Zoroastrian belief system, maintaining that Zurvan, the highest deity of its pantheon, was not a god, but merely a human being who lived in the time of the Titans and was later deified by the Persians, and that it was the human founder of the Persian religion who, as a part of his *Religionsgründung* project, introduced "the creation of the stars by the shamefulness with mother and sisters."[133] As Eznik claims further on, it was a "certain Zradašt" (Զրադաշտ ոմն), who, driven by his own licentiousness and looking for a way to legitimize it, introduced the myth of cosmogonical incest among the Persians so that "observing this the nation will thus be indifferent to the same impurity."[134] Moreover, in the sixth century, this theory was expressed very unequivocally by Barḥadbešabbā, who relates that among the ordinances established by the "Persian Magus Zoroaster" for his followers was one stipulating that "it is necessary for a son to take his mother in marriage, his daughter or his sister."[135]

It is remarkable that CT's author follows none of these traditions, but offers his own unique explanation of the origins of *xwēdōdah*. This choice, whether it is the result of sheer ignorance or a conscious decision, sets him apart from the rest of the ancient Christian writers on Zoroastrianism and thus deserves to be carefully examined. With that goal in mind, let us address the question of the possible identity of that Persian priest and Magus to whom CT gives the credit of introducing the custom of close-kin marriage.

---

130 *Chron.* 1.10; ed. Thurn 2000, p. 11; trans. Jeffreys et alii 1986, p. 7. This tradition also appears in John of Nikiu (*Chron.* 8.1–3) and *Chronicon Paschale* (ed. Dindorf 1832, v. 1, p. 67).
131 On this, see section 2.1.2 below.
132 *Graec. affect. cur.* 9.33: τοὺς μὲν Ζαράδου νόμους; ed. Canivet 1958, v. 2, p. 346.
133 *De Deo* 158; ed. Mariès & Mercier 1959, pp. 463–464; trans. Blanchard & Young 1998, p. 107.
134 *De Deo* 192; ed. Mariès & Mercier 1959, p. 472; trans. Blanchard & Young 1998, pp. 119–120.
135 ܐܡܗ ܕܢܣܒ ܠܒܪܐ ܘܠܐ ܒܪܬܗ ܐܘ ܚܬܗ; ed. Scher 1908, pp. 365–367; trans. Becker 2008, pp. 135–136.

The Syriac form of the personal name "Ardashir" borne by this person is derived from *Ardašīr*, a Middle Persian form of the Old Persian name "Artaxerxes" (*Artaxšaçā*).¹³⁶ Meaning "one whose rule is through truth/order," it was assumed as a throne name by several kings of the Achaemenid dynasty. This name also retained its popularity during the Sasanian period, when it was borne by various representatives of the Iranian nobility, including monarchs, beginning with the founder of the Sasanian empire, Ardašīr I (d. 242 CE).¹³⁷

It is difficult to explain why CT's author gave this particular name to the inventor of *xwēdōdah*. In the historical sources, the name "Ardashir" is very rarely mentioned in connection with this practice. One such example comes from Plutarch's *Life of Artaxerxes*, which relates how this Achaemenian monarch married one of his two daughters.¹³⁸ Yet several considerations prevent us from regarding Plutarch's account as a possible source of CT. First of all, the form of the Magus' personal name in CT can hardly have been derived from *Arṭaḥšašt* (or *Arṭaḥšištā*), which was a standard way of spelling Artaxerxes' name in Syriac.¹³⁹ Moreover, there are important differences between the portrayals of these two figures. Contrary to CT, no mention of Artaxerxes being a priest is found in Plutarch's narrative. Nor does Plutarch ascribe any paradigmatic significance to the king's act of close-kin marriage regarding the marital laws or mores of the Persians.

An additional difficulty is posed by the fact that CT's author associates the Persian custom of close-kin marriage first and foremost with the priestly class. This stands at odds with the fact that during the Sasanian period, *xwēdōdah* was also practiced by the common people. This may be seen from discussion of this practice in Middle Persian legal works that reflect the realities of this period, such as the *Mādayān ī Hazār Dādestān*.¹⁴⁰

The association of *xwēdōdah* with the priestly caste in CT might reflect the general notion of Zoroastrian priests as the guardians par excellence of the native Iranian religious tradition. According to some scholars, it was Zoroastrian priests who exerted particular efforts to preserve the practice of

---

136 In its correct form, it appears in the West Syrian mss of CT (22.15,17): Oc^a ܐܪܕܫܝܪ; Oc^c ܐܪܕܫܝܪ.
137 For non-royal bearers of this name, see Gignoux 1986, #126; Gignoux 2003, p. 23, #37.
138 Art. 23; ed. Perrin 1914–1926, v. 11, pp. 182–183.
139 This is the case in both the Peshitta's rendering of the Hebrew-Aramaic אַרְתַּחְשַׁשְׂתְּא / אַרְתַּחְשַׁסְתְּא (Ezra 4:7 *et passim*) and in the Syro-Hexapla's rendering of the Greek Ἀρταξέρξης (1(3) Ezra 2:16 *et passim*) into Syriac. For occurrences of this form in non-biblical Syriac sources, see Gignoux et alii 2009, p. 43, ##63a–e.
140 For a convenient collection of the relevant passages, translated and discussed, see Hjerrild 2003, pp. 171–203.

close-kin marriage during the difficult period of the Seleucid domination over Persia, when Greek ideas and customs began to gain a foothold in the region.[141] Whether this suggestion is correct or not, it can hardly be doubted that at least during the Sasanian period and afterwards, it was the Zoroastrian priestly class who took upon themselves the task of the active promotion of this custom among the Persians.

In addition to this, it should be kept in mind that several high-ranking Zoroastrian priests from the late Sasanian period bore the name "Ardashir." Thus, in Ferdowsī's *Šāh-nāma*, there are two "chief priests" (Mid. Pers. *mowbedān mowbed*) from the late Sasanian period who were named Ardashir, one of whom was active during the reign of Pērōz I (r. 459–484) and the other during the reign of Khosrow I (r. 531–579).[142] While it is quite possible that CT's author may have been aware of the latter, our knowledge of his *Sitz im Leben* is too limited to warrant any speculation on a possible connection between this historical person and the figure of Ardashir in CT.

In attempting to solve the riddle of the name "Ardashir," it might be helpful to turn to the most famous bearer of this name: Ardašīr I, the founder of the Sasanian empire. Of particular relevance for our purpose is evidence provided by the numismatic material from this monarch's reign. There are numerous gold and silver coins issued by Ardašīr I that feature the king's profile on the obverse and an image of a fire altar accompanied by the legend "the fire of Ardašīr" (NWR' ZY 'rthštr = *ādur ī Ardašīr*) on the reverse.[143] Ardašīr only began to issue coins featuring fire altars during the second stage of his career, after his victory over Artabanus IV, the last Arsacid "King of Kings," in the year 223/224. Before this, when Ardašīr was the vassal king of Fars and issued his own coins, they did not feature representations of fire altars. The appearance of an image of a fire altar on Iranian coins during the first year of the Sasanian era when Ardašīr came to power thus became one of the most apparent expressions of the difference between the new dynasty's policy and the previous Parthian tradition of coinage, where such imagery appears to be virtually absent.[144] The

---

141   See Hjerrild 2003, p. 169.
142   See Khaleghi-Motlagh 1987.
143   See Alram & Gyselen 2003, pp. 91–152. This legend refers to the king's personal sanctuary built in the city of Ardašīr Xwarrah/Fīrūzābād. In al-Ṭabarī's *History*, it is mentioned as "Ardashīr's fire temple"; ed. de Goeje et alii 1879–1901, v. I.2, p. 1067; trans. Bosworth 1999, p. 410.
144   For a general introduction to Parthian numismatics, see Sellwood 1983. The only significant instance of a pre-Sasanian use of iconography related to the cult of fire in the tradition of Iranian coinage is that of the rulers of the post-Achaemenian *frataraka* dynasty, who issued coins bearing images of structures that are considered by many scholars to represent fire temples or altars. Yet it seems that this was a local phenomenon, limited to

introduction of this iconographical motif was part of Ardašīr's "radical reordering of Iranian coinage," the main purpose of which was to emphasize the special role that the Zoroastrian religion would play under the Sasanians.[145] In light of this highly visible shift in the iconography of Iranian coinage under Ardašīr, it is not difficult to imagine how an outsider might have come up with the idea of a close connection between this monarch and the Zoroastrian cult of fire.[146]

It should be conceded, however, that this identification of the Ardashir in CT with Ardašīr I involves an element of speculation. Given the limitations of our knowledge, it seems impossible at present to come up with a satisfactory explanation for our author's choice of this particular Iranian name for the supposed founder of close-kin marriage. For this reason, a more productive line of approach in dealing with the story of Ardashir, whether he was a real historic person or a purely fictional figure, would be to focus on how this character serves the author's agenda.

As has been noted already, the main thrust of CT 27.12–16 is directed against the Persian custom of close-kin marriage. While the etiological story to which CT's author resorts in order to delegitimize this practice might be unique and developed by him especially for such a purpose, some of its elements do find parallels in other Christian works from late antiquity. Thus, Syriac Christian parallels to the association of close-kin marriage with demonic forces have been pointed out above. In fact, the theory of the demonic origins of *xwēdōdah* advanced by CT's author and other Syriac writers may be a result of the intentional polemical inversion of the genuine Zoroastrian beliefs according to which this custom constituted one of the most powerful weapons in the ongoing struggle against demons.

In addition to this, a comparison with other specimens of Christian anti-Zoroastrian polemic can help us to recognize another polemical strategy that CT's author employs in this passage—one that underlies the connection between the practice of *xwēdōdah* and a specific historical figure, the Zoroastrian priest Ardashir.

---

the province of Fārs where this dynasty ruled, and too remote in time from CT's author's personal experience. There is also no scholarly consensus about whether the tower-like buildings on *frataraka* coins are at all connected to the cult of fire. On this, see Potts 2007.

145 Alram 2008, pp. 17–19.

146 Cf. Agathias of Myrina (*Hist.* 4.26.3), who makes note of the unprecedented privileges acquired by the Zoroastrian priestly caste under Ardašīr while describing the king as "a devotee of the magian religion and an official celebrant of its mysteries"; ed. Keydell 1967, p. 75; trans. Frendo 1975, p. 60.

In order to better appreciate this strategy, let us turn to the portrayal of the Persians and their religion found in the work of Agathias of Myrina, a sixth-century Byzantine historian. In the second book of the *History*, Agathias describes the burial practice of corpse exposure common among the Persians.[147] This gives him an opportunity for a general discussion of the nature and genesis of the Iranian religion, including the question of how peculiar customs such as this and that of close-kin marriage came into existence. According to Agathias, both the bizarre funeral rites and the abominable marriage customs of the present-day Persians are the detrimental results of the latter having abandoned their "old ways" (τὰ μὲν πρότερα ἔθη), practiced by the earliest inhabitants of their land such as the Assyrians, Chaldeans, and Medes, and adopting "alien and degenerated manners" under the influence of Zoroaster, the true founder of the Magian religion.[148]

It is this polemical strategy of deconstructing religious practices peculiar to Zoroastrianism as later innovations and distortions of a more ancient religion of "Persia" that CT's author shares with Agathias. In a manner similar to that of the Byzantine historian, our author repudiates the custom of Iranian close-kin marriage by presenting it not as part of the legacy of Nimrod, whom he promotes as the cultural hero of the region, but as a later perversion of the original mores.

We should also not overlook a potentially apologetic dimension of this strategy. This may be illustrated by the attitude taken by some Muslim intellectuals of Persian extraction with respect to ancient pre-Islamic customs of their nation such as *xwēdōdah* that were considered particularly offensive from the point of view of the new religion.[149] Thus, in his *Kitāb al-āṯār al-bāqīa*, the eleventh-century scholar and polymath al-Bīrūnī transmits the oral testimony of Marzbān b. Rustam, a noble and learned Persian man, according to whom Zoroaster did not actually legislate this custom for his followers. Rather, he had approved it for a very specific and hypothetical situation in which no other woman save a man's mother was available for him to ensure the survival of his line.[150]

What this Persian savant and the author of CT share is that both of them, although in different ways, attempt to dissociate the founding figure of Persian culture, be that Zoroaster or Nimrod, from the reprehensible practice of

---

147 *Hist.* 4.23.1–25.3; ed. Keydell 1967, pp. 70–73; trans. Frendo 1975, pp. 56–59.
148 *Hist.* 4.24.5; ed. Keydell 1967, p. 72; trans. Frendo 1975, p. 58.
149 On the popularity of the topic of close-kin marriage as an anti-Persian invective motif in Arabic literature, especially in the context of the *šu'ūbīya* polemics, see van Gelder 2005, pp. 36–77.
150 Ed. Fück 1952, p. 75.

close-kin marriage. Such reinterpretations of Iranian primeval history provided an ingenious way out of the "double bind" into which a Persian follower of a monotheistic religion would sometimes be caught as a result of the clash of loyalties to the two different frames of reference—his religious and his ethnic identities.

One further question in connection with CT's author's presentation of Iranian close-kin marriage needs to be addressed. Should we look at this polemic from a purely rhetorical angle, as one of the literary strategies employed in the text, or it is possible to relate it to the social reality of the author's time? In order to answer this question, let us turn to the evidence on the impact of this practice on the lives of Iranian Christians.

There are several written sources that tell us about Christians of Iranian origin who had practiced *xwēdōdah* before they embraced the new faith. One such testimony is provided by the *Life of Mār Benjamin*, which was composed during the fifth or sixth century. While speaking about Benjamin's descent, the author reports that his mother had been married to her brother Goršāh, the saint's father, "according to the foul law of the Magians."[151] It is also related that following their conversion to Christianity and baptism, Benjamin's parents ceased any conjugal relations.[152] Another such case comes from a slightly later hagiographical composition, the *Life of George Mihr-Māh-Gušnasp*, an Iranian Christian of noble descent, who suffered a martyr's death during the reign of Khosrow II, in the year 615. According to the saint's biographer, the famous East Syrian theologian Babai the Great, Mihr-Māh-Gušnasp had been married to his sister Hazārōy prior to his conversion.[153] Needless to say, after his conversion and choice of the monastic way of life, this marriage was terminated.

Hagiography is not the only literary corpus that throws light on the influence exerted by the custom of close-kin marriage on the Christians of Sasanian Iran. Additional evidence on this subject is provided by the normative documents that were produced in their midst. Several of these works contain an explicit prohibition of this practice. The importance of this evidence should not be missed given the regulatory function of such texts, which were produced with the aim of forming a coherent religious community, ideologically shaped around written dogmatic texts, distinctive rites, and a clear scheme of hierarchy.

---

151 Ed. Scheil 1897, p. 68.
152 Ed. Scheil 1897, pp. 68–69.
153 Ed. Bedjan 1895, pp. 436–437.

An interdiction on *xwēdōdah* appears in the so-called *Regulations for an Association of Artisans*. This Syriac composition, which seems to have been produced during the late Sasanian period, is a secular legal text regulating the activities of a professional guild, whose members were exclusively Christians. It was preserved in the collection of laws compiled in the ninth century by the East Syrian bishop Gabriel of Basra. There, on the long list of guidelines meant to regulate the lives and behavior of the guild members, we find a pledge to keep away "from the disgusting practice of intercourse with mother, daughter, daughter-in-law, mother-in-law, brother's wife, uncle's wife, along with other such abominable things which are abhorred by Christian law."[154]

More information on close-kin marriage among Iranian Christians is provided by the East Syrian tradition of canon law. Of particular importance are regulations connected with the catholicos Mār Abā I, who systematically contested this practice.[155] Mār Abā's polemic against *xwēdōdah* in his tractate on the laws of marriage and sexual intercourse has already been mentioned. Moreover, one of the ordinances of the council, which he convened in the year 544, is explicitly directed against various forms of close-kin marriage that were supposedly practiced by at least some members of the community.[156] To these should be added the testimony of the *Life of Mār Abā*, where we find the story of a dispute between the catholicos and the *mowbedān-mowbed* of the district of Bēt Aramāyē that revolves around the issue of close-kin marriage. It is noteworthy that during this exchange, the Zoroastrian priest asks Mār Abā to allow those of his flock who had been joined in *xwēdōdah* marriage before having converted to Christianity to remain in this state. The catholicos, however, instantly rejects this compromise.[157]

Analyzing the material connected with Mār Abā, Manfred Hutter comes to the conclusion that close-kin marriage "was a well-known practice during the middle of the 6th century also among Iranian members of the Church of the East."[158] According to him, it was one of the distinguishing features of a syncretistic "Zoroastrianized" version of Christianity, whose adherents strove

---

154 ܘܡܬܪܚܩܝܢ ... ܡܢ ܬܫܡܫܬܐ ܐܝܟ ܕܒܐܡܐ ܘܒܪܬܐ ܘܟܠܬܐ ܘܚܡܬܐ ܘܐܢܬܬ ܐܚܐ ܘܐܢܬܬ ܕܕܐ ܥܡ ܫܪܟܐ ܕܣܢܝܬܐ ܕܕܐܝܟ ܗܠܝܢ ܕܣܢܝܢ ܒܢܡܘܣܐ ܕܟܪܣܛܝܢܘܬܐ; ed. Kaufhold 1976, p. 177; trans. Brock 2009, p. 58.
155 On Mār Abā's polemic against *xwēdōdah*, see Hutter 2003; Panaino 2008.
156 Ed. Chabot 1902, pp. 82–83 [Syr.], 335–336 [trans.]. This prohibition was reaffirmed at the Council of Išoyahb I (585); ed. Chabot 1902, pp. 149–150 [Syr.], 410–411 [trans.]. For the Islamic period, cf. canons ##19, 25 of the Nestorian patriarch Timothy I (780–823); ed. Sachau 1907–1914, v. 2, pp. 72–73, 75.
157 Ed. Bedjan 1895, pp. 235–236; trans. Braun 1915, pp. 200–202.
158 Hutter 2003, p. 172.

to combine some native Iranian practices with the regulations of their new faith. While discussing the possible reasons for the popularity of *xwēdōdah* among Iranian Christians lies beyond the scope of our investigation, it should be noted here that, cultural and religious considerations aside, some people may have resorted to this option for purely economic reasons.[159]

This relative prominence of close-kin marriage as an element of the syncretism between Iranian beliefs and Christianity was not unique to Syriac Christianity. Comparable evidence comes from Armenia, another late antique Christian society that developed under the strong influence of Iranian culture.[160] Similarly to the Syriac Christian tradition, polemic against this practice became a constitutive element of Armenian Christian identity.[161] Thus, in the fourth century, we find Nersēs the Great exhorting Armenian nobles "to refrain from incestuous marriages with close family relations within the clan, especially from intimacy with daughters-in-law or anything of the kind, as had once been [the custom]."[162] Later, this custom was formally condemned at the Council of Shahapivan, which was held in the year 444.[163]

At the same time, promotion of *xwēdōdah* among already Christianized Armenians formed part of the Sasanians' efforts to bring them back under the Iranian sphere of influence. Some evidence on this is provided by Ełišē Vardapet in the *History of Vardan*, where, among other things, he describes the measures the Sasanians imposed on the Christian Armenians after their army was defeated in June 451. Some of these measures were aimed at bringing the matrimonial customs of the Armenian nobility into accordance with Zoroastrian norms, including that "Daughters shall be [wives] for fathers, and sisters for brothers. Mothers shall not withdraw from sons, and grandchildren shall ascend the couch of grandparents."[164]

As the first-century Greek epigraphic material from the Macedonian settlers of Dura-Europos suggests, the spread of close-kin marriage among the non-Iranian population of the Near East could be traced back well into the pre-Sasanian period.[165] Moreover, from the third century on, references to this

---

159   Thus a too-small inheritance might induce a man to marry his mother or sister. On this, see Frandsen 2009, p. 83, who relies on the testimony of Išoʿboxt, an eighth-century East Syrian jurist.
160   On this, see Garsoïan 1976; Russell 1987.
161   See Russell 1987, pp. 94–95.
162   Pseudo-Faustus of Byzantium, *Epic Histories* 4.4; trans. Garsoïan 1989, p. 114. Cf. also Moses of Khoren, *Hist.* 3.20; trans. Thomson 1978, p. 275.
163   Canon #13; ed. Akinian 1949, pp. 156–159.
164   *Hist.* 2; trans. Thomson 1982, pp. 103–104.
165   See Cumont 1924.

practice begin to appear in the Roman legal tradition. Thus, a prohibition of incest is found in the edict of Diocletian that was issued at Damascus in the year 296.[166] Later, we find one of the laws promulgated by Emperor Justinian (r. 527–565) and preserved in the *Corpus Iuris Civilis* to be aimed against the "unlawful marriages" (γάμοις ἀθεμίτοις) practiced in the provinces of Mesopotamia and Osrhoene.[167] Justinian's successor, Justin II (r. 565–578), also issued a law against the same practice in the same regions.[168] As has been convincingly argued by several scholars, these laws were promulgated in order to eradicate the custom of close-kin marriages that was apparently practiced throughout the Eastern provinces of the late Roman empire.[169]

All this evidence testifies that during late antiquity, close-kin marriage was practiced among some of the Iranian converts to Christianity as well as among the non-Iranian population of those regions that fell within the sphere of direct or indirect influence from the Persian empire. The testimony of Syriac and Armenian sources demonstrates that the renunciation of this practice became an important marker of Christian identity in late Sasanian Iran. The upsurge of such polemics may be related to the fact that from the fifth century on, more and more ethnic Iranians began to convert to Christianity, bringing with them Zoroastrian religious and cultural baggage. Consequently, it seems warranted to suggest that CT's polemic against *xwēdōdah* should be considered not merely as an expression of its author's ethnographical curiosity, but as an attempt to handle the practical issue of confronting this aspect of Iranian culture that was apparently relevant for his community.

1.4   *Astrology*

The discussion of Zoroastrian close-kin marriage is followed by a complementary narrative that likewise purports to deal with Persian customs and features the figure of Ardashir (CT 27.17–22):

> And this Ardashir the Magian first began to deal with the signs of the Zodiac, and fortunes, and fate, and misfortunes, and palpitations, as well as with all the other aspects of Chaldeanism. And all this learning is the error of demons, and those who exercise it shall receive the punishment of judgement, together with the demons. However, because this

---

166   *Mosaicarum et Romanarum legum collatio* 6.4; ed. Hyamson 1913, pp. 86–89.
167   *Novel* 154; ed. Schoell & Kroll 1895, pp. 729–730.
168   *Novel* 3; ed. von Lingenthal 1857, pp. 8–9.
169   See Chadwick 1979; Lee 1988.

> revelation of Nimrod was taught to him by Yonṭon, none of the orthodox doctors have rejected it, since even they have practiced it. For the Persians call it "revelation" and the Romans "astronomy." But that astrology, which the Magians cling to, comes from sorcery and from the deceitful learning. There are, however, some who say that fortune and misfortunes and fate do truly exist, but they are in error.[170]

The main focus of this account is on the practice of astrology, its origins, and its possible relevance for Christians. Similarly to the case of close-kin marriage, CT's author ascribes the invention of this branch of knowledge to the Zoroastrian priest Ardashir. The author's attitude to this practice is likewise expressly negative, as he draws a close connection between it and the activity of demonic powers. In order to determine how this narrative is related to our author's Iranian context, I will analyze some of its elements from a source-critical angle and compare it to the centuries-old tradition of Christian polemic against astrology.

In CT 27.17–22, the author brings together a number of concepts and practices relevant to the art of prognostication, all of which, for him, fall into the broad category of "Chaldeanism" (*kaldāyutā*). As to the specific kinds of divination he denounces, it is possible to single out two practices—astrology, which regards human life to be influenced by the "signs of the Zodiac" (*malwāšē*), and palmomancy, a mode of prognostication that derives meaning from observation of "palpitations" (*rpāpē*), i.e. involuntary movements of the human body.[171]

Some of the divinatory practices listed in CT 27.17 are discussed earlier, in CT 26.1–10, where the author advances an evolved narrative that explains the origins of idolatry and human sacrifice. According to this story, these reprehensible practices began in the days of Abraham's father Terah in the city of Ur due to Satan's machinations. After the death of a certain rich citizen of this city, his son erected a golden statue on his father's grave. Satan then entered

170 Or^A: ܘܗܘ ܗܢܐ ܐܪܕܫܝܪ ܟܘܡܪܐ ܚܙܐ، ܠܗܘܢ ܡܬܚܙܝܢ ܒܡܠܘ̈ܫܐ ܘܒܚܕ̈ܪܐ ܘܒܫܘܠܩ̈ܐ ܘܒܦܓ̈ܥܐ ܘܒܪ̈ܦܦܐ ܘܒܢܝܫܐ ܗܕܐ ܘܒܗܠܝܢ ܟܠܗܝܢ ܕܟܠܕܝܘܬܐ. ܘܗܢܐ ܟܠܗ ܝܘܠܦܢܐ ܕܛܥܝ̈ܢ ܕܕܘ̈ܝܐ ܐܢܘܢ، ܘܐܝܠܝܢ ܕܦܠܚܝܢ ܠܗ ܒܗ ܕܝܘܐ ܡܫܡܠܝܢ ܡܣܡܟ ܒܢ̈ܝܐ ܕܕܝܢܐ. ܗܢܐ ܕܝܢ ܓܠܝܢܐ ܕܢܡܪܘܕ ܡܛܠ ܕܝܘܢܛܘܢ ܐܠܦܗ ܠܢܡܪܘܕ ܠܐ ܐܢܫ ܡܢ ܡ̈ܠܦܢܐ ܬܪ̈ܝܨܝ ܫܘܒܚܐ ܐܣܠܝܘܗ. ܡܛܠ ܕܐܦ ܗ̈ܢܘܢ ܐܬܕܒܪܘ ܒܗ. ܦܪ̈ܣܝܐ ܕܝܢ ܡܩܪܝܢ ܠܗ ܓܠܝܢܐ. ܘܪ̈ܗܘܡܝܐ ܐܣܛܪܘܢܘܡܝܐ. ܗܝ ܕܝܢ ܕܐܚܝܕܝܢ ܗܘܘ ܡܓܘ̈ܫܐ ܐܣܛܪܘܠܘܓܝܐ ܡܢ ܐܢܘܢ ܕܚܪܫܘܬܐ ܘܕܝܘܠܦܢܐ ܕܛܥܝܝ. ܐܝܬ ܕܝܢ ܕܐܡܪܝܢ ܕܓܕܐ ܠܗ ܐܝܬ ܒܝ̈ܫܐ ܘܦܓ̈ܥܐ ܘܫܠܩܐ. ܘܗܠܝܢ ܛܥܝܢ.

171 On this practice, see Hopfner 1949. On its occurence in the Sasanian context, see the evidence of later Arabic sources, discussed by Inostrantsev 1907, pp. 50–52. For medieval Syriac treatises on palmomancy, see Furlani 1917.

this statue and persuaded the man to sacrifice his own child to him. As the man did so and bathed in his son's blood, Satan left the statue, entered him, and thus "taught him sorcery, and incantation, and oracles, and Chaldeanism, and fortunes, and misfortunes, and fate."[172] It should be noted, however, that while this narrative offers a general etiological explanation for pagan divination, it does not mention astrology, which appears as a distinctive practice for the first time in CT 26.1–10.

The abstract noun "Chaldeanism," which, according to CT, includes the practice of astrology, is derived from the ethnonym "Chaldean" (*kaldāyā*), which in its turn goes back to the Akkadian *kaldu*, used to designate both a people and a land. Originally, it referred to the tribal groups of West Semitic origin that were closely involved in Babylonian social and political life and active in southern Mesopotamia during the first half of the millennium BCE. Having originated as an ethnonym, in the course of time the noun "Chaldean" acquired a broader range of meanings. Thus, the association of Chaldeans with the art of prognostication, especially astrology, became commonplace in the Greco-Roman tradition, where the terms "Chaldean" and "Babylonian" seem to be virtually synonymous.[173] In fact, from around the mid-second century BCE, the ethnonym "Chaldean" was often used by classical authors as a synonym for astrologers, irrespective of their ethnic origin.[174] This Greco-Roman notion of Chaldeans, strengthened by their biblical image as a group of prognostication specialists summoned by the Babylonian king Nebuchadnezzar (Daniel 2:2–10, 4:7, 5:7–11), was adopted and further developed by Jewish and Christian authors, including Syriac-speaking ones.[175]

Although the Chaldeans' priority as astrologers par excellence was occasionally disputed, and some gave this honor to the Egyptians,[176] the reputation of Babylonia-Mesopotamia as the birthplace of astronomy and the art of divination, including astrology, remained probably the most popular view during Greco-Roman and Christian antiquity. Needless to say, this belief does not contradict the modern scholarly consensus on the origins of scientific astronomy

---

172 Or^A: ܡܠܟܐ ܘܚܪܫܐ ܘܐܘܕܥܗ ܩܨܡܐ ܘܟܠܕܝܘܬܐ ܘܓܕܐ ܘܒܝܫܬܐ ܘܚܠܩܐ.
173 Cf. Strabo, *Geogr.* 16.1.6; Cicero, *De div.* 1.2, 91; Diogenes Laertius, *Vit.* 1.6. On the history of this ethnonym, see Dandamaeva 1999–2000; Wong 1992.
174 For examples, see Liddell & Scott 1996, p. 1971.
175 Cf. *Jubilees* 1:8; Philo of Alexandria, *De Abr.* 69; *Quaest. in Gen.* 3.1; Josephus, *Ant.* 1.138; 10.195–203, 234–235; *Sybilline Oracles* 3.226–230; Hippolytus, *Ref.* 4.1.1–13; Origen, *C. Cels.* 6.80; Pseudo-Clementines, *Rec.* 9.22. For Syriac sources, see Payne Smith 1879–1901, v. 1, col. 1745.
176 Cf. Diodorus Siculus, *Bib.* 1.50.1, 81.6. For additional references and discussion, see van der Horst 2002, pp. 140–143.

and astral prognostication in ancient Mesopotamia.[177] Thus, the earliest evidence that mentions astronomical phenomena in the context of divination comes from Sumerian literature produced in the late third millennium and is connected with Gudea, the ruler of Lagash.[178]

The Chaldeans' high prestige as astrologers found natural expression in the opinion that they had invented the practice.[179] CT's author, however, does not follow this popular view and instead offers his own peculiar theory of the origins of divination. While some of the structural elements of the narrative of the invention of astrology in CT 27.17–22 do have parallels in earlier classical and Christian sources, as a whole it has no precedents.

By ascribing the discovery of astrology to the Zoroastrian priest Ardashir, CT's author shifts the focus from the Chaldeans to the Persians as the inventors of this branch of prognostication. The fact that the Persians—who adopted many local practices, including the science of omens, after the Achaemenids took over the Near East—were known in antiquity for being practitioners of divination might have contributed to this shift. For instance, in his book *On Divination*, Cicero reports that "among the Persians augury and divination are practiced by the Magi."[180] Among Christian authors, Agathias of Myrina, in his description of Zoroastrian fire-worship, says of the Magians that by gazing into this element, "they perform their secret rites and scrutinize the course of future events," while suggesting that "they took over this practice from the Chaldaeans or some other people."[181]

The association of astrology with Persians in CT may also reflect the influence of Greco-Roman traditions of ethnography, where "Chaldeans" were often confused with "Persians" as a result of geographical proximity.[182] This association between Persians and Chaldeans is also found in Syriac sources. Thus, John bar Penkāyē describes the Persian Magians as descendants of Chaldeans, who "attribute the entire governance of God to the stars and signs of the Zodiac."[183]

---

177 For a general introduction to Mesopotamian prognostication and astrology, see Maul 2007; Rochberg 2004; Hunger & Pingree 1999.
178 See Rochberg 2004, p. 64.
179 Cf. Chaeremon *apud* Michael Psellus; ed. van der Horst 1984, pp. 8–13; Origen, *C. Cels.* 6.80.
180 *De div.* 1.91; trans. Wardle 2006, p. 75.
181 *Hist.* 2.25.1–2; ed. Keydell 1967, p. 73; trans. Frendo 1975, p. 59.
182 Cf. Diogenes Laertius, *Vit.* 9.35; Pseudo-Nonnus, *Invect.* 1.70; PG 36, col. 1021. See Kingsley 1995, pp. 200–203.
183 *Chron.* 9: ܟܠܗ ܕܐܠܗܐ ܡܕܒܪܢܘܬܗ ܟܠܗ ܘܠܡܘܙܠܬܐ ܠܟܘܟܒܐ ܕܝܗܒܝܢ; ed. Furman 2011, p. 59.

The most remarkable aspect of CT's account of the origins of astrology, however, is its attribution to Ardashir the Magian. There were different opinions among ancient writers regarding the precise moment in the history of the human race when this practice came into existence, and the honor of its invention was given to a wide range of figures.

In classical sources, the discovery of astronomy/astrology is sometimes ascribed to the Greek mythological hero Atlas, the legendary king of Mauretania, although alternative opinions on the subject were also expressed.[184] Thus, Pliny the Elder (1st c.) states that the science of astronomy was discovered by the Assyrian king Belus, who ruled in Babylon.[185]

Another influential Greco-Roman view on the origins of astronomy/astrology connected their discovery with the name of Zoroaster. In the abridgment of the universal history of the Roman historian Pompeius Trogus (1st BCE) by Junianus Justin, Zoroaster is said to be "the first that invented magic arts, and to have investigated, with great attention, the origin of the world and the motions of the stars."[186] This notion had gained popularity among Christian writers as well. The author of Pseudo-Nonnus' *Scholia* says of astronomy that it was first discovered by "the Babylonians through Zoroaster."[187] Procopius of Gaza refers to the opinion of certain "Greeks" according to whom it was Zoroaster who "had discovered astrology" (ἐξεῦρεν ἀστρολογίαν).[188]

This association of Zoroaster with astronomy/astrology is hardly surprising given the aforementioned confusion between Chaldeans and Persians. Sometimes, even Zoroaster himself was characterized as "Chaldean." Hippolytus of Rome transmits a testimony on Pythagoras by certain Aristoxenus, according to whom the legendary philosopher had once visited "Zaratas the Chaldean" (Ζαράταν τὸν Χαλδαῖον), who explained his dualistic doctrine to him.[189] A similar idea is expressed in Pseudo-Nonnus' *Scholia*, where it is stated that the movements of the heavens and their influence on humans had been recognized by "the Chaldeans, first—by Zoroaster and after him—by Ostanes."[190] It should

---

184 Cf. Herodorus of Heracleia, #31, frg. 13; ed. Jacoby 1923–1958, v. 1, p. 218; Xenagorus of Heracleia, #240, frg. 32; Ibid., v. 2B, p. 1010; Dionysius Scytobrachion, #32, frg. 7; Ibid., v. 1, p. 237; Diodorus Siculus, *Bib.* 2.60.2; 4.27.5; Pseudo-Eupolemus, *apud* Eusebius, *Praep. ev.* 9.17.9.
185 *Hist. nat.* 6.122; ed. Rackham et alii 1938–1962, v. 2, pp. 430–431.
186 *Epit.* 1.1.9: *primus dicitur artes magicas invenisse et mundi principia siderumque motus diligentissime spectasse*; ed. Rühl & Seel 1935, p. 4; trans. Watson 1853, p. 4.
187 *Invect.* 1.70: Τὴν δὲ ἀστρονομίαν λέγονται πρῶτοι εὑρηκέναι Βαβυλώνιοι διὰ Ζοροάστρου; PG 36, col. 1021. For the Syriac version of this text, see Brock 1971, pp. 253 [Syr.], 115 [trans.].
188 *Comm. in Gen.* 11; PG 87.1, col. 312.
189 *Ref.* 1.2.12; ed. Marcovich 1986, p. 60.
190 *In Epiph.* 16; ed. Brock 1971, p. 169; for the Syriac version, see Ibid., pp. 187 [Syr.], 67 [trans.].

also be noted that in the rich corpus of pseudepigraphic Zoroastrian writings that were composed in Greek and circulated under the names of Zoroaster and Ostanus, the former was primarily associated with astrological lore.[191]

Turning to Jewish and Christian authors, there are a number of opinions on the origins of astronomy/astrology, whose main distinction from the classical sources is that they ascribe this honor to various figures from the Hebrew Bible. One of the earliest traditions of this sort claims that it was invented by Enoch. This notion is expressed, among others, by the author of *Jubilees* (4:17), who says of the patriarch that he "was the first of mankind ... who wrote down in a book the signs of the sky in accord with the fixed patterns of each of their months."[192]

Besides Enoch, the discovery of astronomy/astrology was associated with several other biblical figures. For instance, according to Josephus, "the science of the heavenly bodies and their orderly array" was discovered by Seth's progeny.[193] In some circles, the tradition of Enoch as the inventor of astronomy had influenced the image of Seth as the first scribe, and so the discovery of this science was ascribed to the latter.[194] In the fourth century, Epiphanius of Salamis blames Nimrod for being the originator of "wrong doctrine, astrology (ἀστρολογίας) and magic," while rejecting the opinion of those who identify him with Zoroaster.[195] Later, Procopius of Gaza mentions the opinion of some unspecified "others" according to whom astrology had been invented by Arphaxad.[196] The seventh-century historian John of Antioch, relying on the authority of Josephus, says of Cainan that "after the Flood he wrote a book of astronomy, having found the names of the stars engraved on a stone slab."[197]

As to the native Zoroastrian sources, there are not many references to the origins of astronomy/astrology in the surviving Pahlavi corpus. One such tradition claims that astrology was invented by a certain Babel, who was active during the reign of the legendary Iranian monarch Yima/Jamšīd. The Middle Persian *Provincial Capitals of Ērānšahr* relates that Bābēl, who built the city of Babylon during the reign of Yima, "bound the planet Mercury there and he showed the seven planets and the twelve constellations and the eighth portions

---

191 See Boyce & Grenet 1991, pp. 493–495.
192 Ed. VanderKam 1989, p. 26 [trans.]. Cf. also *1 Enoch* 72:1; Pseudo-Eupolemus *apud* Eusebius, *Praep. ev.* 9.17.8.
193 *Ant.* 1.69–71; ed. Thackeray 1926–1965, v. 4, pp. 32–33.
194 Cf. John Malalas, *Chron.* 1.1. On this development, see Klijn 1977, pp. 49–51.
195 *Panar.* 1.3.2–3; ed. Holl 1915–1933, v. 1, p. 177; trans. Williams, F. 2009, p. 18.
196 *Comm. in Gen.* 11; PG 87.1, col. 312.
197 Καϊνάν, ὅστις μετὰ τὸν κατακλυσμὸν συνεγράψατο τὴν ἀστρονομίαν, εὑρηκὼς τὰς τῶν ἄστρων ὀνομασίας ἐν πλακὶ λιθίνῃ γεγλυμμένας, ὡς Ἰώσηπος συνεγράψατο; ed. Roberto 2005, pp. 6–7.

by sorcery to the Sun and to those below (mankind)."[198] A very similar tradition ascribed to the Persian astronomer Ibn Nawbakht (ob. 815) is transmitted by the tenth-century Arab scholar Ibn al-Nadīm, according to whom people learned about "the positions of the heavenly bodies and their routes, degrees, minutes, and stations, both high and low, and with their courses and all of their directions" during "the period of Jam ibn Awijhān, the king."[199]

This overview demonstrates the great variety of opinions about the origins of astrology in antiquity. CT's author, however, deliberately stays away from all these options and comes up with his own theory. By associating astrology with the Zoroastrian priest Ardashir, he resorts to the same polemical strategy that he employed in the previously discussed case of close-kin marriage. The connection between astrology and Ardashir is meant to enhance the author's general claims about the demonic etiology of this branch of knowledge. Aiming to denounce astrology, in CT 27.17–22 he combines two previously introduced polemical themes—the general condemnation of divinatory practices as Satanic inventions from CT 26.1–10 and the negative image of Ardashir as the inventor of reprehensible Persian customs from CT 27.12–16.

In proposing a demonic etiology for astrology, CT's author follows a well-trodden path. The association of astrology with demonic forces was a recurrent motif in the rich tradition of Christian condemnation of this practice, which was often denounced in the context of polemic against astrolatry or defense of free will.[200] The roots of this particular motif could be traced back to ancient Jewish works such as 1 Enoch 8:3, which reports that humans were taught astrology by the fallen angels Baraqiel, Kokabel, and Tamiel.[201] The first Syrian Christian author to use it was Tatian, writing in the second century. Waging an attack against the pagan concept of fatalism, this apologist claims that humanity was subjected to the necessity of fate through the agency of demons, who "showed men a chart of the constellations."[202] Later, the author of the Pseudo-Clementines informs us that astrologers, who rely on the notion of climacteries, are in fact deceived by demons.[203]

---

198   u-š tīr abāxtar ānōh be bast ud mārīg [ī] haft [ud] dwāzdah ī axtarān ud abāxtarān [ud] haštom bahrag pad jādūgīh ō mihr ud azērīg be nimūd; ed. Daryaee 2002, pp. 14 [text], 18 [trans.].
199   Fihrist 7.1; ed. Flügel 1871–1872, p. 238; trans. Dodge 1970, v. 2, p. 572.
200   On this tradition, see Hegedus 2007, esp. pp. 125–137 on the motif of the demonic origins of astrology.
201   Ed. Knibb 1978, v. 2, pp. 82–83 [trans.].
202   Orat. 8.1; ed. Whittaker 1982, pp. 14–15.
203   Rec. 9.12.2–3; ed. Rehm & Strecker 1994, p. 264. Cf. also Severus of Antioch, Hom. 109; ed. Brière 1943, pp. 774–775.

There is an additional aspect of CT's author's condemnation of astrology that deserves to be explicated. It is noteworthy that in his denunciation, our author takes care to draw a clear distinction between this reprehensible practice and the legitimate science of astronomy, resorting to using two different terms in order to distinguish the two branches of knowledge dealing with heavenly phenomena. Moreover, in order to legitimate astronomy, he provides it with an appropriate etiology in CT 27.11, claiming that it originated not from Ardashir, but from Nimrod, to whom it had been communicated by Yonṭon.

While approaching this polemically charged dichotomy between "astronomy" and "astrology," it should be recalled that whereas we draw a sharp distinction between the two, in antiquity the latter was seen as a mere extension of the former, and the terms were more or less synonymous up until the late classical period.[204] Nevertheless, first attempts to draw a demarcation line between these branches of knowledge can already be found in the works of ancient authors, pagan as well as Christian.

An explicit and scientific distinction between astronomy and astrology appears in the works of the second-century Egyptian scientist Claudius Ptolemy. Ptolemy distinguishes between astronomy and astrology as two different methods of prognostication through ἀστρονομία and treats these two branches of knowledge in two separate works, astronomy in *Almagest* and astrology in *Tetrabiblos*. For Ptolemy, astronomy proper inquires into "the aspects of the movements of sun, moon, and stars in relation to each other and to the earth," while the subject of astrology is "the changes which they (i.e. the movements) bring about in that which they surround."[205] This distinction is Aristotelian insofar as astrology is associated with material things in the sublunar realm, where unpredictable changes occur constantly, while the planets and stars, with their regular and therefore predictable motions, are the subject of astronomy.[206] It should be stressed that although in this system astrology is considered to be somewhat inferior to astronomy because it is less predictable and less certain, Ptolemy acknowledges it as a legitimate and even beneficial practice, defending it from those colleagues who argue against it.[207]

As the example of Ptolemy's apologetic efforts on behalf of astrology shows, condemnation of this practice was hardly a Jewish or Christian prerogative. From the second century BCE on, astrology begins to come under attack

---

204   On the Greek terms ἀστρονομία and ἀστρολογία, see Hübner 1989.
205   *Tetrab.* 1.1; ed. Robbins 1940, pp. 2–3. For an earlier, less articulated expression of this distinction, see Cicero. *De div.* 1.2.
206   Cf. *Tetrab.* 1.2; ed. Robbins 1940, pp. 4–9.
207   Cf. *Tetrab.* 1.2–3; ed. Robbins 1940, pp. 12–33.

from philosophers who attempted to undermine the legitimacy that this science received within the Greek philosophical tradition as a result of the influence of Platonic astral theology and Stoic determinism and pantheism.[208] Occasionally, the distinction between astronomy and astrology is evoked in the context of philosophical denunciations of the latter.

For instance, the late second-century Skeptic philosopher Sextus Empiricus devoted the entire fifth book of his tractate *Against the Mathematicians* to the refutation of astrology. He begins his attack on astrology by clearly distinguishing it from the science of astronomy proper.[209] In what follows, astrology is denied any validity on the grounds of its inability to establish the time of a man's conception or birth with sufficient exactness, as well as because of the lack of precision in human observance of stellar constellations. As a result, he accuses astrologers of being charlatans and comes to the conclusion that there is absolutely no reason to suggest that "life is ordered according to the motions of the stars."[210]

The practice of differentiating astronomy from astrology was continued and further developed in the Christian tradition of anti-astrological polemic from late antiquity on. We find it at work in a passage of the *Hexaemeron* by Basil of Caesarea, where he distinguishes between those who practice legitimate observation of the signs provided by heavenly bodies and those who "overstep the borders" and engage in the "vain science" of astrology, according to which human lives depend on the motion of the stars and planets.[211] In the sixth century, Severus of Antioch explains the difference between the practice of "astronomy" (*'asṭrānāmiya'*), "the true and established science of stars" that directs the minds of those who observe the stars' beauty to their creator, and that of the "vain astrologers" (*'asṭrālāgu sriqē*) who, in relying on the misleading motion of the stars, devise "certain fate and compulsory lot" and thus drive people away from divine providence.[212] Thus, by making a distinction between the two manners of studying the stars, one legitimate and one prohibited, CT's author follows an established motif from the repertoire of Christian polemic against astrology.

Having examined CT's author's relationship to the earlier tradition of Christian discourse on astrology, a question should be asked as to his motives in forging

---

208 On this, see Long 1982.
209 *Adv. math.* 5.1–2; ed. Bury 1933–1949, v. 4, pp. 322–323.
210 *Adv. math.* 5.87, 95; ed. Bury 1933–1949, v. 4, pp. 360–361, 364–365.
211 *Hexaem.* 6.4–5; ed. Giet 1968, pp. 346–349.
212 *Hom.* 9.8; ed. Brière et alii 1976, p. 340.

his own version of the origins of this practice. Why does he emphasize its association with Zoroastrianism, and why does he bother to differentiate between astrology and astronomy, denouncing the former and defending the latter?[213] In order to answer these questions, we shall set the depiction of astrology in CT 27.17–22 against the contemporary Iranian cultural background.

The ancient Mesopotamian tradition of science and prognostication began to penetrate Iran as early as the Achaemenid period. However, it was during late antiquity that the Iranian tradition of astronomy and astrology reached its full development, primarily due to the efforts of Sasanian scholars, who mastered both the Greco-Roman and the Indian sciences of the heavens and accommodated them with the traditional Zoroastrian world-view.[214] Similarly to the classical tradition, in ancient Iranian culture astronomy and astrology were considered to form one science, which was termed "star-telling" (*star-gōwišnīh*).[215] This science inquires both into the "motion" (*rawišn*) of the celestial bodies, i.e. astronomy, and into their "work and function" (*kār ud rāyēnišn*), i.e. astrology.[216]

Far from being a purely theoretical enterprise, the Iranians' interest in the luminary bodies, considered to be living divinities, was deeply grounded in the belief that all human affairs are affected by them, both positively and negatively. This notion is expressed, for example, by the author of *Dādestān ī Mēnōg ī Xrad*, who states that "every good and evil that occurs to men, and also the remaining creatures, occurs through the Seven planets and the Twelve constellations" (8.17–21).[217] As he explains further, this influence is determined by the fact that these two groups of heavenly bodies participate in the ongoing struggle between good and evil. The seven planets fight on the side of Ahriman and act as mediators of his malevolent conspiracy against humanity, while the twelve signs of the Zodiac are under the command of Ohrmazd and thus protect the well-being of his creatures.[218]

---

213 This choice is not as obvious as one might think at first. There are enough examples of both these sciences being condemned by Christian authors. For instance, in the *Testament of Our Lord*, a Greek apocryphal work translated into Syriac by Jacob of Edessa, "astronomy" (*nāmusāyut kawkbē*) is condemned along with "astrology" (*mmallut kawkbē*) as belonging to "the weapons of the devil," such as magic, witchcraft, idolatry etc.; ed. Vööbus 1975–1976, v. 1, pp. 35 [Syr.], 53 [trans.].
214 For a general review of astrology in pre-Islamic Iran, see Brunner 1987; Pingree 1989; Raffaelli 2001, esp. pp. 13–49; Panaino 2015.
215 *Dēnkard* 4; ed. Madan 1911, v. 1, p. 412.
216 *Dādestān ī Mēnōg ī Xrad* 49.2–3; ed. West 1871, v. 1, pp. 47 [text], 174–175 [trans.].
217 Ed. West 1871, v. 1, pp. 17 [text], 142–143 [trans.].
218 Cf. also Iranian *Bundahišn* 5.4–5, 5a.3–9, 5b.12–13. On this aspect of Zoroastrian mythology, see Zaehner 1955, pp. 158–163.

CATEGORIZING THE IRANIAN "OTHER"

The prominent place of astrology in Iranian culture during late antiquity is reflected in how deeply this practice permeated the social fabric of the Sasanian empire. Thus, astrological training was considered to be a part of the curriculum in the education of the Iranian nobility. For instance, the young aristocrat hero of the Middle Persian story *King Khosrow and His Page*, while enumerating before the king of kings his credentials, such as his excellent religious and secular education, mastery of horse-riding, martial prowess, etc., boastfully claims:

> And into matters pertaining to the stars and planets (*stāragān ud abāxtarān*) I have so penetrated that those in this profession are, in comparison with me, something mean.[219]

Among the most visible expressions of the importance ascribed to astrology in late ancient Iran was the office of court astrologers, to whose services Sasanian monarchs would habitually resort. The *Testament of Ardašīr*, presumably a late Sasanian composition preserved in Arabic, mentions "astrologers" (*al-munaǧǧimūn*) as comprising, together with scribes and physicians, the third of the four main classes into which Sasanian society was divided.[220] According to al-Ṭabarī's *History*, King Khosrow II Parvīz employed at his court "360 men who were prognosticators, these being learned scholars, including soothsayers, magicians, and astrologers."[221] As a rule, Sasanian kings would consult astrologers before making important political or military decisions. The fifth-century Armenian *History* ascribed to Faustus of Byzantium relates that Shapur II summoned astrologers along with other divination specialists to help him decide on the correct course of action towards the Armenian king Arshak.[222] It should also be noted that Persian astrologers were involved in large-scale intellectual projects, such as the translation of Greek and Indian astrological compositions into Pahlavi, as well as the production of original works such as *Wizīdag*, a commentary on Vettius Valens' *Anthologiae*, or the professional astrological compendiums, known as *Zāyč ī šahryārān*.[223] Unfortunately, none of these Pahlavi works has survived.

---

219 Ed. Monchi-Zadeh 1982, p. 65, §14.
220 Ed. Grignaschi 1966, pp. 54 [Arab.], 74 [trans.].
221 Ed. de Goeje et alii 1879–1901, v. I.2, p. 1010; trans. Bosworth 1999, p. 331.
222 *Epic Histories* 4.54; trans. Garsoïan 1989, pp. 170–171. A similar story about Shapur II is found in the Syriac *Romance of Julian* (ed. Sokoloff 2016, pp. 382–385), where the king summons the Magi for such purposes.
223 See Brunner 1987.

Given the high prestige of astrology in Iranian culture under the Sasanians, it is hardly surprising that some of their Christian subjects engaged in it as well. This is especially relevant for those Christians who belonged to the higher ranks of society and thus were more susceptible to the influence of Iranian culture. In the *Chronicle of Seert*, we hear about the court astrologer (*munaǧǧim*) of King Zamasp (r. 496–499), an East Syrian Christian named Moses, who, when the time came to choose a successor to Akak, the current catholicos, interceded with the king on behalf of the Christian community.[224] For the later period, the author of the *Chronicle of Khuzistan* says of Gabriel bar Rūfīn, the East Syrian metropolitan of Nisibis until the year 596, when he was succeeded by Gregory of Kashkar, that he had been forcibly demoted from his see on account of being "greatly immersed in the course of the stars and horoscope."[225] In the first decade of the seventh century, the *Chronicle of Seert* mentions a certain Mār Abā from Kashkar, a personal physician and astrologer of Khosrow II.[226]

The case of Gabriel bar Rūfīn shows that astrology was a matter of concern for Syriac Christian elites in late ancient Iran during the sixth century. This concern, however, was hardly a new development by the time CT was composed. Its roots go back to the earliest period in the history of Christianity in Syria–Mesopotamia, the region in which the ancient Near Eastern astral cults were thriving.[227] Accordingly, polemic against astrology became one of the general lines of argument in the Christian struggle against "paganism" in this area.[228] More fuel was added to the fire of anti-astrological polemic by the fact that astrological speculations figured prominently in the doctrines of heterodox movements, such as those founded by Bardaisan and Mani, which were gaining momentum among Syriac-speaking Christians.[229] As a result of all this, criticism and condemnation of astrology are found in a wide range of Syriac Christian writings produced during late antiquity.

The polemic against astrology waged by CT's author should certainly be regarded as part of this general trend. There is, however, an additional aspect to CT's representation of astrology that could help us to understand the peculiar manner in which our author deals with this practice. This aspect comes to the fore in chapters 45 and 46, which contain a developed account of the Magi mentioned in the New Testament (Mt 2:1–12). At the core of his narrative lies

---

224 *Chron. Seert* 2.15; ed. Scher 1908–1918, v. 3, pp. 128–129.
225 ܣܓܝ ܡܛܒܥ ܗܘܐ ܒܪܗܛܐ ܕܟܘܟܒܐ ܘܕܐܣܛܪܘܠܘܓܝܐ; ed. Guidi 1903, p. 17 [Syr.].
226 *Chron. Seert* 2.80; ed. Scher 1908–1918, v. 4, pp. 521–522.
227 On the astrological component of such cults, see Green, T.M. 1992, pp. 40–43 (on Harran); Brykczyński 1975 (on Palmyra).
228 See Drijvers, H.J.W. 1982, pp. 40–41; Tubach 2008, pp. 249–253.
229 See Jones 1997.

the image of the Magi, who are said to hold expertise in the astronomical science of the "motions of the stars" which enables them "to know and understand the importance of events before they take place" (CT 45.9). The crucial function of the Magi in the overall scheme of *Heilsgeschichte* developed by CT's author is to be the keepers and interpreters of the "revelation" about the future birth of the Messiah left to his posterity by King Nimrod and to transfer the three symbolic gifts deposited by Adam in the "cave of treasures" to the newborn Jesus. It is their proficiency in astronomy that made it possible for the Magi to properly recognize the significance of the star in Matthew 2:9 and fulfill their unique role in the history of salvation.

It should be remembered that for an ancient reader of Matthew 2:1–12, this story, with its focus on the Magi and the astral phenomenon, bore strong astrological overtones. Naturally, this account would easily lend itself to a pro-astrological interpretation. This issue became a cause for concern quite early on among defenders of Christian orthodoxy, who made efforts to neutralize the story's subversive power.[230] For instance, in the fourth century, John Chrysostom wages an attack against those readers of the New Testament who referred to the star of Matthew 2:9 as "a sign that astrology (ἀστρολογίαν) may be depended on."[231]

It is, I believe, this danger of a pro-astrological reading of the Matthean story that might influence CT's author in choosing his unique strategy of denouncing astrology. We do not have to try too hard to imagine such a "misreading" of the canonical narrative of the Magi taking place in the context of late ancient Iranian culture, where astrology was not distinguished from astronomy and where some Christians did not feel constrained to pursue this line of intellectual inquiry. In order to prevent this, CT's author imports the Western dichotomy between astronomy and astrology into his discourse, thus splitting the harmonious whole of the Iranian science of "star-telling" into two diametrically opposed branches, one legitimate and one forbidden. It is telling that he found no original Syriac terms to mark this dichotomy and instead had to resort to the Greek loan-words ʾasṭrānāmiun and ʾasṭrālāgiyaʾ. The main narrative purpose of this distinction between astronomy and astrology is to dissociate the respectable figures of the Matthean Magi from any connection whatsoever to the pagan practices of divination, while at the same time preserving their ability to function as faithful interpreters of celestial phenomena.

---

230 See Riedinger 1956, pp. 130–146; Hegedus 2007, pp. 201–211.
231 *Hom. in. Matth.* 6.1; PG 57, col. 61; trans. Prevost & Riddle 1888, p. 36. Cf. also Augustine, *Serm.* 199.2, 201.1.

CT's author strengthens the negative evaluation of astrology through this polarized dichotomy still further by establishing a close connection between this practice and Zoroastrianism through the figure of Ardashir. At the same time, a complementary reversal is applied to the figures of the Matthean Magi, whom he dissociates from the Persian religion by maintaining that their true identity was that of Iranian kings and not of Zoroastrian priests.[232] As in the case of close-kin marriage, CT's author resorts to the polemical strategy of associating astrology with Zoroastrianism and demonic forces in order to discredit it as belonging to that part of Iranian culture with which, for a Christian, no compromise is apparently possible.

2 Iranian Kingship

2.1 Nimrod

The biblical information about the figure of Nimrod is rather scarce. In the only substantial account of him—in Genesis 10:8–12, where he is introduced as a descendant of Cush–Nimrod is presented as a native Babylonian monarch who was also the first ruler of the neighboring kingdom of Assyria.[233] Perhaps the most conspicuous aspect of Nimrod's portrayal in Genesis is his representation as a paragon of military and venatic prowess, conveyed through the description of the king as "a mighty warrior" (*gibbōr*) in verse 8 and as "a mighty hunter before God" (*gibbôr ṣayid lip̄nê 'ăḏōnāy*) in verse 9. Moreover, in verses 10–12, Nimrod is credited with exercising rule over several cities in the "land of Shinar," most importantly Babylon, as well as with building a number of cities in Assyria, among which Nineveh should be singled out. The original function of the figure of Nimrod in the biblical narrative is not immediately obvious to a modern reader. As has been suggested by some scholars, the author of Genesis introduced him in order to critically engage with the contemporary imperialistic Assyrian ideology.[234]

Given the elliptical character of the description of Nimrod in the Bible, it is no wonder that the enigmatic figure of the hunter-king aroused the curiosity of the ancient readers of Genesis. In the course of time, a body of exegetical

---

232 Cf. CT 45.18; 46.3–4. This aspect of the Magi's portrayal in CT is analyzed in section 2.3 below.

233 A connection between Nimrod and Assyria is also found in Micah 5:6, where the phrase the "land of Nimrod" (אֶרֶץ נִמְרֹד) is used as a synonym for this region.

234 On this aspect of the portrayal of Nimrod in the Bible, see van der Kooij 2006; Hom 2010. For the general background of this biblical figure, see Uehlinger 1999; Levin 2002.

speculations on this biblical character developed.[235] What is important for our discussion is that in all three monotheistic traditions of biblical interpretation, Nimrod is usually presented in a negative light. In exploring the ambiguity that resides in the Hebrew preposition *lipnê* that describes his relationship to God in Genesis 10:9, the possible etymological connection between his name and the Hebrew/Aramaic verb *mrd*, "to rebel," or his perceived resemblance to the "mighty men" (MT הַגִּבֹּרִים, LXX γίγαντες) of Genesis 6:4, many Jewish and Christian authors depicted Nimrod as a sinner and a villainous rebel against God.[236]

The most developed and widespread negative exegetical tradition about Nimrod presented him as the initiator of the Tower of Babel building project. Regardless of whether the biblical author intended a connection between the account of Nimrod in Genesis 10:8–12 and the story of the Tower of Babel in Genesis 11:1–9, this option was certainly explored by many ancient readers of Scripture, mostly to the detriment of the hunter-king. An example of such a reading of Genesis 10–11 comes from the works of Philo, who, while explaining the spiritual meaning of the figure of Nimrod, draws a parallel between him and the rebellious Giants and Titans of Greek mythology, as both strive for earthly things and build "walls and towers on earth against heaven."[237] Slightly later, we find Josephus presenting Nimrod as "an audacious man of doughty vigour," who incited the people against God and persuaded them to build a tower in case of another flood.[238] This exegetical motif became quite popular in the later Jewish and Christian traditions of biblical interpretation.[239]

A significant exception to this mainstream negative view of Nimrod, however, is found in late antique Syriac Christian writings which throws light on the genesis of the peculiar portrayal of this figure in CT. Before turning to it,

---

235 For a general overview of the treatment of Nimrod in Jewish and Christian traditions in antiquity, see van der Horst 1990; in addition to this, see Hayward 1992; Hahn 1988. For Muslim views of Nimrod, see Heller 1993; Schützinger 1962; Lowin 2012.
236 For Jewish sources, cf. Philo, *De gig.* 65–66; Pseudo-Philo, *Lib. ant.* 4.7; *Genesis Rabbah* 23.7, 26.4, 37.2–3, 42.4, 44.2; *Targum Neofiti* on Gen 10:9; *Targum Pseudo-Jonathan* on Gen 10:9; *Targum Chronicles* on 1 Chr 1:10; *Fragment-Targum of the Pentateuch* on Gen 10:9, ed. Klein 1980, v. 1, pp. 49, 131. For Christian sources, cf. John Chrysostom, *Hom. in Gen.* 29.30; an unidentified commentator on Gen 10:8–9 in the catena ed. Petit 1991–1996, v. 2, p. 190, #813; Augustine, *De civ. Dei* 16.3–4; Victorinus, *Comm. in Apoc.* 7.2; Prudentius, *Hamart.* 144–148.
237 *Quaest. in Gen.* 2.82; trans. Marcus 1953, v. 1, p. 173.
238 *Ant.* 1.113–115; ed. Thackeray et alii 1926–1965, v. 4, pp. 54–55.
239 For Jewish sources, cf. Pseudo-Philo, *Lib. ant.* 6.14; *b.Hullin* 89a; *b.Abodah Zarah* 53b; *Pirke de-Rabbi Eliezer* 24. For Christian sources, cf. Eusebius, *Onom.*, ed. Klostermann 1904, p. 40; Eustathius of Antioch, *Comm. in Hex.*, PG 18, col. 753; Procopius of Gaza, *Comm. in Gen.*, PG 87.1, col. 309; Augustine, *De civ. Dei* 16.4.

I would like to point out that the common negative view of Nimrod is also represented in the works of Syriac authors. An early example of this kind is provided by Aphrahat, who describes the biblical kingdom of the Babylonians as "the kingdom of the sons of boastful Nimrod."[240] Moreover, an etymological argument that Nimrod's name was derived from the noun "rebel" (*mārudā*) appears in Syriac works on biblical onomastica.[241] The image of Nimrod as the initiator of the building of the tower of Babel is likewise found in Syriac sources. It is possible that this exegetical motif developed in Syriac exegetical tradition under the influence of Western Christian sources, such as, for example, Eusebius' *Onomasticon*, the Syriac translation of which features Josephus' report of Nimrod as the leader of the tower builders.[242] This account of Nimrod's depravity enjoyed considerable popularity among Syriac writers, especially during the medieval period.[243]

At the same time, alongside these traditions, a more positive approach to the figure of Nimrod may be discovered in ancient Syriac sources. Perhaps the most manifest expression of this tendency is the propensity of several Syriac authors to dissociate Nimrod from the building of the Tower of Babel. We come across this phenomenon in Ephrem's *Commentary on Genesis*, according to which Nimrod had no part in this building project. On the contrary, he plays a positive role as the instrument of divine will in the story of the tower by scattering its builders after their languages were confused and seizing their city, i.e. Babel, for himself.[244] A less conspicuous method of dissociating Nimrod from the building of the tower was to not mention him in this context at all. This strategy finds its most exemplary expression in the homilies on the Tower of Babel by Narsai and Jacob of Serugh, neither of whom refers to Nimrod in connection with this event, although both poets do indulge in the paronomastic word-play based on the root *mrd*, "to rebel."[245]

The dissociation of Nimrod from the building of the tower was not the only exegetical strategy used by these Syriac authors in order to improve his image.

---

240   *Dem.* 5.13: ܠܡܠܟܘܬܐ ܕܒܢܝ ܢܡܪܘܕ ܫܒܗܪܢܐ; ed. Parisot 1894, col. 209; trans. Valavanolickal 2005, v. 1, p. 108.

241   Cf. the Syriac onomasticon preserved in ms. British Library, Add. 17167 (6th to 7th cc.); ed. Wutz 1915, v. 2, p. 812.

242   Ed. Timm 2005, pp. 16–17.

243   Cf. *Acts of Mār Mari* 32, ed. Harrak 2005, pp. 74–75; *Revelations and Testimonies about Our Lord's Dispensation* (c. 8th c.) *apud* Desreumaux 1995–1996, p. 138; Theodore bar Koni (8th c.), *Lib. schol.* 2.112; Cyriacus of Tagrit (9th c.), *On Divine Providence* 19.2–3; ed. Oez 2012, v. 2, pp. 200–203; Michael the Great, *Chron.* 2.2–3.

244   *Comm. in Gen.* 8.4.1–2; ed. Tonneau 1955, p. 66; trans. Mathews & Amar 1994, p. 148.

245   For Narsai's homily, see ed. Frishman 1992, pp. 69–86 [Syr.]; for Jacob's, ed. Bedjan 1905–10, v. 2, pp. 1–27.

Thus, Ephrem interprets the proverbial saying about Nimrod in Genesis 10:9 as bearing a positive meaning of blessing, as "one used to bless (*mbarāku mbarak*) a chief or a ruler by saying, 'May you be like Nimrod, a mighty hunter who was victorious in the battles of the Lord'."[246] In his turn, in the *Homily on Noah's Blessings*, Narsai emphasizes that Nimrod received "primacy and temporal kingship" (*rišānutā w-malkut zabnā*) from God and that it was God who made him "a valiant warrior."[247]

This outstanding deviation from the mainstream negative view of Nimrod stands in obvious need of explanation. Some scholars look for possible external factors that would explain this development. For instance, in his thorough review of the ancient exegetical traditions about Nimrod, Pieter van der Horst has suggested that the positive image of this biblical hero in the writings of Ephrem and some other Syriac authors should be explained by their indebtedness to Jewish sources, namely to the "fairly extensive positive Nimrod haggada" that supposedly existed in early Jewish literature.[248] However, given the scarcity and problematic nature of the sources that Van der Horst used to reconstruct this haggada, his hypothesis is hardly a viable solution.[249]

While not denying the legitimacy of such an approach to idiosyncratic exegetical traditions in principle, I believe that in this particular case the roots of the unusual positive portrayal of Nimrod in the works of Ephrem and similarly minded authors should be sought in the realm of internal Syriac cultural and theological developments. It appears that the rise of the positive image of Nimrod in Syriac Christian tradition was, to a significant degree, an expression of the phenomenon of "local patriotism," that is a marked propensity for putting additional emphasis on and giving a positive treatment of those themes or figures that are related in one way or another to an author's regional context

---

246 *Comm. in Gen.* 8.1.2; ed. Tonneau 1955, p. 65; trans. Mathews & Amar 1994, pp. 146–147.
247 Ed. Frishman 1992, pp. 61 [Syr.], 62 [trans.].
248 See van der Horst 1990, pp. 225–226.
249 Thus, the passage from Pseudo-Eupolemus transmitted by Eusebius (*Praep. ev.* 9.18.2) does not actually refer to Nimrod. A genuine example of a positive view of Nimrod in the rabbinic corpus is indeed provided by the *Targum of Pseudo-Jonathan* on Gen 10:10–12, according to which he left for Assyria before the construction of the tower began in order to avoid participating in the project. Interesting as it is, this exegetical tradition alone can hardly bear the weight of Van der Horst's thesis about existence of the "positive Nimrod haggada" in rabbinic literature. This tradition is arguably marginal, given its incongruence with the more prevalent negative view of Nimrod in this same Targum (cf. Gen 10:9, 11:28, 16:5). Moreover, its relevance for the analysis of the works of Syriac authors from late antiquity, such as Ephrem, is seriously undermined by the fact that the *Targum of Pseudo-Jonathan*, which features references to Islam, seems to be a rather late composition; on this, see Ohana 1975; Shinan 1992, pp. 193–198.

or that of his intended audience.[250] It was because this biblical figure began to be considered as a foundational figure and cultural hero by the Christians of Northern Mesopotamia that they chose to supplant the dominant negative image of him with a more positive one. The primary impetus for this development was provided by the biblical information on the close connection between Nimrod and the cities of Babylonia and Assyria (Gen 10:10–12), which were later identified with several important urban centers of Northern Mesopotamia.[251] Accordingly, it is hardly surprising to discover that each of the three Syriac authors mentioned above as examples of the positive attitude towards Nimrod was personally connected to Edessa and Nisibis, two cities that figure most prominently among the towns believed to have been founded by this hero.

The important role Nimrod played in the development of a distinctive local identity among the Syriac-speaking Christians of Mesopotamia finds an additional illustration in the appeals to him as an ancestral figure. The fact that the inhabitants of this geographical area considered themselves to be Nimrod's descendants is expressed, for instance, in the *Acts of Mār Mari*, whose author, in a rhetorical digression expressing amazement at the apostle's success in converting the peoples of the regions of Bēt Arāmāyē, Seleucia, and Ctesiphon, refers to them as "the sons of powerful Nimrod" (*bnay Nemrud ganbārā*).[252] In the hagiographical account of the life and passion of the Persian martyr Qardag, a native of the city of Arbela, we are told that the saint "was from a great people from the stock of the kingdom of the Assyrians" and that "his father was descended from the renowned lineage of the house of Nimrod."[253] The author of the *History of Karkā d-Bēt Slok* (c. 5th to 6th cc.), while describing the legendary history of the city, ascribes its foundation to the Assyrian monarch "Sardana," who was a "descendant of Nimrod" (*bar Nemrud*).[254] The East Syrian *Vita* of the seventh-century monastic leader Rabban Hormizd, a native of Shiraz who was active in Northern Mesopotamia, features a story in which Satan, after being expelled by the saint, addresses him in an apparently derogatory manner as a "follower of Nimrod" (*Nemrudāyā*).[255] To this evidence may be added examples of the personal name "Nimrod" being used among Syriac-speaking

---

250 On this phenomenon among the Jews and Christians in antiquity, see Pearce & Jones 1998; Gafni 1990; Grosby 1996.
251 On this, see section 2.1.2 below.
252 Ed. Harrak 2005, pp. 74–75.
253 ܐܒܘܗܝ، ܡܢ ܫܪܒܬܐ ܡܫܡܗܬܐ ܕܒܝܬ ܢܡܪܘܕ; ed. Abbeloos 1890, p. 12; trans. Walker 2006, p. 20.
254 Ed. Bedjan 1890–1897, v. 2, p. 507. On this, see Becker 2008, pp. 400–402.
255 Ed. Budge 1902, v. 1, p. 18 [Syr.]; v. 2.1, p. 27 [trans.].

Christians. One of the ten fifth-century Persian martyrs of Bēt Garmai, a region around the city of Kirkuk in Northern Iraq, bore this name.[256]

In his treatment of Nimrod, CT's author definitely belongs to this tradition of positive interpretations of this biblical figure. Thus, like Narsai and Jacob of Sarug, he does not mention Nimrod in connection with the Tower of Babel episode.[257] Moreover, as has been demonstrated above, he refrains from any judgmental comments regarding Nimrod when portraying him as the founder of the Zoroastrian cult of fire, and he presents him in an unquestionably positive light as the originator of the art of astronomy among the Persians.

An additional expression of CT's author's positive attitude towards Nimrod can be recognized in his treatment of his genealogy. According to the biblical account (Gen 10:6–8), Nimrod descends from Noah's son Ham, through Cush. This genealogical tradition was a matter of common scriptural knowledge among Western Christian authors.[258] It is also found in the works of Syriac writers. Thus, Aphrahat describes the Babylonians, mentioned in the book of Daniel, as "the children of Ham, the seed of Nimrod."[259] Our author, however, makes no mention of this aspect of Nimrod's scriptural background, notwithstanding his deep interest in genealogical information, as well as the considerable attention he pays to this figure. In light of what we know about the highly negative image of black people in the ancient world, including Iran,[260] this silence might be interpreted as the result of an intentional omission of the information that might tarnish Nimrod's reputation.[261] Later, we find the strategy of ameliorating Nimrod's genealogy being employed in a more ingenious manner by the Syriac author of the *Apocalypse of Pseudo-Methodius*, who traces his lineage to Shem, in direct disregard of the biblical text.[262]

---

256 Ed. Bedjan 1890–1897, v. 4, p. 184. For later examples, cf. the West Syrian patriarch Philoxenus Ignatius Nimrod (ob. 1292) in Wright, W. 1901, p. 986.
257 Cf. CT 24.12–16.
258 Cf. Eusebius, *Chron.*, ed. Aucher 1818, v. 1, p. 109; Epiphanius of Cyprus, *Panar.* 1.3.2–3; John of Nikiu, *Chron.* 5.1–4; *Chronicon Paschale*, ed. Dindorf 1832, v. 1, p. 50.
259 *Dem.* 5.10: ܒܢܝ ܚܡ ܙܪܥܗ ܕܢܡܪܘܕ; ed. Parisot 1894, col. 205; trans. Valavanolickal 2005, v. 1, p. 106. A similar view of Nimrod's descent is expressed in Narsai, *Homily on Noah's Blessings*; ed. Frishman 1992, p. 62.
260 See Snowden 1970; Byron 2002; Shapira 2002.
261 For examples of Nimrod's Hamite descent being used against him, cf. Philo, *Quaest. in Gen.* 2.82; *Pirke de-Rabbi Eliezer* 24.
262 *Apoc.* 3.5; ed. Reinink 1993, pp. 5 [Syr.], 7 [trans.]. For an earlier expression of this notion, see John Malalas (*Chron.* 1.7), who says of Nimrod's father that he was "of the tribe of Shem, named Cush, an Ethiopian"; ed. Thurn 2000, p. 9; trans. Jeffreys et alii 1986, p. 5. Cf. also John of Antioch, *Hist. chron.*; ed. Roberto 2005, pp. 8 [Gr.], 9 [trans.]; *Chronicon Paschale*; ed. Dindorf 1832, v. 1, p. 64.

In light of this, it appears that local patriotism constitutes a systemic feature of the manner in which CT's author reworked the biblical account of Nimrod.[263] In what follows, I intend to focus on those aspects of the image of Nimrod in CT in which this tendency comes to the fore most prominently. Moreover, particular attention will be paid to those cases where our author goes beyond the conceptual horizons of this particular hermeneutic strategy and uses biblical material in order to address issues that bring him into closer contact with the dominant culture of Iranian society, including those related to the institution of kingship.

2.1.1 Nimrod as the Founder of Monarchy

When he mentions Nimrod for the first time in CT 24.24, the author introduces him in the following way:

> And in the days of Reu, in his one hundred and thirtieth year, the first king began to reign upon the earth, the mighty Nimrod. And he reigned sixty-nine years, and the beginning of his kingdom was Babel.[264]

It is the characteristic of Nimrod as the "first king" (*malkā qadmāyā*) in the history of the human race that is of particular importance for our discussion. The biblical account of Nimrod presents him as a royal figure (cf. Gen 10:10). However, it merely points out that Babylon, together with several other cities, formed his original kingdom, without claiming that Nimrod was actually the founder of the institution of monarchy itself. This idea only appears in the later tradition of scriptural exegesis. An early attestation of the image of Nimrod as the first monarch in Christian tradition comes from the works of Jerome, who casts him in a negative light as "the first to seize despotic rule over the people, which men were not yet accustomed to."[265]

As to the Syriac exegetical tradition, it appears that the writers who lived prior to CT's time preferred to follow the general biblical view of Nimrod's royal status. The author of the Pseudo-Clementines mentions that Nimrod was

---

263 Besides the figure of Nimrod, this tendency is also expressesed in the favorable treatment of the Magi from the Gospel of Matthew and in the assertion of the primacy of the Syriac language, which are analyzed further in section 2.3 below and section 2 of chapter 4 respectively.

264 Or^A: ܘܒܝܘܡܝ̈ ܪܥܘ ܒܪ ܡܐܐ ܘܬܠܬܝܢ ܫܢܝ̈ܢ ܐܩܝܡ ܡܠܟܐ ܩܕܡܝܐ ܥܠ ܐܪܥܐ ܢܡܪܘܕ ܓܢܒܪܐ. ܘܐܡܠܟ ܫܬܝܢ ܘܬܫܥ ܫܢܝ̈ܢ. ܘܪܝܫ ܡܠܟܘܬܗ ܒܒܠ.

265 *Quaest. in Gen.* 10.8–10: *Nemrod filius Chus arripuit insuetam primus in populo tyrannidem regnauitque*; ed. de Lagarde 1868, p. 16; trans. Hayward 1995, p. 41.

the first to reign in Babylon.²⁶⁶ In a similar vein, Ephrem, in his discussion of Nimrod in the *Commentary on Genesis*, states that he became "the first to rule" over Babel.²⁶⁷ By the end of late antiquity, the image of Nimrod as the first monarch in the history of humanity had become widespread among Syriac Christians. Besides CT, a positive account of Nimrod as the first king, appointed by God, appears in the seventh-century *Chronicle* of John bar Penqāyē.²⁶⁸

In order to better appreciate the author's strategy in presenting Nimrod as the first king, we should set it against the background of a wide range of opinions on the issue of the origins of monarchy that were current in late antique Christian historical thought. Some writers ascribed this honor to Kronos. For instance, Julius Africanus relates regarding this figure that "he first revealed how to rule and exercise kingship over the Assyrians."²⁶⁹ Other historiographers pointed to Belus as the first king of Babylon and/or Assyria.²⁷⁰ According to another influential view, the first monarch was Belus' son Ninus.²⁷¹ Thus, the sixth-century Byzantine historian Agathias of Myrina relates that "Ninus was, it seems, the first to establish a settled kingdom hereabout."²⁷² Alternatively, the author of the Syriac chronological work in ms. BL Add. 14643 singles out Sichon as "the first king who received crown from God."²⁷³ Moreover, we should not forget that there was an indigenous Zoroastrian tradition about the origins of monarchy which connected this social institution with Hōšang, the founder of the Pēšdādian dynasty in the Iranian historical traditional.²⁷⁴

Regarded against this background, CT's portrayal of Nimrod as the founder of monarchy emerges as a conscious authorial choice, aimed at forging a new perspective on the history of human culture that was independent from both the Western Christian historiographical tradition and the native Iranian views

---

266 *Rec.* 1.30.7: *septima decimal generatione apud Babyloniam Nebroth primus regnavit*; ed. Rehm & Strecker 1994, p. 26. Cf. the Syriac version: ܘܒܬܪ ܕܝܢ ܒܬܪܝܢܥܣܪ ܕܪܝܢ ܐܡܠܟ ܢܡܪܘܕ; ed. Frankenberg 1937, p. 38.
267 *Comm. in Gen.* 8.4.2; ed. Tonneau 1955, p. 66; trans. (modified) Mathews & Amar 1994, p. 148.
268 Cf. mēmrā 2; ms. Mingana Syr. 179, fol. 8v.
269 Ed. Wallraff et alii 2007, #F24a, pp. 52–53. Cf. also John Malalas, *Chron.* 1.8.
270 Cf. Eusebius, *Chron.*, ed. Aucher 1818, v. 1, pp. 81–82; Augustine, *De civ. Dei* 12.11, 18.2; Isidore of Seville, *Etym.* 8.11.23. For traces of this figure in the Syriac literary tradition, see the *History of Karkā d-Bēt Slok*, where Belus is characterized as "first king of the Assyrians"; ed. Bedjan 1890–1897, v. 2, p. 507.
271 On this figure, see Weidner 1936; Nagel 1982.
272 Agathias, *Hist.* 2.25.4; ed. Keydell 1967, p. 73, trans. Cameron 1969–70, p. 85. Cf. also Orosius, *Hist.* 2.2.
273 Trans. Cowper 1861, p. 80.
274 For him, see Shahbazi 2004b; Christensen 1917, pp. 131–164.

on the origins of kingship. This perspective, based first and foremost on the biblical master narrative, allows our author to create a unique vision of the past, tailored to the needs of his own Syriac-speaking Christian community as it aims to boost its self-image. Furthermore, this aspect of Nimrod's portrayal provides a basis for the further development of this character within CT itself.

2.1.2 Nimrod as the Founder of Cities

In CT 27.23, the author relates that Nimrod "built strong cities in the east—Babylon, and Nineveh, and Rāsān, and Seleucia, and Ctesiphon, and Ādurbādagān; and he made three fortresses."[275] He adds in CT 30.19 that "in the fiftieth year of Reu, Nimrod went up and built Nisibis, and Edessa, and Harran."[276]

These passages are directly related to the biblical description of Nimrod as the founder of several cities in the Near East. In Genesis 10:10–12, it is said of Nimrod that "the beginning of his kingdom was Babel, Erech, and Accad" in the land of Shinar, and that he built "Nineveh, Rehoboth-ir, Calah, and Resen between Nineveh and Calah" in the land of Assyria. Whereas the Syriac translator of the Peshitta of Genesis closely followed the Hebrew version of the cities' names, in the later Syriac tradition of scriptural exegesis they were often changed in order to bring them up to date with the contemporary geography of the Near East.[277] One of the first Syriac authors to resort to such "modernization" of Genesis 10:10–12 was Ephrem. In the *Commentary on Genesis*, he explains the biblical city of Erech as Edessa, Accad as Nisibis, Calah as Seleucia-Ctesiphon, Rehoboth as Adiabene, the second Calah as Hatra, and Resen as Reshaina.[278]

In general, CT's author follows Ephrem's suggested interpretation of Genesis 10:10–12. This is consistent with his general strategy of presenting CT as a genuine Ephremian work.[279] He also adds something new to the Ephremian list by including the cities of Ādurbādagān in West Iran and Harran in Mesopotamia. There is, however, an important aspect of this image of Nimrod which, although it is not obvious, should be taken into consideration in order to understand the author's strategy of cultural identity. As he ascribes

275 Or[A]: ܗܘ ܕܝܢ ܢܡܪܘܕ ܒܢܐ ܡܕܝܢ̈ܬܐ ܚܣܝܢ̈ܬܐ ܒܡܕܢܚܐ. ܠܒܒܠ ܘܢܝܢܘܐ ܘܪܣܢ ܘܣܠܝܩ ܘܩܛܝܣܦܘܢ ܘܐܕܘܪܒܝܓܢ. ܘܬܠܬܐ ܡܚܣܢ̈ܐ ܥܒܕ.

276 Or[A]: ܘܒܫܢܬ ܚܡܫܝܢ ܠܐܪܥܘ ܗܠܟ ܗܘܐ ܢܡܪܘܕ ܘܒܢܐ ܗܘܐ ܠܢܨܝܒܝܢ ܘܠܐܘܪܗܝ ܘܠܚܪܢ.

277 For a general overview of this material, see Jullien, Ch. 2011.

278 *Comm. in Gen.* 8.1; ed. Tonneau 1955, p. 65; trans. Mathews & Amar 1994, p. 147. The same phenomenon occurs in rabbinic literature; cf. *Genesis Rabbah* 37.4, *Targum Neofiti* and *Targum Pseudo-Jonathan* on Gen 10:10–12.

279 On this, see section 5 of chapter 4.

the foundation of these Mesopotamian cities to Nimrod, CT's author is not simply copying Ephrem, but promoting a covert ideological agenda by giving preference to one of several alternative traditions on the origins of urban centers that circulated in the Near East during late antiquity.

On the one hand, there was a long-standing and influential tradition in Greco-Roman historiography and ethnography in which discussion of the origins of various institutes and centers of culture, including cities, was an important topic.[280] In this tradition, the city of Nineveh was thought to have been founded by the legendary Near Eastern monarch Ninus. This opinion was expressed by the Greek historian Ctesias (5th BCE) and later appears in a wide range of classical authors.[281] From Eusebius onwards, it becomes well attested among the Greek Christian authors.[282]

There was a somewhat wider range of opinions on the question of the foundation of Babylon. According to some classical historians, this city was established by Ninus' wife, Queen Semiramis.[283] Others ascribed this honor to King Chaldaios or King Belos.[284] The personal opinion of Stephen of Byzantium (6th c.) that Babylon was founded not by Semiramis, but by the wise man Babylon, son of Medos, may be added to these.[285] As to the cities of Seleucia and Edessa, some Greco-Roman authors ascribed their establishment to Seleucos I Nicator (c. 358–281 BCE), the famous general of Alexander the Great and founder of the Seleucid dynasty.[286]

As a result of the centuries-long Hellenistic and Roman hegemony over the Near East, local communities developed a wide gamut of foundation myths, including those about the origins of cities, in which native traditions were often blended with and adapted to Western cultural patterns.[287] Syriac-speaking Christians were no exception to this development. One of the main channels

---

280 For general information, see Thraede 1962; Gruen 2011, pp. 223–252; Smith, J.M. 1991. On the cities of Mesopotamia, see esp. Vlaardingerbroek 2004.
281 For Ctesias, see Diodorus Siculus, *Bib.* 2.3.1–4.1. Cf. also Strabo, *Geogr.* 16.1.2; Ammianus Marcellinus, *Res gest.* 23.6.22.
282 *Praep. ev.* 10.9.10. Cf. also John Malalas, *Chron.* 1.11; Stephen of Byzantium, *Ethn.* N.63 (ed. Billerbeck et alii 2006–2017, v. 3, p. 388); John of Antioch, *Hist. chron.* 1.5 (ed. Roberto 2005, p. 10); John of Nikiu, *Chron.* 6.3.
283 Thus Ctesias *apud* Diodorus Siculus, *Bib.* 2.7.2–8.7. Cf. also Strabo, *Geogr.* 16.1.2.
284 For the former, see See Dicaearchus of Messina (4th BCE) *apud* Stephen of Byzantium, *Ethn.* Ch.10; ed. Billerbeck et alii 2006–2017, v. 5, p. 76. For the latter, see Pseudo-Eupolemus *apud* Eusebius, *Praep. ev.* 9.18.2.
285 *Ethn.* B.5; ed. Billerbeck et alii 2006–2017, v. 1, p. 320.
286 On Seleucia, see Pliny the Elder, *Hist. nat.* 6.122. On Edessa, see Eusebius' *Chronicle* as reflected in Jerome's *Chronicle*; ed. Helm 1913–1926, p. 127. Cf. also John Malalas, *Chron.* 17.15.
287 See Belayche 2009; McCants 2011, pp. 85–105; de Bellefonds 2011.

through which Hellenistic traditions of this kind entered the Syriac-speaking milieu was apparently the works of Greek Christian historians such as Eusebius or John Malalas, which were translated into Syriac or otherwise influenced Syriac authors.[288] To the examples listed above may be added a tradition that Nineveh was founded by King Assur, which may be found in the early Syriac translation of Eusebius' *Onomasticon*.[289] Due to the high prestige of Greek Christian culture, Western founding figures also begin to appear in original works written in Syriac. For instance, the East Syrian author of the *Chronicle of Khuzistan* (7th c.) presents the monarch Nin as the founder of Edessa, Nisibis, Ctesiphon, and Nineveh.[290] He also names Queen Semiramis as the founder of Babylon and Seleucos as another founder of Edessa.[291] Similarly, another East Syrian historiographer, Mār Abā, ascribes the founding of Seleucia to Seleucos.[292]

At the same time, there were native Iranian traditions on the origins of several of the cities mentioned by CT's author. The main source of our knowledge on this subject is the so-called *Provincial Capitals of Ērānšahr*. This brief Middle Persian composition, which at least partially seems to transmit material from the late Sasanian period, provides a description of the main cities in the "domain of the Iranians." According to this work, the city of Babylon was built "by Bābēl during the reign of Jam,"[293] the city of Nisibis "by Warāzag the son of Gēw,"[294] the city of Ctesiphon "by the order of Tūs, the son of Warāz from

---

288 On Eusebius in Syriac, see Toda 2011; Debié 2006. On Malalas' influence on Syriac writers, see Witakowski 1990b; Debié 2004.

289 ܣܘܢ, ܕܒܢܝܬܐ ܗܘ ܐܪܝܘܟ, ܗ. ܐܪܝܘܟ ܕܒܢܝܗ ܗܕ ܢܘܗ ܡܢ ܡܠܟ ܐܬܘܪ; ed. Timm 2005, p. 76; cf. also p. 92.

290 ܣܘܡ ܒܢ ܥܠܡ ܟܕ ܐܝܪ ܢܝܢ ܕܗܘ ,ܐܘܪܗܝ, ܘܐܪܒܐ ܕܐܬܘܪ ܘܢܨܝܒܝܢ. ܡܚܠܟ ܕܗ, ܡܩܕܘܢܝܐ <...> ;ed. Guidi 1903, p. 35 [Syr.]. Cf. also the mention of Nin as the founder of Nineveh in the Syriac chronological work from ms. British Library, Add. 14643, translated by Cowper 1861, p. 81, and the *Chronicle of Ps.-Dionysius of Tel-Mahre* on Ninus and Semiramis as the founders of Nineveh and Babylon respectively; ed. Chabot 1927–1949, v. 1, pp. 13, 17 [Syr].

291 Ed. Guidi 1903, p. 35 [Syr.]. The same tradition about Semiramis appears in ms. British Library, Add. 14643; trans. Cowper 1861, p. 81.

292 Ed. Macler 1903, p. 507, §42. The same opinion on the origins of Seleucia-Ctesiphon is expressed by the author of the *History of Karkā d-Bēt Slok*, who ascribes the foundation of five cities in Syria to Seleucus, including Antioch and his own city; ed. Bedjan 1890–1897, v. 2, p. 510.

293 §24: *šahrestān ī bābēl, bābēl pad xwadāyīh [ī] jam kard*; ed. Daryaee 2002, pp. 14 [text], 18 [trans.].

294 §22: *šahrestān [ī] *nasībīn *warāzag [ī] gēwagān kard*; ed. Daryaee 2002, pp. 14 [text], 18 [trans.].

the family of Gēw,"[295] the city of Edessa "by Narseh the Arsacid,"[296] and the city of Ādūrbādagān "by Ērān-Gušasp who was the general of Ādūrbādagān."[297] Moreover, it is possible that several alternative Iranian traditions on the foundation of the cities of Mesopotamia existed in antiquity.[298]

An awareness of the variety of foundation myths that circulated in the late ancient Near East helps us to gain a better understanding of the ideological message implicit in CT's portrayal of Nimrod as the founder of the cities of Syria and Mesopotamia. Much like in the case of the image of Nimrod as the first monarch discussed above, this biblical figure becomes instrumental for CT's author's assertion of an independent position vis-à-vis both the Hellenistic body of knowledge on the origins of culture and its Iranian counterpart. As to the former, the tendency towards cultural independence could also be recognized in the peculiar way our author reworked those Greek traditions and motifs that he chose to integrate into his narrative.[299]

When the list of Nimrod's cities in CT is compared with those of other writers, it becomes apparent that by giving Nimrod the credit for founding Ādūrbādagān, our author expands the domain of his symbolic authority as a cultural hero from Northern Mesopotamia further to the East, to the heartlands of Iran. This is consistent with CT's general trend of establishing a close connection between Nimrod and Iran. Thus, in CT 45.5–7, the author uses the phrase "the land of Nimrod" (*'arʿēh d-Nemrud*) as a synonym for "the land of Persia" (*'arʿā d-Pāres*). This identification of Nimrod with Persia, which has no precedent in the biblical narrative, is rooted in the close association between Assyrians and Persians that developed during the post-biblical period.[300] By the time of CT's composition, the Persian empire is habitually referred to as the

---

295 §21: *šahrestān ī tīsifōn az framān ī tūs ī *warāzag ī gēwagān kard*; ed. Daryaee 2002, pp. 14 [text], 18 [trans.].

296 §23: *šahrestān ī ōrhāy narsēh ī aškānān kard*; ed. Daryaee 2002, pp. 14 [text], 18 [trans.].

297 §56: *šahrestān ādūrbādagān ērān-gušasp ī ādūrbādagān spāhbed [kard]*; ed. Daryaee 2002, pp. 16 [text], 20 [trans.].

298 Cf. *Annals* of Ḥamza al-Iṣfahānī (10th c.) on the foundation of Babylon by Ṭahmūrath and of Ctesiphon by Jamshīd; ed. Gottwaldt 1844–1848, v. 1, pp. 29, 31.

299 Cf. the story of the invention of purple dye in CT 36.1–8. Originally a piece of Hellenistic cultural lore (cf. Julius Pollux, *Onomast.* 1.45; John Malalas, *Chron.* 2.9), which was also known in Syriac (cf. Diocles' fragment, ed. de Lagarde 1858, pp. 201–202), this etiological myth appears in CT in a de-Hellenized and biblicized form, i.e. with the Tyrian king Phoinix substituted with the biblical monarch Hiram and the name of Heracles as the inventor of the practice omitted.

300 On this, see Harrak 2005, pp. 52–53.

"land of Nimrod" in Syriac sources. As typical examples, one can mention the Syriac *Julian Romance*,[301] Jacob of Serugh,[302] and several others.

2.1.3 Nimrod as the Prophet of the Star of Bethlehem

Another important and innovative aspect of CT's author's portrayal of Nimrod is that he ascribes to him the authorship of the prophecy concerning the star that guided the Magi on their way to Bethlehem in the Gospel of Matthew. A basis for this narrative line is laid in CT 27.6–11, where our author relates a story about Nimrod's discipleship under Yonṭon, the fourth son of Noah. According to this account, the king went to Yokdora in the region of Nōd, where he found Yonṭon at Lake Aṭras.[303] After Nimrod bathed in the lake and "made obeisance" (*sged*) to Yonṭon, acknowledging his superiority, the king remained at his side for three years. During that time, Yonṭon taught him "wisdom and the book of revelation" (*ḥekmtā we-spar gelyānā*). The subject of "revelation" (*gelyānā*) which Yonṭon taught Nimrod is raised again in CT 27.17–22, where the author identifies it with the legitimate practice of astronomy while distinguishing it from the forbidden art of astrology.

The theme of Nimrod's "revelation" finds its resolution in the story of the appearance of the star of Bethlehem, and how the inhabitants of Persia reacted to it, found in CT 45.2–12. In this relatively long narrative, we are informed that the star appeared to the Magi two years before Jesus was born. Disturbed by this unusual celestial phenomenon, "the Magi and the Chaldeans" of Persia "consulted their books of wisdom (*sepray ḥekmathun*), and through the might of the wisdom of their books they understood and learned, and stood upon the strength of the truth." As our author points out, it was the book entitled "The Revelation of Nimrod" (*gelyānēh d-Nemrud*) that made them realize that the appearance of the new star signified that "a king was born in Judah." Having thus understood "the whole path of the dispensation of Christ," the Magi acted in accordance with "the tradition (*mašlmānutā*) which had been handed down to them by their fathers" and went up to the mountains of Nōd, where they took the gifts of gold, frankincense, and myrrh and embarked on their journey to Palestine.

These passages demonstrate how CT's author further enhances the positive image of Nimrod by ascribing to him the authorship of the revelation that enabled the Magi of the Gospel of Matthew to correctly interpret the meaning of the star of Bethlehem and thus to fulfill their part in God's providential plan.

---

[301] Ed. Sokoloff 2016, pp. 211, 221, 325, 333, 337.
[302] Ed. Bedjan 1905–1910, v. 1, p. 114.
[303] For discussion of this obscure geographical setting, see Ri 2000, pp. 319–327.

This portrait of Nimrod has no immediate analogs in the Christian sources from late antiquity. The closest parallel to the notion of Nimrod's "revelation" is found in a passage from the Syriac *Romance of Julian* in which an apology for the Zoroastrian art of astral prognostication is put into the mouth of King Shapur. The reliability of this practice, referred to as "revelation," is illustrated by the claim that it was given to the "house of Nimrod," i.e. the Persians, when Nimrod "received the crown from heaven through its revelation (*b-gelyānāh*)."[304] However, whereas both CT's author and the author of the *Romance* share the basic notion of Nimrod as the founder of astral prognostications among the Persians, the latter makes no explicit connection between this art and the New Testament episode of the Magi.

In order to appreciate the originality of CT's author's association between Nimrod and the star of the Magi in Matthew 2:1–12, one should consider it in connection with another much more influential exegetical tradition that presented Balaam as the prophet of this star, based on the prophecy of this pagan diviner in Numbers 24:17.[305] One of the earliest Christian authors to make this connection was Justin Martyr, who, in the *Dialogue with Trypho the Jew*, relates that the Magi were able to recognize the star of Bethlehem as a sign of the coming of God's Son because of the Mosaic prophecy in Numbers 24:17.[306] Later, we find Origen claiming that "the star which appeared at the birth of Jesus was prophesied by Balaam."[307] By the fourth century, the identification of the star of Balaam with the star of the Magi becomes commonplace in the exegetical tradition of Western Christianity, in Greek as well as in Latin.[308]

A similar situation characterizes the Syriac Christian tradition before the time of CT. Thus, in one of Eusebius of Caesarea's questions about the Gospels, which is preserved only in Syriac, the Magi are presented as descendants of Balaam (*men bnawhi d-Bel'am*) who preserved their ancestor's prophecy of the star in written form.[309] Moreover, the author of the Pseudo-Eusebian *On the Star*, also preserved only in Syriac, presents a developed narrative according to which Balaam's prophecy regarding the star was recorded and transmitted

---

304 Ed. and trans. (modified) Sokoloff 2016, pp. 212–213.
305 On the development of this exegetical motif, see Dorival 1999; Hegedus 2007, pp. 204–206; Nicklas 2008.
306 *Dial.* 106.4; ed. Marcovich 1997, p. 253; trans. Falls 1948, p. 160.
307 *C. Cels.* 1.59; ed. Marcovich 2001, p. 60; trans. Chadwick 1965, p. 54. Cf. also *Hom. in Num.* 18.4.2.
308 Cf. Gregory of Nyssa, *Oratio in diem natalem Christi*, PG 46, col. 1133; Ambrose, *Expos. ev. Luc.* 2.48; Ambrosiaster, *Quaest.* 63; Jerome, *Comm. in Matt.* 1.2; Caesarius of Arles, *Serm.* 113.2. For the iconographic evidence, see Kirschbaum 1954.
309 Ed. Mai 1847, pp. 281–282; Germ. trans. Beyer 1925–1927, pp. 4–9.

through generations of Assyrian kings, who bequeathed it to their Persian successors.[310] As to the native Syriac authors, the connection between the star of Bethlehem and Numbers 24:17 was already known to Ephrem.[311] Closer to the time of CT's composition, Jacob of Serugh develops this exegetical motif in the *Homily on the Star That Appeared to the Magi*. While describing the Magi's reaction to the appearance of the new star, Jacob emphasizes several times that they could not make sense of this unusual celestial phenomenon by consulting "their own books" of Chaldeanism, i.e. astrology.[312] It is only when they turn to the prophecy of Balaam in Numbers 24:17 that the Magi are able to identify the geographical location where the new king would appear.[313]

These examples demonstrate that Balaam being the prophet of the star of Bethlehem was the prevailing exegetical opinion in late antiquity. CT's author, however, breaks with this tradition and dissociates Balaam and his prophecy from the New Testament episode of the Magi. Only a distant echo of Balaam's reputation as the prophet of the Bethlehem star can be recognized in CT 35.18–21. There, a story is told of the altar to the sun, which was built in Baalbek by the three envoys sent by Nimrod to Balaam, the "priest of the mountain of Seir," because he had heard that the latter "[was] familiar with the signs of Zodiac."[314] Interestingly, the names of Nimrod's envoys reflect the influence of Iranian onomastics, which seems to strengthen the image of their master as a Persian monarch.[315] The exact motivation behind Nimrod's interest in Balaam's astrological expertise is, however, unclear from the text. Yet regardless of whether CT's author did or did not envisage Nimrod and Balaam as two equally knowledgeable experts in the science of the stars, what is important for us is that neither in this passage nor anywhere else in his work does he ascribe any role

---

310   Ed. Wright, W. 1866–1867, pp. 9–17 [Syr.], 157–162 [trans.].
311   Cf. *De Nat.* 24.4, 20; ed. Beck 1959, pp. 122, 125.
312   Ed. Bedjan 1905–1910, v. 1, pp. 93, 96.
313   Ed. Bedjan 1905–1910, v. 1, p. 97.
314   Or^A: ܘܡܢ ܒܬܪ ܗܕܐ ܫܕܪ ܢܡܪܘܕ ܬܠܬܐ ܐܝܙܓܕܐ ܗܘ ܕܐܝܬܘܗܝ ܒܠܥܡ ܟܗܢܐ ܕܛܘܪܐ ܕܣܥܝܪ، ܕܫܡܗ ܦܝܘܪܙܟܪ ܘܦܝܘܪܙܢܝ ܘܢܙܢܕܘܪ. ܡܛܠ ܕܫܡܥ ܕܗܘ ܝܕܥ ܗܘܐ ܒܐܬܘܬܐ ܕܡܠܘܫܐ، ܘܡܚܕܐ ܫܕܪ ܠܗ ܪܒܝܥܐ. ܘܗܘ ܒܠܥܡ ܟܗܢܐ ܫܠܚ ܠܗ ܒܗ ܒܐܬܪܐ ܕܒܥܠܒܟ ܥܠ ܛܘܪܐ ܠܒܪܐ.
315   The names of the first two envoys, PYWRZKR and PYWRZNY, have recently been interpreted as *Pērōzak* and *Pērōz-dād* by Gignoux et alii 2009, pp. 114–115, ##339–340. It is also possible to explain them as artificially constructed names that evoke the Middle Persian personal name *Pīr*, "old, aged, ancient," which was used both as a separate name and as part of composite names; for examples, see Gignoux 1986, pp. 148–149, ##770–774; Gignoux et alii 2009, p. 116, ##345–347. The name of the third envoy, NZNDWR, is more difficult to interpret. On the basis of its manuscript variants—Or^B ܢܙܢܕܘܪ, Or^D ܢܙܢܕܘܪ, Oc^a ܢܙܢܕܘܪ—it can be explained as a derivative of *Yazd*, *Yazid*, or *Yazdēn*; for examples, see Gignoux et alii 2009, pp. 140–147.

to Balaam in the transmission of the astronomical lore that enabled the Magi to correctly interpret the star of Bethlehem.

Instead of Balaam, CT's author promotes the figure of Nimrod as the provider of the supernatural knowledge which allowed the Magi to grasp the true meaning of the unusual astral phenomenon as a sign of the coming of Jesus. By connecting Nimrod with Yonṭon and thus with Noah, our author indirectly endows him with the legitimacy of the antediluvian succession of righteous men. This aspect of his portrayal of Nimrod is consistent with our author's general tendency to present this biblical figure in a positive light, promoting him as the cultural hero of Northern Mesopotamia and Iran.

As to the Iranian connotations of this aspect of Nimrod's portrayal in CT, these were noted by Mary Boyce and Frantz Grenet, who point out that by presenting Nimrod as the author of a book, the Syriac author blends "the Semitic concept of a written literature" with the Zoroastrian notion of "a teaching transmitted orally for generations."[316] I believe, however, that there is additional evidence to support this suggestion and develop it even further. For this, we should pay closer attention to the Syriac word *gelyānā*, "revelation," chosen by CT's author to refer to the divinatory practice which Nimrod learned from Yonṭon, as well as to the literary medium through which its outcome was articulated and transmitted to posterity. This choice is not as obvious as one might think. For instance, in a comparable narrative situation, the author of another Syriac apocryphon, the *Testament of Adam*, uses the noun "testament" (*diyatiqi*) in order to describe Adam's prophetic message to his descendants, in which he details Christ's future redemption of the world.[317]

Although translating *gelyānā* as "revelation" is certainly correct, it is important to be attentive to the wide range of meanings that this Syriac word conveys, including "appearance" and "manifestation." Thus, in the texts translated from Greek, *gelyānā* is used to render such nouns as ἀποκάλυψις, ἐπιφάνεια, φανέρωσις, and χρηματισμός.[318] In searching for an adequate analog to the Syriac *gelyānā* in the religious vocabulary of Zoroastrianism, it is probably the Middle Persian adjective *paydāg*, "visible, manifest, revealed" and its derivatives—the noun *paydāgīh*, "appearance, revelation" and the denominative verbs *paydāgēnīdan*, "to manifest, reveal," and *paydāgīhistan*, "to have appeared, have been revealed"—that constitute the closest match.[319] These words figure prominently as a means of referring to sacral or otherwise important

---

316 Boyce & Grenet 1991, p. 453.
317 *Test. of Adam* 3.6; ed. Robinson, S.E. 1982, p. 64.
318 For the references, see Payne Smith 1879–1901, v. 1, col. 721.
319 On these words, see Nyberg 1964–1974, v. 2, p. 149; MacKenzie 1986, pp. 66–67.

knowledge in the Zoroastrian tradition. For example, in the corpus of Pahlavi literature, material from the authoritative bulk of the Zoroastrian religious tradition is often introduced with the help of reference formulas that include the word *paydāg*—"it is revealed" (*paydāg*), "it is revealed in the religion" (*pad dēn paydāg*), or "it is revealed from the Avesta" (*az Abestāg paydāg*).[320] The derivative verbal noun *paydāgēnīdarīh* may denote an act of revelation, as in the *Dēnkard*, where it describes the manifestation of spiritual mysteries via corporal forms.[321] It is particularly significant that on several occasions, we find Pahlavi sources resorting to this vocabulary in order to describe knowledge obtained through oracles or omens, including astrological ones. For instance, the Pahlavi *Vendīdād* speaks about the visible "sign" (*daxšag*) that shall serve as a "manifestation" (*paydāgīh*) of the calamities to come.[322] The word *paydāg* appears in the *Book of the Deeds of Ardašīr* in the court astrologers' answers to King Ardawān, who interrogates them on the matters related to his young rival Ardašīr.[323] In light of this prominence of the word *paydāg* and its derivatives as the markers of revealed knowledge, it may be tempting to recognize CT's author's description of Nimrod's message to his successors as *gelyānā* as an attempt to mimic this native Iranian vocabulary.

The notion of Nimrod's "revelation" as part of the native lore of the "Persians" in CT resonates with the genuine Iranian belief that the birth of a new monarch could be signaled by omens such as astral phenomena. The most explicit evidence of this kind comes from *Zand ī Wahman Yasn*, a Middle Persian apocalyptic composition that purports to be a translation of the lost Avestan treatise *Bahman Yašt*.[324] In chapter 7 of this work, which describes events that inaugurate the eleventh millennium of Ušēdar, the author introduces the figure of the eschatological king Wahrām ī Warzāwand from the Kayanian dynasty, who, together with the priest Pišyōtan, will overcome the hostile armies and restore Iran and its religion, i.e. Zoroastrianism, to their glory.[325] It is related that the birth of this savior-king shall be announced by a celestial omen,

---

320 Cf. *Dēnkard* 5.13.12, 5.19.7; ed. Amouzgar & Tafazzoli 2000, pp. 52, 62. For a list of such formulae, see Widengren 1983, pp. 101–103. For a discussion of the nature of these Avestan quotations, see Cereti 2010.
321 *Dēnkard* 5.7.3; ed. Amouzgar & Tafazzoli 2000, p. 38. Cf. also *Dādestān ī Dēnīg* 36.47; ed. Jaafari-Dehaghi 1998, p. 128.
322 *Vendīdād* 1.14; ed. Moazami 2014, pp. 36–39.
323 *Kār-nāmag* 4.7; ed. Grenet 2003, p. 70.
324 For general information, see Sundermann 1988; Cereti 1995, pp. 1–27.
325 On this figure, see Cereti 1996.

a falling star—"the night when the *kay* will be born a sign will reach the world, a star will fall from the sky. When that *kay* will be born a star will reveal the sign."[326]

One cannot fail to notice the similarity between this passage and the New Testament story of the star of Bethlehem. There is still ongoing discussion among scholars as to whether the author of the Gospel of Matthew was influenced by an indigenous Iranian tradition, such as the one reflected in *Zand ī Wahman Yasn*, or whether both the Christian and the Persian sources developed independently under the influence of the common Hellenistic beliefs about a close connection between astral phenomena and earthly rulers.[327] This issue, however, is of a lesser importance for our discussion than the question of whether the notion of astral omens in connection with the accession of monarchs was familiar in the Sasanian cultural milieu during the time of CT's composition. I believe that there are reasonable grounds for thinking so. On the one hand, Iranists agree that *Zand ī Wahman Yasn* as a whole is a post-Islamic composition. At the same time, however, most of the students of this work seem to accept that a significant portion of it goes back to the pre-Islamic period.[328] According to Carlo Cereti, the cluster of traditions about Kay Wahrām to which this astral omen belongs could be dated to the late Sasanian period.[329] Additional support for this dating may be found in the fact that the author of the *Zand ī Wahman Yasn* introduces this omen with the formula "it is revealed in the religion" (*pad dēn paydāg*), thus presenting it as part of the already established authoritative body of Zoroastrian knowledge.

The importance of astral phenomena as omens of political change related to the birth of a new ruler during the Sasanian period is also expressed in the *Book of the Deeds of Ardašīr*. There, King Ardavān's chief astrologer informs him, upon examining the current position of the "star" (*stārag*) Jupiter in the horoscope, that "a new lord and ruler (*xwadāy-ēw ud pādixšāy-ēw ī nōg*) shall appear, who will kill many potentates and subject the world to single rule once more."[330] To this may be added the evidence of several East Syrian astrological texts that seem to reflect the political situation of pre-Islamic Iran, in which there are discussions of the heavenly omens presented by shooting

---

326 *Zand ī Wahman Yasn* 7.6: *kū ān šab ka ān kay zāyēd nišān ō gēhān rasēd, stārag az asmān wārēd. ka ōy kay zāyēd stārag nišān nimāyēd*; ed. Cereti 1995, pp. 142 [Pahl.], 162 [trans.].
327 See Davies & Allison 1988, pp. 230–236; Hultgård 1977–1981, v. 1, pp. 326–328; Hultgård 1998.
328 For an overview of scholarly opinions on this subject, see Cereti 1995, pp. 15–27.
329 Cereti 1995, p. 26.
330 *Kār-nāmag* 3.5–6; ed. Grenet 2003, p. 64. For an analysis of this passage, see Panaino 1994.

208   CHAPTER 3

stars, i.e. comets, some of which predict changes of government or military disturbances.³³¹

2.1.4   Nimrod's Investiture

In chapter 24, CT's author presents the following account of Nimrod's royal investiture, which took place in the days of Reu, at the end of the third millennium after the creation of the world (CT 24.25–26):

> This one (i.e. Nimrod) saw the likeness of a crown in the heavens. And he called Sasan, the weaver, and he wove him a crown like that. And he set it on his head. And because of that people used to say that the crown came down to him from heaven.³³²

In this passage, CT's author offers an etiological gloss on what appears to be a popular belief about the heavenly origins of Nimrod's crown. According to him, this crown was made by an artisan named Sasan, whom Nimrod summoned after he saw a pattern of it in the sky. There are several features in this short story that betray our author's indebtedness to the world of Iranian ideas, images, and literary tropes related to the institution of kingship.

The Iranian setting of this account is indicated by the mention of "Sasan the weaver." This person bears the same name as "Sasan the king" in CT 27.4–5, the originator of the Persian horse cult discussed above. Since these two figures fulfill different narrative functions, it is difficult to definitively establish whether CT's author considered them to be identical. However, taking into account the fact that they are both active during Nimrod's lifetime and bear the same personal name, this possibility seems to be very likely.

The motif of Nimrod's crown and its modeling after a celestial pattern is especially important for unpacking the Iranian background of this narrative unit. In order to understand the genesis and function of this motif, we shall turn to the rich tradition of Iranian royal ideology, in which the crown functioned as one of the essential elements of visual expression. It is this cultural context that provides us with a key to our story.

While referring to Nimrod's headdress, CT's author uses not only the common Syriac word *kalilā*, "diadem," but also the noun *tāgā*, which is a Syriac

---

331   See ed. Budge 1913, v. 2, pp. 520–522, 652–655 [trans.].
332   Or^A: ܘܐܝܟ ܗܘ ܕܚܙܐ ܕܡܘܬܐ ܕܟܠܝܠܐ ܒܫܡܝܐ. ܘܩܪܐ ܠܣܣܢ ܓܪܕܝܐ. ܘܐܪܩܡ ܠܗ ܟܠܝܠܐ. ܘܣܡܗ ܒܪܝܫܗ. ܘܡܛܠ ܗܕܐ ܗܘܘ ܐܡܪܝܢ ܕܡܢ ܫܡܝܐ ܢܚܬ ܠܗ ܟܠܝܠܗ.

loan-word from the Middle Persian *tāg*, "crown."³³³ By doing so, he is apparently relying on an existing tradition about Nimrod's royal crown. The author himself acknowledges this indebtedness in the concluding sentence of the unit, from which it follows that the story of Sasan the craftsman was meant to provide an explanation for this tradition.

In the Syriac texts produced during the fifth and sixth centuries, Nimrod's name is not infrequently found being used metonymically to refer to the Sasanian empire or to the Persians as a nation. On certain occasions, a more specific image of Nimrod's "crown" (*tāgā*) is evoked for this purpose. Thus, in the Syriac *Romance of Julian*, Emperor Julian's dream of military victory over Persia is described as his intention to annex "the crown of the house of Nimrod" (*tāgā d-bēt Nemrud*).³³⁴ Jacob of Serugh evokes the image of "the crown of Nimrod" (*tāgēh d-Nemrud*) in the *Homily on the Star That Appeared to the Magi*, where he treats the Matthean Magi as representatives of the Persian nation whose visit and bringing of gifts are presented as an act of recognizing the supreme authority of the newborn messianic king Jesus.³³⁵

There is one particular attestation of the motif of the celestial origins of Nimrod's crown that might predate CT. It comes from the third part of the Syriac *Romance of Julian* mentioned above, which deals with the infamous emperor's campaign against Persia. There, we find an account of how, after having read the threatening letter from Julian, the Persian king Shapur II turns to Jovian, who at that time served as a military commander. Trying to persuade Jovian of his future destiny as Julian's successor to the Roman throne, Shapur relates that he obtained this knowledge through the "revelation of Magianism" (*gelyānāh da-mgušutā*). In the king's words, the reliability of this art of prognostication, also described as "exalted wisdom" (*ḥekmat rawmā*), is supported by the fact that Nimrod himself "received the crown from heaven through its revelation."³³⁶ From the offhand manner of the mention of Nimrod's celestial crown in this passage, it can be deduced that this motif was not invented by the author of the *Romance of Julian*, but that it was in circulation before the time of its composition, i.e. the first decades of the sixth century.³³⁷ As there are no signs that CT's author was dependent on the *Romance of Julian* or vice

---

333   See Sokoloff 2009, p. 1623. This loan-word is only attested in the Eastern Middle Aramaic dialects, i.e. Syriac, Mandaic, and Jewish Babylonian Aramaic.
334   Ed. Sokoloff 2016, p. 155.
335   Ed. Bedjan 1905–1910, v. 1, pp. 93, 120. Cf. also the *Homily on Vainglory*; Ibid., v. 2, p. 795.
336   ܡܨܕ ܐܬ ܡܢ ܬܓܐ ܕܓܠܝܢܗ; ed. and trans. (modified) Sokoloff 2016, pp. 212–213.
337   This relatively late dating of the *Romance of Julian* was first proposed by Nöldeke 1874, pp. 281–283; recently, it has been supported by Wood 2010, pp. 140–142. For attempts to date this work earlier, to the fourth century, see Drijvers, H.J.W. 1994; Muravjev 1999.

versa, the appearance of this motif in both these works leads us to suggest that it was part of the common lore related to the biblical figure of Nimrod that circulated among the Syriac-speaking Christians in the Byzantine–Persian contact zone during the late fifth and early sixth century.[338]

Let us turn now to the problem of the Iranian background of the depiction of Nimrod's royal headgear and the rite of his investiture in CT 24.25–26. The crown and the coronation ritual occupied a central position in the ideology and practice of Iranian kingship.[339] As the Muslim historian al-Maʿsūdī testifies, the Persians "attach a mysterious significance to the custom of putting on the crown."[340] We know that until the fifth century, every Sasanian monarch had his own uniquely designed crown, sometimes more than one, that distinguished him from his predecessors and was faithfully represented in his official images. This crown was usually encircled by the diadem that symbolized the divine blessing of the king's rule. The importance of crown imagery for Sasanian royal ideology is confirmed by the fact that the scene of royal investiture was habitually conveyed to the general population through highly visible media such as coins and rock reliefs, which depicted the highest divinites of the Zoroastrian pantheon performing the coronation ceremony.[341]

The royal crown, together with some other material expressions of Iranian kingship, was meant to convey the idea of the central position of the king as the pivot of the universe.[342] For this purpose, for instance, the interior of the royal throne hall during the late Sasanian period was designed in such a way as to represent an image of the celestial world.[343] It is this aspect of Iranian royal symbolism, in which a close visual connection is established between the royal crown and the heavenly realm, that seems to reverberate in CT 24.25–26.

A good example of this connection comes from Ibn Isḥāq's *Life of Muhammad*, where a story is narrated about a certain Sayf ibn Dhū Yazan, a

---

338   The author of the *Romance of Julian* also resorts to this motif in his account of the coronation of Emperor Jovian (ed. Sokoloff 2016, pp. 408–409). On the later (i.e. post-CT) reception of this image, see Desreumaux 2003.
339   See Peck 1993; Shahbazi 1993; Rose 2006.
340   *Murūǧ al-ḏahab* 21: ولهم فى وضع التاج على الراس اسرار يذكرونها; ed. de Meynard et alii 1966–1979, v. 1, pp. 261–262; trans. Modi 1935, p. 17.
341   For images, see Ghirshman 1962, pls. 65, 67, 152, 167, 168, 211, 233, 235. For discussion of this material, see Rose 2006; Vanden Berghe 1988. For an alternative interpretation of these scenes as representing not the royal coronation *per se*, but rather the act of establishing a "covenant" (*mithra*) between the king and his deity, see Kaim 2009.
342   See Panaino 2004a, pp. 563–572.
343   See L'Orange 1953, pp. 18–27.

local leader from Yemen, who traveled to the court of Khosrow I in order to obtain military assistance against the Abyssinian invasion. During his visit, Dhū Yazan was given an audience by the king. Part of the description of this audience deals with the king's audience chamber, of which the royal crown constituted the central element. According to Ibn Isḥāq, this crown looked "like a huge grain-measure with rubies, pearls, and topazes set in gold and silver" and was so heavy that it hardly could be worn by a human, so that it had to be suspended from the top of the dome of the hall by a "golden chain."[344] Besides the utilitarian purpose, there is a recognizable symbolic dimension in this spatial arrangement of the king's crown that purports to visualize the notion of the celestial origins of this emblem of royal power and thus to convey the general idea of a divine authorization of kingship. This vivid description provides a visual gloss for the motif of the royal crown descending from heaven known to us from CT 24.26 and the *Romance of Julian*.

Moreover, Ibn Isḥāq's depiction of the golden royal crown suspended from the heaven-like ceiling offers us a possible clue as to the iconographical identity of "the likeness of a crown" (*dmutā da-klilā*) in the sky after which Nimrod's headgear was fashioned according to CT 24.25. I believe that by referring to this "likeness," CT's author connects Nimrod with the solar aspect of Iranian royal imagery.

The sun played an important role in the royal ideologies of the ancient world, and Iran was no exception to this trend. Solar features had already been attributed to Iranian kings during the Achaemenid epoch.[345] Under the Sasanians, this tradition was continued and further developed. There is rich evidence for the profound influence exercised by solar imagery on royal ideology during the Sasanian period. The association with the sun was such an important element of the self-image of the Sasanian kings that it was evoked even in diplomatic documents. According to Ammianus Marcellinus, Shapur II, in his official letter to Constantine, gives himself the title of "partner with the stars, brother of the sun and moon" (*frater solis et lunae*).[346] A similar testimony comes from the report of John Malalas, who quotes a letter from Kawād I to Justinian in which the Persian king calls himself "the sun of the East" (ἡλίου ἀνατολῆς) while referring to the Roman emperor as "the moon of the West" (σελήνης δύσεως).[347]

---

344   Ed. Wüstenfeld 1858–1860, v. 1, p. 42; trans. Guillaume 1955, p. 30. This story appears also in al-Ṭabarī's *History*; ed. de Goeje et alii 1879–1901, v. I.2, p. 946.
345   See Nagel & Jacobs 1989.
346   *Res gest.* 17.5.3; ed. Rolfe 1935–1940, v. 1, pp. 332–333.
347   *Chron.* 18.44; ed. Thurn 2000, p. 378.

It is particularly important that we find the motif of the sun-like radiating royal headgear among the iconographical attestations of the influence of solar imagery on the public performance of Sasanian kingship. Representations of the radiate crown shaped in a distinctively sun-like form appear on the coinage of Sasanian kings such as Bahrām I (r. 273–276).[348] Another example of the publicly visible function of the solar crown was that of royal audiences held on certain festive occasions. For instance, in his *Chronology of Ancient Nations*, al-Bīrūnī reports that on the day of Mihragān, the great autumn festival, Sasanian kings would crown themselves with "a crown on which was worked an image of the sun (*ṣūrat al-šams*) and of the wheel on which it rotates."[349]

As to the origins of this particular iconographical motif of the radiate royal headgear, al-Bīrūnī's mention of the king's solar crown in the context of the celebration of Mihragān suggests that it might have developed as a result of the influence of Mithraic imagery on the Iranian ideology of kingship.[350] The visual motif of the radiate crown is well attested in the iconography of Mithra, the ancient Indo-European deity associated with the sun.[351] There is a substantial amount of archaeological material from the Sasanian period in which Mithra is represented with a nimbus with rays.[352] Mithra's solar crown is also mentioned in the literary sources. For instance, in the Syriac version of the *Alexander Romance* (2.6), when Darius meets Alexander the Great for the first time, the Persian king imagines him to be the god Mithra, "for his aspect resembled that of the gods; for the crown that was fastened on his head resembled the rays (of the sun)."[353]

This evidence shows that the application of solar imagery to the royal crown played a significant role in the ideology and iconography of Iranian kingship during late antiquity. It should be added that the close symbolic and visual connection between the sun and the royal headgear could also work in the opposite direction, so the former could also be likened to the latter. For example, the author of the *Bundahišn* describes the sun as a "crown" (*abesar*) that revolves around the world.[354] Taking all this into consideration, I would like to

---

348 See Gyselen 2004, pp. 76, 102–105.
349 Ed. Sachau 1878, p. 222, ln. 9–10; trans. Sachau 1879, p. 207.
350 On this influence, see Piras 2010, pp. 260–263.
351 In Middle Persian, *mihr* was used to refer both to the deity Mithra and to the sun.
352 See Callieri 1990; Shenkar 2014, pp. 102–114; Adrych et al. 2017, pp. 81–105.
353 ܡܛܠ ܕܗܘܐ ܚܙܘܗ ܕܡܐ ܠܕܐܠܗܐ܂ ܘܟܠܝܠܐ ܕܐܣܝܪ ܗܘܐ ܒܪܫܗ ܕܡܐ ܗܘܐ ܠܙܠܝܩܐ ܕܫܡܫܐ; ed. Budge 1889, pp. 128 [Syr.], 72 [trans.].
354 Iranian *Bundahišn* 5b.1: *xwaršēd gardišn čiyōn abesar pērāmōn ī gēhān*; ed. Pakzad 2005, p. 81.

suggest that the celestial "likeness" after which Sasan manufactured the royal crown for Nimrod according to CT 24.25 was that of the sun.

Some scholars have suggested that the image of Nimrod's heavenly crown in CT is related to the Iranian notion of royal "glory" (Avest. *xᵛarənah*, Mid. Pers. *xwarrah*).[355] This rich and complex notion constituted one of the central elements of the Iranian ideology of kingship.[356] This was an important notion in Zoroastrian cosmology and ethics and was generally conceived as a luminous and fiery magical power that pervaded the supernatural, natural, and human worlds while directing and motivating every being towards the fulfillment of its respective duties. In its function as a guarantee and a sign of success, *xwarrah* also came to bear the meaning of "(good) fortune." Understood as royal "fortune," i.e. a hereditary dynastic charisma, it became a fundamental element of the Iranian discourse of kingship.

There are several arguments in favor of such an interpretation of Nimrod's solar crown. First of all, there seems to be a direct etymological connection between the word *xwarrah* and the Iranian noun *xu̯ar/n* "sun" (Avest. *hvar*, Mid. Pers. *xwar*).[357] There is also a tendency among scholars of Iranian royal iconography to interpret the kings' diadems on Sasanian coins and reliefs and the beribboned ring in the Sasanian investiture scenes as visual expressions of the royal *xwarrah*.[358] However, since no scholarly consensus has yet been reached regarding the exact nature of the relationship between the notion of *xwarrah* in the written Zoroastrian sources and its possible iconographical representations, this avenue of research should be pursued with caution.[359]

There are two additional aspects of the description of Nimrod's investiture in CT 24.25–26 that deserve to be elucidated in connection with the problem of our author's acquaintance with the ideology and practice of Iranian kingship. One of these aspects concerns the exact meaning of the sentence "and he set it on his head," which describes the act of bestowing the royal crown on Nimrod's head. This phrase is ambiguous with respect to the identification of the act's subject, so this operation could therefore be ascribed to Nimrod himself as

---

355   Cf. Götze 1922, p. 64; Ri 2000, p. 304.
356   This notion has been extensively discussed by scholars. For a concise survey and bibliography, see Gnoli 1999.
357   See Rastorgueva & Edelman 2007, pp. 438–443.
358   See, for example, Soudavar 2003.
359   See remarks by de Jong 2004, pp. 364–365.

well as to his subordinate Sasan. The situation is complicated by the fact that both these coronation scenarios have parallels in Iranian tradition.³⁶⁰

There were some instances when the Sasanian king would crown himself. One such case involves Shapur I, who according to the *Cologne Mani Codex* (18.7–8) "crowned himself with the grand diadem."³⁶¹ The use of the verb ἀναδέω, "to crown," in the Middle Voice indicates that the subject, i.e. the king, performed the action of crowning on himself.³⁶² However, there is ample evidence of the Sasanians following the earlier Parthian practice of being crowned by a representative of one of the great Iranian aristocratic families, such as the Sūrēns.³⁶³ During the later Sasanian period, the role of "bestower of the crown" was assumed by the Zoroastrian chief priest (*mōbadān mōbad*). Thus, according to al-Ṭabarī's *History*, it was the "chief mōbadh" who was "responsible for placing the crown (*al-tāǧ*) on the head of every king who was invested with royal power."³⁶⁴ In light of the fact that the practice of a representative of the nobility performing the coronation of the Iranian kings is much better attested than that of self-coronation, it seems more likely that Nimrod's crowning in CT 24.25 should be understood as being performed by Sasan, who thus functions as a "bestower of the crown."

Secondly, the context of Iranian royal imagery may provide a solution to the difficulty posed by the rather strange identification of Sasan as a "weaver" (*zāqurā*). Since he is said to be responsible for manufacturing Nimrod's crown, one would rather expect him to be designated by one of the Syriac words that refer to artisans who work with precious metals, such as *qaynāyā*, *ḥašālā*, or *ṣrāpāyā*. However, whereas we are accustomed to thinking about kings' crowns as the handiwork of goldsmiths par excellence, in the Iranian context this attribute of royal power formed a rather elaborate artifact in which metal elements were combined with those made of textile.

Images of a diadem tied at the back of the head with two ribbons may already be found on coins produced by the Parthians, who in this respect emulated their Seleucid predecessors.³⁶⁵ This tradition was continued and further elaborated during the Sasanian period, when the fillet with floating pleated ribbons became a persistent element of the royal headgear.³⁶⁶ Moreover,

---

360 For an overview of the development of the Iranian coronation ceremony, see Shahbazi 1993.
361 διάδημα μέγιστον ἀνεδήσατο; ed. Cameron & Dewey 1979, pp. 18–19.
362 For additional references to Shapur's self-coronation, see Shahbazi 1993, p. 277.
363 See Christensen 1944, p. 107.
364 Ed. de Goeje et alii 1879–1901, v. I.2, p. 861; trans. Bosworth 1999, p. 91.
365 See Peck 1993, p. 408–412.
366 See Peck 1993, p. 413–416.

another important element of the Sasanian royal headgear was the *korymbos*, the silky tiara around which the gold ornament or "crown" was built. From the fifth century on, the simpler early crowns developed into more complex versions that featured multiple symbols of gods and were composed of many elements. By the time of Khosrow II, the ceremonial crown had evolved into a very elaborate headgear that was too heavy for the king to wear and so it had to be suspended from the ceiling of the throne hall at Ctesiphon.

From this evidence, it is possible to conclude that the process of manufacturing royal headgear in the late Sasanian empire would have involved the joint efforts of goldsmiths and craftsmen working with textiles. Accordingly, it is easy to imagine how the process of assembling such a composite crown would be described as "weaving" and the artisan who carried out this work as a "weaver."[367]

Following these observations on the interplay of traditional and innovative elements in CT's author's portrayal of Nimrod's investiture, as well as his indebtedness to the symbolic world of Iranian royal ideology, the question of the authorial intent behind this narrative should be addressed. In what follows, I would like to suggest that the story of Sasan and Nimrod in CT 24.25–26 is apologetically motivated and that it allows our author to subtly subvert the official Sasanian ideology of kingship. As was noted earlier, the figure of Sasan played an important role in the self-image of the Sasanian dynasty and was often evoked to support their claim to royal power. It is this aspect of the Sasanian royal ideology that CT's author engages by forging his own story of the relationship between Sasan and Nimrod.

In order to better comprehend the apologetic strategy that underlies CT 24.25–26, let us turn to a striking parallel to the scene of Nimrod's investiture found in the *Book of the Deeds of Ardašīr*. In this work, Ardašīr's glorious future is signaled by a portent when his father Pāpag has a dream in which he beholds a whilte elephant and "the sun ... shining from the head of Sāsān" (*xwaršēd az sar ī Sāsān bē tābēd*) and illuminating the whole world. The dream interpreters to whom Pāpak turns explain this vision as a propitious omen, whose recipient, either himself or one of his descendants, is destined to come

---

367 The same argument is valid with respect to the beribboned ring conferred upon a king that frequently appears in scenes of royal investiture in Parthian and Sasanian monumental art. On this artifact, which should not be confused with the royal crown in *sensu stricto*, see Kaim 2009.

to "sovereignty over the world" (*pādixšāyīh ī gēhān*) because these natural objects are the signs of "bravery and power and victory."³⁶⁸

It is the motif of Sasan's solar aura which functions as a symbolic expression of his royal status in the *Book of the Deeds of Ardašīr* and thus lends legitimacy to the dynasty named after him that provides us with a key to the apologetic dimension of CT 24.25–26. When we compare this portrayal of Sasan with that of CT, it turns out that the Christian author resorts to a functional inversion of the image of Sasan as the paradigmatic originator of Sasanian kingship. According to his vision of ancient history, Sasan is merely an attendant of Nimrod, who is the true founder of Iranian kingship.

Two polemical techniques may be seen at play in this apologetic inversion in the depiction of Sasan. First of all, by associating Sasan with Nimrod, CT's author dischronologizes him. Taking Sasan out of the context of Sasanian royal mythology and subjugating him to the reference frame of biblical history deprives him of his symbolic weight. Moreover, there is a perceptible tint of irony in the portrayal of Sasan as the manufacturer of Nimrod's crown. CT's author demotes him from the exalted position of the legitimate possessor of this primary insignia of royal power to that of merely its manufacturer, who acts on behalf of a higher authority.

CT's author symbolically reverses the established hierarchical order when he represents the semi-mythical eponym of the Sasanian dynasty as a servant of Nimrod, who is the true cultural hero of Northern Mesopotamia. Taking into account that Christians constituted a disempowered minority group in the Sasanian empire, it seems epistemologically justified to analyze this aspect of Nimrod's portrayal in CT using the optics of postcolonial theory. An illuminating way to approach the socio-political dimension of this portrayal is to conceptualize it in terms of the critical theory of domination and subordination developed by James Scott.³⁶⁹ Following Scott's analysis of different patterns of domination and resistance, it seems justifiable to regard the association of Nimrod with the world of Iranian kingship as an element of "hidden transcript": a discourse "that represents a critique of power spoken behind the back of the dominant."³⁷⁰ The hidden transcript is one of the "hidden forms of resistance" to ideological dominance that are created by subordinate groups and are intended first and foremost for internal consumption. The application of this analytical approach to the description of Nimrod in CT is valid for two

---

368 *Kār-nāmag* 1.8–13; ed. Grenet 2003, pp. 54–56.
369 See Scott 1990. For an attempt to apply Scott's insights to the ancient world, see the works collected in Horsley 2004.
370 Scott 1990, p. xii.

reasons: first, because we are dealing here with a text that was produced by a subordinate minority group, and second, because our author consciously chooses to engage the dominant majority culture by using its own symbols and images.

It is the subversive strategy of "symbolic inversion" that may be recognized at work in the scene of Sasan's subordination to Nimrod. According to Scott, this strategy constituted a useful weapon in the arsenal of "hidden transcripts" employed by subservient groups in order to respond critically to the public discourse.[371] Through the symbolic inversion of Sasan's status, CT's author contests the hegemony of the public transcript of Sasanian royal propaganda and offers his community a vision of the past in which the current pattern of domination is reversed.

The conceptual apparatus of postcolonial theory can help us to throw light on another remarkable aspect of the prominent role ascribed to the figure of Nimrod in CT. What strikes an Iranist reading this work is the complete absence of Zoroaster from the passages that deal with the origins of the Persians' religion and customs. In light of our author's noticeable acquaintance with Iranian culture, it is hard to believe that he knew nothing about the founder of the Zoroastrian religion. His silence about Zoroaster is thus as conspicuous as his silence about the Exodus and giving of the Torah in his retelling of Old Testament history discussed in the previous chapter. It should be regarded as a conscious authorial decision, another instance of the author's selective approach to the past. However, the gap in the mythological history of Persia created by the absence of Zoroaster is different from that of Jewish history in that it is filled by Nimrod, who functions as a substitute figure for Zoroaster.

The identification of Nimrod with Zoraster is attested in several Christian sources that were produced before the time of CT.[372] For instance, as we have already seen, the author of the Pseudo-Clementine *Homilies* connected these two figures in his account of the origins of the Persian cult of fire, while noting that after his death from the heavenly fire, Nimrod–Zoroaster began to be worshipped as a god among the Persians.[373] Slightly later, Epiphanius of Cyprus mentions that this opinion was held by some unidentified "Greeks," although he himself does not share it and argues that "the two, Nimrod and Zoroaster, are far apart in time."[374]

---

[371] See Scott 1990, pp. 166–182.
[372] See Bousset 1907, pp. 369–373; Schoeps 1950, pp. 19–23.
[373] *Hom.* 9.4–5; ed. Rehm & Strecker 1992, p. 133. On the Persians' deification and worship of Nimrod, cf. also John Malalas, *Chron.* 1.7; John of Nikiu, *Chron.* 5.1–4.
[374] *Panar.* 1.3.2–3; ed. Holl 1915–1933, v. 1, p. 177; trans. Williams, F. 2009, p. 18.

CT's author deviates from this tradition in that he does not explicitly identify Nimrod with Zoroaster. However, we can hardly avoid noticing that the figure of the legendary founder of the Persian religion lurks behind the depiction of Nimrod in CT. The most obvious aspect that Nimrod shared with Zoroaster is his role as the founder of astronomy and the cult of fire among the Persians discussed above. In connection with the former, it should be mentioned that a number of late Syriac sources transmit the tradition about Zoroaster predicting the birth of Jesus.[375] While there is no unquestionable evidence for this story having been invented by Syriac Christians during late antiquity, this scenario appears most plausible to me. To this, we should add the connection between Nimrod and Ādurbādagān, which is only attested in CT. It is noteworthy that the region of Ērān-wēz and the river Dāityā, which figure as the place of Zoroaster's birth and public ministry in the Avestan corpus, were interpreted during the later periods as being located in Azerbaijan/Atropatene.[376]

It thus becomes apparent that CT's author produced his own image of Nimrod by merging biblical material with the native Iranian traditions, some belonging to the imaginaire of Iranian kingship and others relating to the figure of Zoroaster. This innovative blending of elements that come from the two different cultural systems, i.e. from the Christian minority and the Zoroastrian majority, brings us once more to the tenets of postcolonial theory. The notion of colonial mimicry, a part of the more general anti-colonial strategy of "hybridity," which I will discuss in more detail at the conclusion of this chapter, allows us to understand the cultural work performed by the unusual and innovative portrayal of Nimrod in CT. As we have seen, in both the case of the Nimrod–Sasan connection and the Nimrod–Zoroaster fusion, CT's author mimics the native Iranian tradition. The main objective of this mimicry is to subvert the discourse of the dominant and oppressive non-Christian culture by creating an alternative in-between space of hybridity where its heroes and symbols are subjected to those of the disempowered Christian minority.

2.2 Cyrus

A concise but important development of the theme of Iranian kingship appears in chapter 42, where the author narrates events from biblical history

---

375 Cf. Theodore bar Kōnī (8th c.), *Lib. schol.* 7, ed. Scher 1910–1912, v. 2, pp. 74–75; Išodad of Merv (9th c.), *Commentary on Matthew*, on Mt 2:2, ed. Gibson 1911–1916, v. 1, p. 19 [trans.]; Ḥasan bar Bahlūl (10th c.), *Lexicon*, ed. Duval 1888–1901, v. 2, cols. 1825–1826; Solomon of Basra (13th c.), *Book of the Bee* 37, ed. Budge 1886, pp. 81–82 [trans.]. For more references, see Gottheil 1894.

376 Cf. Iranian *Bundahišn* 29.16; ed. Pakzad 2005, p. 343. For a useful overview of the Pahlavi and Muslim evidence, see Jackson 1899, pp. 193–201.

such as the first destruction of Jerusalem by Nebuchadnezzar, the Babylonian exile, and Cyrus' liberation of the Jewish people. The latter incident occupies a significant part of the narrative space (CT 42.11–22). In full agreement with the biblical account, our author presents Cyrus in a favorable manner by emphasizing his role as the liberator of the exiled Judaeans. CT's narrative, however, features a remarkable elaboration of the story of this Iranian monarch that is completely absent from his canonical portrayal.

According to the biblical account (cf. Ezra 1:1–4; 2Chr 36:22–23), it was God himself who "stirred up the spirit" of Cyrus so that he made a proclamation throughout his kingdom in which the Judaean exiles were allowed to return to their native land and rebuild their temple. This explanation became the basis for the later Jewish and Christian accounts of the king's decree. For instance, Josephus explains this event in a manner similar to that of Scripture and further elaborates it by adding that Cyrus was seized by the desire to implement God's will after reading the divine prophecy about himself in the book of Isaiah (cf. Is 45:13).[377]

CT's author, however, offers a more narratively sophisticated explanation of the king's decision by ascribing his willingness to release the exiles to the influence of his Jewish wife. Cyrus decides to allow the Jews to return to their homeland and rebuild their sanctuary because he is persuaded to do so by his queen, who, according to CT 42.12, was "the daughter (*bart*) of Salathiel, the sister (*ḥāteh*) of Zerubbabel." This explanation of Cyrus' motivation in releasing the Jews has no exact analogs in the surviving Jewish and Christian writings from antiquity and is most likely the result of our author's creativity.

CT's claim that Cyrus' wife was of Jewish decent is not found in any other ancient Jewish or Christian source. The Syriac form of her name, mentioned in CT 42.19, poses certain difficulties, since the manuscript witnesses differ significantly at this point.[378] It should first be noted that CT's version of the queen's name appears to be completely unrelated to the classical tradition on this subject. For instance, Herodotus names the Achaemenian princess Cassandane as Cyrus' beloved wife.[379] Another Greek historian, Ctesias, relates that Cyrus married Amytis, the daughter of the Median king Astyages, after he had executed her husband Spitamas.[380] As to the original form of Cyrus' wife's name in CT, this could be reconstructed in different ways. Su-Min Ri prefers the reading MŠḤT and explains it as "la femme messianique," apparently based on Cyrus'

---

377 *Ant.* 11.1–7; ed. Thackeray et alii 1926–1965, v. 6, pp. 314–317.
378 Textual variants: Or^{AELOPSUV} ܡܫܝܚܬܐ, Or^{BCDHM}Oc^d ܡܫܝܚܬܐ, Or^F ܡܠܝܟܬܐ, Oc^{abce} ܚܙܝܬܐ.
379 *Hist.* 2.1, 3.2–3; ed. Godley 1926–1930, v. 1, pp. 170–171.
380 *Apud* Photius, *Bibl.* 72; ed. Henry 1959–1977, v. 1, p. 106.

Syriac title *mšiḥā*.[381] While this explanation certainly seems plausible, given our author's propensity to make Aramaic puns, we should not be too quick to discard the form MŠYNT as secondary. It may be derived from the Middle Persian name "Mašyāne," which, as mentioned above, was the name borne by the female half of the first human couple in the Zoroastrian mythological tradition.[382]

Without going into detailed analysis of her story, I would like to single out two literary parallels that may shed some light on the genesis of the depiction of Cyrus' wife in CT. One is provided by the biblical account of Esther, a Jewish queen of the Persian king Ahasuerus, who likewise pleaded before her royal husband on behalf of her kinsmen. Another important parallel to CT 42.11–22 is found in the *Chronicle* of John Malalas, who offers an extensive account of the events that resulted in Cyrus' release of the Jews.[383] According to him, this happened in the aftermath of the military crisis caused by the unexpected invasion of Cyrus' enemy, the Lydian king Croesus. Demoralized in the face of imminent danger, Cyrus is helped by his wife Bardane (Βαρδάνη). The queen suggests that he turn to the Jewish prophet Daniel for help, whom she knows from the time when she was married to Cyrus' predecessor, King Darius. Following Bardane's advice, Cyrus summons Daniel and, after recognizing the prophet's supremacy, receives assistance from him. Daniel prays for the king's victory over his enemy and promises that God shall be on his side while acquainting him with Isaiah's prophecy about his role in the future restoration of Jerusalem. Reassured, Cyrus promises Daniel that he will release the Israelites. True to his word, he fulfills his pledge after he defeats Croesus and allows the Jews to leave Persia for their homeland. There are significant differences between this account and that of CT which make it very unlikely that there was any direct literary relationship between the two compositions. It seems more likely that CT's author created his own version of the events surrounding Cyrus' edict by combining an account similar to that of Malalas with the biblical story of Esther.

Whatever the sources that CT's author used to forge this story may have been, one extraordinary detail in the portrayal of Cyrus, which is unique to this work, deserves our particular attention. It appears in CT 42.19, where the author offers an explanation of the two remarkable epithets applied to Cyrus

---

381   Ri 2000, p. 413.
382   Cf. Iranian *Bundahišn* 14.11; ed. Pakzad 2005, p. 183. For more on these figures, see Christensen 1917, pp. 7–105.
383   *Chron.* 6.7–11; ed. Thurn 2000, pp. 119–122; trans. Jeffreys et alii 1986, pp. 81–84. Cf. also John of Nikiu, *Chron.* 51.4–12.

in Scripture: "my (i.e. God's) shepherd" (Heb. *rōʿî*) from Isaiah 44:28 and the "anointed one" (Heb. *māšîaḥ*, Gr. χριστός, Syr. *mšiḥā*) from Isaiah 45:1:[384]

> And the name of Cyrus was called "My shepherd, the anointed of the Lord," because his seed was received into the seed of David through Mšaynat, the sister of Zerubbabel, whom he had married.[385]

The primary purpose of this sentence is apparently to demonstrate that the titles "shepherd" and "anointed one," which in this context have strong royal connotations, could be rightfully applied to a non-Israelite figure such as Cyrus. As CT's author argues, by marrying the daughter of Salathiel and the sister of Zerubbabel, both of whom were descendants of King David (cf. the genealogical list in CT 44.42–45),[386] the Persian monarch was, so to speak, grafted onto the Davidic lineage and thus became a rightful partaker of the Israelite royal dignity.

There were other attempts to provide Cyrus with a Jewish pedigree, seemingly motivated by the wish to find an explanation for the king's pro-Jewish decree. One example of this sort is found in the Judaeo-Persian poem *Ardašīr-nāmah* by Shahin of Shiraz (14th c.), where Cyrus is presented as a son of the Persian king Ardashir/Ahasuerus and his Jewish queen Esther.[387] This genealogical motif may be traced back as far as the eighth century, when al-Ṭabarī, in his *History*, reported an allegedly Christian tradition according to which Cyrus was Ardashir and Esther's son and later "embraced the faith of the Israelites" and began the reconstruction of Jerusalem.[388] The tradition of Cyrus being Esther's son also appears in the *First Targum to Esther* (7:2). This rabbinic composition features a story of the Persian king Ahasuerus/Xerxes refusing Esther's request to rebuild the Temple on account of his pledge to the pagan subjects and asking the queen to wait until her son Cyrus "will grow up and will inherit the kingdom and it shall be done."[389] While most scholars date

---

384 On this aspect of Cyrus' portrayal in Deutero-Isaiah, see Fried 2002.
385 Or^A: ܐܠܗܝܡ, ܡܫܝܚܐ ܕܡܪܝܐ ܪܥܝܝ ܩܪܝܗܝ ܠܟܘܪܫ ܫܡܐ. ܘܐܬܩܪܝ ܙܪܥܗ ܒܙܪܥܐ ܕܕܘܝܕ ܒܝܕ ܡܫܝܢܬ ܚܬܗ ܕܙܘܪܒܒܠ, ܕܢܣܒܗ.
386 For the biblical reference to their Davidic lineage, see 1 Chronicles 3:1–19.
387 On this, see Netzer 1974, pp. 43–52.
388 Ed. de Goeje et alii 1879–1901, v. I.2, pp. 653–654; trans. Perlmann 1987, p. 51. Cf. also al-Ṭabarī's account of Cyrus' Kayanian counterpart, King Bahman, whose mother was also Esther and who appointed Zerubbabel over the Israelites and allowed him to return to Judaea; ed. de Goeje et alii 1879–1901, v. I.2, p. 688; trans. Perlmann 1987, p. 82.
389 ברם אוריכי עד ירבי כרש בריך ויחסן מלכותא ותיתעבד; ed. Grossfeld 1983, pp. 28 [Aram.], 64 [trans.].

this Targum to the late sixth or early seventh century,[390] there is a difficulty in dating the particular tradition about Cyrus in this work. Several manuscripts of the *First Targum* mention the Persian king Darius, not Cyrus, as the son of Esther who will restore the Temple.[391] The *Leviticus Rabbah* (13.5), an Amoraic Midrash from Byzantine Palestine, which relates that "the latter Darius," i.e. Darius the son of Ahasuerus from Daniel 9:1, was "the son of Esther,"[392] indicates that this reading should be preferred as the original. It thus appears that the motif of Cyrus' descent from a Jewish mother is not securely attested in the genuine Jewish sources from late antiquity,[393] which makes it not immediately relevant to the discussion of our author's position on this subject.

Returning to the genealogical connection between Cyrus and David in CT, I would like to suggest that besides its purely exegetical function as a solution for the problem of the king's unusual titles in Isaiah, this effort to present the great Persian monarch as a kinsman of David has wider implications for our understanding of the particular apologetic agenda pursued by the author in his dealing with the subject of Iranian kingship. To comprehend this agenda, the notion of the Davidic descent of Jesus, which was important in Christian belief, should be taken into account. It should also be mentioned that the authors of the New Testament not only refer to Jesus as the "son of David," but include both Salathiel and Zerubbabel in the lists of his Davidic ancestors (cf. Mt 1:12–13; Lk 3:27). Accordingly, the inevitable conclusion is that by including Cyrus in the Davidic line of descent, CT's author turns this Iranian king into a kinsman of Jesus.

The genealogical connection between Cyrus and David could therefore rightfully be considered another element in our author's series of apologetic efforts to naturalize Christianity in the world of Iranian culture by presenting it as an ancestral Persian faith, which I shall discuss in more detail later. It should be noted at this point that CT's author was not the only Syriac-speaking Christian in late antiquity who attempted to recruit the figure of Cyrus for such purposes. For instance, in the Syriac version of Eusebius' *On the Star*, this king is included in the list of other ancient monarchs of the Near East who transmitted Balaam's prophecy about the star and looked forward to its fulfillment.[394] Even more significant is the mention of Cyrus in the proceedings of the East Syrian synod of Mār Abā I (540–552), which took place in the year 544. In this

---

390   See Grossfeld 1991, pp. 19–20.
391   See variant readings in ed. Grossfeld 1983, p. 28.
392   Ed. Margulies 1993, p. 290.
393   On the rabbis' treatment of Cyrus, see Urbach 1961; Mokhtarian 2010.
394   Ed. Wright, W. 1866–1867, pp. 12 [Syr.], 159 [trans.].

public document, we find the contemporary Sasanian monarch Khosrow I extolled as the "second Cyrus" (*Kureš da-trēn*), who is established and supported by God to act for the benefit of the Christian community.[395]

2.3 The Magi

Two chapters of CT (45 and 46) present an extended narrative of the New Testament Magi. They are introduced as one of several groups in Persia who become disturbed after witnessing the appearance of a new bright star in the sky within which the image of "a maiden carrying a child" with "a crown set upon his head" was depicted. The Magi, characterized as experts in astronomy, consult their books, including the one entitled "The Revelation of Nimrod," from which God's providential plan for Christ to be born in Judea becomes apparent to them. Carrying out their own part in this plan, the Magi, who are said to be three in number, travel to the "mountains of Nod." There, they take three gifts from the "cave of treasures"—gold, frankincense, and myrrh, which Adam brought out of Paradise and deposited there. With these gifts, the Magi travel to Bethlehem in Judea, where they find the infant Jesus, worship him, and offer him the gifts. The Magi's story concludes with their acknowledgment of Jesus as God and their departure back to their homeland. This narrative is ultimately based on Matthew 2:1–12, but contains a considerable amount of non-biblical material. In what follows, I am going to discuss those extra-canonical features in the Magi's portrayal that put a particular emphasis on their Iranian background.

2.3.1 The Origins and Number of the Magi

The Gospel of Matthew (2:1–12) is the only document in the New Testament corpus that contains a story about certain "wise men from the East" (Gr. μάγοι ἀπὸ ἀνατολῶν) who come to Judea following a star in order to worship the newborn king of the Jews and offer him gifts of gold, frankincense, and myrrh. Throughout the centuries, the figures of the mysterious Eastern visitors captured the imagination of many Christians and brought to life a rich tradition of representations of the Magi in literature and art.[396]

The word μάγοι, which the Gospel's author employed to describe these visitors, had a wide range of meanings in Greek. This noun could indicate "members of the Persian priestly caste," or "any possessor or user of supernatural powers," or, properly speaking, "magicians, sorcerers," or, figuratively,

---

395 Ed. Chabot 1902, pp. 69–70 [Syr.], 320 [trans.].
396 For a general overview of traditions about the Magi, see Kehrer 1908–1909; Élissagaray 1965; Trexler 1997.

"a deceiver or seducer."[397] The question of which of these meanings was intended by the author of the Gospel has occupied scholars for generations.[398] It is less relevant, however, for our study than the problem of the translation and reception of Matthew 2:1–12 in the Syriac-speaking milieu. In all the Syriac versions of the New Testament, from the Old Syriac Gospels up to that of Thomas of Harkel, the Greek μάγοι in Matthew 2:1–12 is translated as *mgušē*.[399] In the native Syriac sources, this noun is primarily used to refer to members of the Persian priestly class, or occasionally to non-priestly adherents of the Zoroastrian religion.[400] That the Greek noun μάγος was not translated as the Syriac noun *mgušā* by default can be seen from the Peshitta version of Acts 13:6 and 13:8, where it is rendered as *ḥarāšā*, "magician, sorcerer." It is possible that the Syriac translators of Matthew 2:1–12 wanted to remove the ambiguity present in the Greek μάγος and to unequivocally identify the Eastern visitors as followers of Zoroastrianism. Later, the identification of the Matthean Magi as *mgušē* became standard in the Syriac Christian tradition, where these figures enjoyed considerable popularity.[401]

As to the origins of the Magi, it is related in CT 45.12 that they come from the "East" (*madnḥā*) and more specifically, in CT 45.5, from "the land of Persia" (*'ar'ā d-Pāres*).[402] The New Testament account of the Magi provides no exact information about their homeland save the brief mention that they came "from the East." During late antiquity, Christian exegetes came up with a number of solutions for the problem of the "East" in Matthew 2:1. The most popular of them was the understanding of this geographical term as referring to "Persia," apparently developed under the influence of the Iranian connotations of the noun "Magi."[403] Occasionally, the Magi were thought to have come from "Arabia," "Babylon," or even "Ethiopia."[404] By connecting the Magi to "Persia," CT's author

---

397 Delling 1967, pp. 356–358. See also de Jong 1997, pp. 387–403.
398 See Luz 2007, pp. 101–116; Delling 1967, p. 358; Powell 2000a, 2000b.
399 Ed. Kiraz 1996, v. 1, p. 15.
400 On the word's range of meanings, see Payne Smith 1879–1901, cols. 2008–2009. Its etymology goes back to the Old Persian *maguš*; see Sokoloff 2009, p. 707.
401 On the Magi in Syriac tradition, see Monneret de Villard 1952; Witakowski 2008; Debié 2008; Haelewyck 2011.
402 Ed. Ri 1987, pp. 362, 366.
403 Cf. Clement of Alexandria, *Protr.* 5.65.1, *Strom.* 1.15; Origen, *C. Cels.* 1.24; Basil of Caesarea, *Hom. in Chr. gen.* 5; John Chrysostom, *De beato Philogonio.* 6.4; Cyril of Alexandria, *Comm. in Is.* 4.4 (PG 70, col 1061).
404 For "Arabia," cf. Justin, *Dial.* 77.4, 78.2, 88.1, 106.4; Epiphanius, *De fide* 8.1; on this tradition, see Maalouf 1999. For "Babylon," cf. Balai, *Madrasha on the Dedication of the Newly Built Church in Qenneshrin* 49, 51, 54, 59; ed. Overbeck 1865, pp. 256–257. For "Ethiopia," cf. Caesarius of Arles, *Serm.* 194.1.

followed an already centuries-old tradition of interpreting Matthew 2:1 that was especially popular among Syriac-speaking Christians.[405]

In CT 45.19, the author lists the Magi, mentioning both their names and the regions under their authority. It is apparent from this list that the Magi were three in number. This stands in contrast with the view that the Magi were twelve in number that was much more common among Syriac-speaking Christians. One of the earliest Syriac sources that expresses such a view is the so-called *Revelation of the Magi*, an extended apocryphal narrative embedded in the West Syrian *Chronicle of Zuqnin* (8th c.) which may go back to the fifth or even fourth century.[406] The antiquity of this tradition is confirmed by its appearance in the *Opus Imperfectum in Matthaeum*, an anonymous fifth-century Latin commentary on the Gospel of Matthew. The author of this work recounts the story of the twelve Magi and their gifts, relying on an apocryphal book ascribed to Seth as his source.[407] There is no other Syriac Christian source predating or contemporary to CT in which the Magi are three in number, and it is not clear where CT's author received this idea. In light of my hypothesis that CT had West Syrian origins, it may be reasonable to regard this motif as one of the "Western" exegetical traditions that reached its author via the Miaphysite network. Another possibility would be that our author was influenced by the iconography of Nativity and Adoration scenes, which usually include a depiction of the three Magi. There are several artistic representations of the three Magi that come from Syria or Mesopotamia, such as, for example, the scene of the Adoration of the Magi on a sixth-century slab from Rasm al-Qanāfez.[408] This scenario is further supported by later Syriac authors such as Jacob of Edessa, who, while defending the opinion that the Magi were twelve in number,

---

405   Cf. Jacob of Serugh, *Homily on the Nativity*, ed. Bedjan 1902, p. 786; *Homily on the Star That Appeared to the Magi*, ed. Bedjan 1905–1910, v. 1, p. 86, ln. 3; p. 87, ln. 11; p. 97, ln. 16; p. 114, ln. 1; Simeon the Potter, *Hymns on the Nativity* 5.2, ed. Euringer 1913, p. 228; Pseudo-Ephremian *Soghitha on Mary and the Magi* 4.4–8, 49, 52, ed. Beck 1959, pp. 210, 216 [Syr.].
406   See Landau 2008. For later Syriac traditions on the twelve Magi, see Witakowski 2008.
407   PG 56, col. 637–638.
408   See Nasrallah 1961, pp. 45–48. Cf. also the scene of the Adoration of the Magi on the two incense burners: one from Qamishli (6th to 7th cc.) described by de Jerphanion 1939, p. 308, fig. 3–4 and one from Takrit (8th to 9th cc.) described by Harrak 2006. For numerous examples of representations of the three Magi in the Western Christian (i.e. Greek and Latin) art in late antiquity, see Leclercq 1931. In the Armenian tradition, the three Magi feature in the scene of the Adoration from the Ejmiacin Gospels (late 6th to early 7th cc.); see Mathews 1982, pp. 205–206.

mentions iconographical representations featuring the three Magi as the source of an alternative view.[409]

2.3.2 The Royal Status of the Magi

Another noteworthy feature of the narrative of the Magi in CT is that they are described as "kings, the sons of kings" (*malkē bnay malkē*) in 45.18. No royal features are attributed to the Magi in the canonical account and it is only in the later tradition of Christian exegesis that we find them invested with such dignity.[410] The depiction of the Magi as "kings," although attested from the second century, was not particularly widespread during late antiquity. One of the earliest writers to suggest this was Tertullian, who on several occasions offers a messianic interpretation of the Psalm verses that feature "the kings of Arabia and Saba" and their offerings (Ps 72:10–11, 15) as referring to the Magi's visit and even notes that "the East regards the Magi almost as kings."[411]

The marginal character of the Magi's royal status in the Christian tradition of late antiquity is confirmed by the evidence provided by Christian art, where the scene of the Adoration of the Magi was one of the most popular subjects.[412] The first images of the Magi's visit, already attested in the second century, are found in the catacombs of Rome. By the fourth century, this scene becomes very popular. The earliest artistic representations of the Magi in frescoes, mosaics, and sculptures would usually render them featuring general Orientalizing traits, such as the Phrygian cap, Oriental-style chlamys or chiton, and anaxyrides.[413] Their iconography is often modeled after that of the triumphal monuments of imperial Rome, where representatives of the defeated barbarian nations were depicted presenting gifts, especially golden crowns. One of the best-known representations of the Magi that illustrates this tendency is that of the sixth-century mosaic from the basilica church of Sant' Apollinare Nuovo in Ravenna.[414] Nevertheless, representations of the Magi as kings, so

---

409 *Letter (# 14) to John of Litarba*; the relevant fragment was published by Nestle 1881, pp. 83–84.
410 On the development of this tradition, see Powell 2000a.
411 *Adv. Marc.* 3.13.8: *Nam et magos reges habuit fere oriens*; ed. Kroymann 1954a, p. 525. This sentence, along with an identical interpretation of Ps 72:10,15, also appears in his *Adv. Jud.* 9.12.
412 Most of the artistic representations of the Magi from antiquity are conveniently collected in Leclercq 1931. For an analysis of the early iconography of the Magi, see Vezin 1950; Deckers 1982; Trexler 1997, pp. 21–38.
413 See Vezin 1950, pp. 65–70.
414 See von Simson 1987, pp. 89–95.

popular in medieval European art, were virtually unknown to the late antique and early Byzantine traditions of Christian art.[415]

Notwithstanding Tertullian's statement about the East regarding the Magi as kings, no such imagery seems to be found in the surviving Greek Christian writings from late antiquity. While a messianic interpretation of Psalm 72:10–11 [LXX 71:10–11] in which the bringing of gifts by "the kings of Arabia and Saba" (βασιλεῖς Ἀράβων καὶ Σαβα) was regarded as a prefiguration of the Magi's visit became quite popular among Greek-speaking Christian exegetes from the fourth century,[416] it had no recognizable impact on how the Magi were perceived in the Eastern Christian imagination.

The situation is almost the same in the Syriac Christian tradition prior to CT's time. It is remarkable that the majority of ancient Syriac writers who mention the Magi or address Matthew 2:1–12 do not employ any royal imagery at all. Ephrem, in those of his *Hymns on the Nativity* that repeatedly evoke the story of Matthew 2:1–12, characterizes the Eastern visitors only as *mgušē*.[417] In the Syriac *Commentary on the Diatessaron*, which is ascribed to Ephrem, there is an extended discussion of the Magi's visit where they are consistently referred to as *mgušē* and at are one point likened to the prophets, but they are never represented as "kings."[418] No royal characteristics are attributed to the Magi in Jacob of Serugh's several poems about the Nativity.[419]

One of the rare cases of the recognition of the Magi's royal status in Syriac sources from late antiquity is found in the *Testament of Adam*. In the "Prophecy" section of this apocryphal composition, where Adam foretells the future coming of Christ to Seth, he mentions the Magi and characterizes them as "the sons of kings" (*bnay malkē*).[420] Stephen Robinson, the editor of the *Testament*, dates the "Prophecy" part of it to the third century.[421] However, there are some con-

---

415   See Trexler 1997, pp. 35–36, 46.
416   On this, see below.
417   Cf. Hymns ##22–24; ed. Beck 1959, pp. 109–127 [Syr.]. The phrase *malkē rhibin* in Hymn 26.2 (ed. Beck 1959, p. 133 [Syr.]), which could be taken as being related to the Magi, should rather be understood, in light of the poetic parallelism Ephrem employs in this stanza, as referring to the malevolent local rulers of Judaea, such as Herod. To avoid ambiguity, it would be better to translate it not as "kings are hastening" (trans. McVey 1989, p. 206), but as "kings are disquieted/alarmed." Cf. also the *Soghitha on Mary and the Magi* attributed to Ephrem, where the envious "local kings" (*malkē d-'ar'ā*) are mentioned in the context of the Magi's visit (ed. Beck 1959, p. 214, ln. 32 [Syr.]).
418   Cf. *Comm. Diat.* 2.18–25; trans. McCarthy 1993, pp. 68–73. For a discussion of this tradition, see de Halleux 1991.
419   Ed. Bedjan 1902, pp. 720–808; ed. Rilliet 1986, pp. 538–549.
420   *T. Adam* 3:7 (Recension #1 and 3); ed. Robinson, S.E. 1982, pp. 64–65, 100–101.
421   Robinson, S.E. 1982, p. 151.

siderations that make us suspect this particular tradition to be a later addition. These are based on the evidence provided by the Syriac versions of another apocryphal work, the *Transitus Mariae*, into which the part of the *Testament* that mentions the Magi is incorporated. We have two early manuscripts of the *Transitus* at our disposal, one from the fifth century and one from the sixth. It is remarkable that while in the sixth-century Syriac version of this work the Magi are called "the sons of kings" (*bnay malkē*), the fifth-century version contains no such characteristic.[422]

Another early mention of the Magi's royal status is found in the writings of Isaac of Antioch, a fifth-century Syriac poet. In his still-unpublished *Homily on the Magi Who Came from the East*, preserved in the sixth-century manuscript Vatican Syriac 120, we come across a scene of Herod's interrogation of the Magi during which they entreat the king not to mistake them for Persian spies and reveal their true identity, claiming that "we are from the chiefs of Persia, and even kings and sons of kings."[423] Although there is still much work to be done on Isaac's corpus and the place of this homily within it, in the meantime it would be not unreasonable to suggest the second half of the fifth century as the earliest likely date of the Magi being described in royal terms in Syriac Christian tradition.

2.3.3 The Names of the Magi

The Magi's royal status is strengthened even further by the fact that all three of them are represented as bearers of characteristically royal Iranian names. In CT 45.18–19, the author describes the Magi in the following way:

> These are the kings, the sons of kings, who bore the offerings to the King: Hormizd of Makhozdi, the king of Persia, who was named "king of kings" and who used to dwell in the lower Azerbaijan, and Yazdgird, the king of Saba, and Perozad, the king of Sheba, which is in the East.[424]

There is a certain difficulty in deciphering the Magi's names due to the fact that there are many textual variants for each name. In my translation, I follow the

---

422 For the sixth-century Syr. *Transitus*, see Wright, W. 1865, pp. 27 [Syr.]; 145 [trans.]; for the fifth-century version, see Lewis 1902, pp. 68 [Syr.], 41 [trans.].

423 ܡܢ ܪܫܝ ܦܪܣ ܐܝܬܝܢ ܘܐܦ ܡܠܟܐ ܘܒܢܝ ܡܠܟܐ; ms. Vatican Syr. 120, fol. 199r. This is homily #106 in the list in Mathews 2003. I thank Kristian Heal for drawing my attention to this text.

424 Or^A: ܗܘܡܙܕܝܘܢ.

reconstruction of these names offered by Carl Bezold in his German translation of CT as the most philologically convincing.[425]

The name of the first Magus is perhaps the most problematic. Its two main variants in the manuscripts of CT are "Hormizd" and "Hormizdād."[426] Both these theophoric names, derived from the name of Ohrmazd, the highest deity of Zoroastrianism, are attested in the original Iranian sources.[427] Accordingly, it is difficult to decide which of these two forms, which are both supported by the manuscript evidence, should be preferred as the original form of the king's name. The form "Hormizd" seems to be a more likely option. This choice is based on the fact that the two other Magi bear distinctive royal names. While we know of several Sasanian kings named Hormizd,[428] there are no examples of the personal name "Hormizdād" being borne by an Iranian monarch. It is noteworthy, however, that in the historiographical work of Agathias of Myrina, the names of Kings Hormizd I and II are spelled as Ὁρμισδάτης.[429]

The name of the second Magus does not present particular difficulties and should without doubt be established as "Yazdgird."[430] Its meaning is also theophoric—"made by God." We know of three Sasanian kings who bore this name—Yazdgird I (r. 399–421), Yazdgird II (r. 438–457), and Yazdgird III (r. 632–651), the last ruler from the Sasanian dynasty.

The form of the third Magus' name also varies considerably in different manuscripts of CT.[431] Given the fact that—with the exception of PYRWZ—none of these variants has parallels in the corpus of indigenous Iranian onomastics, the form "Pērōz" ("victorious") seems most likely to be the original form of

425 See ed. Bezold 1883–1888, v. 1, p. 57.

426 Textual variants: Or[ABDMO] ܗܘܪܡܝܙܕܕ, Or[EHLPSU] ܗܘܪܡܙܕܕ, Or[C]Oc[d] ܗܘܪܡܝܙܕ, Or[V] ܗܘܪܡܝܙܕܪ, Oc[c] ܗܘܪܡܐܙܕܪ.

427 See Justi 1895, pp. 7–9; Gignoux 1986, pp. 98, 137–139. An attempt to reconstruct the original name of the first Magus as *Hormizd-farr* by J. Marquart, who interpreted the Magi's names in the light of the Iranian names of the three envoys sent by Nimrod to Balaam according CT 35.18–21 (Marquart 1907, p. 7), is seriously flawed due to his reliance on the limited textual basis of Bezold's edition of CT, and thus can hardly be accepted as satisfactory.

428 There were five Sasanian kings that bore this name: Hormizd I (r. 272–273), Hormizd II (r. 303–309), Hormizd III (r. 457–459), Hormizd IV (r. 579–590), and Hormizd V (r. 630–632).

429 See *Hist.* 4.24.5; 4.25.1; ed. Keydell 1967, p. 154.

430 Textual variants: Or[A] ܐܝܙܕܓܪܕ, Or[BCDOPSV] ܐܙܕܓܪ, Or[EHLMU] ܐܙܪܓܕ, Oc[abc] ܐܙܕܓܕܪ, Oc[d] ܝܙܕܓܪܕ. Cf. this name spelled as ܝܙܕܓܪ and ܐܝܙܕܓܪܕ in other Syriac sources; for the references, see Gignoux et alii 2009, pp. 143–144, ##453a–j. For examples of this name in Iranian sources, see Justi 1895, pp. 148–149; Gignoux 1986, pp. 189–190.

431 Textual variants: Or[AELOPSUV] ܦܝܪܘܙܕ, Or[BCD] ܦܝܪܘܙ, Or[H] ܦܝܪܘܙܕܕ, Or[M] ܦܝܪܘܕܕ, Oc[a] ܦܘܪܙܕܢ, Oc[d] ܦܝܪܘܙܕܢ. He is also mentioned by name in CT 46.22, where only the form ܦܝܪܘܙܕܕ is attested.

this name.⁴³² There were two Sasanian monarchs who bore this name—Pērōz I (r. 459–484) and Pērōz II (ob. after 661). It thus seems reasonable to accept a suggestion made by Witold Witakowski that the rule of Pērōz I, the first Sasanian king bearing this name, might serve as a *terminus post quem* for the story of the Magi in CT.⁴³³

This tradition of the Magi's names has no parallels in other sources from late antiquity and is unique to CT. It is completely independent from the contemporary Western tradition, where the Magi were named Gaspar, Melchior, and Balthasar.⁴³⁴ A legitimate question arises as to the reason behind the attribution of these particular Sasanian royal names to the Magi in CT. We could attempt to find a common denominator that would bring together three Sasanian kings bearing these names and thus throw light upon the author's choice. One answer to this question could be that CT's author named the Magi after those Sasanian kings who had recently ruled and would therefore be easily recognized by his intended audience. One possible configuration of three Sasanian kings whose names correspond to those of the three Magi was offered by Albrecht Wirth. He suggested that the prototypes of the Magi in CT were the three following Sasanian monarchs, who ruled consecutively from the middle to the second half of the fifth century: Yazdgird II (r. 438–457), Hormizd III (r. 457–459), and Pērōz I (r. 459–484).⁴³⁵

One could, however, think of another possible common denominator that seems to provide a better solution to the problem of the Magi's names. The author's choice of these particular names might have been determined by the fact that the Sasanian kings who bore these names had a positive attitude towards Christianity. This explanation is certainly appropriate for the first Magus, whose name may be understood as alluding to Hormizd IV (r. 579–590). This Sasanian king, during whose reign CT's author may well have lived, pursued a policy of religious tolerance towards Christians and hindered attempts by the Zoroastrian clergy to launch anti-Christian persecution.⁴³⁶

---

432   For examples of the name *Pērōz* and its derivates in Iranian sources, see Justi 1895, pp. 247–251; Gignoux 1986, pp. 147–148; Gignoux 2003, p. 55. Marquart's attempt to derive the name of the third Magus from the Persian name *Farr-vindād* (Marquart 1907, p. 4) is too arbitrary to be useful.
433   Witakowski 2008, pp. 815–816.
434   For the references and discussion, see Metzger 1970, pp. 80–81.
435   Wirth 1894, p. 203, n. 2.
436   On him, see Shahbazi 2004a. On Hormizd's policy towards Christians in his empire, see Labourt 1904, pp. 200–203; Christensen 1944, pp. 442–443.

CATEGORIZING THE IRANIAN "OTHER" 231

The second Magus, whose name may have been derived from Yazdgird I (r. 399–420), also conforms to this pattern. Reviled by the non-Christian Persian and Arabic sources as a "sinner," for the greatest part of his rule this king treated his Christian subjects favorably, legalizing public Christian worship in Persia and sponsoring the first synod of the Church of the East.[437] Although the last year of Yazdgird's reign saw a renewal of anti-Christian persecution, this fact did not blacken the king's image in the later Christian tradition, where the negative aspect of his rule was often de-emphasized, either through disregard, explanation, or justification.[438]

The case of the third Magus is the most problematic. The only Sasanian king who could have served as his prototype was Pērōz I. In distinction from Hormizd IV and Yazdgird I, this king's loyalty to the official Zoroastrian religion was staunch and unquestionable. He is said to have initiated persecutions against the Christians of his empire.[439] Yet the existing evidence on Pērōz's policy towards Christians is contradictory. Thus, in a number of East Syrian sources, he is presented in a positive light, mainly on account of his role as the patron of Barṣauma of Nisibis.[440] The *Chronicle of Arbela* even said of Pērōz that "although he was a pagan, he greatly helped the Christians during his lifetime."[441] This positive picture of his reign also seems to be supported by the *Martyrdom of Gregory Pīrān-Gušnasp*, a late sixth-century hagiographical work, where it is reported that the Christians of Iran enjoyed a period of peace "from the reign of King Pērōz until the tenth year of King Khosrow."[442] While Stephen Gerö may be correct in his refusal to accept the reliability of these two sources as witnesses to Pērōz's real policy towards Christians,[443] it is important for our argument that at least some sixth-century Iranian Christians saw nothing wrong with the image of Pērōz as a king who was favorably disposed to the Christian minority.

Another aspect of the Magi's portrayal in CT that deserves attention is their association with particular geographical regions. The first Magus, Hormizd,

---

437 See Labourt 1904, pp. 87–103; Christensen 1944, pp. 269–273.
438 On this, see McDonough 2008a.
439 See Gero 1981, pp. 17–20.
440 See Labourt 1904, pp. 149–150; Gero 1981, pp. 36–37.
441 ܐܦܢ ܚܢܦܐ ܐܝܬܘܗܝ ܗܘܐ ܣܓܝ ܥܕܪ ܗܘܐ ܠܟܪܣܛܝܢܐ ܒܚܝܘܗܝ; ed. Mingana 1908, p. 67, ln. 36–37.
442 ܡܢ ܫܠܡܘܬܗ ܕܦܝܪܘܙ ܡܠܟܐ ܥܕܡܐ ܠܫܢܬ ܥܣܪ ܕܟܘܣܪܘ ܡܠܟܐ; ed. Bedjan 1895, p. 348, ln. 13–15.
443 See Gero 1981, p. 20.

is characterized as "the king of Persia" (*malkā d-Pāres*), and in order to reinforce this claim, he is referred to by the distinctively Iranian royal title "king of kings"—*mlek malkē* in Syriac, which is a calque of the Persian *šāhān šāh*. Hormizd's origins are related to MKWZDY, a toponym (or possibly patronym) which is difficult to identify with a reasonable degree of certainty.[444] Another toponym connected with Hormizd is easily recognizable, since it derives as a calque from "Ādurbādagān," the Middle Persian name for the province of Azerbaijan.[445] There were several possible reasons for mentioning Azerbaijan in connection with a Sasanian king. As stated above, Azerbaijan served as the religious center of the Sasanian empire, since the principal royal sanctuary of Ādur Gušnasp, to which every newly crowned Sasanian monarch had to pay homage, was located there. Moreover, the city of Ganzak, the capital of the province, functioned as an important center of Sasanian administration.[446] In fact, the puzzling phrase that Hormizd "used to dwell (*yāteb hwā*) in the lower Azerbaijan," which stands in contradiction to the pre-eminent status of Seleucia-Ctesiphon as the official capital of the Sasanian empire, may be explained as a reflection of the fact that Ganzak at times served as the Iranian rulers' summer residence.[447]

While the association of Hormizd with Persia does not present particular problems, the mention of "Saba" and "Sheba" as the kingdoms of the two other Magi is in need of explanation. It would be counterproductive to look for a connection between those historical Sasanian kings who were named Yazdgird and Pērōz and these geographical regions, which are located in Arabia. Rather, as Witakowski has suggested,[448] this association should be understood as the result of a purely literary development, i.e. as an example of embedded exegesis of the following messianic prophecy from Psalm 72:10–11:

---

444   Textual variants: Or^ABCDELMSUV Oc^d ܡܟܘܙܕܝ, Or^OP ܡܟܘܙܕܝ, Or^H ܟܘܙܕܡܝ. An attempt to explain this noun as being composed of the Persian noun *māh*, "month," and Armenian *kʿowsti*, derived from the Middle Persian *kust* ("district"), in de Lagarde 1888, p. 841, is hardly convincing. Likewise, I see no compelling reason to accept Marquart's emendation of this *hapax* into the relative clause ܗܘ ܡܙܕܝ, "who is Mazdai" (Marquart 1907, p. 7).
445   The correct form is found in Or^P ܐܬܪܒܝܓܢ and Oc^d ܐܬܪܒܝܓܢ.
446   Mani is said to visit Ganzak during one of his missionary journeys (see *Cologne Mani Codex* 121.4–15). It was to this city that the catholicos Mār Abā I was sent to be kept under house arrest by Khosrow I. On this affair, see Labourt 1904, pp. 181–185; Macuch 2014.
447   Thus, in *Geogr.* 11.13.3, Strabo says of the Parthians that "their royal summer palace is situated in a plain at Gazaca" (βασίλειον δ' αὐτῶν θερινὸν μὲν ἐν πεδίῳ ἱδρυμένον Γάζακα); ed. Jones, H.L. 1917–1949, v. 5, pp. 304–305.
448   Witakowski 2008, p. 815. Marquart seems to have been the first scholar to notice this scriptural allusion; see Marquart 1907, p. 2.

The kings of Tarshish and of the isles will bring him offerings. The kings of Sheba and Saba will offer gifts. And all kings will bow down before him, and all nations will worship him.[449]

CT's author was not the first Christian writer to read Matthew 2:1–12 in the light of Psalm 72:10–15. Here, he follows a well-established tradition of Christological interpretation of this Psalm. In the passage mentioned above, Tertullian interprets Psalm 72:10–15 as referring to the Magi's visit and their gifts. By the fourth century, this understanding of Psalm 72:10–15 became widespread throughout the Greek-speaking part of Christendom. Athanasius of Alexandria, in the *Expositions on the Psalms*, interprets "the gold of Arabia" in Psalm 72:15 as referring to the Magi's offerings.[450] This exegetical tradition appears in the works of later Greek exegetes, and its wide distribution makes it difficult to definitively establish how it reached the Syriac-speaking milieu of CT.[451] Putting aside the possibility of its oral circulation or of CT's author being directly acquainted with the aforementioned Greek works, we may point to the Syriac translation of Athanasius' *Expositions* that was already in existence by the sixth century as a plausible source of inspiration for our writer.[452]

2.3.4   The Clothing of the Magi

As the story of the Magi advances, the author presents the following description and explanation of the particular manner in which the Magi were dressed during their visit to Bethlehem (CT 46.3–4):

> They were called "Magi" because of the garb of Magianism, which the pagan kings used to wear whensoever they offered up a sacrifice and brought offerings to their gods. They used two different kinds of apparel: that of royalty—inside, and that of Magianism—outside. Likewise also

---

449   Peshitta: ܟܠܗ ܡܠܟܘܬܐ ܕܬܪܫܝܫ ܘܕܓܙܪܬܐ ܩܘܪܒܢܐ ܢܝܬܘܢ ܠܗ. ܡܠܟܐ ܕܫܒܐ ܘܕܣܒܐ ܡܘܗܒܬܐ ܢܩܪܒܘܢ. ܘܢܣܓܕܘܢ ܠܗ ܟܠܗܘܢ ܡܠܟܐ. ܘܟܠܗܘܢ ܥܡܡܐ ܢܦܠܚܘܢܝܗܝ.
450   Καὶ δοθήσεται αὐτῷ χρυσίον Ἀραβικὸν, δηλοῖ σαφῶς ἃ προσήνεγκαν οἱ μάγοι δῶρα; PG 27, col. 325.
451   Cf. Didymus the Blind, *Comm. in Zech.* 3.305; Cyril of Alexandria, *Comm. in Is.* 4.4; Eusebius of Caesarea, *Comm. in Ps.* (PG 23, col. 813); Amphilochius of Iconium, *Or.* 4.7. It may be noted that no such interpretation of Ps 72:10–15 is attested in the commentaries on the Psalms from the Antiochene tradition by Theodore of Mopsuestia and Theodoret of Cyrrhus and later East Syrian works such as the *Commentary on Psalms* by Išoʿdad of Merv. This may serve as an additional example of the dissimilarity between CT and the East Syrian exegetical tradition discussed above, in section 4 of chapter 1.
452   See ed. Thomson 1977, pp. 143 [Syr.], 116 [trans.].

> those, who went up to Christ prepared to offer their gifts, were arrayed in the two kinds of apparel.[453]

As in the case of the Magi's names, no similar tradition about their particular manner of dress is attested in any other ancient Christian source. Nor do ancient Greco-Roman or Oriental sources provide explicit descriptions of Iranian kings being clothed in the two distinctive kinds of attire, royal and priestly, during their participation in Zoroastrian rites. The unique character of this tradition calls for close attention and obliges us to attempt to grasp the message conveyed by means of this imagery.

One solution to this problem has been proposed by Witakowski, according to whom the Magi's description in CT 46.3–4 should be understood as a purely literary development: by combining these two kinds of garment, CT's author "makes an effort to reconcile the tradition of their being kings with Matthew's term *magoi*."[454] This explanation provides an obvious but only partial solution to the problem, because it does not analyze this unique tradition in the context of CT's general literary strategy. It explains *how* the double image of the Magi's dress came into existence, but not *why* the author decided to use it.

There are good reasons to regard this aspect of the Magi's depiction as something more than the merely ingenious invention of an exegetically oriented mind whose sole purpose was to resolve real or apparent contradictions in the authoritative texts or to close a "gap" in the tradition.[455] While it is clear that our author is relying on the existing tradition of Christian scriptural exegesis in his work, he is far from being an antiquarian who collects different opinions about biblical figures and attempts to harmonize them. On the one hand, we do find examples of different exegetical traditions being "reconciled" in CT, such as the case of the threefold characteristics of Adam as king, prophet, and priest.[456] However, such examples demonstrate that the author felt it necessary to harmonize only those traditions that would advance his own agenda. Thus, in the case of Adam, his threefold status is conditioned by the author's supersessionist anti-Jewish theology, according to which the Jewish

453 Or[A]: ܡܓܘ̈ܫܐ ܕܝܢ ܐܬܦܪܣܘ ܡܛܠ ܐܣܟܝܡܐ ܕܡܓܘܫܘܬܐ ܕܠܒܝܫܝܢ ܗܘܘ ܡܠ̈ܟܐ ܣܢ̈ܝܩܐ. ܕܐܡܓܘ̈ܫܐ ܕܒܒܝܬ ܕܚܫܘܬܐ ܘܡܟܘܪܝܢ ܘܡܘܪ̈ܒܐ ܠܐܠܗܘܬܗܘܢ. ܢܗܘܘܢ ܡܬܚܙܝܢ ܒܬܪܝܢ ܐܣܟܝ̈ܡܝܢ. ܟܕ ܗܘܘ ܕܡܠܟܘܬܐ ܡܢ ܠܥܠ ܘܕܡܓܘܫܘܬܐ ܡܢ ܠܬܚܬ. ܗܟܢܐ ܐܦ ܗܢܘܢ ܕܣܠܩܘ ܗܘܘ ܠܘܬ ܡܫܝܚܐ ܟܕ ܡܛܝܒܝܢ ܠܡܩܪܒܘ ܩܘܪ̈ܒܢܝܗܘܢ ܠܒܝܫܝܢ ܗܘܘ ܕܬܪ̈ܝܗܘܢ ܐܣܟܝ̈ܡܝܗܘܢ.

454 Witakowski 2008, pp. 815–816.

455 On the latter, see Vevaina 2010.

456 Cf. CT 2.18; 48.29. Each of the three traditions circulated separately in Jewish and Christian exegesis before the time of CT.

people were deprived of the gifts of kingship, prophecy, and priesthood after the coming of Jesus.[457] In fact, instead of trying to "reconcile" those exegetical traditions that could not be integrated into his version of biblical history, CT's author was perfectly capable of ignoring or even explicitly rejecting them.[458] In light of all this, the reason for the author's decision to preserve both aspects of the Magi's identity, royal and priestly, is in need of explanation.

As pointed out above, the tradition that the Magi were royal had a rather limited currency in the late ancient Near East. CT's author seems to be one of the earliest writers to develop a consistent and full-fledged image of the Magi on this foundation. My suggestion would be that CT's unique dual image of the Magi as both royal and priestly is a result not only of the author's reliance on the previous tradition of New Testament exegesis, but also of his acquaintance with some indigenous Iranian ideas of monarchy. Parallels provided by Iranian sources oblige us to seriously consider the possibility that CT's author refashioned the traditional image of the Magi in light of the ideology of an inseparable connection between "religion" (*dēn*) and "state" (*xwādayīh*) that was prevalent in Sasanian political discourse.

One of the first scholars to comment on the possibility of an Iranian background for the description of the Magi's dress in CT was Geo Widengren.[459] According to him, the double apparel of the Magi is related to the ancient Iranian idea of sacred kingship, which was conveyed in a most visible manner through the dress code of the Iranian kings, who, from the Achaemenian times onwards, used vestments distinguished by the combination of red and white, thus indicating a union of the two highest offices of Indo-European society, that of the warrior class (red/purple) and that of the priestly caste (white), in the person of the king. In what follows, I am going to expand this thesis, which, although it seems to be basically convincing, is nonetheless in need of certain adjustments.

Similarly to many other ancient cultures, the Iranians considered the institution of kingship to be intimately connected with the realm of the divine.[460]

---

457 Cf. CT 48.29; 50.13–14; 52.17. For discussion of this anti-Jewish argument, see section 4.1 of chapter 2.
458 Cf. his rejection of the interpretation of the "sons of men" of Gen 6:1–9 as angels (CT 15.4–8); the rejection of the idea of Hebrew as the primeval language (CT 24.11); the polemic against the Melchizedekians (CT 30.11–17); and the disagreement with the incorrect genealogy of the Twelve Tribes (CT 33.1).
459 See Widengren 1959, p. 254.
460 For an overview of ancient theories of kingship, see Oakley 2006. On sacral kingship in Sasanian Iran, see Widengren 1959; Choksy 1988; Daryaee 2008; Panaino 2009, esp. pp. 216–227.

The origins of the principle of royalty were traced back to the beginning of the world, as it was believed to have been created by Ohrmazd himself.[461] There is an ongoing debate among Iranists over the exact meaning of the Middle Persian formula *kē čihr az yazdān* found in official Sasanian inscriptions and coins as a characteristic of the king.[462] Regardless of whether this formula should be understood as the kings' claim of direct divine descent or as an expression of their iconic resemblance to gods, it functions as a public assertion of Zoroastrian divinities being the ultimate source of Sasanian royal power.

Unfortunately, we possess only limited evidence for the cultic activity of Iranian kings and their participation in sacrificial ceremonies.[463] For example, in Philostratus' account of Apollonius of Tyana's visit to the Parthian court, it is the king who is represented as carrying out the ritual of horse sacrifice in the presence of the Magi.[464] Occasionally, the quality of *magus* is attributed to Sasanian kings. In the Syriac *Romance of Julian*, Shapur II is referred to as "the great king, the Magus, and the mighty god."[465] According to Agathias of Myrina, the founder of the Sasanian dynasty, Ardashir, was "a devotee of the magian religion and an official celebrant of its mysteries."[466] On the basis of this and similar evidence, Antonio Panaino comes to the conclusion that Sasanian monarchs "behaved as natural members of the clergy with a different function and with a number of proper privileges."[467]

Given the extreme scarcity of evidence about actual Zoroastrian ritual practice during the Sasanian period in general and on the cultic duties performed by kings in particular, it is difficult to validate or disprove Panaino's claim. It is important for our argument that at least in the realm of discourse, religious devotion and close collaboration with the priestly caste were considered to be the essential characteristics of a Sasanian monarch. On this foundation, a

---

461 Cf. *Dēnkard* 3.289; for the Pahlavi text and French translation of this passage, see Molé 1963, pp. pp. 48–49.
462 The main problem is the multivalency of the noun *čihr*, which could be translated as "likeness," "form," "seed," or "stock." For a recent treatment of this problem, see Daryaee 2008, pp. 65–67; Panaino 2009, pp. 227–246.
463 See Widengren 1959, pp. 251–254.
464 Philostratus, *Vit. Apol.* 1.29–31; ed. Jones, Ch.P. 2005, v. 1, pp. 104–109.
465 ܡܠܟܐ ܪܒܐ ܡܓܘܫܐ ܘܐܠܗܐ ܚܝܠܬܢܐ; ed. and trans. (modified) Sokoloff 2016, pp. 370–371. The epithet *'alāhā* ("god") looks strange in this context and is most likely the result of a too-literal rendering of the Persian title *bay* ("lord") by the Syriac-speaking author of the *Romance*; see Panaino 2009, p. 222, n. 71.
466 *Hist.* 2.26.3: ἦν δέ γε οὗτος τῇ μαγικῇ κάτοχος ἱερουργίᾳ καὶ αὐτουργὸς τῶν ἀπορρήτων; ed. Keydell 1967, p. 75; trans. Frendo 1975, p. 60. Cf. also George Synkellos' report on Ardashir; ed. Mosshammer 1984, p. 440.
467 Panaino 2009, p. 233.

well-attested doctrine of concordat developed between the Sasanian state and the Zoroastrian religion.[468] This fundamental principle of Sasanian political ideology is memorably expressed in the *Letter of Tansar*, possibly composed during the sixth century, whose author states that "Church and State were born of the one womb, joined together and never to be sundered."[469] Similar statements are also scattered throughout various Zoroastrian texts written in Pahlavi. In the third book of the *Dēnkard*, it is proclaimed that "kingship is built on religion, and religion on kingship" and that "kingship and religion, religion and kingship are [fellow-] countrymen to each other."[470] The author of the *Dēnkard* offers Zoroaster as a paradigm of this union when he praises the prophet for the two sublime qualities that were combined in his person—"the Kayanian Glory" (*kayān xwarrah*), i.e. the glory of kingship, and "the glory of priesthood" (*hērbed xwarrah*).[471] Another exemplary embodiment of these two qualities is Yima, the mythical king of the primeval Paradise, in whom, like in Zoroaster, "the Glory of lordship" (*xwarrah ī xwadāyīh*) is united with "the Glory of Good Religion" (*xwarrah ī weh dēn*).[472]

In light of all this evidence, it seems very likely that CT's author was aware of the double royal and priestly function of kingship in Sasanian Iran when formulating his description of the Magi's vestments, and that he consciously evoked this imagery in order to express the Iranian identity of the New Testament Magi even more emphatically. As to the question of the author's purpose in creating this unique portrayal of the Magi that blends together royal and priestly features, the answer to this lies, I would argue, in his strategy of promoting a covert political agenda of dissociating the institution of the Iranian monarchy from the Zoroastrian religion, which is discussed in more detail below.

2.3.5 The Magi's Anticipation of Jesus

There is one more manifestation of the Magi's Iranian background in our work that deserves to be discussed. It comes into view in CT 46.8, where the following account of what the Magi expected to see when they came to the newborn "king of the Jews" is offered:

---

468   On this notion, see Zaehner 1961, pp. 296–299; Shaked 1984, pp. 31–40. Most of the relevant primary sources are collected in Molé 1963, pp. 37–58.
469   Trans. Boyce 1968a, p. 33.
470   *Dēnkard* 3.58: *pad awēšān xwadāyīh abar dēn, dēn abar xwadāyīh winārdagīh ... xwadāyīh dēn [ud] dēn xwadāyīh [ham-]dehān*; text and translation *apud* Shaked 1984, p. 39.
471   *Dēnkard* 7.3.46; for the Pahlavi text and French translation of this passage, see Molé 1967, pp. 36–39.
472   *Dēnkard* 3.129; for the Pahlavi text and French translation see Molé 1963, pp. 37–38.

> Thus did they think that they would find in the land of Israel a royal palace, and couches of gold covered [with carpets and tapestries],[473] and the king and the son of the king arrayed in purple, and hastening soldiers and companies of royal troops, and nobles of the kingdom paying him honor by presenting gifts, and furnished tables with food fit for the king, and delicacies in rows, and men servants and women servants serving in fear.[474]

This description contains a number of characteristic features that point to the ceremony of the Iranian royal audience as the basic pattern after which the Magi's expectations are modeled. The institution of the royal audience had great significance in the ancient Iranian system of government and was regarded as an indispensable element of the monarch's office.[475] Whereas CT's author explicitly places the Magi's expectations of Jesus against the background of the royal court by mentioning the "royal palace" (*pālāṭin d-malkutā*), in addition to this general remark there are several more specific elements in his description of this setting that betray its Iranian origins.

One such element is the "couches of gold" (*ʿarsātā d-dahbā*), which refers to the ceremonial couch or throne that was used by the king and magnates of Iran and neighboring Armenia during feasts and banquets. We already find this luxurious object mentioned in the Young Avesta, when, in the hymn addressed to the goddess Aši, couches with "golden feet" (*zaraniiapaχšta.pāδā̊ŋhō*) are listed among the rewards of those who praise her.[476] Later, Josephus relates that one of the exclusive privileges of the Parthian kings was "to lie down on a bed of gold" (ἐπὶ κλίνης χρυσῆς καθεύδειν).[477] The Sasanian high priest Kerdir mentions a "golden couch" (*zarrēn bazm*) in the context of a banquet scene when describing his heavenly vision in a section of the Middle Persian inscription at

473 While absent from Or^A, this pair of nouns appears in many manuscripts of the Eastern recension. The sentence's syntax and the fact that "tapestries" are mentioned in the Western recension indicate that there is a high probability that at least one of these objects featured in the original text of CT.

474 Or^A: ܗܟܢܐ ܡܣܬܒܪ ܗܘܐ ܠܗܘܢ ܕܡܫܟܚܝܢ ܗܘܘ ܒܐܪܥܐ ܕܐܝܣܪܝܠ ܦܠܛܝܢ ܕܡܠܟܘܬܐ. ܘܥܪܣܬܐ ܕܕܗܒܐ ܟܕ ܡܟܣܝܢ [ܒܣܛܝܠܬܐ ܘܐܪܓܠܐ]. ܘܡܠܟܐ ܘܒܪ ܡܠܟܐ ܟܕ ܡܬܥܛܦܝܢ ܒܐܪܓܘܢܐ. ܘܚܝܠܘܬܐ ܘܗܦܪܐ ܕܚܝܠܐ ܡܠܟܝܐ ܟܕ ܪܗܛܝܢ. ܘܪܘܪܒܢܐ ܕܡܠܟܘܬܐ ܟܕ ܣܓܕܝܢ ܠܗ ܒܩܘܪܒܢܐ. ܘܦܬܘܪܐ ܕܡܛܝܒܘܬܐ ܕܡܠܟܐ ܟܕ ܡܬܩܢܝܢ. ܘܡܛܥܡܐ ܟܕ ܣܕܝܪܝܢ. ܘܥܒܕܐ ܘܐܡܗܬܐ ܕܡܫܡܫܝܢ ܒܕܚܠܬܐ.

475 On this ceremony, see Khaleghi-Motlagh 1989.

476 *Yašt* 17.9; *apud* Bailey 1943, p. 6.

477 *Ant.* 20.67; ed. Thackeray et alii 1926–1965, v. 9, p. 424.

Sar Mašhad.[478] This object features prominently in images of kings' banquets, which were very popular in Sasanian silverwork. In many of these scenes, the king is depicted sitting on a couch, either alone or with a consort.[479]

Another noteworthy element of CT 46.8 that brings to mind imagery related to the setting of the Iranian royal audience or banquet is the mention of the "carpets/mattresses" (*milātā*) that are spread upon the couches. These mattresses, called *wistar(ag)* in Middle Persian, were a particularly important element of the adornment of the royal throne during Sasanian times.[480] A vivid description of these luxurious items can be found in al-Ṭabarī's *History*, in the account of the audience given by Khosrow II (r. 591–628) when he was held captive by his own son. While visited by a military commander, the imprisoned monarch is said to be "seated on three Khusrawānī rugs woven with gold, which had been laid on a silken carpet, and he was lolling back on three cushions likewise woven with gold."[481] Like the royal couch mentioned above, this accessory also features prominently in scenes of royal banquets on Sasanian silverwork, where the couch upon which the king sits is usually covered with several layers of mattresses.[482]

An additional detail bearing connotations of Iranian kingship is the "purple" (*purpārān*) in which the baby Jesus was supposedly wrapped. An important part of the Iranian dress code, the color purple distinguished the clothing of the warrior class, to which kings and the nobility belonged, from Median and Achaemenian times onwards.[483] This practice continued during the Sasanian period, as there are several mentions of Persian kings and their soldiers being dressed in red.[484] Several Greek sources describe Persian kings or their armies

---

478   Ed. Gignoux 1991, pp. 91, §25 [Pahl.], 96 [trans.]. I have translated the Middle Persian noun *bazm* as "couch" and not as "throne," as Gignoux's French translation "trône" would suggest, following the lead of N.G. Garsoïan, who renders its Armenian cognate *bazmakan* as "banqueting-couch, feasting-couch"; see Garsoïan 1989, p. 515.
479   Cf. silver plates in Ghirshman 1953, pp. 60–61, 63, 66–67. See also Dentzer 1971; Harper 1979.
480   See Sperber 1982, pp. 91–93; Shaked 1986, pp. 77–79. As has been pointed out by G. Herman, one should distinguish between *mattresses*, upon which the king sat, and *cushions*, against which he leaned; see Herman 2008, p. 74.
481   وكان كسرى جالسا على ثلاثة انماط ديباج خسرواني منسوج من ذهب قد فرشت على بساط من ابريسم متكأ على ثلث وسائد منسوجة بذهب; ed. de Goeje et alii 1879–1901, v. I.2, p. 1048; trans. Bosworth 1999, p. 385.
482   See Ghirshman 1953, pp. 60–61, 63, 67.
483   See Reinhold 1970, pp. 18–20; Shahbazi 1992, pp. 723–735.
484   See Tafazzoli 2000, p. 1.

being dressed in purple.[485] Similar descriptions are found in Zoroastrian sources, such as the *Dēnkard*, where the attire proper to the warriors is described as "the garment which is red (*suxr*) and wine-coloured (*may-gōn*), adorned with all kinds of ornament, with silver and gold, chalcedony, and shining ruby."[486]

Some of the images employed in CT 46.8 suggest that the author may not have had an ordinary royal audience in mind while constructing this fictitious scene, but rather one of those ceremonies that were performed with much greater pageantry during Nowrūz and Mihragān, the two most important festivals of the Zoroastrian year.[487] There were two different kinds of royal audience that were held during these holidays—the private, for the reception of foreign dignitaries and the Persian nobility, and the public, for the reception of other members of Iranian society.[488]

One of the elements that recalls such festival settings is the mention of the "gifts" (*mawhawātā*) being offered by the "nobles of the kingdom" (*rawrbānē d-malkutā*). The presentation of gifts to the Sasanian monarch by his subjects of every rank, from foreign rulers down to commoners, constituted one of the central elements of these two festivals.[489] As related in the Arabic *Book of Crown* ascribed to al-Jāḥiz, "it is proper to offer to the king presents on Mihragān and Nowrūz, and the reason for this is that they divide the year."[490] The mention of "delicacies" (*paṭbāgē*) arranged on the tables also suggests a possible festival context for this imaginary audience. During both Nowrūz and Mihragān, it was customary to offer to the king particular sorts of food associated with each of these festivals—new milk and cheeses for the former and ripe fruits and nuts for the latter.[491] Eating sugar candies as an auspicious omen for the New Year was another ancient Iranian custom.[492] According to the *Book of Beauties and Antitheses*, another pseudo-Jāḥizian work, at Nowrūz Iranian kings were offered "white sugar with pared fresh Indian nuts" to eat.[493] There

---

485 Cf. Eunapius, *Vitae sophist.* 6.5.8 (on Shapur II); Julian, *Orat.* 2.63B (on the Persian army).
486 *Dēnkard* 3.192.3; *apud* Tafazzoli 2000, p. 1.
487 On these festivals, see Boyce 1983.
488 See Khaleghi-Motlagh 1989, p. 733.
489 See Boyce 1983, pp. 799–803; Ehrlich 1930.
490 ومن حق الملك هدايا المهرجان والنيروز والعلة فى ذلك أنهما فصلا السنة; ed. Zéki Pasha 1914, p. 146. This phrase opens a section that describes exchanges of gifts between the king and his subjects during these two festivals. For a French translation, see Pellat 1954, pp. 165–168.
491 See Boyce 1983, p. 802.
492 See Carter 1974, p. 192.
493 سكّر ابيض وجوز هندوىّ مقشّر; ed. van Vloten 1898, p. 362.

was also a tradition of putting seven different sorts of grains on the king's table during this festival.[494]

∴

Having observed the close connection that CT's author established between the Magi of the Gospel of Matthew and several ideas and images characteristic of Iranian royal culture, we are faced with the question of his motives for undertaking such a particular and innovative reinterpretation of these biblical characters.

First of all, it should be noted that the story of the Magi has an important narrative and theological function within the overall framework of the Christian history of salvation that CT's author advances. The three Iranian kings serve as indispensable mediators who channel God's promise of universal salvation given at the very beginning of human history in the Old Testament to its fulfillment in the New Testament. It is through them that our author is able to develop the general notion of the unbroken continuity of sacred history into a coherent and vivid narrative. By delivering the three symbolic gifts—gold, frankincense, and myrrh—to the infant Jesus, the Magi confirm his status as the "Last" or "New" Adam and signal the commencement of his redemptive ministry, thus bringing the circle of *Heilsgeschichte* to its completion (cf. CT 45.13–15).[495] The considerable attention paid to the figures of the Magi, as well as their thoroughly positive portrayal that culminates in the confession of Jesus as God (cf. CT 46.19–26), also agrees with the consistent anti-Jewish agenda that CT's author pursued, as his supersessionist theology required an example of good Gentiles in order to cast a deeper shadow over the unbelieving Jewish people.[496]

Another avenue for understanding the particular attention paid to the Magi in CT is provided by the aforementioned notion of local patriotism. The case of the Magi should be added to that of the Syriac-speaking Christians' positive image of Nimrod as a founding figure of Northern Mesopotamia. The fact of their origins in the "East," in the "land of Persia," would naturally dispose the Christians of these regions to regard the Magi as their compatriots and representatives, and, as a consequence, to hold them in high esteem.

---

494   Cf. Pseudo-Jāḥiz, *Book of Beauties*; ed. van Vloten 1898, p. 361; al-Dimašqī, *Cosmography* 9.8; ed. Mehren 1866, p. 278.
495   Adam took these offerings from Paradise after his expulsion and deposited them in "the cave of treasures" (cf. CT 5.17; 13.6; 16.14, 21; 45.12). See also Ruzer & Kofsky 2010, pp. 117–118.
496   On this aspect of CT, see section 4.1 of chapter 2.

These arguments alone do not suffice, however, to account for several unique features of the Magi's portrayal in CT, such as the use of the names of Sasanian monarchs and other distinctively Iranian royal attributes, which set CT's author apart from the majority of late ancient Syriac and other Christian writers who dealt with the Magi. When taken seriously, this emphatic stress on the *royal* identity of the Magi in CT makes us pose the question of a possible political dimension behind this narrative.

Appealing to the figures of the Magi was a popular means of legitimizing earthly lordship during the Middle Ages, both in the Latin West and the Byzantine East.[497] When, however, we turn to late antiquity, it seems that the Magi were only rarely used for this purpose in the Christian political discourse of this epoch. There are only a few instances of politically charged utilizations of the Magi from this period. One such instance is found in the works of Augustine. In one of his sermons for Epiphany, Augustine uses this festival as an occasion to implore earthly kings to "have a pious and filial fear" of Jesus, extolling the Magi as the models of such behavior.[498] In addition to this, some scholars point out the possible political implications of the image of the Magi in the sixth-century mosaics in San Vitale church in Ravenna. In the mosaic panel in the apse of this church, there is an image of Theodora, the wife of Emperor Justinian, with a picture of the Magi on the embroidered border of her chlamys. As has been suggested by Natalia Teteriatnikov, the royal couple consciously adopted the figures of the Magi in order to enhance their image as wealthy donors to the church.[499] Another explanation of the Magi's appearance on the empress' vestment has been offered by Matthew Canepa, who suggests that this iconographical detail should be analyzed in the context of Roman–Persian rivalry and understood as an effort to visually assert "the subjection of Iranian religion and sovereign to the Roman religion—Christianity."[500]

When comparing the image of the Magi in CT with these attempts to deploy them for political purposes, the different socio-political context of CT's author and his community should be taken into account. The manner in which the biblical figures of the Magi functioned in the political discourse of the late Roman empire, which had adopted Christianity as its official religion, would not be the same as that of the Sasanian state, where Christians formed a minority group, persecuted or, at best, tolerated.

---

497   See Trexler 1997, pp. 44–75; Geary 1994, pp. 243–256.
498   *Serm.* 200.2; PL 38, col. 1029–1030; trans. Hill 1993, pp. 83–84. For an analysis of this passage, see Powell 2000a, pp. 475–478.
499   Teteriatnikov 1998, p. 382.
500   Canepa 2009, p. 120. For a non-political interpretation of the Magi on Theodora's dress, see McClanan 2002, pp. 133–134.

As we turn to the Iranian milieu, it becomes apparent that the particular interpretation of the Magi in CT should be examined in light of the discursive tendency to Christianize Sasanian rulers exhibited by some of their Syriac-speaking subjects. This phenomenon has recently been analyzed by Christelle Jullien, who defines it as "un processus graduel de mutation du roi barbare en un allié ou tout au moins en un souverain favorable aux chrétiens."[501] It finds expression in a number of Syriac literary sources produced within the confines of the Sasanian empire during the sixth and early seventh centuries, where several Iranian monarchs are extolled as enlightened or even Christian kings whose rule is divinely sanctioned. An outspoken example of this attitude is the aforementioned case of the acts of the synod of Mār Abā I, where King Khosrow I is praised as the benevolent patron through whom Christ conveys many benefits upon his Church.[502]

Whereas in her article Jullien mostly limits herself to the East Syrian sources and does not take into consideration the material provided by CT, the treatment of the Magi in this work deserves to be regarded as another expression of this tendency. This is shown by the fact that for CT's author, it was important to give the Magi not just any Iranian names, but names that were characteristic of Sasanian kings, notwithstanding the obvious anachronism that was involved in this naming, as the Sasanian dynasty commenced two hundred years after Jesus' birth in Bethlehem.

This observation brings us again to Scott's theory of domination and subordination. As in the case of Nimrod, the image of the Magi in CT is an amalgam of different elements, some of which belong to the culture of the Christian minority, while others are borrowed from the dominant culture of Sasanian Iran. In accordance with Scott's analytical approach, representations of the Magi in the context of the Christian empire could be considered as belonging to the realm of "public transcript," i.e. as forming part of the public performance of mastery and command by the dominant class, whose symbolic subjugation to Jesus, through identification with the Magi, was intended to bolster the emperors' own self-image as justifying their position of dominance over their Christian subjects and thus to legitimate the existing social order. However, in the different political context of the non-Christian Sasanian empire in which CT was composed, it seems justifiable to regard the Magi's identification with the world of Iranian kingship as an element of "hidden transcript." In analyzing the narrative of the Magi in CT as a part of the "hidden transcript" forged by the author in order to engage the dominant Iranian culture, we may discern

---

501   Jullien, Ch. 2009, p. 120. See also McDonough 2008; Schilling 2008.
502   Ed. Chabot 1902, pp. 69–70 [Syr.], 320 [trans.].

the two main interpretative strategies of subversion that he employs towards that goal—a reinterpretation of the Magi's identity from Zoroastrian priests to Sasanian kings, and their conversion to Christianity.

The former strategy has already been examined in detail above. As to the latter, CT's author introduces an elaborated story of the Magi's conversion into the canonical narrative of the Epiphany (CT 46.19–26). After they have offered the infant Jesus their gifts, the Magi stay with him for three more days. During that time, they witness a magnificent spectacle of the angelic host coming down from heaven and singing the threefold Sanctus from Isaiah 6:3 in front of Jesus. This angelophany has an immediate effect on the Eastern visitors and makes them believe in Christ. The third Magus, King Pērōz, explains the vision to his companions by pointing out that when he studied "in the school of the Hebrews" (*b-ʾeskulē d-ʿEbrāyē*), he read prophesies in the book of Isaiah about the future king of angels and men who would come from heaven.[503] The subsequent conversion of the Magi culminates in a public act of recognizing Jesus as God. Performed at the conclusion of their visit, it is represented by the author as a cultic act of "worshipping."[504]

The subversive power of these narratives lies firstly in the fact that by presenting the Magi to be more like Sasanian kings than Zoroastrian priests, CT's author marginalizes the religious aspect of their identity, while subjugating it to the secular one. He explicitly stresses in CT 46.3–4 that although it may look as though the New Testament Magi were members of the Zoroastrian priestly caste, their true identity was that of Iranian monarchs. This shift in the Magi's identity aims to dissociate the venerated scriptural figures—and, by extension, the Sasanian kings—from Zoroastrianism, the official religion of the Persian empire, with which no compromise was possible for CT's author.[505] This dissociation of the Sasanian monarchy from Zoroastrianism is further strengthened and finally sealed by the act of the Magi's conversion. CT's author dresses the Magi in the Sasanian royal garb only in order to "baptize" them. The purpose of this double-staged reinterpretation of the scriptural figures is clearly apologetic, as it conveys the idea that the Iranian kings had already acknowledged Jesus a long time ago. Accordingly, an implied message of the Magi's story in CT is that it presents the option of conversion to Christianity for Sasanian kings not as an innovation or an adoption of a foreign religion, but as a legitimate

---

503 In his speech (CT 46.22–23), he quotes Isaiah 7:14 and 9:6 as proof-texts.
504 In CT 46.26, he uses the verb *sged*, "to worship," analogous to the Greek προσκυνέω, in order to describe the Magi's respectful reaction to the infant Jesus.
505 This is evident from the open polemic against several aspects of Zoroastrian religion that our author wages elsewhere in his work; cf. CT 27.12–16 for polemic against close-kin marriage and CT 27.17–22 against divination and astrology.

CATEGORIZING THE IRANIAN "OTHER" 245

return to the faith of their forefathers. It is thus difficult to miss the subversive political dimension of this reinterpretation of the Magi, which is fueled by the dream of royal conversion and of a new Sasanian Constantine that was ever-present in the psyche of the Christians of Iran.[506]

As a final point in this discussion, it should be noted that CT is not the only example of politically charged deployment of the Magi in the late antique Near East. There are at least two more ancient sources where a similar connection is forged between these scriptural figures and the Sasanians.

Thus, Barhebraeus, a thirteenth-century West Syrian scholar, reports in the *Ecclesiastical Chronicle* a story of the religious dispute that supposedly took place between the already mentioned sixth-century East Syrian catholicos Mār Abā I and the Sasanian king Khosrow I.[507] During this dispute, the king, who acts as a spokesperson for the West Syrian theological position, cites a number of arguments intended to prove the divine nature of Jesus and Mary's right to be called the "mother of God." Among the proofs offered by the king, who turns out to be well versed in the New Testament, is that "our fathers the Magi, unless they knew that he who was born from the virgin in Bethlehem is God, would not have come from the East to worship him and would not have brought him the offerings."[508]

There are serious reasons to doubt the historicity of this story of the meeting between the king and the catholicos, which clearly betrays a West Syrian bias as it includes several stock motifs of anti-Nestorian polemic. However, even if we discard the whole story as fictional, its building blocks may still be useful for reconstructing the discursive world of the Syriac-speaking Christians under Sasanian rule. As far as our case is concerned, it is remarkable that the Syriac Christian who invented this story, whoever he was, found it rhetorically persuasive to present the Sasanian king acknowledging the Magi of the New Testament as his ancestors, even if he did so for the sake of polemics.

Another story that evokes the motif of Persians identifying themselves with the Magi of the Gospel of Matthew appears in the Greek composition known as the *Letter of the Three Patriarchs*. This apologetic document in defense of icons, which is addressed to the Byzantine emperor Theophilus (r. 829–842), was allegedly written in Jerusalem in the year 836 by the three

---

506 On this, see Schilling 2008, esp. pp. 159–234; Jullien, Ch. 2009, pp. 127–131.
507 Ed. Abbeloos & Lamy 1872–1877, v. 3, col. 91–95. For an English translation of this story and discussion, see Casartelli 1888.
508 ܘܐܒܗܬܢ ܡܓܘܫܐ ܐܠܘ ܠܐ ܝܕܥܝܢ ܗܘܘ ܕܐܠܗܐ ܗܘ ܗܘ ܕܐܬܝܠܕ ܡܢ ܒܬܘܠܬܐ ܒܒܝܬ ܠܚܡ. ܠܐ ܐܬܝܢ ܗܘܘ ܡܢ ܡܕܢܚܐ. ܘܣܓܕܘ ܠܗ ܘܩܪܒܘ ܠܗ ܩܘܪܒܢܐ; ed. Abbeloos & Lamy 1872–1877, v. 3, col. 93.

eastern patriarchs—Christopher of Alexandria, Job of Antioch, and Basil of Jerusalem.[509] Among other arguments and stories about the miraculous power of icons, this letter describes an incident from the Persian conquest of Palestine in the year 614, in which, we are informed, the Sasanian army took over the city of Bethlehem and it was only by a miracle that the church of the Nativity was not destroyed. This miracle was brought about by the image of the Magi in the scene of the Adoration on the mosaic that was located on the western part of the basilica's exterior façade. It was the Persian conquerors' spontaneous reaction to this image that made them spare the building:

> when they gazed at the pictures of their compatriots, the Persian astrologers and Magi, they stood in awe before their picture, as if they were still alive, and out of reverence and love for their forefathers, they preserved this great church intact and completely unharmed for their sake.[510]

It seems certain that the author of the *Letter* did not invent this story, but borrowed it from some older source which is unknown to us. However, as in the case of the account from Barhebraeus' *Chronicle*, we may wonder whether this story possesses any historical value. It is doubtful whether the *Letter* should be trusted in its ascription of the production of the mosaics in the church of the Nativity to the initiative of Empress Helen, mother of Constantine. Some scholars suggest that these mosaics were made later, as part of the basilica renovation carried out by Justinian.[511] Even more suspicious is the miraculous story itself, not only on account of the unlikely aesthetic reaction ascribed to the Persians, but also because it is not supported by any other Christian source on the Byzantine–Persian conflicts during the seventh century. Yet its historical unreliability notwithstanding, I believe that this story, like the one transmitted by Barhebraeus, still retains its value as a witness to the close connection between the New Testament Magi and the Sasanian Persians that emerged as an important element of the symbolic discourse in the Christian culture of the late antique Near East.

When read alongside these stories, CT's account of the Magi provides us with an insight into the particular socio-political imaginaire that had crystallized among the Christians of the Roman–Persian contact zone during late antiquity. Living under the constant threat of the Sasanian military machine, they were looking for a means of domesticating the hostile superpower, even if

---

509 The text was edited by Munitiz et alii 1997. See also Brubaker & Haldon 2001, pp. 279–280.
510 Ed. and trans. (modified) Munitiz et alii 1997, pp. 42–43.
511 See Clermont-Ganneau 1898, pp. 139–140. See also Vincent & Abel 1914, pp. 127–128.

only on a symbolic level. One such means was the dissemination of stories in which the sworn enemies of the Christian faith are transformed into its friends as they recognize themselves in the mirror provided by the canonical figures of the Magi. It was the combination of the Magi's Iranian pedigree with their liminal position in the New Testament history of salvation that made it possible for the Christian imagination of late antique Syria–Mesopotamia to deploy them as a catalyst that facilitated the symbolic transformation of the Sasanian rule from a hostile and alienating oppressor into an obedient and respectful patron of Christianity.

3   Concluding Observations

The cases from CT examined here demonstrate that its author was deeply rooted in the world of Iranian culture and did not hesitate to introduce those of its elements that he found useful into his retelling of biblical history. While the origins of some of the Iranian themes and images in CT could be traced to the previous periods of Syriac Christian literary activity, such as, for example, some aspects of the portrayal of Nimrod, several of them are attested for the first time in CT. This bears witness to our author's considerable degree of liberty and selectiveness in his dealing with the canonical narrative as well as with the previous Christian tradition of scriptural exegesis.

These examples of distinctively Iranian motifs and images incorporated into CT indicate the relatively advanced level of acculturation to Iranian society that our author and, arguably, his community, had attained. This shows that acculturation was an essential part of the Syriac-speaking Christian minority's stance vis-à-vis Iranian culture in the context of the late Sasanian empire.

CT's author's relationship to Persian culture was not limited to that of quiescent adoption. His selective inclusion of Iranian traditions comprises only one pole of the wider spectrum, at the opposite end of which we find the straightforward rejection of those aspects of Iranian religion and culture that seem to be especially objectionable to him. Continuing the established tradition of classical and Christian anti-Persian discourse, he wages polemics against such Iranian customs as the institution of close-kin marriage and various divinatory practices, especially astrology. Yet even while reproducing these common anti-Zoroastrian topoi, the author handles them creatively by connecting both of these negative aspects of Iranian culture with Zoroastrianism through the fictional figure of Ardashir the Magian.

Besides quiescent appropriation and straightforward rejection, CT's author resorts to another, subtler strategy of coping with the challenge posed to his audience by Iranian culture. Perhaps the most interesting group of Iranian motifs in CT is comprised by those cases where he engages with the institution of Iranian kingship. To this group belong the portrayal of Nimrod, the genealogy of Cyrus, and the account of the New Testament Magi.

Despite the obvious differences in CT's author's treatment of these biblical characters, it is possible to recognize a particular common agenda that determines the way he reworks the canonical material in all three cases. To understand it, we should pay attention to the shared narrative characteristic of their association with Christianity. All these biblical figures stand in close relation with the founder of the Christian religion: Nimrod is the author of the prophecy about Jesus' future coming, Cyrus becomes his kinsman through David and Zerubbabel, and the Magi bring him the gifts and subsequently embrace Christianity.

This observation allows us to single out the apologetic strategy of Christianizing the past as the main driving factor behind CT's author's handling of these characters. In a manner similar to the case of anti-Jewish polemic discussed above, he projects Christianity back into the distant past of Iranian history. For that purpose, he chooses the figures of Nimrod, Cyrus, and the Magi, each of whom also represents the world of Iranian kingship in one way or another.

The main objectives of this apologetic strategy can be understood by analyzing it against the background of the Iranian ideas about Zoroastrianism as the Persians' ancestral religion. This notion had deep roots in the political philosophy of the Sasanian kings, who inaugurated a major shift in the history of Iranian civilization by turning Zoroastrian orthodoxy into the state religion of their empire and thus facilitated the crystallization of a new, religion-based Iranian identity.[512] Far from being an abstract concept, the understanding of Zoroastrianism as the Iranian ancestral faith penetrated deeply into the tissue of social life in Sasanian Iran through a variety of ritual and commemorative practices. The cult of the ancestors was one of the most important elements of Zoroastrian religious life. Among its main expressions was sacrificial worship "on behalf of the souls" (Mid. Pers. *pad ruwān*) of the departed that involved offerings of consecrated food and clothing in order to benefit them in the underworld kingdom of the dead. The administration of the pious foundations for religious services *pad ruwān* is well attested during the Sasanian period.[513] Another important ritual focus of ancestral worship was Frawardīgān, the ten-day celebration at the end of the year in honor of the *fravašis*, the spirits of the

---

512 On this, see Gnoli 1989, pp. 129–174.
513 See Modi 1922, pp. 75–80; de Menasce 1964; Boyce 1968c.

dead.⁵¹⁴ The basic purpose of this elaborate festival was to welcome the souls of the departed ancestors into the home and treat them with rites of hospitality.

The conversion of an ethnic Persian to Christianity, which automatically involved the repudiation of the rituals of ancestral worship,⁵¹⁵ disrupted the spiritual bond (*paywan*) between the generations of Zoroastrian believers and thus undermined the cohesion of Iranian society. It is no wonder that such cases were usually perceived by the convert's relatives and fellow citizens as a blatant betrayal of the Iranian social contract and provided a major cause of friction between the Christian minority and the Zoroastrian majority.

The theme of conversion to Christianity as a betrayal of the Iranian ancestral religion recurs throughout a number of hagiographical sources that stem from Sasanian Iran. It appears, for instance, in the *Acts of Shirin*, an originally Syriac composition preserved only in Greek translation. In his description of a confrontation between Shirin, who became a Christian at the age of eighteen, and her Zoroastrian family, the hagiographer describes the latter's unsuccessful efforts to bring her back to her "paternal religion" (πατρικὴν θρησκείαν).⁵¹⁶ At one point, he presents the devil appearing to the saint in a dream and rebuking her for disregarding "paternal tradition" (πατρῷαν παράδοσιν).⁵¹⁷ In the Syriac *Martyrdom of Gregory Pīrān-Gušnasp*, the angel God sends to encourage this Persian nobleman to embrace Christianity asks him how long he will cling to "the ancestral piety of Magianism" (*deḥltā d-ʾabāhayk da-mgušutā*).⁵¹⁸ In the Syriac account of the martyrdom of another Persian martyr, Bishop Mār ʿAbdā, King Yazdgird I reprimands the Christians for their apostasy from Zoroastrianism and the destruction of fire temples while referring to the Iranian religion as "the doctrine that we received from our forefathers" (*yulpānā d-men ʾabāhayn mqabal lan*) and describing its cultic buildings as the heritage that "we received from our ancestors to be held in honour" (*d-men ʾabāhē d-ʾabāhayn d-netyaqrun mqablin lan*).⁵¹⁹

There is good reason to believe that this aspect of the Zoroastrian-Christian conflict is not merely a hagiographical topos, but reflects the genuine

---

514 See Malandra 2001; Boyce 1977, pp. 212–235. Panaino 2004b, pp. 66–75.
515 Cf. the *Martyrdom of Gregory Pīrān-Gušnasp*, where, as a result of his conversion, the saint refuses to participate in the Frawardīgān celebrations; ed. Bedjan 1895, pp. 351–356. On this episode, see also Becker 2009, pp. 327–328.
516 *Acts of Shirin* 8; ed. Devos 1946, p. 117.
517 *Acts of Shirin* 6; ed. Devos 1946, p. 116. Cf. also §11, where the saint's native religion is described as the "devilish tradition of Zoroaster" (Ζωροάστρου δαιμονιώδη παράδοσιν); ed. Devos 1946, p. 119.
518 Ed. Bedjan 1895, p. 353.
519 Ed. Bedjan 1890–1897, v. 4, p. 251.

concerns of Zoroastrian Persians about the spread of Christianity in their midst. Important evidence on this is provided by the Armenian author of the *History of Sebeos* (7th c.) in the description of the anti-Christian persecution launched by Khosrow II, motivated by the king's desire to preserve the *status quo* in the religious sphere. According to him, in order to stop conversions from Zoroastrianism to Christianity and vice versa, this Sasanian king issued a declaration in which he addressed his subjects thus: "Let each one remain firm in his own ancestral tradition (*hayreni awrēnkʿ*). And whoever does not wish to hold his ancestral religion, but in rebellion abandons his ancestral traditions, shall die."[520] Khosrow's self-image as the protector of the ancestral faith of the Persians finds confirmation in the native Iranian tradition. Thus, in Ferdowsī's *Šāh-nāma*, a story is told of the conflict that developed after Khosrow received a set of lavish Western garments adorned with Christian symbols as a gift from a Byzantine prince. The Sasanian king's public donning of this outfit was perceived by some of his courtiers as a blatant attempt to betray their native religion. Khosrow, however, had instantly rebuffed this charge, exclaiming: "God forbid that I should abandon the faith of grandfathers (*din-e niyāgān*), chosen and pure lords of the earth, and go over to the faith of Christ (*din-e masiḥā*)!"[521]

What is particularly remarkable about Khosrow's reply is that while explaining his refusal to embrace the faith of the Romans, he finds it necessary to cite the example of the primeval heroes of Iranian mythology, who adhered to "the faith of God" (*din-e yazdān*) and knew nothing about Christianity, as an argument supporting his choice: "From Gaiumart and from Jamshid to Kai Kubad none mentioned Christ."[522] This argument, which might well belong to the most ancient literary stratum of the *Šāh-nāma*, i.e. the Sasanian royal epic *Xwadāy-nāmag*,[523] provides us with another hermeneutic key for understanding CT's author's efforts of to present Christianity as the ancestral religion of the whole of humanity, including the Persians.

Considered against this background, CT's author's association of Nimrod, Cyrus, and the Magi with Christianity emerges as a covert apologetic effort aimed at promoting Christianity instead of Zoroastrianism as the true ancestral faith of the Persians. By forging a close connection between these

---

520 *Hist.* 13; trans. Thomson & Howard-Johnston 1999, pp. 29–30.
521 Ed. Khaleghi-Motlagh et alii 1988–2008, v. 8, p. 133; trans. (modified) Warner & Warner 1905–1925, v. 8, p. 310. On this episode in the context of Khosrow's Christian policy, see Loukonin 1987, pp. 180–181.
522 گیومرت وجمشید با کیقباد کسی از مسیحا نکردند یاد ; ed. Khaleghi-Motlagh et alii 1988–2008, v. 8, p. 133; trans. (modified) Warner & Warner 1905–1925, v. 8, p. 310.
523 On this lost work, see Yarshater 1983; Shahbazi 1990; Hämeen-Anttila 2018.

representatives of Iranian kingship and Jesus, our author seeks to legitimize Christianity as the religion native to Iranian soil in the eyes of those of his audience who may have doubts in this regard. Thus, in the case of the Magi, he explicitly emphasizes the traditional character of Christianity in Persia by pointing out in CT 45.12 that in following the prophecy of the star, they acted in accordance with "the tradition which had been handed down to them by their fathers."[524]

The development of the theme of Iranian kingship in CT has another important aspect that should be addressed here. It has been demonstrated that in his handling the scriptural figures of Nimrod and the Magi, our author relied heavily on imagery and concepts rooted in the world of Sasanian royal ideology. Reading some of these narratives through the critical lens of postcolonial cultural studies has enabled us to apprehend a subversive literary strategy behind them. As has been suggested, this strategy reflects the values and aspirations of a Christian minority group that seeks to actively engage the dominant culture of the Sasanian empire.

The figures of Nimrod, Cyrus, and the Magi provided CT's author with an opportunity to address, albeit in a covert manner, the complicated issue of the relations between the Christian minority and the Sasanian state. The peculiar and often innovative treatment of these scriptural characters in CT serves as an example of a rather sophisticated and nuanced approach towards the symbols of imperial culture among the Syriac-speaking Christians of Sasanian Iran, which goes beyond the simplistic dichotomy of adoption/rejection. By inventively rewriting the canonical narratives, CT's author creates a discursive space that enables him to renegotiate the meaning of Christian identity in the context of late Sasanian society and its culture.

This renegotiation involves the strategy of drawing a sharp and axiologically charged dichotomy between the religious and political dimensions of the dominant culture of Sasanian Iran in which the two converged. CT's author demonizes and rejects those aspects of Iranian culture that are, from his point of view, closely associated with Zoroastrianism, the state religion. At the same time, he abstains from any negative remarks in relation to the institution of Iranian kingship and the practices associated with it. Our author presents even such salient expressions of Zoroastrian religiosity as the cult of fire and alleged horse-worship in a neutral nonjudgmental manner when they are mentioned in connection with Iranian royal figures. In a most sophisticated manner, however, this dichotomy is enforced in the hermeneutic move of reinterpreting

---

524 Or^A: ܐܝܟ ܥܝܕܐ ܕܐܫܠܡܘ ܗܘܘ ܠܗܘܢ ܡܢ ܐܒܗܬܗܘܢ.

the New Testament Magi from Zoroastrian priests into Iranian kings. As to the purpose of this narrative strategy, the most plausible explanation seems to be that by doing so, CT's author strives to express his loyalty to the institution of Iranian kingship and thus to legitimate it in the eyes of his readers.

At the same time, we should not be oblivious to the fact that CT's author carries out this legitimization of Iranian kingship on his own, rather peculiar, terms. It is highly significant that at the two crucial moments in his retelling of biblical history, he places the characters that symbolize Iranian kingship into a subjugated position vis-à-vis the figures from the scriptural metanarrative. First, he does so in his depiction of the very beginnings of the institution of monarchy, by presenting Sasan, the eponymous founder of the ruling Iranian dynasty, as a subject and servant of Nimrod. He resorts to this strategy again when he reinterprets the Matthean Magi as Iranian kings only in order to make them worship Jesus and acknowledge him as their God. These subversive uses of symbols and images that belong to the culture of the dominant majority by a member of a subaltern minority group allow us to recognize a discursive layer of "hidden transcript" in CT.

From a methodological point of view, a promising way to approach this subaltern intellectual's discursive strategy of subverting the symbols of the dominant culture would be to look at it through the prism of the dialectics of colonial mimicry and hybridity, concepts introduced into the field of postcolonial studies by Homi Bhabha.[525] Originally developed to address the modern cultural and political situation of European imperialistic dominance, these notions retain their epistemological value for analyzing narratives that were shaped by and in response to imperial power in the ancient world.[526]

Scholars distinguish between the two basic modes of mimicry, i.e. the natives' attempts to adopt and internalize the forms and habits of their colonial master: properly speaking, colonial mimicry, when the dominated native strives to imitate his master in an effort to access his power, and subversive mimicry, when he does so in order to contest his authority. According to Bhabha, the subversive power of the latter kind of mimicry resides in the situation of ambivalence that it creates when the imitation of the colonizer fails to reach its final goal of a complete harmonization and always remains a repetition with a difference, teetering thus on the brink of mockery, parody, and menace.[527]

By contesting the authority of colonial discourse through its partial repetition, subversive mimicry results in the cultural form of colonial hybridity

---

525 See Bhabha 1994.
526 See, for example, Boyarin & Burrus 2005; Barclay 2005; Charles, R. 2009; Leander 2010.
527 See Bhabha 1994, pp. 85–92.

that produces ambivalence in the colonial masters and alters the authority of power. The notion of "hybridity" is a key concept of postcolonial theory that allows us to go beyond the simplistic antithesis of assimilation/antagonism in the analysis of the immensely complex relations between colonized and colonizer.[528] It does not simply refer to a perfunctory commixture of the elements of two cultures, dominant and subjected; it stresses ambivalence as the main feature of the new cultural formation, which emerges in a situation of cultural contact under conditions of inequality. Such hybridity involves not only a radical transformation of the minority's "original" native culture, but at the same time undermines the power of the colonizing discourse due to the ambiguity that characterizes the new cultural product.

The concepts of subversive mimicry and colonial hybridity enable us to make sense of the peculiar manner in which CT's author portrays biblical figures associated with Iranian kingship: Nimrod, Cyrus, and the Magi. The hybrid character of their representation in CT may be recognized in the authorial strategy of purposefully blending scriptural and Iranian motifs and images into a new mélange of Syriac Christian cultural memory. In the case of Cyrus, this hybridity becomes almost literally present in the narrative, as the author resorts to imagery of the commixture of seeds in order to express the novel genealogical idea of this Persian king as a kinsman of Jesus.

We have seen how CT's author implemented this subversive strategy through a subtle reinterpretation of several basic symbols and ideologems from the dominant Iranian culture. He both separates the institution of Iranian kingship from its Siamese twin, the Zoroastrian religion, and simultaneously subjugates it to the framework of a new "hybrid" discourse of the past based on the biblical master narrative. By doing so, our author, a representative of the Syriac-speaking Christian minority, attempts to subvert the hierarchy of power that existed in the contemporary Persian society and thus to provide his community with a viable identity that would ensure its self-confidence and survival in the particular social and cultural circumstances of late Sasanian Iran.

528 See Bhabha 1994, pp. 102–122.

CHAPTER 4

Identifying the Syriac Christian "Self"

As pointed out in the introduction, there are two basic aspects of collective internal definition that determine its dynamics: the categorization of others and the self-identification of the group. The previous two chapters have analyzed the two principal strategies of identification that belong to the former kind, aimed at constructing otherness through the exclusion of those who are located outside of the writer's community of faith, understood here in the most general terms as the Christian religion. In this chapter, I will focus on another, internally oriented strategy of self-identification, which our author employs in order to ensure the cohesion of his own group through articulating its distinctiveness within the Christian world.

There were various ways to achieve and maintain internal group cohesion in antiquity. As far as the world of Christianity is concerned, one of the most common and powerful principles of group identification was based on confessional considerations, i.e. it was a group's interpretation of Christian teaching that served as the primary criterion for belonging. However, from a study of Christian societies of late antiquity and the Middle Ages, it becomes apparent that other strategies of collective identification could be employed as well.

There is no doubt that CT's author was a Christian himself and that he was writing for a Christian audience. Christian theology and imagery form the backbone of his program of rewriting the biblical past. Yet while performing the important function of establishing continuity with the previous tradition of Christian self-identification, this dimension of CT by itself is not enough to explain how our writer intended to mobilize the sense of groupness in his community. The fact that he does not find it necessary to evoke Christianity as a distinctive phenomenon or Christians as a separate group even once throughout his entire work testifies to this.[1] Instead, as I will propose, in the case of CT, it is not the notion of "Christianity" as such that serves as a catalyst for the crystallization of the sense of group solidarity, but rather the discourse of ethnicity, articulated through the rhetoric of "Syrianness."

It is only relatively recently that students of Syriac Christianity have begun to pay closer attention to the role played by ethnic factors in the development

---

1 The most explicit expression of Christian identity in the text of CT is found in 44.17, where the narrator, Ephrem, addresses his interlocutor Nāmusāyā as "our brother in Christ."

of Christian group identities in Syria and Mesopotamia during late antiquity.[2] However, until now the original contribution made by CT's author in this regard has remained mostly unnoticed. So far, it has only been looked at by Philip Wood, who briefly dealt with some elements of CT's ethnic reasoning in his recent monograph on the formation of "Edessene" Christian identity.[3] Illuminating as these observations are, they do not present us with a comprehensive picture of the ethnic identification in CT, since Wood is more interested in those aspects of collective identity that are related to the tradition of Edessene local patriotism.

I intend to fill this gap by providing a detailed discussion of how CT's author pursues a strategy of collective identification based on ethnic principles. As was already mentioned in the introduction, CT satisfies the criteria for the minimalist conception of ethnicity as it contains an awareness of "Syrian" peoplehood, which manifests itself in the author's use of the ethnonym *Suryāyē*. Taking that as a starting point, I am going to analyze the following narrative elements of his composition that mark it as an expression of the ethnically distinctive "Syriac" version of Christian collective identity: the use of the ethnonym "Syrians"; the double claim of Syriac supremacy, based on the Syriac language; the mention of the Edessene king Abgar; and the choice of "Ephrem the Syrian" as the author's *nom de plume*.

1   The Ethnonym "Syrians"

The existence of a recognizable group name is a *sine qua non* condition for the formation of a viable collective identity. Such a name does indeed appear more than once in the text of CT, whose author advances an apologetic agenda on behalf of the group whom he calls *Suryāyē*, "Syrians," as can be seen from CT 24.11 and 53.26 (discussed in detail below). There are several additional passages where this ethnonym is mentioned, such as in CT 42.6 and 44.14, where the narrator refers to the three main traditions of historiography with which he claims to be acquainted and lists "the writers of Syrians" (*maktbānē d-Suryāyē*) alongside those of "Jews" and "Greeks."[4]

---

[2] Cf. studies by Millar 2007, 2013; Salvesen 2008; Wood 2010; Andrade 2010–2011; ter Haar Romeny 2012.
[3] Wood 2010, pp. 117–124.
[4] In some textual witnesses, such as Oc^d, *Suryāyē* appear in the list of Shem's descendants in CT 24.19, while other manuscripts, such as Or^A, have "Aram" (*Ārām*) instead.

In what follows, I will address the complicated question of what the sociohistorical and socio-cultural reality behind this label might have been. The corresponding English term "Syriac" is frequently used indiscriminately by modern scholars for referring to all groups of Aramaic- or Syriac-speaking Christians of the Near East, regardless of their own self-perception. However, as I shall demonstrate further, at least during the period of late antiquity, this group label was not as universal and neutral as one might suppose. This demonym deserves to be closely examined in order to contextualize the particular version of Christian identity that our author promotes. What exactly was the nature of this group, one among many others in the intricate ethnic mosaic of the late antique Near East?

In order to clarify this issue, it is necessary to undertake a brief excursus into the history of the term "Syrian": *Suryāyā* (sg.), *Suryāyē* (pl.).[5] It should be stressed from the outset that given the intrinsically context-bound nature of ethnic labels, the task of finding a common denominator that would bring together all meanings of this particular label in a comprehensive and non-contradictory way seems very difficult, if not impossible.[6] Hence, I shall limit myself to focusing only on those aspects of the ethnonym *Suryāyē* that may shed light on its function during late antiquity, with a particular focus on the context of CT.

To begin with, it should be pointed out that *Suryāyā* is not a native Aramaic word, but a loan-word from Greek. It is derived from the noun Σύρος, "Syrian," whose stem is augmented with the Syriac gentilic ending -*āyā*, which indicates belonging to something. In Syriac sources, the term *Suryāyā* as a group designation is only attested from the fifth century on. Among its earliest attestations, one can mention such fifth-century works as the Syriac version of Eusebius' *On the Theophany*, where the "Syrians" (*Suryāyē*) are mentioned on several occasions,[7] or the canons of Marutha of Maipherqat, where it is related that "the Syrians (*Suryāyē*) have the custom of calling one subject by two terms."[8]

It is important to bear in mind that the noun *Suryāyā* was not the first term that speakers of what we now call "Syriac" chose to refer to themselves and their language. In fact, *Suryāyā* is an etic ethnic label (or exonym) that gradually

---

5 Various aspects of this term have been discussed by Nöldeke 1871a, 1871b; Fiey 1965; Nasrallah 1974; Frye 1992; Sauma 1993; Rollinger 2006; Messo 2011.
6 To get a glimpse of the polysemous and fluid nature of this label during the Middle Ages, see Nasrallah 1974.
7 Cf. *De Theoph*. 2.67, 3.79, 5.52; ed. Lee 1842, pp. 2.65, 3.79, 5.52. The oldest Syriac manuscript that contains this work, i.e. BL Add. 12150, comes from Edessa and is dated to the year 411; see Wright, W. 1870–1872, v. 2, pp. 631–633.
8 Ed. Vööbus 1982, p. 34 [Syr.], 30 [trans.].

supplanted the indigenous emic label (or endonym) *Ārāmāyā*, "Aramaean." Before the fifth century, Syriac speakers only use the term *Ārāmāyā* in order to describe themselves. It is well attested in the works of Ephrem, who, in his polemical passages aimed against Bardaisan, refers to this native of Edessa as "the philosopher of the Aramaeans" (*pilāsupā d-Ārāmāyē*)[9] or "the Aramaean philosopher" (*pilāsupā Ārāmāyā*).[10] Remarkably, the author of the Syriac version of the anti-Manichaean tractate by Titus of Bostra, one of the earliest translations from Greek to Syriac carried out during the last decades of the fourth century, renders the phrase "the language of Syrians" (τῇ Σύρων φωνῇ), describing the language of Mani's writings, as "the Aramaic language" (*lešānā Ārāmāyā*).[11]

From the fifth century on, however, Syriac-speaking Christians of the Roman Near East tend to refer to themselves more and more using the etic label *Suryāyē* instead of the emic *Ārāmāyē*. A good example of this transition is provided by the figure of the Aramaean general Naaman from 2 Kings 5, who is described as "Syrian" (Ναιμὰν ὁ Σύρος) in Luke 4:27. In early Syriac translations of the New Testament, such as the Old Syriac Gospels (Sin) and the Peshitta, Naaman's gentilic is rendered as "Aramaean" (*Ārāmāyā*).[12] Moreover, it is very likely that this was also the reading of the Syriac version of Tatian's *Diatessaron*.[13] However, in the later Syriac translations of the Gospels, such as the seventh-century Harklean version, Naaman's title is translated as "Syrian" (*Suryāyā*).[14] The same rendering also appears in the Syriac translation of the *Homilies* of Severus of Antioch carried out by Paul of Callinicum (6th c.) and later revised by Jacob of Edessa (7th to 8th cc.).[15]

It has been suggested by several scholars that this shift in self-reference occurred as a result of the intensive Hellenization that accompanied the

---

9 *Against Bardaisan's "Domnus"*; ed. Mitchell 1912–1921, v. 2, pp. 7–8 [Syr.], p. iii [trans.; modified]. Cf. also another passage from this work, where Bardaisan is said to have "made himself a laughing-stock among Aramaeans (*Ārāmāyē*) and Greeks"; ed. Mitchell 1912–1921, v. 2, p. 7, ln. 47–48 [Syr.], p. iii [trans.; modified].

10 *Against Mani*; ed. Mitchell 1912–21, v. 2, pp. 225 [Syr.], cvi [trans.].

11 Ed. Roman et al. 2013, pp. 40–41.

12 Ed. Kiraz 1996, v. 3, p. 71.

13 This may be inferred from the Arabic version of this work (ch. 17), where Naaman has the nisba *al-Nabāṭī*, "Nabataean" (ed. Ciasca 1888, p. 79), a regular word for referring to "Aramaeans" in Arabic sources, and not *al-Šāmī*, "Syrian," as in the standard Arabic versions of the New Testament (cf. ed. de Lagarde 1864, p. 73). On the Arabic ethnonym *Nabāṭ*, see Graf & Fahd 1993.

14 Ed. Kiraz 1996, v. 3, p. 71. This is also found in the Syro-Palestinian version of Luke. See the lectionary, edited by Lewis & Gibson 1899, p. 283.

15 *Hom.* 42; ed. Brière & Graffin 1971, p. 68.

Christianization of the Syriac-speaking realm.[16] Without going into a detailed discussion of this proposition, I would like to add that while in general this connection between the changes in the identity vocabulary of Syriac-speaking Christians and the Hellenization of the Roman Near East seems to be convincing, it might be further developed and conceptualized as another expression of the complex and multi-dimensional Westernization of Syriac Christianity that took place during the fifth and sixth centuries.[17]

That this replacement of the indigenous ethnic categories by their Westernized analogs constituted one of the side effects of the Greek political and cultural hegemony in the Hellenistic and Roman Near East had already been noted by some intellectuals native to the region. This point was explicitly made by Josephus in his discussion of the division of languages at the Tower of Babel. As he describes the phenomenon of some nations not preserving the original names given to them by their founders but changing them "to make them more intelligible to their neighbours," he holds the Greeks ("Ἕλληνες) responsible for this apparently detrimental development—"for when in after ages they rose to power, they appropriated even the glories of the past, embellishing the nations with names which they could understand and imposing on them forms of government, as though they were descended from themselves."[18]

At some point, Syriac-speaking Christians also internalized the fact that the ethnonym *Suryāyā* had taken hold as a result of the influence of external political forces. For example, in his *Lexicon*, the East Syrian scholar Ḥasan bar Bahlūl (10th c.) explains the toponym "Syria" as being derived from the name of the king named "Syros" and thus comments on the name "Syrian": "At first Syrians were called 'Aramaeans'; and after Syros began his reign over them they began to be called 'Syrians.'"[19]

As far as the shift from "Aramaean" to "Syrian" is concerned, it is noteworthy that while making reference to the "Syriac" language in CT 24.11, the author finds it necessary to explain this term to his audience by commenting that it is none other than the "Aramaean" language: *lešānā Suryāyā d-itaw Ārāmāyā*. The necessity of this gloss and its phrasing allow us to reconstruct a linguistic situation in which the Syriac-speaking community behind CT made use

---

16   See Witakowski 1987, p. 76; Messo 2011, pp. 118–125.
17   On this phenomenon, see Wood 2012, pp. 182–186.
18   *Ant.* 1.121; ed. Thackeray 1926–1965, v. 4, pp. 58–59. This passage should be regarded in the broader context of Josephus' apologetic attempt to challenge the Greek cultural hegemony (cf. *C. Ap.* 1.6–18).
19   Ed. Duval 1888–1901, v. 2, col. 1324. This tradition also appears as a gloss to the lexicographical work of Išoʿ bar ʿAli (9th c.); ed. Gottheil 1908–1928, v. 1, p. 155, n. 12.

of both these ethnic labels simultaneously while still perceiving the gentilic "Aramaean" as a default term for referring to their language.

1.1 Territorial Aspects of Suryāyā

To disentangle the complicated sociolinguistic aspects of the Syriac ethnic labels, I shall focus on the question of how the term *Suryāyā* functioned in the context of Syriac-speaking communities during late antiquity. First of all, regarding its Greek prototype Σύρος, it is not always obvious what the authors of the classical period and late antiquity meant when they referred to "Syrians," since this name could be evoked to convey a wide range of meanings such as a person's origin, language, or culture.[20] It is, however, the territorial connotations that appear to determine the most basic level of meaning for this label. In the majority of cases, when the context allows us to establish the meaning of this term, the word "Syrian" functions as a demonym, i.e. it refers to a person who originated from or inhabited the geographical region of "Syria." In this regard, one may recall the words of the author of the fourth-century *Commentary on Job*, ascribed to a certain Julian, who remarks that a person reveals his "nation" when he speaks about his "country."[21] One can recognize the predominance of the territorial connotations of the label Σύρος in the fact that when it is not used alone, it often appears in combination with the noun γένος, which in such contexts would be best translated not as "race," but as "origin."[22]

This territorial definition of the label "Syrian," however, raises more difficulties than it solves. The main problem with it is that during the period of classical antiquity, the geographical term "Syria" was far from being exact and well defined. Rather, it was a general word used to refer to the vast geographical space that extended from the eastern shores of the Mediterranean Sea to the Taurus Mountains in the north-west, the river Euphrates in the east, the Arabian desert in the south-east, and the Sinai Peninsula in the south. Accordingly, during the period of Roman dominance in the Middle East, any native or inhabitant of such provinces of *Dioecesis Orientis* as *Palaestina Prima*, *Palaestina Secunda*, *Phoenice*, *Phoenice Libanensis*, *Syria Prima*, *Syria Secunda*, *Euphratensis*, *Osroene*, and *Mesopotamia* could be referred to as "Syrian."

---

20 A comprehensive study of this term in classical sources is still a desideratum. In the meantime, see Isaac 2004, pp. 335–351.

21 εἶπεν τὴν πατρίδα, ἐσήμανε τὸ ἔθνος; ed. Hagedorn 1973, p. 311.

22 Cf. Epiphanius, *Panar.* 46.1.6 (ed. Holl 1915–1933, v. 2, p. 204); Hesychius of Jerusalem, *Hom. in Luc.* 10 (ed. Aubineau 1978–1980, v. 2, p. 948); *Vit. Thecl.* 1.15 (ed. Dagron 1978, p. 228); Agathias of Myrine, *Hist.* 2.29.1 (ed. Keydell 1967, p. 78). As an alternative to γένος, the noun πατρίς, "fatherland," is occasionally used; cf. Lucian, *Toxaris* 28 (ed. Harmon et alii 1913–1967, v. 5, p. 148).

Some examples are in order to illustrate this broad geographical spectrum. Starting from the north-east, we see Lucian introducing the figure of a "Syrian from the banks of Euphrates" (Σύρος τῶν Ἐπευφρατιδίων) in one of his dialogues.[23] Eusebius describes Bardaisan, a native of Edessa, as a "Syrian by origin" (Σύρου μὲν τὸ γένος).[24] Moving down to the south-west, we find Porphyry transmitting an earlier tradition about Pythagoras' father Mnesarchos being "a Syrian from Tyre of Syria" (Σύρον ἐκ Τύρου τῆς Συρίας).[25] To this may be added the case of the "Syro-Phoenician woman" (Συροφοινίκισσα) whom Jesus met in the region of Tyre (Mk 7:24–37). Regarding the inhabitants of Palestine proper, we see Alexander Polyhistor (1st c. BCE), as quoted by Eusebius, referring to the Jewish émigrés to Egypt in the days of the biblical patriarch Joseph as "Syrians."[26] At some point, Eusebius himself presents Jesus as "the Syrian fisherman" (ὁ ἁλιεύς, ὁ Σύρος).[27] Moving further south, Mark the Deacon describes Porphyry, the bishop of Gaza, as speaking "the language of Syrians" (τῇ Σύρων φωνῇ).[28]

Even from this brief list of examples, one may conclude that far from being a well-defined demonym, the label "Syrian" served as an umbrella term for referring to diverse ethnic groups of the Roman Levant. This had already been noted by the second-century grammarian Aelius Herodianus, who explains the word "Syrian" as "the name common to many peoples."[29] Used in such a broad sense, this label implied no mastery of "Syriac" language, whichever dialect of Aramaic that might be. As an example, one can mention the famous fourth-century rhetor Libanius, whom the Church historian Socrates Scholasticus characterizes as "the Syrian Sophist" (τῷ Σύρῳ σοφιστῇ).[30] However, there is no evidence whatsoever to suggest that Libanius was acquainted with Syriac.

When we turn to Syriac sources, it becomes apparent that here the label *Suryāyā* could also be—and actually was—used to convey a comparably broad territorial range of meanings. Quite expectedly, it happens thus in the works translated into Syriac from Greek, such as Eusebius' already mentioned *Theophany* where Jesus is described as "the Syrian fisherman" (*ṣayādā*

---

23 *Fisherman* 19; ed. Harmon et alii 1913–1967, v. 3, pp. 30–31.
24 *Praep. ev.* 6.9.32; ed. Mras & des Places 1982–1983, v. 1, p. 334.
25 *Vita Pythag.* 1; ed. Nauck 1886, p. 17.
26 *Praep. ev.* 9.23.3; ed. Mras & des Places 1982–1983, v. 1, p. 517.
27 *De theoph.* 4.6; ed. Gressmann & Laminski 1991, fragm. 6, p. 19. He also applies this label to Jesus' Galilean followers, as he describes the apostle Matthew as "the Syrian man" (Σύρος ἀνήρ), although "Hebrew by speech" (τὴν φωνὴν Ἑβραῖος). *Supplementa ad quaestiones ad Stephanum*; PG 22, col. 961. Cf. also Julian, *Comm. in Hiob.* on the Hebrew language being called "Syriac" and Judaea being called "Syria"; ed. Hagedorn 1973, pp. 311–312.
28 *Vita Porph.* 66; ed. Lampadaridi 2016, p. 146.
29 *De prosodia catholica* 8: Σύρος κοινὸν ὄνομα πολλῶν ἐθνῶν; ed. Lentz 1867, p. 192.
30 *Hist.* 3.1.13; ed. Hansen 1995, p. 188.

Suryāyā).³¹ This usage is also found in the works of native Syriac authors such as John of Ephesus, who says of John, the bishop of Hephaestus in Egypt, that he "was by his origin (*ba-gensēh*) a Syrian, that is a Palestinian (*Palisṭināyā*), from the city of Gaza."³²

It seems, however, that for the majority of Syriac-speaking authors during late antiquity and the early Middle Ages, the demonym *Suryāyā* had a somewhat more territorially restricted frame of reference. Thus, the Syriac historiographical tradition provides us with several testimonies that the region called "Syria" did not indiscriminately include all areas of the Near East that were inhabited by Semitic- or even Aramaic-speaking peoples, but rather referred to the territories situated to the west of the Euphrates, along the Antioch—Edessa axis.

This outlook is articulated, for instance, by the West Syrian historian Dionysius of Tell-Maḥrē (9th c.), who speaks about "Syria" as the region located "to the west of the Euphrates."³³ A similar opinion is expressed by another ninth-century Syriac author, the East Syrian lexicographer Išoʿ bar ʿAli, who defines "Syria" as "all of the land from Antioch to Edessa."³⁴ This picture is also confirmed by the *Chronicle of Zuqnin* (8th c.), in the third part of which may be found a list of the episcopal sees in "Syria" from which the West Syrian bishops had been expelled during the anti-Monophysite persecutions of the sixth century.³⁵ On the basis of this evidence, it can be concluded that there was a well-established geographical viewpoint among Syriac-speaking Christians according to which the region of "Syria" was comprised of such provinces of the late Roman empire as *Syria Prima, Syria Secunda, Phoenice Libanensis, Euphratensis, Osroene,* and *Mesopotamia.*

This territorially restricted understanding of "Syria" and "Syrian," i.e. as terms relating only to the Western part of the Aramaic-speaking world located within the borders of the Roman empire, is also reflected in some non-Syriac sources. Apparently, it underlies a passage from the *Ecclesiastical History* of Theodoret of Cyrus in which he mentions the city of Antioch-in-Mygdonia and

---

31 *De theoph.* 4.6; ed. Lee 1842, p. iv.6.
32 *Lives* 25; ed. Brooks 1923–1925, v. 2, p. 527.
33 ܣܘܪܝܐ ܐܝܬܝܗ ܕܝܢ ܡܢ ܡܥܪܒܐ; *apud* Michael the Great; ed. Chabot 1899–1910, v. 4, p. 750.
34 ܣܘܪܝܐ ܗܘ ܟܠܗ ܐܬܪܐ ܕܡܢ ܐܢܛܝܘܟܝܐ ܘܥܕܡܐ ܠܐܘܪܗܝ; ed. Gottheil 1908–1928, v. 1, p. 155.
35 The list includes the following cities: Antioch, Laodicea, Aleppo, Seleucia, Mabbug, Apamea, Qenneshrin, Amida, Damascus, Abila, Yabrud, Palmyra, Hawarin, Cyrrhus, Germanicia, Edessa, Harran, Hemerion, Perrhe, Reshaina, Circesion, Callinicos, Shura, Tella, Dara, and Arsamosata. Ed. Chabot 1927–1949, v. 2, pp. 17–18; trans. Harrak 1999, pp. 50–51.

comments on its indigenous name by adding that both "Syrians and Assyrians call it Nisibis."[36] This division of the Aramaic-speaking world into "Syrians" and "Assyrians" has a close parallel in the geographical and administrative terminology of Sasanian Iran, such as that of the third-century trilingual inscription of Shapur I on Ka'ba-ye Zardošt that distinguishes between the Persian province of *Asūrestān* (Mid.-Pers./Parth. ʾSWRSTN; Gr. Ἀσσυρίας) and the Roman province of *Sūriyā* (Mid.-Pers. SWLYʾY/ʾSWLYʾY; Parth. SWRYʾ/ʾSWRYʾ; Gr. Συρίας).[37]

A distant echo of this geographical division may be recognized in the linguistic vocabulary of the Babylonian Talmud. Here, in the tractate *Sotah*, a brief discussion of the validity of the use of the Aramaic language is presented in which the famous rabbi Judah the Patriarch (3rd c.) says "Why use the Syriac language in the land of Israel? Either use the holy tongue or Greek!" and is answered by Rav Joseph saying "Why use the Aramaic language in Babylon? Either use the holy tongue or Persian!"[38] What is remarkable about this exchange of opinions is that it comprises a parallel construction wherein the Palestinian rabbi refers to the Aramaic language as "Syriac" (*Sursi*) whereas his Babylonian colleague, a third-generation Amora, makes use of the term "Aramaic" (*Arami*). Furthermore, a cursory examination of the Bavli's corpus shows that it seems to have a predilection for referring to the Aramaic language as "Aramaic" while the label "Syriac" appears only on rare occasions and only in connection with the figures of Western, i.e. Palestinian, provenance.[39]

Regarding the label "Syrian" as a marker of territorial identity in the first place, it should be mentioned that as such it indicates only one of several levels in the hierarchy of territorial identities through which a person could describe himself/herself or be described by others. The way that inhabitants of the late Roman Near East expressed their territorial identity may be visualized through a series of expanding circles or as a Matryoshka doll comprised of three principal levels: the micro level of the exact place of origin, the middle level of

---

36 *Hist.* 1.7.4: Σύροι δὲ αὐτὴν καὶ Ἀσσύριοι Νίσιβιν ὀνομάζουσι; ed. Parmentier & Hansen 2009, p. 31.

37 Huyse 1999, v. 1, pp. 22–23 (§2), 25–26 (§6), 28 (§10), 38 (§23), 43 (§30).

38 *b.Sotah* 49b: הָא אמ' רבי בארץ ישראל לשון סורסי למה או לשון קודש או לשון יוני ואמ' רב יוסף בבבל לשון ארמי למה או לשון קודש או לשון פרסי. I am quoting from ms. Oxford-Bodl. heb. d. 10 (2833). In one manuscript, Munich 95, the second saying is attributed to Rav Assi. However, in the majority of the passage's textual witnesses, it is transmitted under Rav Joseph's name. This tradition also appears in *b.Bava Qamma* 82b–83a, where the second saying is attributed to Rav Joseph.

39 Cf. also *b.Pesahim* 61a, where the same Judah the Patriarch explains the difficult verbal form *tākōssû* of Exodus 12:4 as לשון סורסי הוא, i.e. a "Syriac expression."

the province or region, and the macro level of the state.[40] Thus, depending on the context, a Syriac-speaking native of the city of Amida in Northern Mesopotamia could refer to himself as "Amidene," "Syrian," or "Roman."

The basic level of a person's territorial identification is comprised by the city or village from which he originates. Examples of this sort abound, for instance, in the hagiographical compendium of John of Ephesus, who appears to be particularly fond of pointing out his holy men's places of origin. He often does so using demonyms derived with the help of the gentilic suffix -āyā that usually go together with the noun *gensā*, a Syriac calque from the Greek γένος. Maro, "an Amidene by origin,"[41] or Paul, "an Antiochene by his origin," can be mentioned as illustrations of this.[42]

The middle level of territorial identity, to which the term "Syrian" also belongs, in the context of the Roman empire usually refers to a territorial unit that is bigger than a city but smaller than a state, such as a province or district. Again, John of Ephesus provides us with plenty of examples of this kind, such as Aaron the presbyter who "was by his origin from Armenia,"[43] or Leontius the presbyter, who "was by his origin from Ingilene."[44]

As to the highest macrolevel of territorial identity, this is determined by belonging to a large geopolitical unit such as a state or empire. In the case of "Syrians," this dimension of their identity is usually conveyed by the label "Romans," a term that bears the primary connotations of being a citizen or subject of the Roman empire.[45] For example, in his letter to the Christians of Najran, Jacob of Sarug turns to his coreligionists in Arabia in the name of "us, Romans" (*Rhumāyē*) who enjoy a peaceful life under the Christian kings.[46] Similar language is employed by John of Ephesus, who in the *Lives of the Eastern Saints* refers to "the commonwealth of us, Romans" (*puliṭiyā dilan Rhumāyē*).[47]

1.2 Linguistic and Cultural Aspects of Suryāyā

At the same time, it appears that alongside this broad semantic range designated by the term "Syrian," there also existed a narrower and more exclusive understanding of this label, one that took into consideration the linguistic and

---

40   For an illuminating discussion of these three levels, corresponding to the categories of *populus, provincialis*, and *civis* from Roman legal terminology, see Mathisen 2015.
41   *Lives* 27; ed. Brooks 1923–1925, v. 2, p. 552.
42   *Lives* 46; ed. Brooks 1923–1925, v. 2, p. 672.
43   *Lives* 38; ed. Brooks 1923–1925, v. 2, p. 641.
44   *Lives* 39; ed. Brooks 1923–1925, v. 2, p. 645.
45   On the broad semantic range of this label in Syriac, see Tannous 2018b.
46   Ed. Olinder 1937, p. 92.
47   *Lives* 48; ed. Brooks 1923–1925, v. 2, p. 689. Cf. also *Hist. eccl.* 3.25; ed. Cureton 1853, p. 188.

cultural dimensions of "Syrianness." This meaning of "Syrian" is amply illustrated by the anonymous gloss found in some manuscripts of Photius' *Bibliotheca* in the chapter on Iamblichus, the second-century Greek novelist. It is reported regarding this person that he was

> a Syrian by origin on both his father's and his mother's side, a Syrian not in the sense of the Greeks who have settled in Syria, but of the native ones, familiar with the Syrian language and living by their customs.[48]

This description is remarkable in that its author finds it necessary to draw a distinction between two different understandings of what it means to be "Syrian." On the one hand, he refers to the superficial "Syrianness," based on a merely territorial dimension, of those Greek settlers and their descendants who inhabit the region but apparently have no knowledge of its language or customs. He contrasts these with the "true" Syrians, i.e. the autochthonous population of Syria that does preserve their native language and ancestral way of life.

It is particularly noteworthy that the anonymous Greek writer singles out language and customs as the key characteristics that define a person's "Syrian" identity. There are additional examples that demonstrate the principal importance of the linguistic factor for defining the notion of "Syrianness" in antiquity. One is provided by Jerome, who points out in his biography of the holy man Malchus that he was "Syrian by origin and tongue" (*Syrus natione et lingua*).[49] A similar description in Greek comes from the *Ecclesiastical History* of Theodoret of Cyrus, where the heresiarch Audaeus is described as "Syrian, both by origin and by speech" (Σύρος καὶ τὸ γένος καὶ τὴν φωνήν).[50]

What emerges from this evidence is that in the sociolinguistic context of the late Roman Near East, it was the pair *natio*/γένος, i.e. place of origin, and *lingua*/φωνή, i.e. language, that constituted the two most salient markers of ethnic identity. It is important to stress, however, that neither of these two markers by itself was sufficient to definitively determine a person's identity. The insufficiency of the territorial marker is illustrated by the above-quoted passage on Iamblichus, where the "Syrianness" of the Greek settlers of the region emerges as superficial in comparison with that of the native Syriac speakers.

---

48 *Bibl.* 94: Οὗτος ὁ Ἰάμβλιχος Σύρος ἦν γένος πατρόθεν καὶ μητρόθεν, Σύρος δὲ οὐχὶ τῶν ἐπῳκηκότων τὴν Συρίαν Ἑλλήνων, ἀλλὰ τῶν αὐτοχθόνων, γλῶσσαν δὲ σύραν εἰδὼς καὶ τοῖς ἐκείνων ἔθεσι ζῶν ἕως αὐτὸν τροφεύς; ed. Henry 1959–1977, v. 2, p. 40, n. 1; trans. *apud* Millar 1993, p. 491.
49 *Vita Malchi* 2.2; ed. Leclerc & Morales 2007, p. 186.
50 *Hist.* 4.9.1; ed. Parmentier & Hansen 2009, p. 228.

In Syriac sources, this aspect of "Syrian" identity comes to the fore most prominently in the context of interaction between the Greek and Syriac cultures. A good example of this use of the label *Suryāyā* comes from the works of Severus Sēbōkht. This seventh-century West Syrian scholar, who was well versed in Greek language and culture, seeks to challenge the Greeks' hegemony in the field of natural sciences, such as astronomy, on several occasions.[51] He does so by drawing a contrast between *Suryāyē* and *Yawnāyē*, i.e. Greeks, placing the main emphasis on the linguistic and cultural connotations of these ethnic labels. At one point, Severus confronts those who believe that "all knowledge exists only in the Greek language" and refers to himself ironically as a "Syrian and ignoramus" (*Suryāyā kit w-lā yalipā*),[52] apparently aiming not at the territorial aspect of his Syriac identity, but at its supposedly inferior cultural aspect.

It is in this sense that the term *Suryāyē* appears in the works of East Syrian writers, who occasionally use it to refer to the Syriac cultural or literary tradition of which they perceive themselves to be a part. Thus, Šemʿon Barqāyā, an East Syrian author of the late sixth to early seventh century, while discussing some calendrical issues in his commentary on the *Chronicle* of Eusebius of Caesarea, relates that the date of the spring equinox "of us, Syrians" falls on the 19th of the month of Ādar.[53] A similar case of the use of *Suryāyē* is provided by Barḥadbešabbā ʿArbāyā, a contemporary of Šemʿon, in the section of his *History* devoted to the Antiochene exegete Diodore of Tarsus. After presenting biographical information drawn from the letters of Athanasius of Alexandria, where this ecclesiastic figure is connected with the city of Tyre, Barḥadbešabbā finds it necessary to point out that there also an alternative tradition about Diodore's Roman origins which is "handed down among us, Syrians."[54]

In these passages, we see how these two East Syrian scholars, who were active during the last decades of the Sasanian rule, indicate their membership of the group of *Suryāyē*. In both of these cases, we are dealing with highly educated authors, one of whom, Barḥadbešabbā, was definitely a member of the School of Nisibis.[55] Furthermore, in both instances we find the term "Syrian" operating within the general dichotomy between "Syrian tradition" and "Greek tradition." Both Šemʿon and Barḥadbešabbā evoke this in order to introduce the indigenous "Syriac" material that poses an alternative to what comes from

51 Cf. Nau 1910, pp. 248–252; Nau 1929–1930, pp. 332–333, 337–338.
52 *Apud* Nau 1910, p. 251.
53 *Apud* Elias of Nisibis, *Chron.*; ed. Chabot & Brooks 1909–1910, v. 2, p. 111 [Syr.]. For what little is known about Šemʿon, see Baumstark 1922, pp. 135–136.
54 *Hist. eccl.* 18; ed. Nau 1932, p. 323.
55 On this figure, see Becker & Childers 2011.

the Greek sources: for the former, the calendrical tradition related to calculating the date of Easter, and for the latter, the biographical material differing from the image of Diodore which emerges from Athanasius' letters. In light of this, it seems justified to regard the term *Suryāyē* in both these cases as a marker of the cultural and scientific tradition expressed and transmitted in the Syriac language, of which the two East Syrian intellectuals consider themselves to be legitimate heirs.

A word might be added here on the deficiency of a linguistic marker alone in establishing a person's ethnic identity. This phenomenon may be observed in the account of a certain John of Amida provided by John of Ephesus in the *Lives of the Eastern Saints*. He relates that this sixth-century Syriac-speaking monk from Amida worked as a missionary in the Armenian district of Anzetene, in the region inhabited by the people called Urṭāyē.[56] As John of Ephesus notes, the holy man "was thought to be an Urṭāyā and was so called." He finds it necessary, however, to comment on this fact and to disclose the misleading character of this description. According to John, concerning his proper identity, the holy man should be categorized as "Syrian," whereas the label *Urṭāyā* was applied to him only figuratively because he mastered the language of the Urṭāyē and actively used it to preach among them: "He was thought to be and was called an Urṭāyā, though by his origin (*ba-gensēh*) he was a Syrian (*Suryāyā*)."[57]

1.3 *The Confessional Aspect of* Suryāyā

As one attempts to establish the sociolinguistic profile of the label *Suryāyā* in late antiquity, it becomes apparent that during this historical period, it was used for the purposes of *self-reference* for the most part, although not exclusively, by those Syriac-speaking Christians who lived within the confines of the Roman empire, i.e. the Western half of the Aramaic-speaking commonwealth.[58] The main reason for this was, of course, the territorial connotations of this term that linked it to the region of "Syria" controlled by the Romans.

Explicit descriptions of "Syrians" as a distinctive Western-based group within the whole of Syriac-speaking Christendom have so far only been found in later sources. For instance, the already mentioned West Syrian historian

---

56 *Lives* 58; ed. and trans. (modified) Brooks 1923–1925, v. 3, p. 208. For a discussion of this ethnic group, see Tubach 1995, who argues that it is related to the ancient Urartians.

57 Ed. and trans. (modified) Brooks 1923–1925, v. 3, p. 208.

58 This is, however, not so as far as referring to their language is concerned. During the period from the fifth to the seventh century, there are references to the "Aramaean language" (*lešānā Ārāmāyā*) and the "Syrian language" (*lešānā Suryāyā*) distributed almost equally in the works of Syriac-speaking authors, who lived within the confines of the Roman empire as well as under Sasanian rule.

Dionysius of Tell-Maḥrē argues that the term "Syrians," in the proper sense of the word, should be applied only to those "Aramaeans" who inhabit territories to the west of the Euphrates and that one can use this label for referring to those of them who live to the east of this river only "metaphorically."[59] There are, however, reasons to believe that such an understanding of "Syrianness" is not an idiosyncratic invention of Dionysius, but an echo of the earlier tradition of perceiving "Syrians" as a group distinctive from (or within) "Aramaeans." One of the earliest expressions of this outlook was that of Išoʿyahb III of Adiabene (ob. 659), an East Syrian catholicos, who in one of his letters mentions "Syrians" and "Aramaeans" separately alongside such groups as "Huzites" and "Persians."[60]

To understand the general reluctance of East Syrian Christians to use the label "Syrians" as a self-reference identity marker, except in contexts that involve appeals to the linguistic or cultural relevance of Syriac heritage, one has to take several considerations into account. First of all, as has been mentioned above, there existed a narrow territorial outlook that conceived "Syria" as the region that extended from Antioch to Edessa in the east and Damascus in the south. It is important to remember that during late antiquity, this territory was under the direct ecclesiastical jurisdiction of the patriarchal see of Antioch.[61] Already during the earliest period of the Christian presence in Antioch, the ecclesiastical body associated with the city had become known as the "Church of Syria."[62] This continued well into the later period and is also attested in Syriac sources. For instance, Jacob of Sarug, in one of his letters where he mentions the affair of Nestorius, refers to the ecclesiastical body, represented by John of Antioch, as the "Church of Syria" (ʿidtā d-Suryā).[63] However, in distinction from the West Syrians, the East Syrian Christians of the Sasanian empire, who had their own autonomous patriarchal see in the capital city of Seleucia-Ctesiphon, never considered themselves to be part of this ecclesiastical body governing the region of "Syria."[64]

---

59 ܘܐܬܚܠܦܘ ܡܢܗܘܢ ܒܗ̇ܠܝܢ ܐ̈ܬܪܘܬܐ ܕܒܗܘܢ. ܐܝܬܝܗܘܢ ܐ̈ܪܡܝܐ ܕܠܐ ܡܬܩܪܝܢ ܣ̈ܘܪܝܝܐ. ܐܠܐ ܡܢ ܥܠܬ ܕܝܬܒܝܢ ܠܥܠ ܡܢ ܦܪܬ ܢܗܪܐ; *apud* Michael the Great; ed. Chabot 1899–1910, v. 4, p. 750.

60 *Ep.* 2.7; ed. Duval 1904–1905, pp. 134 [Syr.], 100 [trans.].

61 See Devreesse 1945.

62 The earliest examples of this formula are found in the letters of Ignatius of Antioch (late 1st to early 2nd cc.). Cf. *Eph.* 21: τῆς ἐκκλησίας τῆς ἐν Συρίᾳ; *Rom.* 9: τῆς ἐν Συρίᾳ ἐκκλησίας; *Pol.* 7: ἡ ἐκκλησία ἡ ἐν Ἀντιοχείᾳ τῆς Συρίας; ed. Ehrman 2003, v. 1, pp. 240, 280, 318.

63 *Ep.* 17; ed. Olinder 1937, p. 83, ln. 9–10.

64 On this, see de Halleux 1978.

Moreover, as a result of the Christological controversies of the fifth and sixth centuries, it happened that a substantial part of the Christian population in the territories under the jurisdiction of the patriarchate of Antioch sided with the Miaphysite theology, the main proponents and defenders of which in this region were figures such as Severus of Antioch, Philoxenus of Mabbugh, and Jacob Baradaeus. It is at this point that, in the words of John Meyendorff, "confessional loyalties become interwoven with ethnicity" and ethnic labels such as "Syrian" or "Egyptian" became designations for those who opposed the Christological doctrine promoted by the Council of Chalcedon.[65] This phenomenon was noted by the Syriac author of the *Life of Jacob Baradaeus*, a West Syrian hagiographical composition ascribed to John of Ephesus, where the following explanation of the self-designation "Jacobites" is offered:

> And hence throughout Syria and in the countries of Persia and of the Armenians the expression became current "We are of the faith of Jacob"; and in Alexandria and in Egypt again the expression became current, "We are of Theodosius" so that on this account the believers of Egypt were named Theodosians, and the Syrians (*Suryāyē*) Jacobites (*Ya'qubāyē*).[66]

It is not clear, however, exactly when the confessional re-interpretation of the label "Syrians" had entered the identity vocabulary of the West Syrians. This meaning is clearly attested during the medieval period, when we find the label *al-Suryān*, i.e. the Arabic calque of *Suryāyā*, being used mainly by the members of the West Syrian community in order to mark their confessional identity.[67]

It has recently been suggested that the ethnonym "Syrians" had already acquired this confessional meaning during the second half of the sixth century. In her analysis of the role played by historiographical works in the formation of West Syrian identity, Muriel Debié discussed a peculiar passage from John of Ephesus' *Lives of the Eastern Saints* in which he presents an account of the four devout deacons: Abraham, Cyriac, Barḥadbešabbā, and Sergius. On the

---

65 Meyendorff 1989, p. 270.
66 Ed. Brooks 1923–25, v. 3, p. 256.
67 Cf. the West Syrian apologetic work entitled *Treatise on the Syrian Faith* (*Mīmar 'alā al-amāna al-Suryāniya*); ed. Cöln 1904, p. 40, or the marginal note in a West Syrian liturgical manuscript, whose owner refers to himself as belonging to "the ancient Syrians" (*al-Suryān al-qadīm*); Harrak 2011, p. 116. Occasionally, one comes across other Arabic-speaking confessional groups of Syriac lineage, such as Melkites, using this label for self-reference; see Nasrallah 1987, p. 167.

IDENTIFYING THE SYRIAC CHRISTIAN "SELF" 269

one hand, John introduces all four as "being by origin from Syria."⁶⁸ Further on, however, he singles out more specific origins for each of them, using the same noun *gensā*: Abraham "by his origin was from the city of Maipherqat," Cyriac "by origin from the country of the Persians," Barḥadbešabbā "by his origin from Ingilene, from a village called Arʻa Rabtha," and Sergius "by his origin was Armenian."⁶⁹ According to Debié, there is an apparent contradiction in the geographical terms that describe the deacons' origins in this account which can be resolved only if we understand the reference to "Syria" here "not as a regional, but as a religious identity, meaning Syrian Orthodox."⁷⁰

While I do not want to reject the possibility that the ethnonym "Syrians" had acquired a confessional meaning during John's own lifetime, I am not persuaded by this particular interpretation of his use of ethnic labels. This apparent contradiction could be resolved even if the reference to the "Syrian" origins of the holy men is interpreted as territorial or linguistic in nature. The cases of Abraham and Barḥadbešabbā do not pose particular difficulties for understanding the "Syrian" identity of these persons in purely geographical terms, since both the city of Maipherqat and the region of Ingilene were located within the confines of the Roman province of Mesopotamia, which was conceived as part of "Syria." The case of Sergius is more problematic, but even here the reference to his "Armenian" origins does not necessitate that he came from Armenia proper. He might also have been a native of one of the five small satrapies that were originally vassal principalities under Armenian suzerainty but had been annexed from the Sasanian empire by the Romans during the reign of Diocletian, in the year 299.⁷¹ These territories constituted a transitional area between Armenia and Syria, where "Armenian" and "Syrian" territorial identities could overlap to a certain degree. Finally, the case of Cyriac could be interpreted along the same lines. As has been suggested above, in the discussion of the use of the term *Suryāyē* by Barḥadbešabbā, the Syriac-speaking Christians of Nisibis, a "Persian" city during John's lifetime but once a part of Roman Mesopotamia, had sound historical reasons to consider themselves to be "Syrian," not only culturally and linguistically, but in the territorial sense as well.

Thus far, the most explicit early attestation of the confessional meaning of the ethnonym *Suryāyē* comes from the works of those East Syrian

---

68 *Lives* 43: ܗܘܘ ܕܐܝܬܝܗܘܢ ܡܢ ܣܘܪܝܐ ܒܓܢܣܐ; ed. Brooks 1923–1925, v. 2, p. 658.
69 Ed. Brooks 1923–1925, v. 2, p. 659.
70 Debié 2009, p. 109.
71 On this, see Williams, S. 1985, pp. 85–86. The principalities in question are Ingilene, Sophanene, Arzanene, Corduene, and Zabdicene.

authors who exhibit an awareness of the intricate nexus between the ethnic and confessional aspects of the label "Syrian" as the self-designation of the Syriac-speaking Miaphysites. One of the earliest examples of this awareness comes from the works of Dādišoʿ Qaṭrāyā, a seventh-century ascetical writer. In the *Commentary on the Book of Abba Isaiah*, he draws a distinction between the two principal kinds of heretics: those who are only wrong in their practice and those who distort the correct doctrine itself. The "Messalians" are mentioned as an example of the former, whereas in order to illustrate the second type of wrongness, Dādišoʿ points to the "Syrians" and their "corruption of faith," evidently aiming at the West Syrians.[72]

A valuable addition to the repertoire of negative reactions towards "Syrians" on the part of East Syrian writers comes from the *Book of Scholia* by Theodore bar Koni (8th c.). In the second mēmrā of his book, Theodore offers his own version of the biblical *tabula gentium*, the catalog of nations from Genesis 10.[73] What is remarkable about his adaptation of the scriptural material is that while numbering "Aramaeans" (*Ārāmāyē*) together with the rest of the descendants of Shem, in complete agreement with Scripture (cf. Gen 10:22–23), Theodore lists "Syrians" (*Suryāyē*) as a separate ethnic entity and includes them among the descendants of Ham, together with Western groups such as "Antiochenes," "Emessenes," and "Tyrians." Given Ham's negative image and his posterity in the Christian ethnographical tradition,[74] this use of the term "Syrian" might be interpreted as an intentional attempt to tarnish the reputation of West Syrian Christians and to widen the distance between them and Theodore's own community even more by articulating it not in religious, but in ethnic categories.

It might be noted here that the use of the label *Suryāyē* by various denominations of Syriac-speaking Christians does not become less complicated during the period that followed the Arab takeover of the Middle East. This name seems to be evoked most often by the West Syrians as one of the standard terms of self-reference.[75] At the same time, it is not completely unattested in the East Syrian sources. However, while there is no doubt that East Syrian writers do make use of the term *Suryāyē* when speaking about their own cultural or literary heritage preserved in the Syriac language,[76] it still remains to be

---

72 *Comm.* 11.13: ܣܘܪܝܝܐ ܐܝܟ ܚܒܠܐ ܡܢ ܗܝܡܢܘܬܐ; ed. Draguet 1972, p. 151 [Syr.].
73 *Lib. schol.* 2.116–118, ed. Scher 1910–1912, v. 1, pp. 115–116.
74 See section 2.1 of chapter 3 above.
75 Cf., for example, Jacob of Edessa, *Encheiridion*; ed. Furlani 1928, p. 226; Dionysius bar Ṣalibi, *Against the Armenians*; ed. Mingana 1931, p. 507 *et passim*; Barhebraeus, *Chron. eccl.* 1.88; ed. Abbeloos & Lamy 1872–1877, v. 2, cols. 485–487 *et passim*.
76 Cf. Elias of Nisibis, *Chron.*, making use of the calendrical system of *Suryāyē*, ed. Chabot & Brooks 1909–1910, v. 1, p. 5 [Syr.]; ʿAbdišoʿ of Nisibis, distinguishing between the writings of "Greek Fathers" and "Syrian Fathers," ed. Assemani 1719–1728, v. 3.1, p. 51.

established whether this label functioned as a genuine autonym among the East Syrians during this period.

Finally, there appears to be a tendency on the part of some West Syrian authors to employ the term "Syrian" in a broader manner, using it to refer to all Syriac-speaking Christians, West Syrian and East Syrian alike. For instance, Barhebraeus, in his fundamental grammar of the Syriac language, evokes the term "Syrians" while referring to the two distinctive "traditions" of the Syriac language: the "Western" one of Edessa, i.e. West Syrian, and the "Eastern" one of Nisibis, i.e. East Syrian.[77] In this broadening of the meaning of the term "Syrian," we might recognize a reflection of the ecumenical spirit of the so-called "Syriac Renaissance," the period of Syriac cultural and intellectual revival during the twelfth and thirteenth centuries that was characterized by a spirit of openness and cooperation between the two religious communities as well as between Christians and Muslims.[78]

To summarize these observations: looking at the evidence from Syriac sources from late antiquity and the early Middle Ages, we can distinguish three main meanings within the fuzzy semantic field of the ethnonym *Suryāyā*: (a) "territorial," i.e. referring to persons originating from or inhabiting the region of "Syria"; (b) "linguistic," i.e. referring to speakers of the Syriac language; and (c) "confessional," i.e. referring to the Syriac-speaking faction of the Miaphysite movement. Considering the implications of our author's choice of this particular ethnonym as an identity marker, it becomes clear that he does not limit himself to the territorial meaning of this term when addressing the Christian community located within the confines of the Sasanian empire. On the other hand, given the meta-confessional approach to the biblical past that CT pursues, it does not seem warranted to interpret this label as an *intended* marker of West Syrian identity. Accordingly, what remains is to regard the ethnic label "Syrians" in our work as reflecting the "middle ground" of linguistic and thus cultural identification.

2 Syriac Primacy: The Language

CT's author's most conspicuous contribution in the implementation of his agenda of reworking Scripture to forge and promote a version of Syriac-oriented Christian identity that was firmly rooted in the biblical past

---

77 *Book of Rays*, introduction; ed. Moberg 1922, p. 2.
78 See Teule 2009; 2010. For an important discussion of the Muslim contribution to this phenomenon, see Seleznyov 2012.

is the unprecedented stress that he places on the idea of the superiority of Syriac over all other languages. The argument in favor of Syriac as the primeval language is presented in CT 24.9–11, the part of the narrative that retells the biblical account of the division of languages after the destruction of the Tower of Babel which took place after the descendants of Noah migrated to the land of Shinar (Gen 11:1–9):

> And in the days of Peleg all the tribes and families of the children of Noah gathered together, and went up from the East. And they found a plain in the land of Shinar, and they all sat down there, while all speaking in the same language and the same speech. From Adam and until that time all the peoples spoke this language, that is to say, Syriac, which is Aramaic. For this language is the king of all languages. But the ancient writers have erred in that they said that Hebrew was the first (language), and in this matter they have mingled an ignorant mistake with their writing. For all the languages that exist in the world are derived from Syriac, and all the languages in books are mingled with it. In the writing of the Syrians the left (hand) stretches out to the right (hand), and all sons of the left (side) are drawing close to the right (hand) of God. But with the Greeks, and the Romans, and the Hebrews, the right (hand) stretches out to the left.[79]

The main thrust of this passage is to assert that the "one language" (Heb. *śāpāh ʾeḥāṯ*, Syr. *lešānā ḥad*) shared by all humanity before the Tower of Babel was none other than Syriac. To substantiate this bold assertion, our author claims—though without giving any examples—that all the languages in the world are derived from Syriac and thus contain some elements of it.

The notion of a primeval language, while not unknown in the classical world, did not play such a prominent role there as it did in Judaism and related Christian and Islamic traditions.[80] While there is an assortment of Greek

79 OrA: ܘܒܝܘ̈ܡܝ ܦܠܓ ܐܬܟܢܫܘ ܘܣܠܩܘ ܟܠܗܝܢ ܫܪ̈ܒܬܐ ܘܬܘ̈ܠܕܬܐ ܕܒܢ̈ܝ ܢܘܚ ܡܢ ܡܕܢܚܐ: ܘܐܫܟܚܘ ܦܩܥܬܐ ܚܕܐ ܒܐܪܥܐ ܕܣܢܥܪ ܘܝܬܒܘ ܬܡܢ ܟܠܗܘܢ. ܟܕ ܐܝܬܝܗܘܢ ܡܢ ܐܕܡ ܘܥܕܡܐ ܠܬܡܢ ܒܗܢܐ ܠܫܢܐ ܡܡܠܠܝܢ ܗܘܘ. ܗܘܘ ܚܕ ܠܫܢܐ ܘܚܕ ܡܡܠܠܐ ܗܢܐ ܓܝܪ ܠܫܢܐ ܐܝܬܘܗܝ. ܗܢܘ ܕܝܢ ܒܠܫܢܐ ܣܘܪܝܝܐ ܕܐܝܬܘܗܝ ܐܪܡܝܐ. ܟܠܗܘܢ ܒܗܿ ܕܐܡܪܘ ܕܥܒܪܝܐ ܐܝܬܘܗܝ. ܡܟܬ̈ܒܢܐ ܓܝܪ ܩܕ̈ܡܝܐ ܛܥܘ. ܡܠܟܐ ܕܟܠܗܘܢ ܠܫ̈ܢܐ ܟܠܗܘܢ ܓܝܪ ܠܫ̈ܢܐ. ܘܗܪܟܐ ܚܠܛܘ ܠܗܘܢ ܕܠܐ ܝܕܥܬܐ ܒܡܟܬܒܢܘܬܗܘܢ. ܩܕܡܝܐ ܘܒܗ. ܚܠܝܛܝܢ ܒܡܬܚ̈ܠܠܐ ܟܠܗܘܢ ܒܟܬ̈ܒܐ. ܕܐܝܬ ܒܥܠܡܐ ܡܢ ܠܫܢܐ ܣܘܪܝܝܐ ܫܩܝܠܝܢ ܘܡܬܩܪܒܝܢ ܠܝܡܝܢܗ ܕܐܠܗܐ ܟܠܗܘܢ. ܒܟܬܒܐ ܕܣܘܪ̈ܝܝܐ ܣܡܠܐ ܡܬܦܫܛܐ ܠܝܡܝܢܐ ܘܝܘ̈ܢܝܐ ܓܝܪ ܘܪ̈ܗܘܡܝܐ ܘܥܒܪ̈ܝܐ ܠܣܡܠܐ ܡܬܦܫܛܐ ܝܡܝܢܐ. ܒܢ̈ܝ ܣܡܠܐ.

80 For a general overview of various ancient theories on the origins of language(s), see Borst 1957–1963. See also Gera 2003 for a discussion of Greek material; Smelik 2013, pp. 11–99, for the Jewish tradition; and Eskhult 2014.

myths about the invention of language by deities or heroes, such as Hermes or Prometheus, none of these seems to lay particular stress on specifying precisely which language it was, to say nothing of setting it off against other languages. The identity of the first language is only very rarely made explicit by Greco-Roman authors.[81]

It is significant that the author of CT does not simply affirm the primacy of the Syriac language, but does so while explicitly rejecting a similar claim made by some unspecified "ancient writers" concerning Hebrew. In fact, by doing this, he challenges an influential and centuries-old tradition shared by many Jews and Christians in antiquity.

The idea of Hebrew as the primeval language was first formulated in Jewish circles during the Second Temple period. Its earliest attestation comes from the *Book of Jubilees*, where God restores "the language of creation" to Abraham, that is, the Hebrew language, which fell into disuse after the disaster of the Tower of Babel.[82] Another tradition of this kind appears in *4QExposition on the Patriarchs* (= 4Q464), one of the sectarian writings from Qumran, where Hebrew is mentioned in connection with Abraham and is said to triumph at the end of days and become the language of all humanity once more.[83] Later, we see the notion of Hebrew as the language of creation enjoying wide support in rabbinic circles.[84] It reached its pinnacle in the Jewish mystical tradition, where, beginning with the *Sefer Yetzira*, the twenty-two letters of the Hebrew alphabet were interpreted as essential elements in the cosmogonical process.[85]

The notion of Hebrew primacy was one of the many ideas which early Christianity inherited from its Jewish matrix, and it soon became widespread throughout the Christian world. It is attested in a variety of Greek sources, Christian as well as pagan. Among the Greek authors of late antiquity that espoused it were Julius Africanus,[86] Zosimos of Panopolis,[87] John Chrysostom,[88] and the *Apocalypse of Paul* (§30). In the Latin West, one of its earliest

---

81   Cf. the case for Phrygian being the first language, made in Herodotus, *Hist.* 2.2; ed. Godley 1926–1930, v. 1, pp. 274–277. For an analysis of this story, see Gera 2003, pp. 68–111.
82   *Jub.* 12.25–26; ed. VanderKam 1989, p. 73 [trans.].
83   See Eshel & Stone 1993.
84   Cf. *Genesis Rabbah* 31.8; *y.Megillah* 1:8 [71b]; *Targum Neofiti* to Gen 11:1; *Targum Pseudo-Jonathan* to Gen 11:1; *Pirke de-Rabbi Eliezer* 22. For a discussion of this material, see Rubin, M. 1998, pp. 309–317.
85   See Idel 1992.
86   As Agapius of Mabbug testifies, "Africanus the sage claims that Seth, the son of Adam, was the first to bring to light letters and taught writing and the Hebrew language"; ed. Wallraff et alii 2007, p. 43.
87   Ed. Jackson 1978, pp. 28–29.
88   *Hom. 30 in Gen.*; PG 53, col. 279.

attestations comes from Jerome, who considered Hebrew to be "the mother of all languages."[89] A little later, this opinion was further supported by the authority of Augustine.[90] The primacy of Hebrew was apparently also a popular notion among the Christians of Egypt, as evidenced by the *Chronicle* of John of Nikiu and some Coptic magical texts.[91]

The earliest explicit expression of this idea on Syrian soil comes from the third century. The author of the *Pseudo-Clementines*, a Greek work written in Syria, when speaking about the introduction of idolatry after the Flood, remarks that "until that time the Hebrew language, which had been given to the human race by God, predominated."[92] The popularization of this notion among Syriac Christians was facilitated by the early (no later than the first decade of the fifth century) translation of the *Pseudo-Clementines* into Syriac.[93]

Apart from the author of the *Pseudo-Clementines*, one of the earliest Syrian writers to espouse the idea of Hebrew as the primeval language seems to be Eusebius of Emesa, a fourth-century exegete born in Edessa. According to Jacob of Edessa, who quotes an otherwise unattested work of Eusebius, the latter explicitly affirmed the primacy of Hebrew by citing the Hebrew etymological paronomasia involving the nouns "man" (*'îš*) and "woman" (*'iššāh*) in Genesis 2:23 as a scriptural proof-text.[94]

There is no reason to doubt the general accuracy of Jacob's summary of Eusebius' argument. It is, however, far from certain whether the sentence attacking those who hold the view of Aramaic primacy stems from Eusebius. In my opinion, this polemical clause should be regarded as coming from Jacob and not as part of Eusebius' original argument. There is absolutely no evidence whatsoever that the idea of Aramaic as the primeval language existed during Eusebius' lifetime, i.e. the first half of the fourth century. On the other hand, during Jacob's lifetime, i.e. the second half of the seventh century, it enjoyed wide support among Syriac-speaking Christians. Moreover, the thrust of this attack fits well with Jacob's apologetic efforts on behalf of the originality of the Hebrew language.[95]

---

89   *Comm. in Soph.* 3.14–18, ed. Adriaen 1970, p. 708.
90   *De civ. Dei* 16.11.
91   For the former, see *Chron.* 2.1–3; 27.14–17; trans. Charles 1916, pp. 16, 26–27; for the latter, Mirecki 1994, p. 442.
92   *Rec.* 1.30.5: *usque ad illud tempus divinitus humano generi data Hebraeorum lingua tenuit monarchiam*; ed. Rehm & Strecker 1994, p. 25.
93   In the Syriac version of the *Recognitions*, the original Greek sentence is rendered thus: "And until then only one language was in use—Hebrew, beloved by God" (ܘܚܒܝܒܐ ܠܐܠܗܐ ܥܕܡܐ ܠܗܘ ܙܒܢܐ ܗܘܐ ܚܕ ܠܫܢܐ ܒܠܚܘܕ ܐܝܬܘܗܝ ܗܘܐ ܥܒܪܝܐ); ed. Frankenberg 1937, p. 38.
94   *Letter* (#13) *to John of Litarba*; ed. Wright, W. 1867, p. 21.
95   On this, see Adler 1994, p. 154.

It is likely that the notion of Hebrew as the primeval language was also shared by Ephrem the Syrian. Although we do not find it unambiguously expressed in his writings, at least one passage seems best understood in that sense. While discussing Genesis 11:1–9 in his *Commentary on Genesis*, Ephrem states regarding the "first language" (*lešānā qadmāyā*) of humanity that after the Tower of Babel, it "was lost by all the nations and remained with only one."[96] Although Ephrem does not identify the nation that preserved this original language, the most likely interpretation of this sentence seems to be that it refers to the Jewish people, and accordingly to the Hebrew language. This assumption is supported by the fact that Ephrem does not promote the idea of Syriac as the primeval language in any of his authentic writings. Moreover, in the fourth-century intellectual context, where Hebrew was the only attested candidate in discussions of the primeval language, such an ambiguous statement should almost certainly be understood as relating to this language and not, for instance, to Syriac.

The idea of Hebrew primacy was still popular in sixth-century Syria close to the time of CT's composition. Jacob of Sarug bears witness to this in the second of his mēmrē on the Apostle Thomas in India, where he paraphrases the part of the *Acts of Thomas* (§§5–8) in which the apostle meets the Jewish flute-girl. Jacob adds a detail not found in the original text of the *Acts*, saying that the apostle cursed the butler who smote him on his cheek "in Hebrew"— "in that language in which his Lord cursed the serpent in Eden."[97] The notion of Hebrew as the primeval language retained its appeal for at least some Syriac-speaking Christians well after CT's time, as can be seen from the writings of Jacob of Edessa, who was its most prominent apologist during the seventh century.[98] All these examples demonstrate that the prevailing opinion in late ancient Syria was that Hebrew was the original primeval language.

There is a tendency among scholars to underestimate the popularity of the idea of Hebrew primacy among Syriac Christians and to present the notion of Syriac originality as being supported by the majority of Syriac writers. Thus, Milka Rubin notes that Theodoret's view on Syriac primacy was "almost the rule amongst the Syriac writers."[99] A similar assertion about the idea of the originality of Hebrew being "a minority option" among Syriac writers has

---

96   *Comm. in Gen.* 8.3; ed. Tonneau 1955, p. 66 [Syr.]; trans. Mathews & Amar 1994, pp. 147–148 (modified).
97   ܒܗܕܐ ܠܫܢܐ ܕܒܗ ܠܛ ܡܪܗ ܠܚܘܝܐ ܕܒܥܕܢ܀ ed. Strothmann 1976, p. 250.
98   See Adler 1994, pp. 153–154.
99   Rubin, M. 1998, p. 322.

recently been made by Yonatan Moss.[100] While these claims may, perhaps, be true for the medieval period, they are by no means accurate for late antiquity. In fact, the only Syriac writer to affirm the primacy of the Syriac language during this period is the author of CT. In view of the examples asserting Hebrew primacy from late antiquity mentioned above, such undifferentiated claims that project the situation at the later stages of the development of the tradition back to the earlier period should be avoided.

The virtual consensus on the originality of Hebrew began to crack during the fifth century. One of the first Christian thinkers to hold a different opinion on the subject was Theodoret, the bishop of the city of Cyrrhus in Syria and a prolific writer who was active during the first half of the fifth century. In the section of his *Questions on Genesis* dealing with the Tower of Babel and the division of tongues, Theodoret expresses the following opinion about the primeval language:

> Which is the most ancient language (γλῶσσα ἀρχαιοτέρα)? The names give the clue; Adam, Cain, Abel, and Noah belong to Syriac (τῆς Σύρων ἴδια γλώττης). Speakers of Syriac normally refer (ἔθος τοῖς Σύροις καλεῖν) to red earth as "adamtha," so Adam means "earthy" or "made of dust"; Cain "acquisition," for when he sang God's praises, Adam said, "Thanks to God I have acquired a man"; Abel "grief," since his was the first death ever seen and he was the first to cause his parents pain; and Noah "rest."[101]

Further on, Theodoret addresses the issue of Hebrew primacy and disagrees with those exegetes according to whom the name "Hebrews" was derived from Heber (see Gen 10:2–5), the person who supposedly preserved the "original language" (προτέρα φωνῇ), that is, Hebrew.[102] Theodoret offers an alternative etymological explanation for this ethnonym and concludes the discussion on a rather conciliatory note, remarking that the entire issue is irrelevant to matters of faith.

It is noteworthy that Theodoret's argument in favor of Syriac originality seems to be free of any explicit apologetical or polemical overtones and is based purely on linguistic reasoning, such as the similarity between Aramaic words and several personal names in the first chapters of Genesis. The absence of any valorization of the Syriac language on Theodoret's part accords well with the opinion expressed by Henning Lehmann, who in his analysis of Theodoret's

---

100 Moss 2010, p. 120.
101 *Quaest. in Gen.* 60; ed. Petruccione & Hill 2007, v. 1, pp. 122–125.
102 *Quaest. in Gen.* 62; ed. Petruccione & Hill 2007, v. 1, pp. 126–129.

knowledge and use of Syriac comes to the conclusion that his mother tongue was Greek and that he had no deep knowledge of this language, and therefore that he exhibits "no romantic approach to Syriac" and rather considers himself as "the heir to classical Greek."[103]

We may wonder, however, whether in making the claim of Syriac primacy, which was extraordinary for his time, Theodoret might not have been driven by some other agenda than merely scholarly inquisitiveness or personal attachment to it as the language of his upbringing. I believe there are grounds for suggesting that he was. We know that Theodoret had close ties with the Syriac-speaking world. He was familiar with the Syriac language and even spent part of his youth living among Syriac monks. As has been noted by scholars, there is a discernible tendency on Theodoret's part to present and promote himself as a representative of the widely respected Syrian asceticism.[104] Taking this fact into consideration, it seems not unlikely that this expression of Syriac primacy, which at first glance appears purely academic, might ultimately be rooted in Theodoret's personal agenda of self-promotion.

It is possible that even before Theodoret, the cause of Syriac primacy might have been advanced by his teacher Theodore of Mopsuestia. A number of Syriac Christian and Muslim sources transmit this opinion in Theodore's name.[105] In his recent analysis of this tradition, Moss inclines towards accepting the testimony of these sources as genuine.[106] In my view, however, given the late nature of all these witnesses and the lack of unanimity on this issue among East Syrian transmitters of the Theodoretan legacy, it seems impossible at the present time to satisfactorily resolve the question of the authenticity of this tradition. It might just as well be a product of later internal development in which Syrians ascribed this novel idea to Theodore, the ultimate authority for the East Syrian exegetical tradition, in order to provide it with legitimacy.

There is another remarkable ancient witness to the notion of Syriac as the primeval language that until now has gone unnoticed in scholarly discussions of Syriac primacy. It comes from a little-studied Greek work entitled *On the*

---

103 Lehmann 2008, pp. 203, 215–216.
104 On this, see Urbainczyk 2000; for an important discussion of Theodoret's cultural identity, see also Millar 2007.
105 These are: (1) the anonymous *Diyarbekir Commentary* (8th c.); ed. van Rompay 1986, pp. 68–69 [Syr.], 88–89 [trans.]; (2) Išoʿdad of Merv (9th c.), *Comm. in Gen.* 1:1; ed. Vosté & van den Eynde 1950–1955, pp. 135 [Syr.], 147 [trans.]; (3) Ibn al-Nadīm, *al-Fihrist* 1.1; ed. Flügel 1871–1872, v. 1, p. 12. For a discussion of al-Nadīm's testimony, see Samir 1977, pp. 360–363.
106 See Moss 2010, pp. 132–135.

Mystery of Letters, a Christian composition which offers a developed mystical interpretation of the letters of the Greek alphabet. The Greek original of this work, which might be contemporary with CT, has recently been discovered and edited by Cordula Bandt.[107] In §19 of this composition, the following apology for the antiquity of the Syriac language is offered:

> For before all that there were the Syrian letters and the Syrian language, which is the profound language of the Chaldaeans (τὰ Σύρα γράμματα, καὶ ἡ Σύρα γλῶσσα ἡ βαθεῖα τῶν Χαλδαίων). As some historians say, these (i.e. the letters) were learned through divine inspiration in the generation of Enoch; at that time when, as the Scripture says, the descendants of Adam introduced the arts of forging ore and harp-playing. It is this Syrian language and its twenty-two letters that were in use among men until the tower and the confusion of languages. With a view to the Syrian letters, then—they are not from a man and not by men, but these figures of our letters were engraved by the hand and the finger of God on a certain stone tablet, such as the tablets of the Law. The Greek companions of the man called Cadmus found this tablet after the Flood. And from it then the teaching of the letters was revealed in *Palaestina prima* of Phoenicia. And because of that the wise Herodotus called these letters Phoenician.[108]

What we observe here is a powerful argument for Syriac as the primeval language of humanity which has no close parallels in the Greek Christian literature of late antiquity and the early Middle Ages. The author of *On the Mystery* introduces the theme of Syriac primacy in order to buttress the main theological idea that drives his work, i.e. that the letters of the Greek alphabet convey a hidden message about the mystery of Christ, before his (imaginary?) Jewish opponents. In its turn, this is possible only because the Greek alphabet is derived from the "Syrian" one, the first script in the history of the human race, which was revealed by God himself. Like CT's author, the author of *On the Mystery* promotes the primacy of Syriac by declaring it to be the "one language" spoken by humanity before the Tower of Babel.

He substantiates the claim about the primacy of the Syriac language and alphabet over those of the Greeks by creatively adapting the popular Herodotean account of the origins of the Greek alphabet, according to which it was brought to Greece by the Phoenicians, led by Prince Cadmus, who spread

---

107   Bandt 2007, p. 148. Its Coptic version was published earlier by Hebbelynck 1900–1901.
108   Ed. Bandt 2007, p. 148.

this knowledge among the Ionian Greeks.[109] It appears that in doing so, he further develops the idea of the precedence of the "Syrian" alphabet (but not of the "Syrian" language as such!) that had already been espoused by some Greek-speaking intellectuals during late antiquity. The fact that on several occasions Cadmus' account of Herodotus may be found in a slightly modified form in the later tradition of Greco-Roman historiography testifies to this, so that in addition to the "Phoenicians," the honor of inventing the Greek alphabet is also ascribed to the "Syrians."

Thus, Clement of Alexandria, developing the apologetic theme of the Greeks' dependence on barbarian peoples, mentions the opinions of several classical authors regarding the Phoenician origins of the Greek alphabet and summarizes their views by claiming that "they say that the Phoenicians and the Syrians first invented letters."[110] Later, Eusebius of Caesarea modifies this tradition as he pursues a similar apologetic agenda in the *Praeparatio Evangelica*. After mentioning the case of Cadmus and the Phoenicians as the inventors of the Greek alphabet, Eusebius adds that "some say that the Syrians were the first who devised letters."[111] The wording of this sentence suggests that Eusebius is here depending on the passage from Clement quoted just now. However, he reinterprets Clement's words in favor of Hebrew primacy, claiming that "these Syrians would be Hebrews who inhabited the neighboring country to Phoenicia, which was itself called Phoenicia in old times, but afterwards Judaea, and in our time, Palestine."[112]

In her discussion of §19 of *On the Mystery*, Bandt maintains that the "Syrian language" (Σύρα γλῶσσα) in this passage, as well as throughout the whole work, is synonymous with Hebrew, and she regards it as another expression of Hebrew primacy.[113] This interpretation, however, is hardly tenable. A close examination of those instances in *On the Mystery* where the adjectives or nouns "Syrian" and "Hebrew" appear alongside each other reveals that the author made a clear distinction between the two ethnic groups and

---

109 *Hist.* 5.58–59; ed. Godley 1926–1930, v. 3, pp. 62–65. On Cadmus, see Edwards, R.B. 1979.
110 *Strom.* 1.16.75; ed. Stählin 1905–36, v. 2, p. 48; trans. from Roberts & Donaldson 1887, p. 317.
111 *Praep. ev.* 10.5.2: εἰσὶ δὲ οἳ Σύρους γράμματα ἐπινοῆσαι πρώτους λέγουσι; ed. Mras & des Places 1982–1983, v. 1, p. 574; trans. Gifford 1903, v. 3.2, p. 506.
112 *Praep. ev.* 10.5.2; ed. Mras & des Places 1982–1983, v. 1, p. 574; trans. Gifford 1903, v. 3.2, p. 506. Eusebius' claim might have arisen under the influence of a particular trend in Greco-Roman ethnography, in which the ethnonym "the Syrians of Palestine" (Σύροι οἱ ἐν τῇ Παλαιστίνῃ), mentioned by Herodotus (*Hist.* 2.104) alongside the Phoenicians as another nation that learned the custom of circumcision from the Egyptians, began to be interpreted by later intellectuals as referring to the Jews. Cf. Ovid, *Ars. amat.* 1.416; Josephus, *C. Ap.* 1.168–171; *Ant.* 8.262; see Feldman 1996, pp. 554–555.
113 Bandt 2007, p. 31.

their languages. Thus, in §23 he evokes the names of several Christian theologians who mastered both "the language of Hebrews and that of Syrians."[114] Moreover, the author explicitly identifies the "Syrian" language with that of the "Chaldaeans." Besides the above-quoted §19, he does this in §37, where he identifies "Syrian" and "Chaldaean" letters—τὰ Σύρα ἤγουν Χαλδαῖα γράμματα—and also mentions the letters of "Syrians" and those of "Hebrews" as though they are two separate things.[115] All this evidence leaves no doubt that by evoking the "Syrian" language and its letters, the author of *On the Mystery* intended to refer to some form of the Aramaic language and not to Hebrew.

The apology for the Syriac language in *On the Mystery* has several features in common with that of CT. As has already been noted, the author of this work shares with CT the important theme of Syriac being the language spoken by humanity before the division of tongues. Moreover, the claim of CT's author that "all the languages that exist in the world are derived from Syriac, and all the languages in books are mingled with it" (CT 24.11) finds a close counterpart in the declaration of *On the Mystery*'s author that "all languages under heaven" derive their alphabets from the Syrian alphabet.[116] It is also important that in both these works the notion of Syriac as the primeval language serves the purpose of an anti-Jewish apologetic agenda.[117] In addition to §19, the anti-Jewish dimension of the idea of Syriac primacy in *On the Mystery* comes to the surface in §37, where the author castigates the Jews, who do not accept his teaching, by likening them to Canaanites, "deprived of Abraham's Syriac, the time-honored language."[118]

At the same time, there are significant differences between these two expressions of Syriac primacy. First of all, in distinction from CT, the author of *On the Mystery* focuses almost exclusively on the alphabet and the interpretation of the names of its letters. Unlike CT's author, he ascribes no meaning to the form of the Syriac script. Furthermore, in order to support his claim of Syriac primacy, he makes use of the classical myth of Cadmus and the Phoenician origins of the Greek alphabet, which plays no role in CT's narrative. This, as well as some additional minor differences between these affirmations of Syriac primacy, precludes us from suggesting any direct connection between the two

---

114 Bandt 2007, p. 158. Cf. also §26, where he refers to "Hebrews," "Syrians," and "Arabs" as three distinctive groups whose languages feature similar pronominal forms (Bandt 2007, p. 166), and §28, where he lists the "Hebrew," "Syrian," and "Arabic" languages separately (Bandt 2007, p. 168).
115 Bandt 2007, pp. 182–184.
116 §37; Bandt 2007, p. 184.
117 On the anti-Jewish implications of the affirmation of Syriac primacy in CT, see below.
118 ἐκπεσὼν τῆς Ἀβραμιαίας Σύρας καὶ γλώσσης τῆς εὐγενεστέρας; ed. Bandt 2007, p. 184.

works. It seems more likely that the two variations on the theme of Syriac primacy, that of CT and that of *On the Mystery*, developed independently of one another.

Returning to the assertion of the primacy of Syriac in CT, one of the proofs its author gives seems to be based on its being written from right to left, supposedly unique to Syrians, which, it is claimed, sets it apart from the Hebrew, Greek, and Latin scripts, characterized by being written left to right.[119] This quasi-linguistic argument was most likely invented by our author, as no Syriac or other Christian writer makes use of it before the sixth century. Remarkably, it is not based on any actual feature of the four respective scripts as known to us and thus appears to be completely fictitious.[120] Nothing similar to this claim is found in Jacob of Edessa's categorization of languages, which is also based on their way of writing and which draws a distinction between languages written from left to right, such as Greek, Latin, Egyptian, and Armenian, and those written from right to left, such as Hebrew, Syriac, Arabic, and Persian.[121] As can be seen, no unique place is ascribed to the Syriac language in this classification.

This unusual argument makes the polemical intention that underlines our author's claim of Syriac primacy even more evident, as the superior position ascribed to Syriac vis-à-vis Greek, Latin, and Hebrew is based on the superiority of the right side over the left. The dichotomy between left and right is one of the universal constants of human culture. In many religious traditions in antiquity, the distinction between these directions was used to indicate positive and negative values. This distinction, in which the left was marked as the bad side and the right as the good, could already be found in the Hebrew Bible (cf. Eccl 10:2) and becomes quite common in post-biblical Judaism and Christianity.[122]

---

119   The actual meaning of the phrase *semālā mawšeṭā l-yaminā*, lit. "the left stretches out to the right," as characteristic of the Syriac writing in CT 24.11 is obscure. It is understood as referring to the direction of the Syriac script from right to left by the translator of CT into Arabic (ed. Gibson 1901, p. 34), as well as by most modern translators (cf. Toepel 2013, p. 558).

120   An attempt by Jan van Reeth to explain this enigmatic claim by referring to some actual features of the Estrangela script does not seem particularly convincing; see van Reeth 2005, p. 141.

121   See Jacob's note in his translation of Severus' *Cathedral Homilies*; ed. Brière 1960, pp. 196–197.

122   For the Jewish tradition, see Philo, *Quis Her.* 209; *Test. of Benj.* 10:6; *Apoc. of Abraham* 27, 29; *Test. of Abraham* (A) 12:12, 13:9; *Cant. Rabbah* 1.9.1. For Christianity, see Mt 25:31–46; *Hypost. of Archons* 95.34–96.3. See also Grundmann 1964; Court 1985; Lloyd 1962.

Syriac Christian culture inherited this dichotomy from its Jewish and Greek Christian matrixes. Identification with the left side was generally used to mark those who were perceived as enemies of God or Christians. For example, Ephrem says of Judas that he became "the head of the left side" (*rišā l-semālā*).[123] The epithet "sons of the left side" (*bnay semālā*) used by CT's author was also applied to the sinners whom God condemned to eternal punishment in the eschatological scenario described in Matthew 25:31–46.[124]

Identification with the left was applied not only to the human enemies of God, but also to demonic forces. Thus, Ephrem calls the forces of evil, comprised of demons, Satan, Death, and Sheol, "the party of the left side" (*gabā d-semālā*).[125] In the Syriac *Life of Simeon the Stylite*, demons are called "the sons of the left side."[126] In a similar vein, Jacob of Sarug calls Satan "the commander of the left side" (*rabḥaylā d-semālā*) in one of his homilies.[127]

The demonological aspect of the association with the left side in CT might have additional connotations if one takes its Iranian provenance into consideration. In several Semitic languages, the cognates of Syr. *semālā*, in addition to the main meaning of "left," may also designate the north. Thus, in Biblical Hebrew, the noun *śᵉmōl*, besides meaning "left," is at times used to indicate the north.[128] In Classical Arabic, *šimāl* is used both for "left" and for the north wind.[129] At the same time, in the Zoroastrian cosmological model, the north (Mid. Pers. *abāxtar*) was considered to be where hell, the dwelling place of Ahreman and the demonic forces, is located.[130] The Persian *Diatessaron* (4.3) testifies that this connection between the left and the north was known to the Christians of Iran, as it refers to "the North (*šamāl*), that is the left side (*kanār čap*)."[131]

All this suggests that in claiming the superiority of the Syriac language over Hebrew, Greek, and Latin, the author of CT does not limit himself to the idea of Syriac as the primeval language, but resorts to demonizing these three languages and, by implication, their speakers. It is important to stress at this

---

123 *Hymn. adv. Haer.* 22.11; ed. Beck 1957b, p. 81 [Syr.].
124 Cf. Ephrem, *Necrosima* 12; ed. Assemani et alii 1732–1746, v. 3 [Syr.], p. 244; *Martyrdom of Peter 'Abšelama*; ed. Assemani 1748, v. 2, p. 209.
125 *Carm. Nis.* 36.18; ed. Beck 1963, p. 14 [Syr.].
126 Ed. Assemani 1748, v. 2, p. 232.
127 Ed. Rilliet 1986, p. 570, §8.
128 Cf. Gen 14:15; Josh 19:27; Job 23:8–9; Ezek 16:46.
129 See Lane 1863–1893, v. 4, pp. 1600–1601.
130 For the references, see Tafazzoli 1989, p. 539. Cf. also the description of the syncretistic religious system of the Ṣābians of Harran by Ibn al-Nadīm, *al-Fihrist* 9.1; ed. Flügel 1871–1872, v. 1, p. 323. See also, Green, T.M. 1992, pp. 195–203.
131 Ed. Messina 1951, p. 288.

point that our author is attempting to challenge not only the authority of the Hebrew language, but that of Greek and Latin as well. This polemical usage of a linguistic argument based on the formal features of the Syriac script is unique to our author and stands out as one of his contributions to the tradition of Syriac apologetics.

3 Syriac Primacy: The People

In his attempt to raise the prestige of Syrians, the author of CT does not confine himself to declaring the superiority of Syriac as the original language of humanity. He gives the idea of Syriac supremacy another original and unprecedented expression based on its absence from the inscription on Jesus' cross. In CT 53.20–27, the following description of the aftermath of Jesus' death on the cross is presented:

> And when Joseph brought him (i.e. Jesus) down from the Cross, he took away that inscription which was spread out above his head, that is, over the cross of Christ, because it had been written by Pilate in Greek, and Roman, and Hebrew. And for what reason did Pilate not write in it the name of the Syrians? Because the Syrians had no part in (the shedding of) the blood of Christ. And Pilate was a wise man and a lover of the truth, (and) he did not want to write a lie as wicked judges do. But he acted in accordance with what is written in the Law of Moses, that those who condemn the innocent should raise their hand against him first there. And Pilate wrote the names of the murderers of Christ and hung above him: Herod the Greek, Caiaphas the Hebrew, and Pilate the Roman. But the Syrians had no part in his murder. And to this testifies Abgar, the king of Edessa, who wanted to go up to Jerusalem and destroy it because the Jews crucified Christ.[132]

132 Or[A]: ܘܟܕ ܐܚܬܗ ܝܘܣܦ ܡܢ ܙܩܝܦܐ. ܫܩܠ ܟܬܒܐ ܗܘ ܕܦܪܝܣ ܗܘܐ ܠܥܠ ܡܢ ܪܫܗ ܐܘܟܝܬ ܠܥܠ ܡܢ ܙܩܝܦܗ ܕܡܫܝܚܐ. ܡܛܠ ܕܒܝܕ ܦܝܠܛܘܣ ܐܬܟܬܒ ܗܘܐ ܝܘܢܐܝܬ ܘܪܗܘܡܐܝܬ ܘܥܒܪܐܝܬ. ܘܡܛܠ ܐܝܢܐ ܥܠܬܐ ܠܐ ܟܬܒ ܒܗ ܦܝܠܛܘܣ ܫܡܐ ܕܣܘܪܝܝܐ. ܡܛܠ ܕܠܝܬ ܗܘܐ ܠܗܘܢ ܠܣܘܪܝܝܐ ܫܘܬܦܘܬܐ ܒܕܡܗ ܕܡܫܝܚܐ. ܘܦܝܠܛܘܣ ܓܒܪܐ ܗܘܐ ܚܟܝܡܐ ܘܪܚܡ ܩܘܫܬܐ. ܠܐ ܨܒܐ ܕܢܟܬܘܒ ܕܓܠܬܐ ܐܝܟ ܕܥܒܕܝܢ ܕܝܢܐ ܕܥܘܠܐ. ܐܠܐ ܐܝܟ ܕܟܬܝܒ ܒܢܡܘܣܐ ܕܡܘܫܐ ܗܟܢܐ ܥܒܕ. ܕܐܝܠܝܢ ܕܡܚܝܒܝܢ ܙܟܝܐ ܗܢܘܢ ܢܪܡܘܢ ܒܗ ܐܝܕܐ ܩܕܡ ܠܗܘܢ. ܘܦܝܠܛܘܣ ܟܬܒ [ܠܫܡ̈ܗܝܗܘܢ ܕܩ̈ܛܠ ܡܫܝܚܐ] ܘܬܠܐ ܠܥܠ ܡܢܗ: ܗܪܘܕܣ ܝܘܢܝܐ. ܘܩܝܦܐ ܥܒܪܝܐ. ܘܦܝܠܛܘܣ ܪܗܘܡܝܐ. ܠܣܘܪܝܝܐ ܓܝܪ ܠܝܬ ܗܘܐ ܠܗܘܢ ܫܘܬܦܘܬܐ ܒܩܛܠܗ. ܘܣܗܕ ܒܗܕܐ ܐܒܓܪ ܡܠܟܐ ܕܐܘܪܗܝ. ܕܨܒܐ ܗܘܐ ܠܡܣܠܩ ܠܐܘܪܫܠܡ ܘܠܡܚܪܒܗ ܥܠ ܕܙܩܦܘܗܝ ܝܗܘ̈ܕܝܐ ܠܡܫܝܚܐ. The text

The author here offers a peculiar interpretation of the passage from the Gospel of John (19:19–20), relating that at the crucifixion, Pilate placed an inscription on Jesus' cross that featured the phrase "Jesus of Nazareth, the King of the Jews," written in three languages: Hebrew, Latin, and Greek. Deviating from the canonical version, he alleges that this inscription contained the names of the three primary culprits responsible for Jesus' unjust condemnation and execution. This claim is justified by a vague reference to "the law of Moses" regarding the correct procedure in a death penalty case, which Pilate supposedly followed. Most likely, it is an allusion to the biblical prescription according to which a person accused of a crime punishable by stoning could be condemned to death on the testimony of two or three witnesses, who should be first to begin implementing the death penalty (cf. Deut 17:4–7). The role of such witnesses in Jesus' case is ascribed to Herod, Caiaphas, and Pilate.

What is truly remarkable in this treatment of the canonical narrative is that our author uses the absence of the mention of "Syrians" from the trilingual inscription as a pretext for exonerating this group of the crime of deicide. No comparable treatment of John 19:19–20 is found in the works of Syriac or any other Christian exegetes before the time of CT. When this passage is handled by Syrian authors, it mostly serves as an argument in anti-Jewish polemic, when Pilate uses the three languages providentially to inform all the nations of the world that the Jews are guilty of Christ's murder. These verses are explained in this way, for example, by Theodore of Mopsuestia and by the author of the Pseudo-Ephremian *Sermons on the Holy Week*.[133]

Taking the emphasis the author of CT puts on the absence of Syrians from the inscription on Jesus' cross at face value, it could be argued that this or a similar opinion could actually have been held in antiquity. In fact, there is one ancient tradition that might lend itself to such an interpretation. It appears in the Greek *Paraphrase of the Gospel of John* written by Nonnus of Panopolis, a fifth-century poet from Egypt. In this hexametrical retelling of the canonical Gospel narrative, Nonnus relates regarding the inscription of John 19:19–20 that it was written "in the Ausonian, Syrian, and Achaian languages."[134] Whereas the identification of the first and last items on this list as Latin and Greek presents no difficulties, the meaning of the "Syrian language" is open to various explanations. Francis Thomson takes it literally, i.e. as a reference to the Syriac

---

has been emended, with the bracketed passage moved to what appears to be its original position.
133 For Theodore, see ed. Vosté 1940, p. 336 [Syr.]; for the Pseudo-Ephremian text, ed. Beck 1979, pp. 62–63 [Syr.].
134 *Paraphr. Ioan.* 19.109: Αὐσονίῃ γλώσσῃ τε Σύρων καὶ Ἀχαΐδι φωνῇ; ed. Scheindler 1881, p. 222.

or Aramaic language.[135] He bases this interpretation on the claim that the true meaning of the Greek adverb Ἑβραϊστὶ in John 19:20 is not actually "in Hebrew," but "in Aramaic," correctly pointing out that in all cases when this adverb is used by the Gospel's author to introduce Semitisms, it describes borrowings from Aramaic and not from Hebrew.[136] According to Thomson, Nonnus was aware of this correct meaning of Ἑβραϊστὶ, which is confirmed by the fact that on two occasions when the poet decides to include John's "Hebraisms" in his paraphrase, Γαββαθα in John 19:13 and Γολγοθα in John 19:17, he changes them into "Syriacisms."[137]

While Thomson is certainly right regarding the true etymology of the "Hebraisms" in the Gospel of John, his proposal regarding Nonnus' awareness of this fact does not seem very likely. It presupposes an advanced level of linguistic competence in comparative Semitics in a Greek poet from Byzantine Egypt that is not attested in antiquity even among the native Syriac-speaking translators and interpreters of the New Testament or, for that matter, among the majority of the ancient exegetes of the Gospel, who failed to recognize "Syriacisms" behind John's "Hebraisms." Instead, I would argue that the Egyptian writer simply does not distinguish between the two Semitic languages spoken in Palestine and employs the label "Syrian" as a synonym for "Hebrew." This suggestion is corroborated by the fact that in antiquity the ethnic label "Syrian" was often used in a broad territorial sense and could be applied to the inhabitants of Palestine, including Jews, without difficulty.[138]

Our author's proleptic rhetoric about the Syrians' innocence of Christ's execution can hardly, then, be taken as an attempt to rebuff any actual claim in that regard. This straw argument serves rather as a rhetorical pretext for claiming the superiority of the "Syrians" over three other groups: Jews, Greeks, and Romans. Noteworthily, all four ethnic groups are defined here through their language. In this regard, it is significant that we see how the author of CT makes two attempts to challenge the prestige of the three particular languages—Hebrew, Greek, and Latin—while putting them in opposition to Syriac. Whereas in CT 24.9–11 he denounces these languages on the basis of their external features, in CT 53.20–27 his negative rhetoric against them escalates as he takes it to an even deeper theological level by blaming the speakers of Hebrew, Greek, and Latin for the murder of Christ. The polemical intention

---

135   Thomson, F.J. 1992, p. 76.
136   Cf. John 5:2 (Βηθζαθὰ); 19:13 (Γαββαθα); 19:17 (Γολγοθα); 20:16 (ραββουνι).
137   Paraphr. Ioan. 19.64–65: ἐνδαπίῳ δὲ Γαββαδὰ παφλάζοντι Σύρων κικλήσκετο μύθῳ; ed. Scheindler 1881, p. 218; Paraphr. Ioan. 19.91: Γολγοθὰ τὸν καλέεσκε Σύρων στόμα; ed. Scheindler 1881, p. 220.
138   On this, see section 1 above.

of these barely disguised attacks on these three languages is manifest. Making sense of the goals our author was pursuing in waging this polemic, which has no precedent in the works of Christian writers before him, poses, however, a certain difficulty.

The presence of the Hebrew language in this list is not surprising, given the general anti-Jewish thrust of CT and the supersessionist ideology of its author.[139] The denunciation of Hebrew fits well with the author's strong anti-Jewish rhetoric, which portrays the Jews as the killers of Christ.[140] The negative portrayal of the other two languages, Greek and Latin, however, is striking and needs explanation. One possible way of explaining this rhetoric would be to suggest that its main thrust lies in the challenge our author is attempting to pose to the doctrine of Hebrew, Greek, and Latin as the three sacred languages. This doctrine received its most developed expression in Europe during the Middle Ages, but its earliest attestations can already be found in late antiquity.[141] One of its earliest formulations belongs to Isidore of Seville, a Latin Church Father who was active from the second half of the sixth century to the first decades of the seventh. In the section dealing with languages in his *Etymologies*, Isidore claims:

> There are three sacred languages (*linguae sacrae*)—Hebrew, Greek, and Latin—which are preeminent throughout the world. On the cross of the Lord the charge laid against him was written at Pilate's command in these three languages. Hence—and because of the obscurity of the Sacred Scriptures—a knowledge of these three languages is necessary, so that, whenever the wording of one of the languages presents any doubt about a name or an interpretation, recourse may be had to another language.[142]

The roots of the idea of the privileged position held by the three languages of the superscription on Jesus' cross go back to the fourth and fifth centuries, when the notion of their special merit began to develop in the Latin West. Thus, in one of his letters, Jerome, while boasting about the universal dissemination and success of the Gospel, draws particular attention to its dissemination among the Jews, Greeks, and Romans, "peoples which the Lord

---

139 Cf. CT 19.13; 31.28; 43.9; 48.29 [Oc]; 50.13–14; 52.1; 52.17. See chapter 2 above.
140 Cf. CT 48.13–14; 50.4; 51.12; 53.6 [Or].
141 See Hilhorst 2007, pp. 782–783; Thomson, F.J. 1992.
142 *Etym.* 9.1.3; ed. Lindsay 1911, v. 1, p. 343; trans. Barney et alii 2006, p. 191. Isidore repeats this idea in *Liber numerorum* 4.17: *sacrae legis triplex est, Hebraea, Graeca et Latina*; PL 83, col. 182.

had dedicated to his faith by the title written on his cross."[143] Later, Augustine characterizes these three languages as "the most excellent in the whole world."[144] For Augustine, these three languages were singled out because of their importance: Hebrew because of the Jews' glory in the Law of God, Greek because of the wisdom of the Greeks, and Latin because of the Romans' world dominion.[145]

It could be that this notion of the exclusive status of the three languages on the cross also received some degree of recognition in the Christian East. For example, for Cyril of Alexandria, the reason for the trilingual inscription on the cross is that these languages are "the most widely known of all."[146] In the Syriac version of *Transitus Mariae*, the account of the end of Mary's earthly existence is said to miraculously appear written in these same three languages.[147] Nevertheless, despite these expressions recognizing the importance of Hebrew, Greek, and Latin, which are contemporary with or even predate CT, it is far from certain that people in the Sasanian part of Mesopotamia, where our work was composed, would have known about it. And even if it was, it is debatable whether this notion was popular enough to provoke such an emphatic rebuttal. Since there seems to be no conclusive evidence in that regard, the explanatory force of this hypothesis is rather weak.

There is yet another direction of thought that may help us to better appreciate the driving force behind our author's challenge to the Greek language. In order to follow it, the issue of the status of the Syriac language vis-à-vis Greek during the fifth and sixth centuries should be briefly addressed.[148] As has been noted by scholars, beginning from the second half of the fourth century, after the Roman empire's official conversion to Christianity, the Syriac Christians came to be more and more influenced by the patterns of life and thought of their Western Greek-speaking coreligionists. The Westernization of Syriac Christianity proceeded on different levels.[149] One of its main manifestations was a dramatic increase in translations from Greek into Syriac.[150] In order to adequately convey Greek words and concepts for which no original Syriac equivalents existed, translators introduced many Greek loan-words into the

---

143   *Ep.* 60.4; ed. Hilberg 1996, pp. 552–553.
144   *In Psalmum LVIII enarratio* 1.1; ed. Dekkers 1956, pp. 729–730.
145   *In Iohannis Evangelium Tractatus CXXIV* 117.4; ed. Willems 1954, p. 653. Cf. also *Sermo de Passione Domini in Parasceve* (#218.6); PL 38, col. 1085.
146   *Comm. in Ioan.* 12; ed. Pusey 1872, v. 3, p. 85.
147   Ed. Lewis 1902, pp. 32 [Syr.], 19 [trans.].
148   For a discussion of this subject, see Brock 1994; Taylor, D.G.K. 2002; Millar 2008, 2011, 2012.
149   On the important aspect of this process as normalization of Syrian asceticism, see Wood 2012, pp. 183–186; Minov 2014a, pp. 259–260.
150   On this, see especially Brock 1994.

Syriac vocabulary. Sometimes, especially in the later stages of this translation movement, even the Syriac syntax itself was violated in order to bring it closer to that of the Greek original.

Apparently, this process provoked a negative reaction from those Syrians who saw it as a threat to the purity of their native language. One of the earliest objections to this aspect of the expansion of Greek culture comes from the *Commentary on Ecclesiastes* ascribed to John of Apamea, a fifth-century Syriac author.[151] In this work, we find the following expression of resentment towards the detrimental results of the Greek language's influence on Syriac:

> One should say also this, that even the Syriac language was greatly corrupted by contact with and closeness to the Greek language. And the manners of its eloquence were forgotten even by the people for whom it was the native language.[152]

A similar feeling of nostalgia for the lost purity of the Syriac language seems to underlie the words of the anonymous author of the preface to the Syriac *Book of Steps*, when he praises the book's composer for "the simplicity of his style" (*pšiṭut meltēh*) which reminds him of the style of "the ancient Syriac language" (*meltēh ʿatiqtā hi b-lešānā Suryāyā*).[153] It is this simple and unskilled style, uncorrupted by scholastic jargon, that allows the writer of the preface to extol the author of the *Book of Steps* as a prophet and "one of the last disciples of the Apostles," whose doctrine was derived not "from the teachings of wise men," but was directly inspired by the Holy Spirit.[154] Although the exact time and identity of the preface's writer are not known, it is evident that he lived during the period in which the major translations of patristic works from Greek into Syriac had already been carried out, as he himself refers to Greek authors such as Gregory of Nazianzus, Basil of Caesarea, and Evagrius Ponticus.[155]

The purity of the Syriac language was not the only issue at stake. Occasionally, antagonism between advocates of the Syriac and Greek languages would

---

151 John's authorship of this work is far from certain; see Strothmann 1973, pp. 213–214; van Rompay 1996, pp. 631–632. It should be emphasized, however, that the earliest textual witness of this work, ms. British Library, Add. 14597, is dated to the year 569; see ed. Strothmann 1988b, p. xxi.

152 ܢܐܡܪ ܕܝܢ ܐܦ ܗܕܐ. ܕܐܦ ܗܘ ܠܫܢܐ ܣܘܪܝܝܐ ܣܓܝ ܐܬܚܒܠ ܡܢ ܩܪܝܒܘܬܗ ܕܠܫܢܐ ܗܘ ܝܘܢܝܐ. ܘܐܫܬܟܚܘ ܕܛܥܘ ܙܢܝ̈ ܡܡܠܠܗ ܐܦ ܡܢ ܐܝܠܝܢ ܕܗܘ ܠܗܘܢ ܠܫܢܐ; ed. Strothmann 1988b, p. 4.

153 Ed. Kmosko 1926, col. 4; trans. Kitchen & Parmentier 2004, p. 4.

154 Ed. Kmosko 1926, cols. 1–4; trans. Kitchen & Parmentier 2004, pp. 3–4.

155 Ed. Kmosko 1926, col. 5; trans. Kitchen & Parmentier 2004, p. 4.

develop on another, more significant level of theological discourse. This tension is most visibly expressed by Philoxenus of Mabbug in the *Letter to the Monks of Senoun*, written in the third decade of the sixth century, where he explains his Miaphysite Christology to a Syriac-speaking monastic community. In this letter, Philoxenus complains about the Syriac language's inability to adequately express the Christological terminology originally coined in Greek.[156] Philoxenus' situation is complicated by the fact that the Syriac monks whom he is addressing seem to adhere to the traditional Christological vocabulary supported by the authority of none other than the great Ephrem the Syrian, who, as it turned out, had expressed the mystery of the Incarnation in terms no longer acceptable by the standards of the new post-Chalcedonian theology almost 200 years later. As has been demonstrated by Lucas van Rompay, there was a noticeable change in Philoxenus' attitude to Ephrem which reflects a general tendency among the West Syrian theologians of the sixth century towards the marginalization of this Church Father as an authority in Christological discussions.[157]

As emerges from this evidence, one of the side effects of the profound Westernization and Hellenization which Syriac-speaking society underwent during the fifth and sixth centuries was the feelings of inferiority and threat experienced by at least some Syriac speakers in relation to the Greek language and culture. This observation calls into question the rather optimistic picture of Greco-Syriac sociolinguistic and cross-cultural interaction presented by David Taylor. In his thorough investigation of the dynamics of Greco-Aramaic bilingualism in the late Roman Near East, Taylor comes to the conclusion that the "new hybrid form of Syriac," i.e. the artificial form of the Syriac language that developed as a result of the massive translation of Greek works carried out by the Syrians during the sixth and seventh centuries, should not be interpreted as "evidence for the cultural and linguistic dominance of Greek and the decline in prestige of Aramaic."[158]

The example of John of Apamea makes it clear, however, that the profound Hellenization of the Syriac language also had a downside: it caused discontent among some of the Syriac-speaking Christians, who perceived it as a threat to their cultural identity. Bearing in mind this ambivalence in reaction to the impact of the Greek culture among Syriac speakers, we might be justified in reading the barely concealed antipathy towards the Greek and Latin languages evident in the passages from CT analyzed above as an attempt to challenge

---

156   Ed. de Halleux 1963, pp. 51 [Syr.], 42 [trans.]; cf. also pp. 54–55 [Syr.], 45 [trans.].
157   See van Rompay 2004, pp. 99–102.
158   Taylor, D.G.K. 2002, p. 331.

the cultural hegemony of Western Christendom over the indigenous Syriac Christian culture, with the Greek language as its most important vehicle. This aspect of Syriac identity in CT has been pointed out by Serge Ruzer and Aryeh Kofsky, who interpret our author's anti-Western rhetoric as an expression of "exclusiveness in the self-perception of the author's community," whose geographical and cultural remoteness was conducive to the development of its self-image as "the true spiritual elite vis-à-vis a hegemonic Greco-Roman Christendom."[159]

4   The Figure of Abgar

In CT 53.26–27, the author concludes his argument that "Syrians" had nothing to do with Jesus' murder by bringing up the figure of the Edessene king Abgar as the historical example meant to confirm this truth: "But the Syrians had no part in his murder. And to this testifies Abgar, the king of Edessa, who wanted to go up to Jerusalem and destroy it because the Jews crucified Christ." The author's decision to utilize this particular personage as the representative of "Syrians" is not accidental and deserves closer attention.

Before proceeding with the discussion of Abgar, it should be noted that there is an element of anachronism in the author's choice of this figure as the representative of "Syrians." He is not aware that the mention of the term *Suryāyē* and the figure of Abgar stand in contradiction with his choice of Ephrem as a pen-name: it seems that neither of these two names had been ever mentioned by the historical Ephrem himself, as far as we can judge from the preserved corpus of his genuine writings.[160]

The royal dynasty of the Abgarids ruled over the small kingdom of Osrhoene, with its capital city Edessa, during the period from 132 BCE to 242 CE.[161] There is a possibility, based on evidence from onomastics and some aspects of the religious life of pre-Christian Edessa, that the Abgarids might originally have been Arabs.[162] The figure of "King Abgar" looms large in the history of early

---

159   Ruzer & Kofsky 2010, p. 116.
160   This, along with the complete absence of the related figure of the apostle Addai from Ephrem's authentic works, is in need of explanation, since by Ephrem's time, i.e. the middle and second half of the fourth century, the local Edessene legend that focused on these two characters was already in circulation. While this subject lies beyond the scope of this investigation, I would merely like to suggest in passing that it was perhaps due to his Nisibene upbringing that Ephrem was reluctant to accept this local Edessene tradition.
161   See Ross 2001.
162   See Drijvers, H.J.W. 1980, pp. 153–154; Retsö 2003, pp. 440–442.

Christianity in Syria. No later than the first half of the fourth century, a local Edessene legend developed according to which Christianity was introduced into the city by the apostle Addai as early as the first century, during the reign of King Abgar V "the Black" (r. 4 BCE to 7 CE, 13–50 CE).[163] The earliest witness to this tradition is Eusebius of Caesarea, who incorporated the text of the apocryphal correspondence between Abgar and Jesus into his *Ecclesiastical History* (1.13.1–22; 2.1.6–8), claiming that he had obtained its original from the public archive of Edessa where it was preserved in the Syriac language.[164] In Syriac literature, this legend appears in its most developed form in the *Teaching of Addai*, an apocryphal composition that was produced in Edessa, apparently during the fifth century.[165]

Even a perfunctory examination of Syriac sources from late antiquity reveals that the figure of Abgar constituted a very important element in the self-image of the Christian community of Edessa. Thus, besides the *Teaching of Addai*, we find this monarch mentioned throughout a wide range of Syriac compositions that are connected with the city. The third-century *Book of the Laws of Countries* contains a positive reference to Abgar in connection with his abolition of the pagan custom of ritual self-castration among the inhabitants of Edessa, which may be understood as implying the king's conversion to Christianity.[166] Abgar's conversion is mentioned in the fifth-century *Acts of Šarbel*,[167] and the memory of the Edessene king is evoked by the author of the Syriac *Julian Romance*, composed during the fifth or sixth century, when he describes the triumphal entrance of Emperor Jovian to the city.[168]

This evidence demonstrates that the image of Abgar as the first believing king and mediator of God's blessing and protection to the city became an integral part of Edessene Christian identity at a relatively early stage. This intimate connection between the king and his city was amply expressed by Jacob of Sarug, who in the mēmrā on the Edessene martyr Ḥabib figuratively refers to the city of Edessa as the "daughter of Abgar" whom the apostle Addai betrothed to Christ.[169]

---

163 On the early stages of the development of this legend, see Drijvers, H.J.W. 1987; Mirkovic 2004; Desreumaux 2009.
164 Ed. Lake et alii 1926–1932, v. 1, pp. 86–87.
165 For the Syriac text and an English translation, see Howard 1981.
166 Ed. Cureton 1855, pp. 20 [Syr.], 31–32 [trans.]. When he describes what had brought Abgar to this measure, the Syriac author uses the verb *haymen*, "to believe."
167 Ed. Cureton 1864, pp. 43 [Syr.], 43 [trans.].
168 Ed. Sokoloff 2016, pp. 464–465.
169 Ed. Cureton 1864, pp. 92 [Syr.], 92 [trans.]. Cf. also mēmrā *On Edessa and Jerusalem*; ed. Bedjan 1905–1910. v. 5, p. 733.

The high respect for Abgar continues well into the period after the Syriac-speaking world's split into the East and West Syrian communities of faith. What should be pointed out, however, is that during this period the king was apparently celebrated first and foremost by those "Syrians" who regarded Edessa as their spiritual and cultural metropolis. Quite naturally, this description applies to the West Syrians most of all, since in the aftermath of the enforced closure of the "School of the Persians" and the migration of its teachers across the Roman–Persian border to Nisibis in the year 489,[170] it was they who, apparently, constituted one of the largest groups within the Edessene population from the confessional point of view.

Some time ago, Alain Desreumaux argued that the *Teaching of Addai* itself was produced during the last decades of the fifth century by the Miaphysite Christians of Edessa, who used the legendary story of the portrait of Christ as a Christological argument.[171] While a re-examination of this hypothesis lies beyond the scope of this investigation, I would like to note that it may be strengthened further if one takes the reception history of Abgar's legend among Syriac-speaking Christians during the period after the last decades of the fifth century into account.[172] As may be instantly seen, there is a certain disproportion in the amount of attention paid to the figure of the king between the two main confessional traditions.

On the one hand, there is ample evidence for the high regard in which Abgar was held by the West Syrian authors of late antiquity and the Middle Ages. Among the earliest examples of this kind is that of the author of the *Chronicle of Pseudo-Joshua the Stylite*, composed c. 507, who refers to Jesus' promise to Abgar to keep Edessa from its enemies.[173] The figure of Abgar was of considerable importance for another West Syrian author from the turn of the sixth century, Jacob of Sarug, who devotes two separate mēmrē to celebrating the king, *On Abgar* and *On Addai and Abgar*,[174] and often evokes him in his other poetical works and letters.[175] Abgar's importance as an exemplary

---

170 See Becker 2006, pp. 41–76.
171 See Desreumaux 1987.
172 This subject has not yet been thoroughly investigated. For some useful information, see Wood 2010, pp. 82–127. On the treatment of Abgar in the West Syrian historiographical tradition, see van Rompay 1999.
173 §§ 5, 60; ed. Wright, W. 1882, pp. 7, 59–60 [Syr.], 5–6, 51 [trans.].
174 Ed. Akhrass & Syryany 2017, v. 1, pp. 230–260.
175 Cf. mēmrā *On Edessa and Jerusalem*; ed. Bedjan 1905–10. v. 5, pp. 737–738, 741–743. Cf. also letter #20, where God's promise to Abgar to preserve Edessa is evoked (ed. Olinder 1937, pp. 129–135); letter #32, where Abgar is mentioned alongside Constantine (ed. Olinder 1937, p. 245); letter #35, where Jacob presents the king as a paragon of Christian faith (ed. Olinder 1937, p. 260).

Christian monarch finds confirmation in his liturgical commemoration in the West Syrian tradition,[176] in which we see him, together with Constantine and Helene, being celebrated in the category of "pious kings."[177]

Compared with the rich tradition of Abgar's veneration among the West Syrians, the East Syrian sources from late antiquity and the Middle Ages strike an observer with a conspicuous lack of interest in the Edessene monarch which borders on deliberate disregard. Of course, the silence of the East Syrian tradition in regard to Abgar is not absolute. A significant exception to this rule in the late antique East Syrian literary tradition is the *Acts of Mār Māri*, a legendary account of the Christianization of Mesopotamia and Babylonia that was produced in the East Syrian Monastery of Qunni in the vicinity of Baghdad, most likely during the sixth century.[178] The author of this composition devotes a significant part of the narrative space (§§2–5) to the king and his correspondence with Jesus.[179] It might be noted, however, that the figure of Abgar plays no independent role in the overall narrative scheme of this work. In fact, the king only appears in the introductory part of the *Acts*, and only because of his connection to the apostle Addai. It is the latter character who appears to be of much greater importance for the author of the *Acts*, who introduces Addai in order to strengthen the credentials of the main hero of his narrative, Mārī, by presenting him as the disciple and legitimate heir of the apostle of Edessa and consequently demonstrating how the Christian faith traveled from Edessa to Babylonia.[180] If Amir Harrak is correct in tracing the origins of the tradition of Mārī's missionary enterprise back to the earliest period of the history of Christianity in Babylonia,[181] the notion of the close connection between him and Addai might belong to a more archaic stratum in the self-image of the Persian church, formed before the confessional division of the second half of the fifth century. It is these considerations that prevent me from accepting the evidence of the *Acts of Mār Māri* alone as decisive proof that the figure of Abgar continued to enjoy high regard among the East Syrians even during the period after the fifth century.

As has been suggested above, this disproportion in the importance assigned to the person of Abgar between the West Syrian and East Syrian traditions is related to the crucial role played by this royal figure in the Edessene local myth. The main objective of the apocryphal story that connected Abgar

---

176 See medieval martyrologies and menologies published by Nau 1912, pp. 41, 45, 77, 95, 100.
177 Ed. Nau 1912, p. 44.
178 See Harrak 2005, pp. xiv–xix.
179 Ed. Harrak 2005, pp. 4–11.
180 Ed. Harrak 2005, pp. 10–13.
181 See Harrak 2005, pp. xxxiii–xxxvi.

with Jesus himself was to enhance the status of the Christian congregation in Edessa and to provide a firm basis for its position of pre-eminence over other Syriac-speaking communities of the late antique Near East.

By choosing to evoke the figure of King Abgar as an exemplary representative of "Syrianness," the author of CT perpetuates the foundation myth of Edessene Christianity. Incidentally, this concords with the suggestion that he was a member of the West Syrian community of late Sasanian Mesopotamia, as it is in native Syriac sources coming from the West Syrian cultural milieu that the ethnic "Aramaean" aspect of Abgar's identity is noted and emphasized. For instance, on several occasions, Jacob of Sarug characterizes the legendary king as "the son of the Aramaeans" (*bar Ārāmāyē*).[182] It is this aspect of the king's image that helps our author to pursue his own agenda of forging a new inclusive kind of Syrian Christian identity based on a shared culture and language.

5 Attribution to Ephrem

In most Syriac manuscripts of CT, its authorship is ascribed to Ephrem, the famous fourth-century Syriac Church Father.[183] Although undoubtedly Ephrem could not have been the real author of CT, this attribution still deserves our serious attention as an essential element of its actual author's literary and ideological agenda. This pseudepigraphic strategy should be analyzed in the context of Ephrem's growing importance among Syriac-speaking Christians during the sixth and seventh centuries.

Before discussing this aspect of CT, I shall briefly address the issue of whether the attribution to Ephrem belongs to the oldest stratum of the work, since there are scholars who consider it to be a later addition to what was originally an anonymous composition. This position is taken by Su-Min Ri, who dismisses the attribution to Ephrem and considers it to be an outcome of later efforts to legitimize CT made by its transmitters.[184] I believe, however, that this attribution should be regarded as an original and integral element of our work.

The presence of the attribution to Ephrem in the majority of the work's manuscripts, including its most important textual witness, Or^A, testifies first and

---

182 Cf. mēmrā *On Gurya and Shamuna* (ed. Cureton 1864, pp. 97 [Syr.], 97 [trans.]); mēmrā *On Edessa and Jerusalem* (ed. Bedjan 1905–1910, v. 5, p. 738).

183 For general information on Ephrem, see de Halleux 1983; Mathews & Amar 1994; McVey 2000.

184 Ri 2000, p. 100.

foremost to its originality.¹⁸⁵ This evidence is further strengthened by some internal literary features that support the view that CT was devised by its author not as an anonymous work, but as a pseudepigraphic one. One such feature is the appearance of several sentences throughout the work in which the narrator becomes visible by speaking in the first person when he addresses the interlocutor named "Namusāyā" or makes aside comments.¹⁸⁶ It would be against the logic of narrative for a supposedly anonymous work to feature such first-person utterances. Among these passages, a special position is occupied by CT 44.16, where the narrator refers to divine grace as the source of his authority. This claim resonates well with the image of Ephrem as a divinely inspired teacher, an image that had gained great popularity among Syriac Christians by the time of the CT's composition.¹⁸⁷ The Ephremian attribution is also corroborated by external evidence, which includes several ancient translations of CT and references to it in later Syriac compositions. Concerning the former, Ephrem is mentioned as the author of the work in the still-unpublished Karshuni recension of CT,¹⁸⁸ as well as in its Georgian version.¹⁸⁹

As for the ancient Syriac writers who quote CT under Ephrem's name, one of the earliest examples comes from the *Gannat Bussame*, an East Syrian commentary on biblical pericopes composed around the tenth century. There we find an exposition of Mary's genealogy according to which Eleazar had two sons, Matthan and Jotham, the former being Joseph's grandfather (cf. Mt 1:15) and the latter Mary's, which is said to be declared by "Mar Ephrem in the succession of generations."¹⁹⁰ While absent from the examined Syriac manuscripts of CT, this tradition is found in its Arabic version.¹⁹¹ Later on, the author of the anonymous West Syrian *Chronicle to the Year 1234* cites a piece of biblical genealogy related to Zerubbabel which is identical to that of CT 43.15 under Ephrem's name.¹⁹²

---

185 The Ephremian attribution is attested in all manuscripts of the Western recension and in 80% of the complete manuscripts of the Eastern recension (Or^{ADELOPSU} vs Or^{MV}) in Ri's edition. Ephrem is also indicated as the author in six out of twelve unpublished manuscripts of CT that are preserved in their entirety; see Minov 2021b. In many East Syrian manuscripts of CT, the attribution to Ephrem appears not in the title, but in the concluding sentence, i.e. 54.16.
186 Cf. CT 15.6 (Or^{A}); 43.14; 44.16–19, 50–51; 45.1; 47.6; 48.5 [Or.]; 50.3; 52.14; 53.11.
187 On this, see below.
188 It is found in ms. Mingana Syr. 32, fol. 89v–145v; see Ri 2000, p. 58.
189 See trans. Mahé 1992, p. 1.
190 Ed. Reinink 1988, pp. 53 [Syr.], 63 [trans.].
191 Ed. Bezold 1883–1988, v. 2, p. 229. Cf. CT 43.23–25, where Eleazar's son Matthan is the grandfather of both Joseph and Mary.
192 Ed. Chabot 1916–1937, v. 1, p. 103.

That CT was devised as an Ephremian pseudepigraphon from the outset is important for grasping the particular agenda pursued by its author. To understand what cultural work this attribution might perform in the context of sixth-century Syriac Christianity, let us take a brief look at the role that the figure of Ephrem played at that time.

The process of Ephrem's canonization began soon after his death around the year 373, and by the sixth century it had reached its zenith. His life and achievements were celebrated and widely disseminated in the Syriac *Vita* that was already in circulation by that time.[193] Ephrem was the first native Syriac writer to be highly revered, and not only by his compatriots; his fame spread throughout the Christian world.[194] Turning Ephrem into an international celebrity might have catalyzed the process of pseudepigraphic creativity under his name.[195]

By the late fifth century and the beginning of the sixth, Ephrem's authority was already firmly established among West Syrians. Thus, Jacob of Sarug dedicated a special mēmrā to him in which he extolled Ephrem as "an amazing orator who surpassed the Greeks in his manner of speech" and as "the crown of the entire Aramaeandom."[196] Philoxenus of Mabbugh quotes Ephrem extensively in his early theological works.[197] For Philoxenus, who characterizes Ephrem as "the teacher of us Syrians," he is the only Syriac Church Father who meets the standards represented by such Greek-speaking touchstones of orthodoxy as Athanasius, the Cappadocians, and Cyril of Alexandria.[198]

When it comes to the East Syrian tradition, it might seem that during the sixth century the figure of Ephrem was overshadowed to a certain extent by that of Theodore of Mopsuestia, especially in biblical exegesis. Regardless of whether this is true or not, there are still enough references that show Ephrem to be a highly respected figure among the East Syrians as well. For example, Barḥadbešabbā ʿArbāyā, in his *Cause of the Foundation of the Schools*, makes

---

193 For the text and discussion, see Amar 2011.
194 See Griffith 1989–1990, pp. 7–17; Taylor, D.G.K. 1998.
195 The corpus of writings attributed to Ephrem is truly impressive both in size and in geographical distribution. The Ephremian dossier was transmitted in practically all the literary languages of ancient Christianity: Greek, Latin, Armenian, Georgian, Christian Arabic, Geez, Coptic, and Church Slavonic. For an overview of this diverse material, see Hemmerdinger-Iliadou & Kirchmeyer 1960; Blanchard 1993; Outtier 1975; Samir 1978; Vaillant 1958.
196 Ed. Amar 1995, pp. 32–33, 64–65.
197 For an insightful analysis of Philoxenus' attitude to Ephrem, see van Rompay 2004. It may be noted here that as van Rompay demonstrates, Philoxenus became more ambivalent about Ephrem's legacy over time. For more on this, see section 3 above.
198 Ed. de Halleux 1962, pp. 38 [Syr.], 44 [trans.].

mention of Ephrem's contribution to the development of the educational system.[199] We hear also about the liturgy ascribed to Ephrem being celebrated in the city of Nisibis until the first half of the seventh century, when the catholicos Išoʿyahb III abolished this custom as part of his program of standardizing the East Syrian rite.[200] Furthermore, in the seventh century, Martyrius-Sahdona refers to Ephrem as "the great teacher ..., who in the Church of God is relied upon as a prophet."[201]

Martyrius' praise of Ephrem as a prophet belongs to the popular tradition of representing him as a divinely inspired teacher reflected in a number of Syriac works. In the fictitious correspondence of Papa of Seleucia, Ephrem is referred to as a prophet several times.[202] Similar statements appear in the Syriac *Life of Ephrem* (§14) and in the Syriac version of Palladius' *Lausiac History* (ch. 40), where Ephrem's prolific teachings are described as "a fountain flowing from his mouth" and it is said of him that "the words which were coming from his lips were from the Holy Spirit."[203]

It is this traditional image of Ephrem as a quasi-prophetic teacher that seems to stand behind the explicit claim to authority made by the narrator of CT, which is based less on scholastic values such as book learning or adherence to tradition than on immediate inspiration from God. This claim is expressed most clearly in CT 44.16, where the narrator refers to the "grace of Christ" (*ṭaybutēh da-mšiḥā*) as the source of his confidence as a writer and his superiority over the other ecclesiastical and non-ecclesiastical writers in being able to present the true succession of the generations from Adam to Jesus. While one might regard these words as an expression of the topos of God's assistance that was widespread among the Christian writers of late antiquity, there is a difference between the author of CT and other Syriac authors who resort to this literary convention.[204] In distinction from these writers, God's assistance in CT 44.16 is not marked in terms of modality, as something the narrator desires to obtain, but is presented in a matter-of-fact way as something he already possesses, when he declares that "the grace of Christ" already "has granted" (*yehbat*) him the knowledge that the previous Christian writers "were

---

199   Ed. Scher 1908, pp. 381–382.
200   *Chronicle of Seert* 1.26; ed. Scher 1908–1918, v. 1, p. 295.
201   Ed. de Halleux 1960–1965, v. 2, p. 82 [Syr.].
202   See trans. Braun 1894, pp. 167, 176, 178.
203   For the former, see Amar 2011, pp. 29 [Syr.], 33 [trans.]; for the latter, Draguet 1978, v. 2, pp. 286–289 [Syr.]; v. 4, pp. 190–192 [trans.].
204   For examples, see Riad 1988, pp. 214–215.

deprived of" (*etbaṣar menhun*). This attitude to God's grace is different from what we find in Ephrem's genuine writings.[205]

Moreover, when our author resorts to another popular literary convention, that of presenting his writing not as his own initiative, but as a response to a request (cf. CT 44.17),[206] no expression of modesty or reservation—which usually accompanies such assertions—is found in CT.[207] This stands in contrast with a more attenuated approach from Ephrem himself, who often engages in self-abasement and expresses reservations concerning his ability to convey the divine truth.[208] These particular aspects of CT's claim to authority are conditioned by the image of Ephrem as a prophet, whose possession of divine charisma is already assured.

The author of CT deliberately chooses to hide behind Ephrem's name in order to avail himself of his authority as a universally revered Church Father. By doing so, he resorts to a centuries-old literary strategy which early Christianity inherited from both its Jewish and its Greco-Roman matrixes and which remained much in vogue among Christians throughout late antiquity.[209] He was not the first Syriac Christian to do so. Although it is difficult to give a precise date for the different works that constitute the rich pseudo-Ephremian dossier in Syriac, it is very likely that Ephrem's name was already being used for such a purpose before the sixth century.[210]

The choice of Ephrem as a pen-name might have been conditioned not only by his universal fame, but also by him being the only Syrian theologian equally recognized and celebrated by the two main factions within Syriac-speaking Christianity during the sixth century. By ascribing his work to this foundational figure of Syriac Christendom, the author of CT was aiming to spread his message across the entire community of Syriac speakers. As is evident from the

---

205 Cf. *Hymns on Paradise* (1.15), where Ephrem turns to God with a plea to protect him by "the wings of your grace"; ed. Beck 1957a, p. 4 [Syr.]. Cf. also *Hymns on the Church* 9.2.
206 Ephrem himself uses this topos on several occasions; cf. *Commentary on Genesis*, Prologue 1; trans. Mathews & Amar 1994, p. 67; *Discourses to Hypatius* 1; ed. Mitchell 1912–1921, v. 1, p. i [trans.].
207 For examples of these two topoi in the works of Syriac writers, see Riad 1988, pp. 191–202.
208 Cf. *Hymns on the Church* 9.1,7; *Hymns on Paradise* 1.2,16; *Letter to Publius* 24–25; *Discourses to Hypatius* 1; ed. Mitchell 1912–1921, v. 1, pp. ii–iii [trans.]. For an analysis of this motif in the context of Ephrem's theological hermeneutics, see den Biesen 2006, pp. 112–117, 215–216.
209 On this, see Aland 1961; Speyer 1971; Meade 1986; Beatrice 2002; Gray, P.T.R. 1988.
210 For an overview of Pseudo-Ephremian writing in Syriac, see Melki 1983, pp. 44–88. One of the earliest works of this kind is the so-called *Testament of Ephrem*. For this text, see ed. Beck 1973, pp. 43–69 [Syr.].

rich history of the reception and translation of his work, this choice turned out to be a successful one.

By attributing his work to Ephrem, our author projects his argument far back into that period in the history of Syriac Christianity when the Syriac œcumene was united and not yet split along dogmatic lines. This search for a common ground on his part may also be seen in his avoidance of explicit Christological discussions[211]—the main cause of the division in Syrian Christianity during this period—as well as in his use of the old-fashioned incarnational language of "clothing into body" that was traditional to Syria.[212]

The Ephremian attribution also fits well with what might be characterized as an archaizing and anti-Hellenistic tendency in the way our author reworks the biblical narrative. In a manner that sets him apart from many other Syrian writers of his time, CT's author remains oblivious to the influential tradition of Greek Christian chronography and historiography and builds his version of the primeval history mainly on biblical foundations.[213] Although aware of the existence of the Greek historiographical tradition, he pays no attention to the figures and events of the Greco-Roman past. It appears that even in those rare cases when he does make use of classical Greek motifs, he reworks them by removing any traits that might betray their origins.[214] Who else but Ephrem, whom Jacob of Sarug characterized as "an amazing orator who surpassed the Greeks in his manner of speech,"[215] would be a more fitting representative and spokesman for such an indigenist agenda?

---

211   Such cases as the explicit anti-Miaphysite statements found in the two passages of the Eastern recension (CT 21.19 and 29.10) are, in my view, later interpolations.

212   Cf. CT 5.8: "He shall sojourn in a Virgin, and shall put on a body" (*w-lābeš pagrā*). On this Christological language, see Brock 1982c; Shchuryk 2007. On a similar strategy in the use of this archaizing terminology by another sixth-century Syriac writer, Daniel of Ṣalah, see Taylor, D.G.K. 2009, pp. 76–77.

213   It is uncertain whether the author of CT knew Greek. On several occasions, he does refer to unidentified "Greek writers" (cf. CT 42.6; 44.14). In CT 17.22, he refers to the Septuagint. However, these references are hardly sufficient to serve as proof of his mastery of the Greek language.

214   The story of the invention of purple from CT 36.1–8 may be mentioned as an example of such reworking. This tradition is well attested in classical and Christian sources (cf. Julius Pollux, *Onom.* 1.45; John Malalas, *Chron.* 2.9; *Chronicon Paschale*; ed. Dindorf 1832, v. 1, pp. 78–79). It is also found in Syriac literature; cf. the fragment from Pseudo-Diocles; ed. de Lagarde 1858, pp. 201–202. However, in distinction from all these sources that credit the philosopher Heracles and the Tyrian king Phoenix with having discovered the dye, the author of CT connects this event with the biblical king Hiram.

215   Ed. Amar 1995, pp. 32–33. Cf. also Sozomen, *Hist. eccl.* 3.16.

6   Concluding Observations

This chapter demonstrates how the author of CT integrates several elements that might be categorized as ethnic into his reworking of the biblical narrative. He does so on behalf of the group referred to as "Syrians," creating a holistic picture of the biblical past by tailoring it to the unique needs and sensibilities of this group. It is with this purpose in mind that the author promotes the notion of Syrian primacy based on the Syriac language, introduces the legendary figure of the Edessene king Abgar as the representative of Syrianness, and ascribes the authorship of his work to Ephrem, the most famous Syriac writer of all time. His retelling of the sacred history emerges, therefore, as a narrativized embodiment of Christian cultural memory that enhances the status of the "Syrians" as a distinctive ethnic group.

Having observed how our author implements a particular strategy of internal group identification that involves the ethnicization of biblical history, it remains to be asked whether he was original in doing so. Let me first address the question of whether the notion of "Aramaeans" or "Syrians" as an ethnically distinct group existed at all prior to the time of CT's composition. To answer this definitively would require a large-scale investigation that cannot be undertaken here. Instead, I shall confine myself to pointing out some important aspects of the development of Syriac Christian self-identification during late antiquity that may bring us closer to understanding the place of the ethnic factor in its dynamics.

On the one hand, from the very beginning of the new religion in Syria and Mesopotamia, the Syriac-speaking Christians of these regions regarded themselves as an integral part of the Christian commonwealth and would habitually resort to the rhetoric of universalism. For instance, during the third century, we come across the following celebration of Christian unity that transcends the division of local customs in the *Book of the Laws of Countries*, a work that stems from the circles of Bardaiṣan: "What, then, shall we say respecting the new race (*šarbtā ḥadtā*) of ourselves who are Christians, whom in every country and in every region the Messiah established at His coming; for, lo! wherever we be, all of us are called by the one name of the Messiah—Christians."[216] A century later, Aphrahat proclaims that "on account of Jesus the peoples and all languages praise the One, who had delivered his Son."[217]

---

216   Ed. Cureton 1855, pp. 20 [Syr.], 32 [trans.].
217   *Dem.* 21.19; ed. Parisot 1907, cols. 977–980; trans. Valavanolickal 2005, v. 2, p. 224. Cf. also *Dem.* 16.2.

At the same time, however, we may observe that alongside these expressions of Christian unity a parallel system of self-understanding began to develop among Syriac-speaking Christians that was based on narrower principles of local or regional identification. It should be pointed out that from the perspective of the basic anthropological model of ethnic identification, there is a fundamental difference between this construction of groupness and the ethnic one. Richard Jenkins, who offers a provisional classification of the ideologies of group identification, distinguishes between ideologies based on the principle of *co-residence*, such as communalism, localism, and regionalism, and those based on the principle of *ethnicity*, such as ethnicism, nationalism, and racism.[218] This conceptual distinction, I believe, is of particular importance for any attempt to differentiate between the various expressions of collective self-understanding that were in use among Syriac Christians during late antiquity.

The phenomenon of local or regional identity is something that has only recently begun to capture the interest of scholars of the ancient Mediterranean and Near East.[219] In the socio-cultural context of the late antique Near East, such local or regional ideologies of identification would often take the form of local patriotism, that is, a conscious and positive relationship to the place that one inhabits. Among the various peoples of this region, it is perhaps Jewish local patriotism that has been most intensively studied so far.[220] There is, however, sufficient evidence to suggest that other local groups, including Syrians, were also able to resort to this strategy of identification.

Vestiges of this type of group identification gaining currency among the inhabitants of Syria and Mesopotamia may be found even before the arrival of Christianity.[221] Thus, during the first century BC, Meleager of Gadara, a Greek writer of Syrian origin, attempts to reclaim Homer's prestige for his native homeland by arguing that the legendary poet "was a Syrian by birth" (Σύρον ὄντα τὸ γένος), basing his argument on the observation that Homer's Achaeans do not eat fish, an animal considered to be sacred in this region.[222] In a similar manner, Syrian or Phoenician descent was claimed for famous Greek philosophers such as Thales and Pythagoras.[223]

This strategy of identification continued later, during the period that followed the introduction and spread of Christianity among the Syriac-speaking

---

218 See Jenkins 2008, pp. 86–88.
219 See, for instance, articles in Whitmarsh 2010.
220 See Gafni 1990b, 2009; articles in Jones & Pearce 1998.
221 The subject of pre-Christian "Syrian" identity is still relatively understudied. For a recent contribution to this field, see Andrade 2013.
222 Athenaeus, *Deipn.* 4.45; ed. Kaibel 1887–1890, v. 1, p. 355.
223 See Clement of Alexandria, *Strom.* 1.62.2–4; cf. also Herodotus, *Hist.* 1.170.

population of the Roman Near East. Now, however, it was not Homer, but the Bible to which Syrians would turn as the ultimate source for gaining cultural prestige. A good example of such use of Scripture comes from the *Hymns on Julian Saba* ascribed to Ephrem. As he engages in a supersessionist interpretation of the biblical past, the Syriac poet asserts that the land of Aram, referred to as "our land," is superior to Zion because the biblical patriarchs and matriarchs, such as Abraham, Jacob, Sarah, and others, walked through it, and he moreover suggests that salvation comes from Aram because the patriarch Judah, from whom Christ is descended, was born there.[224] In a similar vein, the author of the Ephremian *Commentary on the Diatessaron* makes use of the canonical story of the Magi in order to construct a supersessionist dichotomy that asserts the superiority of the "Easterners" (*madnḥāyē*), who recognized the true meaning of the star, over "Israel," who failed to do so, and proudly proclaims that "the East (*madnḥā*) adored the Messiah first."[225]

The urban context was apparently the most prevalent site for the crystallization of local identities during antiquity.[226] As far as the late Roman Near East is concerned, a particularly rich and manifold tradition of local patriotism among Syriac-speaking Christians developed during this period in connection with the city of Edessa, one of the earliest centers of Christianity in the region.[227] As has been mentioned above, the apocryphal tradition of correspondence between King Abgar and Jesus, through which the local Christian community claimed a special connection between their city and the founder of Christianity himself, was forged there as early as the first half of the fourth century. From that time on, the legend of Abgar became the most important element of Edessene local patriotism. It is on the basis of this myth that Jacob of Sarug was able to extoll Edessa as "the first bride of Christ."[228]

Prominent as it is, the account of Abgar was not the only manifestation of the Edessene citizens' local pride. During the third century, a claim about the chastity of the city's inhabitants was made by the author of the *Book of the Laws of Countries*.[229] Later, in the fifth century, we see in a petition that was preserved in the Syriac version of the acts of the second Council of Ephesus, the

---

224 *De Juliano Saba* 4.8–11; ed. Beck 1972, pp. 46–47 [Syr.]. For a discussion of this passage, see Salvesen 2009, pp. 217–218.
225 *Comm. Diat.* 2.21a; ed. Leloir 1990, p. 8; trans. McCarthy 1993, p. 69.
226 For the Roman imperial context, see Revell 2009; Raja 2012.
227 For an overview of the city's history, see Segal 1970. A thorough analysis of Edessa's prominent role in Syriac-speaking Christians of the Roman empire gradually asserting their cultural independence has been recently undertaken by Wood 2010.
228 *Letter* 32; ed. Olinder 1937, p. 245.
229 Ed. Cureton 1855, pp. 17 [Syr.], 26–27 [trans.].

so-called Robber Council convened in the year 449, that the citizens of Edessa boast that "from the very beginning our city, by the grace of God, excelled in faith," basing this claim not only on the unique blessing Jesus bestowed on Edessa according to the legend of Abgar, but also on the fact that the apostle Thomas was buried there.[230] It seems appropriate to conclude this list with the *Life of Ephrem* (c. 6th c.), whose author quotes a hymn that was presumably composed by the saint himself where Edessa is praised as "the city which is a shadow (*ṭelālā*) of that heavenly Jerusalem."[231]

Edessa, however, was not the only Syriac-speaking urban center that promoted its own locally customized version of Christian identity. Richard Payne has recently discussed how the Syriac Christian elite of the city of Karkā d-Beit Slōk in Northern Mesopotamia developed a particular self-understanding, based on the claim of belonging to the royal lineage of the ancient Assyrian and Iranian kings, that would facilitate their integration into the dominant culture of Sasanian Iran.[232]

A broader version of regional patriotism surfaces in the works of some Syriac Christians who lived in the territory of Sasanian Iran. The author of the *Acts of Mār Māri* extols this apostle of Mesopotamia and Babylonia and seeks to secure his prominent position by pointing out that Mārī converted "the summit of the lands of the (four) quarters of the world" (*rišā d-atrawātā d-penyātēh d-ʿālmā*).[233] A similar expression of territorial grandiloquence is attested in the *Ecclesiastical History* of Barḥadbešabbā Arbayā.[234]

These expressions of territorial identification among Syriac-speaking Christians in Iran may be related to the contemporary imperial self-image of Sasanian Persians, who regarded their country to be the center and the best part of the inhabited world. Thus, the author of the *Letter of Tansar* extols Persia as "the land of the humble" (*bilād al-kāḍiʿīn*) and asserts its central position by claiming that "our land (*zamīn*) lies in the midst (*miyān*) of other lands and our people are the most noble and illustrious of beings."[235]

A comparison of the identity strategy employed by the author of CT with these expressions of territorial self-identification among Syriac Christians of late antiquity reveals a complex picture. On the one hand, his narrative does contain certain vestiges of local patriotism, such as the Edessene myth of Abgar or the image of Nimrod as the cultural hero of Northern Mesopotamia. Our

---

230   Ed. Flemming 1917, p. 22; trans. Doran 2006, p. 146.
231   §38; ed. Amar 2011, pp. 88 [Syr.], 96 [trans.].
232   Payne 2012, pp. 127–163.
233   §10; ed. Harrak 2005, p. 22.
234   See *Hist. eccl.* 31; ed. Nau 1913, p. 613.
235   Ed. Minovi & Rezwani 1975, pp. 89–90; trans. Boyce 1968a, pp. 63–64.

author, however, transcends the limitations of group identification based on the principle of co-residence when he resorts to the innovative strategy of ethnicization by placing the ultimate stress on language as the essential marker of "Syriac" identity. It is the choice of the trans-territorial element of language as the primary factor in establishing cultural similarity and difference that allows our author to offer his community an inclusive version of "Syrianness" which is not constrained by local or regional agendas.

As far as the limitations imposed by the incomplete nature of the surviving evidence allow us to judge, it is rarely, if at all, that one finds this strategy of group identification being employed by Syriac-speaking Christians prior to the time of CT's composition. It is true that from the second half of the fifth century on we do occasionally come across the language of "Syrian" or "Aramaean" peoplehood used by Syrian or Syriac-speaking authors. Thus, in the acts of the second Council of Ephesus, the presbyter Pelagios of Antioch speaks about his origins thus: "I am from the people of Syrians (ʿamā d-Suryāyē), from Antioch, the city located towards sunrise."[236] In the mēmrā on Jacob of Sarug written by his disciple George, the former is praised as the source of spiritual sustenance for "the nation of Syrians" (gensā d-bēt Suryāyē).[237] In addition to the language of "Syrianness," the closely related ethnic term Ārmāyutā, "Aramaeandom," is sometimes used. It appears that Jacob of Sarug was the first to use it when, in the mēmrā on Ephrem, he praised the poet as "the crown of the entire Aramaeandom" (klilā l-kulāh Ārmāyutā).[238] Later, Jacob himself was extolled in similar language by the author of an anonymous mēmrā dedicated to him which relates that "the whole party of Aramaeandom (kulēh gabā d-Ārmāyutā) was illuminated through him."[239] Yet notwithstanding the existence of this language of "Syrian" or "Aramaean" groupness, it appears that none of the Syriac-speaking authors before the time of CT attempted to formulate its content explicitly to indicate how the "Syrians" differ from other ethnic groups.

The author of CT stands out as one of the first authors writing in Syriac in late antiquity to fill the notion of "Syrianness" with more than purely territorial content. It is highly remarkable that he does so by choosing language as the main focal point of the Syrian collective identity. By entangling the Syriac language with the two highest points of the Christian *Heilsgeschichte*, Paradise and Golgotha, our author imbues it with a deep religious meaning and thus turns it into a powerful leverage that makes it possible for his imagined community of

---

236 Ed. Flemming 1917, p. 86.
237 Ed. Abbeloos 1867, p. 48.
238 Ed. Amar 1995, pp. 64 [Syr], 65 [trans.] (modified).
239 Ed. Krüger 1972, p. 113.

"Syrians" to assume an attitude of superiority not only vis-à-vis non-Christian rivals such as Jews or Persians, but also vis-à-vis their Greek and Roman coreligionists. He thus emerges as a true innovator among Syriac Christian writers of late antiquity, none of whom attempted to define the supremacy of their own community over others in terms of language during this period. In this respect, our author also stands alone in the general context of late ancient Christianity, where no comparable blending of religious and linguistic components within the framework of ethnic identity seems to be firmly attested.

This is not to say that there are no examples of a Christian author extolling the language of his ethnic group at the expense of other languages. For instance, Ełishe, a fifth-century Armenian writer, takes pride in his native tongue as he lists the negative features of various languages and claims that Armenian combines the positive qualities of all of them.[240] This expression of linguistic patriotism, however, cannot be equated with the position of CT's author, since it is based on the subjectively perceived qualities of the language itself and not on extra-linguistic religious or ontological considerations.

The closest example of the use of a linguistic argument for the purposes of ethnic identification in antiquity is provided by the Jews. Many scholars have pointed out that a conscious attachment to the Hebrew language was paramount in the construction of Jewish identity beginning from the Second Temple period, both in Palestine and, to a certain extent, in the Diaspora.[241] It may also be noted that the stress the author of CT lays on the linguistic factor in his construction of "Syriac" Christianity echoes the statements of those late ancient thinkers who considered language to be the most important constituent of ethnicity. This idea was given lapidary expression by Claudius Marius Victor, a fifth-century Christian Latin poet who proclaimed that "languages make peoples" (*gentem lingua facit*).[242] Or, as Isidore of Seville, another late antique Christian writer, put it: "Peoples arose from languages, not languages from peoples."[243]

By valorizing the Syriac language in religious terms, our author lays the cornerstone for his vision of "Syrian" peoplehood, deeply embedding this novel notion into his community's cultural memory. This emphasis on language as the marker of collective identity *par excellence* reflects a significant shift in the West Syrian Christians' self-understanding taking place during the sixth

---

240 See Thomson, R.W. 2004, p. 384. It is noteworthy, however, that Ełishe does not go so far as to claim Armenian to be the primeval language.
241 See Schwartz, S. 1995; de Lange 1996; Weitzman, S. 1999; Goodblatt 2006, pp. 49–70.
242 *Alethia* 3.274; ed. Petschenig et alii 1898, p. 416.
243 *Etymologia* 9.1.14: *ex linguis gentes, non ex gentibus linguae exortae sunt*; ed. Lindsay 1911, v. 1, p. 345.

and seventh centuries, which has been characterized by Bas ter Haar Romeny as the development "from a religious association to a community that gradually acquired the sense of being an ethnic community."[244] As we have seen, this ethnicization of Syriac Christian identity entailed a switch from territorial strategies of identification to those based on a shared culture, of which the Syriac language was one of the most important constitutive elements.

In order to better understand CT's author's choice of ethnicization as the primary strategy of group identification, we should, I believe, apply to it postcolonial optics and situate it within the broader imperial context of cultural dynamics in the Sasanian empire, while bearing in mind the specific political situation of the community behind the text. This community could best be described as a minority group, active in the part of the Roman–Persian contact zone in Mesopotamia that was under Sasanian control. As has been discussed above, this background points to the author's close acquaintance with Iranian culture, manifest in the polemic against Zoroastrianism and in his use of certain Iranian ideas and images.[245]

The main challenge that all Christians living in the territories ruled by the Sasanians had to face in dealings with their overlords was that of political loyalty.[246] It was a general perception among the inhabitants of the Roman–Persian frontier that becoming a Christian might or should entail pledging loyalty to the Roman state. An example of this attitude is the story of the conversion of the Arab tribal leader Naaman from the Syriac *Life of Simeon Stylite*, a late fifth-century work. The text relates that he initially attempted to prevent those among the Arabs under his command who used to visit the famous holy man from converting to Christianity. The reason for this is made explicit by one of Naaman's chieftains, who warned his commander that these admirers of Simeon "will become Christians and follow the Romans (*w-dābqin le-Rhumāyē*)," and as a result, "they will defy you and desert you."[247]

Accusations of disloyalty or espionage on behalf of Romans, whether actual or imaginary, were among the most common charges leveled by Sasanians against their Christian subjects from the fourth century on. Suspicious of their allegiance, the Sasanians attempted to prevent any uncontrolled contact between the Iranian Christians and their Roman coreligionists. Traveling to the Roman territory is presented as something that could be perceived by the

---

244   ter Haar Romeny 2012, p. 196.
245   See chapter 3.
246   See Brock 1982a.
247   Ed. Assemani 1748, v. 2, p. 327; trans. Doran 1992, p. 147.

Persians as an act of disloyalty in a fictitious argument for secession from the ecclesiastical authority of Antioch put into the mouth of the East Syrian catholicos Akak by Philoxenos in his *Letter to Abu 'Afr*.[248] This picture is supported by John bar Penkaye, who, in the discussion of how the See of Ctesiphon gained ecclesiastical autonomy from Antioch, explains that this was achieved primarily because of the difficulties in communication between the two ecclesiastical centers, as the Persians had accused the bishops who traveled from Persia to Antioch of espionage.[249]

It took time for the Persian Christians to accommodate to the Sasanians' demands for loyalty, mainly through the gradual process of asserting their administrative and theological independence from the Church in the Roman empire which took place during the fifth century. The crucial points on this road were the Church of the East's affirmation of its autocephaly at the synods of Isaac (410) and Dadisho (424) and the adoption of a "Nestorian" Christological profession at the synods of Barṣauma (484) and Acacius (486).[250] The desire to placate the Persian authorities could also be recognized in other areas of ecclesiastical law. Thus, it seems to underlie one of the canons of Narsai that forbids students of the School of Nisibis to enter Roman territory without special permission from their superiors.[251] We may wonder, however, whether the Christians of Sasanian Iran ever succeeded in gaining the complete trust of their masters. For example, reports such as that from the year 573, when the Persian military governor of Nisibis expelled all Christians from the city while making preparations to withstand a siege from the Romans, seem to speak against this.[252]

As relative latecomers to the Sasanian territories, West Syrians faced the same challenge. Given the fact that their main power base was in the Roman-controlled part of Mesopotamia, they had to demonstrate their loyalty to the Persians in order not to be treated as a fifth column. There is enough evidence to show that they did attempt to gain favor and lobby their interest with the Sasanian kings while making efforts to accommodate to the new political context. The most remarkable achievement of West Syrians in that regard was the activity of the court physician Gabriel of Singar, who succeeded in lobbying

---

248 Ed. Harb 1967, pp. 213–214.
249 *Chronicle* 14; ed. Mingana 1908, v. 2, pp. 123*–124*.
250 See Baum & Winkler 2003, pp. 15–32.
251 Canon #4; ed. Vööbus 1962, pp. 75–77.
252 See *Chronicle of 1234* 65; ed. Chabot 1916–1937, v. 1, pp. 202–203; trans. Greatrex & Lieu 2002, pp. 143–144. Cf. also a report by Evagrius Scholastiucs (*Hist. eccl.* 5.8–9) that Paul, the city's bishop at that time, collaborated with the Romans, providing them with intelligence; see Lee 1993.

Khosrow II on behalf of his community by winning the king's favored wife Shirin to their side.[253] As for the accommodation, we see how Aḥudemmeh of Tagrit, a West Syrian bishop who was active in Sasanian Mesopotamia during the second half of the sixth century, built a church dedicated to St Sergius in the province of Bet ʿArabaye to serve as an alternative to the famous shrine of St Sergius in Ruṣafa in order to prevent his Christian Arab flock from going to the Roman territory on pilgrimage.[254] The political importance of this enterprise has been recognized by Elizabeth Key Fowden, who points out that when the new church was burnt down by zealots from the rival East Syrian party, its reconstruction was sponsored by none other than King Khosrow I himself.[255]

Seen against this background, the polemic waged by the author of CT against the Greek and Latin languages reveals an additional undertone: that of subaltern accommodation to the imperial expectations of loyalty. The question of how issues related to language, and, more generally, to cultural or religious allegiance were treated in the Sasanian empire, especially in the frontier regions, deserves much more extensive analysis than can be attempted here.[256] I shall limit myself to pointing to the evidence that suggests that sometimes the Sasanians pursued a deliberate policy of preventing the spread of the Greek language and culture in the territories they controlled. The most conspicuous examples of this policy come to us from Armenia, another frontier zone that—much like Northern Mesopotamia—served as an arena where the two superpowers, the Roman and the Sasanian empires, competed for dominance during late antiquity.

Moses of Khoren, a medieval Armenian historian, reports on the anti-Greek policy pursued by a certain Mehrujan, an Armenian noble from the family of Artsruni whom Shapur II sent as commander of the Persian army that invaded Armenia in the 360s. According to Moses of Khoren, Mehrujan

> ordered that Greek letters should not be studied but only Persian, and that no one should speak or translate Greek, on the pretext that it was to prevent the Armenians from having any acquaintance or friendly relations with the Greeks.[257]

---

253   See Hutter 1998.
254   *History of Aḥudemmeh* 4; ed. Nau 1905, p. 29; for a discussion of Aḥudemmeh's mission, see Fowden, E.K. 1999, pp. 121–128.
255   Fowden, E.K. 2015, p. 184.
256   For some insights, see Brock 1982a; Fisher 2011; Fowden, E.K. 1999; Frendo 1997, 2008; Garsoïan 2004; Greatrex 2003; Toral-Niehoff 2014. A holistic analysis of religious and cultural dynamics across the entire length of the Sasanian side of the Roman–Persian frontier, from Caucasus to Arabia, remains, however, a desideratum.
257   *Hist.* 3.36; trans. Thomson 1978, pp. 294–295.

In the same chapter, Moses offers another description of the cultural situation in the eastern (i.e. the Persian) part of Armenia after the signing of a treaty between Theodosios I and Shapur III in the year 387, according to which the country was divided between the two empires. Among other things, Moses mentions Mehrujan's destruction of Greek books and adds that "at the division of Armenia, the Persian governors did not allow anyone to learn Greek in their part but only Syriac."[258]

Later in the same section of Moses' *History*, we find an indication that it was not only the Persians who played an active role in the clash of cultures in the frontier zone; this issue was also of importance to the Romans. Thus, in the (fictional?) letter of Emperor Theodosius I to the Armenian catholicos Sahak the Great quoted by Moses of Khoren, the Roman monarch reproaches the catholicos for having commissioned translations of important Church writings into Armenian from Syriac instead of turning to Constantinople for help.[259]

A noteworthy detail of Moses' account is that while the Persian administration in Armenia banned the Greek language, it allowed the use of Syriac, apparently perceiving the latter as having nothing to do with their enemy's culture. These two sides of the linguistic policy of the Sasanian administration in Armenia provide us, I believe, an additional clue for understanding the motivation behind the glorification of Syriac at the expense of the three languages, i.e. Hebrew, Greek, and Latin, and, implicitly, their bearers, in CT. Despite the defensive and apologetic garb of this rhetoric, our author is not so much trying to exculpate the Syrian nation of the fictitious accusation of Jesus' murder, but rather seeks to incriminate the three nations represented by the three languages, i.e. the Jews, Greeks, and Romans. By tarnishing the two latter groups, he particularly aims at creating a cultural distance between his community and these representatives of the Sasanians' Western enemies.

The novel emphasis on the ethnicized "Syriac" communal self-image, different from and superior to Western Christianity, emerges therefore as a successful acculturation strategy. It enabled the West Syrian community behind CT not only to assert its own uniqueness and superiority within the Christian world, but also at the same time to position themselves within the cultural space of the Sasanian empire in a way that would signal their loyalty to the state.

---

258 *Hist.* 3.54; trans. Thomson 1978, pp. 322–323.
259 *Hist.* 3.57: "And we especially blame you for this, that disdaining the learned men in our city, you have sought scholarly inventions from certain Syrians"; trans. Thomson 1978, p. 329.

General Conclusion

The mythological past was a hotly contested terrain in the clash of cultures that characterized the intellectual climate of Sasanian Mesopotamia in late antiquity. Narratives of origins served as the primary basis of self-legitimation for both the Jewish and Christian minorities in their confrontation with each other, as well as their engagement with the dominant Iranian culture. In the course of this book, CT has emerged as an original and imaginative contribution to the development of Christian cultural memory during late antiquity due to its author's deployment of the biblical past for the needs of communal identity building.

I have argued that CT was produced during the second half of the sixth century or the first decades of the seventh century by a West Syrian Christian author, perhaps of the Julianist persuasion, who was active in the part of Northern Mesopotamia that was controlled by the Sasanian empire. Attentiveness to the social and cultural context of late Sasanian Mesopotamia enables us to better appreciate the kind of cultural work that this composition performs.

At the center of this book is the combination of the three major strategies of identification, the use of which defines the unique character of this work as an indispensable witness to the process of collective identity formation among Syriac-speaking Christians in Sasanian Iran. As we have seen, CT's author offers his community a discursive form of cultural difference based on a collective internal definition, which entails both the externally oriented strategy of categorizing others and the internally oriented strategy of self-identification. The former strategy results in our author's construction of two principal categories of otherness: one comprised of Jews, a competing minority, and another of Persians, the politically dominant group. As for the latter strategy, it manifests itself in the rhetoric of "Syrianness."

As far as the strategies of identification involving CT's author's paradigmatic "others," i.e. Jews and Persians, are concerned, we have seen that they primarily operate on the level of religious argumentation, i.e. they are aimed at the construction of otherness through the exclusion of those who are located outside the author's community of faith, understood here in the most general terms as the Christian religion. In both of these cases, CT's author pursues the mutually related narrative policies of appropriation and subversion. In the case of the Jews, we see how he appropriates the canonical biblical narratives in order to create his own version of the foundational Christian past while simultaneously subverting it through careful ideological revision that includes anti-Jewish rhetoric, Christianization of the primeval history, and supersessionist theology. In the case of the Persians, he appropriates the symbols and images of Iranian kingship while confronting this social institution by dissociating it from Zoroastrianism and reimagining it within the Christian cultural framework.

We have seen that anti-Jewish polemic occupies an important place in CT as a whole. This evidence, as well as the author's explicit statement about the apologetic goal of his work, allows us to conceptualize CT as an exercise in apologetic historiography. By presenting Christianity as the original religion of the human race and rewriting biblical history along supersessionist lines, CT's author participates in what Doron Mendels has described as the "long process of new hermeneutics," through which the Church "created a new collective memory out of the old Jewish heritage."[1] CT thus emerges as an original contribution to the ongoing interpretation of communal tradition through which a Syriac Christian writer demonstrates his own community's continuity with the foundational past while excluding their Jewish rivals from it. In addition to this, by evoking the Christ-killing charge, our author sought to establish the ultimate boundary between Christianity and Judaism, making these two categories mutually exclusive. In light of the French sociologist Pierre Bourdieu's observation on the role of difference in the construction of social identity that "difference is asserted against what is closest, which represents the greatest threat,"[2] there is good reason to suspect that the pervasiveness of anti-Jewish rhetoric in CT somehow reflects the real-life situation of intercommunal competition between the two closely related religious minorities of Sasanian Mesopotamia.

The battle for the past, which CT's author waged on two fronts, against both Jews and Persians, aims at dispelling any uncertainty regarding his community's origins. This uncertainty may, perhaps, have some relation to the important rupture in the transmission of historical knowledge among the Aramaic population of the Near East. Prior to the dawning of the modern era, only faint echoes of the former glory and rich history of the Assyro-Babylonian empires and ancient Aramaean kingdoms had penetrated the historical consciousness of the Syriac-speaking Christians of the Middle East.[3] Since they had no indigenous historiographical tradition to rely on, their knowledge about this aspect of the region's past was almost entirely derived from the Bible and, to a lesser degree, from Greco-Roman sources.[4] This dependence on the

---

1 Mendels 2004, p. 115.
2 Bourdieu 1984, p. 479.
3 On this, see Salvesen 1998; Harrak 2001, pp. 181–182.
4 See Becker 2008.

Bible as the primary source of information on their own "national" past made Christians in late antique Mesopotamia particularly vulnerable in the context of rivalry for prestige with the Jews and thus required an original solution.

CT's author demonstrates a considerable degree of creativity in his apologetically driven rewriting of biblical history. Far from limiting himself to a passive retranslation of the canonical biblical narratives, he exercises a remarkable degree of independence and resourcefulness in adapting them to fit his agenda. We have also observed his innovative approach regarding the inherited repertoire of anti-Jewish polemic. A comparable level of originality is evident in the way our author makes use of Iranian ideas and imagery, especially in his reinterpretation of the scriptural figures of Nimrod, Cyrus, and the Magi.

In the discussion of the representation of Persian religion and culture in CT, the insights of postcolonial studies, especially the notions of mimicry and hybridity, proved to be particularly useful. This approach to the study of cultural production in situations of competition and inequalities of power enables students of Syriac Christianity in Iran to be more attentive to how this subaltern group's self-representation was shaped by the hegemonic discourse of Sasanian imperial culture. The creative association of the biblical figures mentioned above (i.e. Nimrod, Cyrus, and the Magi) with the symbolic world of Iranian kingship undertaken by CT's author reveals how the collective memory of a religious minority group could be turned into a space of negotiation with the dominant culture. Our analysis of the subaltern politics of memory and identity in CT thus throws additional light on the manifold nature of the "sociopolitical instrumentality of the past" in antiquity, to use the words of Bruce Lincoln.[5]

CT's major contribution to the development of a new model of Syriac Christian collective memory manifests itself in the author's resort to an ethnic strategy of identification, integral elements of which are the work's ascription to Ephrem the Syrian, its evocation of the legendary Edessene king Abgar, and its advocacy of Syriac primacy. By attributing his text to Ephrem, who was revered by virtually every Syriac-speaking Christian in antiquity, CT's author could claim this divinely inspired teacher's high spiritual authority on its behalf. Although he was not the first Syriac writer to resort to this pseudepigraphic strategy, CT's author is innovative in that no one before him had used Ephrem's authority for a large-scale rewriting of biblical history. The most remarkable novelty in the author's advancement of an ethnic argument, however, is his original use of the notion of the primacy of the Syriac language. It should be stressed that this is the first known example of this idea being

---

5 Lincoln 1989, p. 17.

expressed by a Christian author writing in Syriac. What is perhaps even more significant is that he seems to be the first to resort to it for markedly apologetic purposes, using language as the most salient marker of collective identity.

Of course, as has been mentioned above, there are expressions of Syriac cultural pride or local patriotism that predate our composition, but none of them contains the element of confrontation with other non-Syriac Christian cultures. This aspect of CT makes it one of the earliest expressions of "ethnic argumentation" in Syriac; that is, "the concern to formulate ethnic identities strategically as the basis for an apologetic argument."[6] Our author transcends the limits of the territorially based notion of "Syrianness" by ethnicizing it, as he chooses the Syriac language to serve as the primary marker of cultural difference and communal belonging. In using the Syriac language to inscribe its speakers into the two axial points of the history, i.e. the moments of the world's creation and its redemption at Jesus' crucifixion, CT's author does not limit himself to celebrating the antiquity of his native tongue, but turns it into leverage to assert the superiority of his ethno-religious community of "Syrians" over other religious and ethnic groups such as Jews, but also over Greek- and Latin-speaking Christians.

As we have seen, for Christians living under Sasanian rule, the choice of language was not only a matter of cultural preference, since it could easily be reframed in terms of political loyalty. CT's author's ethnicization of Syriac Christian identity can be regarded as a response to the challenges posed to his community by the particular socio-political situation. Thus, the creation of a new "Syriac" collective self-awareness, based not only on the religious principle, but also on the ethnic one, would provide the Christian community behind CT with a convenient way out of the disadvantageous and potentially dangerous situation of "divided loyalties" in which Syriac-speaking Christians of Sasanian Iran would often find themselves as a result of their adherence to the official religion of the Roman empire, the perpetual enemy of their Sasanian overlords. By assuming the ethnicized "Syriac" identity, which was not only distinctive from but also superior to that of the "Greeks" and "Romans," the Syriac-speaking Christians of Sasanian Mesopotamia could distance themselves from the world of Western Christendom and thus demonstrate their loyalty to their Persian sovereigns. The manifestation of a specifically Syriac identity in CT could thus be imagined as a wave interference effect that emerges in the liminal "third space" of postcolonial theory, the space of

---

6 Johnson, A.P. 2006, p. 10.

cultural negotiation and resistance in the situation of a minority group caught in the clash of the two competing imperial hegemonies, Roman and Sasanian.[7]

It may not be by chance that this new model of collective identification based on ethnicity emerged among the West Syrian Christians and not among their East Syrian coreligionists. Geographically divided between the territories of the two rivaling empires, the West Syrians may have been feeling a more acute need for an ideology that would guarantee their unity. There was also an inner-Christian integrative potential in ethnicity as the basis of group identity. By employing the self-designation of "Syrians," evoking the authoritative figure of Ephrem, and stressing the superiority of the Syriac language, CT's author offered a supra-confessional and trans-territorial vision of Syriac Christian identity that was able to bypass the deep denominational division of the Syriac-speaking world.

It is thus the dual ethno-religious character of Syriac Christian group identity promoted by CT's author that represents the major innovation in the repertoire of identity formation among Syriac Christians of late antiquity. This interpretation of CT appears to be fully compatible with the general model of collective identity formation among West Syrians proposed by Bas ter Haar Romeny, who envisages it as a movement from a purely religious to an ethno-religious modus of identification. The Leiden group's model requires only one small adjustment, which is related to the question of when exactly the ethnicization of the West Syrian collective identity began. The results of my investigation suggest that its earliest manifestations are attested not in the aftermath of the Muslim conquest of the Near East, but somewhat earlier, already during the late sixth or early seventh century.

The prominence of ethnic self-identification in CT forces us to critically reassess the position on Syriac Christian identity in Sasanian Iran taken by Sebastian Brock, according to whom it was religion that comprised the primary and only basis of collective identification for the Christians of the Sasanian empire. CT's case makes it apparent that for at least some Syriac-speaking Christians in Sasanian Iran, ethnicity was becoming an essential element in the construction of their self-representation.[8] Nevertheless, I believe that the model Brock suggested could still be useful, if it is modified by limiting its applicability to the earlier, pre-sixth-century period of the Christian presence in Iran. As a matter of fact, there are reasons to assume that from the sixth

---

7   On the notion of the "third space" as the place of cultural production in the context of power inequality, see Bhabha 1994, pp. 31–38. For an application of this concept to the study of ancient Judaism and Christianity, see Boyarin & Burrus 2005.
8   A similar point in connection with CT has been made recently by Wood 2010, p. 124.

century on, the ethnic factor had begun to take hold not only among the West Syrian Christians of the Sasanian empire, as exemplified by CT, but also among their East Syrian coreligionists. It has recently been argued by Antonio Panaino that even within the mainstream East Syrian church of Sasanian Iran, there are indications of its gradual Iranization and transformation into a "national Church" of Persia.[9] While Panaino's hypothesis certainly appears plausible to me, this aspect of the East Syrian identity formation is in need of further investigation.

The strategies of representing the biblical past in CT discussed in this book reveal the innovative character of this work as a vehicle of cultural memory and its significance as a site for the production of a Christian collective identity in the late antique Near East. By converting the canonical texts of the Old and New Testaments into a shared cultural knowledge through the two-sided process of appropriation and contestation, its author develops a unique version of the foundational past, specifically tailored to meet his community's needs.

Unfortunately, we do not know how CT's author's vision of Syriac Christian collective memory was received by its intended audience. From the later history of the work's reception during the Islamic period, we can conclude that it was sufficiently appealing to cross the confessional borders, as it can be found being read and transmitted by both West and East Syrians.[10] Some of its novel ideas gained considerable popularity. For example, the notion of Syriac as the primeval language would become a stock motif in the repertoire of Syriac pride for centuries to come. However, more systematic research remains to be carried out on CT's impact on the medieval historiographical tradition among Syriac Christians, including works produced in Arabic.

As a concluding caveat on the role of cultural memory in the formation of Syriac Christian identity in late antique Mesopotamia, we ought to keep in mind that CT provides us with access to only one aspect of this process. This composition opens a window to the dynamics of an *internal* collective definition that took place within the Christian community behind it, while the necessary *external* counterpart of these dynamics, i.e. this social group's categorization by other groups, Christian and non-Christian alike, remains invisible. Regardless of whether or not these limitations imposed by the nature of our sources could be overcome, this avenue of research should receive its due attention in future research on the evolution of Syriac Christian identity. Such research would also have to account for how universalistic and integrative

---

9   See Panaino 2010.
10   See Götze 1924.

trends in the making of Christian cultural memory like the one manifested in CT interplayed with more particularistic and factional identity strategies; most importantly, those rooted in Christological controversies. This book should be regarded, then, as merely a first step towards producing a comprehensive history of Christian collective identity in the Sasanian empire, in which the particular perception of the past in CT would be placed within the wider context of the "shared symbolic universe" of Iranian society and its culture, constituted by "common practices and representations."[11]

11 Here, I am evoking the methodological observations on the future of memory studies made by Confino 1997, p. 1399.

Bibliography

Primary Sources

Abbeloos, J.B. (1867), *De vita et scriptis Sancti Jacobi, Batnarum Sarugi in Mesopotamia episcopi* (Lovanii: Vanlinthout Fratres).

Abbeloos, J.B. (1890), "Acta Mar Kardaghi Assyriae praefecti qui sub Sapore II martyr occubuit: syriace juxta manuscriptum Amidense una cum versione latina," *AB* 9, 5–106.

Abbeloos, J.B., and Lamy, Th.J. (1872–1877), *Gregorii Barhebræi Chronicon ecclesiasticum*. 3 vols (Paris: Maisonneuve).

Adriaen, M. (1970), *S. Hieronymi Presbyteri Opera. Pars I: Opera Exegetica, 6: Commentarii in Prophetas minores* (CCSL 76A; Turnhout: Brepols).

Akhrass, R.-Y., and Syryany, I. (2017), *160 Unpublished Homilies of Jacob of Serugh*. 2 vols (Damascus: Syriac Orthodox Patriarchate).

Akinian, N. (1949), "Die Kanones der Synode von Shahapiwan," *Handes Amsorya* 63:4–12, 79–170 [in Armenian].

Albert, M. (1976), *Jacques de Saroug. Homélies contre les Juifs* (PO 38.1; Turnhout: Brepols).

Albl, M.C. (2004), *Pseudo-Gregory of Nyssa. Testimonies against the Jews* (SBL Writings from the Greco-Roman World 8; Atlanta, Ga.: Society of Biblical Literature).

Amar, J.P. (1995), *A Metrical Homily on Holy Mar Ephrem by Mar Jacob of Sarug* (PO 47.1; Turnhout: Brepols).

Amar, J.P. (2011), *The Syriac Vita Tradition of Ephrem the Syrian*. 2 vols (CSCO 629–630, Syr. 242–243; Louvain: Peeters).

Assemani, G.S., Benedictus, P., and Assemani, S.E. (1732–1746), *Sancti patris nostri Ephraem Syri opera omnia quae exstant, Graece, Syriace, Latine*. 6 vols (Roma: Typographia Pontificia Vaticana).

Assemani, S.E. (1748), *Acta sanctorum martyrum Orientalium et Occidentalium in duas partes distributa, adcedunt Acta S. Simeonis Stylitae*. 2 vols (Roma: Typis Josephi Collini).

Athanassiadi, P. (1999), *Damascius. The Philosophical History* (Athens: Apamea).

Aubineau, M. (1978–1980), *Les homélies festales d'Hésychius de Jérusalem*. 2 vols (Subsidia Hagiographica 59; Bruxelles: Société des Bollandistes).

Aucher, I.B. (1818), *Eusebii Pamphili Caesarensis episcopi Chronicon bipartitum*. 2 vols (Venetiis: Typis coenobii PP. Armenorum in insula S. Lazari).

Azéma, Y. (1955–1998), *Théodoret de Cyr. Correspondance*. 4 vols (SC 40, 98, 111, 429; Paris: Cerf).

Bandt, C. (2007), *Der Traktat "Vom Mysterium der Buchstaben". Kritischer Text mit Einführung, Übersetzung und Anmerkungen* (TUGAL 162; Berlin: Walter de Gruyter).

Bardy, G. (1927), *Les Trophées de Damas. Controverse judéo-chrétienne du VIIe siècle* (PO 15.2 [73]; Paris: Firmin-Didot).

Barney, S.A., Lewis, W.J., Beach, J.A., and Berghof, O. (2006), *The Etymologies of Isidore of Seville* (Cambridge: Cambridge University Press).

Battista, A., and Bagatti, B. (1979), *La Caverna dei Tesori: testo arabo con traduzione italiana e commento* (Studium Biblicum Franciscanum Collectio Minor 26; Jerusalem: Franciscan Printing Press).

Bausi, A. (1992), *Il Qalēmenṭos etiopico: La rivelazione di Pietro a Clemente, I libri 3-7* (Studi Africanistici, Serie Etiopica 2; Napoli: Istituto Universitario Orientale).

Bausi, A. (2017), "Il Gadla 'Azqir," *Adamantius* 23, 342–380.

Beck, E. (1955), *Des heiligen Ephraem des Syrers Hymnen de Fide*. 2 vols (CSCO 154–155, Syr. 73–74; Louvain: L. Durbecq).

Beck, E. (1957a), *Des heiligen Ephraem des Syrers Hymnen de Paradiso und contra Julianum*. 2 vols (CSCO 174–175, Syr. 78–79; Louvain: Peeters).

Beck, E. (1957b), *Des heiligen Ephraem des Syrers Hymnen contra Haereses*. 2 vols (CSCO 169–170, Syr. 76–77; Louvain: L. Durbecq).

Beck, E. (1959), *Des heiligen Ephraem des Syrers Hymnen de Nativitate (Epiphania)*. 2 vols (CSCO 186–187, Syr. 82–83; Louvain: Secrétariat du Corpus SCO).

Beck, E. (1961), *Des heiligen Ephraem des Syrers Carmina Nisibena, I*. 2 vols (CSCO 218–219, Syr. 92–93; Louvain: Secrétariat du CorpusSCO).

Beck, E. (1962), *Des heiligen Ephraem des Syrers Hymnen de Virginitate*. 2 vols (CSCO 223–224, Syr. 94–95; Louvain: Secrétariat du CorpusSCO).

Beck, E. (1963), *Des heiligen Ephraem des Syrers Carmina Nisibena, II*. 2 vols (CSCO 240–241, Syr. 102–103; Louvain: Secrétariat du CorpusSCO).

Beck, E. (1964), *Des heiligen Ephraem des Syrers Paschahymnen: De azymnis, de crucifixione, de resurrectione*. 2 vols (CSCO 248–249, Syr. 108–109; Louvain: Secrétariat du CorpusSCO).

Beck, E. (1966), *Des heiligen Ephraem des Syrers Sermo de Domino Nostro*. 2 vols (CSCO 270–271, Syr. 116–117; Louvain: Secrétariat du CorpusSCO).

Beck, E. (1970), *Des heiligen Ephraem des Syrers Sermones, II*. 2 vols (CSCO 311–312, Syr. 134–135; Louvain: Secrétariat du CorpusSCO).

Beck, E. (1972), *Des heiligen Ephraem des Syrers Hymnen auf Abraham Kidunaya und Julianos Saba* (CSCO 322, Syr. 140; Louvain: Secrétariat du CorpusSCO).

Beck, E. (1973), *Des heiligen Ephraem des Syrers Sermones, IV*. 2 vols (CSCO 334–335, Syr. 148–149; Louvain: Secrétariat du CorpusSCO).

Beck, E. (1979), *Ephraem Syrus. Sermones in Hebdomadam Sanctam*. 2 vols (CSCO 412–413, Syr. 181–182; Louvain: Secrétariat du Corpus SCO).

Becker, A.H. (2008), *Sources for the Study of the School of Nisibis* (TTH 50; Liverpool: Liverpool University Press).

Bedjan, P. (1890–1897), *Acta martyrum et sanctorum*. 7 vols (Paris–Leipzig: Otto Harrassowitz).

Bedjan, P. (1895), *Histoire de Mar-Jabalaha, de trois autres patriarches, d'un prêtre et de deux laïques nestoriens* (2nd rev. ed.; Paris: Otto Harrassowitz).

Bedjan, P. (1902), *S. Martyrii, qui est Sahdona, quæ supersunt omnia* (Paris–Leipzig: Otto Harrassowitz).

Bedjan, P. (1905–1910), *Homiliae selectae Mar-Jacobi Sarugensis*. 5 vols (Paris–Leipzig: Otto Harrassowitz).

Bensly, R.L., and Barnes, W.E. (1895), *The Fourth Book of Maccabees and Kindred Documents in Syriac First Edited on Manuscript Authority* (Cambridge: Cambridge University Press).

Berger, D. (1979), *The Jewish-Christian Debate in the High Middle Ages: A Critical Edition of the Niẓẓaḥon Vetus* (Judaica 4; Philadelphia: Jewish Publication Society of America).

Beyer, G. (1925–1927), "Die evangelischen Fragen und Lösungen des Eusebius in jakobitischer Überlieferung und deren nestorianische Parallelen," *OC* II.12–14, 30–70; III.1, 80–97, 284–292; III.2, 57–69.

Bezold, C. (1883–1888), *Die Schatzhöhle aus dem syrischen Texte dreier unedirten Handschriften ins Deutsche übersetzt und mit Anmerkungen versehen*. 2 vols (Leipzig: J.C. Hinrichs).

Billerbeck, M., Kambylis, A., and Neumann-Hartmann, A. (2006–2017), *Stephani Byzantii Ethnica*. 5 vols. (Corpus fontium historiae Byzantinae 43.1–5; Berlin: Walter de Gruyter).

Blanchard, M.J., and Young, R.D. (1998), *A Treatise on God Written in Armenian by Eznik of Kołb (floruit c.430-c.450)* (Eastern Christian Texts in Translation 2; Leuven: Peeters).

Bosworth, C.E. (1999), *The History of al-Ṭabarī. Vol. 5: The Sāsānids, the Byzantines, the Lakmids and Yemen* (SUNY Series in Near Eastern Studies; Albany, N.Y.: State University of New York).

Boyce, M. (1968a), *The Letter of Tansar* (Serie Orientale Roma 38, Literary and Historical Texts from Iran 1; Roma: Istituto Italiano per il medio ed estremo oriente).

Boyce, M. (1975a), *A Reader in Manichaean Middle Persian and Parthian: Texts with Notes* (Acta Iranica 9, Troisième série: Textes et mémoires 2; Leiden: E.J. Brill).

Braun, O. (1894), "Der Briefwechsel des Katholikos Papa von Seleucia. Ein Beitrag zur Geschichte der ostsyrischen Kirche im vierten Jahrhundert," *Zeitschrift für katholische Theologie* 18, 163–182, 546–565.

Braun, O. (1915), *Ausgewählte Akten persischer Märtyrer* (Bibliothek der Kirchenväter 22; München: Jos. Kösel).

Brière, M. (1943), *Les Homiliae Cathedrales de Sévère d'Antioche: traduction syriaque de Jacques d'Édesse (suite). Homélies CIV à CXII* (PO 25.4; Paris: Firmin-Didot).

Brière, M. (1960), *Les Homiliae Cathedrales de Sévère d'Antioche: traduction syriaque de Jacques d'Édesse (suite). Homélies CXX à CXXV* (PO 29.1; Paris: Firmin-Didot).

Brière, M., and Graffin, F. (1971), *Les Homiliae Cathedrales de Sévère d'Antioche: traduction syriaque de Jacques d'Édesse (suite). Homélies XL à XLV* (PO 36.1 [167]; Turnhout: Brepols).

Brière, M., and Graffin, F. (1982), *Sancti Philoxeni episcopi Mabbugensis dissertationes decem de Uno e sancta Trinitate incorporato et passo (Mêmrê contre Habib). V. Appendices: I. Tractatus; II. Refutatio; III. Epistula dogmatica; IV. Florilegium* (PO 41.1 [186]; Turnhout: Brepols).

Brière, M., Graffin, F., Lash, C.J.A., and Sauget, J.-M. (1976), *Les Homiliae Cathedrales de Sévère d'Antioche: traduction syriaque de Jacques d'Édesse. Homélies I à XVII* (PO 38.2 [175]; Turnhout: Brepols).

Brock, S.P. (1971), *The Syriac Version of the Pseudo-Nonnos Mythological Scholia* (University of Cambridge Oriental Publications 20; London: Cambridge University Press).

Brock, S.P. (1987), *The Syriac Fathers on Prayer and the Spiritual Life* (Cistercian Studies Series 101; Kalamazoo, Mich.: Cistercian Publications).

Brock, S.P. (1995), *Isaac of Nineveh (Isaac the Syrian). "The Second Part", Chapters IV–XLI*. 2 vols (CSCO 554–555, Syr. 224–225; Louvain: Peeters).

Brock, S.P. (2008a), *The History of the Holy Mar Ma'in, With a Guide to the Persian Martyr Acts* (Persian Martyr Acts in Syriac: Text and Translation 1; Piscataway, N.J.: Gorgias Press).

Brock, S.P. (2009), "Regulations for an Association of Artisans from the Late Sasanian or Early Arab Period," in: P. Rousseau and E. Papoutsakis, eds., *Transformations of Late Antiquity: Essays for Peter Brown* (Farnham, England: Ashgate), 51–62.

Brock, S.P. (2011), "A West Syriac Life of Mar Shabbay (Bar Shabba), Bishop of Merv," in: D. Bumazhnov, E. Grypeou, T.B. Sailors and A. Toepel, eds., *Bibel, Byzanz und Christlicher Orient: Festschrift für Stephen Gerö zum 65. Geburtstag* (OLA 187; Leuven: Peeters), 259–279.

Brooks, E.W. (1907), *Vitae virorum apud Monophysitas celeberrimorum. Pars prima.* 2 vols (CSCO Syr. III.25 [7–8]; Paris: Typographeo Reipublicae).

Brooks, E.W. (1915–1920), *A Collection of Letters of Severus of Antioch from Numerous Syriac Manuscripts*. 2 vols (PO 12.2, 14.1; Paris: Firmin-Didot).

Brooks, E.W. (1919–1924), *Historia ecclesiastica Zachariae Rhetori vulgo adscripta*. 4 vols (CSCO Syr. III.5–6; Louvain: Typographeo Reipublicae).

Budge, E.A.W. (1886), *The Book of the Bee: The Syriac Text Edited from the Manuscripts in London, Oxford, and Munich with an English Translation* (Anecdota Oxoniensia, Semitic Series 1.2; Oxford: Clarendon Press).

Budge, E.A.W. (1889), *The History of Alexander the Great, being the Syriac Version of the Pseudo-Callisthenes* (Cambridge: Cambridge University Press).

Budge, E.A.W. (1902), *The Histories of Rabban Hôrmîzd the Persian and Rabban Bar-'Idtâ.* 3 vols (Luzac's Semitic Text and Translation Series 9–11; London: Luzac and Co.).

Budge, E.A.W. (1913), *Syrian Anatomy, Pathology and Therapeutics, or "The Book of Medicines."* 2 vols (London: Oxford University Press).

Budge, E.A.W. (1927), *The Book of the Cave of Treasures: A History of the Patriarchs and the Kings, Their Successors, from the Creation to the Crucifixion of Christ, Translated from the Syriac Text of the British Museum MS. Add. 25875* (London: The Religious Tract Society).

Bury, R.G. (1933–1949), *Sextus Empiricus*. 4 vols (LCL; London: William Heinemann).

Butts, A.M., and Gross, S. (2016), *The History of the 'Slave of Christ': From Jewish Child to Christian Martyr* (Persian Martyr Acts in Syriac: Text and Translation 6; Piscataway, N.J.: Gorgias Press).

Cameron, R., and Dewey, A.J. (1979), *The Cologne Mani Codex (P. Colon. inv. nr. 4780) "Concerning the Origin of his Body"* (SBL Texts and Translations 15, Early Christian Literature Series 3; Missoula, Mont.: Scholars Press).

Canivet, P. (1958), *Théodoret de Cyr. Thérapeutique des maladies helléniques.* 2 vols (SC 57; Paris: Cerf).

Cereti, C.G. (1995), *The Zand ī Wahman Yasn: A Zoroastrian Apocalypse* (Serie Orientale Roma 75; Roma: Istituto italiano per il Medio ed Estremo Oriente).

Chabot, J.B. (1899–1910), *Chronique de Michel le Syrien, patriarche jacobite d'Antioche (1166–1199)*. 4 vols (Paris: Ernest Leroux).

Chabot, J.B. (1902), *Synodicon orientale ou recueil de synodes nestoriens* (Paris: Imprimerie Nationale).

Chabot, J.B. (1916–1937), *Anonymi auctoris Chronicon ad annum Christi 1234 pertinens*. 3 vols (CSCO 81, 82, 109, Syr. 36, 37, 56; Paris: Typographeo Reipublicae).

Chabot, J.B. (1927–1949), *Incerti auctoris Chronicon Pseudo-Dionysianum vulgo dictum*. 3 vols (CSCO 91, 104, 121, Syr. III.1–2 [43, 53, 66]; Louvain: Secrétariat du Corpus SCO).

Chabot, J.B., and Brooks, E.W. (1909–1910), *Eliae metropolitae Nisibeni opus chronologicum* (CSCO 62–63, Syr. 21–24; Paris: Secrétariat du CorpusSCO).

Charles, R.H. (1916), *The Chronicle of John, Bishop of Nikiu* (Oxford: Williams & Norgate).

Ciasca, A. (1888), دياطاسارون الذي جمعه طظيانوس من المبشرين الأربعة *seu Tatiani Evangeliorum harmoniae arabice nunc primum ex duplici codice edidit et translatione latina* (Roma: Typographia Polyglotta).

Cöln, F. (1904), "Die anonyme Schrift "Abhandlung über den Glauben der Syrer"," *OC* 4:1, 28–97.

Coquin, R.-G., and Godron, G. (1990), "Un encomion copte sur Marie-Madeleine attribué à Cyrille de Jérusalem," *Bulletin de l'Institut Français d'Archéologie Orientale* 90, 169–212.

Cowper, B.H. (1861), *Syriac Miscellanies, or Extracts Relating to the First and Second General Councils, and Various Other Quotations, Theological, Historical, and Classical* (London: Williams and Norgate).

Cureton, W. (1853), *The Third Part of the Ecclesiastical History of John Bishop of Ephesus* (Oxford: Oxford University Press).

Cureton, W. (1855), *Spicilegium Syriacum Containing Remains of Bardesan, Meliton, Ambrose and Mara Bar Serapion* (London: F. & J. Rivington).

Cureton, W. (1864), *Ancient Syriac Documents Relative to the Earliest Establishment of Christianity in Edessa and the Neighbouring Countries, from the Year after Our Lord's Ascension to the Beginning of the Fourth Century* (London: Williams and Norgate).

Dagron, G. (1978), *Vie et miracles de sainte Thècle* (Subsidia hagiographica 62; Bruxelles: Société des Bollandistes).

Dagron, G., and Déroche, V. (1991), "Juifs et Chrétiens dans l'Orient du VIIe siècle," *Travaux et mémoires* 11, 17–273.

Darmesteter, J. (1883), *The Zend-Avesta. Part 2: The Sîrôzahs, Yasts, and Nyâyis* (The Sacred Books of the East 23; Oxford: Clarendon Press).

Daryaee, T. (2002), *Šahrestānīhā i Ērānšahr: A Middle Persian Text on Late Antique Geography, Epic, and History* (Bibliotheca Iranica: Intellectual Traditions 7; Costa Mesa, Calif.: Mazda Publishers).

de Boor, C. (1883–1885), *Theophanis Chronographia*. 2 vols (BSGRT; Leipzig: B.G. Teubner).

de Goeje, M.J. et alii (1879–1901), *Annales quos scripsit Abu Djafar Mohammed Ibn Djarir at-Tabari*. 15 vols (Leiden: E.J. Brill).

de Halleux, A. (1960–1965), *Martyrius (Sahdona). Œuvres spirituelles*. 8 vols (CSCO 200–201, 214–215, 252–255, Syr. 86–87, 90–91, 110–113; Louvain: Secrétariat du Corpus SCO).

de Halleux, A. (1962), "Nouveaux textes inédits de Philoxène de Mabbog. I: Lettre aux moines de Palestine; Lettre liminaire au synodicon d'Éphèse," *Le Muséon* 75:1–2, 31–62.

de Halleux, A. (1963), *Philoxène de Mabbog. Lettre aux moines de Senoun*. 2 vols (CSCO 231–232, Syr. 98–99; Louvain: Secrétariat du CorpusSCO).

de Lagarde, P.A. (1858), *Analecta syriaca* (Leipzig: B.G. Teubner).

de Lagarde, P.A. (1864), *Die vier Evangelien arabisch aus der Wiener Handschrift herausgegeben* (Leipzig: F.A. Brockhaus).

de Lagarde, P.A. (1868), *Hieronymi Quaestiones Hebraicae in Libro Geneseos* (Leipzig: B.G. Teubner).

de Menasce, J.-P. (1973), *Le troisième livre du Dēnkart* (Travaux de l'Institut d'études iraniennes de l'Université de Paris III 5, Bibliothèque des œuvres classiques persanes 4; Paris: C. Klincksieck).

de Meynard, B., de Courteille, P., and Pellat, Ch. (1966–1979), *Mas'ūdī. Les prairies d'or.* 7 vols (2nd rev. ed.; Publications de l'Université Libanaise, Section des études historiques 11; Beyrouth: Publications de l'Université Libanaise).

Dekkers, E. (1956), *Sancti Aurelii Augustini Enarrationes in Psalmos LI–C* (CCSL 39, Aurelii Augustini opera 10.2; Turnhout: Brepols).

Detoraki, M., and Beaucamp, J. (2007), *Le martyre de Saint Aréthas et de ses compagnons (BHG 166)* (Paris: Association des amis du Centre d'histoire et civilisation de Byzance).

Devos, P. (1946), "Sainte Šīrīn, martyre sous Khosrau Ier Anōšarvān," *AB* 64, 87–131.

Dewing, H.B. (1914–1961), *Procopius.* 7 vols (LCL; Cambridge: William Heinemann).

Dhalla, M.N. (1908), *The Nyaishes or Zoroastrian Litanies: Avestan Text with Pahlavi, Sanskrit, Persian and Gujarati Versions* (Columbia University Indo-Iranian Series 6; New York: Columbia University Press).

Dindorf, L. (1832), *Chronicon Paschale.* 2 vols (Corpus Scriptorum Historiae Byzantinae; Bonn: Weber).

Dodge, B. (1970), *The Fihrist of al-Nadīm: A Tenth-Century Survey of Muslim Culture.* 2 vols (New York: Columbia University Press).

Doran, R. (1992), *The Lives of Simeon Stylites* (Cistercian Studies Series 112; Kalamazoo, Mich.: Cistercian Publications).

Doran, R. (2006), *Stewards of the Poor: The Man of God, Rabbula, and Hiba in Fifth-Century Edessa* (Cistercian Studies Series 208; Kalamazoo, Mich.: Cistercian Publications).

Dörries, H., Klostermann, E., and Kroeger, M. (1964), *Die 50 Geistlichen Homilien des Makarios* (PTS 4; Berlin: Walter de Gruyter).

Draguet, R. (1972), *Commentaire du livre d'Abba Isaïe (logoi I–XV) par Dadišo Qatraya (VIIe s.).* 2 vols (CSCO 326–327, Syr. 144–145; Louvain: Secrétariat du CorpusSCO).

Draguet, R. (1978), *Les formes syriaques de la matière de l'Histoire lausiaque.* 4 vols (CSCO 389–390, 398–399, Syr. 169–170, 173–174; Louvain: Secrétariat du CorpusSCO).

Drijvers, H.J.W., and Drijvers, J.W. (1997), *The Finding of the True Cross—The Judas Kyriakos Legend in Syriac: Introduction, Text and Translation* (CSCO 565, Subs. 93; Louvain: Peeters).

Duval, R. (1888–1901), *Lexicon syriacum auctore Hassano bar Bahlule: voces syriacas græcasque cum glossis syriacis et arabicis complectens.* 3 vols (Collection orientale 15–17; Paris: Typographeo Reipublicae).

Duval, R. (1904–1905), *Išō'yahb Patriarchae III Liber epistularum.* 2 vols (CSCO Syr. II.64; Paris: Typographeo Reipublicae).

Ehrman, B.D. (2003), *The Apostolic Fathers.* 2 vols (LCL 25; Cambridge: Harvard University Press).

Euringer, S. (1913), "Die neun "Töpferlieder" des Simeon von Gêšîr," *OC* II.3, 221–235.

Falls, T.B. (1948), *Saint Justin Martyr. The First Apology; The Second Apology; Dialogue with Trypho; Exhortation to the Greeks; Discourse to the Greeks; The Monarchy or The*

Rule of God (The Fathers of the Church: A New Translation 6; Washington, D.C.: The Catholic University of America Press).

Ferrar, W.J. (1920), *The Proof of the Gospel, being the Demonstratio Evangelica of Eusebius of Cæsarea.* 2 vols (Translations of Christian Literature, Series I: Greek Texts; London: Society for Promoting Christian Knowledge).

Flemming, J.P.G. (1917), *Akten der Ephesinischen Synode vom Jahre 449: Syrisch* (Abhandlungen der Königlichen Gesellschaft der Wissenschaften zu Göttingen, Philologisch-Historische Klasse, N.F. 15.1; Berlin: Weidmann).

Flügel, G. (1871–1872), *Kitâb al-Fihrist.* 2 vols (Leipzig: F.C.W. Vogel).

Flusin, B. (1992), *Saint Anastase le Perse et l'histoire de la Palestine au début du VIIe siècle.* 2 vols (Le Monde Byzantin; Paris: Centre National de la Recherche Scientifique).

Frankenberg, W. (1937), *Die syrischen Clementinen mit griechischem Paralleltext. Eine Vorarbeit zu dem literargeschichtlichen Problem der Sammlung* (TUGAL 48.3; Leipzig: J.C. Hinrichs).

Frendo, J.D. (1975), *Agathias. The Histories* (Corpus fontium historiae Byzantinae 2a; Berlin: Walter de Gruyter).

Friedlander, G. (1916), *Pirḳê de Rabbi Eliezer: The Chapters of Rabbi Eliezer the Great, according to the Text of the Manuscript Belonging to Abraham Epstein of Vienna* (London: Kegan Paul, Trench, Trübner & Co.).

Frishman, J. (1992), *The Ways and Means of the Divine Economy: An Edition, Translation and Study of Six Biblical Homilies by Narsai* (Ph.D. dissertation; Universiteit Leiden).

Fück, J. (1952), "Sechs Ergänzungen zu Sachaus Ausgabe von al-Bīrūnīs "Chronologie Orientalischer Völker"," in: *Documenta Islamica Inedita* (Berlin: Akademie-Verlag), 69–98.

Furlani, G. (1928), "L"Εγχειρίδιον di Giacomo d'Edessa nel testo siriaco," *Rendiconti della Reale Accademia Nazionale dei Lincei. Classe di scienze morali, storiche e filologiche* VI.4, 222–249.

Furman, Yu.V. (2011), *Девятая книга "Всемирной истории" Йо̄ханна̄на Бар Пенкāйē: исследование и перевод* (дипломная работа; Российский Государственный Гуманитарный Университет, Институт восточных культур и античности).

Gaisford, Th. (1842), *Eusebii Pamphili episcopi Cæsariensis Eclogæ propheticæ, e codice manuscripti Bibliothecæ Cæsareæ Vindobonensis nunc primum edidit* (Oxonii: E typographeo Academico).

Garsoïan, N.G. (1989), *The Epic Histories Attributed to P'awstos Buzand (Buzandaran Patmut'iwnkʿ)* (Harvard Armenian Texts and Studies 8; Cambridge, Mass.: Harvard University Press).

Gibson, M.D. (1901), *Apocrypha Arabica: Kitāb al-Magāll, or The Book of the Rolls; The Story of Aphiḳia; Cyprian and Justa, in Arabic; Cyprian and Justa, in Greek* (Studia Sinaitica 8; London: C.J. Clay and Sons).

Gibson, M.D. (1911–1916), *The Commentaries of Isho'dad of Merv, Bishop of Hadatha (c. 850 A.D.), in Syriac and English.* 5 vols (Horae Semiticae 5–7, 10–11; Cambridge: Cambridge University Press).

Giet, S. (1968), *Basile de Césarée. Homélies sur l'Hexaéméron* (SC 26bis; 2nd rev. ed.; Paris: Cerf).

Gifford, E.H. (1903), *Eusebii Pamphili Evangelicae Praeparationis libri XV.* 4 vols (Oxford: Clarendon Press).

Gignoux, Ph. (1968), *Homélies de Narsaï sur la création* (PO 34.3–4; Turnhout: Brepols).

Gignoux, Ph. (1991), *Les quatre inscriptions du mage Kirdīr: textes et concordances* (Cahiers de Studia Iranica 9; Collection des sources pour l'histoire de l'Asie centrale pre-islamique 11.1; Paris: Union académique internationale).

Gignoux, Ph., and Tafazzoli, A. (1993), *Anthologie de Zādspram* (Cahiers de Studia Iranica 13; Paris: Association pour l'avancement des études iraniennes).

Ginsburger, M. (1903), *Pseudo-Jonathan (Thargum Jonathan ben Usiël zum Pentateuch) nach der Londoner Handschrift (Brit. Mus. add. 27031)* (Berlin: S. Calvary & Co.).

Gismondi, H. (1896–1899), *Maris Amri et Slibae de patriarchis nestorianorum commentaria ex codicibus vaticanis.* 4 vols (Roma: C. de Luigi).

Godley, A.D. (1926–1930), *Herodotus.* 4 vols (LCL; 2nd rev. ed.; London: William Heinemann).

Gollancz, H. (1928), *Julian the Apostate, now Translated for the First Time from the Syriac Original* (London: Oxford University Press).

González Casado, P. (2004), *La Cueva de los Tesoros* (Apócrifos cristianos 5; Madrid: Ciudad Nueva).

Gottheil, R.J.H. (1908–1928), *The Syriac-Arabic Glosses of Īshōʿ bar ʿAlī, Part II.* 2 vols (Atti della Reale Accademia Nazionale dei Lincei, Memorie V, 13; Roma: Tipografia della R. Accademia Nazionale dei Lincei).

Gottwaldt, J.M.E. (1844–1848), *Hamzae Ispahanensis Annalium libri X.* 2 vols (Petropoli: L. Voss).

Greatrex, G., and Lieu, S.N.C. (2002), *The Roman Eastern Frontier and the Persian Wars. Part 2: AD 363–630. A Narrative Sourcebook* (London: Routledge).

Grébaut, S. (1911–1913), "Littérature éthiopienne pseudo-clémentine. III. Traduction du Qalêmentos," ROC 16, 72–81, 167–175, 225–233; 17, 16–31, 133–144, 244–252, 337–346; 18, 69–78.

Grenet, F. (2003), *La geste d'Ardashir fils de Pābag: Kārnāmag ī Ardaxšēr ī Pābagān* (Die: A Die).

Gressmann, H., and Laminski, A. (1991), *Eusebius. Die Theophanie: Die griechischen Bruchstücke und Übersetzung der syrischen Überlieferung* (GCS, Eusebius Werke 3.2; 2nd rev. ed.; Berlin: Akademie Verlag).

Griffin, C.W. (2016), *The Works of Cyrillona* (Texts from Christian Late Antiquity 48; Piscataway, N.J.: Gorgias Press).

Grignaschi, M. (1966), "Quelques spécimens de la littérature sassanide conservés dans les bibliothèques d'Istanbul," *Journal Asiatique* 254:1, 1–142.

Grossfeld, B. (1983), *The First Targum to Esther, according to the ms. Paris Hebrew 110 of the Bibliothèque nationale* (New York: Sepher-Hermon Press).

Grossfeld, B. (1991), *The Two Targums of Esther* (The Aramaic Bible 18; Edinburgh: T.&T. Clark).

Grypeou, E. (2010), *Η Σπηλιά των Θησαυρών* (Συριακή Εκκλησιαστική Γραμματεία 6; Θήρα: Θεσβίτης).

Guidi, I. (1881), "La lettera di Simeone vescovo di Bêth-Arśâm sopra i martiri omeriti," *Atti della Reale Accademia Nazionale dei Lincei, Serie Terza: Memorie della Classe di Scienze morali, storiche e filologiche* 7, 471–515.

Guidi, I. (1903), *Chronica minora, Pars prior*. 2 vols (CSCO Syr. III.4; Paris: Typographeo Reipublicae).

Guignard, Ch. (2011), *La lettre de Julius Africanus à Aristide sur la généalogie du Christ. Analyse de la tradition textuelle, édition, traduction et étude critique* (TUGAL 167 Berlin: Walter de Gruyter).

Guillaume, A. (1955), *The Life of Muhammad: A Translation of Isḥāq's Sīrat rasūl Allāh* (London: Oxford University Press).

Häberl, Ch.G., and McGrath, J.F. (2020), *The Mandaean Book of John: Critical Edition, Translation, and Commentary* (Berlin: Walter de Gruyter).

Hagedorn, D. (1973), *Der Hiobkommentar des Arianers Julian* (PTS 14; Berlin: Walter de Gruyter).

Hall, S.G. (1979), *Melito of Sardis. On Pascha and Fragments* (Oxford: Clarendon Press).

Hansen, G.Ch. (1995), *Sokrates Kirchengeschichte* (GCS NF 1; Berlin: Akademie Verlag).

Harb, P. (1967), "Lettre de Philoxène de Mabbūg au Phylarque Abū Yaʿfūr de Ḥīrtā de Bētnaʿmān (selon le manuscrit no 115 du fonds patriarcal de Šarfet)," *Melto* 3, 183–222.

Harkins, P.W. (1979), *Saint John Chrysostom. Discourses against Judaizing Christians* (The Fathers of the Church: A New Translation 68; Washington, D.C.: The Catholic University of America Press).

Harmon, A.M., Kilburn, K., and MacLeod, M.D. (1913–1967), *Lucian*. 8 vols (LCL; London: William Heinemann).

Harrak, A. (1999), *The Chronicle of Zuqnīn, Parts III and IV: A.D. 488-775* (Mediaeval Sources in Translation 36; Toronto: Pontifical Institute of Mediaeval Studies).

Harrak, A. (2005), *The Acts of Mār Mārī the Apostle* (SBL Writings from the Greco-Roman World 11; Atlanta, Ga.: Society of Biblical Literature).

Hayward, Ch.T.R. (1995), *Saint Jerome's Hebrew Questions on Genesis: Translated with Introduction and Commentary* (Oxford Early Christian Studies; Oxford: Clarendon Press).

Hebbelynck, A. (1900–1901), "Les Mystères des lettres grecques d'après un manuscrit copte-arabe de la bibliothèque Bodléienne d'Oxford: texte copte, traduction, notes," *Le Muséon* NS 1 [19], 5–36, 105–136, 269–300; NS 2 [20], 5–33, 369–415.

Heikel, I.A. (1913), *Eusebius Werke, Band 6: Die Demonstratio Evangelica* (GCS 23; Leipzig: J.C. Hinrichs).

Heimgartner, M. (2012), *Die Briefe 42–58 des Ostsyrischen Patriarchen Timotheos I.* 2 vols (CSCO 644–645, Syr. 248–249; Louvain: Peeters).

Helm, R. (1913–1926), *Eusebius Werke, Band 7: Die Chronik des Hieronymus*. 2 vols (GCS 24, 34; Leipzig: J.C. Hinrichs).

Henry, R. (1959–1977), *Photius. Bibliothèque.* 8 vols (Collection byzantine; Paris: Les Belles Lettres).

Hilberg, I. (1996), *Sancti Eusebii Hieronymi epistulae. Pars I: Epistulae I–LXX* (CSEL 54; Wien: Verlag der Österreichischen Akademie der Wissenschaften).

Hill, E. (1993), *Saint Augustine. Sermons on the Liturgical Seasons (184–229Z)* (The Works of Saint Augustine: A Translation for the 21st Century 3.6; Brooklyn, N.Y.: New City Press).

Hoffmann, J.G.E. (1880), *Iulianos der Abtruennige. Syrische Erzaehlungen* (Leiden: E.J. Brill).

Holl, K. (1915–1933), *Epiphanius. Ancoratus und Panarion*. 3 vols (GCS 24, 31, 37; Leipzig: J.C. Hinrichs).

Hotchkiss, R.V. (1974), *A Pseudo-Epiphanius Testimony Book* (SBL Texts and Translations, Early Christian Literature Series 1; Missoula, Mont.: Scholars Press).

Howard, G. (1981), *The Teaching of Addai* (SBL Texts and Translations 16, Early Christian Literature Series 4; Chico, Calif.: Scholars Press).

Huyse, Ph. (1999), *Die dreisprachige Inschrift Šābuhrs I. an der Kaʿba-i Zardušt (ŠKZ)*. 2 vols (Corpus inscriptionum Iranicarum III, Pahlavi Inscriptions 1.1; London: The School of Oriental and African Studies).

Hyamson, M. (1913), *Mosaicarum et Romanarum legum collatio* (London: Oxford University Press).

Ibn ʿAbd Rabbih (1876), *al-ʿIqd al-farīd li-Šihāb al-Dīn Aḥmad al-maʿrūf bi-Ibn ʿAbd Rabbih al-Andalusī al-Mālikī. Wa-bi-hāmišihi Zahr al-ādāb wa-thamar al-albāb li-Abī Isḥaq Ibrāhīm ibn ʿAlī al-maʿrūf bi-al-Ḥuṣrī al-Qayrawānī al-Mālikī.* 3 vols (Būlāq: al-Maṭbaʿah al-ʿĀmirah).

Jaafari-Dehaghi, M. (1998), *Dādestān ī Dēnīg. Part I: Transcription, Translation and Commentary* (Cahiers de Studia Iranica 20; Paris: Association pour l'avancement des études iraniennes).

Jackson, H.M. (1978), *Zosimos of Panopolis. On the Letter Omega* (SBL Texts and Translations 14, Graeco-Roman Religion 5; Missoula, Mont.: Scholars Press).

Jacoby, F. (1923–1958), *Die Fragmente der griechischen Historiker*. 14 vols (Berlin: Weidmannsche Buchhandlung / Leiden: E.J. Brill).

Jeffreys, E.M., Jeffreys, M., and Scott, R. (1986), *The Chronicle of John Malalas: A Translation* (Byzantina Australiensia 4; Melbourne: Australian Association for Byzantine Studies).

Jones, Ch.P. (2005), *Philostratus. The Life of Apollonius of Tyana*. 2 vols (LCL; Cambridge, Mass.: Harvard University Press).

Jones, H.L. (1917–1949), *The Geography of Strabo*. 8 vols (LCL; London: William Heinemann).

Kaibel, G. (1887–1890), *Athenaei Naucratitae Dipnosophistarum libri XV*. 3 vols (Leipzig: B.G. Teubner).

Kaufhold, H. (1976), *Die Rechtssammlung des Gabriel von Basra und ihr Verhältnis zu den anderen juristischen Sammelwerken der Nestorianer* (Münchener Universitätsschriften—Juristische Fakultät, Abhandlungen zur rechtswissenschaftlichen Grundlagenforschung 21; Berlin: J. Schweitzer).

Kawerau, P. (1985), *Die Chronik von Arbela*. 2 vols (CSCO 467–468, Syr. 199–200; Leuven: Peeters).

Kazan, S. (1961–1965), "Isaac of Antioch's Homily against the Jews," *OC* 45, 30–53; 46, 87–98; 47, 89–97; 49, 57–78.

Keydell, R. (1967), *Agathiae Myrinaei historiarum libri quinque* (Corpus Fontium Historiae Byzantinae 2; Berlin: Walter de Gruyter).

Khaleghi-Motlagh, D., Omidsalar, M., and Khatibi, A. (1988–2008), *Abu'l-Qasem Ferdowsi. The Shahnameh (The Book of Kings)*. 8 vols (Persian Text Series: New Series 1; New York: Persian Heritage Foundation).

Kiraz, G.A. (1996), *Comparative Edition of the Syriac Gospels: Aligning the Sinaiticus, Curetonianus, Peshîttâ and Harklean Versions*. 4 vols (New Testament Tools and Studies 21.1–4; Leiden: E.J. Brill).

Kitchen, R.A., and Parmentier, M.F.G. (2004), *The Book of Steps: The Syriac Liber Graduum* (Cistercian Studies Series 196; Kalamazoo, Mich.: Cistercian Publications).

Klein, M.C. (1980), *The Fragment-Targums of the Pentateuch according to Their Extant Sources*. 2 vols (Rome: Biblical Institute Press).

Klostermann, E. (1904), *Eusebius. Das Onomastikon der biblischen Ortsnamen* (GCS, Eusebius Werke 3.1; Leipzig: J.C. Hinrichs).

Klostermann, E. (1935), *Origenes Matthäuserklärung*, I. *Die griechisch erhaltenen Tomoi* (GCS 40, Origenes Werke 10; Leipzig: J.C. Hinrichs).

Kmosko, M. (1907), "S. Simeon bar Sabba'e," in: *Patrologia Syriaca* (Paris: Firmin-Didot), vol. 1.2, 659–1055.

Kmosko, M. (1926), *Liber Graduum e codicibus syriacus Parisiis, Londini, Romae, Hierosolymis alibique asservatis edidit, praefatus est* (Patrologia Syriaca 1.3; Paris: Firmin-Didot).

Knibb, M.A. (1978), *The Ethiopic Book of Enoch: A New Edition in the Light of the Aramaic Dead Sea Fragments*. 2 vols (Oxford: Clarendon Press).

Kotwal, F.M. (1969), *The Supplementary Texts to the Šāyest nē-šāyest* (Det Kongelige Danske Videnskabernes Selskab, Historisk-filosofiske Meddelelser 44.2; København: Munksgaard).

Kotwal, F.M., and Kreyenbroek, Ph.G. (1992), *The Hērbedestān and Nērangestān. Vol. 1: Hērbedestān* (Cahiers de Studia Iranica 10; Paris: Association pour l'avancement des études iraniennes).

Kourcikidzé, C., (1992), *La Caverne des Trésors: version géorgienne* (CSCO 526, Iber. 23; Louvain: Peeters).

Kroymann, E. (1954a), "Q.S.Fl. Tertvlliani Adversvs Marcionem," in: *Qvinti Septimi Florentis Tertvlliani Opera. Pars 1: Opera Catholica; Adversvs Marcionem* (CCSL 1; Turnhout: Brepols), 437–726.

Kroymann, E. (1954b), "Q.S.Fl. Tertvlliani Adversvs Ivdaeos," in: *Qvinti Septimi Florentis Tertvlliani Opera. Pars 2: Opera Montanistica* (CCSL 2; Turnhout: Brepols), 1337–1396.

Krusch, B., and Levison, W. (1951), *Gregorii episcopi Turonensis Libri historiarum X* (Monumenta Germaniae historica, Scriptores rerum Merovingicarum I.1; 2nd ed.; Hannover: Hahnsche Buchhandlung).

Lake, K., Oulton, J.E.L., and Lawlor, H.J. (1926–1932), *Eusebius. The Ecclesiastical History.* 2 vols (LCL; London: William Heinemann).

Lampadaridi, A. (2016), *La conversion de Gaza au christianisme: La Vie de S. Porphyre de Gaza par Marc le Diacre (BHG 1570). Édition critique, traduction, commentaire* (Subsidia hagiographica 95; Bruxelles: Société des Bollandistes).

Land, J.P.N. (1875), *Anecdota Syriaca IV: Otia Syriaca* (Leiden: E.J. Brill).

Lang, D.M. (1976), *Lives and Legends of the Georgian Saints* (2nd rev. ed.; Crestwood, N.Y.: St Vladimir's Seminary Press).

Le Strange, G., and Nicholson, R.A. (1921), *The Fársnáma of Ibnu'l-Balkhí* (E.J.W. Gibb Memorial, New Series 1; London: Luzac and Co.).

Leclerc, P., and Morales, E.M. (2007), *Jérôme. Trois vies de moines: Paul, Malchus, Hilarion* (SC 508; Paris: Cerf).

Lee, S. (1842), *Eusebius, Bishop of Caesarea. On the Theophania or Divine Manifestation of Our Lord and Saviour Jesus Christ: A Syriac Version, Edited from an Ancient Manuscript Recently Discovered* (London: Society for the Publication of Oriental Texts).

Leloir, L. (1963), *Saint Éphrem. Commentaire de l'Évangile Concordant: texte syriaque (Manuscrit Chester Beatty 709)* (Chester Beatty Monographs 8; Dublin: Hodges Figgis).

Leloir, L. (1990), *Saint Éphrem. Commentaire de l'Évangile Concordant: texte syriaque (Manuscript Chester Beatty 709). Folios additionnels* (Chester Beatty Monographs 8; Louvain: Peeters).

Lentz, A. (1867), *Herodiani technici reliquiae. Vol. 1: Praefationem et Herodiani prosodiam catholicam continens* (Grammatici graeci 3.1; Lipsiae: B.G. Teubner).

Lewis, A.S. (1902), *Apocrypha Syriaca: The Protevangelium Jacobi and Transitus Mariae, with Texts from the Septuagint, the Corân, the Peshitta, and from a Syriac Hymn in a Syro-Arabic Palimpsest of the Fifth and Other Centuries* (Studia Sinaitica 11; London: C.J. Clay and Sons).

Lewis, A.S., and Gibson, M.D. (1899), *The Palestinian Syriac Lectionary of the Gospels, Re-Edited from Two Sinai Mss. and from P. de Lagarde's Edition of the "Evangeliarium Hierosolymitanum"* (London: Kegan Paul, Trench, Trübner & Co.).

Lieu, S.N.C., and Lieu, J.M. (1989), "From Ctesiphon to Nisibis: Ephrem the Syrian, Hymns against Julian," in: S.N.C. Lieu, ed., *The Emperor Julian: Panegyric and Polemic—Claudius Mamertinus, John Chrysostom, Ephrem the Syrian* (TTH 2; 2nd rev. ed.; Liverpool: Liverpool University Press), 89–128.

Lindsay, W.M. (1911), *Isidori Hispalensis episcopi Etymologiarum sive originum libri XX*. 2 vols (Scriptorum classicorum bibliotheca Oxoniensis; Oxford: Clarendon Press).

Macomber, W.F. (1974), *Six Explanations of the Liturgical Feasts by Cyrus of Edessa, an East Syrian Theologian of the Mid Sixth Century*. 2 vols (CSCO 355–356, Syr. 155–156; Louvain: Secrétariat du CorpusSCO).

Madan, D.M. (1911), *The Complete Text of the Pahlavi Dinkard*. 2 vols (Bombay: Fort Printing Press).

Mahé, J.-P. (1992), *La Caverne des Trésors: version géorgienne* (CSCO 527, Iber. 24; Louvain: Peeters).

Mai, A. (1847), *Novae patrum bibliothecae. Tomus 4: Sancti Gregorii Nysseni, Eusebii Caesariensis, Dydimi Alexandrini, Iohannis Chrysostomi et aliorum nova scripta* (Roma: Typis Sacri Consilii Propagando Christiano Nomini).

Marcovich, M. (1986), *Hippolytus. Refutatio omnium haeresium* (PTS 25; Berlin: Walter de Gruyter).

Marcovich, M. (1997), *Iustini Martyris Dialogus cum Tryphone* (PTS 47; Berlin: Walter de Gruyter).

Marcovich, M. (2001), *Origenes. Contra Celsum libri VIII* (Supplements to Vigiliae Christianae 54; Leiden: Brill).

Marcus, R. (1953), *Philo. Supplement I-II*. 2 vols (LCL; London: W. Heinemann).

Margulies, M. (1993), *Midrash Wayyikra Rabbah: A Critical Edition Based on Manuscripts and Genizah Fragments with Variants and Notes*. 2 vols (3rd ed.; New York: The Jewish Theological Seminary of America) [in Hebrew].

Mariès, L., and Froman, L. (1959), "Mimré de saint Ephrem sur la bénédiction de la table," *L'Orient Syrien* 4, 73–109, 163–192, 285–298.

Mariès, L., and Mercier, Ch. (1959), *Eznik de Kołb. De Deo* (PO 28.3; Paris: Firmin-Didot).

Martin, J.-P.P. (1875), "Discours de Jacques de Saroug sur la chute des idoles," *ZDMG* 29, 107–147.

Mathews, E.G., Jr., and Amar, J.P. (1994), *St. Ephrem the Syrian. Selected Prose Works: Commentary on Genesis, Commentary on Exodus, Homily on Our Lord, Letter to*

Publius (The Fathers of the Church: A New Translation 91; Washington, D.C.: The Catholic University of America Press).

McCarthy, C. (1993), *Saint Ephrem's Commentary on Tatian's Diatessaron: An English Translation of Chester Beatty Syriac MS 709 with Introduction and Notes* (JSS Supplement 2; Oxford: Oxford University Press).

McLeod, F.G. (1979), *Narsai's Metrical Homilies on the Nativity, Epiphany, Passion, Resurrection and Ascension: Critical Edition of Syriac Text* (PO 40.1 [182]; Turnhout: Brepols, 1979).

McNamara, M., Hayward, Ch.T.R., and Maher, M. (1994), *Targum Neofiti 1: Exodus; Targum Pseudo-Jonathan: Exodus* (The Aramaic Bible 2; Collegeville, Minn.: The Liturgical Press).

McVey, K.E. (1989), *Ephrem the Syrian. Hymns on the Nativity, Hymns Against Julian, Hymns on Virginity and on the Symbols of the Lord* (Classics of Western Spirituality; New York: Paulist Press).

Meerson, M., and Schäfer, P. (2014), *Toledot Yeshu: The Life Story of Jesus*. 2 vols (Texte und Studien zum antiken Judentum 159; Tübingen: Mohr Siebeck).

Mehren, A.F. (1866), *Cosmographie de Chems-ed-Din Abou Abdallah Mohammed ed-Dimichqui* (Saint-Pétersbourg: Académie Impériale des sciences).

Messina, G. (1951), *Il Diatessaron persiano: Introduzione, testo, traduzione* (Biblica et Orientalia 14; Roma: Pontificio Istituto Biblico).

Metzger, B.M. (1985–1987), *Les constitutions apostoliques* (SC 320, 329, 336; Paris: Cerf).

Milikowsky, Ch.J. (1981), *Seder Olam: A Rabbinic Chronography* (Ph.D. dissertation: Yale University).

Mingana, A. (1908), *Sources syriaques. Vol. 1: Mšiḥa-Zkha (texte et traduction); Bar-Penkayé (texte)* (Leipzig: Otto Harrassowitz).

Mingana, A. (1931), *Woodbrooke Studies: Christian Documents in Syriac, Arabic, and Garshūni, Edited and Translated with a Critical Apparatus. Vol. 3: Vision of Theophilus; Apocalypse of Peter* (Cambridge: W. Heffer & Sons).

Minovi, M., and Rezwani, M.E. (1975), *Tansar's Letter to Goshnasp* (2nd ed.; Tehran: Kharazmie Publishing and Distribution,) [in Persian].

Mitchell, Ch.W. (1912–1921), *S. Ephraim's Prose Refutations of Mani, Marcion, and Bardaisan*. 2 vols (London: Williams and Norgate).

Moazami, M. (2014), *Wrestling with the Demons of the Pahlavi Widēwdād: Transcription, Translation, and Commentary* (Iran Studies 9; Leiden: Brill).

Moberg, A. (1922), *Le Livre des Splendeurs: la grande grammaire de Grégoire Barhebraeus. Text syriaque édité d'après les manuscrits avec une introduction et des notes* (Acta Regiae Societatis Humaniorum Litterarum Lundensis 4; Lund: C.W.K. Gleerup).

Moberg, A. (1924), *The Book of the Himyarites: Fragments of a Hitherto Unknown Syriac Work* (Acta Regiae Societatis Humaniorum Litterarum Lundensis 7; Lund: C.W.K. Gleerup).

Modi, J.J. (1935), "Mas'udi's Account of the Pesdadian Kings," *Journal of the K.R. Cama Oriental Institute* 27, 6–32.

Molé, M. (1967), *La legende de Zoroastre selon les textes pehlevis* (Travaux de l'Institut d'études iraniennes de l'Université de Paris 3; Paris: C. Klincksieck).

Monchi-Zadeh, D. (1982), "Xusrōv ī Kavātān ut rētak: Pahlavi Text, Transcription and Translation," in: *Monumentum Georg Morgenstierne II* (Acta Iranica 22, Hommages et Opera Minora 8; Leiden: E.J. Brill), 47–91.

Monferrer-Sala, J.P. (2003), *Textos apócrifos árabes cristianos: introducción, traducción y notas* (Pliegos de Oriente; Madrid: Trotta).

Morris, J.B. (1847), *Selected Works of S. Ephrem the Syrian, Translated out of the Original Syriac* (A Library of Fathers of the Holy Catholic Church 41; Oxford: J.H. Parker).

Mosshammer, A.A. (1984), *Georgii Syncelli Ecloga chronographica* (BSGRT; Leipzig: B.G. Teubner).

Mras, K., and des Places, É. (1982–1983), *Eusebius Werke, Band 8: Die Praeparatio Evangelica*. 2 vols (GCS 43.1–2; 2nd rev. ed.; Berlin: Akademie-Verlag).

Munitiz, J.A., Chrysostomides, J., Harvalia-Crook, E., and Dendrinos, Ch. (1997), *The Letter of the Three Patriarchs to the Emperor Theophilus and Related Texts* (Surrey, England: Porphyrogenitus).

Nau, F. (1905), *Histoires d'Ahoudemmeh et de Marouta, métropolitains jacobites de Tagrit et de l'Orient (VIe et VIIe siècles), suivies du traité d'Ahoudemmeh sur l'homme* (PO 3.1 [11]; Paris: Firmin-Didot).

Nau, F. (1912), *Martyrologes et ménologes orientaux, I-XIII. Un martyrologie et douze ménologes syriaques édités et traduits* (PO 10.1 [46]; Paris: Firmin-Didot).

Nau, F. (1913), *La seconde partie de l'Histoire de Barhadbešabba 'Arbaïa et controverse de Théodore de Mopsueste avec les Macédoniens* (PO 9.5 [45]; Paris: Firmin-Didot).

Nau, F. (1916), *Documents pour servir à l'histoire de l'Église nestorienne* (PO 13.2 [63]; Paris: Firmin-Didot).

Nau, F. (1929–1930), "Le traité sur les "constellations" écrit, en 661, par Sévère Sébokt, évêque de Qennesrin," *ROC* III, 7 [27], 327–410.

Nau, F. (1932), *La première partie de l'Histoire de Barhadbešabba 'Arbaïa* (PO 23.2; Paris: Firmin-Didot).

Nauck, A. (1886), *Porphyrii philosophi Platonici opusula selecta* (BSGRT; 2nd ed.; Leipzig: B.G. Teubner).

Nestle, E. (1881), *Brevis linguae syriacae grammatica, litteratura, chrestomathia cum glossario* (Porta Linguarum Orientalium 5; Karlsruhe: H. Reuther).

Oez, M. (2012), *Cyriacus of Tagrit and his Book on Divine Providence*. 2 vols (Gorgias Eastern Christianity Studies 33; Piscataway, N.J.: Gorgias Press).

Olinder, G. (1937), *Iacobi Sarugensis Epistulae quotquot supersunt* (CSCO, Syr. II.45; Paris: Typographeo Reipublicae).

Overbeck, J.J. (1865), *S. Ephraemi Syri, Rabulae episcopi Edesseni,* Balaei *aliorumque Opera selecta e codicibus syriacis manuscriptis in museo Britannico et bibliotheca Bodleiana asservatis primus edidit* (Oxford: Clarendon Press).

Pakzad, F. (2005), *Bundahišn: Zoroastrische Kosmogonie und Kosmologie. Band 1: Kritische Edition* (Ancient Iranian Studies Series 2; Tehran: Centre for the Great Islamic Encyclopaedia).

Palmer, A., Brock, S.P. and Hoyland, R.G. (1993), *The Seventh Century in the West-Syrian Chronicles* (TTH 15; Liverpool: Liverpool University Press).

Parisot, J. (1894), *Aphraatis Sapientis Persae Demonstrationes* (Patrologia Syriaca 1.1; Paris: Firmin-Didot).

Parisot, J. (1907), "Aphraatis Sapientis Persae Demonstratio XXIII De Acino," in: *Patrologia Syriaca,* Vol. 1.2 (Paris: Firmin-Didot), 1–489.

Parmentier, L., and Hansen, G.Ch. (2009), *Theodoret. Kirchengeschichte* (GCS NF 5; 3rd ed.; Berlin: Walter de Gruyter).

Patrick, J. (1906), "Origen's Commentary on the Gospel of Matthew," in: A. Menzies, ed., *The Ante-Nicene Fathers: Translations of the Writings of the Fathers down to A.D. 325. Vol. 9* (New York: Charles Scribner's Sons), 410–512.

Pearse, R. (2010), *Eusebius of Caesarea. Gospel Problems and Solutions = Quaestiones ad Stephanum et Marinum (CPG 3470)* (Ancient Texts in Translation 1; Ipswich, Suffolk UK: Chieftain Publishing).

Pedersen, N.A. (2006), *Manichaean Homilies, with a Number of Hitherto Unpublished Fragments* (Corpus Fontium Manichaeorum, Series Coptica 2; Turnhout: Brepols).

Pellat, Ch. (1954), *Le livre de la Couronne, Kitāb at-Tāǧ (fī Aḫlāq al-Mulūk), ouvrage attribué à Ǧāḥiẓ* (Paris: Les Belles Lettres).

Perlmann, M. (1987), *The History of al-Ṭabarī. Vol. 4: The Ancient Kingdoms* (SUNY Series in Near Eastern Studies; Albany, N.Y.: State University of New York).

Perrin, B. (1914–1926), *Plutarch's Lives.* 11 vols (LCL; London: William Heinemann).

Pertusi, A. (1959), *Giorgio di Pisidia. Poemi, I. Panegirici epici* (Studia patristica et Byzantina 7; Ettal: Buch-Kunstverlag).

Petit, F. (1991–1996), *La chaîne sur la Genèse. Édition intégrale I-IV.* 4 vols (Traditio Exegetica Graeca 1–4; Louvain: Peeters).

Petruccione, J.F., and Hill, R.Ch. (2007), *Theodoret of Cyrus. The Questions on the Octateuch.* 2 vols (Library of Early Christianity 1–2; Washington, D.C.: The Catholic University of America Press).

Petschenig, M., Ellis, R., Brandes, G., and Schenkl, K. (1898), *Poetae Christiani minores, pars 1* (CSEL 16; Vindobonae: F. Tempsky).

Prevost, G., and Riddle, M.B. (1888), *Saint Chrysostom. Homilies on the Gospel of Saint Matthew* (A Select Library of Nicene and Post-Nicene Fathers of the Christian Church 10; New York: The Christian Literature Company).

Pusey, P.E. (1872), *Sancti patris nostri Cyrilli archiepiscopi Alexandrini in D. Joannis evangelium, accedunt fragmenta varia necnon Tractatus ad Tiberium diaconum duo.* 3 vols (Oxford: Clarendon Press).

Rackham, H., Jones, W.H.S., and Eichholz, D.E. (1938–1962), *Pliny. Natural History.* 10 vols (LCL; London: William Heinemann).

Rehm, B., and Strecker, G. (1992), *Die Pseudoklementinen, I. Homilien* (GCS 42; 3rd rev. ed.; Berlin: Akademie Verlag).

Rehm, B., and Strecker, G. (1994), *Die Pseudoklementinen, II. Rekognitionen in Rufins Übersetzung* (GCS 51; 2nd rev. ed.; Berlin: Akademie Verlag).

Reinink, G.J. (1988), *Gannat Bussame. 1: Die Adventssonntage.* 2 vols (CSCO 501–502, Syr. 211–212; Louvain: Peeters).

Reinink, G.J. (1993), *Die syrische Apokalypse des Pseudo-Methodius.* 2 vols (CSCO 540–541, Syr. 220–221; Louvain: Peeters).

Ri, S.-M. (1987), *La Caverne des Trésors: les deux recensions syriaques.* 2 vols (CSCO 486–487, Syr. 207–208; Louvain: Peeters).

Riessler, P. (1928), *Altjüdisches Schrifttum ausserhalb der Bibel* (Augsburg: Benno Filser).

Rilliet, F. (1986), *Jacques de Saroug. Six homélies festales en prose* (PO 43.4; Turnhout: Brepols).

Robbins, F.E. (1940), *Ptolemy. Tetrabiblos* (LCL; London: William Heinemann).

Roberto, U. (2005), *Ioannis Antiocheni fragmenta ex Historia chronica* (TUGAL 154; Berlin: Walter de Gruyter).

Roberts, A., and Donaldson, J. (1885), *The Ante-Nicene Fathers: Translations of the Writings of the Fathers down to A.D. 325. Vol. 2* (Buffalo: The Christian Literature Publishing Company).

Rolfe, J.C. (1935–1940), *Ammianus Marcellinus.* 3 vols (LCL; London: William Heinemann).

Roman, A., Schmidt, T.S., Poirier, P.-H., Crégheur, E., and Declerck, J.H. (2013), *Titi Bostrensis Contra Manichaeos libri IV graece et syriace* (Corpus Christianorum Series Graeca 82; Turnhout: Brepols).

Rühl, F., and Seel, O. (1935), *M. Ivniani Ivstini Epitoma historiarvm Philippicarvm Pompei Trogi accedvnt prologi in Pompeivm Trogvm* (BSGRT; Leipzig: B.G. Teubner).

Sachau, E. (1878), *Chronologie orientalischer Völker von Albêrûnî* (Leipzig: F.A. Brockhaus).

Sachau, E. (1879), *The Chronology of Ancient Nations: An English Version of the Arabic Text of the Athâr-ul-bâkiya of Albîrûnî or "Vestiges of the Past"* (London: W.H. Allen & Co.).

Sachau, E. (1907–1914), *Syrische Rechtsbücher.* 3 vols (Berlin: G. Reimer).

Scheil, J.V., "La vie de Mar Benjamin. Texte syriaque," *Zeitschrift für Assyriologie* 12 (1897), 62–96.

Scheindler, A. (1881), *Nonni Panopolitani Paraphrasis s. Evangelii Ioannei* (BSGRT; Lipsiae: B.G. Teubner).

Scher, A. (1908), *Mar Barhadbšabba 'Arbaya, évêque de Halwan (VIe siècle). Cause de la fondation des écoles* (PO 4.4 [18]; Paris: Firmin-Didot).

Scher, A. (1908–1918), *Histoire nestorienne (Chronique de Séert)*. 4 vols (PO 4.3 [17], 5.2 [22], 7.2 [32], 13.4 [65]; Turnhout: Brepols).

Scher, A. (1910–1912), *Theodorus bar Kōnī. Liber Scholiorum*. 2 vols (CSCO Syr. II.65–66; Paris: Typographeo Reipublicae).

Schoell, R., and Kroll, W. (1895), *Novellae* (Corpus iuris civilis 3; Berlin: Weidmann).

Séd, N. (1981), *Le Candélabre du Sanctuaire de Grégoire Abou'lfaradj dit Barhebræus. Douzième base: Du Paradis, suivie du Livre des Rayons: traité X* (PO 40.3 [184]; Turnhout: Brepols).

Shahîd, I. (1971), *The Martyrs of Najrân: New Documents* (Subsidia Hagiographica 49; Bruxelles: Société des Bollandistes).

Shaked, Sh. (1979), *The Wisdom of the Sasanian Sages (Dēnkard VI) by Aturpāt-i Ēmētān* (Persian Heritage Series 34; Boulder, Colorado: Westview Press).

Skjærvø, P.O. (1983), *The Sassanian Inscription of Paikuli. Part 3.1: Restored Text and Translation* (Wiesbaden: Ludwig Reichert).

Smith, T. (1867), "Recognitions of Clement," in: *The Writings of Tatian and Theophilus; and the Clementine Recognitions* (Ante-Nicene Christian Library 3; Edinburgh: T&T Clark), 135–471.

Sokoloff, M. (2016), *The Julian Romance: A New English Translation* (Texts from Christian Late Antiquity 49; Piscataway, N.J.: Gorgias Press).

Stählin, O. (1905–1936), *Clemens Alexandrinus*. 4 vols (GCS; Leipzig: J.C. Hinrichs).

Stone, M.E. (1996), *Armenian Apocrypha Relating to Adam and Eve* (Studia in Veteris Testamenti Pseudepigrapha 14; Leiden: Brill).

Strothmann, W. (1976), *Jakob von Sarug. Drei Gedichte über den Apostel Thomas in Indien* (Göttinger Orientforschungen, I. Reihe: Syriaca, Bd. 12; Wiesbaden: Otto Harrassowitz).

Strothmann, W. (1988a), *Das syrische Fragment des Ecclesiastes-Kommentars von Theodor von Mopsuestia: Syrischer Text mit vollständigem Wörterverzeichnis* (Göttinger Orientforschungen, I. Reihe: Syriaca, Bd. 28; Wiesbaden: Otto Harrassowitz).

Strothmann, W. (1988b), *Kohelet-Kommentar des Johannes von Apamea: Syrischer Text mit vollständigem Wörterverzeichnis* (Göttinger Orientforschungen, I. Reihe: Syriaca, Bd. 30; Wiesbaden: Otto Harrassowitz).

Taillieu, D. (2004), *The Zoroastrian Polemic against Manichaeism in Škand-Gumānīg Wizār and Dēnkard III* (Thesis for the degree of Doctor in Oriental Studies; Katholieke Universiteit Leuven).

Tanghe, A. (1960), "Memra de Philoxène de Mabboug sur l'inhabitation du Saint Esprit," *Le Muséon* 73, 39–71.

Tavadia, J.C. (1930), *Šāyest-nē-šāyest: A Pahlavi Text on Religious Customs* (Alt- und Neu-Indische Studien 3; Hamburg: Friedrichsen).

Ter Minasyan, E. (1957), *Ełišēi vasn Vardanay ew Hayocʿ paterazmin* (Erevan: Armenian Academy of Science).

Thackeray, H.S.J., Marcus, R., and Feldman, L.H. (1926–1965), *Josephus*. 9 vols (The LCL; London: William Heinemann).

Thelwall, S. (1870), "An Answer to the Jews," in: A. Roberts and J. Donaldson, eds., *The Writings of Quintus Sept. Flor. Tertullianus. Vol. 3* (Ante-Nicene Christian Library: Translations of the Writings of the Fathers down to A.D. 325 18; Edinburgh: T&T Clark), 201–258.

Thomson, R.W. (1977), *Athanasiana Syriaca. Part IV: Expositio in Psalmos: 1. Abbreviated Version; 2. Longer Version*. 2 vols (CSCO 386–387, Syr. 167–168; Louvain: Secrétariat du Corpus SCO).

Thomson, R.W. (1978), *Moses Khorenatsʿi. History of the Armenians* (Harvard Armenian Texts and Studies 4; Cambridge, Mass.: Harvard University Press).

Thomson, R.W. (1982), *Ełishē. History of Vardan and the Armenian War* (Harvard Armenian Texts and Studies 5; Cambridge, Mass.: Harvard University Press).

Thomson, R.W., and Howard-Johnston, J. (1999), *The Armenian History attributed to Sebeos* (TTH 31; Liverpool: Liverpool University Press).

Thurn, H. (2000), *Ioannis Malalae Chronographia* (Corpus Fontium Historiae Byzantinae 35; Berlin: Walter de Gruyter).

Timm, S. (2005), *Eusebius von Caesarea. Das Onomastikon der biblischen Ortsnamen: Edition der syrischen Fassung mit griechischem Text, englischer und deutscher Übersetzung* (TUGAL 152; Berlin: Walter de Gruyter).

Tischendorf, C. (1876), *Evangelia apocrypha adhibitis plurimis codicibus Graecis et Latinis maximam partem nunc primum consultis atque ineditorum copia insignibus* (2nd ed.; Lipsiae: Hermann Mendelssohn).

Toepel, A. (2013), "The Cave of Treasures: A New Translation and Introduction," in: R. Bauckham, J.R. Davila and A. Panayotov, eds., *Old Testament Pseudepigrapha: More Noncanonical Scriptures. Volume 1* (Grand Rapids, Mich.: W.B. Eerdmans), 531–584.

Tonneau, R.M. (1953), "Théodore de Mopsueste. Interpretation (du livre) de la Genèse (Vat. Syr. 120, ff. I-V)," *Le Muséon* 66:1–2, 45–64.

Tonneau, R.M. (1955), *Sancti Ephraem Syri in Genesim et in Exodum commentarii*. 2 vols (CSCO 152–153, Syr. 71–72; Louvain: L. Durbecq).

Tronina, A., and Starowieyski, M. (2011), *Apokryfy syryjskie: Historia i przysłowia Achikara, Grota Skarbów, Apokalipsa Pseudo-Metodego* (Pisma apokryficzne 6; Kraków: Wydawnictwo WAM).

Vahman, F. (1986), *Ardā Wirāz Nāmag: The Iranian 'Divina Commedia'* (Scandinavian Institute of Asian Studies: Monograph Series 53; London: Curzon).

van den Broek, R. (2013), *Pseudo-Cyril of Jerusalem. On the Life and the Passion of Christ: A Coptic Apocryphon* (Supplements to Vigiliae Christianae 118; Leiden: Brill).

van der Horst, P.W. (1984), *Chaeremon, Egyptian Priest and Stoic Philosopher: The Fragments Collected and Translated with Explanatory Notes* (Études préliminaires aux religions orientales dans l'Empire Romain 101; Leiden: E.J. Brill).

van Esbroeck, M. (2001), "L'encyclique de Komitas et la réponse de Mar Maroutha (617)," *OC* 85, 162–175.

van Roey, A. (1975–1976), "Une lettre du patriarche Jacobite Serge I (557-561)," *PdO* 6–7, 213–227.

van Rompay, L. (1986), *Le commentaire sur Genèse—Exode 9,32 du manuscrit (olim) Diyarbakir 22*. 2 vols. (CSCO 483–484, Syr. 205–206; Louvain: Peeters).

van Vloten, G. (1898), *Le Livre des beautés et des antithèses, attribué à Abu Othman Amr ibn Bahr al-Djahiz de Basra* (Leiden: E.J. Brill).

VanderKam, J.C. (1989), *The Book of Jubilees*. 2 vols (CSCO 510–511, Aeth. 87–88; Louvain: Peeters).

Varner, W. (2004), *Ancient Jewish-Christian Dialogues: Athanasius and Zacchaeus, Simon and Theophilus, Timothy and Aquila* (Studies in Bible and Early Christianity 58; Lewiston: Edwin Mellen).

Vasiliev, A.A. (1909–1915), *Kitab al-'Unvan: Histoire universelle écrite par Agapius (Mahboub) de Menbidj*. 4 vols (PO 5.4, 7.4, 8.3, 11.1; Paris: Firmin-Didot).

von Lingenthal, K.E.Z. (1857), *Novellae constitutiones imperatorum post Justinianum* (Jus graeco-romanum 3; Leipzig: T.O. Weigel).

Vööbus, A. (1962), *The Statutes of the School of Nisibis* (Papers of the Estonian Theological Society in Exile 12; Stockholm: Estonian Theological Society in Exile).

Vööbus, A. (1975–1976), *The Synodicon in the West Syrian Tradition*. 4 vols (CSCO 367–368, 375–376, Syr. 161–164; Louvain: Secrétariat du CorpusSCO).

Vööbus, A. (1979), *The Didascalia Apostolorum in Syriac*. 4 vols (CSCO 401–402, 407–408, Syr. 175–176, 179–180; Louvain: Secrétariat du CorpusSCO).

Vööbus, A. (1982), *The Canons Ascribed to Mārūtā of Maipherqaṭ and Related Sources*. 2 vols (CSCO 439–440, Syr. 191–192; Louvain: Peeters).

Vosté, J.M. (1940), *Theodori Mopsuesteni Commentarius in Evangelium Iohannis Apostoli*. 2 vols (CSCO 115–116, Syr. 62–63; Paris: Typographeo Reipublicae).

Vosté, J.M., and van den Eynde, C. (1950–1955), *Commentaire d'Išo'dad de Merv sur l'Ancien Testament, I: Genèse*. 2 vols. (CSCO 126, 156, Syr. 67, 75; Louvain: Secrétariat du Corpus SCO).

Wallraff, M., Roberto, U., Pinggéra, K., and Adler, W. (2007), *Iulius Africanus. Chronographiae: The Extant Fragments* (Die griechischen christlichen Schriftsteller der ersten Jahrhunderte NF 15; Berlin: Walter de Gruyter).

Walters, J.E. (2011), *Hymns on the Unleavened Bread by Ephrem the Syrian* (Texts from Christian Late Antiquity 30; Piscataway, N.J.: Gorgias Press).

Warner, A.G., and Warner, E. (1905–1925), *The Sháhnáma of Firdausí*. 9 vols (Trübner's Oriental Series; London: Kegan Paul, Trench, Trübner & Co.).

Watson, J.S. (1853), *Justin, Cornelius Nepos, and Eutropius* (London: Henry G. Bohn).

West, E.W. (1871), *The Book of the Mainyo-i-Khard: The Pazand and Sanskrit Texts (in Roman Characters), as Arranged by Neriosengh Dhaval, in the Fifteenth Century*. 2 vols (Stuttgart: Carl Grüninger).

Whiston, W., and Donaldson, J. (1870), "The Apostolical Constitutions," in: A. Roberts and J. Donaldson, eds., *Ante-Nicene Christian Library: Translations of the Writings of the Fathers down to A.D. 325*, Vol. 17 (Edinburgh: T&T Clark), 1–280.

Whitby, M., and Whitby, M. (1988), *The History of Theophylact Simocatta: An English Translation* (Oxford: Clarendon Press).

White, H. (1912–1913), *Appian's Roman History*. 4 vols (LCL; London: William Heinemann).

Whittaker, M. (1982), *Tatian. Oratio ad Graecos and Fragments* (Oxford: Clarendon Press).

Willems, R. (1954), *Sancti Aurelii Augustini In Iohannis Evangelium tractatus CXXIV* (CCSL 36, Aurelii Augustini opera 8; Turnhout: Brepols).

Williams, A.V. (1990), *The Pahlavi Rivāyat Accompanying the Dādestan ī Dēnīg*. 2 vols (Historisk-filosofiske Meddelelser 60.1–2; Copenhagen: Munksgaard).

Williams, F. (2009), *The Panarion of Epiphanius of Salamis, Book I (Sects 1-46)* (Nag Hammadi and Manichaean Studies 63; 2nd rev. ed.; Leiden: Brill).

Wilmart, A., and Tisserant, E. (1913), "Fragments grecs et latins de l'Évangile de Barthélemy," *Revue biblique* NS 10, 161–190, 321–368.

Wilson, N.G. (1994), *Photius. The Bibliotheca: A Selection Translated with Notes* (London: Duckworth).

Wright, W. (1865), "The Departure of my Lady Mary from this World," *Journal of Sacred Literature and Biblical Record* NS VI.12, 417–448; VII.13, 110–160.

Wright, W. (1866–1867), "Eusebius of Caesarea on the Star," *Journal of Sacred Literature and Biblical Record* NS IX.17, 117–136; X.19, 150–164.

Wright, W. (1867), "Two Epistles of Mâr Jacob, Bishop of Edessa," *Journal of Sacred Literature and Biblical Record* NS X.20, 430–460.

Wright, W. (1882), *The Chronicle of Joshua the Stylite Composed in Syriac A.D. 507* (Cambridge: Cambridge University Press).

Wright, W., and McLean, N. (1898), *The Ecclesiastical History of Eusebius in Syriac Edited from the Manuscripts* (Cambridge: Cambridge University Press).

Wright, W.C. (1913–1923), *The Works of the Emperor Julian*. 3 vols (LCL; London: William Heinemann).

Wurst, G. (1996), *Die Bema-Psalmen* (Corpus Fontium Manichaeorum, Series Coptica 1; Turnhout: Brepols).
Wüstenfeld, H.F. (1858–1860), *Das Leben Muhammed's nach Muhammed Ibn Ishâk bearbeitet von Abd el-Malik Ibn Hischâm*. 2 vols (Göttingen: Dieterichsche Universitäts-Buchhandlung).
Wutz, F. (1915), *Onomastica Sacra. Untersuchungen zum Liber Interpretationis Nominum Hebraicorum des Hl. Hieronymus*. 2 vols (TUGAL 41.1–2; Leipzig: J.C. Hinrichs).
Zéki Pasha, A. (1914), *Djâḥiẓ. Le Livre de la Couronne (Kitab el-tadj)* (Le Caire: Imprimerie nationale).
Zycha, I. (1895), *Sancti Aureli Augustini Quaestionum in Heptateuchum libri VII, Adnotationum in Iob liber unus* (CSEL 28.2; Vindobonae: F. Tempsky).

Secondary Literature

Adler, W. (1989), *Time Immemorial: Archaic History and its Sources in Christian Chronography from Julius Africanus to George Syncellus* (Dumbarton Oaks Studies 26; Washington, D.C.: Dumbarton Oaks Research Library and Collection).
Adler, W. (1994), "Jacob of Edessa and the Jewish Pseudepigrapha in Syriac Chronography," in: J.C. Reeves, ed., *Tracing the Threads: Studies in the Vitality of Jewish Pseudepigrapha* (SBL Early Judaism and Its Literature 6; Atlanta, Georgia: Scholars Press), 143–171.
Adler, W. (1996), "The Apocalyptic Survey of History Adapted by Christians: Daniel's Prophecy of 70 Weeks," in: J.C. VanderKam and W. Adler, eds., *The Jewish Apocalyptic Heritage in Early Christianity* (Compendia Rerum Iudaicarum ad Novum Testamentum 4; Assen: Van Gorcum), 201–238.
Adrych, P., Bracey, R., Dalglish, D., Lenk, S., and Wood, R. (2017), *Images of Mithra* (Visual Conversations in Art and Archaeology; Oxford: Oxford University Press).
Akbarzadeh, D. (2010), "The Hindūgān of Bundhišn," *Iranica Antiqua* 45, 419–426.
Aland, K. (1961), "The Problem of Anonymity and Pseudonymity in Christian Literature of the First Two Centuries," *Journal of Theological Studies* NS 12:1, 39–49.
Alcoff, L.M. (2003), "Introduction. Identities: Modern and Postmodern," in: L.M. Alcoff and E. Mendieta, eds., *Identities: Race, Class, Gender, and Nationality* (Malden, MA: Blackwell Publishing), 1–8.
Alexander, P.J. (1985), *The Byzantine Apocalyptic Tradition* (Berkeley, Calif.: University of California Press).
Alexander, Ph.S. (1988), "Retelling the Old Testament," in: D.A. Carson and H.G.M. Williamson, eds., *It Is Written: Scripture Citing Scripture. Essays in Honour of Barnabas Lindars* (Cambridge: Cambridge University Press), 99–121.

Alexander, Ph.S. (2007), "The Rabbis and Messianism," in: M. Bockmuehl and J. Carleton Paget, eds., *Redemption and Resistance: The Messianic Hopes of Jews and Christians in Antiquity* (London: T&T Clark International), 227–244.

Alexandre, M. (1998), "Apologétique judéo-hellénistique et premières apologies chrétiennes," in: B. Pouderon and J. Doré, eds., *Les apologistes chrétiens et la culture grecque* (Théologie historique 105; Paris: Beauchesne), 1–40.

Allen, M.I. (2003), "Universal History 300-1000: Origins and Western Developments," in: D.M. Deliyannis, ed., *Historiography in the Middle Ages* (Leiden: Brill), 17–42.

Alram, M. (2008), "Early Sasanian Coinage," in: V.S. Curtis and S.R.A. Stewart, eds., *The Sasanian Era* (The Idea of Iran 3; London: I.B. Tauris), 17–30.

Alram, M., and Gyselen, R. (2003), *Sylloge nummorum Sasanidarum: Paris–Berlin–Wien. Band 1: Ardashir I.-Shapur I.* (Denkschriften der Österreichischen Akademie der Wissenschaften, Philosophisch-Historische Klasse 317; Veröffentlichungen der Numismatischen Kommission 41; Wien: Verlag der Österreichischen Akademie der Wissenschaften).

Ambartsumian, A.A. (2005), ""Конные" имена в Авесте и пехлевийской литературе," in: *Новое в лингвистике и методике преподавания иностранных языков. Материалы научно-методической конференции* (С.-Петербург: ВИТУ), 21–33.

Anderson, G.A. (1988), "The Cosmic Mountain: Eden and Its Early Interpreters in Syriac Christianity," in: G.A. Robbins, ed., *Genesis 1-3 in the History of Exegesis: Intrigue in the Garden* (Lewiston: Edwin Mellen), 187–224.

Anderson, G.A. (1989), "Celibacy or Consummation in the Garden? Reflections on Early Jewish and Christian Interpretations of the Garden of Eden," *HTR* 82:2, 121–148.

Anderson, G.A. (2000), "The Exaltation of Adam and the Fall of Satan," in: G.A. Anderson, M.E. Stone and J. Tromp, eds., *Literature on Adam and Eve: Collected Essays* (Studia in Veteris Testamenti Pseudepigrapha 15; Leiden: Brill), 83–110.

Andrade, N.J. (2010–2011), "Framing the "Syrian" of Late Antiquity: Engagements with Hellenism," *Journal of Modern Hellenism* 28, 1–46.

Andrade, N.J. (2013), *Syrian Identity in the Greco-Roman World* (Cambridge: Cambridge University Press).

Asmussen, J.P. (1983), "Christians in Iran," in: E. Yarshater, ed., *The Cambridge History of Iran. Vol. 3(2): The Seleucid, Parthian and Sasanian Periods* (Cambridge: Cambridge University Press), 924–948.

Assemani, G.S. (1719–1728), *Bibliotheca orientalis Clementino-Vaticana, in qua manuscriptos codices syriacos, arabicos, persicos, turcicos, hebraicos, samaritanos, armenicos, æthiopicos, Graecos, ægyptiacos, ibericos & malabaricos*. 3 vols (Roma: Typis Sacrae Congregationis de Propaganda Fide).

Assmann, J. (2011), *Cultural Memory and Early Civilization: Writing, Remembrance, and Political Imagination*. Trans. by H. Wilson (Cambridge: Cambridge University Press).

[German original: Assmann, J., *Das kulturelle Gedächtnis: Schrift, Erinnerung und politische Identität in frühen Hochkulturen* (2nd ed.; München: Beck, 1999).

Atiya, A.S. (1968), *A History of Eastern Christianity* (Notre Dame, Indiana: University of Notre Dame Press).

Attridge, H.W. (1976), *The Interpretation of Biblical History in the Antiquitates Judaicae of Flavius Josephus* (Harvard Dissertations in Religion 7; Missoula, Mont.: Scholars Press).

Aune, D.E. (2006), *Apocalypticism, Prophecy and Magic in Early Christianity: Collected Essays* (WUNT 199; Tübingen: Mohr Siebeck).

Avalichvili, Z. (1927–1928), "Notice sur une version géorgienne de la Caverne des Trésors, apocryphe syriaque attribué à saint Éphrem," *ROC* III, 6 [26], 381–405.

Bachmann-Medick, D. (2016), *Cultural Turns: New Orientations in the Study of Culture*. Trans. by A. Blauhut (De Gruyter Textbook; Berlin: Walter de Gruyter).

Bailey, H.W. (1943), *Zoroastrian Problems in the Ninth-Century Books* (Ratanbai Katrak Lectures; Oxford: Clarendon Press).

Bamberger, J. (1901), *Die Litteratur der Adambücher und die haggadischen Elemente in der syrischen Schatzhöhle* (Aschaffenburg: C. Krebs).

Barclay, J.M.G. (2005), "The Empire Writes Back: Josephan Rhetoric in Flavian Rome," in: J. Edmondson, S. Mason and J.B. Rives, eds., *Flavius Josephus and Flavian Rome* (Oxford: Oxford University Press), 315–332.

Bardy, G. (1928), "Melchisédéciens," in: *Dictionnaire de théologie catholique* (Paris: Letouzey et Ané), vol. 10, 513–516.

Batey, R.A. (1971), *New Testament Nuptial Imagery* (Leiden: E.J. Brill).

Baum, W., and Winkler, D.W. (2003), *The Church of the East: A Concise History* (London: Routledge).

Baumstark, A. (1922), *Geschichte der syrischen Literatur, mit Ausschluss der christlich-palästinensischen Texte* (Bonn: A. Marcus und E. Weber).

Bausi, A. (2006), "Current Trends in Ethiopian Studies: Philology," in: S. Uhlig, ed., *Proceedings of the XVth International Conference of Ethiopian Studies, Hamburg July 20-25, 2003* (Aethiopistische Forschungen 65; Wiesbaden: Harrassowitz Verlag), 542–551.

Bausi, A. (2008), ""Philology" as Textual Criticism: "Normalization" of Ethiopian Studies," *Ethiopian Philology* 1:1, 13–46.

Bausi, A. (2010), "Qälemǝnṭos," in: S. Uhlig, ed., *Encyclopaedia Aethiopica, Vol. 4* (Wiesbaden: Harrassowitz Verlag), 251–253.

Beatrice, P.F. (2002), "Forgery, Propaganda and Power in Christian Antiquity: Some Methodological Remarks," in: W. Blümer, R. Henke and M. Mülke, eds., *Alvarium: Festschrift für Christian Gnilka* (Jahrbuch für Antike und Christentum, Ergänzungsband 33; Münster: Aschendorff), 39–51.

Beaucamp, J., Briquel-Chatonnet, F., and Robin, Ch.J. (2010), eds., *Juifs et Chrétiens en Arabie aux Ve et VIe siècles: regards croisés sur les sources* (Centre de Recherche d'Histoire et Civilisation de Byzance, Monographies 32; Le massacre de Najrân 2; Paris: Association des amis du Centre d'histoire et civilisation de Byzance).

Becker, A.H. (2002), "Anti-Judaism and Care for the Poor in Aphrahat's *Demonstration* 20," *JECS* 10:3, 305–327.

Becker, A.H. (2003), "Beyond the Spatial and Temporal Limes: Questioning the "Parting of the Ways" Outside the Roman Empire," in: A.H. Becker and A.Y. Reed, eds., *The Ways that Never Parted: Jews and Christians in Late Antiquity and the Early Middle Ages* (TSAJ 95; Tübingen: Mohr Siebeck), 373–392.

Becker, A.H. (2006), *Fear of God and the Beginning of Wisdom: The School of Nisibis and the Development of Scholastic Culture in Late Antique Mesopotamia* (Divinations: Rereading Late Ancient Religion; Philadelphia: University of Pennsylvania Press).

Becker, A.H. (2008), "The Ancient Near East in the Late Antique Near East: Syriac Christian Appropriation of the Biblical East," in: G. Gardner and K.L. Osterloh, eds., *Antiquity in Antiquity: Jewish and Christian Pasts in the Greco-Roman World* (TSAJ 123; Tübingen: Mohr Siebeck), 394–415.

Becker, A.H. (2009), "Martyrdom, Religious Difference, and "Fear" as a Category of Piety in the Sasanian Empire: The Case of the *Martyrdom of Gregory* and the *Martyrdom of Yazdpaneh*," *Journal of Late Antiquity* 2:2, 300–336.

Becker, A.H. (2010), "The Comparative Study of "Scholasticism" in Late Antique Mesopotamia: Rabbis and East Syrians," *AJS Review* 34:1, 91–113.

Becker, A.H. (2015), *Revival and Awakening: American Evangelical Missionaries in Iran and the Origins of Assyrian Nationalism* (Chicago, Ill.: The University of Chicago Press).

Becker, A.H. (2016), "L'antijudaïsme syriaque: entre polémique et critique interne," in: F. Ruani, ed., *Les controverses religieuses en syriaque* (Études syriaques 13; Paris: Paul Geuthner), 181–208.

Becker, A.H., and Childers, J.W. (2011), "Barḥadbshabba 'Arbaya," in: S.P. Brock, A.M. Butts, G.A. Kiraz and L. van Rompay, eds., *Gorgias Encyclopedic Dictionary of the Syriac Heritage* (Piscataway, N.J.: Gorgias Press), 57–58.

Beckwith, R.T. (1981), "Daniel 9 and the Date of the Messiah's Coming in Essene, Hellenistic, Pharisaic, Zealot and Early Christian Computation," *Revue de Qumran* 10:4 [40], 521–542.

Beeston, A.F.L. (2005), "The Martyrdom of Azqir," in: M.C.A. Macdonald and C.S. Phillips, eds., *A.F.L. Beeston at the Arabian Seminar and Other Papers* (Proceedings of the Seminar for Arabian Studies; Oxford: Archaeopress), 113–118.

Belayche, N. (2009), "Foundation Myths in Roman Palestine: Traditions and Reworkings," in: T. Derks and N. Roymans, eds., *Ethnic Constructs in Antiquity: The Role of Power and Tradition* (Amsterdam Archaeological Studies 13; Amsterdam: Amsterdam University Press), 167–188.

Ben Zeev, M.P. (2005), *Diaspora Judaism in Turmoil, 116/117 CE: Ancient Sources and Modern Insights* (Interdisciplinary Studies in Ancient Culture and Religion 6; Leuven: Peeters).

Bernjam, S.-P. (2001), "How to Speak About Early Christian Apologetics? Comments on the Recent Debate," *Studia Patristica* 36, 177–183.

Bhabha, H.K. (1994), *The Location of Culture* (London: Routledge).

Bidez, J., and Cumont, F. (1938), *Les mages hellénisés: Zoroastre, Ostanès et Hystaspe d'après la tradition grecque*. 2 vols (Paris: Les Belles Lettres).

Bilde, P., Engberg-Pedersen, T., Hannestad, L., and Zahle, J. (1992), eds., *Ethnicity in Hellenistic Egypt* (Studies in Hellenistic Civilization 3; Aarhus: Aarhus University Press).

Blanchard, M.J. (1993), "The Coptic Heritage of St. Ephrem the Syrian," in: T. Orlandi and D.W. Johnson, eds., *Acts of the Fifth International Congress of Coptic Studies, Washington, 12-15 August 1992*. 3 vols. (Rome: C.I.M.), vol. 2.1, 37–51.

Boddens Hosang, F.J.E. (2010), *Establishing Boundaries: Christian-Jewish Relations in Early Council Texts and the Writings of Church Fathers* (Jewish and Christian Perspectives 19; Leiden: Brill).

Borgeaud, P. (2010), "'Silent Entrails': The Devil, His Demons, and Christian Theories Regarding Ancient Religions," *History of Religions* 50:1, 80–95.

Borst, A. (1957–1963), *Der Turmbau von Babel: Geschichte der Meinungen über Ursprung und Vielfalt der Sprachen und Völker*. 4 vols (Stuttgart: A. Hiersemann).

Botha, P.J. (1990), "Polarity: The Theology of Anti-Judaism in Ephrem the Syrian's Hymns on Easter," *Hervormde Teologiese Studies* 46, 36–46.

Botha, P.J. (1991), "The Poetic Face of Rhetoric: Ephrem's Polemics against the Jews and Heretics in *Contra haereses* XXV," *Acta Patristica et Byzantina* 2, 16–36.

Botha, P.J. (2007), "The Relevance of the Book of Daniel for Fourth-Century Christianity according to the Commentary Ascribed to Ephrem the Syrian," in: K. Bracht and D.S. du Toit, eds., *Die Geschichte der Daniel-Auslegung in Judentum, Christentum und Islam. Studien zur Kommentierung des Danielbuches in Literatur und Kunst* (Beihefte zur Zeitschrift für die alttestamentliche Wissenschaft 371; Berlin: Walter de Gruyter), 99–122.

Bourdieu, P. (1984), *Distinction: A Social Critique of the Judgement of Taste*. Trans. by R. Nice (Cambridge, Mass.: Harvard University Press).

Bousset, W. (1907), *Hauptprobleme der Gnosis* (Forschungen zur Religion und Literatur des Alten und Neuen Testaments 10; Göttingen: Vandenhoeck & Ruprecht).

Bowersock, G.W. (2004), "The Ḥaḍramawt between Persia and Byzantium," in: *La Persia e Bisanzio. Atti del Convegno internazionale (Roma, 14-18 ottobre 2002)* (Atti dei Convegni Lincei 201; Roma: Accademia Nazionale dei Lincei), 263–273.

Boyarin, D. (2004), *Border Lines: The Partition of Judaeo-Christianity* (Divinations: Rereading Late Ancient Religion; Philadelphia: University of Pennsylvania Press).

Boyarin, D., and Burrus, V. (2005), "Hybridity as Subversion of Orthodoxy? Jews and Christians in Late Antiquity," *Social Compass* 52:4, 431–441.

Boyce, M. (1968b), "On the Sacred Fires of the Zoroastrians," *BSOAS* 31:1, 52–68.

Boyce, M. (1968c), "The Pious Foundations of the Zoroastrians," *BSOAS* 31:2, 270–289.

Boyce, M. (1975b), "Iconoclasm among the Zoroastrians," in: J. Neusner, ed., *Christianity, Judaism and Other Greco-Roman Cults: Studies for Morton Smith at Sixty* (Studies in Judaism in Late Antiquity 12; Leiden: E.J. Brill), vol. 4, 93–111.

Boyce, M. (1977), *A Persian Stronghold of Zoroastrianism* (Ratanbai Katrak Lectures, 1975; Oxford: Clarendon Press).

Boyce, M. (1983), "Iranian Festivals," in: E. Yarshater, ed., *The Cambridge History of Iran. Vol. 3(2): The Seleucid, Parthian and Sasanian Periods* (Cambridge: Cambridge University Press), 792–815.

Boyce, M. (1985), "Alborz. ii. Alborz in Myth and Legend," in: E. Yarshater, ed., *Encyclopaedia Iranica* (London: Routledge & Kegan Paul), vol. 1, 811–813.

Boyce, M. (2001), "Ganzak," in: E. Yarshater, ed., *Encyclopaedia Iranica* (New York: Bibliotheca Persica Press), vol. 10, 289–290.

Boyce, M., and Grenet, F. (1991), *A History of Zoroastrianism. Vol. 3: Zoroastrianism under Macedonian and Roman Rule* (Handbuch der Orientalistik, Erste Abteilung: Nahe und der Mittlere Osten, Bd. 8: Religion, Abschnitt 1: Religionsgeschichte des Alten Orients, 2.2; Leiden: E.J. Brill).

Brakke, D. (2002), "The Early Church in North America: Late Antiquity, Theory, and the History of Christianity," *Church History* 71:3, 473–491.

Braun, O. (1894), "Der Briefwechsel des Katholikos Papa von Seleucia. Ein Beitrag zur Geschichte der ostsyrischen Kirche im vierten Jahrhundert," *Zeitschrift für katholische Theologie* 18, 163–182, 546–565.

Briquel-Chatonnet, F., and Debié, M. (2017), *Le Monde syriaque. Sur les routes d'un christianisme ignoré* (Paris: Les Belles Lettres).

Broadhurst, L. (2005), "Melito of Sardis, the Second Sophistic, and "Israel"," in: W. Braun, ed., *Rhetoric and Reality in Early Christianities* (Studies in Christianity and Judaism 16; Waterloo, Ontario: Wilfred Laurier University Press), 49–74.

Brock, S.P. (1979), "Jewish Traditions in Syriac Sources," *JJS* 30:2, 212–232.

Brock, S.P. (1982a), "Christians in the Sassanian Empire: A Case of Divided Loyalties," in: S. Mews, ed., *Religious and National Identity: Papers Read at the Nineteenth Summer Meeting and the Twentieth Winter Meeting of the Ecclesiastical History Society* (Studies in Church History 18; Oxford: Basil Blackwell), 1–19.

Brock, S.P. (1982b), "Syriac Views of Emergent Islam," in: G.H.A. Juynboll, ed., *Studies on the First Century of Islamic Society* (Papers on Islamic History 5; Carbondale, Ill.: Southern Illinois University Press), 9–21, 199–203.

Brock, S.P. (1982c), "Clothing Metaphors as a Means of Theological Expression in Syriac Tradition," in: M. Schmidt and C.F. Geyer, eds., *Typus, Symbol, Allegorie bei* den östlichen Vätern und ihren Parallelen im Mittelalter. Internationales Kolloquium, Eichstätt 1981 (Eichstätter Beiträge 4; Regensburg: Friedrich Pustet), 11–38.

Brock, S.P. (1990), "Diachronic Aspects of Syriac Word Formation: An Aid for Dating Anonymous Texts," in: R. Lavenant, ed., V Symposium Syriacum, 1988: Katholieke Universiteit, Leuven, 29-31 août 1988 (OCA 236; Roma: Pontificium Institutum Studiorum Orientalium), 321–330.

Brock, S.P. (1994), "Greek and Syriac in Late Antique Syria," in: A.K. Bowman and G. Woolf, eds., Literacy and Power in the Ancient World (Cambridge: Cambridge University Press), 149–160, 234–235.

Brock, S.P. (1999), "The ruaḥ elōhīm of Gen 1,2 and its Reception History in the Syriac Tradition," in: J.-M. Auwers and A. Wénin, eds., Lectures et relectures de la Bible. Festschrift P.-M. Bogaert (Bibliotheca Ephemeridum Theologicarum Lovaniensium 144; Leuven: Leuven University Press), 327–349.

Brock, S.P. (2003), "Some Diachronic Features of Classical Syriac," in: M.F.J. Baasten and W.T. van Peursen, eds., Hamlet on a Hill: Semitic and Greek Studies Presented to Professor T. Muraoka on the Occasion of His Sixty-Fifth Birthday (OLA 118; Leuven: Peeters), 95–111.

Brock, S.P. (2006), "The Genealogy of the Virgin Mary in Sinai Syr. 16," Scrinium 2, 58–71.

Brock, S.P. (2007), "Syria and Mesopotamia: The Shared Term malka mshiḥa," in: M. Bockmuehl and J. Carleton Paget, eds., Redemption and Resistance: The Messianic Hopes of Jews and Christians in Antiquity (London: T&T Clark International), 171–182.

Brock, S.P. (2008b), "[Review of:] A. Toepel, Die Adam- und Seth-Legenden im syrischen Buch der Schatzhöhle (CSCO 618, Subs. 119; Louvain: Peeters, 2006)," OCP 74:2, 554–557.

Brock, S.P. (2010), "A Criterion for Dating Undated Syriac Texts: The Evidence from Adjectival Forms in -aya," PdO 36, 111–124.

Brock, S.P. (2014), "Eleazar, Shmuni and Her Seven Sons in Syriac Tradition," in: M.-F. Baslez and O. Munnich, eds., La mémoire des persécutions: Autour des livres des Maccabées (Collection de la Revue des Études Juives 56; Paris: Peeters), 329–336.

Brock, S.P., Butts, A.M., Kiraz, G.A., and van Rompay, L. (2011), eds., Gorgias Encyclopedic Dictionary of the Syriac Heritage (Piscataway, N.J.: Gorgias Press).

Brok, M.F.A. (1953), "Le livre contre les mages de Théodoret de Cyr," Mélanges de science religieuse 10, 181–194.

Brooke, G.J. (2005), "Between Authority and Canon: The Significance of Reworking the Bible for Understanding the Canonical Process," in: E.G. Chazon, D. Dimant and R.A. Clements, eds., Reworking the Bible: Apocryphal and Related Texts at Qumran (Studies on the Texts of the Desert of Judah 58; Leiden: Brill), 85–104.

Brown, R.E. (1993), The Birth of the Messiah: A Commentary on the Infancy Narratives in the Gospels of Matthew and Luke (The Anchor Bible Reference Library; 2nd rev. ed.; New York: Doubleday).

Brubaker, L., and Haldon, J.F. (2001), *Byzantium in the Iconoclast Era (ca 680–850): The Sources. An Annotated Survey* (Birmingham Byzantine and Ottoman Monographs 7; Aldershot: Ashgate).

Brunner, Ch.J. (1987), "Astrology and Astronomy in Iran. ii. Astronomy and Astrology in the Sasanian Period," in: E. Yarshater, ed., *Encyclopaedia Iranica* (London: Routledge & Kegan Paul), vol. 2, 862–868.

Bruns, P. (2002), "Endzeitberechnungen in der syrischen Kirche," in: W. Geerlings, ed., *Der Kalender. Aspekte einer Geschichte* (Paderborn: Schöningh), 122–139.

Bruns, P. (2014), "Antizoroastrische Polemik in den Syro-Persischen Martyrerakten," in: G. Herman, ed., *Jews, Christians and Zoroastrians: Religious Dynamics in a Sasanian Context* (Judaism in Context 17; Piscataway, N.J.: Gorgias Press), 57–76.

Brykczyński, P. (1975), "Astrologia w Palmyrze," *Studia Palmyreńskie* 6, 47–109.

Bucci, O. (1978), "Il matrimonio fra consanguinei (khvêtûkdâs) nella tradizione giuridica delle genti iraniche," *Apollinaris* 51, 291–319.

Buckley, J.J. (1993), "The Mandaean Appropriation of Jesus' Mother, Miriai," *Novum Testamentum* 35:2, 181–196.

Buell, D.K. (2005), *Why This New Race: Ethnic Reasoning in Early Christianity* (New York: Columbia University Press).

Burgess, R.W. (2006), "Apologetic and Chronography: The Antecedents of Julius Africanus," in: M. Wallraff, ed., *Julius Africanus und die christliche Weltchronik* (TUGAL 157; Berlin: Walter de Gruyter), 17–42.

Byron, G.L. (2002), *Symbolic Blackness and Ethnic Difference in Early Christian Literature* (London: Routledge).

Callieri, P. (1990), "On the Diffusion of Mithra Images in Sasanian Iran: New Evidence from a Seal in the British Museum," *East and West* 40, 79–98.

Cameron, A. (2001), "Remaking the Past," in: G.W. Bowersock, P. Brown and O. Grabar, eds., *Interpreting Late Antiquity: Essays on the Postclassical World* (Cambridge, Mass.: Belknap Press), 1–20.

Cameron, A. (2002a), "Apologetics in the Roman Empire: A Genre of Intolerance?" in: J.-M. Carrie and R. Lizzi, eds., *"Humana sapit": Études d'antiquité tardive offertes à Lellia Cracco Ruggini* (Bibliothèque de l'antiquité tardive 3; Turnhout: Brepols), 219–227.

Cameron, A. (2002b), "Blaming the Jews: The Seventh-Century Invasions of Palestine in Context," *Travaux et Mémoires* 14, 57–78.

Canepa, M.P. (2009), *The Two Eyes of the Earth: Art and Ritual of Kingship between Rome and Sasanian Iran* (Transformation of the Classical Heritage 45; Berkeley, Calif.: University of California Press).

Carleton Paget, J. (1997), "Anti-Judaism and Early Christian Identity," *ZAC* 1:2, 195–225.

Carter, M.L. (1974), "Royal Festal Themes in Sasanian Silverwork and Their Central Asian Parallels," in: *Commémoration Cyrus: Actes du Congrès de Shiraz 1971 et autres* études rédigées à l'occasion du 2500e anniversaire de la fondation de l'Empire perse. Vol. 1: Hommage universel (Acta Iranica 1; Leiden: E.J. Brill), 171–202.

Casartelli, L.Ch. (1888), "Two Discourses of Chosroës the Immortal-Souled. II. Chosroes Argues from the New Testament," Babylonian and Oriental Record 2:2, 33–36.

Castelli, E.A. (2004), Martyrdom and Memory: Early Christian Culture Making (Gender, Theory, and Religion; New York: Columbia University Press).

Cereti, C.G. (1996), "Again on Wahrām ī Warzāwand," in: La Persia e l'Asia centrale da Alessandro al X Secolo. Convegno internazionale, Roma, 9-12 novembre 1994 (Atti dei Convegni Lincei 127; Roma: Accademia Nazionale dei Lincei), 629–639.

Cereti, C.G. (2001), La letteratura pahlavi. Introduzione ai testi con riferimenti alla storia degli studi e alla tradizione manoscritta (Sīmorγ; Milano: Mimesis).

Cereti, C.G. (2010), "Avestan Quotations in Pahlavi Books: On Two Passages Found in Dēnkard Book VII: Dk VII,1,7 and Dk VII,3,6," Studia Iranica 39:2, 171–183.

Chadwick, H. (1979), "The Relativity of Moral Codes: Rome and Persia in Late Antiquity," in: W.R. Schoedel and R.L. Wilken, eds., Early Christian Literature and the Classical Intellectual Tradition: In Honorem Robert M. Grant (Théologie Historique 54; Paris: Beauchesne), 135–153.

Charles, R. (2009), "Hybridity and the Letter of Aristeas," Journal for the Study of Judaism 40:2, 242–259.

Chazan, R. (2010), Reassessing Jewish Life in Medieval Europe (Cambridge: Cambridge University Press).

Chediath, G. (1982), The Christology of Mar Babai the Great (Oriental Institute of Religious Studies India 49; Kottayam, Kerala: Oriental Institute of Religious Studies).

Chilton, B.D. (2007), "Mamzerut and Jesus," in: T. Holmén, ed., Jesus from Judaism to Christianity: Continuum Approaches to the Historical Jesus (Library of New Testament Studies 352; London: T&T Clark), 17–33.

Choksy, J.K. (1988), "Sacral Kingship in Sasanian Iran," Bulletin of the Asia Institute NS 2, 35–52.

Christensen, A. (1917), Les types du premier homme et du premier roi dans l'histoire legendaire des Iraniens. Ie partie: Gajōmard, Masjaγ et Masjānaγ, Hōšang et Taxmōruw (Archives d'etudes orientales 14.1; Stockholm: P.A. Norstedt & Söner).

Christensen, A. (1944), L'Iran sous les Sassanides (2nd rev. ed.; Copenhague: Ejnar Munksgaard).

Ciancaglini, C.A. (2008), Iranian Loanwords in Syriac (Beiträge zu Iranistik 28; Wiesbaden: Ludwig Reichert).

Clark, E.A. (2004), History, Theory, Text: Historians and the Linguistic Turn (Cambridge, Mass.: Harvard University Press).

Clermont-Ganneau, Ch. (1898), "La prise de Jérusalem par les Perses en 614 (J.-C.)," in: Idem, Recueil d'archéologie orientale (Paris: Ernest Leroux), vol. 2, 137–160.

Cohen, J. (1983), "The Jews as the Killers of Christ in the Latin Tradition, from Augustine to the Friars," *Traditio* 39, 1–27.

Cohen, J. (2007), *Christ Killers: The Jews and the Passion from the Bible to the Big Screen* (New York: Oxford University Press).

Cohen, S.A. (1990), *The Three Crowns: Structure of Communal Politics in Early Rabbinic Jewry* (Cambridge: Cambridge University Press).

Cohen, Sh.J.D. (1999), *The Beginnings of Jewishness: Boundaries, Varieties, Uncertainties* (Berkeley, Calif.: University of California Press).

Confino, A. (1997), "Collective Memory and Cultural History: Problems of Method," *American Historical Review* 102:5, 1386–1403.

Cook, J.G. (2000), *The Interpretation of the New Testament in Greco-Roman Paganism* (Studien und Texte zu Antike und Christentum 3; Tübingen: Mohr Siebeck).

Court, J.M. (1985), "Right and Left: The Implications for Matthew 25.31-46," *New Testament Studies* 31:2, 223–233.

Cowley, R.W. (1978), "The Identification of the Ethiopian Octateuch of Clement, and its Relationship to the Other Christian Literature," *Ostkirchliche Studien* 27:1, 37–45.

Crawford, S.W. (2008), *Rewriting Scripture in Second Temple Times* (Studies in the Dead Sea Scrolls and Related Literature; Grand Rapids, Mich.: W.B. Eerdmans).

Croke, B. (1983), "The Origins of the Christian World Chronicle," in: B. Croke and A.M. Emmett, eds., *History and Historians in Late Antiquity* (Sydney: Pergamon Press), 116–131.

Crone, P. (1991), "Kavād's Heresy and Mazdak's Revolt," *Iran* 29, 21–42.

Cumont, F. (1924), "Les unions entre proches à Doura et chez les Perses," *Comptes-rendus des séances de l'Académie des Inscriptions et Belles-Lettres* 68:1, 53–62.

Czachesz, I. (2010), "Rewriting and Textual Fluidity in Antiquity: Exploring the Socio-Cultural and Psychological Context of Earliest Christian Literacy," in: J.H.F. Dijkstra, J. Kroesen and Y. Kuiper, eds., *Myths, Martyrs, and Modernity: Studies in the History of Religions in Honour of Jan N. Bremmer* (Numen Book Series 127; Leiden: Brill), 425–441.

Dandamaeva, M.M. (1999–2000), "Этноним Χαλδαῖοι в античной традиции," *Iran and the Caucasus* 3, 315–320.

Daniélou, J. (1948), "La typologie millénariste de la semaine dans le Christianisme primitif," *VC* 2:1, 1–16.

Darling, R.A. (1987), "The 'Church from the Nations' in the Exegesis of Ephrem," in: H.J.W. Drijvers, R. Lavenant, C. Molenberg and G.J. Reinink, eds., *IV Symposium Syriacum, 1984: Literary Genres in Syriac Literature* (OCA 229; Roma: Pontificium Institutum Studiorum Orientalium), 111–122.

Daryaee, T. (2008), "Kingship in Early Sasanian Iran," in: V.S. Curtis and S.R.A. Stewart, eds., *The Sasanian Era* (The Idea of Iran 3; London: I.B. Tauris), 60–70.

Daryaee, T. (2009), *Sasanian Persia: The Rise and Fall of an Empire* (International Library of Iranian Studies 8; London: I.B. Tauris).

Daryaee, T. (2012), "Mehr-Narseh," in: E. Yarshater, ed., *Encyclopaedia Iranica*, http://www.iranicaonline.org/articles/mehr-narseh [accessed May 9, 2018].

Davies, W.D., and Allison, D.C. (1988), *A Critical and Exegetical Commentary on the Gospel according to Saint Matthew. Vol. 1: Commentary on Matthew I–VII* (The International Critical Commentary; Edinburgh: T&T Clark).

Davis, F.B. (2003), *The Jew and Deicide: The Origin of an Archetype* (Lanham, Md.: University Press of America).

de Bellefonds, P.L. (2011), "Pictorial Foundation Myths in Roman Asia Minor," in: E.S. Gruen, ed., *Cultural Identity in the Ancient Mediterranean:* (Issues & Debates; Los Angeles, Calif.: Getty Research Institute), 26–46.

de Halleux, A. (1978), "Autonomy and Centralization in the Ancient Syriac Churches: Edessa and Seleucia-Ctesiphon," in: *Wort und Wahrheit, Supplementary Issue 4* (Vienna: Herder), 59–67.

de Halleux, A. (1983), "Saint Éphrem le Syrien," *Revue Théologique de Louvain* 14, 328–355.

de Halleux, A. (1991), "L'adoration des Mages dans le Commentaire syriaque du Diatessaron," *Le Muséon* 104:3–4, 251–264.

de Jerphanion, G. (1939), "Un nouvel encensoir syrien et la série des objets similaires," in: *Mélanges syriens offerts à Monsieur René Dussaud*. 2 vols. (Bibliothèque archéologique et historique 30; Paris: Paul Geuthner), vol. 1, 297–312.

de Jong, A. (1997), *Traditions of the Magi: Zoroastrianism in Greek and Latin Literature* (Religions in the Graeco-Roman World 133; Leiden: Brill).

de Jong, A. (2004), "Sub specie maiestatis: Reflections on Sasanian Court Rituals," in: M. Stausberg, ed., *Zoroastrian Rituals in Context* (Numen Book 102; Leiden: Brill), 345–365.

de Jonge, M. and Tromp, J. (1997), *The Life of Adam and Eve and Related Literature* (Guides to the Apocrypha and Pseudepigrapha 4; Sheffield: Academic Press).

de Lagarde, P.A. (1888), "[Review of:] C. Bezold, Die Schatzhöhle aus dem syrischen Texte dreier unedirten Handschriften ins Deutsche übersetzt und mit Anmerkungen versehen. 2 vols (Leipzig: J.C. Hinrichs, 1883, 1888)," *Göttingische gelehrte Anzeigen* 22, 817–844.

de Lange, N.R.M. (1976), *Origen and the Jews: Studies in Jewish-Christian Relations in Third-Century Palestine* (University of Cambridge Oriental Publications 25; Cambridge: Cambridge University Press).

de Lange, N.R.M. (1996), "The Revival of the Hebrew Language in the Third Century CE," *Jewish Studies Quarterly* 3:4, 342–358.

de Lubac, H. (1998–2009), *Medieval Exegesis: The Four Senses of Scripture*. Trans. by M. Sebanc and E.M. Macierowski. 3 vols (Ressourcement; Grand Rapids, Mich.: W.B. Eerdmans).

de Menasce, J.-P. (1964), *Feux et fondations pieuses dans le droit sassanide* (Travaux de l'Institut d'etudes iraniennes de l'Universite de Paris 2; Paris: C. Klincksieck).

Debié, M. (2004), "Jean Malalas et la tradition chronographique de langue syriaque," in: J. Beaucamp and S. Agusta-Boularot, eds., *Recherches sur la chronique de Jean Malalas*. 2 vols. (Travaux et mémoires du Centre de recherche d'histoire et civilisation de Byzance, Monographies 15; Paris: Centre de recherche d'histoire et civilisation de Byzance), vol. 1, 147–164.

Debié, M. (2006), "L'héritage de la chronique d'Eusèbe dans l'historiographie syriaque," *Journal of the Canadian Society for Syriac Studies* 6, 18–28.

Debié, M. (2008), "Suivre l'étoile à Oxford: inédits sur la venue des Mages," in: G.A. Kiraz, ed., *Malphono w-Rabo d-Malphone: Studies in Honor of Sebastian P. Brock* (Gorgias Eastern Christian Studies 3; Piscataway, N.J.: Gorgias Press), 111–133.

Debié, M. (2009), "Syriac Historiography and Identity Formation," *CHRC* 89:1–3, 93–114.

Debié, M. (2015), *L'écriture de l'histoire en syriaque: transmissions interculturelles et constructions identitaires entre hellénisme et islam* (Late Antique History and Religion 12; Leuven: Peeters).

Deckers, J.G. (1982), "Die Huldigung der Magier in der Kunst der Spätantike," in: F.G. Zehnder, ed., *Die Heiligen Drei Könige – Darstellung und Verehrung. Katalog zur Ausstellung des Wallraf-Richartz-Museums in der Josef-Haubrich-Kunsthalle Köln, 1. Dezember 1982 bis 30. Januar 1983* (Köln: Das Wallraf-Richartz-Museum), 20–32.

Delling, G. (1967), "μάγος, μαγεία, μαγεύω," in: G. Kittel, ed., *Theological Dictionary of the New Testament* (Grand Rapids, Mich.: W.B. Eerdmans), vol. 4, 356–359.

den Biesen, K. (2006), *Simple and Bold: Ephrem's Art of Symbolic Thought* (Gorgias Dissertations 26, Early Christian Studies 6; Piscataway, N.J.: Gorgias Press).

Denis, A.M. (2000), *Introduction à la littérature religieuse judéo-hellénistique*. 2 vols. (Turnhout: Brepols).

Dentzer, J.-M. (1971), "L'iconographie iranienne du souverain couché et le motif du banquet," in: *IXeme Congrès International d'archéologie classique* (*Damas, 11-20 octobre 1969*) (Annales archéologiques arabes syriennes 21.1–2; Damas: Direction générale des antiquités et des musées), 39–50.

Déroche, V. (2012), "Forms and Functions of Anti-Jewish Polemics: Polymorphy, Polysémy," in: R. Bonfil, O. Irshai, G.G. Stroumsa and R. Talgam, eds., *Jews in Byzantium: Dialectics of Minority and Majority Cultures* (Jerusalem Studies in Religion and Culture 14; Leiden: Brill), 535–548.

Desreumaux, A. (1987), "La Doctrine d'Addaï, l'image du Christ et les monophysites," in: F. Boespflug and N. Lossky, eds., *Nicée II, 787-1987: Douze siècles d'images religieuses. Actes do colloque international Nicée II, tenu au Collège de France, Paris, les 2,3,4 octobre 1986* (Paris: Cerf), 73–79.

Desreumaux, A. (1995–1996), "The Prophetical Testimonies about Christ: An Unedited Typological Exegesis in Syriac," *The Harp* 8–9, 133–138.

Desreumaux, A. (2003), "La Couronne de Nemrod: quelques réflexions sur le pouvoir, l'histoire et l'Écriture dans la culture syriaque," in: D.H. Warren, A.G. Brock and D.W. Pao, eds., *Early Christian Voices in Texts, Traditions and Symbols. Essays in Honor of François Bovon* (Biblical Interpretation Series 66; Leiden: Brill), 189–196.

Desreumaux, A. (2009), "La figure du roi Abgar d'Édesse," in: L. Greisiger, C. Rammelt and J. Tubach, eds., *Edessa in hellenistisch-römischer Zeit: Religion, Kultur und Politik zwischen Ost und West. Beiträge des internationalen Edessa-Symposiums in Halle an der Saale, 14.-17. Juli 2005* (Beiruter Texte und Studien 116; Würzburg: Ergon Verlag), 31–45.

Devreesse, R. (1945), *Le patriarcat d'Antioche depuis la paix de l'Église jusqu'à la conquête arabe* (Études palestiniennes et orientales; Paris: V. Lecoffre).

Di Segni, R. (1985), *Il Vangelo del ghetto* (Magia e religioni 8; Roma: Newton Compton).

Dirven, L. (2004), "Religious Competition and the Decoration of Sanctuaries: The Case of Dura-Europos," *Eastern Christian Art* 1, 1–19.

Dirven, L. (2008), "Paradise Lost, Paradise Regained: The Meaning of Adam and Eve in the Baptistery of Dura-Europos," *Eastern Christian Art* 5, 43–57.

Dorival, G. (1999), "L'astre de Balaam et l'étoile des Mages," in: R. Gyselen, ed., *La science des cieux: sages, mages, astrologues* (Res Orientales 12; Bures-sur-Yvette: Groupe pour l'Étude de la Civilisation du Moyen-Orient), 93–111.

Draguet, R. (1924), *Julien d'Halicarnasse et sa controverse avec Sévère d'Antioche sur l'incorruptibilité du corps du Christ. Études d'histoire littéraire et doctrinale, suivie des fragments dogmatiques de Julien* (Louvain: P. Smeesters).

Draguet, R. (1977), "Une méthode d'édition des textes syriaques," in: R.H. Fischer, ed., *A Tribute to Arthur Vööbus: Studies in Early Christian Literature and Its Environment, Primarily in the Syrian East* (Chicago, Ill.: The Lutheran School of Theology at Chicago), 13–18.

Draper, J.A. (2004), ed., *Orality, Literacy, and Colonialism in Antiquity* (SBL Symposium 47; Atlanta, Georgia: Society of Biblical Literature).

Drège, J.-P., and Grenet, F. (1987), "Un temple de l'Oxus près de Takht-i Sangin, d'après un témoignage chinois du VIIIe siècle," *Studia Iranica* 16:1, 117–121.

Drijvers, H.J.W. (1980), *Cults and Beliefs at Edessa* (Études préliminaires aux religions orientales dans l'Empire Romain 82; Leiden: E.J. Brill).

Drijvers, H.J.W. (1982), "The Persistence of Pagan Cults and Practices in Christian Syria," in: N.G. Garsoïan, Th.F. Mathews and R.W. Thomson, eds., *East of Byzantium: Syria and Armenia in the Formative Period. Dumbarton Oaks Symposium, 1980* (Washington, D.C.: Dumbarton Oaks), 35–44.

Drijvers, H.J.W. (1985), "Jews and Christians at Edessa," *JJS* 36:1, 88–102.

Drijvers, H.J.W. (1987), "Abgarsage," in: W. Schneemelcher, ed., *Neutestamentliche Apokryphen in deutscher Übersetzung. Band 1: Evangelien* (Tübingen: Mohr Siebeck), 389–395.

Drijvers, H.J.W. (1992), "Syrian Christianity and Judaism," in: J.M. Lieu, J. North and T. Rajak, eds., *The Jews among Pagans and Christians in the Roman Empire* (London: Routledge), 124–146.

Drijvers, H.J.W. (1994), "The Syriac Romance of Julian: Its Function, Place of Origin and Original Language," in: R. Lavenant, ed., *VI Symposium Syriacum, 1992: University of Cambridge, Faculty of Divinity, 30 August-2 September 1992* (OCA 247; Roma: Pontificio Istituto Orientale), 201–214.

Droge, A.J. (1989), *Homer or Moses? Early Christian Interpretations of the History of Culture* (Hermeneutische Untersuchungen zur Theologie 26; Tübingen: Mohr-Siebeck).

Dunn, G.D. (1998), "Tertullian and Rebekah: A Re-Reading of an "Anti-Jewish" Argument in Early Christian Literature," VC 52:2, 119–145.

Dunn, G.D. (2002), "Tertullian and Daniel 9:24–27. A Patristic Interpretation of a Prophetic Time-Frame," ZAC 6:2, 352–367.

Dunn, G.D. (2003), "*Probabimus venisse eum iam*: The Fulfilment of Daniel's Prophetic Time-Frame in Tertullian's *Adversus Iudaeos*," ZAC 7:1, 140–155.

Duval, R. (1907), *La littérature syriaque* (Bibliothèque de l'enseignement de l'histoire ecclésiastique. Anciennes littératures chrétiennes 2; 3rd ed.; Paris: V. Lecoffre).

Edwards, M.J., Goodman, M., and Price, S. (1999), eds., *Apologetics in the Roman Empire: Pagans, Jews, and Christians* (Oxford: Oxford University Press).

Edwards, R.B. (1979), *Kadmos the Phoenician: A Study in Greek Legends and the Mycenaean Age* (Amsterdam: Adolf M. Hakkert).

Ehrlich, R. (1930), "The Celebration and Gifts of the Persian New Year (Nawruz) according to an Arabic Source," in: *Dr. Modi Memorial Volume: Papers on Indo-Iranian and Other Subjects, Written by Several Scholars in Honour of Shams-ul-Ulama Dr. Jivanji Jamshedji Modi* (Bombay: Fort Printing Press), 95–101.

Eldridge, M.D. (2001), *Dying Adam with His Multiethnic Family: Understanding the Greek Life of Adam and Eve* (Studia in Veteris Testamenti Pseudepigrapha 16; Leiden: Brill).

Élissagaray, M. (1965), *La légende des Rois Mages* (Paris: Éditions du Seuil).

Elsner, J. (2001), "Cultural Resistance and the Visual Image: The Case of Dura Europos," *Classical Philology* 96:3, 269–304.

Elukin, J.M. (2007), *Living Together, Living Apart: Rethinking Jewish-Christian Relations in the Middle Ages* (Jews, Chrisitans, and Muslims from the Ancient to the Modern World; Princeton, N.J.: Princeton University Press).

Engberding, H. (1937), "Die Kirche als Braut in der ostsyrischen Liturgie," OCP 3, 5–44.

Erll, A. (2011), *Memory in Culture*. Trans. by S.B. Young (Palgrave Macmillan Memory Studies; New York: Palgrave Macmillan).

Eshel, E. and Stone, M.E. (1993), "The Holy Language at the End of Days in Light of a New Fragment Found at Qumran," *Tarbiz* 62:2, 169–177 [in Hebrew].

Eskhult, J. (2014), "The Primeval Language and Hebrew Ethnicity in Ancient Jewish and Christian Thought until Augustine," *Revue d'études augustiniennes et patristiques* 60:2, 291–347.

Falk, D.K. (2007), *The Parabiblical Texts: Strategies for Extending the Scriptures in the Dead Sea Scrolls* (Library of Second Temple Studies 63, Companion to the Qumran Scrolls 8; London: T&T Clark).

Feldman, L.H. (1996), *Studies in Hellenistic Judaism* (Arbeiten zur Geschichte des antiken Judentums und des Urchristentums 30; Leiden: E.J. Brill).

Feldman, L.H. (1998), *Josephus's Interpretation of the Bible* (Hellenistic Culture and Society 27; Berkeley, Calif.: University of California Press).

Fiey, J.-M. (1960), "Jean de Dailam et l'imbroglio de ses fondations," *Proche-Orient Chrétien* 10, 195–211.

Fiey, J.-M. (1965), "'Assyriens" ou Araméens?,' *L'Orient Syrien* 10, 141–160.

Fiey, J.-M. (1970), *Jalons pour une histoire de l'Église en Iraq* (CSCO 310, Subs. 36; Louvain: Secrétariat du CorpusSCO).

Fiey, J.-M. (1974–1978), "Les diocèses du "Maphrianat" syrien, 629-1860," *PdO* 5, 133–164, 331–393; 8, 347–378.

Fiey, J.-M. (1988), "Juifs et Chrétiens dans l'Orient syriaque," *Hispania Sacra* 40:2, 933–953.

Fisher, G. (2011), *Between Empires: Arabs, Romans, and Sasanians in Late Antiquity* (Oxford Classical Monographs; Oxford: Oxford University Press).

Forshall, J., and Rosen, F. (1838), *Catalogus codicum manuscriptorum orientalium qui in Museo Britannico asservantur. Pars prima: codices syriacos et carshunicos amplectens* (London: Curatores Musei Britannici).

Fowden, E.K. (1999), *The Barbarian Plain: Saint Sergius between Rome and Iran* (Transformation of Classical Heritage 28; Berkeley, Calif.: University of California Press).

Fowden, E.K. (2015), "Rural Converters among the Arabs," in: A. Papaconstantinou, N.B. McLynn and D.L. Schwartz, eds., *Conversion in Late Antiquity: Christianity, Islam, and Beyond. Papers from the Andrew W. Mellon Foundation Sawyer Seminar, University of Oxford, 2009-2010* (Farnham: Ashgate), 175–196.

Fowden, G. (1993), *Empire to Commonwealth: Consequences of Monotheism in Late Antiquity* (Princeton, N.J.: Princeton University Press).

Frandsen, P.J. (2009), *Incestuous and Close-Kin Marriage in Ancient Egypt and Persia: An Examination of the Evidence* (CNI Publications 34; Copenhagen: Museum Tusculanum Press).

Franklin, A.E. (2013), *This Noble House: Jewish Descendants of King David in the Medieval Islamic East* (Jewish Culture and Contexts; Philadelphia: University of Pennsylvania Press).

Fredriksen, P. (1995), "Excaecati Occulta Justitia Dei: Augustine on Jews and Judaism," *JECS* 3:3, 299–324.

Frend, W.H.C. (1972), *The Rise of the Monophysite Movement: Chapters in the History of the Church in the Fifth and Sixth Centuries* (Cambridge: Cambridge University Press).

Frendo, D. (1997), "The Religious Factor in Byzantine-Iranian Relations," *Bulletin of the Asia Institute* NS 11, 105–122.

Frendo, D. (2008 [2012]), "Religious Minorities and Religious Dissent in the Byzantine and Sasanian Empires (590-641): Sources for the Historical Background," *Bulletin of the Asia Institute* NS 22, 223–237.

Fried, L.S. (2002), "Cyrus the Messiah? The Historical Background to Isaiah 45:1," *HTR* 95:4, 373–393.

Frishman, J. (1987), "Narsai's Homily for the Palm Festival—Against the Jews: For the Palm Festival or against the Jews?," in: H.J.W. Drijvers, R. Lavenant, C. Molenberg and G.J. Reinink, eds., *IV Symposium Syriacum, 1984: Literary Genres in Syriac Literature (Groningen—Oosterhesselen 10-12 September)* (OCA 229; Rome: Pontificium Institutum Studiorum Orientalium), 217–229.

Frye, R.N. (1983), "The Political History of Iran under the Sasanians," in: E. Yarshater, ed., *The Cambridge History of Iran. Vol. 3(1): The Seleucid, Parthian and Sasanian Periods* (Cambridge: Cambridge University Press), 116–180.

Frye, R.N. (1985), "Zoroastrian Incest," in: G. Gnoli and L. Lanciotti, eds., *Orientalia Iosephi Tucci memoriae dicata*. 3 vols. (Serie Orientale Roma 56; Roma: Istituto italiano per il Medio ed Estremo Oriente), vol. 1, 445–455.

Frye, R.N. (1992), "Assyria and Syria: Synonyms," *Journal of Near Eastern Studies* 51:4, 281–285.

Fukai, S. (1974), "The Brand Found on the Persian Silver Horse Statue of the Sasanian Period," *Orient* 10, 79–88.

Funkenstein, A. (1993), *Perceptions of Jewish History* (Berkeley, Calif.: University of California Press).

Furlani, G. (1917), "Due trattati palmomantici in siriaco," *Rendiconti della Reale Accademia Nazionale dei Lincei. Classe di scienze morali, storiche e filologiche* v.26, 719–732.

Gafni, I.M. (1990a), *The Jews of Babylonia in the Talmudic Era: A Social and Cultural History* (Jerusalem: Zalman Shazar Center) [in Hebrew].

Gafni, I.M. (1990b), "Expressions and Types of 'Local Patriotism' among the Jews of Sasanian Babylonia," *Irano-Judaica* 2, 63–71.

Gafni, I.M. (2009), "How Babylonia Became "Zion": Shifting Identities in Late Antiquity," in: L.I. Levine and D.R. Schwartz, eds., *Jewish Identities in Antiquity: Studies in Memory of Menahem Stern* (TSAJ 130; Tübingen: Mohr Siebeck), 333–348.

Gager, J.G. (1985), *The Origins of Anti-Semitism: Attitudes toward Judaism in Pagan and Christian Antiquity* (New York: Oxford University Press).

Gajda, I. (2002), "Les débuts du monothéisme en Arabie du Sud," *Journal asiatique* 290:2, 643–650.

Gajda, I. (2010), "Quel monothéisme en Arabie du Sud ancienne?," in: J. Beaucamp, F. Briquel-Chatonnet and C.J. Robin, eds., *Juifs et Chrétiens en Arabie aux Ve et VIe* siècles. *Regards croisés sur les sources* (Centre de Recherche d'Histoire et Civilisation de Byzance, Monographies 32; Le massacre de Najrân 2; Paris: Association des amis du Centre d'histoire et civilisation de Byzance), 107–120.

Garrison, M. (1999), "Fire Altars," in: E. Yarshater, ed., *Encyclopaedia Iranica* (New York: Bibliotheca Persica Press), vol. 9, 613–619.

Garsoïan, N.G. (1976), "Prolegomena to a Study of the Iranian Elements in Arsacid Armenia," *Handes Amsorya* 90, 177–234.

Garsoïan, N.G. (2004), "Frontier–Frontiers? Transcaucasia and Eastern Anatolia in the Pre-Islamic Period," in: *La Persia e Bisanzio. Atti del Convegno internazionale (Roma, 14-18 ottobre 2002)* (Atti dei Convegni Lincei 201; Roma: Accademia Nazionale dei Lincei), 327–352.

Geary, P.J. (1994), *Living with the Dead in the Middle Ages* (Ithaca, N.Y.: Cornell University Press).

Georgia, A.T. (2018), "The Monster at the End of His Book: Monstrosity as Theological Strategy and Cultural Critique in Tatian's *Against the Greeks*," *JECS* 26:2, 191–219.

Gera, D.L. (2003), *Ancient Greek Ideas on Speech, Language, and Civilization* (Oxford: Oxford University Press).

Gerö, S. (1980), "The Legend of the Fourth Son of Noah," *HTR* 73:1–2, 321–330.

Gerö, S. (1981), *Barṣauma of Nisibis and Persian Christianity in the Fifth Century* (CSCO 426, Subs. 63; Louvain: Peeters).

Ghirshman, R., "Notes iraniennes, V: Scènes de banquet sur l'argenterie sassanide," *Artibus Asiae* 16:1–2 (1953), 51–76.

Ghirshman, R. (1962), *Persian Art: The Parthian and Sassanian Dynasties, 249 B.C.–A.D. 651*. Trans. by S. Gilbert and J. Emmons (Arts of Mankind; New York: Golden Press).

Gignoux, Ph. (1984), "Titres et fonctions religieuses sasanides d'après les sources syriaques hagiographiques," in: J. Harmatta, ed., *From Hecataeus to al-Ḥuwārizmī: Bactrian, Pahlavi, Sogdian, Persian, Sanskrit, Syriac, Arabic, Chinese, Greek, and Latin Sources for the History of Pre-Islamic Central Asia* (Acta Antiqua Academiae Scientiarum Hungaricae 28, Collection of the Sources for the History of Pre-Islamic Central Asia I.3; Budapest: Akadémiai Kiadó), 191–203.

Gignoux, Ph. (1986), *Noms propres sassanides en moyen-perse épigraphique* (Iranisches Personennamenbuch, Band II. Mitteliranische Pesonennamen, Fasc. 2; Wien: Verlag der Österreichischen Akademie der Wissenschaften).

Gignoux, Ph. (1998), "Sāsān ou le dieu protecteur," in: N. Sims-Williams, ed., *Proceedings of the Third European Conference of Iranian Studies, Held in Cambridge, 11th to 15th September 1995. Part 1: Old and Middle Iranian Studies* (Beiträge zur Iranistik 17.1; Wiesbaden: Ludwig Reichert), 1–7.

Gignoux, Ph. (2003), *Noms propres sassanides en moyen-perse épigraphique. Supplément [1986-2001]* (Iranisches Personennamenbuch, Band II. Mitteliranische

Pesonennamen, Fasc. 3; Wien: Verlag der Österreichischen Akademie der Wissenschaften).

Gignoux, Ph. (2008), "Comment le polémiste mazdéen du Škand Gumānīg Vīzār a-t-il utilisé les citations du Nouveau Testament?," in: Ch. Jullien, ed., *Controverses des chrétiens dans l'Iran sassanide* (Cahiers de Studia Iranica 36, Chrétiens en terre d'Iran 2; Paris: Association pour l'avancement des études iraniennes), 59–67.

Gignoux, Ph., Jullien, Ch., and Jullien, F. (2009), *Iranisches Personennamenbuch. Band VII: Iranische Namen in semitischen Nebenüberlieferungen. Fasc. 5: Noms propres syriaques d'origine iranienne* (Sitzungsberichte der Österreichische Akademie der Wissenschaften, Philosophisch-Historische Klasse 789, Iranische Onomastik 5; Wien: Verlag der Österreichischen Akademie der Wissenschaften).

Gnoli, G. (1989), *The Idea of Iran: An Essay on its Origin* (Serie Orientale Roma 62; Roma: Istituto italiano per il Medio ed Estremo Oriente).

Gnoli, G. (1999), "Farr(ah)," in: E. Yarshater, ed., *Encyclopaedia Iranica* (New York: Bibliotheca Persica Press), vol. 9, 312–319.

Goldziher, I. (1884), "Renseignements de source musulmane sur la dignité de Resch-Galuta," *Revue des études juives* 8, 121–125.

Goodblatt, D.M. (1994), *Monarchic Principle: Studies in Jewish Self-Government in Antiquity* (Texte und Studien zum antiken Judentum 38; Tübingen: Mohr Siebeck).

Goodblatt, D.M. (2006), *Elements of Ancient Jewish Nationalism* (Cambridge: Cambridge University Press).

Goodenough, E.R. (1953–1968), *Jewish Symbols in the Greco-Roman Period*. 13 vols (Bollingen Series 37; New York: Pantheon Books).

Gottheil, R.J.H. (1894), "References to Zoroaster in Syriac and Arabic Literature," in: *Classical Studies in Honour of Henry Drisler* (New York: Macmillan and Co.), 24–51.

Götze, A. (1922), *Die Schatzhöhle: Überlieferung und Quellen* (Sitzungsberichte der Heidelberger Akademie der Wissenschaften, Philosophisch-historische Klasse 4; Heidelberg: Carl Winter's Universitätsbuchhandlung).

Götze, A. (1923–1924), "Die Nachwirkung der Schatzhöhle," *Zeitschrift für Semitistik* 2, 51–94; 3, 53–71, 153–177.

Graf, D.F., and Fahd, T. (1993), "Nabaṭ," in: C.E. Bosworth et alii, eds., *The Encyclopaedia of Islam: New Edition* (Leiden: E.J. Brill), vol. 7, 834–838.

Graf, G. (1944–1953), *Geschichte der christlichen arabischen Literatur*. 5 vols (Studi e Testi 118, 133, 146, 147, 172; Città del Vaticano: Biblioteca Apostolica Vaticana).

Graffin, F. (1958), "Recherches sur le thème de l'Église-Épouse dans les liturgies et la littérature patristique de langue syriaque," *L'Orient Syrien* 3, 317–336.

Gray, L.H. (1913–1914), "Zoroastrian and Other Ethnic Religious Material in the Acta Sanctorum," *Journal of the Manchester Egyptian and Oriental Society*, 37–55.

Gray, P.T.R. (1988), "Forgery as an Instrument of Progress: Reconstructing the Theological Tradition in the Sixth Century," *Byzantinische Zeitschrift* 81, 284–289.

Greatrex, G. (1998), *Rome and Persia at War, 502-532* (ARCA, Classical and Medieval Texts, Papers and Monographs 37; Leeds: Francis Cairns).

Greatrex, G. (2003), "Khusro II and the Christians of His Empire," *Journal of the Canadian Society for Syriac Studies* 3, 78–88.

Green, R.P.H. (2006), *Latin Epics of the New Testament: Juvencus, Sedulius, Arator* (Oxford: Oxford University Press).

Green, T.M. (1992), *The City of the Moon God: Religious Traditions of Harran* (Religions in the Graeco-Roman World 114; Leiden: E.J. Brill).

Gregerman, A. (2007), *"Have You Despised Jerusalem and Zion after You Had Chosen Them?": The Destruction of Jerusalem and the Temple in Jewish and Christian Writings from the Land of Israel in Late Antiquity* (Ph.D. dissertation; Columbia University).

Grenet, F. (2007), "Religious Diversity among Sogdian Merchants in Sixth-Century China: Zoroastrianism, Buddhism, Manichaeism, and Hinduism," *Comparative Studies of South Asia, Africa and the Middle East* 27:2, 463–478.

Griffith, S.H. (1989–1990), "Images of Ephraem: The Syrian Holy Man and His Church," *Traditio* 45, 7–33.

Grillmeier, A., and Hainthaler, Th. (1995), *Christ in Christian Tradition. Vol. 2: From the Council of Chalcedon (451) to Gregory the Great (590-604). Part 2: The Church of Constantinople in the Sixth Century*. Trans. by J. Cawte and P. Allen (London: A.R. Mowbray & Co.).

Grosby, S. (1996), "The Category of the Primordial in the Study of Early Christianity and Second-Century Judaism," *History of Religions* 36:2, 140–163.

Grosby, S. (2002), *Biblical Ideas of Nationality: Ancient and Modern* (Winona Lake, Ind.: Eisenbrauns).

Gross, S.M. (2017), *Empire and Neighbors: Babylonian Jewish Identity in its Local and Imperial Context* (Ph.D. dissertation; Yale University).

Gruen, E.S. (2011), *Rethinking the Other in Antiquity* (Martin Classical Lectures; Princeton, N.J.: Princeton University Press).

Grundmann, W. (1964), "δεξιός," in: G. Kittel and G. Friedrich, eds., *Theological Dictionary of the New Testament* (Grand Rapids: W.B. Eerdmans), vol. 2, 37–40.

Grypeou, E. (2013), "Kitāb al-majāll," in: D.R. Thomas and A. Mallett, eds., *Christian-Muslim Relations: A Bibliographical History. Volume 5 (1350–1500)* (History of Christian-Muslim Relations 20; Leiden: Brill), 634–639.

Gurtner, D.M. (2006), *The Torn Veil: Matthew's Exposition of the Death of Jesus* (Society for New Testament Studies, Monograph Series 139; Cambridge: Cambridge University Press).

Gyselen, R. (2003), "Les grands Feux de l'empire sassanide: quelques témoignages sigillographiques," in: C.G. Cereti, M. Maggi and E. Provasi, eds., *Religious Themes and Texts of Pre-Islamic Iran and Central Asia: Studies in Honour of Professor Gherardo*

Gnoli on the Occasion of his 65th Birthday on 6th December 2002 (Beiträge zur Iranistik 24; Wiesbaden: L. Reichert), 131–138.

Gyselen, R. (2004), "New Evidence for Sasanian Numismatics: The Collection of Ahmad Saeedi," in: R. Gyselen, ed., Contributions à l'histoire et la géographie historique de l'empire sassanide (Res Orientales 16; Bures-sur-Yvette: Groupe pour l'Étude de la Civilisation du Moyen-Orient), 49–140.

Gyselen, R. (2007), Sasanian Seals and Sealings in the A. Saeedi Collection (Acta Iranica 44; Louvain: Peeters).

Gyselen, R. (2008), Great-Commander (vuzurg-framadār) and Court Counsellor (dar-andarzbed) in the Sasanian Empire (224-651): The Sigillographic Evidence (Conferenze dell'Unione internazionale degli istituti di archeologia, storia e storia dell'arte in Roma 19; Roma: Istituto Italiano per l'Africa e l'Oriente).

Hachlili, R. (1998), Ancient Jewish Art and Archaeology in the Diaspora (Handbuch der Orientalistik, Abt. 1: Der Nahe und der Mittlere Osten 35; Leiden: Brill).

Haelewyck, J.-C. (2011), "Le nombre des Rois Mages. Les hésitations de la tradition syriaque," in: J.-M. Vercruysse, ed., Les (Rois) Mages (Graphè 20; Arras: Artois Presses Université), 25–37.

Hahn, I. (1988), "Nimrod der Perser," in: R. Dán, ed., Occident and Orient: A Tribute to the Memory of Alexander Scheiber (Budapest: Akadémiai Kiadó), 213–227.

Hakola, R. (2006), Identity Matters: John, the Jews and Jewishness (Supplements to Novum Testamentum 118; Leiden: Brill).

Halbwachs, M. (1925), Les cadres sociaux de la mémoire (Paris: F. Alcan).

Halbwachs, M. (1941), La topographie légendaire des Évangiles en Terre Sainte. Étude de mémoire collective (Paris: Presses universitaires de France).

Hall, J.M. (1997), Ethnic Identity in Greek Antiquity (Cambridge: Cambridge University Press).

Hämeen-Anttila, J. (2018), Khwadāynāmag: The Middle Persian Book of Kings (Studies in Persian Cultural History 14; Leiden: Brill).

Harper, P.O. (1979), "Thrones and Enthronement Scenes in Sasanian Art," Iran 17, 49–64.

Harrak, A. (2001), "Tales about Sennacherib: The Contribution of the Syriac Sources," in: P.M.M. Daviau, J.W. Wevers and M. Weigl, eds., The World of the Aramaeans III: Studies in Language and Literature in Honour of Paul-Eugène Dion (Journal for the Study of the Old Testament, Supplement Series 326; Sheffield: Sheffield Academic Press), 168–189.

Harrak, A. (2005), "Ah! The Assyrian is the Rod of My Hand!: Syriac View of History after the Advent of Islam," in: J.J. van Ginkel, H.L. Murre-van den Berg and T.M. van Lint, eds., Redefining Christian Identity: Cultural Interaction in the Middle East since the Rise of Islam (OLA 134; Leuven: Peeters), 45–65.

Harrak, A. (2006), "The Incense Burner of Takrit: An Iconographical Analysis," Eastern Christian Art 3, 47–52.

Harrak, A. (2011), *Catalogue of Syriac and Garshuni Manuscripts: Manuscripts Owned by the Iraqi Department of Antiquities and Heritage* (CSCO 639, Subs. 126; Leuven: Peeters).

Hartman, L.F., and Di Lella, A.A. (1978), *The Book of Daniel* (The Anchor Bible 23; Garden City, N.Y.: Doubleday).

Hayman, A.P. (1985), "The Image of the Jew in the Syriac Anti-Jewish Polemical Literature," in: J. Neusner and E.S. Frerichs, eds., *"To See Ourselves as Others See Us": Christians, Jews, "Others" in Late Antiquity* (Scholars Press Studies in the Humanities; Chico, Calif.: Scholars Press), 423–441.

Hayward, Ch.T.R. (1992), "Inconsistencies and Contradictions in Targum Pseudo-Jonathan: The Case of Eliezer and Nimrod," *JSS* 37:1, 31–55.

Hegedus, T.M.J. (2007), *Early Christianity and Ancient Astrology* (Patristic Studies 6; New York: Peter Lang).

Heidland, H.W. (1968), "ὄξος," in: G. Kittel and G. Friedrich, eds., *Theological Dictionary of the New Testament* (Grand Rapids, Mich.: W.B. Eerdmans), vol. 5, 288–289.

Heller, B. (1993), "Namrūd," in: C.E. Bosworth, E. van Donzel, W.P. Heinrichs and G. Legomte, eds., *The Encyclopaedia of Islam: New Edition* (Leiden: E.J. Brill), vol. 7, 952–953.

Hemmerdinger-Iliadou, D., and Kirchmeyer, J. (1960), "Éphrem (les versions)," in: *Dictionnaire de spiritualité ascétique et mystique: doctrine et histoire* (Paris: Beauchesne), vol. 4, 800–822.

Henning, W.B. (1945), "The Manichæan Fasts," *Journal of the Royal Asiatic Society* 2, 146–164.

Herman, G. (2008), "The Story of Rav Kahana (BT Baba Qamma 117a-b) in Light of Armeno-Persian Sources," in: Sh. Shaked and A. Netzer, eds., *Irano-Judaica VI* (Jerusalem: Yad Izhak Ben Zvi), 53–86.

Herman, G. (2012), *A Prince without a Kingdom: The Exilarch in the Sasanian Era* (TSAJ 150; Tübingen: Mohr Siebeck).

Herman, G. (2014), "The Last Years of Yazdgird I and the Christians," in: G. Herman, ed., *Jews, Christians and Zoroastrians: Religious Dynamics in a Sasanian Context* (Judaism in Context 17; Piscataway, N.J.: Gorgias Press), 77–100.

Herman, G. (2019), "The Syriac World in the Persian Empire," in: D. King, ed., *The Syriac World* (Routledge Worlds; London: Routledge), 134–145.

Herring, E. (2009), "Ethnicity and Culture," in: A. Erskine, ed., *A Companion to Ancient History* (Blackwell Companions to the Ancient World: Ancient History; Malden, MA: Wiley-Blackwell), 123–133.

Hidal, S. (2007), "Evidence for Jewish Believers in the Syriac Fathers," in: O. Skarsaune and R. Hvalvik, eds., *Jewish Believers in Jesus: The Early Centuries* (Peabody, Mass.: Hendrickson Publishers), 568–580.

Hilhorst, A. (2007), "The Prestige of Hebrew in the Christian World of Late Antiquity and Middle Ages," in: A. Hilhorst, É. Puech and E.J.C. Tigchelaar, eds., *Flores Florentino: Dead Sea Scrolls and Other Early Jewish Studies in Honour of Florentino García Martínez* (Supplements to the Journal for the Study of Judaism 122; Leiden: Brill), 777–802.

Hjerrild, B. (2003), *Studies in Zoroastrian Family Law: A Comparative Analysis* (CNI Publications 28; Copenhagen: Museum Tusculanum Press).

Hodge, C.E.J. (2007), *If Sons, Then Heirs: A Study of Kinship and Ethnicity in the Letters of Paul* (Oxford: Oxford University Press).

Hom, M.K.Y.H. (2010), ""… A Mighty Hunter before YHWH": Genesis 10:9 and the Moral-Theological Evaluation of Nimrod," *VT* 60:1, 63–68.

Hopfner, Th. (1949), "Palmoskopia," in: W. Kroll and K. Mittelhaus, eds., *Paulys Real-Encyclopädie der classischen Altertumswissenschaft: neue Bearbeitung begonnen von Georg Wissowa* (Stuttgart: Alfred Druckenmüller), vol. 18.3 [36.2], 259–262.

Horbury, W. (1971), *A Critical Examination of the Toledoth Jeshu* (Ph.D. dissertation; University of Cambridge).

Horn, C.B. (2006–2007), "Anti-Jewish Polemic and Conversion of Jews to Anti-Chalcedonian Asceticism in the Holy Land: The Case of Eugenia of Tyre," *ARAM* 18–19, 33–48.

Horowitz, E.S. (1998), ""The Vengeance of the Jews Was Stronger than Their Avarice": Modern Historians and the Persian Conquest of Jerusalem in 614," *Jewish Social Studies* NS 4:2, 1–39.

Horsley, R.A. (2004), ed., *Hidden Transcripts and the Arts of Resistance: Applying the Work of James C. Scott to Jesus and Paul* (SBL Semeia Studies 48; Leiden: Brill).

Hruby, K. (1971), *Juden und Judentum bei den Kirchenvätern* (Schriften zur Judentumskunde 2; Zürich: Theologischer Verlag).

Hübner, W. (1989), *Die Begriffe "Astrologie" und "Astronomie" in der Antike. Wortgeschichte und Wissenschaftssystematik, mit einer Hypothese zum Terminus "Quadrivium"* (Abhandlungen der Akademie der Wissenschaften und der Literatur, Mainz, geistes- und sozialwissenschaftliche Klasse 7; Mainz: Akademie der Wissenschaften und der Literatur).

Huizinga, J. (1936), "A Definition of the Concept of History," in: R. Klibansky and H.J. Paton, eds., *Philosophy and History: Essays Presented to Ernst Cassirer* (Oxford: Clarendon Press), 1–10.

Hultgård, A. (1977–1981), *L'eschatologie des Testaments des douze patriarches*. 2 vols (Acta Universitatis Upsaliensis, Historia Religionum 6–7; Uppsala: Almqvist and Wiksell).

Hultgård, A. (1998), "The Magi and the Star—the Persian Background in Texts and Iconography," in: P. Schalk and M. Stausberg, eds., *"Being Religious and Living through the Eyes": Studies in Religious Iconography and Iconology* (Acta Universitatis Upsaliensis, Historia Religionum 14; Uppsala: Uppsala University Library), 215–225.

Humbach, H. (1967), "Ātur Gušnasp und Takht-i Suleimān," in: G. Wiessner, ed., *Festschrift für Wilhelm Eilers. Ein Dokument der internationalen Forschung zum 27. September 1966* (Wiesbaden: Otto Harrassowitz), 189–190.

Hunger, H., and Pingree, D.E. (1999), *Astral Sciences in Mesopotamia* (Handbuch der Orientalistik, Erste Abteilung: Der Nahe und der Mittlere Osten 44; Leiden: Brill).

Hutter, M. (1998), "Shirin, Nestorianer und Monophysiten. Königliche Kirchenpolitik in späten Sasanidenreich," in: R. Lavenant, ed., *Symposium Syriacum VII: Uppsala University, Department of Asian and African Languages, 11-14 August 1996* (OCA 256; Roma: Pontificio Istituto Orientale), 373–386.

Hutter, M. (2003), "Mār Abā and the Impact of Zoroastrianism on Christianity in the 6th Century," in: C.G. Cereti, M. Maggi and E. Provasi, eds., *Religious Themes and Texts of Pre-Islamic Iran and Central Asia: Studies in Honour of Professor Gherardo Gnoli on the Occasion of his 65th Birthday on 6th December 2002* (Beiträge zur Iranistik 24; Wiesbaden: Ludwig Reichert), 167–173.

Idel, M. (1992), "Reification of Language in Jewish Mysticism," in: S.T. Katz, ed., *Mysticism and Language* (New York: Oxford University Press), 42–79.

Ilan, T. (2011), *Lexicon of Jewish Names in Late Antiquity. Part 4: The Eastern Diaspora 330 BCE–650 CE* (TSAJ 141; Tübingen: Mohr Siebeck).

Immerzeel, M. (2009), *Identity Puzzles: Medieval Christian Art in Syria and Lebanon* (OLA 184; Louvain: Peeters).

Inostrantsev, K.A. (1907), "Матеріалы изъ арабскихъ источниковъ для культурной исторіи Сасанидской Персіи. Примѣты и повѣрья," *Записки Восточнаго Отдѣленія Императорскаго Русскаго Археологическаго Общества* 18, 113–232.

Iricinschi, E. (2011), "Good Hebrew, Bad Hebrew: Christians as *Triton Genos* in Eusebius' Apologetic Writings," in: S. Inowlocki and C. Zamagni, eds., *Reconsidering Eusebius: Collected Papers on Literary, Historical, and Theological Issues* (Supplements to Vigiliae Christianae 107; Leiden: Brill), 69–86.

Isaac, B.H. (2004), *The Invention of Racism in Classical Antiquity* (Princeton, N.J.: Princeton University Press).

Istrin, V.M. (1898), *Замечанія о составе Толковой Палеи, I–VI* (Сборникъ Отдѣленія Русскаго Языка и Словесности Императорской Академіи Наукъ 65.6; С.-Петербургъ: Типографія Императорской Академіи Наукъ).

Jackson, A.V.W. (1899), *Zoroaster: The Prophet of Ancient Iran* (London: Macmillan and Co.).

Jacobs, A.S. (2004), *Remains of the Jews: The Holy Land and Christian Empire in Late Antiquity* (Divinations: Rereading Late Ancient Religion; Stanford, Calif.: Stanford University Press).

Jacobs, A.S. (2008), "Jews and Christians," in: S.A. Harvey and D.G. Hunter, eds., *The Oxford Handbook of Early Christian Studies* (Oxford: Oxford University Press), 169–185.

Jeffreys, E.M. (2003), "The Beginning of Byzantine Chronography: John Malalas," in: G. Marasco, ed., *Greek and Roman Historiography in Late Antiquity: Fourth to Sixth Century A.D.* (Leiden: Brill), 497–527.

Jenkins, R. (2008), *Social Identity* (Key Ideas; 3rd ed.; London: Routledge).

Jeremias, J. (2002), *Golgotha* (2nd ed.; Allendorf an der Eder: Antigone-Verlag).

Johnson, A.P. (2006), *Ethnicity and Argument in Eusebius' Praeparatio Evangelica* (Oxford Early Christian Studies; Oxford: Oxford University Press).

Johnson, M.D. (1969), *The Purpose of the Biblical Genealogies* (Society for New Testament Studies, Monograph Series 8; Cambridge: Cambridge University Press).

Jones, F.S. (1997), "The Astrological Trajectory in Ancient Syriac-Speaking Christianity (Elchasai, Bardaisan, and Mani)," in: L. Cirillo and A. van Tongerloo, eds., *Atti del Terzo Congresso Internazionale di Studi "Manicheismo e Oriente Cristiano Antico". Arcavacata di Rende—Amantea, 31 agosto–5 settembre 1993* (Manichaean Studies 3; Louvain: Brepols), 183–200.

Jones, S. and Pearce, S. (1998), eds., *Jewish Local Patriotism and Self-Identification in the Graeco-Roman Period* (Journal for the Study of the Pseudepigrapha, Supplement Series 31; Sheffield: Sheffield Academic Press).

Jordan, W.C. (1987), "The Last Tormentor of Christ: An Image of the Jew in Ancient and Medieval Exegesis, Art, and Drama," *Jewish Quarterly Review* NS 78:1–2, 21–47.

Jossa, G. (2006), *Jews or Christians? The Followers of Jesus in Search of Their Own Identity.* Trans. by M. Rogers (WUNT 202; Tübingen: Mohr Siebeck).

Jullien, Ch. (2009), "Christianiser le pouvoir: images de rois sassanides dans la tradition syro-orientale," *OCP* 75:1, 119–131.

Jullien, Ch. (2011), "Dans le royaume de Nemrod. Autour d'interprétations de Gn 10, 10–12," in: M. Loubet and D. Pralon, eds., *Eukarpa / Εὔκαρπα. Études sur la Bible et ses exégètes en hommage à Gilles Dorival* (Paris: Cerf), 159–172.

Jullien, F. (2015), "Contacts et échanges mazdéo-chrétiens sous Husraw Ier. L'apport de textes syriaques contemporains," in: Ch. Jullien, ed., *Husraw Ier: Reconstruction d'un règne. Sources et documents* (Cahiers de Studia Iranica 53; Leuven: Peeters), 175–194.

Justi, F. (1895), *Iranisches Namenbuch* (Marburg: N.G. Elwert).

Kalmin, R. (1996), "Genealogy and Polemics in Rabbinic Literature of Late Antiquity," *HUCA* 67, 77–94.

Kalmin, R. (1999), *The Sage in Jewish Society of Late Antiquity* (London: Routledge).

Kattago, S. (2015), ed., *The Ashgate Research Companion to Memory Studies* (Ashgate Research Companion; Farnham: Ashgate).

Kehrer, H. (1908–1909), *Die Heiligen Drei Könige in Literatur und Kunst.* 2 vols. (Leipzig: E.A. Seemann).

Kelekna, P. (2009), *The Horse in Human History* (Cambridge: Cambridge University Press).

Kettenhofen, E. (1996), "Deportations, ii. In the Parthian and Sasanian Periods," in: E. Yarshater, ed., *Encyclopaedia Iranica* (London: Routledge), vol. 7, 297–308.

Khaleghi-Motlagh, D. (1987), "Ardašīr," in: E. Yarshater, ed., *Encyclopaedia Iranica* (London: Routledge), vol. 2, 382.

Khaleghi-Motlagh, D. (1989), "Bār (Audience). i. From the Achaemenid through the Safavid Period," in: E. Yarshater, ed., *Encyclopaedia Iranica* (London: Routledge), vol. 3, 730–734.

Killebrew, A.E. (2005), *Biblical Peoples and Ethnicity: An Archaeological Study of Egyptians, Canaanites, Philistines, and Early Israel, 1300-1100 B.C.E.* (SBL Archaeology and Biblical Studies 9; Atlanta, Ga.: Society of Biblical Literature).

King, D. (2019), ed., *The Syriac World* (Routledge Worlds; London: Routledge).

Kingsley, P. (1995), "Meetings with Magi: Iranian Themes among the Greeks, from Xanthus of Lydia to Plato's," *Journal of the Royal Asiatic Society* III, 5:2, 173–209.

Kinzig, W. (1997), "[Review of:] M.S. Taylor, Anti-Judaism and Early Christian Identity: A Critique of the Scholarly Consensus (Leiden: Brill, 1995)," *Journal of Theological Studies* NS 48:2, 643–649.

Kirschbaum, E. (1954), "Der Prophet Balaam und die Anbetung der Weisen," *Römische Quartalschrift für christliche Altertumskunde und für Kirchengeschichte* 49, 129–171.

Kister, M. (2001), "'Let Us Make a Man': Observations on the Dynamics of Monotheism," in: *Issues in Talmudic Research: Conference Commemorating the Fifth Anniversary of the Passing of Ephraim E. Urbach, 2 December 1996* (Jerusalem: The Israel Academy of Sciences and Humanities), 28–65 [in Hebrew].

Klijn, A.F.J. (1977), *Seth in Jewish, Christian and Gnostic Literature* (Supplements to Novum Testamentum 46; Leiden: E.J. Brill).

Knowles, L.E. (1944), "The Interpretation of the Seventy Weeks of Daniel in the Early Fathers," *Westminster Theological Journal* 7, 136–160.

Kofsky, A. (1996), "Eusebius of Caesarea and the Christian-Jewish Polemic," in: O. Limor and G.G. Stroumsa, eds., *Contra Iudaeos: Ancient and Medieval Polemics between Christians and Jews* (Texts and Studies in Medieval and Early Modern Judaism 10; Tübingen: Mohr Siebeck), 59–83.

Kofsky, A. (2000), *Eusebius of Caesarea against Paganism* (Jewish and Christian Perspectives Series 3; Leiden: Brill).

Kofsky, A. (2013), "Julianism after Julian of Halicarnassus," in: B. Bitton-Ashkelony and L. Perrone, eds., *Between Personal and Institutional Religion: Self, Doctrine, and Practice in Late Antique Eastern Christianity* (Cultural Encounters in Late Antiquity and the Middle Ages 15; Turnhout: Brepols), 251–294.

Koltun-Fromm, N. (2011), *Jewish-Christian Conversation in Fourth-Century Persian Mesopotamia: A Reconstructed Conversation* (Judaism in Context 12; Piscataway, N.J.: Gorgias Press).

Kraabel, A.T. (1971), "Melito the Bishop and the Synagogue at Sardis: Text and Context," in: D.G. Mitten, J.G. Pedley and J.A. Scott, eds., *Studies Presented to George M. A. Hanfmann* (Mainz: Philipp von Zabern), 77–85.

Kraft, R.A. (1975), "The Multiform Jewish Heritage of Early Christianity," in: J. Neusner, ed., *Christianity, Judaism and Other Greco-Roman Cults: Studies for Morton Smith at Sixty. Part 3: Judaism before 70* (Studies in Judaism in Late Antiquity 12; Leiden: E.J. Brill), 174–199.

Kuzmina, E.E. (1977), "Распространение коневодства и культа коня у ираноязычных племен Средней Азии и других народов Старого Света," in: *Средняя Азия в древности и средневековье: История и культура* (Москва: Наука), 28–52.

La Spisa, P. (2014), "À propos de l'*Apocalypse de Pierre* arabe ou *Livre des Révélations (Kitāb al-Mağāl)*," in: A. Bausi, A. Gori and G. Lusini, eds., *Linguistic, Oriental and Ethiopian Studies in Memory of Paolo Marrassini* (Wiesbaden: Harrassowitz Verlag), 511–526.

Labahn, M., and Lehtipuu, O. (2015), eds., *People under Power: Early Jewish and Christian Responses to the Roman Empire* (Early Christianity in the Roman World; Amsterdam: Amsterdam University Press).

Labourt, J. (1904), *Le christianisme dans l'empire perse sous la dynastie sassanide (224-632)* (Bibliothèque de l'enseignement de l'histoire ecclésiastique 11; Paris: V. Lecoffre).

Landau, B.C. (2008), "The *Revelation of the Magi* in the *Chronicle of Zuqnin*: The Magi form the East in the Ancient Christian Imagination," *Apocrypha* 19, 182–201.

Lane, E.W. (1863–1893), *An Arabic-English Lexicon*. 8 vols (London: Williams and Norgate).

Leander, H. (2010), "With Homi Bhabha at the Jerusalem City Gates: A Postcolonial Reading of the 'Triumphant' Entry (Mark 11.1-11)," *Journal for the Study of the New Testament* 32:3, 309–335.

Leander, H. (2013), *Discourses of Empire: The Gospel of Mark from a Postcolonial Perspective* (SBL Semeia Studies 71; Atlanta, Georgia: Society of Biblical Literature).

Leclercq, H. (1931), "Mages," in: F. Cabrol and H. Leclercq, eds., *Dictionnaire d'archéologie chrétienne et de liturgie* (Paris: Letouzey et Ané), vol. X.1, 980–1067.

Lee, A.D. (1988), "Close-Kin Marriage in Late Antique Mesopotamia," *Greek, Roman and Byzantine Studies* 29, 403–413.

Lee, A.D. (1993), "Evagrius, Paul of Nisibis, and the Problem of Loyalties in the Mid-Sixth Century," *Journal of Ecclesiastical History* 44:4, 569–585.

Lehmann, H.J. (2008), "What was Theodoret's Mother Tongue?—Is the Question Open or Closed?" in: Idem, *Students of the Bible in 4th and 5th Century Syria: Seats of Learning, Sidelights and Syriacisms* (Aarhus: Aarhus University Press), 187–216.

Leonhard, C. (2001), "Observations on the Date of the Syriac *Cave of Treasures*," in: P.M.M. Daviau, J.W. Wevers and M. Weigl, eds., *The World of the Aramaeans III:*

Studies in Language and Literature in Honour of Paul-Eugène Dion (Journal for the Study of the Old Testament, Supplement Series 326; Sheffield: Sheffield Academic Press), 255–293.

Leonhard, C. (2004), "Die Beschneidung Christi in der syrischen Schatzhöhle. Beobachtungen zu Datierung und Überlieferung des Werks," in: M. Tamcke, ed., *Syriaca II. Beiträge zum 3. deutschen Syrologen-Symposium in Vierzehnheiligen 2002* (Studien zur orientalischen Kirchengeschichte 33; Münster: LIT), 11–28.

Levin, Y. (2001), "Understanding Biblical Genealogies," *Currents in Research: Biblical Studies* 9, 11–46.

Levin, Y. (2002), "Nimrod the Mighty, King of Kish, King of Sumer and Akkad," *VT* 52:3, 350–366.

Levine, L.I. (2005), *The Ancient Synagogue: The First Thousand Years* (2nd ed.; New Haven, Conn.: Yale University Press).

Lewis, J.P. (1978), *A Study of the Interpretation of Noah and the Flood in Jewish and Christian Literature* (Leiden: E.J. Brill).

Liddell, H.G., and Scott, R. (1996), *A Greek-English Lexicon* (9th ed.; Oxford: Clarendon Press).

Lieu, J.M. (1996), *Image and Reality: The Jews in the World of the Christians in the Second Century* (Edinburgh: T&T Clark).

Lieu, J.M. (2002), *Neither Jew nor Greek? Constructing Early Christianity* (Studies of the New Testament and its World; London: T&T Clark).

Lieu, J.M. (2004), *Christian Identity in the Jewish and Graeco-Roman World* (Oxford: Oxford University Press).

Limet, H. (2005), "Ethnicity," in: D.C. Snell, ed., *A Companion to the Ancient Near East* (Blackwell Companions to the Ancient World: Ancient History; Malden, MA: Blackwell Publishing), 370–383.

Lincoln, B. (1989), *Discourse and the Construction of Society: Comparative Studies of Myth, Ritual, and Classification* (New York: Oxford University Press).

Livshits, V.A. (2010), *Parthian Onomastics* (St. Petersburg: Linguistic Society of St. Petersburg) [in Russian].

Lloyd, G.E.R. (1962), "Right and Left in Greek Philosophy," *Journal of Hellenic Studies* 82, 56–66.

L'Orange, H.P. (1953), *Studies on Iconography of Cosmic Kingship in the Ancient World* (Oslo: H. Aschehoug & Co.).

Long, A.A. (1982), "Astrology: Arguments Pro and Contra," in: J. Barnes, J. Brunschwig, M.F. Burnyeat and M. Schofield, eds., *Science and Speculation: Studies in Hellenistic Theory and Practice* (Cambridge: Cambridge University Press), 165–192.

Loomba, A. (2015), *Colonialism/Postcolonialism* (The New Critical Idiom; 3rd ed.; London: Routledge).

Loosley, E. (2018), "Cultural Imperialism at the Borders of Empire: The Case of the 'Villa of the Amazons' in Edessa," in: G.J. Brooke, A.H.W. Curtis, M. al-Hamad and G.R. Smith, eds., *Near Eastern and Arabian Essays: Studies in Honour of John F. Healey* (JSS Supplement 41; Oxford: Oxford University Press), 215–230.

Loukonin, V.G. (1987), *Древний и раннесредневековый Иран: Очерки истории культуры* (Москва: Наука).

Lowin, Sh.L. (2012), "Narratives of Villainy: Titus, Nebuchadnezzar, and Nimrod in the ḥadīth and midrash aggadah," in: P.M. Cobb, ed., *The Lineaments of Islam: Studies in Honor of Fred McGraw Donner* (Islamic History and Civilization 95; Leiden: Brill), 261–296.

Luneau, A. (1964), *L'histoire du salut chez les Pères de l'Eglise. La doctrine des âges du monde* (Theologie historique 2; Paris: Beauchesne).

Luz, U. (2007), *Matthew 1–7: A Commentary*. Trans. by J.E. Crouch (Hermeneia; Minneapolis, Minnesota: Fortress Press).

Maalouf, T.T. (1999), "Were the Magi from Persia or Arabia?" *Bibliotheca Sacra* 156, 423–442.

MacKenzie, D.N. (1986), *A Concise Pahlavi Dictionary* (2nd ed.; London: Oxford University Press).

Macler, F. (1903), "Extraits de la Chronique de Maribas Kaldoyo (Mar Abas Katina [?]). Essai de critique historico-littéraire," *Journal asiatique* X.1, 491–549.

Macuch, M. (1991), "Inzest im vorislamischen Iran," *Archäologische Mitteilungen aus Iran* 24, 141–154.

Macuch, M. (2003), "Zoroastrian Principles and the Structure of Kinship in Sasanian Iran," in: C.G. Cereti, M. Maggi and E. Provasi, eds., *Religious Themes and Texts of Pre-Islamic Iran and Central Asia: Studies in Honour of Professor Gherardo Gnoli on the Occasion of his 65th Birthday on 6th December 2002* (Beiträge zur Iranistik 24; Wiesbaden Ludwig Reichert), 231–246.

Macuch, M. (2014), "The Case against Mār Abā, the Catholicos, in the Light of Sasanian Law," *ARAM* 26:1–2, 47–58.

Malandra, W.W. (2001), "Frawardīgān," in: E. Yarshater, ed., *Encyclopaedia Iranica* (New York: Bibliotheca Persica Press), vol. 10, 199.

Malina, B.J. (2007), "Who Are We? Who Are They? Who Am I? Who Are You (Sing.)? Explaining Identity, Social and Individual," *Annali di storia dell'esegesi* 24:1, 103–109.

Marciak, M. (2014), *Izates, Helena, and Monobazos of Adiabene: A Study on Literary Traditions and History* (Philippika 66; Wiesbaden: Harrassowitz Verlag).

Marcus, J. (2012), "Israel and the Church in the Exegetical Writings of Hippolytus," *Journal of Biblical Literature* 131:2, 385–406.

Marincola, J.M. (1999), "Genre, Convention, and Innovation in Greco-Roman Historiography," in: C.S. Kraus, ed., *The Limits of Historiography: Genre and Narrative in Ancient Historical Texts* (Mnemosyne Supplement 191; Leiden: Brill), 281–324.

Marshak, B.I. (2001), "La thématique sogdienne dans l'art de la Chine de la seconde moitié du VIe siècle," *Comptes-rendus des séances de l'Académie des Inscriptions et Belles-Lettres* 145:1, 227–264.

Marquart, J. (1907), "Untersuchungen zur Geschichte von Eran, II (Schluß)," *Philologus, Supplementband* 10, 1–258.

Mathews, E.G., Jr. (1982), "The Early Armenian Iconographic Program of the Ējmiacin Gospel (Erevan, Matenadaran MS 2374, olim 229)," in: N.G. Garsoïan, Th.F. Mathews and R.W. Thomson, eds., *East of Byzantium: Syria and Armenia in the Formative Period. Dumbarton Oaks Symposium, 1980* (Washington, D.C.: Dumbarton Oaks), 199–215.

Mathews, E.G., Jr. (2003), "The Works attributed to Isaac of Antioch: A[nother] Preliminary Checklist," *Hugoye: Journal of Syriac Studies* 6:1, 51–76.

Mathisen, R.W. (2015), "Natio, Gens, Provincialis and Civis: Geographical Terminology and Personal Identity in Late Antiquity," in: G. Greatrex, H. Elton and L. McMahon, eds., *Shifting Genres in Late Antiquity* (Farnham, England: Ashgate), 277–286.

Maul, S.M. (2007), "Divination Culture and the Handling of the Future," in: G. Leick, ed., *The Babylonian World* (The Routledge Worlds; New York: Routledge), 361–372.

McCants, W.F. (2011), *Founding Gods, Inventing Nations: Conquest and Culture Myths from Antiquity to Islam* (Princeton, N.J.: Princeton University Press).

McClanan, A.L. (2002), *Representations of Early Byzantine Empresses: Image and Empire* (New Middle Ages; New York: Palgrave Macmillan).

McDonough, S.J. (2005), *Power by Negotiation: Institutional Reform in the Fifth-Century Sasanian Empire* (Ph.D. dissertation; University of California, Los Angeles).

McDonougha, S.J. (2008a), "A Second Constantine? The Sasanian King Yazdgard in Christian History and Historiography," *Journal of Late Antiquity* 1:1, 127–140.

McDonougha, S.J. (2008b), "Bishops or Bureaucrats? Christian Clergy and the State in the Middle Sasanian Period," in: D. Kennet and P. Luft, eds., *Current Research in Sasanian Archaeology, Art and History: Proceedings of a Conference Held at Durham University, November 3rd and 4th, 2001* (BAR International Series 1810; Oxford: Archaeopress), 87–92.

McDowell, G. (2017), *The Sacred History in Late Antiquity: Pirqe de-Rabbi Eliezer and Its Relationship to the Book of Jubilees and the Cave of Treasures* (thèse de doctorat; Université de recherche Paris Sciences et Lettres).

McKnight, S. (2003), "Calling Jesus Mamzer," *Journal for the Study of the Historical Jesus* 1:1, 73–103.

McVey, K.E. (1990), "The Anti-Judaic Polemic of Ephrem Syrus' Hymns on the Nativity," in: H.W. Attridge, J.J. Collins and T.H. Tobin, eds., *Of Scribes and Scrolls: Studies on the Hebrew Bible, Intertestamental Judaism, and Christian Origins Presented to J. Strugnell on the Occasion of His Sixtieth Birthday* (Lanham, Md.: University Press of America), 229–240.

McVey, K.E. (2000), "Ephrem the Syrian," in: Ph.E. Esler, ed., *The Early Christian World*. 2 vols. (London: Routledge), vol. 2, 1228–1250.

Meade, D.G. (1986), *Pseudonymity and Canon: An Investigation into the Relationship of Authorship and Authority in Jewish and Earliest Christian Tradition* (WUNT 39; Tübingen: J.C.B. Mohr).

Meier, J.P. (1991), *A Marginal Jew: Rethinking the Historical Jesus. Vol. 1: The Roots of the Problem and the Person* (Anchor Bible Reference Library; New York: Doubleday).

Melki, J. (1983), "S. Éphrem le Syrien, un bilan de l'édition critique," *PdO* 11, 3–88.

Mendels, D. (2004), *Memory in Jewish, Pagan and Christian Societies of the Graeco-Roman World* (Library of Second Temple Studies 45; London: T&T Clark).

Menze, V.-L. (2008), *Justinian and the Making of the Syrian Orthodox Church* (Oxford Early Christian Studies; Oxford: Oxford University Press).

Menze, V.-L. (2019), "The Establishment of the Syriac Churches," in: D. King, ed., *The Syriac World* (Routledge Worlds; London: Routledge), 105–118.

Messo, J. (2011), "The Origin of the Terms 'Syria(n)' & *Sūryoyo*: Once Again," *PdO* 36, 111–125.

Metzger, B.M. (1970), "Names for the Nameless in the New Testament: A Study in the Growth of Christian Tradition," in: P. Granfield and J.A. Jungmann, eds., *Kyriakon: Festschrift Johannes Quasten*. 2 vols. (Münster: Aschendorff), vol. 1, 79–99.

Meyendorff, J. (1989), *Imperial Unity and Christian Divisions: The Church, 450-680 AD* (Church History 2; Crestwood, N.Y.: St. Vladimir's Seminary Press).

Millar, F. (1971), "Paul of Samosata, Zenobia, and Aurelian: The Church, Local Culture and Political Allegiance in Third-Century Syria," *Journal of Roman Studies* 61, 1–17.

Millar, F. (1993), *The Roman Near East, 31 BC-AD 337* (Cambridge, Mass.: Harvard University Press).

Millar, F. (2004), "Christian Emperors, Christian Church and the Jews of the Diaspora in the Greek East, CE 379-450," *JJS* 55:1, 1–24.

Millar, F. (2007), "Theodoret of Cyrrhus: A Syrian in Greek Dress?," in: H. Amirav and R.B. ter Haar Romeny, eds., *From Rome to Constantinople: Studies in Honour of Averil Cameron* (Late Antique History and Religion 1; Leuven: Peeters), 105–125.

Millar, F. (2008), "Community, Religion and Language in the Middle-Euphrates Zone in Late Antiquity," *Scripta Classica Israelica* 27, 67–93.

Millar, F. (2011), "Greek and Syriac in Edessa: From Ephrem to Rabbula (CE 363-435)," *Semitica et Classica* 4, 99–114.

Millar, F. (2012), "Greek and Syriac in Fifth-Century Edessa: The Case of Bishop Hibas," *Semitica et Classica* 5, 151–165.

Millar, F. (2013), "The Evolution of the Syrian Orthodox Church in the Pre-Islamic Period: From Greek to Syriac?," *JECS* 21:1, 43–92.

Millar, F. (2015), *Empire, Church and Society in the Late Roman Near East: Greeks, Jews, Syrians and Saracens (Collected Studies, 2004-2014)* (Late Antique History and Religion 10; Leuven: Peeters).

Minorsky, V. (1944), "Roman and Byzantine Campaigns in Atropatene," BSOAS 11:2, 243–265.

Minov, S. (2010), "'Serpentine' Eve in Syriac Christian Literature of Late Antiquity," in: D.V. Arbel and A.A. Orlov, eds., *With Letters of Light: Studies in the Dead Sea Scrolls, Early Jewish Apocalypticism, Magic, and Mysticism in Honor of Rachel Elior* (Ekstasis 2; Berlin: Walter de Gruyter), 92–114.

Minov, S. (2014a), "Marriage and Sexuality in the *Book of Steps*: From Encratism to Orthodoxy," in: K.S. Heal and R.A. Kitchen, eds., *Breaking the Mind: New Studies in the Syriac Book of Steps* (CUA Studies in Early Christianity; Washington, D.C.: Catholic University of America Press), 221–261.

Minov, S. (2014b), "Dynamics of Christian Acculturation in the Sasanian Empire: Some Iranian Motifs in the *Cave of Treasures*," in: G. Herman, ed., *Jews, Christians and Zoroastrians: Religious Dynamics in a Sasanian Context* (Judaism in Context 17; Piscataway, N.J.: Gorgias Press), 149–201.

Minov, S. (2016), "Gazing at the Holy Mountain: Images of Paradise in Syriac Christian Tradition," in: A. Scafi, ed., *The Cosmography of Paradise: The Other World from Ancient Mesopotamia to Medieval Europe* (Warburg Institute Colloquia 27; London: The Warburg Institute), 137–162.

Minov, S. (2017), "Date and Provenance of the Syriac *Cave of Treasures*: A Reappraisal," *Hugoye: Journal of Syriac Studies* 20:1, 129–229.

Minov, S. (2019a), "Jews and Christians in Late Sasanian Nisibis: The Evidence of the *Life of Mar Yāreth the Alexandrian*," in: J. Rubanovich and G. Herman, eds., *Irano-Judaica VII* (Jerusalem: Ben-Zvi Institute), 473–505.

Minov, S. (2019b), "Syriac," in: A. Kulik, G. Boccaccini, L. DiTommaso, D. Hamidović and M.E. Stone, eds., *A Guide to Early Jewish Texts and Traditions in Christian Transmission* (New York: Oxford University Press), 95–137.

Minov, S. (2021a), "The Syriac *Life of Mār Yāret the Alexandrian*: Promoting the Cult of a Monastic Holy Man in Early Medieval Mesopotamia," in: S. Minov and F. Ruani, eds., *Syriac Hagiography: Between Cult and Literature* (Texts and Studies in Eastern Christianity 20; Leiden: Brill), 160–222.

Minov, S. (2021b), "Syriac Manuscripts of the *Cave of Treasures*: Additional Evidence," *Hugoye: Journal of Syriac Studies* ([forthcoming]).

Mirecki, P. (1994), "The Coptic Wizard's Hoard," HTR 87:4, 435–460.

Mirkovic, A. (2004), *Prelude to Constantine: The Abgar Tradition in Early Christianity* (Studies in the Religion and History of Early Christianity 15; Frankfurt am Main: Peter Lang).

Misztal, B.A. (2003), *Theories of Social Remembering* (Theorizing Society; Maidenhead: Open University Press).

Modi, J.J. (1922), *The Religious Ceremonies and Customs of the Parsees* (Bombay: British India Press).

Mokhtarian, J.S. (2010), "Rabbinic Depictions of the Achaemenid King, Cyrus the Great: The Babylonian Esther Midrash (bMeg 10b-17a) in its Iranian Context," in: C. Bakhos and R.M. Shayegan, eds., *The Talmud in Its Iranian Context* (TSAJ 135; Tübingen: Mohr Siebeck), 112–139.

Molé, M. (1963), *Culte, mythe et cosmologie dans l'Iran ancien. Le problème zoroastrien et la tradition mazdéenne* (Annales du Musée Guimet, Bibliothèque d'Études 69; Paris: Presses universitaires de France).

Momigliano, A. (1983), "The Origins of Universal History," in: R.E. Friedman, ed., *The Poet and the Historian: Essays in Literary and Historical Biblical Criticism* (Harvard Semitic Studies 26; Chico, Calif.: Scholars Press), 133–154.

Monneret de Villard, U. (1952), *Le leggende orientali sui Magi evangelici* (Studi e Testi 163; Città del Vaticano: Biblioteca Apostolica Vaticana).

Morony, M.G. (1984), *Iraq after the Muslim Conquest* (Princeton Studies on the Near East; Princeton, N.J.: Princeton University Press).

Morony, M.G. (2004), "Population Transfers between Sasanian Iran and the Byzantine Empire," in: *La Persia e Bisanzio. Atti del Convegno internazionale (Roma, 14-18 ottobre 2002)* (Atti dei Convegni Lincei 201; Roma: Accademia Nazionale dei Lincei), 161–179.

Morony, M.G. (2005), "History and Identity in the Syrian Churches," in: J.J. van Ginkel, H.L. Murre-van den Berg and Th.M. van Lint, eds., *Redefining Christian Identity: Cultural Interaction in the Middle East since the Rise of Islam* (OLA 134; Leuven: Peeters), 1–33.

Mosig-Walburg, K. (2005), "Christenverfolgung und Römerkrieg—Zu Ursachen, Ausmaß und Zielrichtung der Christenverfolgung unter Šāpūr II," *Iranistik* 7, 5–84.

Moss, Y. (2010), "The Language of Paradise: Hebrew or Syriac? Linguistic Speculations and Linguistic Realities in Late Antiquity," in: M. Bockmuehl and G.G. Stroumsa, eds., *Paradise in Antiquity: Jewish and Christian Views* (Cambridge: Cambridge University Press), 120–137.

Moughtin-Mumby, S. (2008), *Sexual and Marital Metaphors in Hosea, Jeremiah, Isaiah, and Ezekiel* (Oxford Theological Monographs; Oxford: Oxford University Press).

Moukarzel, J. (2014), "Maronite Garshuni Texts: On Their Evolution, Characteristics, and Function," *Hugoye: Journal of Syriac Studies* 17:2, 237–262.

Muravjev, A.V. (1999), "The Syriac Julian Romance and its Place in the Literary History," *Христианский Восток* 1 [7], 194–206.

Murray, M. (2004), *Playing a Jewish Game: Gentile Christian Judaizing in the First and Second Centuries CE* (Studies in Christianity and Judaism 13; Waterloo, Ontario: Wilfrid Laurier University Press).

Murray, R. (1975), *Symbols of Church and Kingdom: A Study in Early Syriac Tradition* (London: Cambridge University Press).

Nagel, W. (1982), *Ninus und Semiramis in Sage und Geschichte. Iranische Staaten und Reiternomaden vor Darius* (Berliner Beiträge zur vor- und Frühgeschichte NF 2; Berlin: Spiess).

Nagel, W., and Jacobs, B. (1989), "Königsgötter und Sonnengottheit bei altiranischen Dynastien," *Iranica Antiqua* 24, 337–389.

Najman, H. (2002), *Seconding Sinai: The Development of Mosaic Discourse in Second Temple Judaism* (Supplements to the Journal for the Study of Judaism 77; Leiden: Brill).

Nasrallah, J. (1961), "Bas-reliefs chrétiens inconnus de Syrie," *Syria* 38:1–2, 35–53.

Nasrallah, J. (1974), "Syriens et Suriens," in: I. Ortiz de Urbina, ed., *Symposium Syriacum, 1972: célébré dans les jours 26-31 octobre 1972 à l'Institut Pontifical Oriental de Rome* (OCA 197; Roma: Pontificium Institutum Orientalium Studiorum), 487–503.

Nasrallah, J. (1987), "La liturgie des Patriarcats melchites de 969 à 1300," *OC* 71, 156–181.

Nau, F. (1910), "La cosmographie au VIIe siècle chez les Syriens," *ROC* 5 [15], 225–254.

Nebes, N. (2010), "The Martyrs of Najrān and the End of the Ḥimyar: On the Political History of South Arabia in the Early Sixth Century," in: A. Neuwirth, N. Sinai and M. Marx, eds., *The Qurʾān in Context: Historical and Literary Investigations into the Qurʾānic Milieu* (Texts and Studies on the Qurʾān 6; Leiden: Brill), 27–59.

Netzer, A. (1974), "Some Notes on the Characterization of Cyrus the Great in Jewish and Judeo-Persian Writings," in: *Commémoration Cyrus: Actes du Congrès de Shiraz 1971 et autres études rédigées à l'occasion du 2500e anniversaire de la fondation de l'Empire perse. Vol. 2: Hommage universel* (Acta Iranica 2; Leiden: E.J. Brill), 35–52.

Neusner, J. (1965–1970), *A History of the Jews in Babylonia*. 5 vols (Studia Post-Biblica 9, 11–12, 14–15; Leiden: E.J. Brill).

Neusner, J. (1971), *Aphrahat and Judaism: The Christian-Jewish Argument in Fourth-Century Iran* (Studia Post-Biblica 19; Leiden: E.J. Brill).

Neusner, J. (1972), "Babylonian Jewry and Shapur II's Persecution of Christianity from 339 to 379 A.D.," *HUCA* 43, 77–102.

Neusner, J. (1976), "The Jews East of the Euphrates and the Roman Empire, 1st-3rd Centuries A.D.," *Aufstieg und Niedergang der Römischen Welt* II.9.1, 46–69.

Nickelsburg, G.W.E. (2003), *Ancient Judaism and Christian Origins: Diversity, Continuity, and Transformation* (Minneapolis: Fortress Press).

Nicklas, T. (2008), "Balaam and the Star of the Magi," in: G.H. van Kooten and J.T.A.G.M. van Ruiten, eds., *The Prestige of the Pagan Prophet Balaam in Judaism, Early Christianity and Islam* (Themes in Biblical Narrative, Jewish and Christian Traditions 11; Leiden: Brill), 233–246.

Nöldeke, Th. (1871a), "Die Namen der aramäischen Nation und Sprache," *ZDMG* 25, 113–131.

Nöldeke, Th. (1871b), "Ἀσσύριος Σύριος Σύρος," *Hermes* 5:3, 443–468.

Nöldeke, Th. (1874), "Ueber den syrischen Roman von Kaiser Julian," *ZDMG* 28, 263-292.
Nöldeke, Th. (1888), "[Review of:] C. Bezold, *Die Schatzhöhle, nach dem syrischen Texten der Handschriften zu Berlin, London und Rom, nebst einer arabischen Version nach den Handschriften zu Rom, Paris und Oxford* (Leipzig: J.C. Hinrichs, 1888)," *Literarisches Centralblatt für Deutschland* 8, 233-236.
Noy, D., and Bloedhorn, H. (2004), *Inscriptiones Judaicae Orientis. Vol. 3: Syria and Cyprus* (TSAJ 102; Tübingen: Mohr Siebeck).
Nyberg, H.S. (1964-1974), *A Manual of Pahlavi*. 2 vols (Wiesbaden: Otto Harrassowitz).
Oakley, F. (2006), *Kingship: The Politics of Enchantment* (New Perspectives on the Past; Malden, MA: Blackwell Publishing).
Ohana, M. (1975), "La polémique judéo-islamique et l'image d'Ismaël dans Targum Pseudo-Jonathan et dans Pirke de Rabbi Eliezer," *Augustinianum* 15, 367-387.
Oppenheimer, A. (2009), "Purity of Lineage in Talmudic Babylonia," in: C. Batsch and M. Vârtejanu-Joubert, eds., *Manières de penser dans l'Antiquité méditerranéenne et orientale. Mélanges offerts à Francis Schmidt par ses élèves, ses collègues et ses amis* (Supplements to the Journal for the Study of Judaism 134; Leiden: Brill), 145-156.
Outtier, B. (1975), "Les recueils arméniens et géorgiens d'œuvres attribuées à S. Ephrem le Syrien," in: D. Arnaud, ed., *Actes du 29e Congrès international des orientalistes, Paris, juillet 1973. Assyriologie* (Paris: L'Asiathèque), 53-58.
Palmer, A. (1990), *Monk and Mason on the Tigris Frontier: The Early History of Tur 'Abdin* (University of Cambridge Oriental Publications 39; Cambridge: Cambridge University Press).
Panaino, A.C.D. (1990-1995), *Tištrya*. 2 vols (Serie Orientale Roma 68.1-2; Roma: Istituto italiano per il medio ed estremo Oriente).
Panaino, A.C.D. (1994), "The Two Astrological Reports of the Kārnāmag ī Ardašīr ī Pābagān (III, 4-7; IV, 6-7)," *Die Sprache* 36:2, 181-198.
Panaino, A.C.D. (2004a), "Astral Character of Kingship in the Sasanian and Byzantine Worlds," in: *La Persia e Bisanzio. Atti del Convegno internazionale (Roma, 14-18 ottobre 2002)* (Atti dei Convegni Lincei 201; Roma: Accademia Nazionale dei Lincei), 555-594.
Panaino, A.C.D. (2004b), *Rite, parole et pensée dans l'Avesta ancien et récent* (Sitzungsberichte der philosophisch-historischen Klasse 716, Veröffentlichungen zur Iranistik 31; Wien: Verlag der Österreichischen Akademie der Wissenschaften).
Panaino, A.C.D. (2004c), "La Chiesa di Persia e l'Impero Sasanide. Conflitto e integrazione," in: *Cristianità d'Occidente e cristianità d'Oriente (secoli VI–XI), 24-30 aprile 2003*. 2 vols. (Settimane di studio della Fondazione Centro Italiano di studi sull'alto Medioevo 51; Spoleto: Fondazione Centro italiano di studi sull'alto Medioevo), vol. 2, 765-863.
Panaino, A.C.D. (2006), "References to the Term *Yašt* and Other Mazdean Elements in the Syriac and Greek Martyrologia, with a Short Excursus on the Semantic Value of

the Greek Verb μαγεύω," in: A.C.D. Panaino and A. Piras, eds., *Proceedings of the 5th Conference of the Societas Iranologica Europæa, Held in Ravenna, 6-11 October 2003. Vol. 1: Ancient & Middle Iranian Studies* (Milano: Mimesis), 167–182.

Panaino, A. (2008), "The Zoroastrian Incestuous Unions in Christian Sources and Canonical Laws: Their (Distorted) Aetiology and Some Other Problems," in: Ch. Jullien, ed., *Controverses des chrétiens dans l'Iran sassanide (Chrétiens en terre d'Iran II)* (Cahiers de Studia Iranica 36; Paris: Association pour l'avancement des études iraniennes), 69–87.

Panaino, A.C.D. (2009), "The King and the Gods in the Sasanian Royal Ideology," in: R. Gyselen, ed., *Sources pour l'histoire et la géographie du monde iranien (224–710)* (Res Orientales 18; Bures-sur-Yvette: Groupe pour l'Étude de la civilisation du Moyen-Orient), 209–256.

Panaino, A.C.D. (2010), "The "Persian" Identity in the Religious Controversies: Again on the Case of the "Divided Loyalty" in Sasanian Iran," in: C.G. Cereti, ed., *Iranian Identity in the Course of History: Proceedings of the Conference Held in Rome, 21-24 September 2005* (Serie Orientale Roma 105, Orientalia Romana 9; Roma: Istituto italiano per l'Africa e l'Oriente), 227–239.

Panaino, A.C.D. (2015), "Cosmologies and Astrology," in: M. Stausberg and Y.S.-D. Vevaina, eds., *The Wiley Blackwell Companion to Zoroastrianism* (Wiley Blackwell Companions to Religion; Malden, MA: Wiley-Blackwell), 235–357.

Payne, R.E. (2012), "Avoiding Ethnicity: Uses of the Ancient Past in Late Sasanian Northern Mesopotamia," in: W. Pohl, C. Gantner and R.E. Payne, eds., *Visions of Community in the Post-Roman World: The West, Byzantium and the Islamic World, 300-1100* (Farnham, England: Ashgate), 205–221.

Payne, R.E. (2015), *A State of Mixture: Christians, Zoroastrians, and Iranian Political Culture in Late Antiquity* (Transformation of the Classical Heritage 56; Oakland, Calif.: University of California Press).

Payne, R.E. (2016a), "Iranian Cosmopolitanism: World Religions at the Sasanian Court," in: M. Lavan, R.E. Payne and J. Weisweiler, eds., *Cosmopolitanism and Empire: Universal Rulers, Local Elites, and Cultural Integration in the Ancient Near East and Mediterranean* (Oxford: Oxford University Press), 209–230.

Payne, R.E. (2016b), "Les polémiques syro-orientales contre le zoroastrisme et leurs contextes politiques," in: F. Ruani, ed., *Les controverses religieuses en syriaque* (Études syriaques 13; Paris: Paul Geuthner), 239–260.

Payne Smith, R. (1879–1901), *Thesaurus Syriacus*. 2 vols (Oxford: Clarendon Press).

Pearce, S., and Jones, S. (1998), "Introduction: Jewish Local Identities and Patriotism in the Graeco-Roman Period," in: S. Jones and S. Pearce, eds., *Jewish Local Patriotism and Self-Identification in the Graeco-Roman Period* (Journal for the Study of the Pseudepigrapha, Supplement Series 31; Sheffield: Sheffield Academic Press), 13–28.

Peck, E.H. (1993), "Crown. ii. From the Seleucids to the Islamic Conquest," in: E. Yarshater, ed., *Encyclopaedia Iranica* (Costa Mesa, Calif.: Mazda Publishers), vol. 6, 408–418.

Penner, T. (2004), *In Praise of Christian Origins: Stephen and the Hellenists in Lukan Apologetic History* (Emory Studies in Early Christianity 10; New York: T&T Clark).

Pereswetoff-Morath, A. (2002), *A Grin without a Cat, I. Adversus Iudaeos Texts in the Literature of Medieval Russia (988-1504)* (Lund Slavonic Monographs 4; Lund: Lund University).

Perikhanian, A.G. (1983a), *Общество и право Ирана в парфянский и сасанидский периоды* (Москва: Наука).

Perikhanian, A.G. (1983b), "Iranian Society and Law," in: E. Yarshater, ed., *The Cambridge History of Iran. Vol. 3(2): The Seleucid, Parthian and Sasanian Periods* (Cambridge: Cambridge University Press), 627–680.

Petersen, A.K. (2007), "Rewritten Bible as a Borderline Phenomenon—Genre, Textual Strategy, or Canonical Anachronism?," in: A. Hilhorst, É. Puech and E.J.C. Tigchelaar, eds., *Flores Florentino: Dead Sea Scrolls and Other Early Jewish Studies in Honour of Florentino García Martínez* (Supplements to the Journal for the Study of Judaism 122; Leiden: Brill), 285–306.

Pilhofer, P. (1990), *Presbyteron Kreitton. Der Altersbeweis der jüdischen und christlichen Apologeten und seine Vorgeschichte* (WUNT 2. Reihe 39; Tübingen: Mohr Siebeck).

Pingree, D. (1989), "Classical and Byzantine Astrology in Sassanian Persia," *Dumbarton Oaks Papers* 43, 227–239.

Piras, A. (2010), "Mythology as a Mean of Identity in Sasanian Royal Imagery," in: C.G. Cereti, ed., *Iranian Identity in the Course of History: Proceedings of the Conference Held in Rome, 21-24 September 2005* (Serie Orientale Roma 105, Orientalia Romana 9; Roma: Istituto italiano per l'Africa e l'Oriente), 255–264.

Pohl, W. (2012), "Introduction: Ethnicity, Religion and Empire," in: W. Pohl, C. Gantner and R.E. Payne, eds., *Visions of Community in the Post-Roman World: The West, Byzantium and the Islamic World, 300-1100* (Farnham, England: Ashgate), 1–23.

Poirier, P.-H. (1983), "Fragments d'une version copte de la *Caverne des Trésors*," *Orientalia* 52:3, 415–423.

Poirier, P.-H. (1995), "Note sur le nom du destinataire des chapitres 44 à 54 de la *Caverne des Trésors*," in: *Christianisme d'Égypte. Hommages à René-Georges Coquin* (Cahiers de la Bibliothèque Copte 9; Paris: Peeters), 115–122.

Potts, D.T. (2007), "Foundation Houses, Fire Altars and the Frataraka: Interpreting The Iconography of Some Post-Achaemenid Persian Coins," *Iranica Antiqua* 42, 271–300.

Powell, M.A. (2000a), "The Magi as Kings: An Adventure in Reader-Response Criticism," *Catholic Biblical Quarterly* 62:3, 459–480.

Powell, M.A. (2000b), "The Magi as Wise Men: Re-examining a Basic Supposition," *New Testament Studies* 46, 1–20.

Quispel, G. (1975), *Tatian and the Gospel of Thomas: Studies in the History of the Western Diatessaron* (Leiden: E.J. Brill).

Raffaelli, E.G. (2001), *L'oroscopo del mondo. Il tema di nascita del mondo e del primo uomo secondo l'astrologia zoroastriana* (Sīmorγ; Milano: Mimesis).

Raja, R. (2012), *Urban Development and Regional Identity in the Eastern Roman Provinces, 50 BC–AD 250: Aphrodisias, Ephesos, Athens, Gerasa* (Copenhagen: Museum Tusculanum Press).

Rajak, T. (1999), "Talking at Trypho: Christian Apologetic as Anti-Judaism in Justin's Dialogue with Trypho the Jew," in: M.J. Edwards, M. Goodman and S. Price, eds., *Apologetics in the Roman Empire: Pagans, Jews, and Christians* (Oxford: Oxford University Press), 59–80.

Rastorgueva, V.S., and Edelman, D.I. (2007), *Этимологический словарь иранских языков. Том 3: f–h* (Москва: Восточная литература).

Reinhold, M. (1970), *History of Purple as a Status Symbol in Antiquity* (Collection Latomus 116; Bruxelles: Latomus).

Reinink, G.J. (1992), "Ps.-Methodius: A Concept of History in Response to the Rise of Islam," in: A. Cameron and L.I. Conrad, eds., *The Byzantine and Early Islamic Near East. Vol. 1: Problems in the Literary Source Material* (Studies in Late Antiquity and Early Islam 1; Princeton, N.J.: Darwin Press), 149–187.

Reinink, G.J. (1997), "A New Fragment of Theodore of Mopsuestia's *Contra Magos*," *Le Muséon* 110:1, 63–67.

Reinink, G.J. (2009), "Tradition and the Formation of the 'Nestorian' Identity in Sixth- to Seventh-Century Iraq," *CHRC* 89:1–3, 217–250.

Retsö, J. (2003), *The Arabs in Antiquity: Their History from the Assyrians to the Umayyads* (London: RoutledgeCurzon).

Revell, L. (2009), *Roman Imperialism and Local Identities* (Cambridge: Cambridge University Press).

Rezania, K. (2008), *Die zoroastrische Zeitvorstellung: Eine Untersuchung über Zeit- und Ewigkeitskonzepte und die Frage des Zurvanismus* (Göttinger Orientforschungen, III. Reihe: Iranica, N.F. 7; Wiesbaden: Harrassowitz Verlag).

Rhee, H. (2005), *Early Christian Literature: Christ in Culture in the Second and Third Centuries* (Routledge Early Church Monographs; London: Routledge).

Ri, S.-M. (1998), "La Caverne des Trésors et Mar Éphrem," in: R. Lavenant, ed., *Symposium Syriacum VII: Uppsala University, Department of Asian and African Languages, 11-14 August 1996* (OCA 256; Rome: Pontificio Istituto Orientale), 71–83.

Ri, A.S.-M. (2000), *Commentaire de la Caverne des Trésors: étude sur l'histoire du texte et de ses sources* (CSCO 581, Subs. 103; Louvain: Peeters).

Riad, E. (1988), *Studies in the Syriac Preface* (Acta Universitatis Upsaliensis, Studia Semitica Upsaliensia 11; Stockholm: Almqvist & Wiksell).

Richardson, P. (2006), "The Beginnings of Christian Anti-Judaism, 70-c. 235," in: S.T. Katz, ed., *The Cambridge History of Judaism. Vol. 4: The Late Roman-Rabbinic Period* (Cambridge: Cambridge University Press), 244–258.

Richardson, P., and Granskou, D. (1986), eds., *Anti-Judaism in Early Christianity. Vol. 1: Paul and the Gospels* (Studies in Christianity and Judaism 2; Waterloo, Ontario: Wilfrid Laurier University Press).

Riedinger, U. (1956), *Die Heilige Schrift im Kampf der griechischen Kirche gegen die Astrologie* (Innsbruck: Universitätsverlag Wagner).

Rist, J. (1996), "Die Verfolgung der Christen im spätantiken Sasanidenreich: Ursachen, Verlauf und Folgen," *OC* 80, 17–42.

Roberts, M. (1985), *Biblical Epic and Rhetorical Paraphrase in Late Antiquity* (ARCA Classical and Medieval Texts, Papers and Monographs 16; Liverpool: Cairns).

Robin, Ch.J. (1991), "Du paganisme au monothéisme," *Revue du monde musulman et de la Méditerranée* 61, 139–155.

Robin, Ch.J. (2004), "Ḥimyar et Israël," *Comptes-rendus des séances de l'Académie des Inscriptions et Belles-Lettres* 148:2, 831–908.

Robinson, R.B. (1986), "Literary Functions of the Genealogies of Genesis," *Catholic Biblical Quarterly* 48:4, 595–608.

Robinson, S.E. (1982), *The Testament of Adam: An Examination of the Syriac and Greek Traditions* (SBL Dissertation Series 52; Chico, Calif.: Scholars Press).

Rochberg, F. (2004), *The Heavenly Writing: Divination, Horoscopy, and Astronomy in Mesopotamian Culture* (New York: Cambridge University Press).

Roest, B. (1999), "Mediaeval Historiography: About Generic Constraints and Scholarly Constructions," in: B. Roest and H.L.J. Vanstiphout, eds., *Aspects of Genre and Type in Pre-Modern Literary Cultures* (COMERS/ICOG Communications 1; Groningen: STYX), 47–61.

Roggema, B.H. (2007), "Biblical Exegesis and Interreligious Polemics in the Arabic *Apocalypse of Peter—The Book of the Rolls*," in: D. Thomas, ed., *The Bible in Arab Christianity* (The History of Christian-Muslim Relations 6; Leiden: Brill), 131–150.

Rokeah, D. (1969), "Ben Stara is Ben Pantera: Towards the Clarification of a Philological-Historical Problem," *Tarbiz* 39:1, 9–18 [in Hebrew].

Rollinger, R. (2006), "Assyrios, Syrios, Syros und Leukosyros," *Die Welt des Orients* 36, 72–82.

Rose, J. (2006), "Investiture. iii. Sasanian Period," in: E. Yarshater, ed., *Encyclopaedia Iranica* (New York: Encyclopaedia Iranica Foundation), vol. 13, 184–188.

Ross, S.K. (2001), *Roman Edessa: Politics and Culture on the Eastern Fringes of the Roman Empire, 114-242 CE* (London: Routledge).

Roukema, R. (2006), "The Veil over Moses' Face in Patristic Interpretation," in: R. Roukema, ed., *The Interpretation of Exodus: Studies in Honour of Cornelis Houtman* (Contributions to Biblical Exegesis and Theology 44; Leuven: Peeters), 237–252.

Rubenstein, J.L. (2003), *The Culture of the Babylonian Talmud* (Baltimore, Maryland: The John Hopkins University Press).

Rubin, M. (1998), "The Language of Creation or the Primordial Language: A Case of Cultural Polemics in Antiquity," *JJS* 49:2, 306–333.

Rubin, Z. (1995), "'The Martyrdom of Azqir' and the Struggle between Judaism and Christianity in South Arabia during the 5th Century C.E.," in: A. Kasher and A. Oppenheimer, eds., *Dor Le-Dor: From the End of Biblical Times Up to the Redaction of the Talmud* (Jerusalem: The Bialik Institute), 251–284 [in Hebrew].

Rubin, Z. (2000), "Judaism and Raḥmanite Monotheism in the Ḥimyarite Kingdom in the Fifth Century," in: T. Parfitt, ed., *Israel and Ishmael: Studies in Muslim-Jewish Relations* (Richmond, Surrey: Curzon), 32–51.

Ruether, R.R. (1974), *Faith and Fratricide: The Theological Roots of Anti-Semitism* (New York: Seabury Press).

Ruether, R.R. (1979), "The *Adversus Judaeos* Tradition in the Church Fathers: The Exegesis of Christian Anti-Judaism," in: P.E. Szarmach, ed., *Aspects of Jewish Culture in the Middle Ages: Papers of the Eighth Annual Conference of the Center for Medieval and Early Renaissance Studies, State University of New York at Binghamton, 3-5 May, 1974* (Albany, N.Y.: State University of New York Press), 27–50.

Russell, J.R. (1987), *Zoroastrianism in Armenia* (Harvard Iranian Series 5; Cambridge, Mass.: Harvard University Press).

Rutgers, L.V. (2009), *Making Myths: Jews in Early Christian Identity Formation* (Leuven: Peeters).

Ruzer, S. (2001), "The *Cave of Treasures* on Swearing by Abel's Blood and Expulsion from Paradise: Two Exegetical Motifs in Context," *JECS* 9:2, 251–271.

Ruzer, S., and Kofsky, A. (2010), *Syriac Idiosyncrasies: Theology and Hermeneutics in Early Syriac Literature* (Jerusalem Studies in Religion and Culture 11; Leiden: Brill).

Ryckmans, J. (1989), "A Confrontation of the Main Hagiographic Accounts of the Najran Persecution," in: M.M. Ibrahim, ed., *Arabian Studies in Honour of Mahmoud Ghul: Symposium at Yarmouk University, December 8-11, 1984* (Yarmouk University Publications, Institute of Archaeology and Anthropology Series 2; Wiesbaden: Otto Harrassowitz), 113–133.

Sachau, E. (1899), *Verzeichniss der syrischen Handschriften der Königlichen Bibliothek zu Berlin*. 2 vols (Die Handschriften-Verzeichnisse der Königlichen Bibliothek zu Berlin 23; Berlin: A. Asher & Co.).

Salvesen, A. (1998), "The Legacy of Babylon and Nineveh in Aramaic Sources," in: S. Dalley, ed., *The Legacy of Mesopotamia* (Oxford: Oxford University Press), 139–161.

Salvesen, A. (2008), "The Genesis of Ethnicity? The Role of the Bible in the Self-Definition of Syriac Writers," *The Harp* 23, 369–382.

Salvesen, A. (2009), "Keeping it in the Family? Jacob and his Aramean Heritage according to Jewish and Christian Sources," in: E. Grypeou and H. Spurling, eds., *The*

Exegetical Encounter between Jews and Christians in Late Antiquity (Jewish and Christian Perspectives 18; Leiden: Brill), 205–220.

Samir, S.Kh., "Théodore de Mopsueste dans le "Fihrist" d'Ibn an-Nadīm," *Le Muséon* 90:3–4 (1977), 355–363.

Samir, S.Kh. (1978), "L'Éphrem arabe, État des travaux," in: F. Graffin and A. Guillaumont, eds., *Symposium Syriacum, 1976: célebré du 13 au 17 septembre 1976 au Centre Culturel "Les Fontaines" de Chantilly (France)* (OCA 205; Roma: Pontificium Institutum Orientalium Studiorum), 229–240.

Sanders, E.P. (1977), *Paul and Palestinian Judaism: A Comparison of Patterns of Religion* (Philadelphia: Fortress Press).

Sandmel, S. (1962), "Parallelomania," *Journal of Biblical Literature* 81:1, 1–13.

Satlow, M.L. (2001), *Jewish Marriage in Antiquity* (Princeton, N.J.: Princeton University Press).

Sauma, A. (1993), "The Origin of the Word Suryoyo-Syrian," *The Harp* 6:3, 171–197.

Schäfer, P. (2007), *Jesus in the Talmud* (Princeton, N.J.: Princeton University Press).

Scheinhardt, H. (1968), "Zitate aus drei verlorenen Schriften des Theodor von Mopsuestia," in: *Paul de Lagarde und die syrische Kirchengeschichte* (Göttingen: Göttinger Arbeitskreis für syrische Kirchengeschichte), 185–198.

Schenk, K.L. (2006), *Returning to Zion: The Narrative of the Dura-Europos Synagogue Frescoes* (Ph.D. dissertation; The Johns Hopkins University).

Schick, R. (1995), *The Christian Communities of Palestine from Byzantine to Islamic Rule: A Historical and Archaeological Study* (Studies in Late Antiquity and Early Islam 2; Princeton, N.J.: Darwin Press).

Schiffman, L.H. (1987), "The Conversion of the Royal House of Adiabene in Josephus and Rabbinic Sources," in: L.H. Feldman and G. Hata, eds., *Josephus, Judaism, and Christianity* (Detroit: Wayne State University Press), 293–312.

Schilling, A.M. (2008), *Die Anbetung der Magier und die Taufe der Sāsāniden: Zur geistesgeschichte des Iranischen Christentums in der Spätantike* (CSCO 621, Subs. 120; Louvain: Peeters).

Schippmann, K. (1971), *Die iranischen Feuerheiligtümer* (Religionsgeschichtliche Versuche und Vorarbeiten 31; Berlin: Walter de Gruyter).

Schoeps, H.J. (1950), *Auf frühchristlicher Zeit: Religionsgeschichteliche Untersuchungen* (Tübingen: Mohr).

Schreckenberg, H. (1995), *Die christlichen Adversus-Judaeos-Texte und ihr literarisches und historisches Umfeld (1.-11.Jh.)* (Europaeische Hochschulschriften. Reihe 23, Theologie 172; 3rd revised ed.; Frankfurt am Main: Peter Lang).

Schützinger, H. (1962), *Ursprung und Entwicklung der arabischen Abraham-Nimrod-Legende* (Bonner orientalistische Studien, neue Serie 11; Bonn: Rheinische Friedrich-Wilhelms-Universität in Bonn).

Schwartz, M. (1998), "Sesen: A Durable East Mediterranean God in Iran," in: N. Sims-Williams, ed., *Proceedings of the Third European Conference of Iranian*

Studies, Held in Cambridge, 11th to 15th September 1995. Part 1: Old and Middle Iranian Studies (Beiträge zur Iranistik 17.1; Wiesbaden: Ludwig Reichert), 9–11.

Schwartz, S. (1995), "Language, Power and Identity in Ancient Palestine," *Past & Present* 148, 3–47.

Schwemer, A.M. (2003), "Jesus Christus als Prophet, König und Priester: Das *munus triplex* und die frühe Christologie," in: M. Hengel and A.M. Schwemer, *Der messianische Anspruch Jesu und die Anfänge der Christologie* (WUNT 138; Tübingen: Mohr Siebeck), 165–230.

Scott, J.C. (1990), *Domination and the Arts of Resistance: Hidden Transcripts* (New Haven, Connecticut: Yale University Press).

Segal, J.B. (1964), "The Jews of North Mesopotamia before the Rise of Islam," in: J.M. Grintz and J. Liver, eds., *Studies in the Bible Presented to Professor M.H. Segal* (Jerusalem: Kiryat Sepher), 32*–63*.

Segal, J.B. (1970), *Edessa, 'The Blessed City'* (Oxford: Clarendon Press).

Seleznyov, N.N. (2012), "Средневековый восточнохристианский экуменизм как следствие исламского универсализма," *Философский журнал* 1 [8], 5–13.

Sellwood, D. (1983), "Parthian Coins," in: E. Yarshater, ed., *The Cambridge History of Iran. Vol. 3(1): The Seleucid, Parthian and Sasanian Periods* (Cambridge: Cambridge University Press), 279–298.

Shahbazi, A.S. (1987), "Asb. i. In Pre-Islamic Iran," in: E. Yarshater, ed., *Encyclopaedia Iranica* (London: Routledge), vol. 2, 724–730.

Shahbazi, A.S. (1990), "On the Xuadāy-nāmag," in: *Iranica Varia: Papers in Honor of Professor Ehsan Yarshater* (Acta Iranica 30; Leiden: Brill), 208–229.

Shahbazi, A.S. (1992), "Clothing. ii. In the Median and Achaemenid Periods," in: E. Yarshater, ed., *Encyclopaedia Iranica* (Costa Mesa, Calif.: Mazda Publishers), vol. 5, 723–737.

Shahbazi, A.S. (1993), "Coronation," in: E. Yarshater, ed., *Encyclopaedia Iranica* (Costa Mesa, Calif.: Mazda Publishers), vol. 6, 277–279.

Shahbazi, A.S. (2004a), "Hormozd IV," in: E. Yarshater, ed., *Encyclopaedia Iranica* (New York: Encyclopaedia Iranica Foundation), vol. 12, 466–467.

Shahbazi, A.S. (2004b), "Hōšang," in: E. Yarshater, ed., *Encyclopaedia Iranica* (New York: Encyclopaedia Iranica Foundation), vol. 12, 491–492.

Shaked, Sh. (1984), "From Iran to Islam: Notes on Some Themes in Transmission," *Jerusalem Studies in Arabic and Islam* 4, 31–67.

Shaked, Sh. (1986), "From Iran to Islam: On Some Symbols of Royalty," *Jerusalem Studies in Arabic and Islam* 7, 75–91.

Shaked, Sh. (1994), *Dualism in Transformation: Varieties of Religion in Sasanian Iran* (Jordan Lectures in Comparative Religion 16; London: School of Oriental and African Studies, University of London).

Shapira, D.D.Y. (2002), "Zoroastrain Sources on Black People," *Arabica* 49:1, 117–122.

Shapira, D.D.Y. (2008), "Gleanings on Jews of Greater Iran under the Sasanians (According to the Oldest Armenian and Georgian Texts)," *Iran and the Caucasus* 12, 191–216.

Shchuryk, O. (2007), "*Lᵉbēš pagrāʿ* as the Language of "Incarnation" in the *Demonstrations* of Aphrahat the Persian Sage," *Ephemerides Theologicae Lovanienses* 83:4, 419–444.

Shenkar, M. (2007), "Temple Architecture in the Iranian World before the Macedonian Conquest," *Iran and the Caucasus* 11, 169–194.

Shenkar, M. (2011), "Temple Architecture in the Iranian World in the Hellenistic Period," in: A. Kouremenos, S. Chandrasekaran and R. Rossi, eds., *From Pella to Gandhara: Hybridisation and Identity in the Art and Architecture of the Hellenistic East* (BAR International Series 2221; Oxford: Archaeopress), 117–139.

Shenkar, M. (2014), *Intangible Spirits and Graven Images: The Iconography of Deities in the Pre-Islamic Iranian World* (Magical and Religious Literature of Late Antiquity 4; Leiden: Brill).

Shenkar, M. (2017), "The Great Iranian Divide: Between Aniconic West and Anthropomorphic East," *Religion* 47:3, 378–398.

Shepardson, Ch.C. (2008a), *Anti-Judaism and Christian Orthodoxy: Ephrem's Hymns in Fourth-Century Syria* (Patristic Monograph Series 20; Washington, D.C.: The Catholic University of America Press).

Shepardson, Ch.C. (2008b), "Paschal Politics: Deploying the Temple's Destruction against Fourth-Century Judaizers," *VC* 62:3, 233–260.

Sherwood, P. (1952), "Sergius of Reshaina and the Syriac Versions of the Pseudo-Denis," *Sacris Erudiri* 4, 174–184.

Shinan, A. (1992), *The Embroidered Targum: The Aggadah in Targum Pseudo-Jonathan of the Pentateuch* (Jerusalem: Magnes Press) [in Hebrew].

Shoemaker, S.J. (1999), ""Let Us Go and Burn Her Body": The Image of the Jews in the Early Dormition Traditions," *Church History* 68:4, 775–823.

Sigal, Ph. (1983), "Aspects of Dual Covenant Theology: Salvation," *Horizons in Biblical Theology* 5:2, 1–48.

Silk, J.A. (2008), "Putative Persian Perversities: Indian Buddhist Condemnations of Zoroastrian Close-Kin Marriage in Context," *BSOAS* 71:3, 433–464.

Simon, M. (1996), *Verus Israel: A Study of the Relations between Christians and Jews in the Roman Empire (AD 135-425)*. Trans. by H. McKeating (London: The Littman Library of Jewish Civilization).

Skarsaune, O. (2002), *In the Shadow of the Temple: Jewish Influences on Early Christianity* (Downers Grove, Ill.: InterVarsity Press).

Smelik, W.F. (2013), *Rabbis, Language and Translation in Late Antiquity* (Cambridge: Cambridge University Press).

Smith, A.D. (1986), *The Ethnic Origins of Nations* (Oxford: Basil Blackwell).

Smith, J.M. (1991), *The Foundation of Cities in Greek Historians and Poets* (Ph.D. dissertation; Yale University).

Smith, K.R. (2016), *Constantine and the Captive Christians of Persia: Martyrdom and Religious Identity in Late Antiquity* (Transformation of the Classical Heritage 57; Oakland, Calif.: University of California Press).

Snelders, B. (2010), *Identity and Christian-Muslim Interaction: Medieval Art of the Syrian Orthodox from the Mosul Area* (OLA 198; Louvain: Peeters).

Snowden, F.M. (1970), *Blacks in Antiquity: Ethiopians in the Greco-Roman Experience* (Cambridge, Mass.: Belknap Press).

Sokoloff, M. (2009), *A Syriac Lexicon: A Translation from the Latin, Correction, Expansion, and Update of C. Brockelmann's Lexicon Syriacum* (Winona Lake, Ind.: Eisenbrauns / Piscataway, N.J.: Gorgias Press).

Sommer, M. (2012), "Heart of Darkness? Post-Colonial Theory and the Transformation of the Mediterranean," *Ancient West & East* 11, 235–245.

Soudavar, A. (2003), *The Aura of Kings: Legitimacy and Divine Sanction in Iranian Kingship* (Bibliotheca Iranica: Intellectual Traditions Series 11; Costa Mesa, Calif.: Mazda Publishers).

Soulen, R.K. (1996), *The God of Israel and Christian Theology* (Minneapolis: Fortress Press).

Sperber, D. (1982), "On the Unfortunate Adventures of Rav Kahana: A Passage of Saboraic Polemic from Sasanian Persia," in: Sh. Shaked, ed., *Irano-Judaica I* (Jerusalem: Yad Izhak Ben Zvi), 83–100.

Speyer, W. (1971), *Die Literarische Fälschung im Heidnischen und Christlichen Altertum. Ein Versuch ihrer Deutung* (München: Ch. Beck'sche Verlagsbuchhandlung).

Spurling, H., and Grypeou, E. (2007), "Pirke de-Rabbi Eliezer and Eastern Christian Exegesis," *Collectanea Christiana Orientalia* 4, 217–243.

Stenger, J. (2009), *Hellenische Identität in der Spätantike: Pagane Autoren und ihr Unbehagen an der eigenen Zeit* (Untersuchungen zur antiken Literatur und Geschichte 97; Berlin: Walter de Gruyter).

Sterling, G.E. (1992), *Historiography and Self-Definition: Josephus, Luke-Acts and Apologetic Historiography* (Supplements to Novum Testamentum 64; Leiden: E.J. Brill).

Stockhausen, C.K. (1989), *Moses' Veil and the Glory of the New Covenant: The Exegetical Substructure of II Cor. 3,1-4,6* (Analecta Biblica 116; Roma: Editrice Pontificio Istituto Biblico).

Stone, M.E. (1992), *A History of the Literature of Adam and Eve* (SBL Early Judaism and its Literature 3; Atlanta, Georgia: Scholars Press).

Stork, H. (1928), *Die sogenannten Melchisedekianer, mit Untersuchung ihrer Quellen auf Gedankengehalt und dogmengeschichtliche Entwicklung* (Forschungen zur

Geschichte des neutestamentliche Kanons und der altkirchlichen Literatur 8.2; Leipzig: D.W. Scholl).

Strothmann, W. (1973), "Das Buch Kohelet und seine syrischen Ausleger," in: G. Wiessner, ed., *Erkenntnisse und Meinungen I* (Göttinger Orientforschungen, I. Reihe: Syriaca, Bd. 3; Wiesbaden: Otto Harrassowitz), 189–238.

Stroumsa, G.G. (1996), "From Anti-Judaism to Antisemitism in Early Christianity?," in: O. Limor and G.G. Stroumsa, eds., *Contra Iudaeos: Ancient and Medieval Polemics between Christians and Jews* (Texts and Studies in Medieval and Early Modern Judaism 10; Tübingen: Mohr Siebeck), 1–26.

Stroumsa, G.G. (2005), "Cultural Memory in Early Christianity: Clement of Alexandria and the History of Religions," in: J.P. Arnason, S.N. Eisenstadt and B. Wittrock, eds., *Axial Civilizations and World History* (Jerusalem Studies in Religion and Culture 4; Leiden: Brill), 295–317.

Stroumsa, G.G. (2007), "False Prophet, False Messiah and the Religious Scene in Seventh-Century Jerusalem," in: M. Bockmuehl and J. Carleton Paget, eds., *Redemption and Resistance: The Messianic Hopes of Jews and Christians in Antiquity* (London: T&T Clark International), 285–296.

Stroumsa, G.G. (2016), *The Scriptural Universe of Ancient Christianity* (Cambridge, Mass.: Harvard University Press).

Suermann, H. (2007), "Bedeutung und Selbstverständnis des Katholikos-Patriarchen von Seleukia-Ktesiphon," in: A. Mustafa, J. Tubach and G.S. Vashalomidze, eds., *Inkulturation des Christentums im Sasanidenreich* (Wiesbaden: Ludwig Reichert), 227–236.

Sundermann, W. (1988), "Bahman Yašt," in: E. Yarshater, ed., *Encyclopædia Iranica* (Costa Mesa, Calif.: Mazda Publishers), vol. 3, 492–493.

Speyer, W. (1971), *Die Literarische Fälschung im Heidnischen und Christlichen Altertum. Ein Versuch ihrer Deutung* (München: Ch. Beck).

Swennen, P. (2004), *D'Indra à Tištrya: portrait et évolution du cheval sacré dans les mythes indo-iraniens anciens* (Paris: De Boccard).

Tafazzoli, A. (1989), "Bāḵtar," in: E. Yarshater, ed., *Encyclopaedia Iranica* (London: Routledge), vol. 3, 539–540.

Tafazzoli, A. (1992), "Čēčast," in: E. Yarshater, ed., *Encyclopaedia Iranica* (Costa Mesa, Calif.: Mazda Publishers), vol. 5, 107–108.

Tafazzoli, A. (2000), *Sasanian Society: I. Warriors, II. Scribes, III. Dehqāns* (Ehsan Yarshater Distinguished Lectures in Iranian Studies 1; New York: Bibliotheca Persica Press).

Tannous, J. (2018a), *The Making of the Medieval Middle East: Religion, Society, and Simple Believers* (Princeton, N.J.: Princeton University Press).

Tannous, J. (2018b), "Romanness in the Syriac East," in: W. Pohl, C. Gantner, C. Grifoni and M. Pollheimer-Mohaupt, eds., *Transformations of Romanness: Early Medieval Regions and Identities* (Millennium-Studien 71; Berlin: Walter de Gruyter), 457–480.

Taqizadeh, S.H. (1940), "The Iranian Festivals Adopted by the Christians and Condemned by the Jews," *BSOAS* 10:3, 632–653.

Tardieu, M. (1991), "La nisba de Sisinnios," *Altorientalische Forschungen* 18:1, 3–8.

Taylor, D.G.K. (1998), "St. Ephraim's Influence on the Greeks," *Hugoye: Journal of Syriac Studies* 1:2, 185–196.

Taylor, D.G.K. (2002), "Bilingualism and Diglossia in Late Antique Syria and Mesopotamia," in: J.N. Adams, M. Janse and S. Swain, eds., *Bilingualism in Ancient Society: Language Contact and the Written Text* (Oxford: Oxford University Press), 298–331.

Taylor, D.G.K. (2009), "The Psalm Commentary of Daniel of Salah and the Formation of Sixth-Century Syrian Orthodox Identity," *CHRC* 89:1–3, 65–92.

Taylor, D.G.K. (2019), "The Coming of Christianity to Mesopotamia," in: D. King, ed., *The Syriac World* (Routledge Worlds; London: Routledge), 68–87.

Taylor, M.S. (1995), *Anti-Judaism and Early Christian Identity: A Critique of the Scholarly Consensus* (Studia Post-Biblica 46; Leiden: E.J. Brill).

ter Haar Romeny, R.B. (2004), "The Identity Formation of Syrian Orthodox Christians as Reflected in Two Exegetical Collections: First Soundings," *PdO* 29, 103–121.

ter Haar Romeny, R.B. (2005a), "From Religious Association to Ethnic Community: A Research Project on Identity Formation among the Syrian Orthodox under Muslim Rule," *Islam and Christian-Muslim Relations* 16:4, 377–399.

ter Haar Romeny, R.B. (2005b), "Hypotheses on the Development of Judaism and Christianity in Syria in the Period after 70 C.E.," in: H. van de Sandt, ed., *Matthew and the Didache: Two Documents from the Same Jewish-Christian Milieu?* (Assen: Van Gorcum), 13–33.

ter Haar Romeny, R.B. (2012), "Ethnicity, Ethnogenesis and the Identity of Syriac Orthodox Christians," in: W. Pohl, C. Gantner and R.E. Payne, eds., *Visions of Community in the Post-Roman World: The West, Byzantium and the Islamic World, 300–1100* (Farnham: Ashgate), 183–204.

ter Haar Romeny, R.B., Atto, N., van Ginkel, J.J., Immerzeel, M., and Snelders, B. (2009), "The Formation of a Communal Identity among West Syrian Christians: Results and Conclusions of the Leiden Project," *CHRC* 89:1–3, 1–52.

Teteriatnikov, N. (1998), "The 'Gift Giving' Image: The Case of the Adoration of the Magi," *Visual Resources* 13:3–4, 381–391.

Teule, H.G.B. (2009), "Reflections on Identity. The Suryoye of the Twelfth and Thirteenth Centuries: Bar Salibi, Bar Shakko, and Barhebraeus," *CHRC* 89:1–3, 179–189.

Teule, H.G.B. (2010), "The Syriac Renaissance," in: H.G.B. Teule, C.F. Tauwinkl, R.B. ter Haar Romeny and J. van Ginkel, eds., *The Syriac Renaissance* (Eastern Christian Studies 9; Leuven: Peeters), 1–30.

Thomas, Ch.M. (2003), *The Acts of Peter, Gospel Literature, and the Ancient Novel: Rewriting the Past* (Oxford: Oxford University Press).

Thomson, F.J. (1992), "SS. Cyril and Methodius and a Mythical Western Heresy: Trilinguism. A Contribution to the Study of Patristic and Mediaeval Theories of Sacred Languages," *AB* 110:1–2, 67–121.

Thomson, R.W. (2004), "Armenian Ideology and the Persians," in: *La Persia e Bisanzio. Atti del Convegno internazionale (Roma, 14-18 ottobre 2002)* (Atti dei Convegni Lincei 201; Roma: Accademia Nazionale dei Lincei), 373–389.

Thorpe, T. (2009), *The Power of Silence: The Empty Temple Mount in Late Antique Jerusalem* (Ph.D. dissertation; Harvard University).

Thraede, K. (1962), "Erfinder II (geistesgeschichtlich)," in: Th. Klauser, ed., *Reallexikon für Antike und Christentum* (Stuttgart: Anton Hiersemann), vol. 5, 1191–1278.

Tisserant, E. (1924), *Inventaire sommaire des manuscrits arabes du fonds Borgia à la Bibliothèque Vaticane* (Roma: Tipografia del senato).

Toda, S. (2011), "Eusebius and Syriac Literature," *PdO* 36, 515–524.

Toepel, A. (2006a), "Yonton Revisited: A Case Study in the Reception of Hellenistic Science within Early Judaism," *HTR* 99:3, 235–245.

Toepel, A. (2006b), *Die Adam- und Seth-Legenden im syrischen Buch der Schatzhöhle: Eine quellenkritische Untersuchung* (CSCO 618, Subs. 119; Louvain: Peeters).

Toral-Niehoff, I. (2014), *Al-Ḥīra: Eine arabische Kulturmetropole im spätantiken Kontext* (Islamic History and Civilization: Studies and Texts 104; Leiden: Brill).

Trexler, R.C. (1997), *The Journey of the Magi: Meanings in History of a Christian Story* (Princeton, N.J.: Princeton University Press).

Tromp, J. (1997), "Literary and Exegetical Issues in the Story of Adam's Death and Burial (GLAE 31–42)," in: J. Frishman and Sh. Naeh, eds., *The Book of Genesis in Jewish and Oriental Christian Interpretation* (Traditio Exegetica Graeca 5; Louvain: Peeters), 25–41.

Trouillot, M.-R. (1995), *Silencing the Past: Power and the Production of History* (Boston, Mass.: Beacon Press).

Tsulaja, G.V. (1991), "Из раннесредневековой грузинской агиографии: "Страсти св. Евстафия Мцхетского" (Этнокультурный аспект)," in: *Древнейшие государства на территории СССР. Материалы и исследования, 1990 год* (Москва: Наука), 116–134.

Tubach, J. (1995), "Johannes Urtayas Muttersprache," *Hallesche Beiträge zur Orientwissenschaft* 20, 21–25.

Tubach, J. (1997), "Die Namen von Manis Jüngern und ihre Herkunft," in: L. Cirillo and A. van Tongerloo, eds., *Atti del Terzo Congresso Internazionale di Studi "Manicheismo e Oriente Cristiano Antico", Arcavacata di Rende—Amantea, 31 agosto-5 settembre 1993* (Manichaean Studies 3; Louvain: Brepols), 375–393.

Tubach, J. (2003), "Seth and the Sethites in Early Syriac Literature," in: G.P. Luttikhuizen, ed., *Eve's Children: The Biblical Stories Retold and Interpreted in Jewish and Christian*

Traditions (Themes in Biblical Narrative, Jewish and Christian Traditions 5; Leiden: Brill), 187–201.

Tubach, J. (2008), "Ephraem Syrus and the Solar Cult," in: T. Kaizer, ed., *The Variety of Local Religious Life in the Near East in the Hellenistic and Roman Periods* (Religions in the Graeco-Roman World 164; Leiden: Brill), 247–262.

Uehlinger, Ch. (1999), "Nimrod," in: K. van der Toorn, B. Becking and P.W. van der Horst, eds., *Dictionary of Deities and Demons in the Bible* (Leiden: Brill), 627–630.

Urbach, E.E. (1961), "כורש והכרזתו בעיני חז״ל," *Molad* 19, 368–374.

Urbainczyk, Th. (2000), "'The Devil Spoke Syriac to Me': Theodoret in Syria," in: S. Mitchell and G. Greatrex, eds., *Ethnicity and Culture in Late Antiquity* (London: Duckworth), 253–265.

Vaillant, A. (1958), "Le saint Éphrem slave," *Byzantinoslavica* 19, 279–286.

van Dam, C. (1997), *The Urim and Thummim: A Means of Revelation in Ancient Israel* (Winona Lake, Ind.: Eisenbrauns).

van der Horst, P.W. (1990), "Nimrod after the Bible," in: Idem, *Essays on the Jewish World of Early Christianity* (Novum Testamentum et Orbis Antiquus 14; Göttingen: Vandenhoeck & Ruprecht), 220–232.

van der Horst, P.W. (2002), "Antediluvian Knowledge: Graeco-Roman and Jewish Speculations about Wisdom from Before the Flood," in: Idem, *Japheth in the Tents of Shem: Studies on Jewish Hellenism in Antiquity* (Contributions to Biblical Exegesis and Theology 32; Kampen: Kok Pharos), 139–158.

van der Horst, P.W. (2009), "A Short Note on the *Doctrina Jacobi Nuper Baptizati*," *Zutot: Perspectives on Jewish Culture* 6:1, 1–6.

van der Kooij, A. (2006), "The City of Babel and Assyrian Imperialism: Genesis 11:1-9 Interpreted in the Light of Mesopotamian Sources," in: A. Lemaire, ed., *Congress Volume: Leiden 2004* (Supplements to Vetus Testamentum 109; Leiden: Brill), 1–17.

van Esbroeck, M. (1994), "Invention de reliques comme attribut impérial: la tunique du Christ à Moscou et son symbolisme," in: P. Catalano, ed., *Roma fuori di Roma: istituzioni e immagini (Roma, 21 aprile 1985)* (Da Roma alla Terza Roma: documenti e studi, Studi 5; Roma: Università degli studi "La Sapienza"), 225–243.

van Gelder, G.J. (2005), *Close Relationships: Incest and Inbreeding in Classical Arabic Literature* (Library of Middle East History 9; London: I.B. Tauris).

van Ginkel, J.J. (2005), "History and Community: Jacob of Edessa and the West Syrian Identity," in: J.J. van Ginkel, H.L. Murre-van den Berg and Th.M. van Lint, eds., *Redefining Christian Identity: Cultural Interaction in the Middle East since the Rise of Islam* (OLA 134; Leuven: Peeters), 67–75.

van Ginkel, J.J. (2008), "'Aramaic Brothers or Heretics': The Image of the East Syrians in the Chronography of Michael the Great (d. 1199)," *The Harp* 23, 359–368.

van Ginkel, J.J., Murre-van den Berg, H.L., and van Lint, Th.M. (2005), eds., *Redefining Christian Identity: Cultural Interaction in the Middle East since the Rise of Islam* (OLA 134; Leuven: Peeters).

van Reeth, J.M.F. (2000), "Melchisedech, le roi qui n'a pas d'âge et son grand interprète Jean d'Apamée," in: *Vieillesse, Sagesse et Tradition dans les civilisations orientales* (Acta Orientalia Belgica 13; Bruxelles: Société Belge d'Études Orientales), 135–150.

van Reeth, J.M.F. (2005), "L'araméen: la langue du Paradis," in: *La langue dans tous ses états* (Acta Orientalia Belgica 18; Bruxelles: Société Belge d'Études Orientales), 137–144.

van Rompay, L. (1981), "A Letter of the Jews to the Emperor Marcian concerning the Council of Chalcedon," *Orientalia Lovaniensia Periodica* 12, 215–224.

van Rompay, L. (1982), "The Martyrs of Najran: Some Remarks on the Nature of the Sources," in: J. Quaegebeur, ed., *Studia Paulo Naster oblata II: Orientalia Antiqua* (OLA 13; Leuven: Departement Oriëntalistiek), 301–309.

van Rompay, L. (1996), "The Christian Syriac Tradition of Interpretation," in: M. Sæbø, ed., *Hebrew Bible / Old Testament: The History of Its Interpretation. Vol. I: From the Beginnings to the Middle Ages (Until 1300). Part 1: Antiquity* (Göttingen: Vandenhoeck & Ruprecht), 612–641.

van Rompay, L. (1999), "Jacob of Edessa and the Early History of Edessa," in: G.J. Reinink and A.C. Klugkist, eds., *After Bardaisan: Studies on Continuity and Change in Syriac Christianity in Honour of Professor Han J.W. Drijvers* (OLA 89; Louvain: Peeters), 269–285.

van Rompay, L. (2004), *"Mallpânâ dilan Suryâyâ.* Ephrem in the Works of Philoxenus of Mabbog: Respect and Distance," *Hugoye: Journal of Syriac Studies* 7:1, 83–105.

van Rompay, L. (2005), "Society and Community in the Christian East," in: M. Maas, ed., *The Cambridge Companion to the Age of Justinian* (Cambridge: Cambridge University Press), 239–266.

Vanden Berghe, L. (1988), "Les scènes d'investiture sur les reliefs rupestres de l'Irān ancien: évolution et signification," in: G. Gnoli and L. Lanciotti, eds., *Orientalia Iosephi Tucci memoriae dicata*. 3 vols. (Serie Orientale Roma 56; Roma: Istituto italiano per il Medio ed Estremo Oriente), vol. 1, 1511–1531.

Vasiliev, A.A. (1950), *Justin the First: An Introduction to the Epoch of Justinian the Great* (Cambridge, Mass.: Harvard University Press).

Vasunia, P. (2007), *Zarathushtra and the Religion of Ancient Iran: The Greek and Latin Sources in Translation* (Mumbai: K. R. Cama Oriental Institute).

Vergani, E. (2017), "Il sinodo di Mar Isaac (410). Appunti e alcune linee di indagine," *Cristianesimo nella storia* 38:3, 655–672.

Vevaina, Y.S.-D. (2010), "Relentless Allusion: Intertextuality and the Reading of Zoroastrian Interpretive Literature," in: C. Bakhos and R.M. Shayegan, eds., *The Talmud in Its Iranian Context* (TSAJ 135; Tübingen: Mohr Siebeck), 206–232.

Vevaina, Y.S.-D. (2018), "A Father, a Daughter, and a Son-in-Law in Zoroastrian Hermeneutics," in: T. Daryaee, ed., *Sasanian Iran: In the Context of Late Antiquity* (Ancient Iran Series 6; Irvine, Calif.: UCI Jordan Center for Persian Studies), 121–147.

Vezin, G. (1950), *L'adoration et le cycle des Mages dans l'art chrétien primitif. Étude des influences orientales et grecques sur l'art chrétien* (Paris: Presses universitaires de France).

Vincent, L.-H., and Abel, F.-M. (1914), *Bethléem. Le Sanctuaire de la Nativité* (Paris: J. Gabalda).

Vlaardingerbroek, M. (2004), "The Founding of Nineveh and Babylon in Greek Historiography," *Iraq* 66, 233–241.

von Simson, O.G. (1987), *Sacred Fortress: Byzantine Art and Statecraft in Ravenna* (Princeton, N.J.: Princeton University Press).

Vööbus, A. (1965), *History of the School of Nisibis* (CSCO 266, Subs. 26; Louvain: Secrétariat du Corpus SCO).

Vosté, J.M. (1939), "Catalogue des manuscrits syro-chaldéens conservés dans la bibliothèque de l'archevêché chaldéen de Kerkouk (Iraq)," *OCP* 5, 72–102.

Walker, J.Th. (2006), *The Legend of Mar Qardagh: Narrative and Christian Heroism in Late Antique Iraq* (Transformation of the Classical Heritage 40; Berkeley, Calif.: University of California Press).

Wallraff, M. (2011), "The Beginnings of Christian Universal History: From Tatian to Julius Africanus," *ZAC* 14:3, 540–555.

Weidner, E.F. (1936), "Ninus (2)," in: *Paulys Real-Encyclopädie der Classischen Altertumswissenschaft* (Stuttgart: J.B. Metzler), vol. 17.1 [33], 634–635.

Weitzman, S. (1999), "Why Did the Qumran Community Write in Hebrew?" *Journal of the American Oriental Society* 119:1, 35–45.

Weltecke, D. (2009), "Michael the Syrian and Syriac Orthodox Identity," *CHRC* 89:1–3, 115–125.

Werner, E. (1966), "Melito of Sardis, the First Poet of Deicide," *HUCA* 37, 191–210.

Whitehead, A. (2009), *Memory* (2nd ed.; New Critical Idiom; London: Routledge).

Whitmarsh, T. (2010), ed., *Local Knowledge and Microidentities in the Imperial Greek World* (Greek Culture in the Roman World; Cambridge: Cambridge University Press).

Widengren, G. (1959), "The Sacral Kingship of Iran," in: *La regalità sacra. Contributi al tema dell'VIII Congresso internazionale di storia delle religioni (Roma, aprile 1955)* (Studies in the History of Religions 4; Leiden: E.J. Brill), 242–257.

Widengren, G. (1960), *Iranisch-semitische Kulturbegegnung in parthischer Zeit* (Arbeitsgemeinschaft für Forschung des Landes Nordrhein-Westfalen, Geisteswissenschaften 70; Köln: Westdeutscher Verlag).

Widengren, G. (1983), "Leitende Ideen und Quellen der iranischen Apokalyptik," in: D. Hellholm, ed., *Apocalypticism in the Mediterranean World and the Near*

East: Proceedings of the International Colloqium on Apocalypticism, Uppsala, August 12-17, 1979 (Tübingen: Mohr-Siebeck), 77–162.

Wiessner, G. (1967), *Untersuchungen zur syrischen Literaturgeschichte I: Zur Märtyrerüberlieferung aus der Christenverfolgung Schapurs II* (Abhandlungen der Akademie der Wissenschaften in Göttingen, Philologisch-historische Klasse III.67; Göttingen: Vandenhoeck & Ruprecht).

Wilken, R.L. (1983), *John Chrysostom and the Jews: Rhetoric and Reality in the Late 4th Century* (Transformation of the Classical Heritage 4; Berkeley, Calif.: University of California Press).

Williams, A.L. (1935), *Adversus Judaeos: A Bird's View of Christian Apologiae until the Renaissance* (Cambridge: Cambridge University Press).

Williams, S. (1985), *Diocletian and the Roman Recovery* (New York: Methuen).

Wilson, S.G. (1986), "Melito and Israel," in: S.G. Wilson, ed., *Anti-Judaism in Early Christianity. Vol. 2: Separation and Polemic* (Studies in Christianity and Judaism 2; Waterloo, Ontario: Wilfrid Laurier University Press), 81–102.

Wirth, A. (1894), *Aus orientalischen Chroniken* (Frankfurt am Main: Moritz Diesterweg).

Witakowski, W. (1987), *The Syriac Chronicle of Pseudo-Dionysius of Tel-Mahrē: A Study in the History of Historiography* (Studia Semitica Upsaliensia 7; Uppsala: University of Uppsala).

Witakowski, W. (1990a), "The Idea of Septimana Mundi and the Millenarian Typology of the Creation Week in Syriac Tradition," in: R. Lavenant, ed., *V Symposium Syriacum, 1988: Katholieke Universiteit, Leuven, 29-31 août 1988* (OCA 236; Rome: Pontificium Institutum Studiorum Orientalium), 93–109.

Witakowski, W. (1990b), "Malalas in Syriac," in: E. Jeffreys, B. Croke and R. Scott, eds., *Studies in John Malalas* (Byzantina Australiensia 6; Sydney: Australian Association for Byzantine Studies), 299–310.

Witakowski, W. (1991), "Sources of Pseudo-Dionysius for the Third Part of his Chronicle," *Orientalia Suecana* 40, 252–275.

Witakowski, W. (1993), "The Division of the Earth between the Descendants of Noah in Syriac Tradition," *Aram* 5, 635–656.

Witakowski, W. (1994), "Mart(y) Shmuni, the Mother of the Maccabean Martyrs, in Syriac Tradition," in: R. Lavenant, ed., *VI Symposium Syriacum, 1992: University of Cambridge, Faculty of Divinity, 30 August-2 September 1992* (OCA 247; Roma: Pontificio Istituto Orientale), 153–168.

Witakowski, W. (2008), "The Magi in Syriac Tradition," in: G.A. Kiraz, ed., *Malphono w-Rabo d-Malphone: Studies in Honor of Sebastian P. Brock* (Gorgias Eastern Christian Studies 3; Piscataway, N.J.: Gorgias Press), 809–843.

Wong, Ch.-K. (1992), "Philo's Use of Chaldaioi," *Studia Philonica Annual* 4, 1–14.

Wood, Ph. (2010), *'We Have No King But Christ': Christian Political Thought in Greater Syria on the Eve of the Arab Conquest (c. 400-585)* (Oxford Studies in Byzantium; Oxford: Oxford University Press).

Wood, Ph. (2012), "Syriac and the 'Syrians'," in: S.F. Johnson, ed., *The Oxford Handbook of Late Antiquity* (Oxford: Oxford University Press), 170–194.

Woodward, K. (2004), ed., *Questioning Identity: Gender, Class, Ethnicity* (2nd ed.; London: Routledge).

Wright, W. (1870–1872), *Catalogue of Syriac Manuscripts in the British Museum, Acquired since the Year 1838*. 3 vols (London: Trustees of the British Museum).

Wright, W. (1901), *A Catalogue of the Syriac Manuscripts Preserved in the Library of the University of Cambridge*. 2 vols (Cambridge: Cambridge University Press).

Yamamoto, Y. (1979–1981), "The Zoroastrian Temple Cult of Fire in Archaeology and Literature," *Orient* 15, 19–53; 17, 67–104.

Yamauchi, E.M. (2002), "The Eastern Jewish Diaspora under the Babylonians," in: M.W. Chavalas and K.L. Younger, eds., *Mesopotamia and the Bible: Comparative Explorations* (Journal for the Study of the Old Testament, Supplement Series 341; Sheffield: Sheffield Academic Press), 356–377.

Yarshater, E. (1983), "Iranian National History," in: E. Yarshater, ed., *The Cambridge History of Iran. Vol. 3(1): The Seleucid, Parthian and Sasanian Periods* (Cambridge: Cambridge University Press), 359–477.

Young, R.J.C. (2003), *Postcolonialism: A Very Short Introduction* (Very Short Introductions; New York: Oxford University Press).

Yuval, I.J. (2006), *Two Nations in Your Womb: Perceptions of Jews and Christians in Late Antiquity and the Middle Ages*. Trans. by B. Harshav and J. Chipman (Berkeley, Calif.: University of California Press).

Zaehner, R.Ch. (1955), *Zurvan: A Zoroastrian Dilemma* (Oxford: Clarendon Press).

Zaehner, R.Ch. (1961), *The Dawn and Twilight of Zoroastrianism* (New York: G.P. Putnam's Sons).

Zahn, M.M. (2020), *Genres of Rewriting in Second Temple Judaism: Scribal Composition and Transmission* (Cambridge: Cambridge University Press).

Zellentin, H.M. (2007), "Rabbinizing Jesus, Christianizing the Son of David: The Bavli's Approach to the Secondary Messiah Traditions," in: R. Ulmer, ed., *Discussing Cultural Influences: Text, Context, and Non-Text in Rabbinic Judaism* (Lanham, Md.: University Press of America), 99–127.

Index of Scriptural References

Old Testament

Genesis
- 1:2 — 42, 43
- 2:23 — 274
- 3:1–15 — 75
- 4:1 — 57
- 5 — 20
- 5:1 — 56
- 5:15–20 — 18
- 6:1–9 — 235
- 6:4 — 191
- 7:7 — 18
- 8:6–12 — 102–104
- 8:8 — 101
- 9:20–27 — 43, 104–105
- 10:2–5 — 276
- 10:8–12 — 190–191
- 10:9 — 193
- 10:10 — 196
- 10:10–12 — 194, 198
- 10:22–23 — 270
- 10:25 — 57
- 11:1–9 — 191, 272, 275
- 11:18–21 — 18
- 11:11–32 — 20
- 11:28 — 193
- 14:15 — 282
- 14:18–20 — 125
- 16:5 — 193
- 22:13 — 125
- 25:23 — 107
- 28:11–19 — 106
- 28:12 — 125
- 28:18 — 125
- 29:1–10 — 106
- 29:10 — 125
- 29:15–28 — 106
- 29:17 — 107
- 49:10 — 69

Exodus
- 12 — 97
- 12:4 — 262
- 25:13–15 — 80
- 25:17–21 — 83
- 25:27–28 — 80
- 28:4 — 111
- 28:15–24 — 111
- 28:27 — 111
- 28:29–30 — 111
- 29:5 — 111
- 30:1–10 — 114
- 34:29–35 — 107, 109–110
- 36:35–38 — 83

Leviticus
- 16:12–16 — 83

Numbers
- 4:13 — 82
- 4:15 — 82
- 5:11–31 — 65
- 11:4–5 — 103
- 13:23 — 80
- 24:17 — 203–204

Deuteronomy
- 7:1–3 — 125
- 16:5–6 — 99
- 17–18 — 92
- 17:4–7 — 284
- 32:32–33 — 76, 85
- 32:32–33 — 76, 85
- 33:8 — 111

Judges
- 4:2–24 — 18

Joshua
- 7:1–26 — 80
- 19:27 — 282

1 Samuel
- 6:13 — 84

2 Samuel
- 7:12–14 — 69

INDEX OF SCRIPTURAL REFERENCES

1 Kings
- 6:5 — 83
- 8:1 — 84

2 Kings
- 23:21–23 — 97

1 Chronicles
- 1–9 — 20
- 3:1–19 — 221

2 Chronicles
- 36:22–23 — 219

Job
- 23:8–9 — 282

Psalms
- 72:10–11 — 226–227, 232
- 72:10–15 — 233
- 72:15 — 226, 233
- 80:8–15 — 76, 85
- 118:27 — 35, 113–115

Isaiah
- 6:3 — 244
- 7:14 — 244
- 9:6 — 244
- 9:6–7 — 69
- 11:1–2 — 66
- 44:28 — 221
- 45:1 — 221
- 45:13 — 219
- 50:1 — 100

Jeremiah
- 3:7–9 — 100
- 3:8 — 101

Ezekiel
- 16 — 100
- 16:46 — 282

Hosea
- 2:18 — 100

Micah
- 5:6 — 190

Daniel
- 2:2–10 — 179
- 4:7 — 179
- 5:7–11 — 179
- 9 — 93
- 9:24–27 — 117–118
- 9:26–27 — 115–116, 119–120

Ezra
- 1:1–4 — 219
- 4:7 — 170
- 6:18–22 — 97

2 Maccabees
- 1:18–36 — 148

New Testament

Matthew
- 1:1, 6, 17 — 66
- 1:2–17 — 20, 66
- 1:12–13 — 222
- 1:15 — 295
- 2:1–12 — 188–189, 203, 223–224, 227, 233
- 3:4 — 43
- 3:7 — 75–76
- 3:16 — 102
- 8:20 — 120
- 9:15 — 100
- 9:27 — 66
- 12:23 — 66
- 12:34 — 75
- 15:22 — 66
- 19:7–9 — 100
- 20:30–31 — 66
- 21:15 — 66
- 21:15 — 66
- 21:33–41 — 86
- 21:33–43 — 88
- 22:15–22 — 82
- 22:42–45 — 66
- 23:33 — 75
- 23:34–39 — 88
- 25:1–13 — 100
- 25:31–46 — 281–282
- 26:65 — 96

Matthew (cont.)

27:16–26	100
27:24–25	72
27:27	83
27:28	82
27:34	85
27:47–48	85, 90
27:51	95

Mark

1:10	102
2:19–20	100
7:24–37	260
10:47–48	66
11:10	66
12:1–12	86
12:13–17	82
12:35–37	66
14:63	96
15:15	77
15:15–16	83
15:16–20	81
15:17	77, 81–82
15:24	77
15:35–36	85, 90
15:38	95

Luke

1:36	66
1:27–32	66
1:36	66
2:4–5	66
3:7	75
3:22	102
3:23–38	20, 66
3:27	222
3:31	66
4:27	257
5:34–35	100
16:31	113
18:38–39	66
20:9–19	86
20:20–26	82
20:41–44	66
22:3	74
23:11	83
23:36	85
23:45	95
27:27, 29, 35	77

27:27–31	81
27:28	81

John

1:32	102
5:2	285
8:39–47	75
12:37–43	88
13:2, 27	74
18:12–13	78
19:1–2	83
19:2	77, 82
19:2–5	81
19:13	285
19:17	285
19:19–20	284
19:20	285
19:23–24	77
19:28–29	85, 90
19:34	41, 78

Acts

2:23, 36	72
2:25–31	66
4:10, 27	72
5:30–31	34, 72
10:39	72
13:8	224
13:16	224
13:22–23, 34–37	66
13:27–28	72
13:46	88
18:6	88
28:25–28	88

Romans

1:3–4	66
7:1–4	100
9:6–33	88, 107
15:12	66

Galatians

3:28	9
4:21–31	88, 107, 110
5:4–5	103

1 Corinthians

6:15–17	100

2 Corinthians
- 3:13–16 — 109–110
- 11:12 — 100

Ephesians
- 5:22–32 — 100

1 Thessalonians
- 2:14–15 — 72

2 Timothy
- 2:8 — 66

Hebrews
- 7:3 — 47

1 Peter
- 3:20–21 — 102

Revelation
- 3:7 — 66
- 5:5 — 66
- 12:9 — 75
- 22:16 — 66

Index of Ancient Sources

Ancient Jewish Sources

Apocalypse of Abraham
    27, 29   281

1 Enoch   59
    8:3   183
    72:1   182

1(3) Ezra
    2:16   170

Genesis Apocryphon   22

Josephus
    Ant. 1.5   123
    Ant. 1.69–71   182
    Ant. 1.113–115   191
    Ant. 1.121   258
    Ant. 1.138   179
    Ant. 8.262   279
    Ant. 10.195–203, 234–235   179
    Ant. 11.1–7   219
    Ant. 13.299–300   92
    Ant. 18.42–43   165
    Ant. 20.17–96   137
    Ant. 20.67   238
    C. Ap. 1.6–18   258
    C. Ap. 1.168–171   279
    War 1.68   92

Jubilees   22–23, 56, 59
    1:8   179
    4:17   182
    12:25–26   273

Life of Adam and Eve   56–57, 59

Philo of Alexandria
    De Abr. 69   179
    De gig. 65–66   191
    De spec. leg. 3.13   165
    Quaest. in Gen. 1.53   58
    Quaest. in Gen. 2.82   191, 195
    Quaest. in Gen. 3.1   179
    Quis Her. 209   281

Pseudo-Philo
    Lib. ant. 4.7   191
    Lib. ant. 6.14   191

4Q464   273

11QTemple Scroll   23

Sybilline Oracles
    3.226–230   179

Testament of Benjamin
    10:6   281

Testament of Abraham
    (A) 12:12, 13:9   281

Rabbinic and Medieval Jewish Sources

Mishnah
    Avot 4:13   92

Tosefta
    Hullin 2:23–24   62
    Sotah 5:9   62

Palestinian Talmud
    Avoda Zara 2:2 [40d]   62
    Berakhot 9:1 [12d]   65
    Megillah 1:8 [71b]   273
    Shabbat 14:4 [14d]   62
    Taanit 2:1 [65b]   119

Babylonian Talmud
    Abodah Zarah 53b   191
    Bava Metzia 85b   56
    Ḥullin 89a   191
    Pesahim 61a   262
    Sanhedrin 43a   62
    Sanhedrin 67a   62
    Sanhedrin 106a   62

Shabbat 104b	62
Sotah 49b	262
Sukkah 52a–b	120

First Targum to Esther

7:2	221–222

Fragment-Targum of the Pentateuch

on Gen 10:9	191

Targum Chronicles

on 1 Chr 1:10	191

Targum Neofiti

on Gen 10:9	191
on Gen 10:10–12	198
to Gen 11:1	273

Targum Pseudo-Jonathan

on Gen 10:9	191
on Gen 10:10–12	193, 198
on Gen 11:1	273
on Ex 28:30	111

Avot de-Rabbi Nathan

A 41; B 48	92

Canticles Rabbah

1.9.1	281

Exodus Rabbah

40.2	56

Genesis Rabbah

23.7	191
24.2	56
26.4	191
31.8	273
37.2–3	191
37.4	198
42.4	191
44.2	191

Leviticus Rabbah

13.5	222

Pirke de-Rabbi Eliezer

	55
22	273
24	191, 195

Seder Olam

28	120

Sefer Niẓẓaḥon Yašan   68

Sefer Yetzira   273

Shahin of Shiraz

Ardašīr-nāmah	221

Toledoth Yeshu   62

Mandaean sources

Book of John

34–35	65

Manichaean sources

Bema Psalms

235	153
241	153

Cologne Mani Codex

18.7–8	214
121.4–15	232

Hymn to the Living Soul

(M 95)	147

Manichaean Homilies   153

Middle Persian hymn

M 28 I	146

Sogdian fragment M 197   153

Classical Literature

Aelius Herodianus

De prosodia catholica 8	260

Ammianus Marcellinus

Res gest. 17.5.3	211
Res gest. 23.6.22	199

Appian of Alexandria
Hist. rom. 12.9 (66) — 149

Athenaeus
Deipn. 4.45 — 301

Catullus
90.1 — 165

Chaeremon — 180

Cicero
De div. 1.2 — 179, 184
De div. 1.91 — 179–180

Curtius Rufus
8.2.8, 19 — 165

Diodorus Siculus
Bib. 1.50.1 — 179
Bib. 1.81.6 — 179
Bib. 2.3.1–4.1 — 199
Bib. 2.7.2–8.7 — 199
Bib. 2.60.2 — 181
Bib. 4.27.5 — 181

Diogenes Laertius
Vit. 1.6 — 179
Vit. 9.35 — 180

Dionysius Scytobrachion
#32, frg. 7 — 181

Eunapius
Vitae sophist. 6.5.8 — 240

Herodorus of Heracleia
#31, frg. 13 — 181

Herodotus
Hist. 1.131 — 156–167
Hist. 1.170 — 301
Hist. 2.1 — 219
Hist. 2.2 — 273
Hist. 3.2–3 — 219
Hist. 3.31 — 165, 168
Hist. 5.58–59 — 278–279

Julian
C. Gal. 253D–261E — 67
Orat. 2.63B — 240

Julius Pollux
Onomast. 1.45 — 201, 299

Junianus Justin
Epit. 1.1.9 — 181

Lucian
Fisherman 19 — 260
Toxaris 28 — 259

Nicolaus of Damascus
#90, F 68 — 146

Ovid
Ars. amat. 1.416 — 279

Philostratus
Vita Apol. 1.29–31 — 236
Vita Apol. 1.31 — 159

Pliny the Elder
Hist. nat. 6.122 — 181, 199

Plutarch
Art. 23 — 170

Porphyry
Vita Pythag. 1 — 260

Ptolemy
Tetrab. 1.1 — 184
Tetrab. 1.2–3 — 184

Sextus Empiricus
Adv. math. 5.1–2 — 185
Adv. math. 5.87, 95 — 185

Strabo
Geogr. 11.13.3 — 232
Geogr. 15.3.13–15 — 146
Geogr. 16.1.2 — 199
Geogr. 16.1.4 — 148
Geogr. 16.1.16 — 148, 179

INDEX OF ANCIENT SOURCES

Xenagorus of Heracleia
#240, frg. 32 — 181

Xenophon
Cyrop. 8.3.24 — 159

Christian Greek Sources

Acts of Anastasius the Persian — 158

Acts of Pilate 2:3–5 — 62

Acts of Shirin
6 — 249
8 — 249

Agathias of Myrina
Hist. 2.25.1 — 146
Hist. 2.25.1–2 — 180
Hist. 2.25.4 — 197
Hist. 2.26.3 — 236
Hist. 2.29.1 — 259
Hist. 4.23.1–25.3 — 173
Hist. 4.24.5 — 173, 229
Hist. 4.25.1 — 229
Hist. 4.26.3 — 172

Alexander the Monk
De inventione Crucis — 114

Amphilochius of Iconium
Or. 4.7 — 233

Apocalypse of Paul
30 — 273

Apostolic Constitutions
6.5.4 — 96

Athanasius of Alexandria
Expositions on the Psalms — 233
Hist. Arian. 71.1 — 137

Basil of Caesarea
Hexaem. 6.4–5 — 185

Chronicon Paschale — 146, 169, 195, 299

Clement of Alexandria
Paed. 1.7.55 — 166
Protr. 5.65.1 — 146, 224
Strom. 1.15 — 224
Strom. 1.16.75 — 279
Strom. 1.21.125–126 — 117
Strom. 1.62.2–4 — 301
Strom. 3.11.1 — 165

Cyril of Alexandria
Comm. in Ioan. 12 — 86, 287
Comm. in Is. 4.4 — 224, 233
De ador. — 114
Glaph. in Gen. 2 — 103
Glaph. in Gen. 4 — 108

Dialogue of Timothy and Aquila
35 — 67
121 — 117

Didymus the Blind
Comm. in Zech. 3.305 — 233

Doctrina Iacobi
1.22 — 117
1.41–42 — 67
1.42 — 65
2.5 — 140

Epiphanius of Salamis
De fide 8.1 — 224
De res. — 113
Panar. 1.2.3–7 — 128
Panar. 1.3.2–3 — 182, 195, 217
Panar. 3.40.5.4 — 59
Panar. 4.55.1–9 — 47
Panar. 46.1.6 — 259
Panar. 78.7.5 — 65

Eusebius of Caesarea
Chron. — 195, 197
Comm. in Ps. — 233
De theoph. 4.6 — 260
Dem. ev. 1.1.6 — 105
Dem. ev. 1.2.9 — 127
Dem. ev. 1.2–4 — 127

Eusebius of Caesarea (cont.)

Dem. ev. 1.3–5	128
Dem. ev. 1.4.6	128
Dem. ev. 1.5.2	127
Dem. ev. 6.13	105
Ecl. proph. 3.10	65
Hist. eccl. 1.3.8	92
Hist. eccl. 1.4.4–6	127
Hist. eccl. 1.4.12	127
Onom.	191
Praep. ev. 6.9.32	260
Praep. ev. 6.10	166
Praep. ev. 7.3–8	127
Praep. ev. 9.17.8	182
Praep. ev. 9.17.9	181
Praep. ev. 9.18.2	193, 199
Praep. ev. 9.23.3	260
Praep. ev. 10.5.2	279
Praep. ev. 10.9.10	199

Eustathius of Antioch

Comm. in Hex.	191

Evagrius Scholastiucs

Hist. eccl. 5.8–9	307

George of Pisidia

Expeditio Persica 1.23–26	158
Expeditio Persica 1.149	47
In Restitutionem S. Crucis 73–74	81

Gregory of Nyssa

Oratio in diem natalem Christi	203

Hesychius of Jerusalem

Hom. in Luc. 10	259

Hippolytus

Comm. in Dan. 4.31–32	117
Dem. adv. Jud. 1, 5	86
Ref. 1.2.12	181
Ref. 4.1.1–13	179
Ref. 7.36.1	47
Trad. ap. 5	92

Ignatius of Antioch

Eph. 21	267
Pol. 7	267
Rom. 9	267

Irenaeus of Lyon

Adv. haer. 1.30.6	59
Adv. haer. 3.21.5	66

John Chrysostom

Adv. Jud.	51
Adv. Jud. 1.5.2–8	84
Adv. Jud. 3.3.6	98
Adv. Jud. 3.3.8	98
Adv. Jud. 6.7.1–7	84
Adv. Jud. 6.7.2	84
De beato Philogonio 6.4	224
Hom. 30 in Gen.	273
Hom. in Gen. 29.30	191
Hom. in Chr. gen. 5	224
Hom. in Matth. 6.1	189
Jud. gent.	51–52

John of Antioch

Hist. chron.	195
Hist. chron. 1.5	199

John Malalas

Chron.	133
Chron. 1.1	182
Chron. 1.7	195, 217
Chron. 1.8	197
Chron. 1.10	168–169
Chron. 1.11	199
Chron. 2.9	201, 299
Chron. 2.12	146
Chron. 6.7–11	220
Chron. 17.15	199
Chron. 18.44	211
Chron. 18.54	139

Julian

Comm. in Hiob	259–260

Julius Africanus

Chron.	21, 116–117, 273

Justin III

Novel 3	177

INDEX OF ANCIENT SOURCES

Justin Martyr	25
Dial. 24–26	105
Dial. 43.1	66
Dial. 45.4	66
Dial. 52	105
Dial. 77.4	224
Dial. 78.2	224
Dial. 88.1	224
Dial. 100.3	66
Dial. 106.4	203, 224
Dial. 109–110	105
Dial. 134.3	107–108
Justinian	
Novel 154	177
Letter of Barnabas	
4.6–7	88
Letter of the Three Patriarchs	245–246
Life of Thecla	
1.15	259
Martyrdom of Arethas	140
Mark the Deacon	
Vita Porph. 66	260
Melito	
On Faith	92
Peri Pascha 72–99	73
Peri Pascha 79	78
Nonnus of Panopolis	
Paraphr. Ioan. 19.64–65	285
Paraphr. Ioan. 19.91	285
Paraphr. Ioan. 19.109	284–285
On the Mystery of Letters	
19	277–279
23	280
26	280
37	280
Origen	
C. Cels. 1.24	224
C. Cels. 1.28	62
C. Cels. 1.32	61–62
C. Cels. 1.59	203
C. Cels. 1.69	62
C. Cels. 4.73	105
C. Cels. 5.27	166
C. Cels. 6.80	166, 179–180
Comm. Matt. 12.4	100
Comm. Matt. 14.18–20	100
Palladius	
Hist. Laus. 40	297
Photius of Constantinople	
Bibl. 72	219
Bibl. 81	142
Bibl. 94	264
Bibl. 265	137
Procopius of Caesarea	
Bell. pers. 2.13.7	139
Bell. pers. 2.24.1–2	161
Bell. pers. 2.24.2	146
Procopius of Gaza	
Comm. in Gen.	191
Comm. in Gen. 11	181–182
Protevangelium of James	
10:1	66
16:1–3	65
Pseudo-Clementines	
Hom. 8.5–7	88
Hom. 9.3–6	147
Hom. 9.4–5	217
Hom. 9.4.1	147
Hom. 9.4.2–5.1	147
Hom. 9.5.2	147
Hom. 9.6.1	147
Hom. 19.19	166
Rec. 1.30.5	274
Rec. 1.30.7	147–148, 196–197
Rec. 1.48.5–6	93
Rec. 4.5	88
Rec. 4.27–29	147
Rec. 4.27.2–3	147
Rec. 4.28.5	147
Rec. 4.29.1	147

Pseudo-Clementines (cont.)
 Rec. 9.12.2–3   183
 Rec. 9.22   179
 Rec. 9.29   166

Pseudo-Epiphanius
 Testimony 5.42   117
 Testimony 7   67

Pseudo-Gregory of Nyssa
 Testimonies against
  the Jews 2.7   67

Pseudo-Macarius
 Hom. 17.14   96

Pseudo-Nonnus' Scholia
 In Epiph. 16   181
 Invect. 1.70   180–181

Questions of Bartholomew
 1.21–22   59

Socrates Scholasticus
 Hist. 3.1.13   260

Sozomen
 Hist. eccl. 3.16   299

Stephen of Byzantium
 Ethn. B.5   199
 Ethn. N.63   199
 Ethn. Ch.10   199

Tatian
 Orat. 8.1   183
 Orat. 28   165

Theodoret of Cyrus
 Comm. in Dan. to
  Dan 9:24–27   117
 Ep. 113   143
 Graec. affect. cur. 9.33   169
 Hist. 1.7.4   261–262
 Hist. 4.9.1   264
 Quaest. in Gen. 60   276
 Quaest. in Gen. 62   276
 Quaest. in Gen. 91   108–109
 Quaest. in Lev. 24   166

Theophanes Confessor
 Chron. AM 5817   140
 Chron. AM 6021   139
 Chron. AM 6114   156

Theophylact Simocatta
 Hist. 3.13.14–15   158

Trophies of Damascus
 4.2.1–4.6   117

Zosimos of Panopolis   273

Christian Latin sources

Altercatio Simoni et Theophili
 15   66

Ambrose
 Expos. ev. Luc. 2.48   203
 Jac. 5.25   108

Ambrosiaster
 Quaest. 63   203

Augustine
 De civ. Dei 12.11   197
 De civ. Dei 16.3–4   191
 De civ. Dei 16.11   274
 De civ. Dei 18.2   197
 In Ioh. Ev. Tract.
  CXXIV 117.4   287
 In Ps. LVIII
  enarratio 1.1   287
 Serm. 199.2   189
 Serm. 200.2   242
 Serm. 201.1   189
 Serm. 218.6   287
 Serm. 218.11   86

Caesarius of Arles
 Serm. 113.2   203
 Serm. 194.1   224

Claudius Marius Victor
 Alethia 3.274   305

Cyprian of Carthage
 Test. 1.20   108

Index of Ancient Sources

Gregory of Tours
  Hist. 1.5   147

Isidore of Seville
  Etym. 8.11.23   197
  Etym. 9.1.3   286
  Etym. 9.1.14   305
  Lib. num. 4.17   286

Jerome
  Chron.   199
  Comm. in Dan. 3.9.24   117
  Comm. in Matth. 1.2   203
  Comm. in Soph. 3.14–18   273–274
  Ep. 22.21   108
  Ep. 60.4   287
  Ep. 123.13   108
  Quaest. in Gen. 10.8–10   195
  Vita Malchi 2.2   264
  Vir. ill. 95   51

Maximus of Turin
  Con. Jud. 5   108

Minucius Felix
  Oct. 31.3   166

Mosaicarum et Romanarum legum collatio
  6.4   177

Orosius
  Hist. 2.2   197

Prudentius
  Hamart. 144–148   191

Tertullian
  De bapt. 8   103
  De carne Christi 22   66
  Ad nat. 1.16.5   165
  Adv. Jud. 8   117
  Adv. Jud. 9.12   226
  Adv. Jud. 9.26   66
  Adv. Jud. 13.15   95
  Adv. Marc. 3.13.8   226
  Apol. 9   165

Victorinus
  Comm. in Apoc. 7.2   191

Syriac Literature

'Abdišo' of Nisibis
  Catalogue   51, 143–144, 270

Acts of Mār Abā   175

Acts of Mār 'Abdā   151

Acts of Mār 'Aqebšmā   151

Acts of Mār Mari
  2–5   293
  10   303
  32   192, 194
  33   74

Acts of Mār Qardagh   5, 74, 151

*Acts of Pethion,
Adurhormizd and
Anahid*   166–167

Acts of Thomas
  5–8   212

Acts of Šarbel   291

Alexander Romance
  2.6   212

Aphrahat
  2.6   89, 93, 113–114
  5.10   195
  5.13   192
  5.21   76, 87
  5.22   78–79, 87
  9.8   105–106
  11   132
  12.3   99, 101
  13   132
  14.33   108
  15   132
  15.7   101
  16   89
  16.2   300
  17.10   118
  19.5   101
  19.9–12   119

Aphrahat (cont.)

19.11	93, 101
21.10	73
21.15–20	73
21.19	300
23.3	92
23.20	66

Apocalypse of Pseudo-Methodius

3.2–8	38
3.5	195

Balai

Madrasha on the Dedication of the Newly Built Church

49, 51, 54, 59	224

Bardaisan

Book of the Laws of Countries

	165, 291, 300, 302

Barḥadbešabbā ʿArbāyā

Cause

	51, 143, 166, 296–297
Hist. eccl.	51
Hist. eccl. 18	265
Hist. eccl. 31	303

Barhebraeus

Book of Rays	271
Chron. eccl.	245
Chron. eccl. 1.88	270

Book of the Himyarites   84

Cave of Treasures

1.1	19
1.3	58
1.4–7	42–43, 124
1.8–9	144
1.9–10	58
1.21	58
1.22	56, 58
1.25	58
2.2	58
2.2–3	124
2.6–9	58
2.6–14	34
2.12	58
2.13	58
2.16	124
2.18	89
2.19–21	56
2.20	58
2.25	34
3.1–7	58
3.3	40, 42
3.6	34, 71
3.13	58–59
3.15	144
3.17	124
3.21	124
4.1	40, 58, 124
4.3	125
4.4	58
4.5	34
4.12	71
4.22	35
4.22–23	59
4.23	58
5.1	56
5.5	58
5.7–13	125
5.8	40, 42, 299
5.10–12	126
5.17	126, 241
5.17–20	56
5.19–32	58–59
5.21–27	56
5.28	56
6.1	58
6.2	58
6.8	57
6.9	58
6.9–14	126
6.14	126
6.17–18	125
7.1–4	126
7.11	58
7.18	58
8.1	126
8.2–10	56
8.13	57
8.15	126
8.19	57
9.1	126
9.5	57

INDEX OF ANCIENT SOURCES

9.7–8	126	27.6–20	38
10.1	126	27.11	184
10.5	57	27.12–16	144, 163, 172, 244
10.8	126		
11.10	40	27.12–17	154
12.11	57	27.17–22	144, 177–178, 180, 183, 186, 202, 244
13.3–7	126		
13.6	241		
14.2–3	56	28.11	125
15.4	20	29.8–14	39, 42
15.4–8	235	29.9–10	125
15.6	295	29.10	41
16.8	89	30.11–17	134, 235
16.12–21	126	30.12–13	47
16.14	241	30.19	144, 198
16.15–17	56	31.17–19	125
16.21	241	31.20–24	125
16.24–28	126	31.26–28	106, 110
17.22	21, 299	31.28	286
18.2–7	125–126	32.14	56
19.5	125	33.1	20, 235
19.9–12	101, 104	33.8	19
19.13	101, 286	33.14–15	125
21.18–20	43	33.16	19
21.18	125	34.1	19
21.19	34, 41	34.2	56
21.21–22	104	34.9	56
22.15	170	35.9	122
22.17	170	35.9–10	56
23.13–23	126	35.18	34–35
24.9–11	42, 272, 285	35.18–21	204, 229
24.11	20, 235, 255, 258, 280–281	35.21	152
		35.25–28	56
24.19	33, 255	36.1–8	201, 299
24.21	33	36.10–41.10	34
24.24	196	39.6–12	56
24.24–26	144	39.10	19
24.25	214	40.3–6	56
24.25–26	162, 208, 210–211, 213, 215–216	41.13–22	34
		42.6	20, 255, 299
		42.7	19
25.8–14	162	42.11–22	219–220
26.1–10	178–179, 183	42.12	219
27.1–3	144–145, 147, 149–152, 162	42.12–22	144
		42.19	219–220
27.4–5	38, 71, 144, 152, 154–157, 159, 161–162, 208	43.8–9	97
		43.9	286
		43.13	60
27.6–11	22, 57, 144, 202	43.14	295

Cave of Treasures (cont.)

43.14–25	60	47.6	69, 295
43.15	34, 295	47.20–27	122
43.23–25	295	48.3	43
44.1–2	23, 60	48.5	69, 295
44.1–4	130	48.5–7	116
44.1–5	20	48.12–13	43
44.3	60	48.12–30	125
44.3–4	50, 61	48.13–14	286
44.4	60	48.29	91, 235, 286
44.5–11	61	49.1	125
44.6	122	49.11	77
44.8–16	20	49.20	69
44.12–13	34	50.1	77
44.12–14	61	50.3	295
44.13–51	19	50.4	77, 286
44.14	20, 255, 299	50.8–12	39
44.15–20	61	50.13–14	90, 235, 286
44.16	295, 297	50.15–16	90
44.16–19	295	50.16	78
44.17	69, 71, 254, 298	50.17	95–96
44.19	69	50.18	97
44.21–47	61	50.19	69
44.42–45	221	50.20–21	79
44.48	61	51.1–17	76, 85–86
44.49	20, 61, 69	51.9–10	76
44.50–51	295	51.11	69
44.53	69	51.12	72, 286
44.53–57	115, 120	51.12–13	74, 76
45.1	69, 295	51.15–17	90, 94
45.2–12	144, 202	51.18–19	41
45.5	224	52.1	286
45.5–7	201	52.1–2	99, 112
45.9	189	52.1–6	35
45.12	224, 241, 251	52.1–17	113
45.13	69	52.14	69, 295
45.13–15	241	52.14–17	112
45.16–17	129	52.15	113
45.18	190, 226	52.17	115, 235, 286
45.18–19	154, 228	52.17–18	91, 97
45.19	38, 225	52.18–19	116
46.3–4	190, 233, 244	53.6	79, 286
46.8	237, 239–240	53.11	69, 81, 83, 295
46.16–18	39, 42	53.11–15	79
46.19–26	241, 244	53.12	72, 83, 110
46.22	229	53.20–27	283, 285
46.22–23	244	53.21	69
46.22–25	129	53.25–26	42, 72, 74
46.26	244	53.26	255
		53.26–27	290

54.3	113	**Elias**	
54.16	295	*Life of John of Tella*	46
54.16–17	19	**Elias of Nisibis**	
Chronicle of AD 1234		*Chron.*	265, 270
65	307	**Ephrem**	
936	139	*Adv. Haer.* 22.11	282
Chronicle of Arbela	231	*Against Bardaisan's*	
12	140	*"Domnus"*	257
		Against Mani	257
Chronicle of Khuzistan	140, 188, 200	*C. Jul.* 3.12	80
		Carm. Nis. 32.16	108
Chronicle of Ps.-Dionysius of		*Carm. Nis.* 36.18	282
Tel-Mahre	200, 261, 267	*Carm. Nis.* 67.2	73
		Comm. in Gen.	
Chronicle of Ps.-Joshua the Stylite		Prologue 1	298
5	292	*Comm. in Gen.* 8.1	198
58	139	*Comm. in Gen.* 8.1.2	193
60	292	*Comm. in Gen.* 8.3	275
		Comm. in Gen. 8.4.1–2	192
Chronicle of Ps.-Zachariah Rhetor		*Comm. in Gen.* 8.4.2	197
9.4	139	*De azym.* 5.6	81
9.8	139	*De azym.* 18.4	78
10.1	46	*De azym.* 18.9	75
		De azym. 18.10	75
Chronicle of Zuqnin	46, 225, 261	*De azym.* 21.3–4	99
		De azym. 21.5–7	99
Cyriacus of Tagrit		*De azym.* 21.21–22	99
On Divine Providence 19.2–3	192	*De azym.* 21.24	99
		De crucif. 4.3	81
Cyrillona		*De crucif.* 4.11	94
On the Pasch of Our Lord	78	*De crucif.* 5.14	74
		De Eccl. 9.1	298
Cyrus of Edessa		*De Eccl.* 9.2	298
Explanation of the Pasch 6	98	*De Eccl.* 9.7	298
		De fid. 49.3–4	103
Dādišoʿ Qaṭrāyā		*De fid.* 87.10	74
Commentary on Abba		*De Juliano Saba* 4.8–11	302
Isaiah	270	*De Nat.* 2.11	63
		De Nat. 2.13	66
Didascalia Apostolorum		*De Nat.* 3.8	75
21	73	*De Nat.* 6.3	63
23	88, 96	*De Nat.* 14.13	63
		De Nat. 24.2	93
Dionysius bar Ṣalibi		*De Nat.* 24.4	204
Against the Armenians	270	*De Nat.* 25.7	118
		De Nat. 26.2	227
Diyarbekir Commentary	277	*De Parad.* 1.2	298

Ephrem (cont.)
   De Parad. 1.15 — 298
   De Parad. 1.16 — 298
   De Parad. 3.14 — 94
   De Parad. 3.16–17 — 94
   De Virg. 8.22–23 — 73
   De Virg. 38.11 — 74
   Discourses to Hypatius 1 — 298
   Homily on Our Lord 6 — 73
   Homily on Our Lord 56 — 93
   Letter to Publius 24–25 — 298
   Mēmrē on the Blessing of the Table — 80
   Necrosima 12 — 282

Ephremian *Commentary on the Diatessaron*
   2.1 — 63
   2.2–3 — 65
   2.18–25 — 227
   2.21 — 302
   3.8 — 76
   16.19 — 87
   18.1 — 86
   18.12 — 118
   20.17 — 82
   20.29 — 106
   21.4–6 — 95

Eusebius of Caesarea
   Onom. — 200
   De Theoph. 2.67 — 256
   De Theoph. 3.79 — 256
   De Theoph. 4.6 — 260–261
   De Theoph. 5.52 — 256

Gannat Bussame — 295

George
   Homily on Jacob of Sarug — 304

Ḥasan bar Bahlūl
   Lexicon — 218, 258

History of Aḥudemmeh
   4 — 308

History of Karkā d-Bēt Slok — 194, 197, 200

Isaac of Antioch
   Homily against the Jews — 87
   Homily on the Magi — 228

Isaac of Nineveh
   Hom. 11.4 — 81

Išoʿ bar ʿAli
   Lexicon — 258

Išoʿdad of Merv
   Comm. on Gen. 1:1 — 277
   Comm. on Matt., on Mt 2:2 — 218

Išoʿyahb III of Adiabene
   Ep. 2.7 — 267

Jacob of Edessa
   Encheiridion — 270
   Letter (# 13) to John of Litarba — 274
   Letter (# 14) to John of Litarba — 225–226

Jacob of Serugh
   Ep. 17 — 267
   Ep. 20 — 292
   Ep. 32 — 292, 302
   Ep. 35 — 292
   Homilies against the Jews 1.66–86 — 65
   Homilies against the Jews 1.315–317 — 86
   Homilies against the Jews 2–3 — 132
   Homilies against the Jews 5.149 — 95
   Homilies on the Apostle Thomas — 275
   Homilies on the Nativity — 120–121, 225
   Homily on Abgar — 292
   Homily on Addai and Abgar — 292
   Homily on Edessa and Jerusalem — 291–292, 294
   Homily on Ephrem — 299, 304
   Homily on Gurya and Shamuna — 294

INDEX OF ANCIENT SOURCES

Homily on Ḥabib	291	*Julian Romance*	94–95, 187, 202–203, 209–211, 236, 291
Homily on Our Lord and Jacob	109–110		
Homily on the Fall of Idols	157		
Homily on the Flood	103	*Liber Graduum*	
Homily on the Friday of the Passion	75–77, 82, 101	Preface	288
		22.11	63
Homily on the Holy Mother of God	63	27.1	63
Homily on the Presentation of Our Lord	63	*Life of George Mihr-Māh-Gušnasp*	174
Homily on the Separation of Foods	132	*Life of Ephrem*	
Homily on the Star That Appeared to the Magi	202, 204, 209, 225	14	297
		38	303
Homily on the Sunday of Hosannas 25–30	101	*Life of Jacob Baradaeus*	268
Homily on the Tower of Babel	192	*Life of Mār Awgen*	166
Homily on the Transfiguration	79, 86	*Life of Mār Benjamin*	174
Homily on the Two Goats	86	*Life of Mār Šabbay*	165
Homily on Vainglory	209		
		Life of Mār Yāret the Alexandrian	140
John bar Penkāyē			
Chron. 1	35		
Chron. 2	197	*Life of Rabban Hormizd*	194
Chron. 9	180		
Chron. 14	307	*Life of Simeon the Stylite*	282, 306
John of Apamea		*Life of Theodosius of Amida*	70
Comm. on Eccl.	288		
John of Ephesus		*Martyrdom of ʿAbd al-Masīḥ of Singar*	140
Hist. eccl.	45		
Hist. eccl. 3.25	263		
Lives 25	261	*Martyrdom of Gregory Pīrān-Gušnasp*	231, 249
Lives 27	263		
Lives 38	263		
Lives 39	263	*Martyrdom of Peter ʿAbšelama*	282
Lives 43	268–269		
Lives 46	263		
Lives 48	263	*Martyrdom of Simeon bar Sabbae*	
Lives 58	45, 266	12	140
Judas Kyriakos Legend	74	**Marutha of Maipherqat**	
		Canons	256

Michael the Great
Chron. 2.2–3   192

Narsai
Homilies on the Creation
  4.248–249   35
Homily on Noah's
  Blessings   193
Homily on Passion   75
Homily on the Tower
  of Babel   192

Philoxenus of Mabbug
Comm. Matt. to
  Mt 16:16–17   120
Florilegium   51
Homily on the Indwelling
  of the Holy Spirit   96
Letter to Abu 'Afr   307
Letter to the Monks
  of Senoun   289

Physiologus   103

Pseudo-Ephrem
Sermon against the Jews
  Given on Palm
  Sunday   87, 101
Sermons on the Holy
  Week   284
Soghitha on Mary and
  the Magi   225, 227

Pseudo-Eusebius
On the Star   203, 222

Regulations for an Association of Artisans   175

Revelations and Testimonies about Our Lord's Dispensation   192

Sergius I of Antioch
Letter to the Bishops
  of Persia   46–47

Severus of Antioch
Hom. 9.8   185
Hom. 42   257
Hom. 43   97–98
Hom. 109   183

Simeon of Bēt Aršām
Letters   140

Simeon the Potter
Hymns on the Nativity
  5.2   225

Solomon of Basra
Book of the Bee 37   218

Teaching of Addai   74, 146, 291–292

Testament of Adam   30–31
  3:5 59
  3:6 205
  3:7 227

Testament of Ephrem   298

Testament of Our Lord   186

Titus of Bostra
Adv. Man.   257

Theodore bar Koni
Lib. schol.   161
Lib. schol. 2.112   192
Lib. schol. 2.116–118   270
Lib. schol. 7   218

Theodore of Mopsuestia
Comm. on Eccl.   70
Comm. on Gen.   35
Comm. on John   284

Timothy I
Canons 19, 25   175
Letter 43.11   70

Transitus Mariae   65, 287

INDEX OF ANCIENT SOURCES

Armenian Sources

Agathangelos
  History of the
    Armenians   154

Sebeos
  Hist. 13   250
  Hist. 38   161
  Hist. 42   139

Eznik of Kołb
  De Deo 158   167, 169
  De Deo 187   167
  De Deo 189   167
  De Deo 191–192   167, 169
  De Deo 195   167
  De Deo 227   154
  De Deo 341   129
  De Deo 342   129

Ełiše Vardapet
  Hist.   64
  Hist. 2   176

Moses of Khoren
  Hist. 3.20   176
  Hist. 3.36   308
  Hist. 3.54   308
  Hist. 3.57   308

Pseudo-Faustus of Byzantium
  Epic Histories 4.4   176
  Epic Histories 4.54   187

Question 3   59

Georgian Literature

Martyrdom of Eustathius
  of Mtskheta   138

Coptic Literature

Cyril of Jerusalem
  Homily on Mary
    Magdalene   31

Hypost. of Archons
  95.34–96.3   281

Ethiopic Literature

Book of Clement   31

John of Nikiu
  Chron. 2.1–3   274
  Chron. 5.1–4   195, 217
  Chron. 6.3   199
  Chron. 8.1–3   169
  Chron. 21.14–19   148
  Chron. 21.17–19   146
  Chron. 27.14–17   274
  Chron. 51.4–12   220
  Chron. 95.26   158

Martyrdom of Azqir   140

Christian Arabic and Persian Sources

Arabic Apocalypse of Peter   27, 29–31, 130–131

Chronicle of Seert
  1.26   297
  1.68   51
  2.9   51, 143
  2.15   188
  2.21   46
  2.80   188

Mārī ibn Sulaimān
  Kitāb al-maǧdal   140

Persian *Diatessaron*
  4.3   282

Treatise on the Syrian
  Faith   268

Zoroastrian Literature

Avesta
  Yašt 8.18   159

Avesta (cont.)
   Yašt 14.3   159
   Yašt 17.9   238

Ardā Wirāz-nāmag   165

Ātaš Niyāyišn 14   150

Bundahišn
   5.4–5   186
   5a.3–9   186
   5b.1   212
   5b.12–13   186
   13.22   104
   14.11   220
   18.4–9   146
   18.8   161
   18.19–20   149
   29.16   218

Dādestān ī Dēnīg
   36.47   206
   36.68–69   167

Dādestān ī Mēnōg ī Xrad
   49.2–3   186

Dēnkard
   3.58   237
   3.80   164, 167
   3.129   237
   3.192.3   240
   3.289   236
   4   186
   5.7.3   206
   5.13.12   206
   5.19.7   206
   6.C82   164–165, 168
   7.3.46   237

Hērbedestān
   2.9   164

Kār-nāmag ī Ardašīr ī Pābagān
   1.8–13   154, 215–216
   1.10   161
   3.5–6   207
   4.7   206

King Khosrow and His Page   187

Mādayān ī Hazār Dādestān   170

Pahlavi Rivāyat
   8a1   164
   8a4   168
   8a7–9   164, 167
   8b1–3   164
   8c1–2   150, 164
   8c6   164
   8e10   164
   8f3   164
   8k1–2   165
   8l1   164
   46.31   161

Provincial Capitals of Ērānšahr   182–183, 200

Suppl. Texts to Šāyest-nē-šāyest
   18.1–4   164

Šāyest-nē-šāyest
   2.5   104
   8.18   164

Škand Gumānīg Wizār
   15   64

Vendīdād
   1.14   206

Zādspram
   3.24   156

Zand ī Wahman Yasn
   6.10   156
   7.6   207

Muslim Literature

Qur'ān
   4:156   65
   24:16   65

INDEX OF ANCIENT SOURCES

al-Bīrūnī
Chronology   212
Kitāb al-āṯār al-bāqīa   173

al-Dimašqī
Cosmography 9.8   241

al-Maʿsūdī
Murūǧ al-dahab 21   210
Murūǧ al-dahab 68   155–156, 160

al-Ṭabarī
History   171, 211, 214, 221, 239

Ferdowsī
Šāh-nāma   250

Ḥamza al-Iṣfahānī
Annals   201

Ibn ʿAbd Rabbih
Unique Necklace   135–136

Ibn al-Balkhī
Fārs-nāma   135

Ibn al-Nadīm
Fihrist 1.1   277
Fihrist 7.1   183
Fihrist 9.1   282

Ibn Isḥāq
Life of Muhammad   210–211

Letter of Tansar   135, 237, 303

Pseudo-Jāḥiz
Book of Beauties and Antitheses   240–241
Book of Crown   240

Testament of Ardašīr   187

Chinese Literature

Duan Chengshi
Youyang zazu   157

Printed in the United States
By Bookmasters